THE BRITISH LARDER

I dedicate this book to three special people in my life.

My beloved mother, Dalene Hamel,
my late father, Harlan Hamel,
and to my best friend, Ross Pike, aka Mr. P.

THE BRITISH LARDER

A cookbook for all seasons

Madalene Bonvini-Hamel

BLOOMSBURY ABSOLUTE
LONDON • OXFORD • NEW YORK • NEW DELHI • SYDNEY

BLOOMSBURY ABSOLUTE

Bloomsbury Publishing Plc
50 Bedford Square, London, WC1B 3DP, UK

BLOOMSBURY, BLOOMSBURY ABSOLUTE, the Diana logo and
the Absolute Press logo are trademarks of Bloomsbury Publishing Plc

First published in Great Britain in 2011
This edition published in 2020

A catalogue record for this book is available from the British Library.

Library of Congress Cataloguing-in-Publication data has been applied for.

ISBN:
HB: 9781472970596
ePUB: 9781472978516
ePDF: 9781472978523

2 4 6 8 10 9 7 5 3 1

Printed and bound in China by C&C Offset Printing Co

Bloomsbury Publishing Plc makes every effort to ensure that the papers used in the manufacture of our books are natural, recyclable products made from wood grown in well-managed forests. Our manufacturing processes conform to the environmental regulations of the country of origin.

To find out more about our authors and books visit www.bloomsbury.com
and sign up for our newsletters

Publisher Jon Croft
Commissioning Editor Meg Boas
Art Director Matt Inwood
Cover Design Peter Moffat
Junior Designer Anika Schulze
Editor Anne Sheasby
Editorial Assistant Imogen Fortes
Indexer Zoe Ross
Food Styling and Photography Madalene Bonvini-Hamel

CONTENTS

Why the British Larder?

I was born and brought up in South Africa, and growing up there I remember that we ate well and always enjoyed foods that were in season. Furthermore, because some of our family members owned or worked on farms, we were spoiled with the best foods each season had to offer, and this included plenty of fresh meat, fruit and vegetables. We also lived by the coast, but seafood wasn't very often eaten at home, and I do now wish that we had taken advantage of our location and enjoyed more fish, as the African coast has plenty to offer.

My grandfather tried to grow nearly everything (some things more successfully than others!) from pawpaw (papaya), mangoes, avocados, pecan nuts and cape gooseberries (physalis) to the more humble cucumbers and tomatoes, and this is what formed the foundation of my knowledge. I'm truly grateful for this privilege, which I must admit I took for granted at the time. My grandmother's walk-in larder boasted some of the finest homemade preserves and she made many things, including soap, golden syrup, pressed brawn and quinces preserved in syrup, as well as all her wonderful seasonal jams and marmalades.

Moving my life to Europe (the Netherlands) in 1993 at the age of 20, was a big ordeal, but it was my own choice, of course (I then moved to the UK in 1994). With a fairly naïve and protected upbringing and a pretty good life provided by my parents, I was suddenly (but voluntarily) living on a different continent and I had to fend for myself. I was brought up to be independent and proud and so I had to stand on my own two feet and make ends meet, no matter what.

Growing up eating and enjoying seasonal foods seemed to be so normal to me at home in South Africa, but once I moved to Europe and started to work in restaurants, especially Michelin-starred kitchens, serving foods such as asparagus in December was very much the done thing. I became quite confused and for a period of my life it became the norm to accept and use imported foods and ingredients, not to mention perfectly shaped and sized fruit and vegetables. I did not dare ask any questions as my job was so important to me, but thinking back, it now feels a bit like betrayal. Consequently, ingredients lost so much of their beauty and appeal, and seasonality just didn't seem to be high on the agenda. Thankfully though, nowadays, seasonal ingredients such as the misshapen tomatoes and bent courgettes that I grew up with, are back in our kitchens and to myself and many others, they are so much more appealing.

I'm also pleased to say that these days many restaurants, supermarkets and so on are much more aware and supportive of British grown produce. They are focusing more and more on the foods that we produce in the UK and those that are on offer during the different seasons. Seasonal food and eating is gradually making a comeback, which is great news for all of us, and I do hope it continues this way.

When the British Larder came along I did not 'deliberately' set out to cook seasonally – it was something that just came naturally to me and it often sparked off childhood and other memories for me. I advocate using local seasonal produce but I don't shun more exotic ingredients such as pineapples, bananas and chocolate in my recipes. I acknowledge that although we live in a country with a cooler climate, this should not preclude us from using ingredients grown in warmer climes. We all know that the economics and success of other countries (and our own) depend on their exports, so with the regulated Fairtrade Foundation schemes and Fairtrade certification in place for a wide variety of foods, I believe it's the right thing to support these countries, providing I know it's all above board and that the right people benefit from my purchases.

Local and regional seasonal food became an obsession for us when we moved to Suffolk. I developed a burning desire to shout about British regional seasonal foods and it gave me the opportunity to focus on one specific county, and one that has so much to offer from the surrounding land and sea. With this book, I hope to inspire you to do the same or similar in your local county or region or even in the UK as a whole.

Each season has its own beauty and brings its own glorious collection of goodies to life. Not only do the different seasons mean enjoying the wide range of seasonal foods that are readily available at that time of year, but they also mark special events and occasions on the calendar. The time of the year also influences how we cook and serve some foods. In the warmer summer months, for example, we are able to enjoy al fresco dining with barbecued foods and salads; during the cold of winter months, we are more likely to cook soups, stews and pies and enjoy them in front of a roaring fire.

I am also fanatical about preserving and storing the goodness of each season, squirrelling away the season's best and prolonging it for as long as I possibly can, hence my slight obsession with preserving, pickling, drying and curing, that all play such an integral part in my cooking repertoire.

I sincerely hope this book will inspire you to choose and use British seasonal ingredients and to support your own local community and county as much as you can.

About me

A desire to succeed

My father had a saying: 'Where there is a will, there is a way and Madalene is the living proof of that'. If I wanted something, I would do anything in my power to get it. Even though I was incredibly shy, perseverance and hard work were ingrained in me and I would do anything to succeed in the challenges I set for myself.

Even so, I sometimes find it hard to believe that I am where I am today. I am a successful chef with an outstanding reputation, and that the book you are holding in your hands is proof of having written my first cookbook! These were always my long-term ambitions and to be realising my dreams so soon is magical.

I have a lot of people to thank for helping me to achieve my dreams. Whether it's for their financial help or for their support or knowledge, or simply for giving me the opportunity to give this all a go: I'm very much the lucky one. I had a sheer passion and a drive to want to succeed and, like others did for me, I hope I can inspire this in others too. This desire to succeed, to be a perfectionist in what I do, and to learn more and more about food... all of these things have led me to the creation and development of the British Larder.

You might be surprised to hear that food was once my enemy and I used to hate it – I was bulimic for a year or so in my twenties. It seems bizarre now, but it's absolutely true. When I first starting working with food, although I loved my job, I could not and did not want to taste the food I had cooked, but then Chef's words rang in my ears: 'You cannot be a good cook if you do not taste the food you prepare', and so slowly my attitude changed and I began to enjoy cooking and, more importantly, began eating and enjoying food once again.

A desire to want to know more was ignited within me by chefs such as chef Rowley Leigh (a true advocate for using British seasonal ingredients). The tales and anecdotes he told us when reminiscing of his days as a commis chef, always made us smile. He spoke with such passion and was so knowledgeable.

True passion is so contagious... and that is where my career really began. And it's a career I have grown to truly love. Food and cooking have become my life, a life that is so rewarding and one that I strive to enjoy every moment of. Inspiration for my recipes comes from so many different things and this book contains a wide selection of the recipes that I love to cook and the food that I enjoy eating.

My food ethos

When thinking about my food ethos, at first I found it hard to put it down on paper, as it's simply part of me as an individual. It's the way I live, work and socialise. Subconsciously, my food ethos has naturally formed the foundations of each recipe I write. I can draw inspiration from anywhere and any situation. I think it's perhaps my strongest quality and is truly beneficial to my career as a chef. It does not matter to whom I speak or where I eat or shop as I can see potential in each and every occasion. I am always looking to put my own twist and stamp on a recipe as I have my own style, and as we all know, food and cooking is completely subjective. What works for me might not always work for others. My photography style is unique to the British Larder and me, and so are my recipes and cooking. My aim is to enhance some classic recipes, as well as creating many of my own dishes, and this is very much a reflection of all my past experiences, training and working as a chef.

I'm a true believer of several important things, including using local and seasonal produce, and although I also use and experiment with more exotic and unusual ingredients from all over the world, I always ensure that the 'hero' ingredient in each recipe is British grown and produced.

I support British producers and farmers as they form such an important part of our heritage and culture. They all need our support and the same goes for the county you live in – I believe that my pennies and pounds spent in the county where I live will help to create opportunities and make that county economically stronger and more self-sustainable.

I believe in using the best quality ingredients that I can afford and feel that using cheap and inferior ingredients in the kitchen will result in an inferior and unpleasant dish.

I always seek to do the right thing and consciously make ethically sound decisions where I can – this may be choosing which eggs I'm going to use, or where I buy my pork from, or which bunch of bananas I select, and so on. I have a conscience and want to sleep easy every night knowing that I have done the right thing.

I believe in simplicity and not over-complicating flavours. Having said that though, a well thought through dish with complementing components is a brilliant reflection of passion and understanding for the seasonal ingredients that have been used. I also recommend that you don't rush when cooking and that you take your time – give the recipes the time they deserve to achieve the best results. Allow yourself enough time to relax and enjoy cooking and you will soon be creating the most delicious dishes.

I also feel it's important to arm yourself with knowledge. No one can ever know everything in life, especially not about cooking, but allow yourself to absorb other people's views, methods and opinions and this will make you a stronger individual. I love asking people their views about food and cooking and I think it makes me a much better and wiser cook. I'm a curious individual and always ask lots of questions (which doesn't always make me popular!) and this definitely adds to my wisdom and knowledge.

The British Larder website

The whole concept of the British Larder stemmed from the website that my partner Ross (aka Mr. P) and I created in 2008. We created a platform where we could express ourselves with food photography, writing and cooking.

The British larder was my way of showing my appreciation to each and every individual that has helped me to become the cook I am today. The industry has been good to me, it has given me a career to be proud of and lots of knowledge and happiness.

Indeed, the website was the perfect opportunity for me to explore and practice my love for this hobby. My passion for photography was ignited by late genius Bob Carlos Clarke, with his brilliant black and white photographic work in Marco Pierre White's book *White Heat*. The provocative manner and sheer gritty intensiveness he photographed Marco with grabbed my attention. As a privileged chef, I am used to seeing the most amazing crafted creations from the wonderful seasonal ingredients that Mother Nature provides for us. I always said that the customer loses out as they might be presented with a immaculate dressed palate of food, but they never see the real beauty of the food. I had a burning desire to capture this privilege, sight and essence and show it to everyone that wants to see. I wanted to inspire people and ignite the passion for crating your own, as I was inspired to do. My images are by no means perfect and technically there are plenty of blunders, but each photo is taken with one aim and that is to show the dish , food and ingredients for what they are, without any over-styling and gimmicks. I use natural light as much as possible and a 60mm micro lenses with a simple no-cluttered approach. This was exactly the approach I took when photographing the images for this book; some images was taken especially for the book and some was adopted from the website.

After we launched the website in 2009, it wasn't long before it became a success, and a big one at that. We knew we'd created something special, but we also know we were already laying the foundations for something much bigger. Consequently, in early August 2010, we gave the British Larder a brand new home: the clicks were turned into bricks and we finally opened the doors to the British Larder, Suffolk.

Opposite: Mr. P working in the garden in summer

A taste of Suffolk on a plate

With the British Larder, Suffolk we brought our British Larder ethos of seasonal, local food to life and gave it a slogan of 'A taste of Suffolk on a Plate'. We lived and breathed this slogan as it became the embodiment of our proven success, and within just a couple of years it became an award-winning pub and restaurant.

Our philosophy of using fresh, seasonal ingredients and local produce from farmers, producers and suppliers located in and around our region to support the local economy, was at the heart of the pub's ethos. We wanted to keep things as close to home as possible.

The British Larder, Suffolk signed up to the Freedom Food's Simply Ask restaurant campaign, declaring the use of Freedom Food-approved ingredients and ensuring our commitment to ethical sustainability and animal welfare when sourcing our products.

We adopted a Bartering system at the pub. Where locals with a glut of fruit and vegetables from their own kitchen gardens could bring their wares and in exchange we provided tokens towards food or drink to be enjoyed at the pub and restaurant. We also made a big fuss of these local food heroes by naming them on the ever-changing menu as and when their produce was used. Consequently, we made many good friends over the years.

The best thing about bartering, and why I'm such an ambassador for this activity, is that it's all about what's in season at that time of the year and, most importantly, it's all local, British produce. It's the living and breathing epitome of seasonality and it's what we then do with these items in order to preserve and enjoy them during the coming months, that makes the journey so interesting and exciting.

In 2015 it was time for Mr. P and I to return to the Big Smoke. We sold the pub and website with its wonderful foundations and ethos to a local businessman who supported and loved our ethos and what it stood for.

We both continue to work as professional chefs in the food and drinks industry, focusing on product development and food innovation, championing British seasonal produce. *The British Larder: a Cookbook for All Seasons* is a documented biography of our life as ambassadors for seasonal British ingredients. This body of work was awarded the highest accolade by being awarded *Gourmand International Best Female Chef Author 2012.*

Opposite top: Suffolk-grown corn on the cob piled high on sale at the British Larder Suffolk farmers' market.

Opposite bottom: We adopted a bartering system at the British Larder Suffolk and a regular contributor was local food lover Lin Carter, AKA Lottie Lin. She often supplied us with her allotment-grown surplus herbs and radishes.

Recipe notes

Use large free-range or organic eggs unless otherwise specified.

I recommend buying and using organic or free-range Freedom Food-approved foods, including meat, poultry and fish, whenever possible.

Unsalted butter is used throughout unless otherwise specified.

Use full-fat (whole) milk unless otherwise specified. All other dairy products should also be full-fat unless otherwise specified.

For seasoning, use Maldon Sea Salt, if possible, or another good quality sea salt (perhaps locally produced), if you prefer.

Only use freshly cracked or milled black pepper and avoid pre-ground spices, as they quickly lose their essential oils. You will achieve a much better flavour in recipes by buying whole spices and grinding your own freshly.

The taste of chutneys, pickles, jams and preserves changes with time. Generally speaking, once made, I recommend storing jars of chutney and pickles for at least 1 week before opening, to allow the flavours time to merge, mingle and mellow slightly. I recommend that the chutneys and pickles can be stored in a cool, dry cupboard for up to about 6 months. In reality, if stored correctly, they will probably keep for much longer. Once opened, I recommend storing them in the fridge and using within 1 week.

Jams, marmalades and jellies can be eaten as soon as they are made, but they also keep well. I recommend storing them in a cool, dry cupboard for up to a year or so, and once opened, I recommend storing them in the fridge and using within 1 month.

With fruit curds, because they contain fresh eggs, these can be eaten as soon as they are made or they can be stored for up to 2–3 weeks in the fridge. Once opened, I recommend keeping them in the fridge and using within 3 days. Please refer to the individual recipes for more specific information.

Cook's notes

Sterilising Jars for Jams, Preserves, Chutneys, Pickles

When making homemade jams, chutneys, etc, sterilising the jars is one of the most crucial tasks and one where you should never cut corners. If you don't do this stage properly, you might find that all your hard work is quickly undone and becomes mouldy and ferments sooner than expected.

Preheat the oven to 100°C/Gas Mark ¼. Wash the chosen jars in hot soapy water, rinse thoroughly, then let them drain (do not dry them with a tea towel). Do the same with the utensils that you are planning to use to fill the jars with, for example, ladle/spoon and metal funnel. Place the damp jars, lids and utensils on a clean baking tray (try not to touch the jars and lids on the insides). Place them in the oven for 30-40 minutes to dry out completely and warm through. When you are ready to fill the jars, remove them from the oven, let the cooked jam or chutney cool slightly, then fill the warm, sterilised jars almost to the top. Never pour the hot jam/chutney into cold jars otherwise the jars are likely to crack. Cover the hot jam with wax discs (wax-side down) and cover with the lids (use vinegar-proof lids for chutneys and pickles), then leave to cool. Once cold, label and store as the recipe directs.

Choosing the Right Sugar for Your Jams and Preserves

Preserving sugar is a specialised white sugar made from sugar cane and sugar beet that is coarser than granulated sugar. It is used for making jams and marmalades with fruits that have a high natural pectin content. The larger sugar crystals dissolve slowly and prevent the mixture from catching to the pan so easily. They also create less scum on top of the boiling liquid, thus resulting in a clearer preserve. Jam sugar is a type of preserving sugar that contains added pectin to ensure a good set. It is ideal for jam and jelly-making and is especially good to use with fruits that have a lower natural pectin content, such as strawberries.

Agar Agar Powder

Agar agar powder is a natural gelling agent that is derived from seaweed (so it is suitable for vegetarians) and it is sometimes used instead of gelatine in some recipes. It is available as a white powder (or as threads) and can be found in most supermarkets or health food shops. Agar agar has a high melting point (it will tolerate heat above 83°C) and it should be dissolved in boiling liquid. Agar agar will collapse if it is stirred, shaken or disturbed before it has set completely. You may need to add more agar agar to get a firm set and it doesn't work in all recipes. For example, fruits and foods with a high acidic level will effect the agar agar and you will require more of it to set mixtures containing fruits such as strawberries and citrus fruits.

The following foods will not work with agar agar at all as they contain enzymes that do not agree with it. These include chocolate, raw spinach and fresh raw kiwi fruit, pineapple, mango, pawpaw (papaya), figs and peaches. You have a better chance if you cook the fruits and spinach first, or use cocoa powder instead of chocolate (white chocolate is OK to use with agar agar though, as technically it is not a chocolate).

As a general guide, use the ratio of ½ teaspoon (about 2.5g) agar agar powder to 250ml liquid.

Gelatine

Gelatine is a soluble gelling agent made from a protein derived from boiled pig's skin or beef or veal bones and connective tissues (so it is not suitable for vegetarians nor for people who have dietary restrictions based on their religion or customs). It is virtually colourless and tasteless and is widely used as a gelling or setting agent in cookery, both in savoury and sweet recipes, including jellies, mousses, terrines, cheesecakes and so on. Gelatine is available in powder form or as thin, clear leaves or sheets. Before use, gelatine should be soaked in a small amount of water to soften it, then it should be warmed gently to dissolve it. Powdered gelatine is sprinkled over the surface of cold water and left to soak before then being warmed and dissolved; gelatine leaves or sheets are soaked in cold water for a few minutes to soften and expand (this is called 'blooming') before being gently squeezed to remove the excess water and then added to warm liquid to dissolve.

Some fruits, including fresh raw pineapple (though canned pineapple is fine), pawpaw (papaya), melon and kiwi fruit cannot be used with gelatine as these fruits contain an enzyme that will break the gelatine down and prevent it from setting. However, gelatine will work successfully with these fruits if you cook them first and, for example, make the cooked fruit into a purée or extract the juice from the cooked fruit to make a jelly.

Gelatine sets firm when cold and melts completely at 35°C. Gelatine should only be warmed gently (to a temperature of over 35°C) until it is dissolved and it should not be boiled.

Once the liquid is cooled below 4°C, the gelatine mixture will set and become firm.

You can use powdered gelatine or leaves/sheets of gelatine in recipes and they are interchangeable. Two leaves/sheets of gelatine are equivalent to about 1 teaspoon (5g) powdered gelatine. As a general guide, use 1 leaf/sheet of gelatine for 100ml liquid to achieve a soft set (easy to turn out), or use 1 leaf/sheet of gelatine for 125ml liquid to achieve a wobbly set (for a dessert that you would serve in a glass, for example).

Yeast

I have specified using fresh yeast in all my yeasted-dough recipes. For me, fresh yeast has a distinct and preferable taste and I definitely prefer the baked results, so I would recommend using it if you can. Fresh yeast is easy to use and my preferred method is simply to rub it into the flour (or dry ingredients) before adding the rest of the ingredients and liquid. Fresh yeast is available from some bakers, delicatessens and larger supermarkets and also from some on-line suppliers (such as Shipton Mill). Remember that fresh yeast is alive (it is a living micro-organism), so buy it in small quantities, always keep it in the fridge and use it up fairly quickly – within 1 week. Fresh yeast can be frozen but the freezing process seems to effect the activeness of the yeast and you don't achieve such good results with frozen (defrosted) yeast, so I would always recommend using fresh yeast.

Personally, I prefer not to use fast-action/easy-blend dried yeast as I have had more disasters than successes with it and therefore cannot recommend it. However, I do use it successfully in one recipe in this book and that is in My Grandmother's Gooseberry Ginger Beer (see page 267), where it works perfectly in place of fresh yeast.

If you do find that fresh yeast is difficult to obtain, then you can substitute it for ordinary dried active yeast granules (this is different to fast-action/easy-blend dried yeast), if you wish, but remember to follow the packet instructions on how to use it. As a general guide, use half the quantity of dried yeast granules to the quantity of fresh yeast stated in each recipe, and always dissolve the dried yeast in the warm liquid (around blood temperature or 37°C) used in the recipe first (or according to the packet directions) to reactivate it, before combining it with the flour and the rest of the ingredients.

Gadgets

I am a bit of a gadget queen and this is all down to Ross (Mr. P) as he is the real gadget fanatic in this team. If it's new and it appeals, then he has to have it! I often then find myself quickly growing attached to the new gadget and consequently adopt it as my own. In this book, I use quite a few specialist tools and gadgets, such as a cream whipper, ice-cream maker, jam thermometer, pestle and mortar, mandolin, blowtorch, pasta machine, potato ricer and mincer. On this occasion, I have left a few out of this book that I'm well known for using and these include my beloved Thermomix, vacuum-packing machine, dehydrator and water bath. The reason for this is so that you are inspired to actually be able to cook all of the recipes in this book at home, without having to invest in a whole new array of kitchen gadgets and appliances!

A cream whipper is a metal or hard plastic reusable bottle or container fitted with a special lid and it is charged with nitrous oxide (N2O) gas pellets or cartridges. This is a specialist culinary piece of equipment available from good cook shops or on-line, but they are inexpensive enough for the home cook to have some fun with. With a cream whipper, the nitrous oxide gas is released into the sealed metal bottle or container – this blows gas into a liquid that contains a high fat content (which helps the liquid to set and keep its foamy, mousse-like texture). As the gas expands in the liquid, this also intensifies the flavour, so when you eat the cream, you will experience an interesting texture as well as a more intense flavour. The lid of the cream whipper can come with different styles of attachments/tubes where the culinary foam will be dispensed from, including a plain or star nozzle and sometimes a 'needle' attachment. In most cases, you will have to purchase the 'needle' attachment separately, and this is the finest attachment you can get for a cream whipper. It is used to inject foams into foods such as doughnuts. Make sure you use the correct attachment as specified in the recipe. I have purchased many of these attachments over the years and my advice is to buy the best quality you can afford. The cheaper versions do not always last or give you the correct result. For home use, I would recommend either investing in a 500ml or 1 litre cream whipper. Other sizes are available too. Before first use, carefully read through the usage instructions and always follow the safety advice given. The foam made using a cream whipper in some recipes or on restaurant menus is referred to as an Espuma (Spanish word for 'foam' or 'froth'), Culinary Foam or Air.

British Larder basics

The recipes that follow are just a few of the foundation recipes which you will see referred to later in the book. I hope they serve you well time and again!

Shortcrust Pastry

Makes about 500g

280g plain flour
a pinch of sea salt
140g unsalted butter
80ml ice-cold water

Sift the flour and salt into a bowl. Using your fingertips, lightly rub the butter into the flour until the mixture resembles fine breadcrumbs.

Gradually add the water, stirring with a round-bladed knife, until the mixture begins to come together. Collect the dough together to form a ball. Knead lightly on a lightly floured work surface (but do not overwork the dough), then wrap in cling film and leave to rest in the fridge for 30 minutes before rolling out.

Cook's Note
This recipe can easily be doubled and one half frozen for later use. Double the recipe, divide the pastry in half and wrap each portion in cling film, then chill in the fridge. Freeze the pastry you are not using and use within 3 months. Defrost overnight in the fridge before use.

Sweet Shortcrust Pastry

Makes about 600g

175g unsalted butter, softened
75g caster sugar
1 vanilla pod, split in half lengthways
  and seeds scraped out (optional)
a pinch of table salt
2 eggs, beaten
300g plain flour

Put the butter, sugar, vanilla seeds, if using, and the salt into the bowl of an electric stand mixer and beat together until fluffy and pale in colour. Slowly add the beaten eggs, a little at a time, beating well after each addition. Sift the flour over the creamed mixture, then slowly mix in the flour until the pastry comes together, being careful not to over mix. (If you prefer, the pastry can be made by hand without a mixer, using a wooden spoon to beat and combine the ingredients, as directed.)

Turn the pastry on to a lightly floured work surface, but do not knead the pastry, just push it together. This recipe makes about 600g pastry and you can either use it all or freeze some to use at a later date. It's unwise to make this recipe in a smaller quantity and you can easily freeze half of it (or as much as you have leftover) to use another time.

Wrap the pastry in cling film (either wrap it as one piece, or divide it into two pieces and wrap each piece separately) and then leave it to rest in the fridge for 30 minutes before rolling out. (I like to shape the pastry into flat, even square(s) so that they fit comfortably into my fridge or freezer.) Freeze the pastry you are not using and use within 3 months. Defrost overnight in the fridge before use.

Thick Béchamel Sauce

Makes about 250ml

200ml milk
¼ onion, peeled
2 cloves
a sprig of fresh parsley
30g unsalted butter
30g plain flour
sea salt and freshly cracked black pepper

Put the milk, onion, cloves and parsley in a small pan and bring to the boil over a low heat, then simmer for 2 minutes. Remove from the heat and leave to infuse for 10 minutes, then strain through a fine sieve, reserving the infused milk and discarding the onion, cloves and parsley.

Melt the butter in a saucepan, stir in the flour to form a thick paste (called a 'roux') and then cook gently, stirring, for about 2 minutes or until the roux is cooked but not coloured. Remove from the heat and gradually whisk in the infused milk, then season with salt and pepper.

Return to the heat and cook, stirring continuously, for about 5 minutes or until the sauce is thickened and smooth (the béchamel sauce will be thick – see Cook's Note). Simmer gently for a further 2-3 minutes. Remove from the heat and use immediately, or pour into a heatproof bowl, cover the surface with a piece of greaseproof paper (to prevent a skin from forming) and leave to cool, then use cold as required.

Cook's Note
To make a thinner béchamel sauce, simply add more milk to your taste – you can use up to 300-400ml milk in total. Obviously the volume of sauce made will increase, depending on how much extra milk you use.

Classic Vinaigrette

Makes about 210ml

50ml white wine vinegar or cider vinegar
2 heaped teaspoons Dijon or wholegrain mustard
a pinch of caster sugar
150ml sunflower, groundnut or rapeseed oil
sea salt and freshly cracked black pepper

Measure all the ingredients into a clean, screw-topped jam jar or a Kilner-type jar. Seal the jar tightly and shake vigorously to combine, then serve immediately or store in the fridge and use within 1 week. If storing, shake the vinaigrette just before serving.

White Chicken Stock

Makes about 2 litres

1kg chicken bones (mixed raw or cooked chicken carcasses and chicken wings)
3 litres cold water
¼ teaspoon sea salt
8 ice cubes
1 large onion, peeled and cut into 6 wedges
1 large leek, white part only, washed and cut into 3 pieces
2 sticks celery, each cut into 3 shorter lengths
2 bay leaves
2 large sprigs of fresh thyme
2 large sprigs of fresh parsley
2 cloves garlic, lightly crushed
1 teaspoon coriander seeds
5 white peppercorns

Place the chicken bones in a large stock pot and add the water and salt. Cover and bring to the boil over a high heat, then reduce the heat to a simmer, remove the lid and skim off any scum from the surface. Simmer for 5 minutes, then add the ice cubes – this will shock the stock and the fat particles will float to the surface where you can then easily skim them off (this helps to make a clear fat-free stock).

Once all the fat is removed and the stock is simmering again, add the onion, leek, celery, bay leaves, thyme and parsley sprigs, garlic, coriander seeds and peppercorns. Cover the pan and bring the mixture back to the boil over a high heat, then reduce the heat to a gentle simmer, remove the lid and skim off any scum from the surface. Simmer the stock very gently for about 1½ hours or until it becomes a rich colour (golden yellow but still clear) and well flavoured, skimming off any scum occasionally (do not boil the stock too fast as this will make it cloudy).

Remove from the heat and leave the stock to cool at room temperature for 1 hour, to enable the flavours to infuse further. Pass the stock through a fine sieve lined with muslin cloth into a bowl or suitable container, leave to cool, then cover and chill in the fridge. Use as required. Keep refrigerated for up to 3 days or freeze in batches for up to 3 months. To use the frozen stock, defrost it in the fridge overnight, then use as required.

Brown Chicken Stock

Makes about 2 litres

1.2kg raw or cooked chicken bones or carcasses
1 tablespoon rapeseed oil
1 large onion, peeled and cut into 6 wedges
1 carrot, cut into 3 chunks
1 large leek, white part only, washed and cut into 3 pieces
2 sticks celery, each cut into 3 shorter lengths
2 cloves garlic, lightly crushed
¼ teaspoon sea salt
1 tablespoon tomato purée
a pinch of caster sugar
2 bay leaves
2 large sprigs of fresh thyme
2 large sprigs of fresh parsley
1 teaspoon coriander seeds
5 black peppercorns
3 litres cold water
8 ice cubes

Preheat the oven to 230°C/Gas Mark 8. Place the bones or carcasses in a roasting tin and roast in the oven for 30-40 minutes or until deep golden brown but not burnt (if you are using leftover bones or carcasses from cooked chicken, you will only need to roast the bones for 25-30 minutes). Remove from the oven and set aside.

Heat the rapeseed oil in a large stock pot, add the onion, carrot, leek, celery, garlic and salt and sauté over a high heat for 6-8 minutes or until golden brown. Add the tomato purée and sugar and cook for a further 2 minutes or until the tomato purée is lightly toasted, stirring continuously to prevent the purée from sticking to the base of the pan and turning bitter. Add the roasted bones, along with the bay leaves, thyme and parsley sprigs, coriander seeds and peppercorns, then add the water, cover the pan and bring the mixture to the boil over a high heat. Once the mixture is boiling, reduce the heat to a simmer, remove the lid and skim off any scum from the surface. Simmer for 5 minutes, then add the ice cubes – this will shock the stock and the fat particles will float to the surface where you can then easily skim them off (this helps to make a clear fat-free stock).

Once all the fat is removed, cover the pan and bring the mixture back to the boil over a high heat, then reduce the heat to a gentle simmer, remove the lid and skim off any scum from the surface. Simmer the stock very gently for about 1½ hours or until it becomes a rich colour (light golden brown but still clear) and well flavoured, skimming off any scum occasionally (do not boil the stock too fast as this will make it cloudy).

Remove from the heat and leave the stock to cool at room temperature for 1 hour, to enable the flavours to infuse further. Pass the stock through a fine sieve lined with muslin cloth into a bowl or suitable container, leave to cool, then cover and chill in the fridge. Use as required. Keep refrigerated for up to 3 days or freeze in batches for up to 3 months. To use the frozen stock, defrost it in the fridge overnight, then use as required.

Beef Stock

Makes about 2 litres

1.2kg raw or cooked beef bones (ask your butcher to cut these into smaller pieces, about 10cm in size) (see Cook's Note)
1 tablespoon rapeseed oil
1 large onion, peeled and cut into 6 wedges
1 carrot, cut into 3 chunks
1 large leek, white part only, washed and cut into 3 pieces
2 sticks celery, each cut into 3 shorter lengths
2 cloves garlic, lightly crushed
¼ teaspoon sea salt
2 tablespoons tomato purée
½ teaspoon caster sugar
2 bay leaves
2 large sprigs of fresh thyme
1 teaspoon coriander seeds
5 black peppercorns
4.5 litres cold water
8 ice cubes

Preheat the oven to 230°C/Gas Mark 8. Place the bones in a roasting tin and roast in the oven for 40-50 minutes or until deep golden brown but not burnt (if you are using leftover bones from cooked beef, you will only need to roast the bones for 25-35 minutes). Remove from the oven and set aside.

Heat the rapeseed oil in a large stock pot, add the onion, carrot, leek, celery, garlic and salt and sauté over a high heat for 6-8 minutes or until golden brown. Add the tomato purée and sugar and cook for a further 2 minutes or until the tomato purée is lightly toasted, stirring continuously to prevent the purée from sticking to the base of the pan and turning bitter. Add the roasted bones, along with the bay leaves, thyme, coriander seeds and peppercorns, then add 3 litres of the water, cover the pan and bring the mixture to the boil over a high heat. Once the mixture is boiling, reduce the heat to a simmer, remove the lid and skim off any scum from the surface. Simmer for 5 minutes, then add the ice cubes – this will shock the stock and the fat particles will float to the surface where you can then easily skim them off (this helps to make a clear fat free stock).

(continued on page 22)

(continued from page 21)

Once all the fat is removed, cover the pan and bring the mixture back to the boil over a high heat, then reduce the heat to a gentle simmer, remove the lid and skim off any scum from the surface. Simmer the stock very gently for about 2 hours or until it becomes a rich colour, skimming off any scum occasionally (do not boil the stock too fast as this will make it cloudy). Add the remaining water, then bring the stock back to a gentle simmer and simmer very gently for a further hour or so to create a dark, rich, meaty, brown-coloured stock.

Remove from the heat and leave the stock to cool at room temperature for 1 hour, to enable the flavours to infuse further. Pass the stock through a fine sieve lined with muslin cloth into a bowl or suitable container, leave to cool, then cover and chill in the fridge. Use as required. Keep refrigerated for up to 3 days or freeze in batches for up to 3 months. To use the frozen stock, defrost it in the fridge overnight, then use as required.

Cook's Note
Veal or lamb bones can be used instead of beef bones to make either a veal or lamb stock. Simply follow the recipe above, but for the lamb stock, roast the raw lamb bones in the oven for 30-40 minutes (or roast for 20-30 minutes, if you are using cooked lamb bones). The roasting times for veal bones are the same as for the beef bones.

Vegetable Stock

Makes about 2 litres

2 carrots, each cut into 3 chunks
2 onions, peeled and each cut into 6 wedges
1 leek, washed and cut into 6 pieces
2 celery sticks, each cut into 6 shorter lengths
1 small fennel bulb (if in season), trimmed and cut into 6 pieces
2 cloves garlic, lightly crushed
3 bay leaves
2 large sprigs of fresh thyme
2 large sprigs of fresh parsley
1 teaspoon coriander seeds
3 of each white, black and pink peppercorns
½ teaspoon sea salt
3 litres cold water
1 lemon

Place all the ingredients, except the lemon, in a large stock pot. Cover the pan and bring the mixture to the boil over a high heat, then reduce the heat to a gentle simmer. Remove the lid and cook very gently for about 30 minutes or until it becomes a golden-coloured, clear, rich-flavoured stock, skimming off any scum from the surface occasionally.

Remove the pan from the heat. Cut the lemon in half, squeeze the juice into the hot stock and then add the lemon halves. Leave the stock to cool and infuse at room temperature for 1 hour.

Pass the stock through a fine sieve lined with muslin cloth into a bowl or suitable container, leave to cool, then cover and chill in the fridge. Use as required. Keep refrigerated for up to 3 days or freeze in batches for up to 3 months. To use the frozen stock, defrost it in the fridge overnight, then use as required.

Roasted Game Stock

Makes about 2 litres

1.2kg raw or cooked bird bones or carcasses or game bones (such as pheasant, partridge, wild duck, venison, rabbit, etc)
1 tablespoon rapeseed oil
1 large onion, peeled and cut into 6 wedges
1 carrot, cut into 3 chunks
1 large leek, white part only, washed and cut into 3 pieces
2 sticks celery, each cut into 3 shorter lengths
2 cloves garlic, lightly crushed
¼ teaspoon sea salt
2 bay leaves
2 large sprigs of fresh thyme
1 teaspoon coriander seeds
5 black peppercorns
3 litres cold water
8 ice cubes

Preheat the oven to 230°C/Gas Mark 8. Place the bones or carcasses in a roasting tin and roast in the oven for 30-40 minutes or until deep golden brown but not burnt (if you are using leftover cooked bird bones or carcasses or bones from cooked game, you will only need to roast the bones for 25-30 minutes). Remove from the oven and set aside.

Heat the rapeseed oil in a large stock pot, add the onion, carrot, leek, celery, garlic and salt and sauté over a high heat for 6-8 minutes or until golden brown. Add the roasted bones, along with the bay leaves, thyme sprigs, coriander seeds and peppercorns, then add the water, cover the pan and bring the mixture to the boil over a high heat. Once the mixture is boiling, reduce the heat to a simmer, remove the lid and skim off any scum from the surface. Simmer for 5 minutes, then add the ice cubes – this will shock the stock and the fat particles will float to the surface where you can then easily skim them off (this helps to make a clear fat-free stock).

Once all the fat is removed, cover the pan and bring the mixture back to the boil over a high heat, then reduce the heat to a gentle simmer, remove the lid and skim off any scum from the surface. Simmer the stock very gently for about 1½ hours or until it becomes a rich colour (light golden brown but still clear) and well flavoured, skimming off any scum occasionally (do not boil the stock too fast as this will make it cloudy).

Remove from the heat and leave the stock to cool at room temperature for 1 hour, to enable the flavours to infuse further. Pass the stock through a fine sieve lined with muslin cloth into a bowl or suitable container, leave to cool, then cover and chill in the fridge. Use as required. Keep refrigerated for up to 3 days or freeze in batches for up to 3 months. To use the frozen stock, defrost it in the fridge overnight, then use as required.

The British Larder | January

January marks the beginning of a brand new year, and it's that inevitable time of year where New Year's resolutions are made and then consequently broken in the blink of an eye! Even thought it's cold, damp and grey outside, the body and mind wishes for refreshing, light and healthy dishes; however, the heart and soul longs for hearty recipes that will help to conquer the winter blues.

Rhubarb

The season delivers an abundance of colour, from the multicoloured feathers of the plethora of British game, to the bright colours from imports such as the jewel-like seeds of pomegranates and the vivid colour of Seville oranges. With our own home-grown fresh fruits being on the lighter side, with not many to choose from at this time of year, imported tropical fruits come into their own. January delivers some culinary delights, with the prospect of forced rhubarb coming into season by the middle of the month. Freshly dug, punchy horseradish and a marvellous selection of roots and tubers, such as celeriac, turnips and Jerusalem artichokes, give the home cook plenty of tasty ingredients to get creative with. The game season is slowly coming to an end as we see the last of the pheasants and wild ducks. Every home cook should try to cook game at least once or twice per season. It's one of the very few ingredients that remains strictly seasonal and this makes it so much more exciting when the new season's game arrives.

Season's best during January...

Apples, Bananas, Beetroot, Blood Oranges, Brill, Brussels Sprouts, Cabbages, Cauliflowers, Celery, Celeriac, Chickweed, Chicory, Clams, Clementines, Cockles, Cod, Duck, Golden Plover, Guinea Fowl, Haddock, Hake, Halibut, Hare, Hazelnuts, Horseradish, Jerusalem Artichokes, John Dory, Kale, Leeks, Lemons, Lemon Sole, Monkfish, Mussels, Oranges, Oysters, Parsnips, Partridges, Passion Fruit, Pears, Pheasant, Pineapples, Pomegranates, Potatoes (main crop), Rhubarb (forced), Salsify, Seville Oranges, Shallots, Skate, Teal, Truffles (black and white), Turbot, Turkey, Turnips, Venison, Walnuts, Widgeon, Winkles, Woodcock.

My culinary rituals for January...

The beginning of a new year feels like life has given us a second chance. Whatever your New Year's resolutions might be, one of mine is usually to capture and savour the best of each season. This usually refers to frugal preserving and getting snappy happy with my camera to take lots of new images for my food library.

Making marmalade

Seville oranges come into season during January, but their availability is limited to a short period only. Seville oranges, also known as bitter oranges, are slightly smaller than ordinary oranges. They are very tart and bitter and originate from the Southern province of Seville in Spain. Seville oranges are perfect and the best for making marmalade and they kick off the new year with a bang in the kitchen. After the craziness of the festive season, making marmalade almost feels like a type of therapy, so, during the month of January, I typically prepare a whole year's supply of Seville orange marmalade. While working with this fantastic ingredient, other recipes evolve and add to the splendour of my January seasonal culinary calendar, in my frantic quest to preserve the best the season has to offer.

Try this quick **Seville Orange Vinaigrette** that will go extremely well with any pan-fried fresh fish or perhaps drizzled over a chicory salad. Use a small, clean glass jar with a tight-fitting lid to mix this vinaigrette. Measure 2 teaspoons Dijon mustard, finely grated zest and juice of 2 Seville oranges, 1 tablespoon soy sauce, 2 teaspoons runny orange blossom honey, 100ml rapeseed oil, and sea salt and freshly cracked black pepper to taste, into the jar, secure the lid and shake vigorously for 30 seconds. Taste and adjust the seasoning, if necessary. Use what you need immediately, then replace the lid and keep the rest in the fridge for up to 1 week. Serves 4–6.

Blood oranges

Blood oranges are a variety of orange that have an unusual red-coloured flesh. They are smaller in size than ordinary oranges. The red-coloured flesh is due to the presence of anthocyanins – pigments that are usually found in flowers, but rarely found in fruits, apart from in this particular variety of orange.

For a refreshing and easy **Blood Orange Granita**, measure 500ml freshly squeezed blood orange juice into a small saucepan, add 50g caster sugar and dissolve the sugar over a low heat. Bring briefly to the boil and simmer for 1 minute. Remove from the heat and add the juice of ½ lemon, then transfer the mixture to a 1 litre shallow, freezer-proof container, cover and place in the freezer. After 2 hours, use a fork to stir and break up the ice crystals, then return to the freezer for a further 2 hours. Repeat this process 3 more times. Keep frozen until ready to serve. Serves 4–6.

Preserving the smell of fresh truffles

I keep fresh black truffles in a jar of dry pearl barley to preserve them for as long as possible. We use a lot of pearl

Preserving the smell of fresh truffles

Jerusalem artichokes

barley and cook it with partridge or pheasant, and the truffles add a subtle flavour to the barley. At the same time, the truffles remain dry and keep for longer as the possibility of mouldy truffles is reduced. This can also be done with risotto rice instead of pearl barley. Remember that truffles are a breathing fungus that will absorb liquid easily, so they can go off in a wink.

Walnuts

As the fresh walnut season is coming to an end, gather as many as you can find. Remove them from their shells and freeze the nuts in freezer bags or suitable covered containers. This will stop them going rancid too quickly. You can then simply defrost and use them as required (or use the walnuts from frozen, depending on what you are using them for).

British Larder Heroes

Duck

Farmed ducks are available all year round, but the wild species such as Mallard, Teal and Widgeon are only in season between September and January (although many gamekeepers advise that the season starts properly in October, once the ducks have eaten more and fattened up a bit, otherwise the meat will be very lean). Britain is well known for producing some of the world's finest eating ducks, with our prize home-produced species, so it's incredibly important that we choose the best, not only for the eating quality, but also from a welfare point of view. Aylesbury ducks from Buckinghamshire are perhaps the most widely known, as they have been bred since the 18th century. Pure Aylesbury duck is prized for its tenderness and less stringy meat, but with the introduction of Peking ducks during the 19th century, people started to cross breed. Aylesbury ducks are less fatty than Peking ducks and are also good egg layers, but they are becoming less easy to find for eating. Goosenargh ducks from Lancashire, with their fairytale white feathers and yellow beaks, are a cross between the Aylesbury and Peking duck. They are ideal for the table as there is a good balance of meat to bone on the birds. Gressingham ducks from East Anglia are a cross between wild Mallard and Peking ducks. As duck has a natural thick layer of fat, when cooking it's important to put the breast fat-side down in a dry pan with no added oil, to allow the fat to render well. This will ensure a crisp golden layer of fat and the meat will be moist and tender. If you roast a whole duck, reserve the fat that comes from roasting the bird and pass it through a fine sieve into a sterilised jar, then cover, cool and keep in the fridge for up to 2 weeks. Duck fat is great for roasting potatoes as it will give them a golden brown crisp outside and make them extra delicious.

Jerusalem artichokes

Jerusalem Artichokes are a member of the sunflower family and they are also known as the sunchoke or earth apple. The name is very misleading as it's not really an artichoke at all – it's a tuber, and if left alone, will grow out of control. Some farmers plant Jerusalem artichokes for conservation purposes and leave the fields for wildlife to live and progress. The taste is similar to a water chestnut and contains the carbohydrate inulin (not insulin) instead of starch. For this reason, Jerusalem artichokes are an important source of fructose for the food and pharmaceutical industry. Many people stay clear of Jerusalem artichokes as they have an undesired effect on the digestive system; however, I love them and find them a fascinating ingredient that pairs up unbelievably well with many different ingredients. If Jerusalem artichokes are eaten raw, this decreases the unwanted side affects that many dislike about them. Try grating a few raw Jerusalem artichokes into a simmering stew – once cooked, they will give the stew a creamy texture with an enriched flavour.

Or are you perhaps bored of mashed potato and in need of a bit of culinary inspiration to jazz up your 'sausage and mash supper'? This tasty **Jerusalem Artichoke Crush** recipe is the perfect seasonal tonic for the January blues. Peel 500g Jerusalem artichokes and cut into 1cm thick slices, then place in a saucepan, cover with cold water and season generously with sea salt. Bring to the boil, then cook for about 10 minutes or until the artichokes are cooked and tender. Drain well and return to the pan, then crush them lightly with a potato masher. Add 25g cold unsalted butter, then fold in 1 tablespoon wholegrain mustard and a handful of chopped fresh flat-leaf parsley and season to taste with sea salt and freshly cracked black pepper. Serves 2.

Salsify

Salsify is also known as the oyster plant – it gets this peculiar name from the fact that it has an oyster-like flavour once cooked. Salsify is a perennial plant from the sunflower family and is cultivated as a root vegetable. The roots are generally muddy and no amount of washing and scrubbing will remove all the dirt, so the best way to deal with salsify is a large, clean kitchen sink, a vegetable peeler and a large container of water with the squeezed juice of a lemon, plus the squeezed lemon halves, added to the water. Once peeled, the creamy white interior of the salsify oxidises quickly, so for the best results, place the peeled salsify sticks immediately in the lemon (acidulated) water to prevent browning. Once all the muddy peelings are removed, rinse the peeled salsify under cold running water and drain. Cook the salsify in a pan containing plenty of water with the juice of 1 lemon

Salsify

added (the acid will help the salsify to retain its creamy white colour). Salsify naturally pairs well with fish, but it tastes just as good with white meats such as chicken, turkey and pork.

This easy and tasty recipe for **Salsify and Smoked Mackerel Cakes** is perfect for a light lunch for 2, and it's an ideal way to use up leftover cooked salsify. Peel 400g salsify, add it to a pan of cold water with the juice of 1 lemon, season with sea salt and bring to the boil, then cook for 8–10 minutes or until cooked and tender. Drain well, then place the warm salsify in a large mixing bowl and mash with a fork. Add 1 egg, 125g flaked smoked mackerel fillet, 1 finely sliced spring onion, 1 tablespoon capers (drained and chopped), 1 tablespoon plain flour (sprinkled over the mixture) and 1 tablespoon chopped fresh mixed soft herbs such as chervil, tarragon and parsley, and mix together well. Add the finely grated zest and juice of 1 lime and season to taste with sea salt and fleshly cracked black pepper. Shape the mixture into 4–6 round fishcakes (each about 5cm in diameter), then dip each fishcake into plain flour seasoned with salt and pepper. Heat a dash of sunflower oil in a non-stick frying pan and fry the fishcakes over a medium heat for 3–4 minutes on each side or until golden, turning once. Serve immediately with a fresh chicory salad and a glass of chilled Chardonnay.

Venison

Venison is a descriptive name for animals from the Cervidae (deer) family. The most common varieties here in the UK are fallow, red, roe, sika and muntjac. It does depend on the species, but in general, venison meat has a strong and unique, wild, gamey taste with a coarse texture and grain. The colour of the meat has a deep dark red to almost black red colour, but again this depends on the species. Over the years, venison has become more acceptable and easier to come by. Venison meat is lean, high in protein and lower in cholesterol than grain-fed commercially reared animals such as beef cattle and lambs. Because venison is very lean, it makes it slightly more difficult to cook and perhaps a bit more daunting for the home cook, but follow these guidelines and hopefully this will give you enough confidence to give it a try.

Venison Cooking Guidelines
Prime cuts such as loin, haunch (leg) and saddle should be cooked quickly like beefsteak – the best way is to cook them to medium-rare. The tougher parts such as neck, shoulder, foreleg, ribs and shank require a long, slow cooking time at a low temperature in a good quality stock to prevent the meat from drying out and becoming stringy.

Woodcock

The woodcock is the largest of the wading birds, with a plump body, short legs and long beak. During the autumn, these migrant birds from Russia and Finland make their way to Britain to spend the warmer winters here. The woodcock is a delicacy and is very expensive. Cooking the woodcock with its guts and everything else intact is an age-old tradition and a stalker's delicacy.

For **Classic Roasted Woodcock** serving 1 woodcock per person, preheat the oven to 200°C/Gas Mark 6. Pluck each woodcock, keeping the head on, then press the legs and wings together, draw the head round and use the beak to skewer through the legs and wings to keep it all in place. Brush each bird with melted unsalted butter, season with sea salt and freshly cracked black pepper and lay 2 rashers of fatty smoked streaky bacon over the breasts, tucking the bacon in. Roast the prepared bird(s) in the oven for 20–25 minutes or until cooked and golden brown. Remove from the oven and leave to rest for 2 minutes. Remove the head of each bird and cut the cooked bird in half, then cut the head in half and scoop the soft pâté-like meat out and spread it on to toasted croûtons. Eat like a king and enjoy!

Salsify and Black Truffle Rösti with Duck Eggs

Fresh truffle is a true seasonal gem, a gift from Mother Nature. Its pungent smell fills a room with fragrance like no other. This complex fungus is a seasonal prized ingredient and one that most chefs dream of working with. As it's such a complex and powerful taste, simplicity is required when using truffles in your cooking. Their taste lends itself to being paired with basic ingredients such as eggs and rice.

I could not imagine a single day without eggs in my larder – they are almost as important as milk and butter. It feels as if I can achieve anything with eggs, from a simple meal to a glorious cake. The only question is what kind of egg to use? Goose eggs, duck eggs, quail's eggs and hen's eggs are readily available and one can have plenty of fun choosing different eggs for different dishes. I take immense pride in the quality of ingredients that I buy – there is without a shadow of a doubt, a taste and quality difference between free-range and organic eggs over cage eggs. Eggs are so versatile – for this recipe, the eggs are simply poached.

Serves 4 as a starter or light lunch

juice of 1 lemon
500g salsify
3 tablespoons unsalted butter
1 large onion, sliced
1 clove garlic, crushed
200g Desiree potatoes, peeled
1 teaspoon chopped fresh chervil
1 tablespoon white wine vinegar
4 duck eggs
sea salt and freshly cracked black pepper
1 small fresh black truffle and baby or mini/micro salad leaves, to serve

For the white bean purée

200g dried white beans (such as haricot beans), soaked overnight in cold water
100ml double cream
1 teaspoon truffle oil

For the kale pesto

100g kale, stalks removed
1 clove garlic, crushed
1 tablespoon toasted pine nuts
20g finely grated fresh Parmesan cheese
1 teaspoon Dijon mustard
60ml rapeseed oil

Make the white bean purée. Rinse the soaked white beans in fresh cold water and drain, then place the beans in a saucepan. Cover with plenty of cold water and bring up to a gentle simmer, then cook, uncovered, for 30–40 minutes or until soft (don't add any salt to the water as this will toughen the skins). Once cooked, drain well, then place in a blender with the cream and blend until smooth. Season to taste with salt and pepper, then add the truffle oil. Keep warm, or if making in advance, cool, then chill in the fridge overnight and reheat before serving.

Next, make the kale pesto. Cook the kale in a pan of boiling water for 1–2 minutes or until very soft, then drain well. Put the kale into a blender with the garlic, the pine nuts, Parmesan cheese, mustard, rapeseed oil and a pinch of salt and pepper and blend together until smooth. Taste and adjust the seasoning, if necessary. If the pesto is a bit thick, add an extra dash of rapeseed oil. Transfer to a bowl, then cover and chill until needed.

For the rösti, fill a bowl with cold water and add half of the lemon juice. Peel the salsify, then dip it into the bowl of acidulated water (to prevent browning), then drain and rinse. Cut the salsify into 5–7cm batons, place it in a saucepan, cover with cold water, then add salt and the remaining lemon juice. Bring to the boil and simmer for 8–10 minutes or until tender. Drain, then finely slice 200g of the cooked salsify, and keep the rest for garnishing the plates.

Melt 1 tablespoon of butter in a pan and sauté the onion and garlic, with salt and pepper added, for 5–6 minutes or until the onion is cooked and golden. Using a slotted spoon, transfer the cooked onions to a bowl. Coarsely grate the peeled potatoes and add to the onions, together with the finely sliced cooked salsify, the chervil and salt and pepper.

Heat another tablespoon of butter in a large, non-stick frying pan and, once the butter is foaming, using half of the potato rösti mixture, spoon 4 separate large spoonfuls of the mixture into the pan, keeping each spoonful separate, to make 4 individual rösti. Cook for about 5 minutes or until golden brown on one side, then flip them over and cook the other side for a further 5 minutes or so until golden brown. If the rösti are colouring a bit too quickly, reduce the heat to very low to ensure they are fully cooked. Drain the rösti on kitchen paper, then transfer to a plate and keep warm. Repeat with the remaining potato mixture to make 8 rösti in total.

Just before serving, poach the eggs. Fill a large, deep saucepan with water, add the white wine vinegar and bring to the boil. Crack the eggs into 4 individual cups. Once the water is gently boiling, carefully slide the eggs into the boiling water, one at a time, using a metal spoon to gently turn each egg over 2 or 3 times to 'wrap' the white around the yolk, and poach until the whites are set and the yolks are still soft (about 3–4 minutes).

Carefully remove the poached eggs using a slotted spoon.

Meanwhile, melt the remaining butter in a pan and sauté the reserved salsify batons, with salt and pepper added, for 2–3 minutes or until golden brown, stirring frequently. Drain on kitchen paper. Gently reheat the white bean purée in a small pan until piping hot.

To serve, spoon some white bean purée on to each serving plate, then place 2 rösti on top, followed by a poached egg. Arrange the sautéed salsify around the edge, then drop a few dollops of the kale pesto around each plate. Thinly slice the fresh truffle over the top and scatter with a few salad leaves. Serve.

Jerusalem Artichoke and Roasted Garlic Soup

A cup of sunchoke soup is enough to kiss the winter blues away. This recipe is dedicated to a dear friend of mine, Abigail from Sotby in Lincolnshire. Her father, Mr Lawson, is a farmer who grows Jerusalem artichokes as part of a conservation project on his farm. I regularly receive a bag filled with Sotby's 'chokes and I have made many tasty recipes with them.

As Jerusalem artichokes have a robust and strong flavour, they pair easily with other robust flavours, such as garlic. By roasting the garlic in the oven until soft and sweet, it adds a natural sweetness and intensity to the soup. My theory is that this soup tastes even better the following day, so why not make a double batch to test my theory?!

Serves 4 as a starter or light lunch

½ bulb of garlic, cut in half widthways
1 teaspoon soft light brown sugar
500g Jerusalem artichokes
1 tablespoon unsalted butter
1 banana shallot, sliced
50ml brandy, Madeira or white wine
1.2 litres good quality vegetable or white chicken stock
sea salt and freshly cracked black pepper
fresh thyme leaves and a drizzle of rapeseed oil, to garnish

Preheat the oven to 180°C/Gas Mark 4. Place the garlic halves on a piece of foil, season the cut-sides with salt and pepper, then sprinkle over the sugar and 1 tablespoon of water. Wrap the garlic loosely, transfer to a baking tray and roast in the oven for 25–35 minutes – the garlic will soften, become golden in colour and develop a sweet taste. Remove from the oven and set aside to cool, then squeeze the soft garlic pulp out of the skins.

Peel and slice the Jerusalem artichokes. Melt the butter in a large saucepan and, once the butter starts to foam, add the shallot, garlic pulp and Jerusalem artichokes, together with a little salt and pepper. Sauté over a low heat for 10–12 minutes or until golden brown – the darker the colour of the artichokes and onions, the more intense the flavour will be.

Pour the brandy into the pan and let it bubble, stirring and scraping the base of the pan with a wooden spoon to deglaze it. Cook until the caramelised bits dissolve and the brandy is reduced to a coating syrup. Add the stock and bring slowly to the boil, then cover and simmer gently for 25–30 minutes or until the artichokes are very tender and the soup is thick and a rich, deep colour.

Carefully transfer the soup to a blender and purée until very smooth. Return to the pan and reheat gently, then taste and adjust the seasoning, if necessary.

Serve hot in bowls, garnished with thyme leaves and a drizzle of rapeseed oil. Serve with plenty of fresh crusty bread.

Cook's Notes
Even though this soup is silky and creamy, it does not contain any cream and therefore is the perfect low-fat recipe. However, if you would like to tame the garlic flavour slightly, stir in a little single cream or crème fraîche, just before serving.

You may like to garnish this soup with Jerusalem Artichoke Crisps. See Pan-Roasted Cod with Jerusalem Artichokes recipe on page 40 for details on how to make these crisps.

Duck Pastrami with Chicory and Blood Orange Jelly

The creation of this dish is a labour of love, but it's well worth all the effort. The combination of the citrusy sweetness of the blood oranges and the bitter crunch of the chicory, creates the perfect accompaniment to balance the richness of the duck, especially cold duck that is turned into classic pastrami. It's a festive plate of food, with its vibrant seasonal colours and flavours, and it is fit for a party or any special occasion.

Personally, I lose interest in dishes with a monotone texture, hence when developing recipes I'm looking to combine different textures as well as interesting flavours, to keep the mind and taste buds engaged until the last mouthful. This dish achieves all of that perfectly.

Serves 6 as a starter or light lunch

For the duck pastrami

2 large duck breasts (about 170g each), with fat on
1 tablespoon coriander seeds
½ teaspoon black peppercorns
12 dried juniper berries
25g sea salt
50g soft dark brown sugar
1 clove garlic, peeled
1 tablespoon chopped fresh thyme leaves
300g long-grain white rice
100ml cold water
3 sprigs of fresh thyme

For the blood orange and balsamic jelly

280ml freshly squeezed blood orange juice
4 teaspoons balsamic vinegar
¼ teaspoon agar agar powder (see page 16)

For the medjool date purée

200g medjool dates, stones removed
1 tablespoon olive oil
1 teaspoon sherry vinegar
sea salt and freshly cracked black pepper

For the Jerusalem artichoke purée

300g Jerusalem artichokes
20g unsalted butter
50ml double cream

To serve

2 heads white chicory, washed, drained and separated into leaves
1 blood orange, peeled and segmented
fresh coriander cress

First, prepare the duck pastrami. Score the fat-side of the duck breasts with a sharp knife, being careful not to cut all the way through to the flesh. Remove and discard the silver skin or thin membrane from the underside of each breast.

Use a pestle and mortar to crush the coriander seeds, peppercorns, 6 of the juniper berries, the salt, brown sugar, garlic and chopped thyme together to form a paste. Rub the paste into the duck breasts, massaging it into the meat and fat. Place the duck breasts on a plate, cover and leave to marinate in the fridge for 12 hours or overnight, to allow the flavours to develop, before smoking the duck.

While the duck is marinating, put 200g of the rice into a bowl, cover with the water and set aside at room temperature for 12 hours or overnight.

Meanwhile, make the blood orange and balsamic jelly. Bring the blood orange juice and balsamic vinegar to the boil in a pan, then boil rapidly for 6–7 minutes or until reduced to 250ml. Stir in the agar agar powder, mix well, then bring back to a simmer and cook for 1 minute. Remove from the heat, pour the hot liquid into a small white plastic tray (about 21 x 14 x 1.5cm in size) and leave to set completely at room temperature (don't move the tray again until the mixture is set) – this will take about 2 hours. Once the jelly has set, cover with a lid and refrigerate.

While the jelly is setting, make the medjool date purée. Place all the ingredients in a blender and blend together to form a paste. Taste and adjust the seasoning, if necessary. Transfer the date purée to a dish, cover and keep refrigerated until needed.

Once you are ready to smoke the duck, you will need to make a smoker using a deep roasting tin, a wire cooling rack and some foil. Line the roasting tin with a layer of foil, then spread the soaked rice (water and all, if the rice has not soaked up all the water), the remaining 6 juniper berries and the sprigs of thyme over the foil. Sprinkle the remaining 100g of dry (unsoaked) rice over the top, then position the cooling rack over the rice mixture. Place the duck breasts, fat-side down, on to the cooling rack.

Place the roasting tin on the hob over a high heat and start the smoking process. Heat until the rice starts to smoke. Cover the whole thing with a tent of foil and keep it over the heat for a further 2–3 minutes, then turn the heat off, remove from the heat and leave the duck breasts to smoke for 5 minutes. Return the roasting tin to the heat to create more smoke, then remove it from the heat again once

(continued on page 38)

(continued from page 36)

enough smoke has built up. Leave to smoke for a further 5 minutes, then let the duck breasts cool completely on the rack in the roasting tin (leaving the whole thing covered with foil until cold). Once smoked, the duck meat will become a dark pink colour and the fat will turn yellow and look melted (but it will be soft, not crispy). Serve the smoked duck breasts at room temperature.

For the Jerusalem artichoke purée, peel and slice the artichokes, then cook them in a pan of boiling salted water for about 10 minutes or until soft. Drain the artichokes, then purée them in a blender until very smooth. Add the butter and cream and blend to mix. If the purée is too thick, add a dash more cream, then add salt and pepper to taste. Keep warm.

To serve, finely slice the duck breasts. Cut the jelly into ½cm squares. Spread some date purée over each serving plate, then place small drops of Jerusalem artichoke purée on to the plates. Arrange the duck slices, chicory, orange segments and coriander cress in the centre of the plates. Serve immediately.

Hay-Baked Jerusalem Artichoke Salad with Smoked Salad Cream (opposite)

Hay-baked Jerusalem Artichoke Salad with Smoked Salad Cream

This is confession time. Most chefs work incredibly long, unsociable hours and every chef I know certainly has a secret comfort food that makes them feel human again. In the winter, with the long, cold, dark days, I quite enjoy a baked potato smothered with salad cream. This recipe is my take on a glamorised version of that dish!

Jerusalem artichokes baked over hay are used instead of potatoes, and while they are baking, the cream (which will be used to make the salad cream) is smoked at the same time. This recipe is a far cry from the humble baked potato and shop-bought salad cream, but it's a clever and interesting twist that evokes great memories.

Serves 4 as a starter

25g clean fresh hay
300ml cold water
800g Jerusalem artichokes
150ml double cream
1 clove garlic, crushed
2 pinches of caster sugar
3 teaspoons Dijon mustard
5 tablespoons hazelnut oil
1 teaspoon cider vinegar
3 teaspoons unsalted butter
1 leek, washed and cut into ½cm slices
2 slices sourdough bread, crusts removed and bread torn into small pieces
4 eggs
juice of 1 lemon
2 tablespoons rapeseed oil, plus extra for tossing with the artichokes
sea salt and freshly cracked black pepper
baby or mini/micro salad leaves, to serve

Put the hay into a bowl and cover with the water. Leave to soak for about 30 minutes, then drain thoroughly in a colander. Preheat the oven to 200°C/Gas Mark 6 and find a wire cooling rack that fits over a large roasting tin.

Peel the Jerusalem artichokes and cut them in half, then cook them in a pan of boiling salted water for about 10 minutes or until just tender. Drain well.

Place the drained hay in the bottom of a large roasting tin and place the cooling rack over the hay, then arrange the artichokes on top of the cooling rack in a single layer.

Pour the cream into a small saucepan and season with salt and pepper. Add the garlic and heat gently to just below boiling point, then pour the cream into a small, ovenproof dish. Place the warmed cream on the cooling rack next to the artichokes and cover the whole lot loosely with a tent of foil.

Heat the roasting tin on the hob until the hay starts to smoke, then transfer the foil-covered roasting tin to the oven and cook for 20 minutes. Remove the cream from the oven – it will look like baked set cream, but once you stir it, it will revert to liquid again (a slightly thickened and reduced liquid). Pass the cream through a fine sieve and leave to cool.

Return the artichokes, uncovered, to the oven for a further 10 minutes or until they have turned a deep, creamy colour – they will be dry and will look slightly smoked.

Meanwhile, prepare the hazelnut confit leeks. To make the vinaigrette, put a pinch of sugar, 1 teaspoon of the mustard, the hazelnut oil, cider vinegar and salt and pepper in a small saucepan and heat gently to just warm it through (do not let it boil). Remove from the heat. Heat 1 teaspoon of the butter in a small, non-stick frying pan and, once the butter starts to foam, add the leek slices and salt and pepper and fry over a medium heat for 5–6 minutes or until the leek is golden brown. Transfer the leeks to the warmed vinaigrette and stir, then set aside to infuse for at least 15 minutes.

In the meantime, wipe the frying pan clean, then return it to the heat with the remaining butter. Once the butter starts to foam, add the bread pieces and cook over a medium heat for 3–4 minutes or until golden brown and crisp. Drain on kitchen paper and set aside.

Soft-boil the eggs in a pan of gently simmering water for 5 minutes, then drain and plunge into cold water to cool them quickly. Once cool, drain and then peel the eggs, reserving 2 eggs for the salad cream. Halve the remaining 2 eggs and season with salt and pepper. Set aside until you are ready to serve.

Make the smoked salad cream. Scoop out the soft egg yolks from the 2 reserved eggs into a bowl and discard the egg whites. Add the remaining sugar and mustard, the lemon juice, 100ml of the smoked cream and 2 tablespoons of rapeseed oil and whisk together until smooth and combined. Season to taste with salt and pepper and set aside.

Assemble the dish by tossing the warm, smoked artichokes in a little extra rapeseed oil. Arrange the artichokes on serving plates with the hazelnut confit leeks and salad leaves alongside. Place an egg half on to each plate, then scatter over the golden bread pieces. Pour the smoked salad cream into a small dipping bowl and serve separately.

Pan-roasted Cod with Jerusalem Artichokes

Crisp, crunchy and soft simply describes the textures of this dish. Serving some of the components of this dish warm and some cold gives it an interesting extra dimension. Cod is a flaky and soft, but fairly neutral-flavoured, fish that goes very well with vegetables that have a strong identity, such as Jerusalem artichokes. This dish makes a perfect starter, but it can also be served as a main course, so is ideal for a special dinner party, and it can all be prepared a day in advance.

I also lightly cure the cod – the reason for this is that cod is very flaky and breaks up easily when cooked, especially if the fish is super fresh, so the cure firms up the flesh and holds it together during cooking. The cure of salt and sugar only stays on the fish for 10 minutes, so you can also do this a day in advance and keep it in an airtight container in the fridge for the following day.

Serves 6 as a starter or 4 as a main course

For the pickled Jerusalem artichokes

2 large Jerusalem artichokes
1 teaspoon white wine vinegar
juice of 1 lemon
a pinch of caster sugar
2 tablespoons extra virgin olive oil
sea salt and freshly cracked black pepper

For the Jerusalem artichoke crisps

sunflower oil, for deep-frying
2 large Jerusalem artichokes

For the Jerusalem artichoke purée

200g Jerusalem artichokes
2 teaspoons unsalted butter
50ml white wine
200ml cold water
50ml double cream

For the lightly cured cod

1 tablespoon caster sugar
1 tablespoon table salt
6 x 55–60g even-sized pieces of skinless, boneless cod (or for a main course, use 4 x 100–120g pieces)
1 tablespoon sunflower oil
½ teaspoon mild curry powder
1 teaspoon unsalted butter

To serve

fresh pea shoots or watercress
fresh mustard cress
1 green-skinned eating apple (preferably Granny Smith)

Make the pickled Jerusalem artichokes. Peel the artichokes and slice them as thinly as possible (preferably using a mandolin) into a bowl. Immediately mix the sliced artichokes with the white wine vinegar, lemon juice, sugar, olive oil and salt and pepper. Cover and leave the mixture to macerate for at least 1 hour in the fridge. This can be done a day in advance and just kept in a covered container in the fridge overnight. Drain the artichokes before serving, reserving the artichokes and pickling liquor separately.

Make the Jerusalem artichoke crisps. Heat the sunflower oil in an electric deep-fat fryer or in a deep frying pan to a temperature of 160°C (or until a small piece of bread browns within 20 seconds in the hot oil). Peel the Jerusalem artichokes and slice them as thinly as possible (preferably using a mandolin). Deep-fry the artichoke slices in the hot oil (do this in batches) for 2–3 minutes or until they are golden brown and crisp. Using a slotted spoon, remove and drain the crisps on kitchen paper, then immediately season them with salt. Leave to cool, then store in an airtight container. These can also be made a day in advance.

Make the Jerusalem artichoke purée – this can also be done a day in advance. Peel and slice the artichokes. Melt the butter in a small saucepan, add the sliced artichokes and a little salt, then cover and sweat over a medium heat for about 8 minutes or until the artichokes are tender. The artichokes will be colourless, but as soon as they start to take on colour, add the wine, cover and cook until the wine becomes thick and syrupy.

Add the water, reduce the heat to very low, then cover and cook for 15–20 minutes or until the artichokes are completely soft. Remove the lid, increase the heat and boil rapidly until nearly all the water has evaporated. Add the cream and bring to the boil, then remove from the heat. Purée the mixture in a blender until smooth, then taste and adjust the seasoning, if necessary. Leave to cool, then cover and refrigerate overnight.

Next, make the lightly cured cod. This can also be done a day in advance. Mix the sugar and salt together, then cover the fish with the sugar/salt cure and set aside for 10 minutes. Wash the cure off the fish under cold running water and pat the fish dry with kitchen paper. The cod is now ready to be cooked, so at this stage it can be stored in an airtight container in the fridge until you are ready to cook it – it will keep overnight in the fridge.

When you are ready to assemble the dish the next day, gently reheat the artichoke purée in a pan until it is piping hot. Meanwhile, cook the cod. Heat the sunflower oil in a large, non-stick frying pan until hot. Dust the pieces of cod with the curry powder. Once the pan is hot enough, add the cod pieces, presentation-side down, into the hot oil and then add the butter. Sauté the fish for 2–3 minutes, then carefully flip it over and cook for a further 30 seconds on the reverse side or until cooked and golden brown. Drain on kitchen paper and keep hot.

To serve, mix the pea shoots and mustard cress together. Core the apple and then cut it into small batons. Toss the apple batons with a little of the reserved pickling liquor from the pickled artichokes. Spoon the warmed artichoke purée on to serving plates. Place the pea shoots and cress on top, followed by the cod. Garnish the dish with the pickled artichokes and apple batons and then finally place a few artichoke crisps on top. Lightly drizzle the remaining pickling liquor around each plate and serve immediately.

Cook's Note

When you buy fresh cod, it should be so fresh that it almost smells like freshly grated lime zest, and the colour of the flesh should be almost opaque. If the flesh is milky in colour with a slightly yellow tint and a faint ammonia smell, then you know it's not fresh.

Venison Burgers with Roasted Parsnip Straws and Beetroot and Red Onion Relish

The game season serves us well and it delivers a variety of interesting ingredients with different tastes. Venison is exciting to cook with and can turn an everyday meal, such as a burger, into a gourmet treat. It took us, at the British Larder Suffolk, a little while to find ourselves and establish who we are, and then finally... drum roll please... it happened when the venison burger arrived. Phew! We thought it would never happen. Our customers adore a tasty burger and if it's made with venison meat, then it's even better. The accompanying sweet roasted parsnip fingers also add to the splendour of this feast of a 'burger and chips'. Have a bit of fun by making your own relish; however, if time is running out, just opt for a good quality bought one instead.

How gamey do you like your venison? We opt for roe deer most of the time as it has a subtle venison flavour, but if you want a really gamey taste, ask your butcher for red deer – it's more punchy, and the longer it hangs, the stronger the taste.

Serves 6 as a main course

For the beetroot and red onion relish
30g unsalted butter
300g red onions, finely sliced
350g raw beetroot, peeled and coarsely grated
1 clove garlic, crushed
½ teaspoon crushed dried chillies
100g dark muscovado sugar
100ml malt vinegar
1 teaspoon finely chopped fresh thyme leaves
sea salt and freshly cracked black pepper

For the venison burgers
2 cloves garlic, unpeeled
1 tablespoon olive oil
1 large onion, finely diced
1 carrot, grated
1 stick celery, grated
600g minced venison
200g minced pork (optional – use all minced venison if you prefer, but a bit of fat keeps the burgers moist, and venison is very lean and can dry out easily)
1 tablespoon wholegrain mustard
1 tablespoon grated fresh horseradish (or substitute ready-grated horseradish from a jar or creamed horseradish, if you like)
1 egg
50g fresh breadcrumbs (preferably sourdough)

For the roasted parsnip straws
1kg parsnips
2 tablespoons olive oil
1 tablespoon coriander seeds
1 tablespoon sea salt
1 teaspoon finely chopped fresh thyme leaves
2 tablespoons clear honey
a squeeze of lemon juice (optional)

6 burger buns, cut in half, plus sliced tomatoes and salad leaves, to serve
cooked hot battered onion rings, to garnish (optional)

First, make the relish. Melt the butter in a saucepan over a low heat and gently sauté the onions, beetroot, garlic and crushed dried chillies, with salt and pepper added, until the mixture starts to caramelise. This should take about 10–15 minutes.

Stir in the sugar and cook until dissolved. Pour the malt vinegar into the pan and let it bubble, stirring and scraping the base of the pan to deglaze it, then cook over a high heat for about 20 minutes or until the mixture is thick and glossy (with a bit of syrup, but not too wet), stirring occasionally. Once the relish is ready, stir in the chopped thyme, then taste and adjust the seasoning, if necessary.

Spoon the relish into hot, sterilised jars, cover and seal, then cool. Keep refrigerated until needed. The longer you let the relish mature, the better the flavour will be, but you can use it straightaway, if you like, as it's just as delicious. This relish will keep unopened in the fridge for up to 3 months; once opened it should also be kept refrigerated and used within 3 days.

Make the burgers. Preheat the oven to 180°C/Gas Mark 4. Wrap the garlic cloves in foil and roast in the oven for 20–25 minutes or until soft and golden. Remove from the oven, cool slightly, then squeeze the soft garlic pulp out of the skins and set aside (see Cook's Note). Heat the olive oil in a large, non-stick frying pan and sauté the onion, carrot and celery, with salt and pepper added, over a medium heat for 7–8 minutes or until soft. Do not let the vegetables colour – when the onions turn transparent, they are ready. Remove from the heat and leave to cool completely, then stir in the roasted garlic.

Put the cooled onion mixture, together with all the remaining burger ingredients, into the bowl of an electric stand mixer, attach a dough hook and knead until all the ingredients are well mixed. I prefer to use a mixer for making burgers as it tightens the meat and prevents it from falling apart when cooking – however, if you do not have a mixer, simply combine the ingredients in a bowl and mix thoroughly by hand. Take a small piece of the mixture and cook it in a hot pan until cooked, then taste and adjust the seasoning, if necessary.

Divide the mixture into 6 equal portions and shape each portion into a thick, round burger. Place on a plate and leave to rest in the fridge for at least 4 hours.

When you are ready to serve, make the roasted parsnip straws. Preheat the oven to 200°C/Gas Mark 6. Peel the parsnips and cut each one lengthways into 6–8 even wedges (each about 1cm-thick), then toss them with the olive oil and season lightly with salt and pepper. Spread the parsnip straws out in a single layer on a baking sheet lined with non-stick baking paper, then roast them in the oven for 12–15 minutes or until tender and golden brown, stirring once or twice.

Meanwhile, using a pestle and mortar, crush the coriander seeds, then add the salt and thyme and mix together. Set aside.

While the parsnips are roasting, cook the burgers in a hot griddle pan over a high heat for 5–6 minutes on each side or until cooked all the way through and to your liking.

Once the roasted parsnips are ready, drizzle over the honey, plus a squeeze of lemon juice, if you like, then season with the thyme and coriander-flavoured salt. Serve immediately with the burgers.

Serve each cooked burger in a bun with a spoonful of the beetroot relish, and tomato slices and salad leaves. Garnish with battered onion rings, if you like, and serve with the hot roasted parsnip straws.

Cook's Note

When making the venison burgers, if you prefer, you don't have to roast the garlic, you can simply crush the 2 peeled garlic cloves and use them raw instead. However, raw garlic has a stronger flavour, whereas roasted garlic has a sweeter, more rounded flavour that complements the venison.

Roasted Woodcock with Truffled Celeriac and Boulangère Potatoes

There is something very grown up and sophisticated about this special dish. Cooking woodcock is something I personally do not take lightly. I feel this huge sense of responsibility and respect for these beautiful seasonal birds, partly because they are a delicacy and are hugely expensive, but also because they have a short season that comes around only once a year. When eating woodcock, it should be treated like 'the last supper'. No expenses are spared, and pairing woodcock with other ingredients should be done with plenty of consideration and precision.

Woodcock take me back to the days when I worked as a commis chef in London for the great Rowley Leigh. He evoked the obsession of seasonal cooking in me – a lovely memory of the good old days. Chef Rowley liked his game well hung and smelling and tasting, well, shall we say rather gamey! As a young commis chef, I did not really get it and when cleaning the fridges out after a long and hard day's work, the smell of the matured grouse and woodcock used to get me right in the stomach. In those days, I did not understand the reasoning behind it all. But then I 'grew up' and learned the tradition where they roasted the birds whole and served the brains and guts as a pâté on toasted brioche. I suppose this is where I get the respect for these birds from – the good old days training to become a chef and food lover.

Serves 2 as a main course

For the Boulangère potatoes

1 tablespoon unsalted butter, plus extra for greasing
2 banana shallots, sliced
2–3 sprigs of fresh thyme, leaves only
4 large Desiree potatoes
250ml hot white chicken stock
sea salt and freshly cracked black pepper

For the truffled celeriac

250g celeriac
50g unsalted butter
100ml white wine
1 teaspoon truffle oil

For the roasted woodcock

2 whole woodcocks, plucked
4 rashers streaky bacon (preferably unsmoked)
a little sunflower oil, for cooking
4 banana shallots, finely sliced
a sprig of fresh thyme
1 tablespoon coriander seeds
150ml red wine
500ml game stock
1 tablespoon unsalted butter

Make the Boulangère potatoes first and make this part of the dish a day in advance, if you like.

Preheat the oven to 160°C/Gas Mark 3 and grease two individual 9 x 6cm ovenproof ramekins with butter.

Melt the remaining tablespoon of butter in a saucepan and sweat the shallots, with salt and pepper added, for 7–8 minutes or until the shallots are transparent and tender. Stir in the thyme leaves, then remove from the heat and set aside.

Peel and thinly slice the potatoes (preferably using a mandolin), then rinse them and drain well. Place a single layer of potato slices over the base of each prepared ramekin and season with salt and pepper, top this with a layer of cooked shallots, then pour over some stock. Repeat these layers until the ramekins are full, finishing with a layer of potato slices. Bake in the oven for 40–50 minutes or until cooked, tender and golden brown. Remove from the oven and leave to cool, then cover and chill in the fridge overnight.

The next day, preheat the oven to 180°C/Gas Mark 4 and reheat the potatoes in the oven (either in the ramekins or turned out on to a greased baking tray) for 20–25 minutes or until hot throughout. If the potatoes start to brown too much, simply cover the dishes with foil. Keep hot until ready to serve.

Meanwhile, for the truffled celeriac, peel and cut the celeriac into wedges (as you would cut a cake), then cut each wedge into ½-cm-thick slices. Heat half of the butter in a non-stick frying pan and, once the butter starts to foam, add the celeriac slices, the remaining butter and salt and pepper and sauté over a medium heat for 9–10 minutes or until the celeriac starts to colour. Once it is golden brown, pour the wine into the pan and let it bubble, stirring and scraping the base of the pan to deglaze it. Then cover the pan and cook for 10–12 minutes or until the celeriac is tender. Remove the lid and, if there is a lot of liquid left in the pan, boil until it has reduced enough to coat the celeriac slices. Remove from the heat, stir in the truffle oil, then set aside and keep warm until needed.

In the meantime, for the roasted woodcock, preheat the oven to 200°C/Gas Mark 6. Remove the head from each bird and reserve, then place 1 bacon rasher over each breast. Place both birds in a roasting tin and roast in the oven for 14 minutes. Remove from the oven and transfer the birds to a cooling rack. Remove the legs from the birds, then return the legs to the roasting tin and roast for a further 10 minutes.

Meanwhile, let the roasted birds (now minus the legs) rest for 10 minutes.

While the woodcock are roasting, heat a dash of sunflower oil in a saucepan and sauté the woodcock heads, shallots, thyme and coriander seeds together until the shallots are dark brown, but not burned. Add the red wine and bubble until reduced by half. Add the stock and bring to the boil, then simmer over a low heat for 10 minutes.

Remove the guts from the roasted birds – the guts should have turned into a soft pâté – and stir them into the simmering sauce. Pass the sauce through a fine sieve into a serving jug and season to taste with salt and pepper. Keep hot.

Remove the bacon and breasts from the woodcock crowns, keeping the skin on the breasts. Melt the butter in a hot, non-stick frying pan and once the butter is foaming, add the breasts, skin-side down, and the bacon, and cook for about 2 minutes or until the breasts are crisp.

Serve the roasted woodcock breasts and legs and bacon on serving plates with the warm truffled celeriac and Boulangère potatoes alongside. Serve with purple sprouting broccoli. Serve the hot sauce separately on the side.

Cook's Note

Spare no expense and serve this delicious meal – a real labour of love – with a good quality red wine. You need something with a full body and a robust character.

Braised Beef Ribs with January King Cabbage and Carrot Crush

This dish will kiss you on the lips and give you a warm, homely hug. There is something really satisfying about cooking good old classic recipes such as this one, which is a twist on a timeless classic – beef stroganoff. People who know me will say there is nothing traditional and safe about my cooking. I thrive on twisting and turning recipes to suit my taste and cooking abilities and I feel comfortable with that as a cook. I believe that cooking is subjective and that there are no rights or wrongs in cookery (well, OK, there are certain set rules and formulas that time and time again will deliver the same results). I also believe that one cannot reinvent the wheel and cookery is pretty much like that too, but what we can do is modernise recipes to prevent old favourites from becoming... well, shall I say 'extinct'.

The carrot and mustard crush is a perfect accompaniment to the beef ribs in this recipe – the slight acidity of the wholegrain mustard in the carrot crush sets off the taste of the stroganoff sauce beautifully. This recipe is definitely a treasure and one to consider preparing on a relaxing Saturday afternoon.

Serves 4 as a main course

For the braised January King cabbage
1 medium January King cabbage, outer leaves removed
150ml chicken or vegetable stock
50g unsalted butter
sea salt and freshly cracked black pepper

For the carrot and wholegrain mustard crush
25g unsalted butter
400g carrots, sliced
150ml cold water
1 tablespoon wholegrain mustard

For the braised beef ribs
2 onions
2 carrots
2 sticks celery
3 tablespoons sunflower oil
1.2kg beef short ribs (choose 4 pieces – they will each have one bone)
1 clove garlic, crushed
3 black peppercorns
½ teaspoon coriander seeds
3 bay leaves
a large sprig of fresh thyme
50ml brandy
1.2 litres beef stock

For the stroganoff sauce
10g unsalted butter
8 shallots, cut in half lengthways
125g chestnut mushrooms, cut into quarters
60ml double cream
1 teaspoon smoked paprika

1 tablespoon chopped fresh flat-leaf parsley and 8 cornichons or baby gherkins, to serve

First, make the braised cabbage. Preheat the oven to 200°C/Gas Mark 6. Cut the cabbage in half and then cut each half into quarters. Wash and drain the cabbage, then season with salt and pepper. Melt the butter in a large casserole over a medium heat and once the butter starts to foam, add the cabbage quarters and cook for 8–10 minutes or until light golden brown on all sides. Add the stock and bring to a gentle simmer, then place a piece of non-stick baking paper directly on top of the cabbage and cover with the lid.

Transfer the casserole to the oven and cook for 15–20 minutes or until the cabbage is tender. Remove from the oven and leave to cool slightly, then drain the cabbage quarters on kitchen paper. Leave to cool completely, then chill until you are ready to serve. Before serving, reheat the cabbage in a covered, ovenproof dish in a preheated oven at 180°C/Gas Mark 4 for 10–12 minutes or until piping hot.

Next, make the carrot and wholegrain mustard crush. Melt the butter in a large saucepan and, once the butter starts to foam, add the carrots and salt and pepper. Sauté the carrots for 2 minutes, then reduce the heat to low, cover and cook for 10 minutes, stirring regularly. By cooking the carrots this way you bring out the natural sweetness of them and this adds a depth of flavour to the dish.

Add the water to the carrots and bring to a gentle simmer, then cover and cook for a further 15 minutes, by which time the liquid should have evaporated – if not, remove the lid, turn the heat up and cook until the liquid has evaporated, without letting the carrots catch or brown too much. Remove from the heat, add the mustard and crush the carrots with a potato ricer or potato masher. Leave to cool, then chill until you are ready to serve. Before serving, gently reheat the carrot crush in a small pan over a medium heat for 5–8 minutes or until piping hot.

Make the braised beef ribs. Preheat the oven to 160°C/Gas Mark 3. Cut the onions, carrots and celery into 2cm pieces and set aside. Heat half of the sunflower oil in a large casserole, season the ribs with salt and pepper and brown them all over in the hot oil. Remove the ribs to a plate, then add the remaining oil to the casserole, together with the prepared vegetables, the garlic, peppercorns and coriander seeds and sauté over a high heat for 8–10 minutes or until golden brown. Add the bay leaves and thyme and sauté for a further minute.

Return the beef to the casserole, pour in the brandy and let it bubble, stirring and

scraping the base of the casserole with a wooden spoon to deglaze it. Simmer until the vegetables absorb the brandy, then add the stock and bring to a gentle simmer. Place a piece of non-stick baking paper directly on to the surface of the stock and cover with the lid. Transfer the casserole to the oven and cook for 1½ hours or until the beef is cooked and tender.

Remove from the oven and carefully remove the beef ribs from the stock. Set the beef aside and keep hot while you make the sauce. Pass the stock through a fine sieve and reserve 300ml of the stock.

Make the stroganoff sauce. Melt the butter in a saucepan, add the shallots and mushrooms and sauté over a medium heat for 7–8 minutes or until golden brown and caramelised. Add the reserved stock and bring to a gentle simmer, then simmer for 4 minutes. Stir in the cream and paprika and bring back to the boil, then taste and adjust the seasoning, if necessary. The sauce is now ready to serve.

Meanwhile, reheat the braised cabbage and carrot crush as directed.

To serve, gently cut the meat away from the bones and cut it into slices. Spoon a quenelle (or spoonful) of the carrot crush on to each serving plate, followed by the braised cabbage. Spoon some sauce on to each plate, arrange the beef slices on top, then spoon over more sauce. Sprinkle the parsley over and garnish each plate with 2 cornichons. Serve immediately.

Venison Haunch Steaks with Spelt, Leeks and Red Wine Sauce

If you are a steak lover, then you should find this recipe both interesting and appealing. Cooking venison can be slightly daunting and the risk that you may end up with a dry and stringy piece of meat is more likely than with beefsteak. The secret when cooking venison steak is to ensure that this lean meat retains its succulence and tenderness. My main recommendation is that if you like meat well done then it would be best to avoid this cut of venison. I cook these 150g steaks for 2 minutes on each side, but the most important part is the resting time afterwards – the resting time should be equal to the total cooking time. As it rests, the meat relaxes and the unwanted red protein juices will drain away (do not be fooled, you might think this is blood, but it's not). The well-rested haunch steaks will be tender and succulent.

Venison haunch steaks go incredibly well with the earthiness of wholegrain spelt. This dish is finished off with a deep red wine sauce and a few carrot crisps (these are optional – well, there needs to be a slight compromise on the classic 'steak and chips'). Make the carrot crisps a day in advance as they will keep well in an airtight container, then prepare the red wine sauce as this is the most time-consuming part of the recipe. If you have some sauce leftover, cool, then freeze it for the next time (it will freeze for up to 3 months) – it will be perfect and saves on all the hard work.

Serves 4 as a main course

1 carrot
1 tablespoon sunflower oil, plus extra to fry the carrot crisps
200g wholegrain spelt
1 teaspoon sea salt
50g cold unsalted butter
2 leeks, washed and cut into 1cm slices
4 x 150g venison haunch steaks
a sprig of fresh thyme, finely chopped
sea salt and freshly cracked black pepper

For the red wine sauce
1 carrot
1 onion
1 leek, washed
2 sticks celery
1 raw beetroot, peeled
2 cloves garlic. peeled
1 tablespoon sunflower oil
1 teaspoon coriander seeds
3 dried juniper berries, crushed
3 cloves
2 tablespoons tomato purée
70g redcurrant jelly
2 bay leaves
2 large sprigs of fresh rosemary
2 large sprigs of fresh thyme
500ml red wine
700ml beef or chicken stock

First, make the carrot crisps. Peel the carrot, then use a vegetable peeler to create long carrot ribbons. Heat some sunflower oil in an electric deep-fat fryer or in a deep frying pan to a temperature of 160°C (or until a small piece of bread browns within 20 seconds in the hot oil). Deep-fry the carrot ribbons in the hot oil (do this in batches, a few at a time) for a few minutes until they are golden brown and crisp. Using a slotted spoon, remove and drain the crisps on kitchen paper, then immediately season them with salt and leave to cool. These can be made a day in advance – simply store in an airtight container overnight.

Next, make the red wine sauce. Cut all the vegetables into 2cm pieces and just crush the garlic with the heel of your hand. Heat the sunflower oil in a large saucepan and sauté all the vegetables, the garlic, coriander seeds, juniper berries and cloves over a medium heat for about 10 minutes or until golden brown. Do not let the vegetables burn – the idea is to caramelise them and bring out their natural sweetness.

Add the tomato purée and cook for a further 5 minutes, stirring regularly to prevent the purée from burning. Do not be tempted to add extra oil as it will make the sauce greasy. Add the redcurrant jelly, bay leaves and rosemary and thyme sprigs, then pour in the wine and let it bubble, stirring and scraping the base of the pan with a wooden spoon to deglaze it. Turn the heat up and cook until the wine has reduced by half.

Add the stock and bring the sauce to a gentle simmer – do not boil the sauce too fast (otherwise it will become cloudy) and do not cover the pan either. Simmer gently for 20 minutes, removing any impurities from the surface using a small ladle. Remove from the heat and pass the sauce through a fine sieve into a clean saucepan. Bubble the sauce over a medium heat until it has reduced to a coating consistency. Remove from the heat and set aside until needed.

Meanwhile, soak the spelt in a bowl of cold water for 20 minutes, then rinse thoroughly and drain. Put the drained spelt into a saucepan and add 3 times the volume of water to spelt. Bring to the boil, then reduce the heat to a gentle simmer and cook for about 10 minutes or until the spelt is tender. Add the salt right at the end of the cooking time, then drain using a colander, set aside and keep hot. (Adding the salt at the end of the cooking time for grains and pulses prevents them from becoming tough on the outside and chewy.)

For the sautéed leeks, melt half of the butter in a non-stick frying pan and sauté the leeks for 5–6 minutes or until golden all over. Season to taste with salt and pepper, then remove from the heat and keep warm until needed.

To cook the venison steaks, heat the remaining 1 tablespoon of sunflower oil in a large, non-stick frying pan over a high heat. Season the steaks on both sides with salt and pepper, then place the steaks into the hot pan and do not move them for 2 minutes. After about 1 minute, place three fingernail-sized knobs of the remaining cold butter into the pan. After the 2 minutes cooking time, turn the steaks over and cook them on the other side for another 2 minutes, again adding 3 more small knobs of cold butter halfway through the cooking time. Transfer the steaks to a plate lined with kitchen paper and leave to rest, uncovered, for 4 minutes.

While the steaks are resting, reheat the red wine sauce in a saucepan until it is gently simmering, then add the hot, cooked spelt and chopped thyme. Taste and adjust the seasoning, if necessary.

To serve, spoon the spelt and red wine sauce and the sautéed leeks on to serving plates. Carve the venison steaks into 1cm-thick slices and serve on top of the spelt and leeks. Garnish with the carrot crisps and serve immediately.

Garlic and Lemon Butter-sautéed Salsify

Salsify has become a vegetable that is now more regularly seen at farmers' markets. Working as an au pair in mainland Europe, I often came across salsify but never really understood what to do with it. After joining a two Michelin-starred restaurant in Chelsea, I soon became familiar with the preparation and taste, as I used to prepare about 5 kilos of it a couple of times a week. I quickly learned to wear disposable gloves because, as with globe artichokes, salsify stains your hands and the peel leaves a slightly sticky residue on your hands that even with persistent scrubbing and hot soapy water, does not disappear until a few days later. Salsify also oxidises and discolours as soon as the skin is peeled away, so dip the peeled salsify into acidulated water (made by adding some fresh lemon juice or a teaspoon of vitamin C powder to a bowlful of ice-cold water) as soon as it is prepared.

This recipe is delicious served with pan-roasted fish or roast chicken.

Serves 4 as an accompaniment or side dish

2 lemons, plus an extra squeeze of lemon juice to season
1kg salsify
1 teaspoon sea salt
150g unsalted butter, softened
6 large cloves garlic, crushed
2 tablespoons chopped fresh flat-leaf parsley
2 slices sourdough bread, crusts removed and bread torn into small pieces
2 banana shallots, cut into ½cm slices
sea salt and freshly cracked black pepper

Fill a large container with cold water, add the juice of ½ lemon, then trim and peel the salsify and immediately dunk it in the lemon/acidulated water. Rinse well and drain, then cut the salsify into 5–7cm long batons (cutting them all to an even size).

Transfer the salsify to a large saucepan, cover with cold water and add the juice of the other half of the lemon, together with the salt. Place a cartouche (a circle of greaseproof paper) on the surface of the water and place a small plate on top to weigh the paper down – this will prevent the salsify from floating and coming into contact with air (which would cause it to discolour).

Bring to the boil, then reduce the heat to a gentle simmer and cook for 8–10 minutes or until the salsify is tender. Be wary that it does not need a long cooking time and can easily overcook and fall apart, but you do not want to cook salsify al dente – it should have a firm, but creamy texture, not crunchy. Drain the cooked salsify using a colander.

While the salsify is cooking, make the garlic and lemon butter. Mix together the butter, garlic, three-quarters of the parsley, the finely grated zest and juice of the remaining lemon and salt and pepper to taste, to form a creamy paste.

Heat 1 teaspoon of the garlic butter in a large, non-stick frying pan and fry the pieces of bread for 5–6 minutes or until golden brown and crisp, then drain on kitchen paper and leave to cool.

Wipe the frying pan out with kitchen paper, then return the pan to the heat. Spoon 1 large tablespoonful of the garlic butter into the warm pan and sauté the shallots and drained salsify, with salt and pepper added, for 8–10 minutes or until golden brown. Add another small knob of garlic butter towards the end of the cooking time, and season with a squeeze of lemon juice.

Transfer the salsify and shallots to a serving dish, sprinkle over the remaining parsley and the golden bread pieces and serve immediately.

Cook's Note
Store any leftover garlic and lemon butter in a covered container in the fridge and use within 3 days.

Molasses-roasted Pineapple with Dark Brown Sugar Cream

I had the privilege to grow up in a country (South Africa) that has a suitable climate to grow exotic fruits such as pineapples, mangoes, guavas, passion fruit, paw paws, avocados, bananas, and plenty more. My grandfather experimented with growing most of these exotics and, if it did not work, he would just pull it out and try something else. I loved his approach and have adopted a similar theory and technique in my cooking and gardening. The British Isles do not have the right climate to grow pineapples, so when they are in season and come from a Fairtrade supplier, then I'm more than happy to buy one.

This recipe is fun and with the availability of so many different varieties of Fairtrade sugars on offer, one cannot do anything other than have a good play with the exotics. For this recipe, I use muscovado, dark brown and molasses sugars, all made from cane sugar. These sugars give this recipe its all-important character. I'm also a chef who loves gadgets – in this recipe I'm using one of my favourites, a cream whipper (see Cook's Note).

Serves 6

For the salted peanut brittle biscuits (makes about 26 biscuits)

200g plain flour
½ teaspoon bicarbonate of soda
450g dark muscovado sugar
100g salted roasted peanuts
½ vanilla pod, split in half lengthways and seeds scraped out
250g unsalted butter, softened
250g smooth peanut butter
1 egg

For the dark brown sugar cream

3 leaves of gelatine
400ml milk
250g dark soft brown sugar
100ml double cream

For the molasses-roasted pineapple

120g molasses sugar
1 teaspoon ground ginger
500g fresh pineapple (prepared weight/ flesh only), peeled, quartered lengthways and core removed

400ml natural yogurt, to serve

Make the biscuit dough. Put the flour, bicarbonate of soda, muscovado sugar, peanuts and vanilla seeds into a food processor and process until you have coarse breadcrumbs. Add the butter, peanut butter and egg and process until the mixture forms a soft, sticky dough. Turn the dough on to a lightly floured work surface and push it all together, but do not knead.

Divide the dough in half and roll each portion into a sausage shape, about 5cm in diameter, then wrap each sausage tightly in cling film and refrigerate overnight. (It's very important that the dough rests well, otherwise the biscuits will bake unevenly and will spread a lot during baking with the potential for burnt edges.)

When you are ready to bake the biscuits the next day, preheat the oven to 180°C/ Gas Mark 4. Line 2 large baking trays with non-stick baking paper.

Remove the cling film from the well-rested biscuit dough sausages and slice each one into thirteen ½ cm-thick rounds (to make a total of 26 biscuits), then place the rounds on the prepared baking trays, leaving plenty of room between each one for them to spread (you will probably need to bake them in batches). Bake in the oven for about 12 minutes or until golden brown and crisp.

(continued on page 56)

(continued from page 54)

Remove from the oven and leave the biscuits to cool on the baking trays for 2 minutes, then carefully remove them to a wire rack and leave to cool completely. Repeat to bake the remaining biscuits. If you wish to make the biscuits in advance, they will keep for up to 1 week in an airtight container, stored in a cool, dry cupboard.

Meanwhile, make the dark brown sugar cream. Soak the gelatine in cold water until it has softened. Gently heat the milk, soft brown sugar and cream together in a small saucepan until the sugar has dissolved, then increase the heat, bring to the boil and boil for 1 minute. Remove from the heat. Squeeze the gelatine gently to remove the excess water, then add the gelatine to the hot milk mixture and stir until dissolved. Pass the mixture through a fine sieve and pour into a cream whipper. Charge with 2 gas pellets, shake vigorously, then refrigerate for 4 hours so that the mixture thickens.

While the cream is chilling, make the molasses-roasted pineapple. Preheat the oven to 200°C/Gas Mark 6.

Sprinkle the molasses sugar and ginger evenly over the prepared pineapple quarters and then use your hands to rub the sugar into the pineapple. Transfer the prepared pineapple to a baking tray lined with non-stick baking paper and roast it in the oven for 25 minutes. Glaze the pineapple twice during roasting by spooning the melted sugar back over the fruit.

Remove from the oven and let the pineapple cool for 5 minutes, then shred it using 2 forks. Transfer the shredded pineapple to a sieve and leave it to drain and cool completely Then transfer to a covered container and refrigerate for 4 hours before use.

Shake the cream whipper vigorously and squirt the foam into a glass to check if it is ready. If the mixture has set solidly, then hold the cream whipper under warm running water to loosen the mixture inside, then shake and use as directed.

To serve, spoon the roasted pineapple into the bottom of 6 serving glasses, then divide the yogurt between the glasses. Shake the cream whipper vigorously and squirt the dark brown sugar cream on top. Crush 2 peanut brittle biscuits and sprinkle the crumbs on top of the desserts to decorate, then serve the desserts, serving 4 biscuits with each glass.

Cook's Note

For this recipe, I use a cream whipper and they are inexpensive enough for the home cook to have some fun with. With a cream whipper, nitrous oxide gas is released into a sealed metal container – this blows gas into a liquid that contains a high fat content (which helps the liquid to set and keep its foamy, mousse-like texture). As the gas expands in the liquid, this also intensifies the flavour, so when you eat the cream, you will experience an interesting texture, as well as a more intense flavour. Cream whippers are available from good cook shops or on-line. See page 17 for more on cream whippers.

Orange Tapioca Soufflés

Tapioca pudding seems to have left behind some bad memories for quite a few people. I do many cookery demonstrations and get to meet people from all walks of life. I was demonstrating to a group of old age pensioners – ladies who all remember the original Ministry of Food recipes during the Second World War – and they described tapioca pudding as stodgy and typical of school dinners. My experience is the complete opposite.

My mother used to love making a baked tapioca pudding on a rainy Sunday afternoon. I remember the tapioca pudding emerging from the oven like a big fluffy pillow, all puffed up with a sumptuous creamy centre, and the sweet smell of caramelising meringue used to hang in the air. I was really naughty and used to pinch the caramelised crusty bits before anyone else had a chance to.

After a bit of tinkering and tweaking of mum's original recipe, this one became a fabulous version of the original – a tapioca soufflé spiked with the citrus zing of orange. The smell of the baking soufflés is mouth-watering, but remember to serve these straight from the oven, as they will lose their puffiness once they start to cool down.

Serves 6

100g tapioca, rinsed and drained
500ml milk
1 tablespoon unsalted butter
60g Seville orange marmalade
2 medium eggs, separated
finely grated zest of ½ orange
5 tablespoons caster sugar
icing sugar and finely grated orange zest, to serve

Put the tapioca in a bowl, pour over 250ml of the milk and leave to soak in the fridge overnight before cooking. The longer you soak tapioca, the easier it is to cook.

The next day, place the butter, tapioca mixture and the rest of the milk in a heavy-based saucepan and bring the mixture to a simmer, stirring regularly to prevent it from catching. Lower the heat (the slower the cooking, the less chance there is of the mixture catching and burning), cover and cook very gently for 35–40 minutes, stirring regularly – the cooked tapioca pearls will go completely translucent and the starch in the grains will thicken the milk. Remove from the heat, cover and let the tapioca mixture rest for 10 minutes.

Meanwhile, preheat the oven to 200°C/Gas Mark 6. Lightly grease six 6 x 6cm ovenproof ramekins and spoon a little marmalade into the bottom of each one. Place the ramekins on a baking tray.

Lightly beat the egg yolks, orange zest and half of the caster sugar together in a bowl, then stir this into the warm tapioca mixture. In a separate bowl, whisk the egg whites with the remaining caster sugar to form soft peaks, then gently fold the meringue into the tapioca mixture.

Spoon the tapioca mixture into the prepared ramekins, filling each one about three-quarters full (the mixture will boil over if the dishes are too full). Bake in the oven (on the baking tray) for about 20 minutes or until risen and golden brown.

Remove the soufflés from the oven and dust them heavily with icing sugar, then sprinkle with the orange zest. Serve immediately, as the soufflés will quickly sink as they start to cool down.

Cook's Note
If you like the sound of this pudding and wish to make it for a dinner party, cook the tapioca cream a day in advance; follow the recipe until you get to the egg white stage, then pour the orange tapioca mixture into a dish, cool, cover and chill in the fridge overnight. Grease the ramekins, spoon in the marmalade and chill these in the fridge overnight also. The next day, remove the tapioca mixture and prepared ramekins from the fridge 30 minutes before you wish to continue, then make the meringue as directed and fold into the orange tapioca mixture. Divide the mixture between the prepared ramekins, then bake and serve as directed.

Orange and Cinnamon Honey Buns

There is something soothing and homely about the smell of freshly baked bread, cakes and buns. Baking on a cold and rainy winter's day is not only pleasurable, but somehow makes bleak days that much more tolerable. These orange and cinnamon honey buns are perfect for a lazy weekend brunch or afternoon sweet treat, served slightly warm with a pot of freshly brewed tea.

When developing my recipes, it's important that I cook food I love and create recipes that are not only memorable, but have purpose and meaning. It took me some time to finally devise a recipe for these buns that I was completely happy with. I set out to create a bun that is not only delicious, but also light and fluffy. The addition of suet to the dough gives this recipe the lightness and flakiness I was after.

Makes 9 buns

For the dough
50g unsalted butter
350ml milk
525g strong white bread flour
30g fresh yeast
150g vegetable suet
a pinch of table salt
50g caster sugar
1 egg, beaten

For the orange, sultana and cinnamon filling
100g golden sultanas (or use regular sultanas, if you wish)
100g unsalted butter, softened
100g dark muscovado sugar
4 teaspoons ground cinnamon
finely grated zest of 2 oranges (use the fruit for the glaze – see below)

For the orange honey glaze
4 oranges, peeled and divided into segments (use the 2 oranges leftover from the filling above, plus 2 more)
200ml freshly squeezed orange juice
200g caster sugar
50g clear orange blossom honey

Make the dough. Melt the butter in a small saucepan and then turn the heat off. Add the milk to the pan, then set aside briefly to let the milk warm through to blood temperature.

In a food processor, process half of the flour, the yeast and the suet together until the suet is completely broken down and is as fine as the flour. Transfer the flour, yeast and suet mixture to the bowl of an electric stand mixer (see Cook's Note), add the rest of the flour, the salt and caster sugar, attach the dough hook and turn the machine on to run at a low speed. Add the warm milk and butter mixture and mix to form a dough, then add the egg and knead the dough for 6 minutes. The dough will be very soft and you might think it's a little too wet, but it's perfectly fine – do not add extra flour.

Turn the dough on to a lightly floured work surface and shape it into a ball with a smooth top. Place the dough ball in a lightly oiled bowl, cover with a clean dry tea towel or cling film and leave the dough to prove (rise) in a warm place until it is doubled in size. My dough takes about 1½ hours to prove on a cold rainy day – if you have the central heating on or have an Aga in your kitchen, it will take less time.

While the dough is proving, make the filling. Put the golden sultanas in a bowl, cover with boiling water and leave to soak for 10 minutes. Drain and gently squeeze the sultanas to remove the excess water, then set aside. Cream the butter, muscovado sugar and cinnamon together in a bowl until pale and fluffy. Set aside until needed. Once the dough has proved, turn it on to a lightly floured work surface and knead lightly, then use your fingers to press and spread the dough evenly into a rectangular shape (about 40-45 x 30-35cm in size). You could use a rolling pin to do this if you like, but I don't like using one as it compresses the dough which means it loses its lightness and puffiness.

Spread the cinnamon butter filling evenly over the dough rectangle, then scatter the soaked sultanas over the top, followed by the orange zest. Roll the dough up like a Swiss roll, starting from a long edge, then dip a serrated knife into flour and cut the roll into 9 even slices. Place the buns, cut-side up, on to a baking tray lined with non-stick baking paper, placing them close together (alternatively, place the buns in a greased and lined deep 20cm square cake tin). Cover with a clean dry tea towel and leave to prove in a warm place for 20-30 minutes or until doubled in size.

Meanwhile, preheat the oven to 200°C/Gas Mark 6.

Bake the buns in the oven for about 30 minutes or until well risen and deep golden brown (if the buns start to turn dark brown before the end of the cooking time, place a piece of foil over the top to prevent them from turning too dark).

While the buns are baking, make the orange honey glaze. Put the orange segments, orange juice, caster sugar and honey into a blender and blend to form a smooth purée. Sieve the purée into a small saucepan and bring to a gentle simmer, then continue to cook over a low heat for 7-8 minutes or until the mixture is reduced by half. The glaze will become shiny and sticky, but do not reduce it too far as it should still be of a pouring consistency.

Remove the baked buns from the oven and let them cool for 10 minutes on the baking tray. Use a knife to separate the buns slightly. Pour some of the hot glaze evenly over the buns, then let the glaze soak in briefly before pouring over the remaining glaze. Leave the buns to cool completely on the baking tray (or in the tin) before removing and serving them.

Cook's Note
To make the dough by hand, put the processed flour, yeast and suet mixture into a large bowl, then add the rest of the flour with the salt and sugar and mix. Make a well in the centre, then pour in the warm milk and butter mixture, add the egg and mix with a palette knife to form a lumpy dough. Turn the dough on to a lightly floured work surface and knead for 7–8 minutes or until the dough becomes silky smooth and elastic. Continue as the recipe directs.

200
ml
175
125
75

Poppy Seed and Blood Orange Loaf Cake

The blood orange season is short (it runs from mid-January to mid-March) and the best time to buy them is mid-season when they are at their best both colour- and taste-wise. I love the deep red colour and strong orangey taste, with a pleasant hint of redcurrant.

I have a love-hate relationship with cakes containing poppy seeds; I find the crunchy texture of 'sand' beneath my teeth rather off-putting. After a bit of tinkering with cake recipes, I discovered that soaking the poppy seeds first makes them swell up and become softer and you then get a memorable cake with superb layers of flavour.

While baking this cake, it took me back to when I was a child and when mum used to bake a lemon poppy seed cake. We used to refer to it as the 'ant cake', because we thought the poppy seeds looked like ants!

This cake not only makes the perfect slice to enjoy with a cup of tea, but it also creates a pretty special pudding, served slightly warm with Blood Orange Granita (see page 27) and a dollop of crème fraîche. Delicious!

Serves 10–12

For the poppy seed and blood orange cake
180ml milk
100g poppy seeds
200g soft unsalted butter
140g caster sugar
1 tablespoon finely grated blood orange zest
3 eggs
300g plain flour
1½ teaspoons baking powder
125ml freshly squeezed blood orange juice

For the blood orange marmalade sauce
160g caster sugar
250ml freshly squeezed blood orange juice
50g blood orange peel, pith removed and peel cut into thin julienne (matchstick) sticks

Make the cake. Preheat the oven to 180°C/Gas Mark 4. Grease and line a 27 x 15cm loaf tin with non-stick baking paper.

Put the milk and poppy seeds into a small saucepan and heat gently until almost boiling. Remove from the heat and leave the poppy seeds to soak for about 10 minutes while you prepare the cake mixture.

Cream the butter, sugar and orange zest together in a bowl until pale and fluffy. Add the eggs, one at a time, beating well after each addition. Sift the flour and baking powder together, then gently fold the flour mixture into the creamed mixture. Do not overwork the mixture at this stage. Fold the blood orange juice and poppy seed milk mixture into the cake mixture.

Transfer the mixture to the prepared tin and level the surface. Bake in the oven for about 1 hour or until a fine metal skewer inserted into the centre comes out clean.

Remove from the oven and leave the cake to cool in the tin for 5 minutes, then turn it out on to a wire rack and leave to cool for a further 20 minutes before spooning over the blood orange marmalade sauce (see below).

While the cake is baking, make the blood orange marmalade sauce. Put the sugar into a small saucepan, add the blood orange juice and heat gently, stirring until the sugar has dissolved. Once the sugar has dissolved, turn the heat up to a rolling boil. Add the julienned sticks of orange peel and continue to boil the mixture for 10–15 minutes or until the sauce becomes fairly thick and glossy (the consistency of marmalade) – if you have a jam thermometer, then boil until the sauce reaches 102°C. Do not stir while the marmalade is boiling.

Remove from the heat and let the sauce cool down slightly before spooning it over the warm cake. Serve the cake warm or cold in slices. Store the cake in an airtight container for up to 3 days (it seems to get better with age, when served slightly warm).

Cook's Note
You can substitute the blood oranges for normal oranges, clementines or satsumas, if you like.

Pistachio and Walnut Baklava with Rhubarb and Rose Delights

Living in a country where so many culinary cultures meet, one is bound to be inspired to borrow, exchange and adapt recipes from home and away. The creativity for this recipe is sparked by the very first of the new season's forced rhubarb. The floral fragrance and colour of this cooked rhubarb reminds me of roses and the last time I made Turkish delight. So, filled with inspiration, I set off to create this recipe for a bit of seasonal fun. This recipe only works with forced rhubarb as you rely on the fragrance of the bright pink thin skin – the outdoor rhubarb will not deliver the same effect and the flavour will definitely be earthier.

Baklava is well received in our household – it's so easy to make, but is also so easy to get wrong. My secret is that you must follow the recipe to the letter. The layering of the filo sheets is very important and, before baking, you must cut through the top layers of filo pastry – if you do not do this, your baklava will not be able to absorb the syrup and will be dry. The final secret is in the soaking of the baklava once cooked – it must be covered with the syrup, a ladleful at a time, and then left to rest at room temperature for at least 12 hours. It's a labour of love, but your efforts and patience will be rewarded with this truly delicious dish.

Coriander has a slight citrus fragrance and it works magically with the rhubarb – an unusual but genius combination!

Serves 24

For the rhubarb and rose delights

350ml cold water
225g caster sugar
225g new season forced rhubarb, washed, drained and chopped into small pieces
juice of 1 lemon
5 leaves of gelatine
25g cornflour, plus 1 tablespoon cornflour
2 tablespoons rosewater
2 tablespoons icing sugar

For the rhubarb and apple purée

125g (prepared weight) eating apples (preferably Russet), peeled, cored and chopped
100ml cold water
125g cooked rhubarb pulp from the rhubarb and rose delights (see above)

For the pistachio and walnut baklava

300g shelled pistachios
300g shelled walnuts
2 teaspoons ground cinnamon
300g light soft brown sugar
16 sheets of chilled fresh or frozen (defrosted) filo pastry (each sheet about 40 x 30cm)
150g unsalted butter, melted
750g caster sugar
750ml cold water
1 cinnamon stick
finely grated zest and juice of 1 lime
finely grated zest and juice of 1 lemon
45g clear honey
1 teaspoon whole cloves

additional chopped pistachios and tiny sprigs of fresh coriander cress, to decorate

First, make the rhubarb and rose delights. Put 300ml of the water into a saucepan with the caster sugar, rhubarb and lemon juice. Cook over a low heat, stirring until the sugar has dissolved, then increase the heat a little and simmer for 5 minutes. Remove from the heat and leave the rhubarb mixture to infuse for 10 minutes. Then pass the rhubarb through a sieve, reserving the juices and pulp separately (the pulp will be used for the rhubarb and apple purée).

Line a 22 x 15cm baking tray with cling film and set aside. Soak the gelatine in cold water until it has softened, then gently squeeze the gelatine to remove the excess water. In a small bowl, blend the 25g cornflour with the remaining 50ml of water until smooth. Measure 450ml of the bright pink rhubarb juice into a non-stick saucepan, add the gelatine and the dissolved cornflour and heat gently, stirring until the gelatine has dissolved, then bring up to a rolling boil. Keep the mixture at a steady rolling boil for 12–14 minutes or until the syrup reaches a temperature of 112–115°C (soft ball stage – see Cook's Notes), stirring continuously to prevent the mixture from catching and burning. Remove from the heat and stir in the rosewater. Pour the mixture into the prepared baking tray, then leave to cool and keep at room temperature for about 12 hours or until the mixture is set; do not refrigerate.

Once the rhubarb and rose jelly is set, cut it into 48 pieces. Combine the remaining 1 tablespoon of cornflour and the icing sugar in a bowl, then roll the jellies in this mixture, coating them all over. Keep the jellies in an airtight container in a cool place for up to 3 days; do not refrigerate.

For the rhubarb and apple purée, put the apples in a small saucepan with the water and bring to the boil, then cover and cook gently for 5 minutes or until the apples are soft. Remove from the heat and transfer the apples and juices to a blender, add the rhubarb pulp and blend together until smooth, then pass the purée through a fine sieve into a bowl. Cover and chill the purée until needed (keep refrigerated and use within 3 days).

For the baklava, preheat the oven to 180°C/Gas Mark 4. Put the nuts, cinnamon and brown sugar into a food processor and pulse until the nuts are all finely chopped to roughly the same size – not powdered, but a coarse crumb texture.

Cut the filo pastry sheets in half so they each measure about 20 x 30cm. Assemble the baklava in a greased baking tin measuring 32 x 22 x 3.5cm. Brush 10 filo sheets with melted butter and lay them, one on top of the other, over the base of the baking tin, then spread half of the nuts and sugar mixture evenly over the filo. Brush another 10 filo sheets with melted butter and lay these over the nut mixture, one on top of the other, then press them down gently. Spread the remaining nut and sugar mixture evenly over the top. Brush the remaining 12 filo sheets with the remaining melted butter, lay these over the nut mixture, one on top of the other, then press them down gently.

Using a sharp paring knife, cut through the first 12 layers of filo to make 24 even-sized pieces. Bake the baklava in the oven for about 45 minutes or until golden brown and crisp.

While the baklava is baking, make the syrup. Put the caster sugar and water into a saucepan, together with all the remaining ingredients (except the decoration). Bring to the boil, then reduce the heat and simmer for 15 minutes or until the syrup has thickened to a coating consistency. Pass the syrup through a fine sieve into a jug and keep hot.

Once the baklava is cooked, remove it from the oven and leave to rest for 5 minutes, then cut the baklava all the way through to the base of the baking tin. Gradually ladle the hot syrup over the hot baklava. It will take a bit of time for the baklava to absorb all the syrup, so keep adding it a ladleful at a time, until it's all used up. Leave the baklava to cool and rest at room temperature for a minimum of 12 hours or overnight.

To serve, remove each piece of baklava from the baking tin and place on a serving plate. Spoon 2 teardrops of the rhubarb and apple purée on to each plate, then place 1 or 2 rhubarb and rose delights alongside. Decorate each plate with a few chopped pistachios and tiny sprigs of coriander cress and serve.

Cook's Notes

When making the rhubarb and rose delights, if you don't have a jam thermometer, place a small plate in the freezer, then put a teaspoonful of the hot syrup on to the chilled plate. If the syrup sets and you can roll the mixture into a soft, pliable ball, then it's ready.

Baklava will keep in an airtight container for up to 1 week in a cool, dry cupboard.

Seville Orange and Vanilla Bean Marmalade

Being both a chef and a food lover, part of me constantly wants to stow away food, squirrelling away the season's best to enjoy at a later date. It's almost as if I have a fear of giving up the foods I love from that particular season until they come around again the following year.

Pickling and preserving makes up a large part of my British Larder. The best part is rummaging through the larder in the hope of finding a gem, and then there it is, a jar of last year's Seville Orange and Vanilla Bean Marmalade. It's like finding a pot of gold!

The Seville orange season is short and, before you know it, it's been and gone. Approach the marmalade-making session with military precision and you will be surprised how quickly and easily you stock up the larder with jars of this golden goodness.

Makes 8 x 250g jars

1.1kg Seville oranges, washed
juice of 1 lemon
2 litres cold water
1 vanilla pod
1kg caster sugar
1kg preserving sugar (see Cook's Notes)

Cut away all the peel and pith from the oranges so that you are left with a pile of peel separated from the orange flesh. Put the orange flesh, juice and pips into a food processor and process to form a smooth purée. (The seeds contain lots of natural pectin that will help the marmalade to set perfectly.) Push the purée through a sieve into a preserving pan or a large, heavy-based saucepan.

Remove as much white pith from the orange peel as possible. Slice the peel into very thin matchstick strips and add these to the sieved purée in the pan. Add the lemon juice and water. Split the vanilla pod in half lengthways and scrape out the seeds into the pan, then add the pod to the pan as well for extra flavour.

Bring to the boil, then reduce the heat and simmer, uncovered, for about 1 hour or until the orange peel is very soft and the mixture has reduced by half. Over a low heat, add both sugars and stir until completely dissolved. Bring back to the boil, then boil rapidly for about 10 minutes, stirring gently once or twice and skimming off any scum from the surface. After 10 minutes, spoon a little of the marmalade on to a chilled plate and place in the freezer for about 2 minutes – if it sets to a jelly, the marmalade is ready; if not, boil it for a further 5–10 minutes and test again.

Remove from the heat and allow the marmalade to cool slightly. Remove and discard the vanilla pod, then carefully pour the marmalade into hot, sterilised jars. Cover with wax discs (wax-side down) and seal. When cold, label and store in a cool, dry cupboard. The marmalade should keep well for a year or so.

Cook's Notes

Preserving sugar is a specialised white sugar made from sugar cane and sugar beet that is coarser than granulated sugar. It is used for making jams and marmalades with fruits that have a high natural pectin content. The larger sugar crystals dissolve slowly and prevent the mixture from catching to the pan so easily. They also create less scum on top of the boiling liquid, thus resulting in a clearer preserve.

Make sure you remove all the scum from the top of the boiling marmalade; this will help it to stay very clear and shiny.

You can use other oranges for this marmalade, however, the high seed content in these Seville oranges is the secret to a successful marmalade. The seeds are high in natural pectin, which helps the marmalade to set.

Le Parfait
Le Parfait

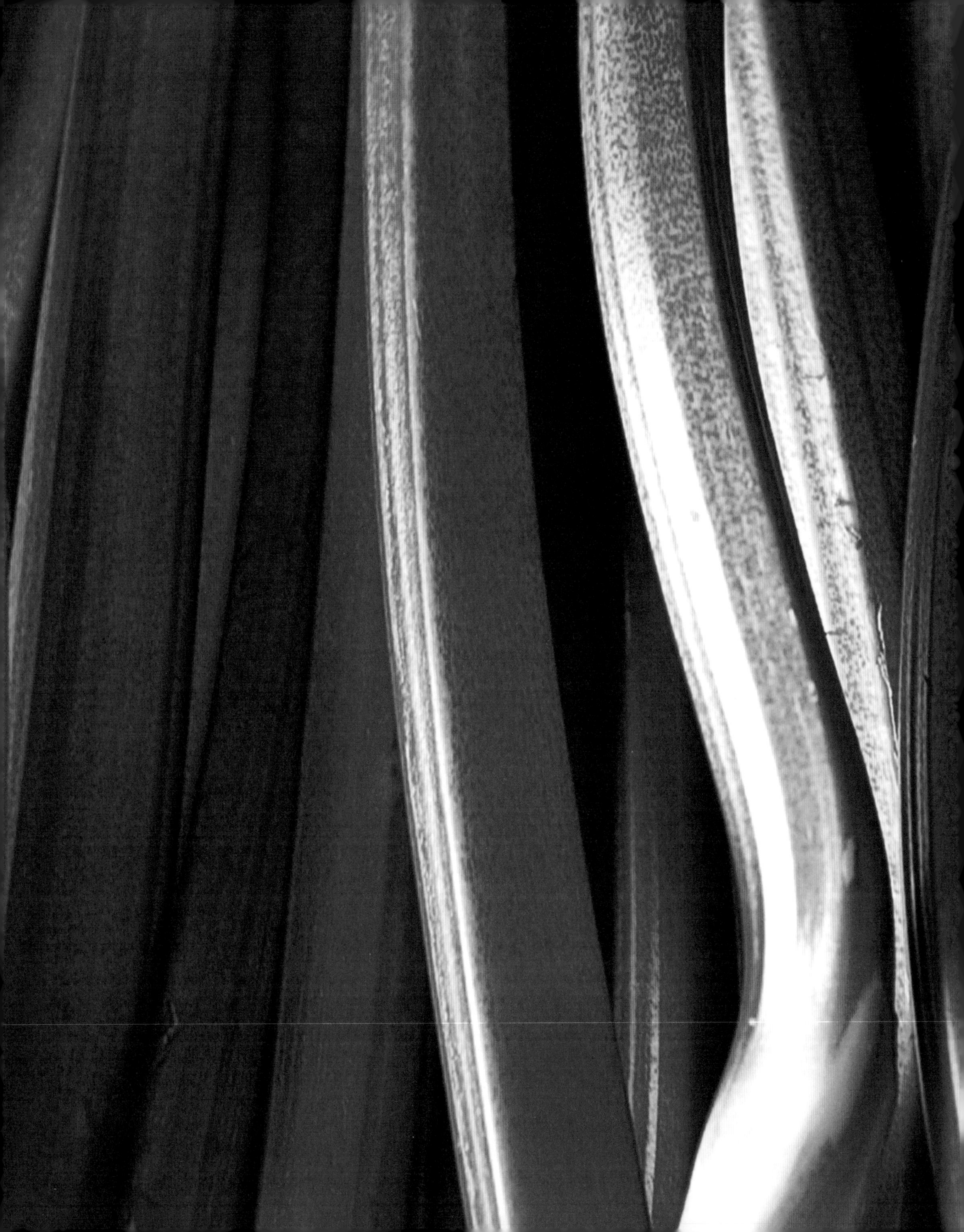

The British Larder | *February*

Winter is coming to an end and the season is slowly changing. The arrival of fresh green plant shoots is noticeable, breaking the predominant shades of brown in the woods. The abundance of winter roots and game is making way for the new season's delights.

The seasonal offerings for the month of February are lean, as Mother Nature takes time to rest, recuperate and replenish for the next season. In search of inspiration, exotics from further afield give us a much-needed boost, along with dried and stored fruits and nuts from the previous season. Reach deep into the larder and find those pickles and preserves from late summer and autumn last year. Dried fruits and nuts not only add extra nutrients, such as iron, fibre and protein, to casseroles, stews, salads and desserts, they also make dishes more interesting and appealing, especially at this time of year. As roots and tubers are finishing, cauliflowers, leeks and kale are still going strong. The ocean is gently warming up as we see the season coming to an end for fish such as turbot, brill and halibut. Shellfish such as oysters, cockles and mussels, are still plentiful, succulent and sweet. The forced rhubarb season continues this month but will come to an end in March, making way for the more robust outdoor rhubarb with its earthy taste. The gamekeepers are cleaning and polishing their guns and putting them away until next season, as the game season is finally at its end.

The beautiful Suffolk coast

Season's best during February…

Bananas, Blood Oranges, Brill, Brussels Sprouts, Cabbages, Cauliflowers, Celeriac, Chickweed, Chicory, Clams, Cockles, Duck, Guinea Fowl, Haddock, Hake, Halibut, Hare, Horseradish, Jerusalem Artichokes, John Dory, Kale, Leeks, Lemons, Lemon Sole, Mussels, Oranges, Oysters, Parsnips, Passion Fruit, Pineapples, Pomegranates, Potatoes (main crop), Purple Sprouting Broccoli, Rhubarb (forced), Salmon, Salsify, Shallots, Skate, Swedes, Truffles (black), Turbot, Venison, Winkles.

My culinary rituals for February…

Food gifts are a great idea for those loved ones who have everything they need. With Valentine's Day approaching, why not bake my delightful Rhubarb Melting Moments (see page 91) for the special person in your life. Amongst the pickling and preserving going on this month, the pancake pan comes out of the cupboard to flip a few pancakes for Shrove Tuesday. For a change from traditional pancakes, try my tempting Buttermilk Pancakes with Pan-Roasted Rhubarb and Blood Oranges (see page 95).

Horseradish

As fresh horseradish is plentiful, I try to preserve as much as possible. Peel and then grate the horseradish, mix it with a few tablespoons of white wine vinegar and freeze in ice cube trays. When needed, pop out as many cubes as you need and defrost, then stir into lightly whipped cream or crème fraîche to enjoy alongside your Sunday roast.

Rhubarb Jam

I believe there is a jam for all seasons and winter is no exception. Make a few jars of my fabulous **Forced Rhubarb Jam** (see page 90) so you can hang on to the vibrant pink colour and wonderful flavour of the new season forced rhubarb for just a little bit longer. Schedule this for February while forced rhubarb is still available. You can also make jam with outdoor rhubarb, but the colour will not be as vibrant pink.

British Larder Heroes

Cauliflower

Cauliflower is a member of the Brassicaceae family. Cauliflowers are at their sweetest and most flavourful when they are at their freshest. Choose a cauliflower with a firm, creamy white head with tight, small florets; once a cauliflower has turned yellow and feels spongy it's definitely past its best. With its strong and very individual taste, cauliflower works well with most cheeses. The natural sweetness of cauliflower also provides an ideal pairing with scallops and mild-tasting white fish such as halibut, turbot and hake.

Cauliflower can be cooked using several cooking techniques. For a delicious and simple side dish try **Roasted Curried Cauliflower**. Preheat the oven to 180°C/Gas Mark 4. Trim, then cut 1 cauliflower into fairly small, even-sized florets. Toss the florets in 2 tablespoons olive oil, a generous pinch or two of mild curry powder, sea salt and freshly cracked black pepper. Place the cauliflower florets in a single layer on a baking tray lined with non-stick baking paper and roast in the oven for 18–20 minutes or until just tender. Transfer to a serving dish, season with the finely grated zest and juice of 1 lemon, scatter over a small handful of chopped fresh parsley, sprinkle with 1 tablespoon toasted flaked almonds and serve. Serves 4.

Chicory or endive

Chicory or endive is a vegetable, which is also known as Belgium witloof. It is available in two colours – red and white. Chicory is grown in sandy peaty soil and the white variety is grown in the dark to keep the colour white. The leaves are bitter in taste and can either be cooked or eaten raw, but chicory is most commonly used in salads. The roots are ground and used as a coffee substitute. Radicchio is a variety of chicory and is also known as Italian chicory or red chicory. Radicchio has distinctive pink-red leaves with white veins and it has a spicy bitter taste, although the leaves become sweeter and milder once cooked.

For a delicious **Chicory Citrus Slaw**, finely shred 1 head of white chicory and place in a bowl, then add 2 tablespoons finely chopped fresh dill. Finely grate the zest from 1 lemon, 1 lime and 1 white grapefruit, then halve all the fruits and remove the segments of flesh. Add all the citrus zest and fruit segments to the chicory. Squeeze out any juice left in the fruit halves (once the segments have been removed) into a small bowl, add ½ teaspoon Dijon mustard, ½ teaspoon clear

Cauliflower

Kale

Forced rhubarb

honey, 1 tablespoon olive oil and 1 teaspoon white wine vinegar and whisk together. Season to taste with sea salt and freshly cracked black pepper. Pour the vinaigrette over the chicory mixture, toss to mix and serve immediately. Serves 2 as an accompaniment with grilled fish or chicken.

Hake

Deep-sea hake comes from the same family as cod and haddock. This mild-tasting fish has a coarse, fibrous, flaky texture and silver-grey skin. Due to its delicate flavour, hake is best paired with strong-tasting flavours such as lemon, capers and anchovies.

For a simple all-in-one baked supper, try my **Hake, Chorizo and Chicory Bake**. Preheat the oven to 180°C/Gas Mark 4 and grease a 25 x 15cm ovenproof dish with 1 tablespoon unsalted butter. Roughly shred 1 head of white chicory and 1 leek and scatter them over the base of the prepared dish. Season with sea salt and freshly cracked black pepper. Chop 80g chorizo sausage into 1cm pieces and scatter over the chicory. Place 2 x 150g skinless, boneless hake fillets, seasoned with salt and pepper, on top of the chorizo, nestling them in and spacing them apart. Pour over 100ml dry white wine and scatter over 1 teaspoon finely chopped fresh thyme. Bake in the oven for 25 minutes or until the fish is cooked and pale golden. Remove from the oven and leave to rest for 2 minutes, then transfer the hake to serving plates. Stir 1 tablespoon crème fraîche into the baked chicory and chorizo, then spoon this over the hake and serve. Serves 2 as a main course or supper.

Horseradish

Horseradish is a perennial plant from the Brassicaceae family, which includes mustard, wasabi, turnips and cabbages. Horseradish grows wild around the British Isles or you can grow it in your garden. The cultivated root can also be bought fresh from some farmers' markets, greengrocers and supermarkets. The root itself has no aroma, but once it is peeled, cut or grated, an enzyme develops that produces 'mustard oil', which is pretty potent and can irritate sinuses

Kale Pesto (page 32)

and eyes. In fact, I find the clean, citrus-like aroma of freshly grated horseradish quite addictive.

There is something rather special about fresh horseradish and I like to use it like a seasoning, especially with oily fish, shellfish and smoked fish. To make a delicious **Smoked Trout and Horseradish** Pâté, remove and discard the skin and bones from 1 whole smoked trout (about 400g whole/unprepared weight) and flake the flesh into a mixing bowl. Add 2 tablespoons crème fraîche, finely grated zest and juice of ½ lemon, sea salt and freshly cracked black pepper and grated (peeled) fresh horseradish to taste, and mix well. (Peel the horseradish like a carrot before grating and add as little or as much as you like to taste.) Serve the pâté with plenty of Melba toast and a glass of your finest English sparkling wine. Serves 2 as a starter or serves 4 as a snack.

Kale

Kale is another vegetable from the Brassicaceae family and is most closely related to wild cabbage in that it does not form a head, unlike the majority of cabbage varieties, but the genetics of kale are very similar to those of spring greens. Kale, sometimes called curly kale, is available in two colours – green or red – and the leaves are the edible part. I tend to use the green variety in cooking, but both types are interchangeable in recipes, so the choice is yours. The stalks of kale are too tough to eat, so they should be removed before cooking. Personally, I prefer all Brassicas cooked well as many are too tough and chewy to serve al dente.

For a pesto with a difference, try my recipe for **Kale Pesto** (see page 32). Stir it into hot cooked pasta or serve with pan-roasted sea bass or turbot.

Mussels

Even though mussels are often regarded as poor man's shellfish, they are probably the only type of shellfish we eat that is plentiful and not endangered, as well as being environmentally sound. Mussels are only good to eat in months with the letter 'r' in the name. The temperature of the sea is also important – the colder the better. To enjoy this wonderful humble food at its best, the secret to success and a happy diner is in the preparation.

To prepare mussels for your favourite recipe, pull off the hairy 'beards', scrub away any barnacles and weed from the shells and wash the mussels thoroughly under cold running water to remove any grit and sand, then drain. Discard any mussels that are heavy, broken or that remain open when tapped sharply with the back of a knife. The prepared mussels are now ready for cooking. Do not overcook them either – the key to moist, succulent mussels is to cook them quickly and briefly, then eat them as soon as they are ready. Once cooked, any mussels that haven't opened should be discarded.

New season forced rhubarb

New season forced rhubarb (available from January to March), with its tender, pink stems, is still considered to be the chef's first choice. Forced rhubarb is grown in the UK in what is known as the Rhubarb Triangle, which is a 23 km^2 (9–square mile) triangle in West Yorkshire, situated between Wakefield, Leeds and Bradford. Forced rhubarb grown in this area is regarded as the very best with its fragrant perfumed taste and beautiful pink colour. In February 2010, after years of petitioning by the producers, Yorkshire Forced Rhubarb was awarded Protected Designation of Origin (PDO) status by the European Commission. Families in Yorkshire have grown forced rhubarb for many generations and what makes this humble vegetable so unique is the method by which it is cultivated and harvested. The rhubarb crowns (roots) are grown outdoors for about 2 years and then they are lifted and left on top of the ground until a frosty spell of weather occurs – this is needed to deceive the crowns into growth once they are in the sheds. The crowns are then moved to heated sheds where they are tricked and forced to grow in the warmth and dark. Depriving rhubarb of light makes the stems shoot upwards in search of light and this produces a more succulent-tasting product. The tender, bright pink stems are then harvested by hand and by candlelight, ready to be packed and sold. Although it's a very labour-intensive process, it's actually a rather romantic story and it really is a labour of love, hence it is such a highly prized and fairly expensive ingredient. I'm obsessed with making curds and as well as believing there is a jam for every season, I also believe there is a curd for each season too. You will find various recipes in this book for making these delicious, rich butter curds.

For a vibrant pink-coloured Rhubarb Curd use new season forced rhubarb, or for a more earthy colour, use outdoor rhubarb – either type will make an equally delicious curd. Use the curd for filling simple blind-baked shortcrust or puff pastry cases, or layer the curd in a glass dish with jelly, custard and sponge cake for the ultimate twist on a classic trifle. To make **Rhubarb Curd**, wash and drain 200g rhubarb, then cut it into 1cm slices. Place in a saucepan with 200g caster sugar and 100ml freshly squeezed lemon juice, then bring to a gentle simmer, cover and cook for 8–10 minutes or until the rhubarb is tender. Carefully transfer the mixture to a blender and purée until smooth. Transfer the warm purée to a heatproof mixing bowl and whisk in 2 whole eggs and 2 egg yolks. Place the bowl over a pan of simmering water (making sure that the bottom of the bowl does not come into contact with the simmering water underneath) and heat gently, stirring continuously with a wooden spoon, until the mixture starts to thicken, then continue to cook gently for a further 10–12 minutes or until the rhubarb curd thickens enough to coat the back of the spoon; do not allow the mixture to boil or it will curdle. Remove the pan from the heat (but leave the bowl set over the pan) and gradually but quickly whisk 125g cold unsalted butter (cut into very small pieces) into the rhubarb curd, a few pieces at a time, until the butter is completely melted and incorporated – by this stage you should have a rich, creamy and glossy rhubarb curd. Use as required or pour the warm curd into a clean bowl, place a piece of cling film directly on the surface to prevent a skin forming, cool and refrigerate for up to 3 days. If you are making the rhubarb curd to serve another time, pour the warm curd into hot sterilised jars (the rhubarb curd will make about 3 x 250g jars). Cover with wax discs (wax-side down) and seal. When cold, label, then store in the fridge and use within 2–3 weeks. Once opened, keep in the fridge and use within 3 days.

Turbot

For most chefs and enthusiastic cooks, turbot is the king of the sea. It is an expensive flat fish with a firm, white flesh and a delicate flavour. The bones make the best quality fish stock. The skin is tough with hard, knobbly bits and should be removed; take extra care when filleting turbot as the knife can get caught in these hard knobbles (alternatively, ask your fishmonger to remove the skin – but do not leave the shop without the bones!).

To make an easy and tasty Fish Stock, chop 500–800g fish bones and trimmings from white fish such as turbot, into large pieces using kitchen scissors (if you use the heads, remove the eyes and gills, otherwise your stock will become bitter and cloudy), wash thoroughly in cold water and drain. Transfer the bones and trimmings to a deep saucepan, add

Turbot

1 stick celery, 1 large onion and 1 leek, all roughly chopped, 2 peeled cloves garlic and a handful of mixed fresh herbs such as thyme, parsley, tarragon and chervil. Add the tops of fresh fennel if you have it available. Fill the pan nearly to the top with cold water and bring slowly to the boil. Remove any scum from the surface with a ladle, then reduce the heat to a gentle simmer and cook, uncovered, for 20 minutes (remember, do not boil, just cook at a gentle simmer – if you boil the stock, it will become cloudy). Remove from the heat and leave to infuse for 1 hour. Pass the stock through a fine sieve into a bowl, then cool completely, cover and refrigerate until needed. The fish stock will keep for up to 2 days in the fridge and for up to 1 month in the freezer. (The amount of fish stock you make will depend on the size of pan you use and how much water you add.) Please note, only use bones and trimmings from white fish (such as cod, haddock, plaice, sole, turbot, etc); do not use bones and trimmings from oily fish (such as salmon, mackerel, herrings, etc) to make the stock.

Cauliflower Soup with Stilton Cream Profiteroles

The well-designed and complicated structure of cauliflowers makes them an impressive vegetable. Have you ever taken the time to study their composition? I find this unique vegetable intriguing as it has so many different dimensions, but then the colour fascinates me even more. When I cook cauliflower, I always try and keep the fresh creamy white colour as I find it warm and inviting.

Creating a soup that packs a punch in flavour is not always easy; my aim when I choose a flavour profile is always to end up with a dish that highlights the flavours of the ingredients I have used. Cauliflowers have a strong fragrant taste, but it's interesting how the addition of other strong flavours such as onions and garlic, can easily mask the fresh taste of the cauliflower. Hence, I only choose simple ingredients when making this kind of soup and I apply this theory to most fragrant vegetables, especially the root varieties such as celeriac and parsnips.

Serves 6 as a starter or light lunch

For the Stilton cream

1 leaf of gelatine
150g Stilton, cut into small pieces
100ml cold water
100ml double cream

For the choux pastry

150ml milk
80g unsalted butter
1 teaspoon table salt
120g plain flour
3 eggs
100ml cold water

For the watercress oil

20g watercress leaves
4 teaspoons olive oil
4 teaspoons sunflower oil
sea salt and freshly cracked black pepper

For the cauliflower soup

1 cauliflower (about 650g total weight)
50g unsalted butter
750ml vegetable or white chicken stock
200ml double cream

a few toasted hazelnuts, to serve (optional)

First, make the Stilton cream (see Cook's Notes). Soak the gelatine in cold water until it has softened. Put the Stilton, water and cream into a small saucepan and heat gently until almost boiling. Transfer the cheese mixture to a blender. Squeeze the gelatine gently to remove the excess water, then add the gelatine to the warm cheese mixture. Blend together until the gelatine has dissolved and the mixture is smooth.

Pass the cheese sauce through a fine sieve, then pour the sauce into a cream whipper (see page 17). Fit the needle attachment to the cream whipper and secure the lid. Charge with 2 gas pellets, shake vigorously, then refrigerate for about 4 hours so that the mixture thickens. Remove the cream whipper from the fridge about 30 minutes before you are ready to fill the choux buns, to allow the Stilton cream to loosen up slightly.

Next, make the choux pastry. Place a shallow roasting tin in the bottom of the oven and preheat the oven to 200°C/ Gas Mark 6. Line 2 baking trays with non-stick baking paper and set aside.

Put the milk, butter and salt into a saucepan and heat gently until the butter has melted, then bring to a gentle simmer. Remove the pan from the heat and immediately sift the flour into the milk mixture, then beat vigorously with a wooden spoon until the mixture is smooth and leaves the sides of the pan to form a ball. Return to a very low heat and cook gently for 5 minutes, stirring continuously, then remove from the heat.

Transfer the dough to an electric stand mixer fitted with a paddle attachment. Turn the mixer on and add the eggs to the dough, one at a time, beating well after each addition, then beat until the mixture becomes silky, smooth and shiny. If you don't have an electric mixer, gradually add the beaten eggs to the dough, beating well with the wooden spoon, until you have a smooth and shiny mixture. Transfer the choux pastry to a piping bag fitted with a 1cm plain nozzle and pipe 18 walnut-sized balls on to the prepared baking trays, leaving a little space between each one.

Place the baking trays in the oven and quickly pour the cold water into the hot roasting tin in the bottom of the oven (be careful as the water will sizzle and spit). Close the oven door quickly. The water will create steam and the buns will each form a crisp outer shell with a cavity inside. Bake the choux buns for 20–25 minutes or until risen, golden brown and crisp. Remove from the oven and poke a small hole in the bottom of each bun with a teaspoon handle to release the steam, then return to the oven and bake for a further 5 minutes to dry out. Transfer to a wire rack and cool completely before filling (see Cook's Notes).

Meanwhile, make the watercress oil. Place all the ingredients in a small jug and use a stick blender to blend everything together until smooth. Taste and adjust the seasoning, if necessary. Cover and refrigerate until needed.

Finally, make the soup. Remove and discard the green outer leaves of the cauliflower, then chop the cauliflower (stalks and florets). Melt the butter in a large saucepan and as soon as the butter starts to foam, add the cauliflower and season with salt and pepper. Sauté the cauliflower over a medium heat for 7–8 minutes or until it starts to take on colour, stirring continuously (don't let the cauliflower take on too much colour as this will turn the soup brown). Add the stock and bring to the boil, then reduce the heat to a gentle simmer, cover and cook for about 12 minutes or until the cauliflower is very soft. Stir in the cream, bring back to a simmer and cook for a further 5 minutes.

Carefully transfer the soup to a blender and purée until smooth. Return to the pan and if the soup is a bit thick for your liking, stir in a little more stock. Reheat gently, then taste and adjust the seasoning, if necessary. Keep hot until you are ready to serve.

To use the Stilton cream, shake the cream whipper vigorously and squirt the foam into a glass to check if it is ready (if the mixture has set solidly, then hold the cream whipper under warm running water to loosen the mixture inside, then shake and use as directed). Insert the needle into the hole in the base of a choux bun and squirt some Stilton cream inside. Repeat to fill all the choux buns.

To serve, ladle the hot soup into bowls, drizzle over the watercress oil and then grate over a few toasted hazelnuts, if you like. Arrange the Stilton cream profiteroles on a separate plate. Serve immediately.

Cook's Notes

Please note that when making the Stilton cream, the cheese sauce does not look great when it is cooking, but once blended, the cheese sauce will be creamy, smooth and appealing. The Stilton cream can be made up to 2 days in advance and kept in the cream whipper in the fridge.

When baking the choux buns, I normally bake one tray at a time, as I find they come out crispier and cook better if there is good air circulation. If you have time, you can do this too.

The unfilled choux buns will keep in an airtight container in a cool, dry cupboard for up to 3 days, although they will be at their very best if made and eaten on the same day. Once filled, the profiteroles should be served immediately as they will soon become soft.

Pan-fried Hake with Garam Masala Mussels

I appreciate the clever use of spices, but combining spices with fish can be tricky. As hake is a fairly mild-tasting fish, it requires strong flavours to give it a lift, and these garam masala mussels do exactly that. You can make your own garam masala spice blend if you like, but good quality ready-made blends will work just as well.

Serves 2 as a main course

For the garam masala mussels
2 tablespoons rapeseed oil
1 leek, washed and sliced
1 onion, chopped
1 clove garlic, crushed
1 heaped teaspoon garam masala
a pinch of crushed dried chillies
500g fresh mussels (in shell), cleaned (see page 72)
200ml dry white wine
150ml double cream
2 tablespoons chopped fresh mixed herbs (such as chervil, parsley, tarragon and chives)
sea salt and freshly cracked black pepper

For the pan-fried hake and wilted spinach
2 x 140g hake fillets, skin on
1 teaspoon olive oil
2 tablespoons unsalted butter
100g fresh spinach, rinsed and drained well
juice of ½ lemon

For the garam masala mussels, heat the rapeseed oil in a large saucepan, then sauté the leek, onion, garlic and spices, with salt and pepper added, over a medium heat for 6–8 minutes or until golden.

Add the mussels to the pan, pour in the wine, then cover with a tight-fitting lid and cook over a high heat for 4–5 minutes or until the shells open. Discard any unopened mussels. Add the cream and bring back to the boil, then remove from the heat, stir in the herbs and taste and adjust the seasoning, if necessary.

Meanwhile, cook the hake. Season the hake with salt and pepper. Heat the olive oil in a non-stick frying pan over a medium heat, place the fish in the pan, skin-side down, then add 1 tablespoon of the butter and fry the fish for about 4 minutes or until the skin is golden and crisp. Flip the fish over and cook for a further 2 minutes or until lightly browned. Remove the fish to a plate and keep warm.

Return the pan to the heat, add the remaining butter and heat until it is melted, then add the spinach and salt and pepper and cook for about 1 minute or until wilted, stirring.

Spoon the wilted spinach on to the centre of 2 bowl plates, place the fish on top and spoon over the mussels and cooking juices. Squeeze the lemon juice over the fish and serve immediately. Serve with boiled new potatoes or mashed potatoes.

Lemon Sole with Orange-baked Chicory and Clam Paper Parcels

This recipe is both magical and impressive and it will intrigue your guests. All the ingredients are wrapped up together in a paper parcel, then oven-baked and served. When you open the puffed-up paper parcels, you will be greeted with the most delicious smells and steam coming from the succulent food inside.

This style of cooking has a purpose, and as with this recipe, the steam will open the clams and cook the fish, capturing all the juices in one place and keeping all the components succulent and moist – a bit of culinary magic indeed. This recipe requires a bit of preparation, as the chicory has to be cooked before it goes into the parcels.

Serves 2 as a main course

2 heads of white chicory
1 tablespoon icing sugar
about 4 tablespoons unsalted butter
finely grated zest and juice of 1 orange
20–24 large fresh clams (in shell)
2 whole lemon sole on the bone (about 400g each), skin and fins removed
200ml dry sherry or dry white wine
sea salt and freshly cracked black pepper
1 tablespoon chopped fresh flat-leaf parsley, plus extra finely grated orange zest, to garnish

First, prepare the chicory. Cut the chicory into quarters, place in a bowl, then sprinkle over the icing sugar and salt and pepper and toss to lightly coat. Melt 2 tablespoons of the butter in a large, non-stick frying pan and once the butter starts to foam and turn a nutty brown colour, add the chicory and fry over a high heat for 8–10 minutes or until golden brown all over. Reduce the heat after a while and add a little extra butter if the chicory is starting to catch. Plenty of colour is good and adds to the flavour, but do not let the chicory burn.

Add the orange zest and juice, reduce the heat to low, then let the chicory cook gently for 8–10 minutes or until tender. You will need to turn the chicory pieces over a few times to get an even glaze all over, as the juices will thicken and become sticky and glossy. Remove from the heat.

Meanwhile, wash the clams thoroughly under cold running water and discard any clams that do not shut firmly when tapped against the edge of the sink. Set aside.

Preheat the oven to 180°C/Gas Mark 4. Cut out two 40 x 40cm pieces of non-stick baking paper and lay them out on a spacious work surface. Divide the chicory between the 2 pieces of paper, placing it in the centre. Spoon over the pan juices.

Wipe the pan clean and return to the heat. Add 1 tablespoon of butter and once it has melted and starts to foam, season the lemon sole with salt (and pepper, if you like – I prefer to use salt only) and place the fish in the pan. Cook over a high heat for 2 minutes, then add the remaining tablespoon of butter to the pan. Immediately remove the fish from the pan, carefully flip the fish over and place a fish on top of each portion of chicory. Pour the warm melted butter and pan juices over the fish. Divide the clams between the 2 portions.

For each parcel, take 2 opposite sides of the paper, bring them together over the top of the ingredients and fold over to seal tightly, then do the same with the other 2 opposite sides, but just before sealing, carefully pour half of the sherry into each parcel and then seal the parcels tightly. Place the parcels on a baking tray and bake in the oven for 12 minutes, by which time the parcels will have puffed-up like big pillows.

Remove from the oven, place each parcel on a serving plate and carefully open (discard any cooked clams that remain unopened). Garnish with the parsley and orange zest and enjoy! Serve with steamed couscous, boiled brown rice or boiled new potatoes and steamed seasonal greens.

Pan-roasted Turbot with Red Wine Sauce and Braised Radicchio

Turbot is the king of the sea and it's very expensive. To give this fish the justice it deserves when cooking, simplicity is the key. Even though turbot is a delicate fish, it's very meaty and the red wine sauce (made with fish stock) in this recipe makes this dish extra special. The quantity of red wine used for the sauce sounds like a lot, but with reduction, it's the right amount to create the perfect flavour.

The cooking time for the turbot will also depend on the thickness of the fillets. The thicker the fillets are, the longer they will take, so adapt the cooking time accordingly.

Serves 4 as a main course

For the red wine sauce
1 teaspoon sunflower oil
6 banana shallots, finely sliced
1 leek, washed and finely sliced
1 bay leaf
1 teaspoon coriander seeds
500ml red wine
500ml fish stock
50g cold unsalted butter, cut into small pieces
sea salt and freshly cracked black pepper

For the braised radicchio
1 large head of radicchio
80g unsalted butter
50ml dry vermouth
250ml white chicken stock

For the pan-roasted turbot
4 x 200g skinless turbot fillets
1 tablespoon olive oil
200g kale, stalks removed

First, make the red wine sauce. Heat the sunflower oil in a heavy-based saucepan and sauté the shallots, leek, bay leaf and coriander seeds over a high heat for about 10 minutes or until the vegetables are golden brown and caramelised.

Pour the wine into the pan and let it bubble, stirring and scraping the base of the pan with a wooden spoon to deglaze it. Simmer for 10–15 minutes or until the wine is reduced by three-quarters of its original volume and it becomes syrupy. Add the stock, bring back to a simmer and simmer gently for 15 minutes.

Pass the sauce through a fine sieve into a clean pan, discard the solids, then return the sauce to a low heat and simmer gently for 10–15 minutes or until the sauce is reduced by half. By this stage, the sauce should be shiny.

Next, cook the radicchio. Cut the radicchio into quarters. Melt the butter in a non-stick frying pan over a high heat and sauté the radicchio on all sides for 7–8 minutes or until it starts to colour. Pour the vermouth into the pan and let it bubble, stirring and scraping the base of the pan with a wooden spoon to deglaze it, then cook over a high heat for about 5 minutes or until it has reduced and becomes syrupy. Add the stock and bring back to a simmer, then cover and simmer gently for about 10 minutes or until the radicchio is tender. Just before serving, drain the braised radicchio on kitchen paper.

Meanwhile, cook the turbot. Season the turbot fillets on both sides with salt only. Heat the olive oil in a non-stick frying pan over a medium heat. Add the turbot fillets and fry for about 2–3 minutes on each side or until cooked and golden, turning once. The cooking time will depend on the thickness of the fillets.

While the turbot is cooking, blanch the kale in a large pan of boiling salted water for about 1 minute or until tender, then drain well. Finish the red wine sauce, whisking in the butter as directed. Keep the sauce hot. Then gradually whisk in the cold butter (away from the heat) once you are ready to serve – the butter will make the sauce glossy (see Cook's Note). Add salt and pepper to taste, if necessary.

To serve, spoon the braised radicchio on to the centre of the serving plates and spoon the blanched kale alongside. Place the golden fried turbot on top, then spoon the red wine sauce around and serve immediately. Serve with buttered new potatoes or crushed new potatoes finished with a splash of olive oil.

Cook's Note
The red wine sauce can be made in advance, if you like. Make it as directed (but do not whisk in the cold butter), then pour the sauce into a bowl and leave to cool. Once cool, cover and refrigerate for up to 3 days. When you are ready to serve, gently reheat the sauce in a saucepan until it comes to a simmer, then gradually whisk in the cold butter to create a glossy sauce.

Mussels with Smoky Bacon, Cider and Horseradish

We are fairly selfish with our approach to what we put on our menus at the British Larder in the sense that we only cook food we love to eat. I'm a mussel lover and it's not often that I get a chance to eat them. There is something rather good about eating with your fingers, food just seems to taste better, and mussels in their shell require a bit of finger action. When I see mussels on a menu I like to order them, but, and this is a big but, I have to trust the restaurant and the chef, because there is nothing worse than dirty mussels. Gritty mussels with beards attached and full of sand can ruin a simple, delicious dish in seconds. At a time of year when we can sometimes feel slightly deprived of warm sunshine and its brightly coloured foods, such as berries, peppers and tomatoes, these mussels and leeks can remind that winter has its own colourful gems. Such beautiful food is enough to put a smile on anyone's face and is a gentle reminder that spring is on its way.

Serves 1 as a main course or 2 as a starter

25ml rapeseed oil
1 small banana shallot, finely diced
80g smoked back bacon rashers, finely diced
½ leek, washed and sliced
1 clove garlic, crushed
1 bay leaf
200ml apple cider
500g fresh mussels (in shell), cleaned (see page 72)
80ml double cream
a handful of fresh parsley and fresh chives, chopped
sea salt and freshly cracked black pepper
peeled fresh horseradish, for grating (to taste), to serve

Heat the rapeseed oil in a large saucepan and sauté the shallot, bacon, leek, garlic and bay leaf, with a little salt and pepper added, over a high heat for 6–8 minutes or until golden brown.

Add the cider to the pan and bring it to a gentle boil. Add the mussels, cover the pan with a tight-fitting lid and cook over a high heat for 4–5 minutes or until the shells open. Discard any unopened mussels.

Add the cream and bring back to the boil, then remove from the heat. Taste and adjust the seasoning, if necessary, then scatter over the chopped herbs.

Serve immediately in a bowl(s) and grate over the fresh horseradish to taste. Serve with plenty of buttered fresh bread.

Venison Meatballs with Red Onion Gravy

This dish meets all the expectations of a hearty and comforting meal and it will easily help you to put a hard day's work well behind you. As venison is very lean it can be fairly dry, therefore wrapping the meatballs in smoked streaky bacon will not only add extra flavour, but it will also keep the meat inside moist and juicy.

The delicious, tangy sweet red onion gravy sets the meatballs off perfectly and the parsnip and kale mash provides an ideal accompaniment.

Serves 4 as a main course

For the red onion gravy
50g unsalted butter, plus 1 tablespoon cold unsalted butter
2 large red onions, finely sliced
125g redcurrant jelly
200ml red wine
500ml chicken stock
sea salt and freshly cracked black pepper

For the venison meatballs
2 slices white bread, crusts removed and bread torn into small pieces
4 tablespoons milk
450g minced venison
2 tablespoons chopped fresh mixed herbs, such as thyme, oregano and parsley
1 egg
2 teaspoons ground coriander
2 teaspoons Worcestershire sauce
8 rashers smoked streaky bacon or 8 slices smoked pancetta
1 tablespoon sunflower oil

For the parsnip and kale mash
500g parsnips (peeled weight), finely sliced
100g kale, stalks removed
50g unsalted butter
50ml double cream

First, make the red onion gravy. Melt the 50g butter in a saucepan and once the butter starts to foam, add the onions and salt and pepper and sauté over a medium heat for 8–10 minutes or until the onions start to turn golden brown. Add the redcurrant jelly and cook for a few minutes or until it has dissolved and becomes liquid.

Pour the wine into the pan and let it bubble, stirring and scraping the base of the pan with a wooden spoon to deglaze it. Simmer for about 5 minutes or until it reduces, becomes syrupy and coats the onions.

Add the stock and bring to the boil, then reduce the heat to a gentle simmer and simmer for 15–20 minutes or until the sauce has thickened slightly. Taste and adjust the seasoning, if necessary. Just before you are ready to serve, whisk in the remaining cold butter to give your gravy a lovely gloss.

Meanwhile, make the venison meatballs. Preheat the oven to 200°C/Gas Mark 6. Line a baking tray with non-stick baking paper and set aside. Put the bread in a shallow dish, pour over the milk and leave to soak for about 10 minutes.

Put the minced venison, soaked bread and milk, chopped herbs, egg, ground coriander, Worcestershire sauce and salt and pepper in a large mixing bowl and mix together thoroughly. Divide the mixture into 8 equal portions and shape each portion into a ball. Wrap 1 rasher of bacon around each ball, then reshape the meatballs a little to make them slightly oblong so that they cook evenly.

Heat the sunflower oil in a large, non-stick frying pan, add the meatballs and cook over a high heat for 8–10 minutes or until browned all over. Transfer the meatballs to the prepared baking tray and roast them in the oven for about 12 minutes or until fully cooked and golden brown. Remove from the oven and let the meatballs rest, uncovered, for 4 minutes before serving.

In the meantime, make the parsnip and kale mash. Cook the parsnips in a pan of boiling salted water for 8–10 minutes or until tender. While the parsnips are cooking, blanch the kale in a separate large pan of boiling salted water for about 1 minute or until tender, then drain well.

Drain the parsnips and push them through a potato ricer or mash them well with a potato masher, then stir in the butter, cream and blanched kale. Taste and add salt and pepper, if necessary. Keep the mash warm until you are ready to serve.

To serve, place a heaped spoonful of the parsnip and kale mash on to each serving plate and place the meatballs (2 per serving) on top. Spoon over a generous amount of the red onion gravy and serve immediately. I serve this dish in shallow bowls so that I can serve a generous helping of sauce for each portion.

Cauliflower and Shallot Piccalilli

Our British Larder piccalilli is the talk of the town! We often get customers who ask to take a jar home with them and I can understand why they want ours instead of making their own or buying inferior versions elsewhere. This piccalilli is at its best once it has been left for about a week after making, as the flavours need a little time to mature and develop. We make large batches of piccalilli at a time, then pot and sell it.

It's a good idea to make a decent amount and then you can give a jar or two to friends and family as a tasty homemade gift – tie a ribbon with a tag around the jars to finish them off. As with all our cooking and recipes, we select the best ingredients we can get, and a local organic farm supplies us with the most wonderful cauliflowers that are firm, sweet and creamy white.

Makes about 4 x 250g jars

180g carrots (peeled weight), cut on the diagonal into ½ cm slices
180g banana shallots (peeled weight), cut into ½ cm slices
300g small cauliflower florets
175g caster sugar
2 star anise
300ml white wine vinegar
150ml malt vinegar
1 large fresh red chilli, deseeded and cut into thin julienne (matchstick) strips
25g mustard powder
15g cornflour
12g turmeric
100ml cold water
1 bay leaf
sea salt and freshly cracked black pepper

Bring a large pan of salted water to the boil. Blanch the vegetables separately in the rapidly boiling water (covering the pan each time). Start with the carrots and blanch them for 5 minutes, then remove using a slotted spoon and refresh in iced water. Next, blanch the shallots for 3 minutes, then remove and refresh in the iced water with the carrots. Finally, blanch the cauliflower florets for 3 minutes, then remove and refresh in the iced water.

Drain the cooled vegetables in a colander; leave them draining for about 30 minutes to ensure that all the water has drained away completely.

Place the sugar, star anise and both vinegars in a heavy-based saucepan, along with salt and pepper, and bring to the boil, then boil rapidly, uncovered, over a high heat for about 8 minutes or until the mixture is slightly reduced and syrupy. Add the chilli strips and cook for a further 2 minutes.

Place the mustard powder, cornflour and turmeric in a small bowl, add the cold water and stir until smooth and blended. Mix 2 ladlefuls of the hot vinegar mixture into the blended cornflour, then stir the cornflour mixture into the remaining vinegar in the pan. Bring back to the boil and cook over a medium heat for 6–8 minutes or until thickened and glossy, stirring continuously.

Add the drained cooled vegetables and bay leaf to the pan, bring the mixture back to the boil and simmer for 1 minute. Remove from the heat, then spoon the piccalilli into hot, sterilised jars. Cover with vinegar-proof lids and seal. Leave to cool, then label and store in a cool, dry cupboard. Store for at least 1 week before using.

The unopened jars of piccalilli should keep well for up to 3 months. Once opened, store in the fridge and use within 1 week.

Cook's Note
Piccalilli is a delicious accompaniment to baked gammon, or it is ideal served as part of a ploughman's platter with mature Cheddar cheese and freshly baked sourdough bread.

Roasted Cardamom Panna Cotta with Stewed Rhubarb Jellies

This recipe is exactly what the British Larder is all about. The combination of flavours, textures and unusual methods is a great explanation of exactly what is going on in my mind. I easily get bored of dishes that have the same texture throughout, hence I like to incorporate a contrast in textures in my recipes. There are several elements to this recipe, so it's your choice to extract what you like from it or you can take the plunge and make the whole lot. Of course, I would recommend trying the latter!

Serves 8

For the roasted cardamom panna cotta
8 cardamom pods
300ml double cream
2 leaves of gelatine
75ml milk
40g icing sugar
300ml natural yogurt

For the stewed rhubarb
500g new season forced rhubarb, washed, drained and cut into 2cm lengths
400ml unsweetened cranberry juice
150g caster sugar
1 vanilla pod, split in half lengthways and seeds scraped out

For the rhubarb jellies
200ml reduced rhubarb syrup from the stewed rhubarb (see above)
½ teaspoon agar agar powder (see page 16)

For the rhubarb and apple sauce
125g new season forced rhubarb, washed, drained and chopped
125g (prepared weight) eating apples (preferably Russet), peeled, cored and chopped
25ml unsweetened cranberry juice
25g unsalted butter

To finish and serve
16 thin slices brioche, cut from a smaller/individual loaf (or cut 8 slices from a larger loaf and then halve each slice)
icing sugar, for dusting
fresh pea shoots and freshly cracked black pepper

First, make the panna cotta. Dry-roast the cardamom pods in a hot, non-stick frying pan over a high heat for 1–2 minutes. Stir or toss the pods continuously until they burst open, but do not let them catch and burn. Remove from the heat.

Place the roasted cardamom pods and the cream in a saucepan and bring gently to the boil, then simmer for a few minutes or until the cream is reduced to 250ml. Remove from the heat, then set the cream aside and leave it to infuse for 1 hour.

Soak the gelatine in cold water until it has softened. Heat the milk in a small saucepan over a low heat until it is almost boiling, then remove from the heat. Squeeze the gelatine gently to remove the excess water, then add the gelatine to the hot milk and stir until dissolved.

Pass the infused cream through a fine sieve to remove the cardamom pods, then stir the cream into the milk mixture.

Sift the icing sugar over the natural yogurt in a bowl, then fold the yogurt mixture into the milk/cream mixture. Pour the mixture into 8 individual 6 x 5cm moulds (each mould about 85ml volume), dividing it evenly. Chill in the fridge for several hours or overnight until set.

Next, make the stewed rhubarb. Place the rhubarb, cranberry juice, caster sugar and vanilla seeds in a saucepan and bring to the boil over a high heat, then cover and cook for about 2 minutes or until the rhubarb is just tender. Remove from the heat and then using a slotted spoon, remove the rhubarb from the juices and lay it out in a single layer on a flat tray. Set aside to cool.

Return the juices in the pan to a high heat and bring to the boil, then boil rapidly for about 5 minutes or until reduced to a thick but runny syrup. Remove from the heat and leave to cool. Measure out 200ml of the cooled syrup for the rhubarb jellies, then set aside a little of the syrup for decoration and chill until needed. Spoon the remaining syrup over the cooked rhubarb to prevent it from drying out and chill in the fridge.

Make the rhubarb jellies. Select a shallow, white plastic tray (about 23 x 18cm in size) to set the jelly mixture in. Put the reduced rhubarb syrup and agar agar powder into a small saucepan and bring to the boil, stirring. Boil for 30 seconds, stirring continuously, then remove from the heat and quickly pour the mixture into the tray to create a very thin layer – you want the mixture to be about 1mm thick. The mixture will set very quickly (please refer to the important tips about using agar agar powder on page 16). Do not move the jelly until it is completely set.

Once set, cut the jelly into 16 even-sized rectangles and remove from the tray. Spoon some of the chilled stewed rhubarb on to each jelly rectangle, dividing evenly, and then carefully roll up each jelly around the rhubarb, to make a cigar shape. Place on a tray and chill in the fridge until needed.

Make the rhubarb and apple sauce. Put the rhubarb, apples and cranberry juice in a saucepan and bring to the boil, then reduce the heat, cover and cook gently for 10 minutes or until the apples are soft – this also gives the flavour time to develop. Add the butter and stir until melted. Remove from the heat, transfer the mixture to a blender and blend until smooth, then pass the purée through a fine sieve into a bowl. Leave to cool, then cover and chill the sauce until needed (keep refrigerated and use within 2 days).

To finish, preheat the grill to medium. Place the brioche slices in a single layer on the rack in a grill pan and toast until golden brown. Turn the slices over and heavily dust each one with icing sugar. Return to the heat and grill for 1–2 minutes or until golden and caramelised.

To serve, spoon a swipe of the rhubarb and apple sauce on to each serving plate. Dip each panna cotta briefly in hot water, then turn out on to the plates. Arrange the rhubarb-filled jellies on the plates (2 per serving), along with the toasted brioche slices (2 per serving), then decorate each serving with a drizzle of the reserved rhubarb syrup. Finish with a sprinkling of pea shoots and a little black pepper. Serve immediately.

Cook's Notes

Use a pipette to drizzle the rhubarb syrup decoratively on to each plate, if you like.

If you have leftovers, these desserts will keep in the fridge for up to 2 days. Refrigerate the panna cotta, rhubarb-stuffed jellies and sauce. Leave the panna cotta in their moulds until you are ready to serve, and prepare and toast the brioche slices just before serving.

Lemon Curd Tartlets

The luxurious and velvety lemon curd in this recipe is very close to my heart. I have had this recipe for over 15 years and it's been used in many of the restaurants I have worked in. I had to think very hard about where I originally obtained this recipe, but if my memory serves me well, it was from a grumpy French pastry chef I once worked with (no, not my friend Fabien, he's French but he's not grumpy… he's lovely and a very good pastry chef indeed!).

I have tweaked and changed this lemon curd recipe over time, but as I was writing this book, I realised that it has become a classic in my recipe collection and one that I shall treasure for many more years to come. I also did a bit of research into other lemon curd recipes, to try and identify what makes mine different and indeed what makes it better than the rest – I concluded that it's the stage when the butter is added, and this makes this recipe unique, glossy and even more irresistible than the rest!

This recipe is also very easy to make, so my theory is to make it fresh, as and when you need it, and enjoy it there and then! OK, it will keep perfectly well in the fridge for 2–3 weeks (unopened in sealed jars), but I'll bet it doesn't last that long!

There are so many things you can do with the lemon curd. For this recipe, I bake the puff pastry cases a day in advance, then cool and store them in an airtight container overnight. I then make the lemon curd the following day and serve it in the crisp pastry cases. Absolutely delicious!

Makes 12 tartlets

375g good quality chilled fresh all-butter puff pastry
2 whole eggs
2 egg yolks
125g caster sugar
a pinch of table salt
125ml freshly squeezed lemon juice
125g cold unsalted butter, cut into very small pieces (keep refrigerated until needed)
icing sugar, to dust

Preheat the oven to 200°C/Gas Mark 6. Grease a 12-hole muffin tin and set aside.

First, make the pastry cases. Roll out the puff pastry on a lightly floured work surface to 2–3mm thickness. Cut out 12 x 8cm rounds, place them on a tray and leave to rest in the fridge for 20 minutes. Line the prepared muffin tin with the pastry rounds and prick them all over with a fork. Place a paper cake case filled with baking beans inside each one and bake blind in the oven for 15 minutes. Remove the beans and paper cases, then return the pastry cases to the oven and bake for a further 5 minutes or until cooked, golden brown and crisp. Remove from the oven and carefully transfer the pastry cases to a wire rack. Leave to cool completely before filling with the warm lemon curd.

Make the lemon curd. Half-fill a saucepan with water and bring up to a gentle simmer. Choose a heatproof mixing bowl that will sit comfortably over the saucepan without slipping down inside the pan (you also want to make sure that the bottom of the bowl does not come into contact with the simmering water underneath). Place the eggs, egg yolks, caster sugar and salt in the bowl and whisk together briefly until well mixed. Whisk in the lemon juice, mixing well.

Place the bowl over the pan of simmering water. Heat gently, stirring continuously with a wooden spoon, until the mixture starts to thicken, then continue to cook gently for a further 10–12 minutes or until the lemon curd thickens enough to coat the back of the spoon; do not allow the mixture to boil or it will curdle.

Remove the pan from the heat (but leave the bowl set over the pan) and gradually but quickly whisk the cold butter into the lemon curd, a few pieces at a time, until the butter is completely melted and incorporated – by this stage you should have a rich, creamy and glossy lemon curd.

While the lemon curd is still warm, pour it into the cooked pastry cases, then leave to cool. Serve at room temperature and just before serving, heavily dust each tartlet with icing sugar.

Cook's Notes
If there is any leftover lemon curd, transfer it to a clean bowl or jar, place a piece of cling film directly on the surface to prevent a skin forming, cool and refrigerate for up to 3 days.

If you are making the lemon curd to serve another time, pour the warm curd into hot sterilised jars (the lemon curd will make about 2 x 200g jars). Cover with wax discs (wax-side down) and seal. When cold, label, then store in the fridge and use within 2–3 weeks. Once opened, keep in the fridge and use within 3 days.

Forced Rhubarb Jam

Making jams and preserves is not only satisfying but it also tells its own seasonal story, and I believe there is a jam for every season. The beauty of forced rhubarb is that the skin is tender so it does not need peeling. It is the tender stems that produce the most beautiful pink colour and fragrant flavour.

As rhubarb is a vegetable and does not contain natural pectin, pectin-rich jam sugar is required for making this jam. Another secret to the success of this bright pink jam is the speed by which it must be cooked. The longer the jam stews and boils, the earthier the taste and browner the colour, so cook it quickly over a high heat and have all your equipment ready before you start. I would also not recommend cooking this jam in large batches: it will destroy the colour and the lovely fresh fragrance that you get from a small batch.

I finish the jam with a little lemon juice to refresh the taste and bring out the sharpness of the rhubarb. I have also added vanilla to accentuate the floral tones in this jam, but if you prefer something spicy, add 6 toasted cardamom pods instead.

Makes about 3 x 200g jars

400g new season forced rhubarb, washed, drained and cut into 1cm pieces
400g jam sugar (see page 16)
1 tablespoon boiling water
1 vanilla pod
juice of ½ lemon

Place the rhubarb, sugar and boiling water in a heavy-based saucepan. Split the vanilla pod in half lengthways and scrape out the seeds into the pan, then add the pod to the pan as well for extra flavour.

Cook over a low heat, stirring until the sugar has dissolved, then turn the heat up to high and bring the mixture to the boil. Boil rapidly for 10–12 minutes or until the jam reaches a temperature of 105°C (setting point), stirring every now and then to prevent it from catching. If you don't have a jam thermometer, check to see if setting point has been reached by spooning a little of the jam on to a chilled small plate. Push a finger across the jam; if the surface wrinkles and it is beginning to set, it has reached setting point. If not, boil it for a further 5 minutes or so and test again. Remember, the longer you cook the jam, the darker and browner the colour will become and the earthier the flavour.

Once the jam has reached setting point, stir in the lemon juice, then remove from the heat and allow the jam to cool slightly. Remove and discard the vanilla pod, then carefully pour the jam into hot, sterilised jars. Cover with wax discs (wax-side down) and seal. When cold, label and store in a cool, dry cupboard. The jam should keep well for a year or so. Once opened, keep in the fridge and use within 1 month.

Rhubarb Melting Moments

I call these my Valentine's biscuits. Mr. P is not a very romantic sort of bloke, but we share something very special and that is a passion for food. Actually, thinking about it, he is a bit of a soppy character after all. One year for Valentine's Day, he bought me a kilo of new season forced rhubarb wrapped in pretty pink tissue paper. I was overwhelmed with this lovely gift and I felt the need to make something that we would both enjoy. So, I made some fantastic Forced Rhubarb Jam (see opposite page) that is bright pink in colour. These biscuits followed shortly afterwards and yes, they are rather pretty and perfect for that special person in your life.

You may also like to try this recipe using other seasonal jams made throughout the year, such as Mulberry Jam (see page 238) or Greengage Jam (see page 292).

Makes about 25 melting moments

For the biscuits
350g unsalted butter, softened
80g icing sugar
½ vanilla pod, split in half lengthways and seeds scraped out
300g plain flour
50g cornflour

For the lemon butter cream
125g unsalted butter, softened
250g icing sugar, sifted
4 teaspoons freshly squeezed lemon juice
finely grated zest of 1 lemon

To assemble
icing sugar, for dusting
125g Forced Rhubarb Jam (see opposite page)

Make the biscuits. Preheat the oven to 180°C/Gas Mark 4. Line 2 baking trays with non-stick baking paper and set aside.

Cream the butter, icing sugar and vanilla seeds together in a bowl until pale and fluffy. Sift the flour and cornflour together, then fold into the creamed mixture to make a dough. The dough will be fairly firm – the softer the butter (not melted though) the easier it will be to work with.

Transfer the biscuit dough to a piping bag fitted with a medium star nozzle. Pipe about 25 rounds (each about 3cm in diameter) on to one of the prepared baking trays to make the round biscuit bases. Pipe about 25 circles (each about 3cm in diameter, with a hole in the centre of each one) on to the second baking tray to make the biscuit tops. Leave enough space between each one as they will spread a little during baking.

Bake in the oven for 18–20 minutes or until pale golden in colour. Carefully transfer the biscuits to a wire rack and leave to cool completely before decorating.

Meanwhile, make the lemon butter cream. Cream the butter in a bowl until it is pale in colour. Add the icing sugar and lemon juice and beat together until the mixture becomes fluffy. Fold in the lemon zest. Transfer the butter cream to a piping bag fitted with a small star nozzle.

To assemble the melting moments, pair up the bases and tops, so you have about 25 pairs of biscuits (each pair consisting of a round base and a round top with a hole in the centre). For each melting moment, place the biscuit top (with the hole in the centre), flat-side down, on the work surface and dust with icing sugar. Turn the biscuit base over so that the flat side is facing upwards and place on the work surface. Pipe a circle of lemon butter cream on to this base, leaving a whole in the centre, then place a teaspoonful of jam into the centre. Place the sugar-dusted biscuit top on top (flat-side down), and now you have a complete melting moment 'sandwich'! Repeat with the remaining biscuit bases and tops, icing sugar, butter cream and jam to make about 25 melting moments.

The melting moments are now ready to eat! They will remain crisp and good for about 2–3 hours, but they will go soggy if you leave them overnight, so I recommend that you do not assemble them until required.

Cook's Note
The biscuits and butter cream can be made in advance. Store the biscuits in an airtight container in a cool, dry cupboard for up to 1 week, and keep the butter cream in an airtight container in the fridge for up to 3 days. Soften the butter cream at room temperature for about 1 hour before use.

Far-left and left: Forced Rhubarb Jam, page 90
Right: Rhubarb Melting Moments, page 91

Banana and White Chocolate Cupcakes with Cream Cheese Frosting

Even though we do not grow bananas in Britain, we do consume a vast quantity of these energy-boosting fruits and they are very much part of our everyday lives. We used to live near a banana depot in the UK and laughed when we first drove past the depot, wondering to ourselves if they really did keep bananas there. As it so happened, I worked at a place where I met the director of that particular banana depot, and it turned out to be a banana ripening plant.

These banana and white chocolate cupcakes are a great way of using up ripe bananas, and baking is the perfect way to keep the winter blues away. The smell of these cupcakes baking is terrific and it lingers lavishingly in the kitchen on chilly days. It's heaven!

I'm a real girl and I love glitz and novel things. Finding edible glitter for the first time at a specialist cake shop made me smile from ear to ear. Ooh, it's like getting a new car; all you want to do is use it. So, I decorated my delicious cupcakes with a fabulous cream cheese frosting, a few silver balls and finally, the pièce de résistance, a sprinkle of my magical hologram white edible glitter.

Makes 12 cupcakes

For the banana and white chocolate cupcakes

150g unsalted butter, softened
150g caster sugar
1 very ripe banana, peeled and mashed with a fork
2 eggs
125g plain flour
1 teaspoon baking powder
25g cornflour
50g white chocolate chips

For the cream cheese frosting

100g cream cheese or full-fat soft cheese (Philadelphia soft cheese is perfect for this)
200g icing sugar, sifted
25g unsalted butter, melted and cooled

silver balls and edible glitter, to decorate (see Cook's Notes)

Make the cupcakes. Preheat the oven to 180°C/Gas Mark 4. Line a 12-hole muffin tin with paper muffin cases and set aside.

Cream the butter and caster sugar together in a bowl until pale and fluffy. Add the mashed banana and beat together until well mixed. Add the eggs, one at a time, beating well after each addition. Sift the flour, baking powder and cornflour over the creamed mixture and fold in, then add the chocolate chips, being careful not to over mix.

Spoon the mixture into the paper cases, filling each case about three-quarters full. Bake in the oven for 20–22 minutes or until well-risen and golden brown and a fine skewer inserted into the centres comes out clean. Transfer the cupcakes to a wire rack and leave to cool completely before decorating.

Meanwhile, prepare the cream cheese frosting (see Cook's Notes). Whisk the cream cheese and icing sugar together in a bowl until light and fluffy (I use a hand-held electric mixer with a whisk attachment for this stage, but it can also be done by hand). While whisking, slowly pour the cooled melted butter into the whisked cream cheese mixture, then whisk for a couple more minutes to incorporate more air. Cover and refrigerate for at least 1 hour before using to allow the frosting to set lightly.

Spread or pipe the frosting over the top of the cupcakes and then make them look extra pretty with some silver balls and a sprinkling of edible glitter. Serve and enjoy!

Cook's Notes

I buy the edible glitter from our local specialist cake craft shop, but you can also buy it online and in some supermarkets too. Please make sure that the glitter is edible; do not use craft glitter. A small tub goes a very long way, providing you apply the glitter with a small brush. I found a very fine brush at the same cake shop, but you could simply buy a cheaper artist's brush from a craft shop or use a cotton bud instead. Dip the dry brush into the glitter and gently shake it over the iced cupcakes to add a bit of glitz and sparkle.

The decorated cupcakes will keep in an airtight container in the fridge for up to 3 days. The undecorated cupcakes will keep in an airtight container in a cool, dry cupboard for up to 3 days.

The cream cheese frosting is best made the day before it is required so that it can set slightly and get a fantastic gloss. Although this frosting is fairly soft, take it out of the fridge about 10 minutes before needed.

Buttermilk Pancakes with Pan-roasted Rhubarb and Blood Oranges

I like a good pancake, and being a chef, I tend to tinker with recipes, so this one has become something rather special. These small pancakes are also sometimes called drop scones, but for me they are puffy pancakes.

They are perfect for breakfast or brunch – cook the pancakes first and keep them warm while you cook the rhubarb and oranges in the same pan. If you are super organised, you can make the pan-roasted rhubarb the evening before and then simply make the pancakes the next morning and reheat the rhubarb and oranges.

Serves 4

For the buttermilk pancakes
135g plain flour
1 teaspoon baking powder
a pinch of table salt
finely grated zest of 1 lime
2 eggs, separated
25g clear honey
130ml buttermilk
25g unsalted butter, melted, plus extra unsalted butter for frying

For the pan-roasted rhubarb and blood oranges
3 blood oranges
4 tablespoons mascarpone
125g caster sugar, plus 1 tablespoon caster sugar
1 vanilla pod, cut in half lengthways and seeds scraped out
25g unsalted butter
500g new season forced rhubarb, washed, drained and cut into ½ cm pieces
25ml Sloe Gin (see page 343)
juice of 1 lime

First, make the pancakes. Sift the flour, baking powder and salt into a bowl, then stir in the lime zest and set aside. In a separate bowl, whisk the egg whites until they become foamy, then add the honey and continue to whisk until soft peaks form.

In another bowl, whisk together the egg yolks, buttermilk and melted butter. Fold the buttermilk mixture into the flour mixture, but do not over mix – a few lumps in the batter will not be a problem. Fold the whisked egg whites into the batter.

Melt a knob of butter in a large, non-stick frying pan and once the butter starts to foam, spoon heaped tablespoonfuls of the batter into the hot pan, shaping each one to about 6cm in diameter, to make 12 pancakes in total (you will need to cook the pancakes a few at a time, in batches, adding another knob of butter to the pan for each batch). Cook over a fairly high heat for a couple of minutes or so until golden underneath and lightly set on top, then flip them over and cook for a further 1–2 minutes or until golden brown on the other side. Drain on kitchen paper, then transfer the pancakes to a clean tea towel or a piece of foil, cover and keep them warm while you prepare the rhubarb.

For the pan-roasted rhubarb and blood oranges, finely grate the zest from the oranges, cut each fruit in half and remove the segments, then squeeze out any juice left in the fruit halves (once the segments have been removed). Set aside.

Place the mascarpone in a small bowl with 1 tablespoon of sugar, one-third of the orange zest and a good pinch of the vanilla seeds and mix well. Cover and refrigerate until needed.

Melt the butter in the same frying pan and once the butter starts to foam, add the rhubarb and the remaining 125g sugar and vanilla seeds and sauté over a medium heat for 8–10 minutes or until the juices have caramelised and become syrupy and the rhubarb is tender.

Pour the sloe gin into the pan and let it bubble, stirring and scraping the base of the pan to deglaze it, then stir in the orange segments, orange juice, the remaining orange zest and the lime juice, bring to a simmer and cook for 1 minute. Remove from the heat.

Serve the warm pancakes (3 per serving) on serving plates and spoon over the pan-roasted rhubarb and blood oranges. Spoon a generous dollop of mascarpone alongside and serve immediately.

Cook's Note
Buttermilk is a versatile ingredient to cook with. It is a soured liquid, thicker than normal milk. Traditional buttermilk is an ideal ingredient for making scones, bread, pancakes and cakes. The lactic acids within buttermilk also contain properties that are useful for the marinating and tenderising of meats such as lamb.

DOROTHY
MAY
IPSWICH

The British Larder | *March*

March signifies the very beginning of spring and the time that Mother Nature prepares to blossom and bloom once again. The sense of connection with nature and the feeling of a new lease of life are in the air. Even though it's still chilly, with the possibility of an unexpected flurry of snow, March is the month that bridges the gap between winter and spring. The days are getting longer and the earth is waking up from a long, cold winter.

It's the time of year when the gardening bug starts to bite and my conscience kindly reminds me that it's time to start planting seeds on my veg patch for my seasonal fruit and vegetables. I make no bones about the fact that I'm an occasional gardener and, much as I'd love to, I'm not fully committed to growing my own fruit and vegetables because my life is too busy and my career too time-consuming to allow me to do that. It sounds like a poor excuse, but that's exactly how it is.

The month of March feels like it should be 'out with the old and in with the new' and the foods in season at this time of year represent just that – plenty of the winter foods are coming to the end of being at their best and they are making way for the new offerings of spring. Having said that though, there is not yet plenty of choice to select from.

During March, the new season salad (spring) onions and purple sprouting broccoli make their appearance, along with sardines and whitebait. Exotics such as pineapples, pomegranates and passion fruits are coming to an end, along with all the varieties of citrus fruit. Shortly we will move on to stored cold room citrus fruits, until they make their way back into season next January. We have become accustomed to these ingredients being available at all times, but we do get an indication of seasonality when the prices fluctuate and this perhaps inspires us to use less of these ingredients when they are out of season.

Season's best during March...

Bananas, Blood Oranges, Cauliflowers, Celeriac, Chickweed, Chicory, Cockles, Hake, John Dory, Kale, Leeks, Lemons, Lemon Sole, Mussels, Nettles, Oranges, Oysters, Passion Fruit, Pineapples, Pomegranates, Purple Sprouting Broccoli, Rhubarb (outdoor), Salad/Spring Onions, Salmon, Salsify, Sea Trout, Shallots, Skate, Sorrel, Spinach, Whitebait, Winkles.

My culinary rituals for March...

Spring has sprung and if you're a keen gardener or even a selective one like me, then the beginning of March is the time to be sowing your sorrel seeds and planting your herbs for the summer months to come.

Mother's Day is fast approaching and planning for this occasion is well worthwhile. With plenty of delicious recipes to choose from it might perhaps be a toss-up between **Lemon, Semolina and Almond Cake** (see page 123), **Rhubarb and Custard Pie-Pudding** (see page 116) or maybe **My Famous Treacle Tart** (see page 120). The choice is yours!

Lemons

Lemons have played a key part in the general British larder for many centuries as they are very versatile and can be used in numerous recipes. The best advice I can give when it comes to choosing lemons is to look out for the organic unwaxed ones. Unwaxed lemons from the Mediterranean are usually large with a thick pith and juicy interior, and the skin is crisp and packed full of flavour. Lemon zest and juice have the magical ability to liven up many dishes. In my opinion, it's a food crime not to use the zest as well as the juice. Invest in a good quality fine grater or Microplane grater and keep it in the top drawer so it is handy to whip out when needed. The Mediterranean citrus season starts in January and finishes by the end of March. However, we can buy lemons all year round as the seasons evolve – as soon as the Mediterranean citrus season comes to an end, then the Southern hemisphere season begins. Preserved lemons are also fairly readily available and are used in cooking. These are whole lemons that are packed into jars and preserved in brine or salt, sometimes with other flavourings (such as herbs and spices) added. They date back centuries in North African-style cooking and are still used widely in North African and Middle Eastern cooking today to impart a fragrant aroma and lemony undertone to dishes such as tagines and stews. You can buy preserved lemons in jars from many supermarkets and delicatessens or you can make your own at home. Use preserved lemons in small amounts to add flavour to casseroles, couscous and rice dishes or salads. Once opened, store in the fridge.

Leeks

To make my recipe for **Traditional Cloudy Lemonade**, cut 5 unwaxed lemons into quarters and place them in a food processor. Add 150g caster sugar and process until the fruits are crushed but are not completely smooth. Transfer the contents to a large container, then stir in 500ml cold water and add a handful of ice cubes. Cover and refrigerate for 2 hours – this will ensure that the lemonade becomes sufficiently chilled. Pass the lemonade through a fine sieve and then serve it in glasses with sprigs of fresh mint and plenty of ice. You might want to adjust the quantity of sugar used to suit your taste and you might like to try using sparkling water instead of still water for an added bit of fizz. Makes about 750ml; serves about 4.

British Larder Heroes

Leeks

Leeks belong to the onion (Allium) family and, once cooked, are milder in flavour compared to onions and garlic. Leeks are not only versatile and delicious to eat, they also have the most beautiful flowers that brighten up any kitchen garden. The white parts are the best for cooking, the dark green parts are bitter and should be used carefully when added to stocks and sauces. Leeks contain natural thickening agents that will help to thicken sauces and stocks. Because their flavour is slightly sweeter and milder than onions, leeks are an ideal aromatic vegetable to use in place of onions in dishes such as soups and stews.

For classic **Leeks Vinaigrette**, trim 12 small leeks, then wash them thoroughly to remove any soil or grit and drain. Add 2 crushed dried juniper berries, 1 bay leaf, 2 sprigs of fresh thyme and 1 crushed clove garlic to a large pan of salted water and bring to the boil. Add the leeks and simmer for 4–5 minutes or until tender. Using a slotted spoon, remove the leeks from the pan and drain on kitchen paper. Transfer the warm leeks to a serving dish and season with sea salt and freshly cracked black pepper, then drizzle generously with French vinaigrette, grate 1 cold (shelled) hard-boiled egg over the top and sprinkle with a small handful of chopped fresh parsley. Serve immediately. This dish is perfect served with poached salmon for an easy mid-week supper. Serves 4 as a side dish.

Oysters

Oysters are seawater bivalves that grow in groups referred to as beds or reefs. There are various types of oysters, many of which are edible. Oysters usually reach maturity in one year, but the native variety (Ostrea edulis), granted as the finest oyster by most, takes 5 years to reach maturity. Due to this, they are protected and cannot be harvested between the spawning season from May to August, so their season (when they are available) runs from September to April. Other oysters such as Pacific and rock oysters are now dominating the market more, as they are easier to farm all year round. Oysters used to be the food of the poor and traditionally, in a beef and oyster pie, the more oysters you had the poorer you would have been, but this has changed and oysters have become a gourmet delicacy and the 'food of the rich'. They are usually eaten raw but are sometimes lightly cooked, however, they are not for everyone; you either love them or loathe them. The term shucking oysters means to open oysters with a special oyster knife. Before you open oysters, check to see if they are safe to eat by tapping them; if they close it means they are alive; if they are already closed and open too easily without any resistance it means they are dead and should not be eaten.

Simplicity is usually the key when serving oysters. Serve freshly shucked oysters with a tasty vinaigrette for the ultimate experience. Try my **Oysters with Shallot and Red Wine Vinaigrette**. Place 2 finely diced banana shallots in a small clean jar that has a tight-fitting lid, add 6 tablespoons red wine vinegar, 2 tablespoons sesame oil and 2 tablespoons sunflower oil, then add sea salt and fresh cracked black pepper and a few drops of Tabasco sauce to taste. Secure the lid and shake the jar vigorously. Shuck 12 washed fresh oysters, then place them on serving plates. Give the vinaigrette a quick shake, then drizzle it over the oysters and serve with crusty bread. Serves 4 as a starter or serves 2 as a light lunch.

Purple sprouting broccoli

This is a member of the Brassicaceae family and it is rich in vitamins A and C and high in fibre. Purple sprouting broccoli has slender, leafy stems of varying lengths with smaller heads of purple-green flowers or florets, compared to the larger heads of the more common green calabrese. A white variety is also available, but the purple variety is the most common. Choose fresh, young and tender purple sprouting broccoli that has firm heads with slender stems; once the flower heads turn slightly yellow it means they are coming to the end of their season and are past their best. Purple sprouting broccoli takes nearly a year to grow and mature enough to be harvested, not great news for impatient gardeners, but the superb taste is worth the wait.

For an accompaniment with sophistication and great taste, try my **Steamed Purple Sprouting Broccoli with Anchovies**. Steam 500g purple sprouting broccoli spears for 4–5 minutes or until tender, then drain and season with sea salt and freshly cracked black pepper. Place in a serving dish, scatter over 10 anchovy fillets in oil (preferably silverskin), drained and cut in half, along with a handful of toasted flaked almonds, and serve. Serves 4.

Rhubarb (outdoor)

Outdoor rhubarb with its thicker stems and large leaves and its earthy and gutsy taste, is starting to come on to the market during March (the season for outdoor rhubarb runs from March–May). Unlike the tender stems of new season forced rhubarb, the thicker stems of outdoor rhubarb need peeling as the skin is stringy, but the taste is still superb. Outdoor rhubarb is easy to grow and every kitchen garden should have a crown or two for personal consumption, as it's a wonderful British seasonal ingredient and a favourite of ours at the British Larder. Rhubarb is in fact classed as a vegetable rather than a fruit, but do remember that the leaves are toxic and should be removed before cooking.

The natural tartness of rhubarb makes it an ideal ingredient for both sweet and savoury dishes, and poached rhubarb with natural yogurt is the perfect recipe to kick-start your day. For my delicious Poached Rhubarb, trim, wash and drain 2 stems of outdoor rhubarb (about 300g) and cut into 1cm slices. Place 150g caster sugar, 1 piece of preserved stem ginger in syrup, drained and finely chopped, and 100ml ginger beer in a small saucepan. Heat gently, stirring regularly, until the sugar has dissolved, then increase the heat slightly and bring to a gentle simmer. Simmer for 2 minutes, then add the rhubarb, cover and simmer for a further 5 minutes or until the rhubarb is tender. Remove from the heat and transfer the poached rhubarb to a clean container. Set aside to cool

Purple-sprouting broccoli

Buckler leaf sorrel

completely, then cover and chill until needed. The poached rhubarb will keep in the fridge for up to 3 days. Serve chilled with natural yogurt and muesli for breakfast. Serves 4.

Skate

Skate are cartilaginous fish belonging to the family of rays. This means they are boneless (they have cartilage instead of bones) and each fish has two wings. Skate wings are the highly prized parts of the fish, with their delicate flavour and soft, melt-in-the-mouth flaky texture (the texture of the cooked wings looks like strings, but is very tender to eat). Skate wings lose their freshness very quickly so should be eaten soon after purchase. Fresh skate has a lime fresh smell and an opaque colour, but once it's past its best, it will smell of ammonia and the flesh will turn milky white in colour.

Skate is commonly cooked and served on the bone (or cartilage, strictly speaking), but if you're not keen on the bones, try this delicious recipe for **Warm Pulled Skate and Steamed Purple Sprouting Broccoli Salad** to serve 2 as a light lunch. Preheat the oven to 200°C/Gas Mark 6. Place 1 skate wing (about 500g) on a baking tray and brush with 2 tablespoons melted unsalted butter, then season with sea salt and freshly cracked black pepper. Bake in the oven for 18–20 minutes or until cooked and golden brown. Remove from the oven and leave to rest for 2 minutes, then using 2 forks, flake the succulent flesh from the bone, flip the fish over (as there is usually plenty of flesh on both sides) and do the same on the other side. Serve the pulled skate flesh with 250–300g steamed purple sprouting broccoli, scatter over a handful of toasted flaked almonds and 1 tablespoon chopped (drained) capers, then drizzle over the pan juices and serve.

Sorrel

Sorrel, with its eye-watering sour tang, is an ingredient that has the 'love it or loathe it' effect. I have fond memories of cooking sorrel omelettes in the 1990's at Kensington Place with Chef Rowley Leigh; it was one of his signature dishes and once it appeared on the menu it was almost as if the arrival of spring had been announced. Because of

Whitebait

its distinctive pungent, sharp taste, sorrel lends itself best towards sauces to accompany fish such as lemon sole. Buckler leaf sorrel is a variety of sorrel with a slightly firmer leaf – it's also known as French sorrel and is native to the mountains of southern and central Europe and southwest Asia. Buckler leaf sorrel is a hardy perennial herb producing small insignificant green flowers in the summer and it has shield-shaped green leaves that taste tart. This variety of sorrel is more succulent and acidic than the common garden sorrel. In traditional folk medicine, buckler leaf sorrel was used as an antiseptic because of its high vitamin C content and was believed to prevent scurvy. In addition to being rich in vitamin C, it is also high in vitamin A and is a good source of iron.

To make a tasty **Sorrel Omelette à la Rowley Leigh**, crack 3 eggs into a small bowl, add sea salt and freshly cracked black pepper and a dash of double cream, then use a fork to lightly whisk the eggs – do not overdo this, just mix until the yolks are just broken. Melt a knob of unsalted butter in a non-stick omelette pan and once the butter starts to foam, pour in the egg mixture and leave it for 30 seconds. Use a wooden spoon to gently stir the eggs over the heat, shake the pan gently to prevent the mixture from catching, stir again briefly and then let the omelette cook until it is set and golden brown underneath but is still creamy on top. Scatter over a large handful of shredded fresh sorrel, fold over a third of the omelette to the centre and then fold over the opposite third. Transfer the omelette to a serving plate and enjoy! Serves 1 as a breakfast, brunch, light lunch or supper.

Whitebait

Whitebait are tiny immature silvery fish from the herring family. They are eaten whole and are usually sold frozen, but fresh whitebait can be found at fresh fish stalls, often near the coast, when they are in season. The sustainability of whitebait is in question as they are harvested in large numbers and this means that the stocks deplete faster than reproduction can take place. The general rule of thumb is to be responsible and buy from suppliers that you can trust to source their products from sustainable resources.

The simplest way to cook whitebait is to coat them in seasoned flour and deep-fry them. For classic **Devilled Whitebait**, heat some sunflower oil in an electric deep-fat fryer or in a deep frying pan to a temperature of 160°C (or until a small piece of bread browns within 20 seconds in the hot oil). Meanwhile, rinse and pat dry 200g whitebait, then place them in a polythene food bag along with 2 tablespoons plain flour, 2 large pinches of cayenne pepper, a large pinch of mustard powder and sea salt and freshly cracked black pepper. Seal the bag and toss to coat the fish all over. Remove the fish from the bag, shake off the excess seasoned flour, then deep-fry the whitebait (in two batches) in the hot oil for about 3 minutes or until golden brown and crisp. Using a slotted spoon, remove and drain the cooked whitebait on kitchen paper, then serve immediately with a wedge of lemon and plenty of buttered brown bread. Serves 2 as a starter or serves 1 as a light lunch served with salad and bread.

Sorrel

Buckler Leaf Sorrel and Spinach Soup

There are many joy to growing your own vegetables. For example, not only do you have the privilege to pick them when they're ready to harvest, but it's also a clear reminder of the season you are currently in.

Growing sorrel is easy, especially the hardier buckler leaf variety. I just stick the plant in a large pot with plenty of fresh compost and it grows happily. When winter comes along it will die back, but then lo and behold next spring it's back up and growing again – a low maintenance plant providing maximum pleasure.

The brightness and beauty of this delicious, vibrant green soup are perfect reminders that spring is in the air. If it's grey and cold outside, serve it hot with a large chunk of freshly baked bread; if it's warm and sunny outside, serve the soup chilled, accompanied by a glass of chilled Pinot gris.

My best tips for how to keep this soup a bright green colour are to ensure that the cooking time for the greens is as short as possible and, if serving the soup chilled, that it is cooled down (preferably over ice) as quickly as possible. I also recommend making this soup in small batches.

Serves 6 as a starter or light lunch

For the buckler leaf sorrel and spinach soup

2 tablespoons olive oil
400g potatoes, finely sliced
1 onion, sliced
1 clove garlic, crushed
a pinch of cayenne pepper
1.2 litres good quality vegetable stock
¼ teaspoon freshly grated nutmeg
finely grated zest and juice of 1 lemon
200g fresh buckler leaf sorrel, rinsed and drained
200g fresh spinach leaves, rinsed and drained
sea salt and freshly cracked black pepper
extra virgin olive oil and a little crème fraîche, to serve
a mixture of edible fresh flowers (such as chive, thyme or nasturtium flowers), if available, and small fresh herb sprigs (such as buckler leaf sorrel leaves, chives or chervil), to garnish

For the sorrel pesto

30g pine nuts
20g golden linseeds
80g fresh buckler leaf sorrel, rinsed and drained
30g finely grated fresh Parmesan cheese
2 tablespoons rapeseed oil
1 clove garlic, crushed
4 sprigs of fresh mint
¼ small bunch of fresh parsley

Make the soup. Heat the olive oil in a large saucepan, then sauté the potatoes, onion and garlic, with the cayenne pepper and salt and pepper added, over a high heat for about 2 minutes or until lightly coloured. Add the stock and bring to the boil, then reduce the heat to a gentle simmer, cover and cook for about 10 minutes or until the potatoes are tender. Add the nutmeg and lemon juice, then remove the pan from the heat.

While the soup is cooking, blanch the sorrel and spinach together in a separate pan of boiling salted water for 1–2 minutes or until just tender, then drain and plunge into iced cold water to ensure they cool rapidly and keep their colour. Drain well and add to the soup, along with the lemon zest.

Carefully transfer the soup to a blender and purée until smooth. If serving the soup cold, pour it into a bowl, then chill over ice in the fridge for about 1 hour before serving. If serving the soup hot, return it to the pan and reheat gently. Taste and adjust the seasoning before serving, if necessary.

Meanwhile, make the sorrel pesto. Toast the pine nuts and linseeds in a hot, dry, non-stick frying pan over a high heat for 2–3 minutes or until golden brown all over, stirring. Remove from the heat and leave to cool completely. Once cool, place the toasted pine nuts and linseeds in a blender, along with all the remaining pesto ingredients and blend together until smooth. Add salt and pepper to taste, then transfer the pesto to a serving dish and leave at room temperature for about 20 minutes before serving, to allow the flavours to develop.

Serve the soup in bowls, either chilled or hot, and serve each portion with a splash of extra virgin olive oil, a few spoonfuls of crème fraîche and a dollop of the sorrel pesto. Garnish with edible flowers and herbs and serve immediately.

Cook's Note

Put any leftover pesto in a clean jar or small airtight container and cover the surface with a little olive oil or place a piece of cling film directly on the surface. Cover and store in the fridge for up to 3 days.

Baked Potato and Leek Soup with Roast Chicken Cigarillos

I love the simplicity of this humble potato and leek soup. The inspiration for this recipe came from standing in front of the fridge one evening with bits of leftover cooked foods staring me in the face. The challenge was to make a tasty supper with leftovers, but it's also a delicious recipe if you cook everything from scratch.

The secret of success for a tasty potato and leek soup is when you add the seasoning. I'm a bit pedantic about the acceptable levels of seasoning when cooking, so I would recommend that some seasoning is added at the start of the cooking process so that the soup can develop flavour. The mistake that most cooks make is not to season their food at all at the beginning or during the cooking process, but then to add a heap of 'raw' salt at the end – at this stage, you need to add so much salt to inject flavour that you end up using too much.

Pepper could perhaps be seen as an enemy of potato and leek soup – you will be surprised how obvious the taste of pepper is with potatoes. I learnt a very valuable lesson once, many moons ago, when I was a commis chef. We used ready-milled pepper at that particular restaurant and I added too much to my potato and leek soup. It tasted like a pot of pepper, potato and leek soup! I was gutted and the chef, understandably, was not happy at all, so I had to start all over again. Lesson learnt for me, so take it easy on the pepper as you can always add extra but you cannot take it away.

The roasted chicken cigarillos add a lovely extra touch and transform a humble dish into a filling and interesting one.

Serves 4 as a starter, light lunch or supper

For the baked potato and leek soup

3 large baking potatoes
2 tablespoons olive oil
20g unsalted butter
375g leeks, washed and cut into 1cm slices
1 litre good quality vegetable or white chicken stock
100ml double cream
sea salt and freshly cracked black pepper

For the roast chicken cigarillos

60g unsalted butter
100g leeks, washed and finely sliced
100g cold roast chicken leg meat, flaked
2 tablespoons snipped fresh chives
4 sheets of chilled fresh or frozen (defrosted) filo pastry (each sheet about 40 x 30cm)

Make the soup. Preheat the oven to 200°C/Gas Mark 6. Wash the potatoes, prick them all over with a fork, then rub them all over with the olive oil. Place the potatoes on a baking tray and bake in the oven for 1–1½hours or until cooked and tender, turning once. Remove from the oven and set aside to cool for 10 minutes, then cut the baked potatoes in half and use a spoon to scoop out the potato flesh from the skins. Set the potato flesh aside.

Rip the potato skins into pieces, return them to the same baking tray, then turn the oven off, place the baking tray in the hot oven and shut the door. Leave the potato skins in the oven as it cools down and then remove them from the oven after about 20 minutes – by which time the pieces of skin will have become roasted and crisp and will make a lovely garnish. Set aside to cool. Meanwhile, melt the butter in a large saucepan and sauté the leeks, with salt and pepper added, over a medium heat for 6–7 minutes or until the leeks start to take on a little colour. Add the baked potato flesh and stock, bring to the boil, then reduce the heat to a gentle simmer, cover and simmer for about 10 minutes or until the soup is thickened and the leeks are tender. Stir in the cream, then remove from the heat.

Carefully transfer the soup to a blender and purée until smooth. Return to the pan (if you like, you can pass the soup through a fine sieve at this stage, but it's not necessary) and reheat gently, then taste and adjust the seasoning, if necessary. Keep the soup hot until you are ready to serve.

In the meantime, make the roast chicken cigarillos. Preheat the oven to 180°C/Gas Mark 4 and line a baking tray with non-stick baking paper.

Melt 20g of the butter in a non-stick frying pan and sauté the leeks, with salt and pepper added, over a medium heat for 6–7 minutes or until softened. Remove from the heat and place the leeks in a bowl, then add the flaked chicken meat and chives and mix well.

Cut the filo sheets in half lengthways to make 8 strips of filo and melt the remaining butter. Lightly brush each strip of filo with melted butter and divide the chicken mixture evenly between each one. Roll up each one tightly from a short end to make 8 cigarillos. Place the cigarillos on the prepared baking tray, brush each cigarillo with melted butter and then bake in the oven for about 15 minutes or until golden brown and crisp.

Serve the hot soup in bowls with the crispy pieces of potato skins and the roast chicken cigarillos served alongside.

Baked Oysters with Bacon and Leeks

I have a love-hate relationship with oysters. It's the opening and shucking of the oysters that is the most hindering part. I like serving them for starters or even at drinks parties, but the thought of having to wrestle them open and get splattered with sea juices is enough to change my mind and prepare other dishes instead.

This method of baking the oysters in their shells in the oven is a slight cheats way of opening the oysters, but it's very effective with no wrestling involved and it's ultimately a cleaner job. Select big oysters for this recipe and serve 3 per person.

Serves 4 as a starter or light lunch

12 large fresh oysters (in shell), washed thoroughly
1 tablespoon unsalted butter
4 rashers smoked back bacon, finely diced
2 leeks, washed and finely shredded
1 clove garlic, crushed
150ml dry white wine
100ml double cream
2 tablespoons chopped fresh mixed soft herbs such as parsley, tarragon and chives
2 tablespoons fresh breadcrumbs
2 tablespoons grated Shipcord cheese (or similar hard Alpine-style cheese, medium-strong in taste – perhaps select a suitable cheese from your region, such as Cornish Yarg, Cheddar, Wensleydale or Caerphilly)
sea salt and freshly cracked black pepper

Preheat the oven to 180°C/Gas Mark 4.

Place the oysters on a baking tray and bake in the oven for 10 minutes. Remove from the oven, then pop the oyster shells open using a butter knife or an oyster knife if you have one and remove the top shells and the meat. Carefully pour the oyster juices through a fine sieve into a cup or jug and then set the oysters and juices aside. Return the empty lower oyster shells to the baking tray and set aside until needed. Discard the top shells. Preheat the grill to its highest setting.

Melt the butter in a non-stick frying pan and once the butter starts to foam, add the bacon, leeks and garlic and sauté over a medium heat for 8–10 minutes or until the bacon becomes crispy and the leeks turn golden.

Pour the oyster juices and wine into the pan and let the liquid bubble, stirring and scraping the base of the pan with a wooden spoon to deglaze it. Cook over a medium heat for about 2 minutes or until the liquid becomes syrupy but has not completely evaporated. Stir in the cream, then bring the mixture to a gentle simmer and cook for 1 minute. Remove from the heat and stir in half of the herbs, then add salt and pepper to taste.

Divide the mixture evenly between the reserved oyster shells and then place an oyster into each shell on top of the bacon mixture. In a small bowl, mix together the breadcrumbs, grated cheese and remaining herbs and then sprinkle this mixture evenly over the oysters. Grill for about 3–4 minutes or until golden brown and bubbling hot. Serve immediately.

Oyster Beignets with Sorrel Velouté

Personally, I'm not fond of raw oysters, but somehow I find cooked oysters easier to eat and more palatable. When I think of oysters, memories come flooding back to me of Marco Pierre White's well-known 'Tagliatelle of Oysters with Caviar' – such a fantastic dish and now a treasured classic, but in those days (in the 1990's) this was cutting edge cuisine of the highest order.

Fresh sorrel and oysters are both truly seasonal treats. The combination of the eye-watering sour tang of sorrel and the sweetness of oysters works a treat. This recipe is what I would describe as a 'show-off' dish that you make for that special occasion. Whether you serve it for 2 or 12, it's a real showstopper and definitely worth the effort. A cream whipper (see page 17) is required for serving the foaming sorrel velouté.

Serves 4 as a starter or 12 as a canapé

For the sorrel velouté

2 teaspoons olive oil
2 banana shallots, finely diced
100ml dry vermouth
200ml fish stock
100ml double cream
juice of ½ lemon
100g fresh sorrel, washed and drained
sea salt and freshly cracked black pepper

For the pickled cucumber

½ cucumber
2 tablespoons cider vinegar
a pinch of sea salt
a pinch of caster sugar

For the oyster beignets

75g self-raising flour
20g cornflour
a pinch of sea salt
1 egg yolk
125ml sparkling water
2 egg whites
12 small-medium fresh oysters (in shell), washed thoroughly
sunflower oil, for deep-frying

edible fresh flowers (such as chive, thyme or nasturtium flowers), if available, and fresh coriander cress, to garnish

First, make the sorrel velouté. Heat the olive oil in a saucepan, add the shallots and salt and pepper, then cover and sweat over a low heat for about 8 minutes or until the shallots turn transparent.

Pour the vermouth into the pan and let it bubble, stirring and scraping the base of the pan with a wooden spoon to deglaze it, then bubble over a high heat for 4–5 minutes or until reduced by half. Add the stock and bring to the boil, then reduce the heat and simmer for 8–10 minutes or until reduced by half. Stir in the cream and bring the velouté back to the boil, then add the lemon juice to taste. Adjust the seasoning, if necessary.

Pour the velouté into a blender, add the sorrel and blend until smooth. Pour the velouté into a cream whipper. Charge with 2 gas pellets, shake vigorously, then refrigerate for 2–3 hours so that the mixture thickens.

Once the sorrel velouté is chilled and ready, make the pickled cucumber. Peel the cucumber, then cut it in half lengthways and remove the seeds. Finely chop the cucumber flesh into 2–3mm dice, then place in a bowl, stir in the cider vinegar, salt and sugar and leave to macerate for 10 minutes. Just before serving, drain the cucumber on kitchen paper.

Meanwhile, make the oyster beignets. Place the flour, cornflour, salt, egg yolk and sparkling water in a bowl and mix together to make a smooth paste. In a separate bowl, whisk the egg whites until they are fluffy, but stop just before the soft peak stage. Fold the egg whites into the beignet batter, then leave to stand for 5 minutes.

Shuck the oysters, rinse the lower shells and oysters in cold water, then drain on kitchen paper and set aside. Discard the top shells.

Heat some sunflower oil in an electric deep-fat fryer or in a deep frying pan to a temperature of 160°C (or until a small piece of bread browns within 20 seconds in the hot oil). Once the oil is hot enough, dip each oyster into the batter, then deep-fry in the hot oil for 1–2 minutes or until golden brown and crisp all over (the cooking time will depend on the size of the oysters) – you will need to deep-fry the oysters in two batches. Using a slotted spoon, remove and drain the cooked oysters on kitchen paper, then season with salt.

To serve, spoon the pickled cucumber into the reserved oyster shells, dividing it evenly. Shake the cream whipper vigorously and squirt some sorrel velouté into each shell, covering the cucumber completely. Place a crisp golden oyster beignet into each shell and garnish with edible flowers and coriander cress. Serve immediately.

Pan-roasted Skate with Anchovy and Purple Sprouting Broccoli Pickle

Nothing beats a delicious, pan-roasted fresh skate wing, with a crisp and golden exterior encasing the delicate, flaky and succulent flesh beneath. The British Larder's values and beliefs are that we choose to only buy ingredients from people who care about food in the same way that we do. Our fish comes from selected suppliers who practice and follow sustainable fishing methods and guidelines. They also bluntly admit when there is no fish to catch or sell to us due to stock levels, but when it is there we are one of the very lucky few to get our hands on fabulous fish, such as skate.

I had never seen a whole skate ray until George Pinney, a local fisherman from Orford, came in with one of these beauties. This did then urge me to learn a bit more about this wonderful fish. As skate is a meaty fish, I serve it simply with an easy and delicious homemade seasonal pickle that is made in minutes.

Serves 2 as a main course

For the anchovy and purple sprouting broccoli pickle

100g purple sprouting broccoli, trimmed
100g kale, stalks removed
8 anchovy fillets in oil (preferably silverskin), drained and chopped
1 clove garlic, crushed
2 tablespoons capers, drained and chopped
80g pitted green olives, chopped
2 tablespoons chopped fresh mixed herbs, such as tarragon, chives and parsley
½ fresh green chilli, deseeded and finely sliced
80ml extra virgin olive oil
25ml sherry vinegar
finely grated zest and juice of 1 lime
sea salt and freshly cracked black pepper

For the pan-roasted skate

2 skate wings (about 450–500g each)
1 tablespoon unsalted butter

First, make the pickle. Blanch the broccoli and kale in a large saucepan of boiling salted water for 2–3 minutes or until just tender. Drain, refresh in iced water, then drain again thoroughly. Roughly chop the broccoli and shred the kale, then place both in a bowl. Add all the remaining pickle ingredients, mixing well, then season to taste with salt and pepper. Cover and leave to marinate at room temperature for 20 minutes (see Cook's Note).

Meanwhile, for the skate, season the skate wings on both sides with salt and pepper. Heat a large, non-stick frying pan over a medium heat until it is warm but not smoking hot (you will need a frying pan that is large enough to cook both skate wings at the same time). Add the butter and when it has melted and starts to foam, add the fish, presentation-side down first, and pan-fry for 5–6 minutes. Turn the fish over and cook for a further 5–6 minutes or until golden brown and the flesh is flaky and soft. Remember, as this fish still has the bone in, make sure it's cooked through, but don't overcook it.

Remove the pan from the heat and leave the skate to rest in the pan for 2 minutes. Transfer the skate to serving plates and spoon the anchovy and purple sprouting broccoli pickle over the top. Serve immediately with boiled new potatoes or baked fennel.

Cook's Note

The pickle is best eaten freshly made, as it does not keep well.

Pan-fried Sea Bass and Crispy Whitebait with Re-fried Spiced Cauliflower Chickpeas

This dish captures and illustrates beautifully my perfect idea for a recipe. It is slightly spicy (not too much heat though), it includes several different textures and it is simple and delicious enough to make time after time. You'll never tire of it!

The re-fried chickpeas and cauliflower are tasty enough on their own, and I would encourage you to make a little bit extra as they are perfect the following day served with toasted pitta shards and a glass of Malbec.

Serves 4 as a main course

For the re-fried spiced cauliflower chickpeas

150g dried chickpeas (see Cook's Note)
1 teaspoon sea salt
80g golden sultanas (or use regular sultanas, if you wish)
100ml dry white wine
80ml rapeseed oil
2 onions, chopped
2 cloves garlic, crushed
1 small cauliflower, cut into small florets (about 300–350g trimmed florets)
2 teaspoons mild curry powder
½ teaspoon turmeric
a pinch of crushed dried chillies
2 tablespoons tahini
2 tablespoons chopped fresh flat-leaf parsley
sea salt and freshly cracked black pepper

For the pan-fried sea bass

4 x 100–120g boneless sea bass fillets, skin on
2 tablespoons rapeseed oil, plus extra for drizzling

For the crispy whitebait
sunflower oil, for deep-frying
100g plain flour
1 tablespoon mild curry powder, plus 1 extra teaspoon
1 teaspoon sea salt
1 teaspoon sesame seeds
a pinch of crushed dried chillies
120g whitebait, rinsed and patted dry

Make the re-fried spiced cauliflower chickpeas. Put the chickpeas in a large bowl and cover with plenty of cold water. Leave to soak for at least 8 hours or preferably overnight.

The next day, drain the chickpeas using a colander and rinse well under cold running water. Transfer the drained chickpeas to a large saucepan and cover with plenty of cold water. Bring to the boil over a high heat, skimming off any scum that forms on the surface, then reduce the heat to a gentle simmer, cover and simmer for about 2 hours or until the chickpeas are tender, stirring once or twice. Add the teaspoon of salt for the last 20 minutes of the cooking time. Drain the chickpeas, then rinse well and drain again. Set aside.

Put the golden sultanas in a bowl. Heat the wine in a small saucepan until it just comes to the boil, then pour it over the sultanas and leave to soak for 15–20 minutes.

Heat the rapeseed oil in a large, non-stick frying pan and sauté the onions, garlic, cauliflower florets, curry powder, turmeric and crushed chillies, with a generous amount of salt and pepper added, over a medium heat for 8–10 minutes or until the onions are transparent and the cauliflower is soft (but do not let the vegetables colour too much).

Add the drained, cooked chickpeas and sauté for a further 5 minutes, stirring occasionally to prevent the onions from catching. Add the soaked sultanas and wine and stir in the tahini, then bring back to a gentle simmer and simmer for 5 minutes.

Remove from the heat and carefully transfer half of the mixture to a blender and blend until smooth. Return the blended mixture to the rest of the cauliflower and chickpeas in the pan, stir in the parsley and taste and adjust the seasoning, if necessary. Keep hot while you cook the sea bass and whitebait.

For the pan-fried sea bass, use a sharp knife to score the skin of the fish fillets, cutting just through the skin and not through the flesh – this will prevent the fish from curling up during cooking and will encourage it to cook evenly. Season the fillets on both sides with salt.

Heat 2 tablespoons of rapeseed oil in a large, non-stick frying pan and once the oil is hot but not smoking, place the fish, skin-side down, into the pan. Cook over a medium heat for about 5 minutes or until the skin is golden brown and crisp (the cooking time will depend on the thickness of the fillets). Carefully flip the fish over and cook for 1 minute on the flesh side or until the fish is just cooked and lightly coloured. Drain on kitchen paper and leave to rest for 1 minute before serving.

Meanwhile, make the crispy whitebait. Heat some sunflower oil in an electric deep-fat fryer or in a deep frying pan to a temperature of 160°C (or until a small piece of bread browns within 20 seconds in the hot oil). In the meantime, place the flour and 1 tablespoon of the curry powder in a bowl, add salt and pepper and mix well.

In a separate small bowl, mix together the remaining teaspoon of curry powder, the teaspoon of salt, the sesame seeds and crushed chillies and set aside.

Once the oil is hot enough, toss the whitebait in the seasoned flour, coating it all over, then shake off any excess. Deep-fry the whitebait in the hot oil for about 3 minutes or until golden brown and crisp. Using a slotted spoon, remove and drain the cooked whitebait on kitchen paper and season generously with the chilli-salt mixture.

To serve, spoon a generous portion of the hot re-fried spiced cauliflower chickpeas on to the centre of each serving plate, place a pan-fried fish fillet on top, followed by some crispy whitebait. Drizzle with a little extra rapeseed oil and serve immediately.

Cook's Note
For this recipe, you need about 400g cooked chickpeas. If you are short of time, you can use canned chickpeas instead of soaking and cooking dried chickpeas. Simply use 400g canned chickpeas (remember this is the drained weight), add them to the sautéed onion/cauliflower mixture and then continue as directed.

Slow-cooked Duck Legs with Pickled Rhubarb

The outdoor rhubarb season takes over from the forced rhubarb season this month. The combination of rhubarb and duck is a match made in heaven. Outdoor rhubarb has a more earthy flavour and the colour is slightly browner in comparison to the bright pink colour of the forced rhubarb, but either type works for this delicious recipe.

Serves 4 as a main course

For the slow-cooked duck legs

4 duck legs, skin on (about 200–250g each)
1 clove garlic, crushed
½ teaspoon coriander seeds, toasted and cooled
1 bay leaf
a large sprig of fresh thyme, leaves only
1kg duck fat
sea salt and freshly cracked black pepper

For the pickled rhubarb

2 tablespoons tamarind pulp
100g caster sugar
50ml freshly squeezed lemon juice
200ml cold water
100ml red wine vinegar
1 bay leaf
200g outdoor rhubarb, washed and drained
100g redcurrant jelly
1 star anise

To make the slow-cooked duck legs, you will need to start a day in advance. Place the duck legs in a shallow plastic container, spread the garlic over the legs, then season with salt and pepper and rub this in. Scatter over the coriander seeds, bay leaf and thyme leaves. Cover and refrigerate overnight or for at least 12 hours.

The following day, cook the marinated duck legs. Preheat the oven to 140°C/Gas Mark 1. Melt the duck fat in a saucepan over a low heat. Wash the duck legs and pat them dry using kitchen paper, transfer the legs to a deep casserole, then pour over the warm duck fat. Place a piece of non-stick baking paper directly on the surface, then place a small plate on top to weigh the legs down (this will ensure the legs remain covered with the fat).

Cover with a tight-fitting lid and cook in the oven for 3 hours. After this time, check to see if the duck is cooked by inserting a metal skewer into the flesh – if it enters and exits easily then it's done; if the duck is slightly resistant, continue cooking for another 30 minutes or so. Once cooked, carefully remove the duck legs to a plate using a slotted spoon. Pass the fat through a sieve into a heatproof bowl and leave to cool, then keep the fat for making delicious roast potatoes (see Cook's Notes).

Meanwhile, make the pickled rhubarb. Place the tamarind pulp in a small saucepan with the sugar, lemon juice, water, red wine vinegar, bay leaf and salt and pepper. Cook over a low heat, stirring until the sugar has dissolved, then turn the heat up, bring to the boil and boil rapidly for about 10 minutes or until the pickling liquid has reduced to a sticky, syrupy mixture.

Remove and discard the bay leaf, then carefully transfer the pickling mixture to a blender and blend until smooth. Pour the pickling syrup back into the saucepan and bring back to the boil.

Cut the rhubarb into batons (each about 6 x 1.5cm in size). Add the rhubarb batons, redcurrant jelly and star anise to the pickling syrup in the pan. Reduce the heat, cover and poach the rhubarb in the syrup over a medium heat for about 5 minutes or until tender. Remove from the heat and set aside to cool. Remove and discard the star anise before serving. Serve at room temperature.

To finish the duck legs, preheat the grill to high. Place the duck legs (hot from the oven) on a baking tray (or on the rack in a grill pan), skin-side up, and place under the grill for 6–8 minutes or until the skin is crispy and golden brown (taking care not to let the skin burn or catch). Serve immediately with sautéed Pink Fir Apple potatoes and buttered kale, and with a generous spoonful of the pickled rhubarb alongside.

Cook's Notes

Once cool, cover the sieved duck fat, then store it in the fridge and use within a few weeks.

Store any leftover pickled rhubarb in an airtight container in the fridge and use within 1 week.

Rhubarb and Custard Pie-pudding

Recipes like this one make my heart flutter and really make me miss my mother! She still lives in South Africa and I truly take after her as she too loves a good pudding and if it includes custard, she's an even happier woman. Although my mum, Dalene, doesn't have a lot of patience, she's a good baker and she follows recipes methodically and always gets good results. Custard, pastry and rhubarb are possibly my mother's favourite ingredients and for me the added rum just brings that extra special touch to this dessert.

It might seem a bit of a long-winded process to make this pie-pudding, but I hope you can trust me enough to give it a go, as it's well worth the effort and is truly delicious. This rustic pudding is perfect for celebrating Mother's Day.

Serves 6

For the pastry
60g unsalted butter, softened
100g caster sugar
1 egg
2 tablespoons dark rum
125g plain flour
1 teaspoon baking powder
25g ground almonds

For the poached rhubarb
50g caster sugar
100ml cold water
½ vanilla pod, split in half lengthways and seeds scraped out
500g outdoor rhubarb, washed, drained and cut into 2cm slices

For the pastry cream
500ml milk
½ vanilla pod, split in half lengthways and seeds scraped out
4 egg yolks
75g caster sugar
50g cornflour
2 tablespoons dark rum

The pastry requires a minimum of 2 hours resting and my suggestion would be to make the pastry a day in advance, then leave it to rest in the fridge and make the rest of the pudding the following day.

Make the pastry. Cream the butter and sugar together in a bowl until pale and fluffy. Add the egg and rum and beat to incorporate. Sift the flour and baking powder over the creamed mixture and fold in, along with the ground almonds, to make a soft dough.

Turn the dough on to a sheet of cling film and bring the dough together, but do not knead it. Wrap the dough tightly in the cling film, then chill in the fridge for a minimum of 2 hours or overnight.

For the poached rhubarb, put the sugar, water and vanilla seeds in a saucepan and cook over a low heat until the sugar has dissolved, then turn the heat up, bring to the boil and boil rapidly for 1 minute. Reduce the heat, then add the rhubarb to the pan, cover and poach over a low heat for 5 minutes. Do not overcook the rhubarb, otherwise it will collapse and lose its shape – it is better if the rhubarb is still a little crunchy at this stage. Drain the rhubarb through a fine sieve, reserving the rhubarb and syrup separately. Spread the rhubarb over the base of a deep 24cm round ovenproof dish. Set aside while you make the pastry cream.

Preheat the oven to 190°C/Gas Mark 5.

Make the pastry cream. Rinse a clean saucepan with cold water and drain, but do not dry the pan. Add the milk and vanilla seeds to the pan and cook over a medium heat until the milk just starts to boil, then remove from the heat.

Meanwhile, in a small bowl, mix the egg yolks, sugar and cornflour together to form a smooth paste. Pour half of the hot milk over the egg mixture, stirring to mix well. Return the egg mixture to the remaining hot milk in the pan, then return to the heat and simmer for about 5 minutes or until the mixture has thickened, stirring continuously. Stir in the rum. Pour the hot pastry cream over the poached rhubarb in the dish.

Roll out the chilled pastry on a lightly floured work surface to 7–8mm thickness. Cut out a 24cm round and carefully place this over the hot pastry cream, tucking in the edges slightly inside the dish, if necessary. Use a metal skewer to make about 6–8 steam holes in the pastry. Bake in the oven for about 30 minutes or until the pastry is cooked, golden brown and crisp.

Remove from the oven and let the pie-pudding cool for 15 minutes, then brush the reserved rhubarb vanilla syrup over the top of the pastry to glaze. Cut into wedges to serve and serve either warm or cold. If there is any leftover reserved rhubarb syrup, reheat it gently and serve with the pie-pudding.

Cook's Note
This pie-pudding is truly delicious and I could happily make one for every season. Replace the poached rhubarb with poached apples and blackberries, pears (poached with saffron), or poached quinces or pineapple, if you like.

Rhubarb, Pecan and Buttermilk Puddings with Buttermilk Ice Cream

Glorious rhubarb! It's amazing how you can taste the change in season with some fruits and vegetables. Rhubarb is one of those magical seasonal taletellers. Early on in the season the forced rhubarb is tender and bright pink with a more delicate, perfumed flavour, then as the season evolves the outdoor rhubarb arrives with its more earthy and robust flavour and slightly browner colour.

At the British Larder we are spoilt with a wide range of fantastic local suppliers, but I'm sure if you have a good look around your area you will find some good local suppliers too. We get our supply of outdoor rhubarb from the charming Piers and Suvie from High House Farm in Sudbourne. They are model farmers with their orchards of apples and cherries groomed to perfection and immaculately grown, just like their wonderful outdoor rhubarb.

Serves 6

For the buttermilk ice cream
700ml buttermilk
120g caster sugar
200ml whipping cream
25ml freshly squeezed lemon juice

For the rhubarb and buttermilk puddings
melted butter, for greasing
115g unsalted butter, softened
150g light soft brown sugar
½ vanilla pod, split in half lengthways and seeds scraped out
2 medium whole eggs
2 medium egg yolks
140ml buttermilk
150g self-raising flour
½ teaspoon bicarbonate of soda
½ teaspoon ground ginger
a pinch of table salt
200g outdoor rhubarb, washed and drained
75g pecan nuts, roughly chopped

First, make the buttermilk ice cream. Place all the ingredients in a bowl and whisk together until well mixed. Cover and leave to rest in the fridge for 1 hour. Pour the mixture into an ice-cream maker and churn until frozen (following the manufacturer's instructions for your particular model). Alternatively, pour the chilled mixture into a shallow, freezer proof container, cover with a lid and freeze until firm, whisking the mixture 3 or 4 times during freezing (every hour or so) to break down the ice crystals and ensure an even-textured result.

Allow the ice cream to soften slightly at room temperature or in the fridge before serving.

Once the ice cream is ready, make the rhubarb and buttermilk puddings. Preheat the oven to 180°C/Gas Mark 4. Grease 6 silicone deep muffin moulds (or a standard 6-hole deep muffin tin) with melted butter and set aside.

Cream the softened butter, brown sugar and vanilla seeds together in a bowl until pale and fluffy. Add the whole eggs, one at a time, beating well after each addition, then beat in the egg yolks. Stir in the buttermilk. Sift the flour, bicarbonate of soda, ground ginger and salt over the creamed mixture and fold in using a large metal spoon to make a fairly thick batter.

Cut the rhubarb into 1cm slices and mix with the pecan nuts. Spoon half of the batter into the prepared moulds, dividing it evenly, and then top this with half of the rhubarb and pecan mixture. Spoon the remaining batter over the top, then divide the remaining rhubarb and pecan mixture between the moulds, placing it on top of the batter.

Bake in the oven for 25–30 minutes or until well-risen, cooked and golden brown. Remove from the oven, transfer to a wire rack and leave the puddings to cool in the moulds for about 10 minutes before serving.

To serve, un-mould each pudding on to a serving plate. Serve warm with scoops of the buttermilk ice cream alongside.

Cook's Note
The buttermilk ice cream will make more than 6 portions, so store any leftovers in the freezer. Once made and frozen, the buttermilk ice cream will keep in the freezer for up to 1 month.

My Famous Treacle Tart

I'm not the best pastry cook around, but I do know a good tart when I see one. This treacle tart is simply one of those perfect recipes that you know you can rely on time after time. It's not very difficult to make, it just requires a bit of quality time.

With fresh seasonal ingredients being fairly limited during the month of March, the store cupboard comes into its own, along with the addition of freshly grated lemon zest – ah, that smell is divine! It's amazing how a grating and squeeze of fresh lemon can transform something so simple into a mouthful of pure pleasure, and this recipe demonstrates that perfectly.

As with our ethos and everything else we believe in at the British Larder, we buy and use the best ingredients we can possibly afford. Moving to Suffolk was in one way very easy, as we knew that the produce, ingredients and suppliers in the area are second to none. When we were first introduced to Chris Brennan, the owner and very capable baker of Pump Street Bakery in Orford, it was like a breath of fresh air and Pump Street Bakery has been a godsend to us ever since. Ross and I believe that we should only buy a product if it's better than one we can make ourselves – Chris's bread is definitely one of those products and one that we use every day in our restaurant.

Inevitably, we do acquire quite a lot of leftover bread, so I tend to whizz it up into breadcrumbs and then start thinking of the tasty recipes I can make to use them all up. I use Chris's sourdough bread in my Christmas puddings and I'm still convinced that it's my secret ingredient in creating the best Christmas puddings I have ever made. I often freeze leftover breadcrumbs to use as and when required, and this recipe is a perfect way of using up some of those breadcrumbs. I have had this treacle tart recipe for years and it's been a popular dessert on many occasions in the past, like a trusty old friend, so here it is for you to make and enjoy for yourself.

Serves 6–8

100g day-old sourdough bread, crusts removed (weight given is for crust-less bread)
1 egg
125ml double cream
300g golden syrup
40g clear honey
finely grated zest and juice of 1 small lemon
60g ground almonds
300g Sweet Shortcrust Pastry (see page 18)

The breadcrumb mixture is prepared then chilled overnight in the fridge, so you will need to start this recipe a day in advance (see Cook's Notes).

Whizz the sourdough bread in a food processor to make fine breadcrumbs. Set aside. Whisk the egg and cream together in a mixing bowl. Set aside. Gently heat the golden syrup and honey together in a small saucepan, just enough to make them runnier and easier to mix. Remove from the heat. Whisk the warmed golden syrup and honey and lemon zest and juice into the egg mixture, then stir in the ground almonds and breadcrumbs. Cover and leave the mixture to rest in the fridge overnight.

The following day, roll out the pastry on a lightly floured work surface to about 2mm thickness and use it to line a (loose-bottomed, if you like) 35 x 10 x 2.5cm fluted oblong flan tin (leaving a slight overhang of pastry). Leave to rest in the fridge for 30 minutes.

Meanwhile, preheat the oven to 160°C/ Gas Mark 3.

Whisk the chilled breadcrumb mixture and pour it into the chilled pastry case. Bake in the oven for 40–45 minutes or until lightly set and golden – the tart will still have a gentle wobble in the centre but this will firm up once cooled.

Remove from the oven to a wire rack and leave the tart to cool completely in the tin. Once cold, trim the overhanging pastry from the top edges of the tart with a small serrated knife, then carefully remove the tart from the tin and cut it into slices. Serve with whipped Chantilly cream, crème fraîche or vanilla ice cream.

Cook's Notes

I recommend using an oblong fluted flan tin instead of a round one for this recipe, so that the tart cooks more evenly and is easier to cut and handle.

Use fresh bread that is a day old, cut the crusts off and use the inside of the loaf only. You can use regular white bread for this recipe, but I prefer sourdough as it gives the tart that extra special taste. Do not use dried breadcrumbs.

Be patient when making this tart and follow the recipe – leave the breadcrumb mixture to rest overnight in the fridge, do not overcook the tart, and leave it to cool completely before cutting and eating.

Lemon, Semolina and Almond Cake

This cake is a celebration cake. It is rich, with a zesty lemon flavour and is an ideal way to say thank you to your loved ones. It's perfect for Mother's Day and if made a day in advance, the taste develops and it is even better. The amaretto liqueur is optional, but as it's a celebration cake, I suggest adding it. The flaked almond and brown sugar topping also adds delicious crunch and texture to the baked cake.

Serves 8–12

finely grated zest and juice of 4 lemons
225g unsalted butter, softened
225g caster sugar
1 vanilla pod, split in half lengthways and seeds scraped out
225g ground almonds
3 eggs
1 teaspoon amaretto liqueur (optional)
115g semolina
1 teaspoon baking powder
a pinch of table salt
50g flaked almonds
50g light soft brown sugar

Preheat the oven to 160°C/Gas Mark 3. Grease and line a 20cm springform cake tin and set aside.

Strain the lemon juice though a fine sieve to remove the pips and set aside.

Cream the butter, caster sugar and vanilla seeds together in a bowl until pale and fluffy. Fold in the ground almonds, then add the eggs, one at a time, mixing well after each addition. Add the lemon zest and juice and amaretto, if you like, and mix well. Sprinkle the semolina, baking powder and salt over the egg mixture and lightly fold in, but do not overwork the mixture – the mixture will be runny. Pour the mixture into the prepared cake tin.

Bake in the oven for about 1½ hours or until cooked and golden brown and a fine metal skewer inserted into the centre comes out almost clean with a light oily residue.

Remove from the oven, sprinkle the flaked almonds and brown sugar evenly over the top of the cake, spray the top with cold water a couple of times and then return the cake to the oven for a further 8 minutes or until the nuts are lightly toasted.

Remove from the oven to a wire rack and leave the cake to cool in the tin for 20–25 minutes or until it is just warm. Remove from the tin and cut into fairly thin slices to serve. This cake has a fine texture and is very rich, so only small portions are needed. Serve just warm with crème fraîche or mascarpone.

Cook's Notes

This cake can be made a day in advance and it will keep in an airtight container at room temperature for up to 2 days. If you have leftovers, reheat portions in a low oven for a few minutes or in a microwave oven on Medium for 20–30 seconds, to just warm the cake through before serving.

The British Larder | *April*

Spring has finally sprung and there is a noticeable seasonal change with new shoots and blossom appearing on the shrubs and trees. Occasional frosty mornings are still around, making gardeners and farmers slightly nervous, but the earth is finally beginning to warm up and we can enjoy the fact that the days are getting longer and the nights are getting shorter.

Radishes

Jersey Royals are starting the new potato season off triumphantly this month as their short season begins. Watercress is beginning to grow in ponds and streams and the fragrance of wild garlic lingers in the woods on warmer, brighter days. Depending on the weather, we may also see a short flurry of wild mushrooms – if the weather is damp and slightly warmer than usual, this creates the perfect conditions for a good crop of spring wild mushrooms. New season spring lamb is also back in time for the all-important Easter celebrations. The season for cockles and winkles is coming to an end, but the ocean is delivering fantastic John Dory, crab and sea trout.

Season's best during April...

Bananas, Broccoli, Chickweed, Chicory, Chives and Chive Flowers, Cockles, Crab, Dill, Jersey Royal New Potatoes, John Dory, Lamb, Mangoes, Nettles, Parsley, Purple Sprouting Broccoli, Radishes, Rhubarb (outdoor), Rocket, Rosemary, Salad/Spring Onions, Salmon, Sea Bass, Sea Beet, Sea Trout, Sorrel, Spinach, Watercress, Whitebait, Wild Garlic, Wild Mushrooms (spring), Woodpigeon.

My culinary rituals for April...

The warmer spring weather is welcomed with open arms. Pretty blossoms on the trees and daffodils poking their sunny yellow faces through the grass are a joyful sight. After a good downpour during the night, a long walk through the forest or woods might result in a fruitful discovery of woodland

Happy pigs!

mushrooms – look out for varieties such as beefsteak fungus, St George's mushrooms, fairy ring mushrooms, field mushrooms and morels.

Once I have used all the fresh mushrooms we can possibly eat within a short period of time, I dry the rest to preserve them for use later in the year. To do this, clean the mushrooms without washing them in water, dusting them well and using a wet piece of kitchen roll to wipe off any soil, then cut them into 1cm-thick slices. Preheat the oven to 110°C/Gas Mark ¼. Scatter the mushrooms over a baking tray lined with non-stick baking paper, then place in the oven to dry for 2–3 hours. Make sure they are completely dry before removing them from the oven, then leave to cool. You will notice that the mushrooms have shrunk a lot and are discoloured, but be assured that the dried mushrooms will provide lots of robust flavour. Once completely cold, store them in an airtight container or jar until needed and use within 3 months.

Other wild foods also make their appearance this month, with wild garlic, chickweed and nettles being the early starters. Head towards the coast to seek out sea beet and sea kale and look out for potential sites to find sea purslane and samphire later on in the summer.

Plant a good selection of nasturtium flowers, borage and chives in your garden if you can, as they will provide plenty of pretty flowers for use in the kitchen, and if you look after them well, you should have a good supply for most of the summer.

I love to give everything a good spring clean around Easter time and the feeling of satisfaction when it's all done is wonderful. Finding a collection of jam jars and clearing out old crockery and the things that you no longer need is a great feeling!

The other side to the culinary season...

Not only does the time of year determine what we eat, special events and celebrations are also an important part of the seasonal calendar and they steer us towards specific recipes suited to the different occasions. Many celebrate Easter during spring for religious reasons and Easter either takes place at the end of March or sometime during April. It marks the end of Lent, a 40-day period of fasting and prayer. Many Christians give up chocolate during Lent. Traditionally, lamb and other indulgent seasonal foods are eaten during the Easter celebrations, once the fast is broken. Many recipes have a special meaning, such as hot cross buns, that are traditionally baked and eaten on Good Friday. As Easter approaches, I find myself doing a lot of baking. To enjoy the Easter celebrations in style, try sweet temptations such as my **Cardamom and Golden Sultana Hot Cross Buns** (see page 154) or **Salted Peanut Chocolate Whoopie Pies** (see page 156).

British Larder Heroes

Broccoli

This is a member of the Brassicaceae family and it is rich in vitamin C and high in fibre. There are two main types of broccoli – the common green variety known as calabrese, with its larger flower heads on thicker stems, and purple sprouting broccoli with its slender, leafy stems of varying lengths with smaller heads of purple-green flowers or florets (a white variety is also available, but the purple variety is the most common). Another variety of broccoli that is also now readily available is Tenderstem broccoli, but this is typically harvested from June–November. It has characteristic long tender stems with small florets that are tender from stem to tip, so it can all be eaten. Tenderstem broccoli has a mild and sweet, but quite distinctive flavour and a texture that is similar to asparagus. There is also another type of broccoli known as Romanesco broccoli or Roman cauliflower, which is in fact a variant form of cauliflower. Romanesco is pale green in colour and has a very decorative and striking appearance, as each floret rises to a peak, and its entire shape approximates a natural fractal appearance. Choose firm heads of broccoli with a good colour and avoid limp heads with open, slightly yellow flowers (in the case of calabrese, purple sprouting broccoli or Tenderstem broccoli). Broccoli can be eaten raw or cooked, but is most often steamed, boiled or stir-fried.

Cockles

Crab

For a tasty **Chopped Broccoli and Stilton Salad**, cut a head (about 300g) of green broccoli (calabrese) into florets, discarding most of the thick stem. Finely chop the florets and mix them with 1 finely diced red onion, 1 finely diced stick of celery and a small handful of chopped roasted pecan nuts in a bowl. In a separate bowl, combine 4 tablespoons mayonnaise, 1 teaspoon malt vinegar, a pinch of caster sugar and 50g crumbled Stilton cheese, mixing well. Add the Stilton mayonnaise to the broccoli salad, toss together to mix well and serve with a little extra Stilton crumbled over the top. If you like, chop 2 cold cooked crispy rashers of smoked back bacon and scatter the bacon over the salad just before serving. Serves 4 as a starter or as an accompaniment with sliced cold meats or poached salmon or trout.

Cockles

Cockles are edible bivalves belonging to the clam family and they live along our coastal shorelines. They are small and it might feel like hard work retrieving the salty sweet cockle flesh from the shells, but they are delicious. Cockles served with vinegar and brown bread is synonymous with going to the seaside. They can be eaten raw or cooked (usually steamed or boiled) and are delicious served in soups and sauces. As they live in the sand, cockles should be washed thoroughly in cold running water to remove as much sand as possible before eating. Discard any cockles that are heavy, broken or that remain open when tapped sharply with the back of a knife. Once cooked, any cockles that haven't opened should be discarded.

For a tempting **Warm Cockle and Bacon Butty**, butter 4 thick slices of granary bread and place 1 slice on each of 2 serving plates. Melt 1 tablespoon unsalted butter in a non-stick frying pan, then add 2 finely diced smoked streaky bacon rashers and sauté over a medium heat for 7–8 minutes or until cooked and golden. Add 250g cooked cockle meat, scatter over 2 finely shredded wild garlic leaves and cook for about 1 minute or until heated through. Remove from the heat and splash over a little malt vinegar to taste. Spoon over the buttered bread slices on the plates, top with the remaining buttered bread slices to make 2 sandwiches and serve immediately. Serves 2 as a breakfast, light lunch or snack.

Crab

The edible parts of the crab (which must be cooked in salted water before eating) consist of the dense, sweet, flaky white muscular tissue or meat, and the softer brown tissue or meat, which is distinctly stronger in flavour and slightly pasty in texture. Usually around a third of the total weight of an adult edible crab is made up of meat, of which one-third is white meat from the claws and two-thirds is brown meat from the body. There are thousands of crab species available in all shapes and sizes. The European Brown Crab or Common Crab is the most widely available and can be enjoyed all year round. Cromer Crab from Norfolk is particularly popular due to its high ratio of white meat to brown.

Waste not, want not is my motto, so, once you have removed the meat from the crab shells, use the shells to make a rich and indulgent **Crab Bisque**. Preheat the oven to 240°C/Gas Mark 9. You will need about 50g cooked crab meat per person for this recipe, so a total of 200g (use the rest of the crab meat for another recipe or dish). Put the empty crab shells (from a 1.2–1.5kg crab or from two 1kg crabs) in a roasting tin and roast in the oven for 20 minutes, stirring once or twice. Meanwhile, heat 1 tablespoon sunflower oil in a large saucepan, add 1 diced carrot, 1 diced leek, 1 diced stick of celery, 1 diced onion and 2 crushed cloves garlic and sauté over a medium heat for 8–10 minutes or until dark golden. Add 1 teaspoon coriander seeds, 5 black peppercorns, 2 sprigs of fresh thyme and the roasted crab shells, together with 1 tablespoon tomato purée. Add 80ml brandy and 100ml dry white wine to the pan and let the liquid bubble, stirring and scraping the base of the pan with a wooden spoon to deglaze it. Boil rapidly over a high heat for 8–10 minutes or until the alcohol has evaporated. Add 1.2 litres fish stock, bring to a simmer, then simmer, uncovered, for 30 minutes or until the stock is dark brown and rich. Using a slotted spoon, remove and discard the crab shells. Carefully transfer the bisque to a blender and blend until smooth, then pass it through a fine sieve back into the pan. Reheat gently until hot, add a dash or two of double cream and then add sea salt and freshly cracked black pepper to taste. Serve in bowls with the flaked cooked crab meat scattered over the top. Serve with buttered brown bread. Serves 4 as a starter or light lunch.

Jersey Royal new potatoes

Jersey Royals are the first crop of new potatoes and they mark the beginning of the new potato season. These well-flavoured, kidney-shaped potatoes, with their wafer-thin skins, are a cultivated type of new potato grown only in Jersey. The Jersey soil is light and well drained and many farmers still use seaweed harvested from the local beaches as a natural fertiliser. The season usually begins in April and runs through to the end of June, with the peak of the season occurring during May. The potatoes are carefully harvested, packed and shipped overnight so they reach markets and supermarkets the next day to ensure they are at their freshest. All genuine Jersey Royals enjoy The Protected Designation of Origin (PDO) which is an official recognition granted by the EU to protect the product and make sure it is produced in its country of origin. These fine and unique potatoes are delicious to eat, but they do tend to command a premium price, although I must say they are well worth it.

Try this delicious **Jersey Royal New Potato and Spinach Salad**. Served either hot or cold, it makes the perfect accompaniment for the Pan-Roasted Salmon with Wild Garlic Butter (see page 133). Cut 10 boiled (drained and cooled slightly) Jersey Royal new potatoes in half. Heat 2 tablespoons olive oil in a non-stick frying pan and sauté the potatoes, with sea salt and freshly cracked black pepper added, over a high heat for 5–7 minutes or until golden brown and crisp. Add 2 handfuls of baby spinach and another dash of olive and sauté for 1 minute or until the leaves start to wilt. Season with the juice of 1 lemon and serve immediately. Serves 2 as an accompaniment.

John Dory

Also known as St Pierre, John Dory is an attractive seawater flatfish with a large head and two distinguishing large black spots on each side below the head, said to be the thumbprints of St Peter. The white flesh is slightly sweet with a nearly transparent colour when super fresh. John Dory graces many chefs' menus and can be served whole or filleted, and baked, steamed, poached, braised or pan-fried. The bones make an excellent fish stock (remember, to make a clear and delicious stock, wash the bones and remove the eyes and guts).

You will need a good quality stock for this fantastic **John Dory and Sea Beet Broth**. Pour 500ml fresh fish stock into a saucepan, add 2 tablespoons soy sauce (preferably dark) and bring up to a gentle simmer. Gently poach 4 skinless John Dory fillets (65–85g each) in the warm stock for 3 minutes or until just cooked, then remove from the heat. Meanwhile, cook 40g rice noodles in a separate pan of boiling water for 2–3 minutes or until tender, then drain. Divide the warm rice noodles between 2 bowls, add a small handful of julienned fresh sea beet leaves (stalks trimmed) and fresh bean sprouts to each bowl. Place 2 fish fillets into each bowl, then ladle the hot broth over the top. Sprinkle over a small handful of chopped fresh coriander and season with freshly squeezed lime juice. Serve immediately with chilli oil to taste. Serves 2 as a light lunch or light supper.

Radishes

Radishes, another member of the Brassicaceae family, are root vegetables which are used mainly as a salad ingredient. There are plenty of radish varieties available, the most common spring variety being the French Breakfast Radish, with the Daikon being the most common type of winter radish. The whole plant is edible and both the leaves and the root can be shredded and served in salads. Radishes are normally eaten raw but can also be cooked in recipes such as stir-fries, or they can be pickled. With their distinctive crisp flesh and peppery flavour, radishes add an interesting texture and taste to dishes.

To make **Soused Radishes**, remove and discard the stalks and leaves from 2 bunches of French breakfast radishes, then cut the radishes in half, and wash and dry them. Put 50g caster sugar, 50ml white wine vinegar, ½ teaspoon mustard powder and sea salt and freshly cracked black pepper in a small saucepan. Heat gently until the sugar has dissolved, then whisk in 100g cold unsalted butter, until the butter has melted into the vinegar, but do not let the mixture boil. Remove from the heat. Meanwhile, blanch the radishes in a separate pan of boiling salted water for 2 minutes, then drain. Add the warm blanched radishes to the sousing liquid and mix. Serve warm or at room temperature with hot smoked fish dishes or grilled lamb chops. Serves 4 as an accompaniment.

Sea beet

Sea beet, also known as sea spinach or wild spinach, grows wild along the seashores of Great Britain. Sea beet is a member of the Chenopodiaceae family of flowering plants and is a wild ancestor of common vegetables such as beetroot, sugar beet and Swiss chard. Prepare sea beet leaves as you would prepare fresh spinach, then shred and either blanch the sea beet briefly in a pan of boiling salted water, then drain, or sauté it in a hot pan with a little melted unsalted butter for a minute or so until wilted, then serve.

Try my delicious seasonal recipe for **Sea Beet and Hot Smoked Peppered Mackerel Pancakes**. Either warm 4 ready-made plain (unsweetened) pancakes (each 15–18cm in diameter) according to packet directions, or cook 4 similar-sized pancakes from scratch (using a

basic homemade pancake batter) and keep them warm. Meanwhile, melt 2 teaspoons unsalted butter in a non-stick frying pan, then add 1 diced onion and sea salt and freshly cracked black pepper and sauté over a medium heat for 4–5 minutes or until the onion is golden and transparent. Remove the skin and bones from 1 whole smoked peppered mackerel (about 350g total weight), then flake the flesh and add to the onion in the pan, together with 2 handfuls of shredded fresh sea beet leaves (stalks trimmed). Add 4–6 tablespoons double cream, then bring up to a simmer and cook for 2 minutes. Remove from the heat. Divide the mackerel mixture evenly between the 4 pancakes, then roll up each pancake to enclose the filling. Serve 2 pancakes per portion with a fresh mixed leaf salad or steamed green beans. Serves 2 as a supper.

Spring wild mushrooms

The main edible wild mushroom season is during the autumn, apart from St George's mushrooms and morels, which appear during mid-late spring. There are many wonderful mushroom varieties, too many for me to write about, but one of my favourites are morels. Treasured by many cooks, these highly prized wild mushrooms are a true seasonal delicacy. Their distinctive honeycomb-like shape can harbour soil, grit and other forest debris, so they should be washed well and carefully before use (but preferably not soaked in water, as they will become waterlogged and unpleasant to eat). Morels must be cooked before consumption, as they are mildly toxic if eaten raw. With their distinctive, natural earthy flavour, morels pair up beautifully with robust and strong-flavoured meats such as beef, veal, guinea fowl and woodpigeon, and fish such as John Dory or turbot. Morels are possibly one of the most expensive mushrooms, as they are not easy to come by and are only available for a short period of time. Dried and canned morels are also available.

For something special, prepare this delicious recipe for **Chicken Breasts Stuffed with Morels**. Soak 40g dried morels in warm water for 1 hour, then drain and squeeze to remove the excess water. Set aside. Melt 1 tablespoon unsalted butter in a non-stick frying pan, add the soaked mushrooms, 1 finely chopped banana shallot and sea salt and freshly cracked black pepper and sauté over a medium heat for 7–8 minutes or until golden brown and soft. Remove from the heat and set aside to cool. Meanwhile, preheat the oven to 200°C/Gas Mark 6. Remove the skin from 2 organic or free-range boneless chicken breasts (120–140g each), then use a sharp knife to butterfly each breast (see page 187 for instructions on how to butterfly chicken breasts). Set aside. Chop the cooled mushroom mixture and drain off any excess liquid, then combine the mushroom mixture with 2 tablespoons mascarpone and 1 teaspoon finely chopped fresh tarragon. Divide the mixture evenly between the butterflied chicken breasts, spreading it out slightly. Fold the breasts over to enclose the filling, then wrap each breast in a thin slice of Parma ham, so that the main part of the chicken is covered. Place the wrapped chicken breasts in an ovenproof dish and bake in the oven for 20–22 minutes or until the chicken is cooked and the Parma ham is crispy. Serve with steamed broccoli and buttered new potatoes. Serves 2 as a main course.

Watercress

Watercress is yet another member of the Brassicaceae family and it has a distinct sharp, peppery flavour. It's said to be one of the oldest known leaf vegetables consumed by humans. Watercress is a hardy aquatic perennial with fleshy stems and small, tender, dark green leaves. Watercress is widely cultivated and grows best in running water that is slightly alkaline. If you are lucky enough and look carefully, you might come across wild watercress growing in running streams of fresh water often shadowed by large trees and foliage. It can also sometimes be found growing in larger garden ponds.

Watercress has many uses and is delicious eaten either raw or cooked. It is excellent in salads, sandwiches and soups and is often used as a garnish. A classic recipe that comes to mind, and a great little reminder that spring really has sprung, is this fairly traditional **Potato and Watercress Soup**. Melt 2 tablespoons unsalted butter in a saucepan, add 350g finely sliced potatoes, 1 finely chopped onion and sea salt and freshly cracked black pepper and sauté over a low heat for about 10 minutes or until the vegetables are soft but have not taken on too much colour. Add 150ml dry white wine to the pan and let the liquid bubble, stirring and scraping the base of the pan with a wooden spoon to deglaze it. Boil rapidly over a high heat for 7–8 minutes or until the wine has evaporated, then add 600ml vegetable stock. Bring up to a simmer, then cover and simmer for about 10 minutes or until the potatoes are completely soft. Add 200ml double cream and bring back to the boil, then remove from the heat. Carefully transfer the soup to a blender, add 200g watercress and blend until smooth, then return to the pan and reheat gently. Season with freshly squeezed lemon juice and then taste, adding more salt and pepper, if needed. Serve immediately. Serves 4 as a starter or 2 as a light lunch.

Wild garlic

Wild garlic, also known as ramsons, is a wild relative of chives. It grows in woodlands, typically in semi-shaded, moist conditions, and can be identified by its long lush green leaves (similar in appearance to those of Lily of the Valley), garlic-like smell and white flowers that appear towards the end of the season. The leaves, flowers and bulbs are edible, but it's the leaves that are used most readily in cooking. It tastes similar to a milder version of normal garlic and can be used raw or cooked in many dishes, including salads, soups, quiches, risottos and pesto.

For a simple but tasty midweek supper, prepare my recipe for **Pan-roasted Salmon with Wild Garlic Butter**. First, make the wild garlic butter by mashing together 3 tablespoons softened unsalted butter, 8 finely sliced wild garlic leaves, 4 finely sliced fresh mint leaves and a pinch of sea salt and freshly cracked black pepper in a pestle and mortar. Set aside. Heat a tiny dash of olive oil in a non-stick frying pan. Season 2 skinless salmon fillets (120–150g each) with salt and pepper. Pan-fry the salmon over a high heat for 3 minutes on one side, then turn them over, turn the heat off and spoon the wild garlic butter over the salmon. Let the residual heat of the pan continue to finish cooking the salmon while the butter is melting into the fish. After 2 minutes, remove the salmon from the pan and serve on a few crushed boiled new potatoes. Spoon the melted garlic butter over, squeeze over freshly squeezed lemon juice to taste and serve immediately. Serves 2 as a main course or supper.

Woodpigeon

Woodpigeons might be a nuisance during spring in the garden and in freshly sown fields, but they taste delicious with their rich, dark meat. It's great to see that they are more widely available and are now regularly sold at many farmers' markets and quality butchers. Choose fresh young birds if you can, but if in doubt about their age, braising them is the best option. Tender young woodpigeons require very little cooking and you should avoid overcooking them as the meat then becomes chewy and tastes livery.

The distinct and robust, almost gamey taste of woodpigeon pairs up beautifully with earthy flavours such as nettles and wild mushrooms, so for a delicious and inspired dish, try my recipe for **Woodpigeon, Nettle and Wild Mushroom Gratin**. Remove the breasts from 2 plump (plucked and gutted) woodpigeons (about 250–300g each, unprepared weight), remove the skin and cut the breast meat into quarters, then season with sea salt and freshly cracked black pepper. Melt 1 tablespoon unsalted butter in a large, non-stick frying pan and sauté the woodpigeon meat over a high heat for 1 minute on each side or until sealed all over. Remove the woodpigeon meat to a plate, then add 2 finely sliced banana shallots and a large handful of cleaned, sliced, mixed fresh wild mushrooms to the same pan, along with 1 tablespoon unsalted butter and sauté over a high heat for 4–5 minutes or until lightly browned. Add a handful of washed, shredded wild garlic leaves and a handful of washed tender nettle tops, season with salt and pepper and then sauté for 30–60 seconds or until the leaves are just wilted. Add 2 tablespoons Madeira, then bring up to a simmer. Remove from the heat and stir in 4 tablespoons crème fraîche, then stir in the woodpigeon meat. Transfer the mixture to a shallow, flameproof baking dish, sprinkle over a generous amount of fresh breadcrumbs. Preheat the grill to high. Place the dish under the grill for 5–8 minutes or until the breadcrumbs are golden and the crème fraîche is bubbling. Serve immediately with plenty of fresh bread. Serves 2 as a supper.

Morels

Forager's Mushroom Soup with Beefsteak Mushroom Croustades

Foraging for food is currently a very popular activity and it's amazing how much free food there actually is out there to collect. However, it's not always as simple as it may seem. Arm yourself with as much knowledge as possible and ideally go foraging with someone who knows what they are looking for. Books will help, as will plenty of common sense, and remember, if in doubt, leave it out. Don't collect and eat things that you are not completely sure are edible.

The wild mushroom season comes around twice a year and the early spring flurry brings us delights such as morels, St George's mushrooms, flat field mushrooms and beefsteak fungus. Later on in the year, during the autumn, other varieties will follow. If you're lucky enough to find beefsteak fungus, which grows on trees (usually oak or sweet chestnut trees), then soak them in cold milk or water for 10 minutes and drain before cooking. This will draw out the bitterness from the mushrooms. Once fried in butter and seasoned with salt, they taste just like a piece of steak.

Serves 4 as a starter or 12 as a canapé (served in espresso cups)

For the mushroom soup

1 tablespoon unsalted butter
300g fresh mixed wild mushrooms, cleaned and sliced
2 banana shallots, finely sliced
200g celery, finely diced
1 clove garlic, crushed
150ml Madeira
600ml vegetable or chicken stock
200ml double cream
sea salt and freshly cracked black pepper

For the beefsteak mushroom brioche croustades

200g fresh beefsteak fungus/mushrooms
100ml milk
2 teaspoons unsalted butter
1 tablespoon olive oil
300g fresh mixed wild mushrooms (such as field mushrooms, fairy ring mushrooms, etc), cleaned and sliced
1 banana shallot, thinly sliced
1 clove garlic, crushed
1 teaspoon chopped fresh thyme
6 large slices of brioche, cut about 1cm thick

small sprigs of fresh chickweed, rinsed and drained, to garnish

First, prepare the soup. Melt the butter in a large saucepan and once the butter starts to foam, add the mushrooms, shallots, celery, garlic and salt and pepper and sauté over a high heat for 8–10 minutes or until the vegetables are deep golden brown. Add the Madeira to the pan and let the liquid bubble, stirring and scraping the base of the pan with a wooden spoon to deglaze it. Boil rapidly over a high heat for 3–4 minutes or until the Madeira turns syrupy and coats the vegetables. Add the stock and bring to the boil, then reduce the heat, cover and simmer gently for about 20 minutes or until the stock is rich and deep-coloured.

Meanwhile, start the croustades. Thinly slice the beefsteak mushrooms, then put them in a dish, cover with the milk and leave to soak for 10 minutes. Drain, discarding the milk, then wash the mushrooms under cold running water, drain and pat dry. Set aside.

Heat the butter and olive oil in a large, non-stick frying pan and as soon as the butter starts to foam, add the beefsteak and mixed wild mushrooms, shallot, garlic and salt and pepper and sauté over a high heat for 7–8 minutes or until the vegetables are golden brown. Stir in the thyme. Remove from the heat and keep hot.

Toast the brioche slices until golden brown on both sides – either under a preheated medium-hot grill or using a toaster. Using a 4cm round cutter, cut 12 rounds out of the toasted brioche slices, then set aside and keep warm. (Use the leftover toasted brioche to make breadcrumbs for another use.)

Finish the soup. Add the cream to the soup in the pan and simmer for a further 5 minutes. Carefully transfer the soup to a blender and blend until very smooth and frothy (see Cook's Note), then return it to the pan and reheat gently.

Finish the croustades. Divide the mushroom mixture evenly between the toasted brioche croustades and then garnish each one with a small sprig of chickweed.

Serve the hot, frothy soup in bowls with the warm croustades alongside. Serve 3 croustades per portion, if serving as a starter; serve 1 croustade per portion, if serving as a canapé.

Cook's Note

For extra cappuccino foaminess, return the blended soup to a deep saucepan and reheat, then use a stick blender to aerate the soup further. The soup must be hot and I find it aerates best if the soup is just below boiling point. If the soup is too thick, it will not foam, so if this is the case, add a dash more double cream to thin the soup down slightly. I also find adding a small knob of cold unsalted butter also does the trick. Fatty components help the soup to aerate. As soon as the soup is aerated and foamy, serve it immediately.

Jersey Royal New Potatoes with Cockles, Sorrel and Smoked Eel

This is a spectacularly beautiful seasonal plate of food, well balanced with the acidity of the sorrel, the natural sweetness from the cockles, the earthy taste of the Jersey Royals and the smokiness from the smoked eel. It is delicious in so many ways.

Serve this dish either completely cold or keep the potatoes warm and toss the salad together at the very last minute. The leftover sorrel pesto can be kept in a covered jar in the fridge (with a piece of cling film placed directly on the surface of the pesto). It will keep for up to 5 days in the fridge and is ideal for tossing with freshly cooked pasta.

Serves 4 as a starter or light lunch

For the sorrel pesto

1 bunch of fresh sorrel (120–150g), washed and patted dry
30g pine nuts, toasted and cooled
20g golden linseeds, toasted and cooled
2 tablespoons finely grated fresh Parmesan cheese
2 tablespoons rapeseed oil
1 clove garlic, crushed
4 sprigs of fresh mint, leaves only
¼ small bunch of fresh parsley
sea salt and freshly cracked black pepper

For the salad

200g purple sprouting broccoli, trimmed
500g Jersey Royal new potatoes, rinsed
2 tablespoons rapeseed oil
1 teaspoon malt vinegar
1 teaspoon chopped fresh tarragon
200g cooked cockle meat
1 lime, cut into quarters
1 bunch of fresh sorrel (120–150g), washed, patted dry and shredded
120g skinless, boneless smoked eel, flaked
10 anchovy fillets in oil (preferably silverskin), drained

First, prepare the sorrel pesto. Place all the pesto ingredients in a blender and blend together until smooth. Taste and adjust the seasoning, if needed, then transfer the pesto to a bowl, cover and refrigerate for about 20 minutes to let the flavours develop.

Make the salad. Blanch the broccoli in a pan of boiling salted water for 2–3 minutes or until just tender or al dente. Drain, refresh in iced cold water, then drain again and set aside.

Put the Jersey Royals in a pan of salted water and bring to the boil, then simmer for 10–15 minutes or until tender. Drain and then leave to cool for 10 minutes.

Put 1 tablespoon rapeseed oil, the malt vinegar and tarragon in a bowl, add the cockle meat and stir to mix. Season lightly with salt and pepper. Cover and leave to marinate at room temperature for 10 minutes.

While the cockles are marinating, finish the potatoes. Cut the potatoes in half. Heat the remaining oil in a non-stick frying pan and sauté the potatoes over a high heat for 7–8 minutes or until golden, then season to taste with salt and pepper. At the same time, pan-fry the lime quarters in the same pan for 6–8 minutes or until golden brown on each side, turning once – this will give them a delicious, tangy seasoned flavour.

In a large serving bowl, toss the broccoli, sautéed potatoes, marinated cockles, shredded sorrel, flaked eel and anchovies together. Drizzle over 1 tablespoon of the sorrel pesto and toss to mix, then taste and add a little more pesto, if you like. Arrange the pan-fried lime wedges on top and serve immediately.

Crab and Sea Beet Salad

Freshly cooked crab meat is sweet and refreshing, and this recipe is a pretty and dainty dish that is easy to make for two or twenty. If you're planning to serve this dish for a special occasion, make all the separate components and store as directed, then simply assemble it all at the last minute and serve.

Serves 6 as a starter or light lunch

200g fresh sea beet leaves, washed and drained, stalks trimmed
1 large bunch of watercress (about 100g)
150ml cold water
½ teaspoon agar agar powder (see page 16)
4 sheets of chilled fresh or frozen (defrosted) filo pastry (each sheet about 40 x 30cm)
2 tablespoons unsalted butter, melted
400g cooked white crab meat, picked over and flaked
1 tablespoon mascarpone
1 tablespoon finely chopped fresh chervil
finely grated zest and juice of 1 lime
sea salt and freshly cracked black pepper
additional fresh sea beet leaves (stalks trimmed), washed, drained and cut into julienne (matchstick) strips, and watercress leaves, to serve

For the sea beet purée and jelly, blanch the sea beet leaves and watercress in a large saucepan of boiling salted water for 1 minute, then drain, refresh in iced water and drain again. Place the blanched sea beet and watercress in a blender and blend to a smooth purée, adding a tablespoon of iced water to thin the purée a little if it's too thick. Pass the purée through a fine sieve and set aside.

Select a shallow, white plastic tray (about 23 x 18cm in size) to set the jelly mixture in. Pour the cold water into a small saucepan, add the agar agar powder and 100ml of the sea beet purée and bring to the boil over a high heat, stirring continuously, then reduce the heat and simmer for 1 minute, stirring. Pour the hot mixture into the plastic tray and leave to set completely at room temperature, then refrigerate until needed. Pour the remaining sea beet purée into a bowl and keep it chilled in the fridge to prevent discoloration.

Next, make the filo waves. Preheat the oven to 180°C/Gas Mark 4. Lightly brush 1 sheet of filo pastry with melted butter and season with black pepper, then place another sheet of filo on top, lightly brush this with melted butter and season with black pepper. Continue in the same way until all 4 sheets of filo are stacked on top of each other, then use a sharp knife to cut the filo stack into six 15 x 5cm rectangles. Make 3 long sausage shapes out of foil and place these on a baking tray with a 10cm gap in between each one. Drape the buttered filo rectangles over the foil sausages to create 6 'waves'. Bake the filo in the oven for 8–10 minutes or until crisp and golden. Remove from the oven and carefully transfer the filo waves (still on the foil sausages) to a wire rack and leave to cool completely. Once cool, carefully remove them from the foil sausages and store in an airtight container until needed.

For the crab salad, in a bowl, mix the crab meat with the mascarpone and chervil and season to taste with the lime zest and juice and salt and pepper. Cover and chill for at least 10 minutes before serving.

To serve, chill the serving plates beforehand. Spread the reserved sea beet purée on the plates, dice the sea beet jelly and scatter about half of it over the plates. Arrange some julienned sea beet leaves on the plates with the watercress leaves. Place the crisp filo waves on top and place quenelles (or spoonfuls) of crab salad on to each filo wave, dividing the crab salad evenly between each portion. Garnish with the remaining sea beet jelly, julienned sea beet leaves and watercress leaves. Serve immediately.

Jersey Royal New Potato and Pig Hash

This recipe warms the cockles of your heart and it is ideal for a hearty breakfast in preparation for a long day ahead. At the British Larder, this dish creates the perfect staff lunch. Staff food at the British Larder does not consist of dishes from the menu, but it's cooked fresh every day using trimmings and leftovers. It's also a great opportunity for all the chefs to experiment with ingredients and to get creative. Most days, it's a bit of a 'Ready, Steady, Cook!' affair.

This tasty Pig Hash is one of Steven Miles' creations – Steve is our sous chef at the British Larder. This recipe started off as a staff meal using leftovers and then it turned into a 'real' dish that we now offer as a lunchtime special on our menu.

Serves 2 as a breakfast, brunch or lunch

2 tablespoons rapeseed oil
1 small onion, sliced or diced
1 clove garlic, crushed
6 cooked Jersey Royal new potatoes, cut into even-sized pieces
150g cooked pork, flaked
150g cooked smoked ham knuckle meat, flaked
2 spring onions, sliced
10 small cornichons or baby gherkins, chopped
finely grated zest and juice of 1 lemon
1 tablespoon chopped fresh mixed herbs (such as chervil, chives, rosemary, thyme and tarragon)
2 eggs
sea salt and freshly cracked black pepper

Heat 1 tablespoon rapeseed oil in a large, non-stick frying pan over a medium heat and sauté the onion, garlic and potatoes, with salt and pepper added, for 6–8 minutes or until golden brown. Add the flaked meat and sauté for a further 8–10 minutes, stirring occasionally.

Remove the pan from the heat, stir in the spring onions, cornichons, lemon zest and juice and chopped herbs. Adjust the seasoning to taste.

Spoon the pig hash on to serving plates and keep it warm while you fry the eggs. Heat the remaining oil in a separate non-stick frying pan over a medium heat. Carefully crack the eggs into the hot oil and fry them 'sunny side up' for 3–4 minutes or until cooked to your liking. Season with salt and pepper.

Place 1 fried egg on top of each portion of pig hash and serve immediately.

Smoked Bacon, Binham Blue and Wild Garlic Breakfast Muffins

These tasty muffins are quick and very easy to make. The smell of them baking is absolutely fantastic, especially on a chilly spring morning, with the lingering aromas of blue cheese, bacon and a hint of garlic – yum, yes please!

These are ideal for breakfast or served as canapés and they are best eaten on the day they are made. However, if there are any leftover, they are great for a lunchbox treat. Select blue cheese from your local area – I have used a local cheese that I love.

Makes 15 small muffins

100g smoked back bacon rashers, chopped
175g plain flour
75g fine polenta
1 teaspoon baking powder
4 fresh wild garlic leaves, washed, drained and finely shredded
100g blue cheese, crumbled (such as Binham Blue or a blue cheese from your local region)
150ml milk
1 egg
50g unsalted butter, melted
sea salt and freshly cracked black pepper
smoked paprika, for dusting

Preheat the oven to 200°C/Gas Mark 6 and grease a 15-cup flexible silicone small muffin mould or small muffin tin (each cup measuring about 5cm wide x 3cm deep).

Heat a non-stick frying pan over a high heat until hot, then sauté the bacon for about 8 minutes or until golden brown and cooked. Remove from the heat, drain on kitchen paper and set aside to cool completely.

Place the flour, polenta, baking powder, wild garlic, blue cheese and cooked cooled bacon in a mixing bowl, add a very small pinch of salt and a grinding of black pepper and mix together using your fingers.

Put the milk, egg and melted butter into a separate bowl and whisk together well. Add the egg mixture to the flour mixture and stir to combine, but do not over mix – the secret to making light muffins is not to stir the mixture too much.

Spoon the muffin mixture into the prepared mould cups, dividing it evenly – you can fill the cups to the top as the muffins do not rise much and they will just puff up a bit.

Bake in the oven for 18–22 minutes or until cooked and golden brown. Turn the muffins out on to a wire rack, lightly dust the tops with smoked paprika and let them cool slightly before serving. Serve warm or cold.

Cook's Notes

I am a great believer that cooks should use their own initiative to adjust recipes and experiment with different flavours. However, I have made the classic mistake with this particular recipe in the past where I have tried to add too many alternative exciting ingredients, and have consequently made the muffins too greasy or heavy. Do not be constrained by a recipe and feel free to experiment, but do remember that less is sometimes more. It's easy to over-complicate flavours and it can ruin your dish completely if you're not careful.

Also, bear in mind that if you substitute the Binham Blue cheese, use a blue cheese with a similar crumbly texture, otherwise a softer cheese may make the muffins too wet if the cheese becomes too runny during baking.

Pan-fried John Dory and Gnocchi with Cockle Velouté

This dish is a perfect celebration of spring and is a reminder of the wonderful edible gifts that Mother Nature provides us with, for which we are very thankful.

I love cockles for their flavour, especially the way I cook them, because they fill the pan with the 'taste of the sea'. For this recipe, the cockles are steamed quickly in a hot pan with white wine and lots of sliced shallots, and then the cooking liquor is used to make a creamy cockle velouté.

The lightly cooked and delicate flesh of the John Dory, served with golden nuggets of pan-fried gnocchi, crisp, salty samphire and juicy cockles, combines various flavours and textures of the sea to create this rich and flavourful dish.

Serves 4 as a main course

For the potato gnocchi

250g Desiree potatoes, cut into chunks
1 egg
70g type '00' pasta flour
2–3 teaspoons semolina
a splash of olive oil
sea salt and freshly cracked black pepper

For the cockle velouté

1kg fresh cockles (in shell)
4 banana shallots, finely sliced
2 large sprigs of fresh flat-leaf parsley, chopped
250ml dry white wine
1 tablespoon olive oil
20g unsalted butter
½ teaspoon coriander seeds, crushed
250ml fish stock
100ml double cream

For the pan-fried John Dory and samphire

1 tablespoon unsalted butter
100g samphire, washed
2 teaspoons small capers, drained
juice of ½ lemon
1 teaspoon chopped fresh flat-leaf parsley
1 tablespoon olive oil
8 skinless John Dory fillets (65–85g each)
coarse sea salt, to taste
20g cold unsalted butter, diced

First, prepare the potato gnocchi. Preheat the oven to 120°C/Gas Mark ½ and line a baking tray with non-stick baking paper. Cook the potatoes in a pan of boiling salted water for 15–20 minutes or until tender, then drain and transfer them to the prepared baking tray.

Place the tray of potatoes in the oven for 10 minutes to dry them out and remove excess moisture, then remove from the oven and push the potatoes through a ricer into a large mixing bowl (or mash them until very smooth using a potato masher). Add the egg, flour and salt and pepper and mix together to form a soft dough. Wrap the dough in cling film and chill in the fridge for 2 hours.

Meanwhile, prepare the cockle velouté. Place the cockles in a colander and wash thoroughly under cold running water, then drain well. Discard any cockles that are heavy, broken or that remain open when tapped sharply with the back of a knife. Heat a large saucepan over a high heat and as it approaches 'smoking hot', add the cockles, half of the shallots and the parsley sprigs to the pan and shake the pan, then add the wine and cover with the lid. Steam the cockles over a high heat for about 2 minutes or until the shells open, shaking the pan once or twice.

Remove from the heat and immediately transfer the cockle mixture to a muslin-lined fine sieve placed over a bowl to collect the cooking juices. Reserve 150ml of the cooking liquor and discard the rest. Pick the cockle meat from the shells, discarding any unopened cockles. Set the cockle meat aside, then cool and refrigerate until needed.

Heat the olive oil and butter in a large saucepan over a medium heat and once the butter starts to foam, add the remaining shallots and the coriander seeds, then cover and sweat for 8–10 minutes or until the shallots are transparent but with no colour. Remove the lid and increase the heat, then add the reserved cockle cooking liquor and boil rapidly for 5–8 minutes or until the liquid has reduced by half. Add the stock and bring to the boil over a high heat, then boil rapidly for 10–15 minutes or until reduced by half. Add the cream, then bring the sauce back to the boil and simmer for 2 minutes.

Remove from the heat and pass the velouté sauce through a fine sieve into a bowl. Add salt and pepper to taste, if needed. Cool, then cover and chill in the fridge until required, then, just before you are ready to serve, gently reheat the velouté in a small saucepan until hot.

Continue making the gnocchi. Once the dough is rested, place on a lightly floured work surface, divide into 4 equal pieces and roll each piece into a sausage shape, about 2cm wide. Using a sharp knife, cut each sausage into 2cm-thick slices. Sprinkle the semolina over a baking tray and place the gnocchi pieces on the tray.

Bring a large saucepan of salted water to the boil. Add the gnocchi, all at once, to the pan, then cover and return the water to a rapid boil. Cook for about 4 minutes or until all the gnocchi float to the surface, carefully stirring once or twice. Remove the gnocchi with a slotted spoon and transfer to a bowl of iced water to cool them quickly, then drain well. Toss the gnocchi in the olive oil, then transfer them to a clean, lightly oiled baking tray. Set aside in the fridge until needed.

Once you are ready to serve, finish the gnocchi and pan-fry the John Dory. To finish the gnocchi, melt the tablespoon of butter in a large, non-stick frying pan over a medium heat. Once the butter starts to foam, add the gnocchi and sauté for about 4 minutes or until golden brown all over. Add the reserved cockle meat, the samphire and capers and sauté for 1 minute, then add salt and pepper, a squeeze of fresh lemon juice and the chopped parsley.

Meanwhile, pan-fry the John Dory. Heat the olive oil in a separate large, non-stick frying pan over a high heat. Season the John Dory fillets with the coarse salt, then place the fillets, presentation-side down, into the hot pan and add the knobs of cold butter. Pan-fry for 2 minutes, then carefully flip the fish over and cook for a further 1 minute or until cooked and flaky. Drain the fish fillets on kitchen paper. In the meantime, gently reheat the velouté as directed.

To serve, spoon some of the gnocchi mixture on to serving plates, place 2 pan-fried John Dory fillets on top of each portion and then spoon over the remaining gnocchi mixture. Froth the velouté using a stick blender, then spoon the foaming sauce over the fish and serve immediately.

Roasted Woodpigeons with Pickled Morels and Watercress Emulsion

Everyone has probably used the old cliché of 'don't judge a book by its cover' more than once in his or her lifetime. I used to cast this judgment on pigeons. I could not think of them as food! My thoughts went from them being someone's pet to being the flying rats in the cities, pooping on statues and all and sundry (urgh!). We get angry with these birds, especially as they raid the freshly sown fields throughout the countryside. Farmers try their utmost to keep them at bay and I have seen some incredibly funky and clever tricks that farmers use to scare them off, from dangling glimmering old CDs to scarecrows and even a fake shotgun sound randomly clapping away at all hours of the day. The truth is nothing really works. There are too many of them and if you can't beat them, eat them!

Woodpigeons are delicious and have been a delicacy served in many restaurants for generations. The saddest thing was that when I used to work as a young chef in a top London restaurant, back then we used to import these plump birds from France, even though we had a plentiful supply in Britain. The memory for me is still very clear in my mind. We received them as whole birds, with their heads and feet on and insides intact, and my first job of the morning at 6:30am was to gut these birds (and you could still see the food they had recently eaten). You might think this is a bad memory but, in fact, it's a beautiful memory for me to savour, even though I wasn't too keen on it at the time, especially so early in the morning!

Woodpigeons can be awful if they are overcooked, so the trick is to cook them lightly and serve them pink or medium-rare. Resting is just as important as the cooking; the normal rule of thumb is to rest the meat for the same length of time as the cooking time. This allows the meat to relax and stay juicy and tender. I also recommend that you buy woodpigeons from a reputable supplier or someone you know – you do not want to purchase a bird riddled with lead pellets.

Serving woodpigeon with earthy grounded flavours, such as watercress and morels, also underlines the fact that they come from the woods.

Serves 2 as main course or 4 as a starter

For the roasted woodpigeons

4 raw elongated Cheltenham beetroots (or raw standard round beetroots), about 450–500g total weight
2 tablespoons olive oil, plus a dash of olive oil
120g spelt
½ teaspoon sea salt
1 tablespoon chopped fresh mixed soft herbs (such as parsley, chives, chervil and tarragon)
1 teaspoon sherry vinegar
2 teaspoons unsalted butter
2 plump woodpigeons (250–300g each), plucked and gutted
sea salt and freshly cracked black pepper

For the pickled morels

100ml rapeseed oil
200g fresh morels, cleaned and sliced
a sprig of fresh thyme, leaves only
2 teaspoons sherry vinegar
a pinch of caster sugar

For the watercress emulsion

50g watercress leaves
1 teaspoon Dijon mustard
a pinch of caster sugar
50ml rapeseed oil

fresh rosemary flowers and watercress sprigs, to garnish

Start by cooking the beetroot for the roasted woodpigeons. Preheat the oven to 160°C/Gas Mark 3. Wash the beetroots, scrub the skin and remove the leaves, but leave a small piece of the leaf stalk attached to each beetroot. Season the beetroots generously with salt and pepper and lay them on a baking tray. Bake in the oven for about 1½ hours or until cooked and tender. Remove from the oven and set aside to cool. Once cool, cut the beetroots into halves or quarters, brush all over with 1 tablespoon olive oil and set aside until needed.

Next, prepare the pickled morels. Heat 1 tablespoon rapeseed oil in a non-stick frying pan over a medium heat and sauté the morels, with salt and pepper added, for 2 minutes. Remove the pan from the heat, then add the thyme leaves, sherry vinegar, sugar and the remaining oil. Let the oil heat through from the residual heat of the pan and set aside at room temperature for 20 minutes.

Meanwhile, prepare the watercress emulsion. Put the watercress leaves, mustard and sugar into a small blender and blend together until smooth. With the motor running, slowly add the rapeseed oil to form an emulsion. Pour into a small bowl, cover and chill until needed (see Cook's Note).

To cook the spelt for the roasted woodpigeons, place the spelt in a saucepan and cover with four times as much cold water. Cover with a lid and bring to the boil, then remove the lid, reduce the heat and simmer for 18 minutes. Add the ½ teaspoon of salt and cook for a further 2 minutes or until the spelt is cooked and tender. Drain well, then place the spelt in a bowl, add the herbs, sherry vinegar, a dash of olive oil and salt and pepper and mix well. Keep warm.

Meanwhile, for the woodpigeons, preheat the oven to 200°C/Gas Mark 6. Heat the remaining tablespoon of oil and the butter in a non-stick frying pan until the butter is foaming. Season the prepared woodpigeons with salt and pepper and add them to the pan, then cook over a high heat for 1 minute on each breast until golden brown. Transfer the woodpigeons to a roasting tin and roast in the oven for 4 minutes.

Remove from the oven and let the woodpigeons rest for 6 minutes, then remove the breasts from the birds using a sharp knife. The woodpigeon breasts are now ready to serve. (Discard the bird carcasses or use them with chicken bones to make stock.)

Divide the beetroot pieces between 2 serving plates (placing them towards the edges), then spoon the spelt salad into the centre of the plates. Drain the morels (discarding the pickling liquor) and place them on the plates, drizzle with a little of the watercress emulsion and then place 2 roast woodpigeon breasts on top of each portion of salad. Garnish the plates with rosemary flowers and watercress sprigs and serve immediately.

Cook's Note

Keep any leftover watercress emulsion in an airtight container in the fridge and use within 3 days. Serve as a salad dressing or drizzled over grilled sardines or herrings.

Fiery Broccoli and Chestnut Mushroom Salad

The inspiration for this recipe came from a visit to our local farmers' market. I saw these beautiful-looking heads of broccoli cut freshly from the surrounding fields. Next to them was a box filled with plump fresh red chillies and fresh root ginger, so I felt the urge to create something delicious that combined these colourful ingredients.

I acknowledge that ingredients such as fresh chillies and root ginger are now an integral part of our everyday lives. They are definitely not native to Britain, but finding them at this very busy farmers' market in a secluded spot in the heart of Suffolk, brought it home to me that on a daily basis we embrace the ingredients and cooking styles of many other cultures from all over the world. By doing this and by combining the 'traditional' with the more 'contemporary', we end up with a wide range of spectacular, individual and rather wonderful dishes.

As I source local organic mushrooms and broccoli, I need to use as much of each vegetable as possible, because part of our ethos is to limit the amount of food waste that we generate. Hence, in recipes such as this one, we use nearly the entire head of broccoli – florets, stalks and all.

Broccoli stalks are in fact delicious and they certainly add an extra dimension to this dish. The best part is that you end up with nearly a quarter more in volume, than if you had only used the florets – a bonus in my eyes.

Serves 4 as a side dish

1 head of broccoli (about 300g total weight)
2 tablespoons olive oil
3 shallots, sliced
1 large fresh red chilli, deseeded and cut into julienne (matchstick) strips
2 tablespoons caster sugar
2 tablespoons white wine vinegar
finely grated zest and juice of 1 lemon
15 fresh chestnut mushrooms, quartered
sea salt and freshly cracked black pepper
poppy seeds, to garnish

Remove the broccoli florets from the stalk and cut them all to the same size. Cook the florets in a saucepan of boiling salted water for 4–5 minutes or until tender. Drain, refresh in iced water, then drain again and set aside.

Peel off the outer layer from the broccoli stalk, then use a mandolin to finely slice the stalk into wafer-thin discs. Set aside.

Heat 1 tablespoon olive oil in a large, non-stick frying pan over a high heat and sauté the shallots for about 5 minutes or until golden. Add the chilli, then reduce the heat and sauté for a further 3 minutes. Add the sugar, white wine vinegar and lemon zest and stir to dissolve the sugar, then bring to the boil. Once the mixture starts to boil, remove the pan from the heat, add the broccoli stalk discs, stir and then transfer to a bowl. Set aside to cool and infuse.

To cook the mushrooms, wipe the frying pan clean, then heat the remaining oil in the same frying pan over a high heat, add the mushroom quarters and salt and pepper and sauté for about 8 minutes or until golden brown. Stir in the lemon juice.

Mix the sautéed mushrooms, broccoli florets and pickled broccoli stalk discs together. Arrange the salad in your chosen bowl or on individual serving plates and garnish with a sprinkling of poppy seeds. The salad is now ready to be served slightly warm, or it can be cooled and chilled before serving, if you like.

Crispy Quack Eggs with Radish Mayonnaise

Scotch eggs have enjoyed something of a comeback and are currently at the height of food fashion once again. When the idea of making a quail's egg coated in duck meat came about, this ridiculous name automatically rolled off the tongue. We had a giggle and hope that you will find it funny too!

At the pub, we cook the duck legs in a water bath for 8 hours, but at home it's best to roast the duck legs in the oven, then flake the meat and add a freshly ground aromatic five spice blend to flavour the meat.

The radish mayonnaise is also a true delight. Making homemade mayonnaise is always special – you can adapt, adjust and play, make up your own flavours and have bundles of fun in the process too.

Makes 12 quack eggs (or 2 per person for a drinks party)

For the crispy quack eggs

1 teaspoon coriander seeds
1 star anise
½ cinnamon stick
3 white peppercorns
3 cloves
200g cooked duck leg meat, flaked
3 hen's eggs
1 tablespoon Worcestershire sauce
1 teaspoon roughly chopped fresh thyme leaves
½ teaspoon coarse sea salt, plus extra for serving
12 quail's eggs
100g plain flour
100g fresh or dried breadcrumbs
sea salt and freshly cracked black pepper
sunflower oil, for deep-frying

For the radish mayonnaise

15g grated fresh horseradish (or substitute 1 tablespoon ready-grated horseradish from a jar or creamed horseradish, if you like)
1 teaspoon wholegrain mustard
2 teaspoons Raspberry Cider Vinegar (see page 238)
2 hen's egg yolks
200ml olive oil
3 French breakfast radishes, with leaves on

First, prepare the crispy quack eggs. Make the five-spice blend. Place the coriander seeds, star anise, cinnamon stick, peppercorns and cloves into a spice grinder or use a pestle and mortar and grind the spices to a powder. It's best to grind your own spices as it releases their essential oils in time for you to capture the flavours in your meal.

Place half of the duck meat into a food processor, along with the ground spices. Add 1 hen's egg, the Worcestershire sauce, thyme and ½ teaspoon of coarse salt and process for 10 seconds. Add the rest of the duck and pulse until just combined. Transfer the duck mixture to a bowl, then cover and refrigerate for 30 minutes so that the mixture becomes firmer.

Cook the quail's eggs in a covered pan of boiling water for 1½ minutes, then remove the eggs using a slotted spoon and place them in a bowl of iced water to cool. Once cold, peel the eggs carefully.

Divide and shape the duck mixture into 12 equal balls. Press each ball of duck mixture flat, place a quail's egg in the centre of each one and then wrap the duck mixture around the egg, enclosing each egg completely. Place the quack eggs on a plate and chill in the fridge for 10 minutes.

Place the plain flour in a small bowl and season with salt and pepper. Crack the remaining 2 hen's eggs into another small bowl and whisk lightly. Place the breadcrumbs in a third small bowl.

First, roll a duck-covered egg in the seasoned flour, tapping off the excess flour, then roll it in the whisked eggs and then finally in the breadcrumbs, making sure it is evenly coated all over. Repeat this process until all 12 duck-covered eggs are coated. Return to the plate and chill in the fridge for 15–20 minutes to rest and firm up.

Meanwhile, prepare the radish mayonnaise. Place the horseradish, mustard, raspberry cider vinegar and egg yolks in a bowl and season lightly with salt and pepper. Whisk together until blended using a balloon whisk, then very slowly whisk in the olive oil, adding it in a slow, steady drizzle. If the mayonnaise becomes a bit thick before you have added all the oil, whisk in 1 tablespoon hot water, then continue slowly adding the oil until it is all incorporated. Taste and adjust the seasoning, if needed.

Wash the radishes and leaves and pat dry. Finely slice the radishes and cut the leaves into thin julienne (matchstick) strips, then fold both into the mayonnaise. Cover and chill until needed.

To cook the quack eggs, heat some sunflower oil in an electric deep-fat fryer or in a deep frying pan to a temperature of 160°C (or until a small piece of bread browns within 20 seconds in the hot oil). Once the oil is hot enough, deep-fry the breadcrumbed eggs in the hot oil for about 3 minutes or until golden brown and crisp all over – you will need to deep-fry the eggs in two batches. Using a slotted spoon, remove and drain the cooked eggs on kitchen paper.

Serve the deep-fried quack eggs hot or warm, sprinkled with coarse sea salt, and serve the radish mayonnaise spooned alongside.

Cook's Note

If there is any leftover radish mayonnaise, store it in an airtight container in the fridge and use within 3 days.

Mango and Orange Blossom Pudding with Polenta Shortbread

It's the time of year when our home-grown fruits are thin on the ground and so the taste of the exotics is welcomed with open arms. I grew up with mangoes being readily available and mum used to buy boxes at a time and ripen them between dad's socks. Bizarre as this might sound, his wardrobe was the coolest and darkest place, and to ripen mangoes quickly you need to keep them in a dark, well-ventilated area and dad's socks provided the perfect place!

There are many varieties of mango, but the finest one of them all is the Alphonso mango from India. Alphonsos are small, but once ripe, they pack a magnificent flavoursome punch. Their season is short and they are available for about 6 weeks from mid-April until the end of May.

I also love finding new ingredients, not necessarily new in the true sense of invention, but those forgotten ingredients from the past, which may have fallen out of food fashion. Orange blossom water is one of those ingredients that I remember using in top London restaurants about 15 years ago. Use it sparingly as it's pretty powerful stuff. I am using it to make an orange blossom air for this recipe and it goes perfectly with the mango jellies and crumbly shortbread to create interesting textures in this truly delicious pudding.

The orange blossom air can be made up to 2 days in advance and kept in the cream whipper in the fridge until needed.

Serves 6 (makes about 24 shortbread biscuits)

For the mango jellies
3 leaves of gelatine
150g prepared mango flesh (preferably Alphonso)
150ml chilled fresh unsweetened mango juice or orange juice
80g caster sugar
50ml double cream

For the polenta shortbread
125g unsalted butter, softened
55g caster sugar, plus extra for rolling and sprinkling
finely grated zest of 2 oranges
50g fine polenta
100g plain flour
30g cornflour
1 teaspoon ground sumac (see Cook's Notes)

For the orange blossom air
2 leaves of gelatine
100ml double cream
50g caster sugar
300ml natural yogurt
2 teaspoons orange blossom water, or to taste

To serve
1 large mango (300–325g unprepared weight), peeled, stoned and diced
2 oranges, peeled and segmented
½ teaspoon chopped fresh thyme leaves
a pinch of ground sumac (see Cook's Notes)

To make the mango jellies, place 6 serving glasses in the fridge. Soak the gelatine in cold water until it has softened.

Put the mango flesh, mango juice, sugar and cream into a blender and blend together until smooth. Transfer the mixture to a small saucepan and bring to the boil over a medium heat, then reduce the heat and simmer gently for 5 minutes. Remove from the heat.

Squeeze the gelatine gently to remove the excess water, then add the gelatine to the hot mango mixture and stir until dissolved. Pass the mixture through a fine sieve, then pour the mango mixture into the chilled serving glasses, dividing evenly. Carefully transfer the glasses to the fridge and leave to set completely – this will take 4–6 hours.

While the jellies are setting, make the polenta shortbread. Cream the butter, 55g sugar and the orange zest together in a bowl until pale and fluffy. Add the polenta and beat together for 1 minute, then fold in the flour and cornflour to make a soft dough. Place the dough on a piece of cling film and form it into a sausage shape about 3cm in diameter. Wrap in the cling film and chill in the fridge for 2 hours (see Cook's Notes).

Make the orange blossom air. Soak the gelatine in cold water until it has softened, then squeeze it gently to remove the excess water. Place the cream, soaked gelatine and sugar in a heatproof bowl set over a pan of simmering water (making sure that the bottom of the bowl does not come into contact with the simmering water underneath), and stir until the sugar and gelatine have dissolved. Remove the bowl from the heat, stir in the yogurt, then add the orange blossom water to taste. Pour the mixture into a cream whipper (see page 17 for more details on a cream whipper). Charge with 2 gas pellets, shake vigorously, then refrigerate for about 2 hours so that the mixture thickens and chills completely.

Meanwhile, bake the polenta shortbread. Preheat the oven to 160°C/Gas Mark 3 and line a large baking tray with non-stick baking paper.

Remove the cling film from the chilled shortbread dough and cut the sausage of dough into 5mm-thick slices, then roll the edges of each shortbread disc in caster sugar. Place on the prepared baking tray, leaving a little space between each one, then sprinkle with the sumac. Bake in the oven for 12–14 minutes or until cooked and very pale golden. Remove from the oven and sprinkle the biscuits with more caster sugar, then transfer them to a wire rack and leave to cool completely (see Cook's Notes).

Shake the cream whipper vigorously and squirt the orange blossom air into a glass to check if it is ready (if the mixture has set solidly, hold the cream whipper under warm running water to loosen the mixture inside, then shake and use as directed).

To serve, mix the diced mango and orange segments together in a bowl, then divide the mixed fruit between the jelly glasses. Shake the cream whipper vigorously and squirt the orange blossom air on top of the fruit, then decorate with the chopped thyme and sumac. Serve immediately with 2–3 polenta shortbreads served alongside each portion.

Cook's Notes

The sumac bush grows throughout the Middle East and in parts of the Mediterranean and it produces small red berries. These berries are picked and dried (the colour of the dried berries darkens to a deep red) and they are used either whole or ground, mainly in Middle Eastern-style cooking. Sumac has a sharp, sour, lemony flavour. I use ground sumac to enhance or substitute citrus flavours and it works well in both sweet and savoury dishes.

The shortbread dough can be made a day in advance, rolled into a sausage shape and wrapped, then kept in the fridge overnight, before slicing and baking the next day, if you like. Alternatively, it can be made, shaped and wrapped, then frozen for up to 1 month. Simply defrost in the fridge overnight, then slice and bake as directed.

Store any leftover baked shortbread biscuits in an airtight container in a cool, dry cupboard for up to 5 days.

OPINEL
FRANCE

Milk Pie

This book would not have been complete unless I included at least one recipe from my roots. This recipe takes me back to my childhood. South Africans call this melk tart and, not so surprisingly, the direct English translation is Milk Tart, or perhaps Milk Pie would be a better description. There are some British versions of this recipe (I'm not sure who borrowed the recipe from whom), but the classic English custard tart is the closest.

With the season changing slowly, the milk becomes richer and more floral in taste as the cattle graze on the new spring pastures. Capturing the taste of that fresh rich milk in a recipe like this is rather special, but the free-range eggs also lend an important hand to the successful and great-tasting results.

Serves 6–8

500g good quality chilled fresh all-butter puff pastry
500ml milk (if you can get raw milk it's even better, or use Jersey milk)
40g unsalted butter
1 vanilla pod, split in half lengthways and seeds scraped out
100g caster sugar
25g plain flour
20g cornflour
a pinch of table salt
2 eggs, separated
ground cinnamon and freshly grated nutmeg, to taste

Roll out the puff pastry on a lightly floured work surface to 2–3mm thickness. Use the pastry to line a 20cm pie dish, then chill in the fridge for 30 minutes. Preheat the oven to 200°C/Gas Mark 6. Prick the pastry case all over, line with non-stick baking paper and fill with baking beans. Bake blind in the oven for 15 minutes, then remove the baking beans and paper. Return the pastry case to the oven and bake for a further 10–15 minutes or until golden and crisp. Remove from the oven and leave to cool. Reduce the oven temperature to 180°C/Gas Mark 4.

Put 400ml of the milk in a saucepan with the butter and vanilla seeds and bring to the boil over a medium heat. Meanwhile, place 50g of the sugar, the flour, cornflour, salt, egg yolks and the remaining milk in a bowl and mix together to form a thick, smooth paste. Place the egg whites in a separate grease-free mixing bowl, add the remaining sugar and whisk together to form soft peaks, then set aside.

Once the milk is boiling, reduce the heat, then pour half of the hot milk over the egg yolk paste, whisking continuously, and then return the egg yolk mixture to the remaining hot milk in the pan. Return to the heat and bring back to the boil, stirring, then reduce the heat and simmer gently for about 5 minutes or until the mixture has thickened, stirring continuously.

Remove from the heat and set aside to cool for 5 minutes, then gently fold in the whisked egg whites. Pour the mixture into the pastry case and generously dust with cinnamon and nutmeg.

Bake in the oven for 20–25 minutes or until the filling is golden. The filling will rise slightly during baking but it will settle back down once cooled. Typically this pie has a slightly sunken filling that looks a little bit wrinkly, unlike the smooth surface of a traditional English custard tart.

Remove from the oven and leave the pie to cool at room temperature before serving. If you serve it while it is still warm, the filling may be too soft and runny. This pie is best eaten fresh on the day it is made, but any leftovers can be kept in an airtight container in the fridge for up to 2 days (but the pastry will become soggy).

Cardamom and Golden Sultana Hot Cross Buns

Oh, it's that time of the year again to enjoy hot cross buns. The smell of them baking in the oven provokes fond childhood memories for me and they are a clear reminder of the season we are in. There is nothing more pleasing than a toasted hot cross bun served with a mug of hot coffee on a sunny spring morning, as you plan the 'to do' list for the day.

For this recipe, I use one-third standard plain flour and two-thirds strong bread flour. Most recipes call for all plain flour but I find the texture of the cooked buns too close to the texture of cakes.

If you believe in superstitions, then it's said that if you share a hot cross bun with another person, this will ensure friendship for the year to come. Well, I hope it's true, and, for that reason, I could not keep this delicious recipe to myself without wanting to share it with you! Happy Easter!

Makes 12 large hot cross buns

For the bun dough
375ml milk
4 green cardamom pods, crushed
240g golden sultanas (or use regular sultanas, if you wish)
15g fresh yeast
440g strong white bread flour
200g plain flour
100g caster sugar
a pinch of table salt
2 teaspoons ground mixed spice
2 teaspoons ground cinnamon
50g unsalted butter, melted
1 egg

For the cross paste
75g plain flour
80ml cold water

For the glaze and decoration
100g clear honey
100ml cold water
3 green cardamom pods, crushed
juice of ½ lemon
1 tablespoon chopped pistachio nuts (optional)

Make the bun dough. Put the milk and crushed cardamom pods into a small saucepan and bring just to the boil, then remove from the heat and leave to infuse for 10 minutes. Pass the milk through a fine sieve, then return the milk to the saucepan, add the sultanas and leave to infuse for 5 minutes. Stir in the yeast until dissolved.

Put both flours, the sugar, salt, mixed spice and cinnamon into the bowl of an electric stand mixer with the dough hook attached. Turn the machine on to run at a low speed and add the melted butter and egg, then slowly add the infused milk mixture and mix to form a dough. Knead the dough on a low speed for 8 minutes.

Turn the dough on to a lightly floured work surface and shape it into a ball. Place the dough ball in a lightly oiled bowl, cover with a clean dry tea towel or cling film and leave the dough to prove (rise) in a warm place for about 1 hour or until it is doubled in size. Grease 2 baking trays and set aside. Once the dough has proved, turn it on to a lightly floured work surface and knead lightly. Divide the dough into 12 equal portions and roll each portion into a smooth ball. Place on the prepared baking trays, leaving space between each one, then cover with clean dry tea towels and leave to prove in a warm place for 15–20 minutes or until doubled in size. Meanwhile, preheat the oven to 200°C/Gas Mark 6.

For the cross paste, mix the flour and water together in a bowl until smooth, then transfer the mixture to a piping bag fitted with a small plain nozzle (2–3mm diameter). Pipe thin lines to represent crosses on top of each bun.

Bake the buns in the oven for 18–22 minutes or until well risen and golden brown. Remove from the oven and let the buns cool on the trays for a few minutes, then transfer them to a wire rack and leave to cool completely. Once cool, return the buns to the baking trays to apply the glaze.

While the buns are baking, make the glaze. Put the honey, water, crushed cardamom pods and lemon juice into a small saucepan, bring to the boil over a medium heat, then simmer for 1 minute. Pass the glaze through a fine sieve into a bowl and let the mixture cool.

Generously brush the glaze over the cooled buns and then sprinkle with the chopped pistachios to decorate, if you like. Serve.

Cook's Note
To make the bun dough by hand, warm, strain, then infuse the milk and sultanas, as directed. Stir in the yeast. Put the flours, sugar, salt, mixed spice and cinnamon into a large bowl. Make a well in the centre, then pour in the melted butter and egg, followed by the warm milk, sultana and yeast mixture and mix with a palette knife to form a lumpy dough. Turn the dough on to a lightly floured work surface and knead for 7–8 minutes or until the dough becomes smooth and elastic. Continue as the recipe directs.

Salted Peanut Chocolate Whoopie Pies

Every now and then something chocolaty is needed and Easter is that time when a bit of chocolate is much appreciated. Food fashions and trends change pretty regularly – the recipe that was 'the bee's knees' a couple or so years ago is now passé and old-hat and there is a new 'fad' doing the foodie fashion rounds. Whoopie pies have been the talk of the town for a while now and yes, I have joined the bandwagon too. Indeed, there is no harm in that.

Apparently whoopie pies stem from the heartland of America where Amish wives used to bake small cakes from their leftover cake batters, then sandwich them together with butter cream and pack them into lunch boxes. The name is claimed to have originated from when the children and husbands opened their lunch boxes and cried 'whoopie' at the sight of these delights! Well, even if this is untrue and only a myth, I want it to be true.

Making whoopie pies entertains and keeps me happy for hours and I love to spend time creating them. For this recipe, the traditional butter cream filling is replaced with a salted peanut cream cheese filling. It's delicious, as the salty sweet flavour with a touch of crunch, makes these naughty little cakes into an even more heavenly treat.

Makes 12–14 whoopie pies

For the salted peanut cream cheese filling
50g unsalted butter (melted weight – see method)
100g salted roasted peanuts
500g icing sugar
200g cream cheese or full-fat soft cheese (Philadelphia soft cheese is perfect for this)

For the whoopie cakes
150g soft light brown sugar
280g plain flour
30g cocoa powder
1 teaspoon baking powder
½ teaspoon bicarbonate of soda
125ml crème fraîche or natural yogurt
1 egg
60ml sunflower oil or groundnut oil
60ml boiling water

For the chocolate glaze
2 leaves of gelatine
110g caster sugar
80ml cold water
80ml double cream
40g cocoa powder

edible glitter, edible gold or silver leaf, silver balls or sugar sprinkles, to decorate (optional)

First, make the salted peanut cream cheese filling as this needs to be made in advance and left to set before use, otherwise your whoopie pies will have a runny filling. I normally make this filling the day before I need it, simply to speed things up. Alternatively, if you make it on the day when you need it, make sure you leave enough time for the filling to set in the fridge before using.

To make the cream cheese filling, melt the butter and then set it aside to cool – it does not matter if it starts to set, as long as it's still soft and pliable. I always melt a bit extra too, as you will find that it sticks to the bowl. Weigh the 50g of melted butter required. Meanwhile, crush the peanuts either by pulsing them in a food processor to resemble coarse breadcrumbs or crush them using a pestle and mortar. Set aside.

Using a balloon whisk, whisk the icing sugar and cream cheese together in a bowl until smooth. Whisk in the cooled butter, then fold in the crushed peanuts. Transfer the mixture to a piping bag fitted with a medium star nozzle (5–6mm diameter) and then chill in the fridge for 2–3 hours or until set, before using.

Meanwhile, make the whoopie cakes. Preheat the oven to 200°C/Gas Mark 6 and line 2 large baking trays with non-stick baking paper. At this stage, on the reverse side of the paper, I draw round a small glass to create circles, each about 5cm in diameter – these will be my guide for the cakes. You will need to draw a total of 24–28 circles, leaving a space between each one.

Place the brown sugar in a large mixing bowl and break up any lumps. Sift the flour, cocoa powder, baking powder and bicarbonate of soda over the sugar and mix together. In a separate bowl, whisk the crème fraîche, egg and sunflower oil together, then whisk in the boiling water. Immediately stir the crème fraîche mixture into the sifted flour mixture and mix just until it all comes together (do not overwork the mixture). Leave the cake batter to rest for 5 minutes – this stage is important as it makes the cake batter easier to work with and the whoopie cakes turn out more evenly and helps them retain their shape.

Transfer the cake batter to a piping bag fitted with a large plain nozzle (I have tried shaping the cake batter using 2 spoons, but have found that the piping bag gives me the best results). Pipe the cake batter into 5cm rounds on the prepared baking trays, using the circles marked on the baking paper as a guide, and filling each circle with cake batter (but remember that they will expand and spread during baking, so your baked cakes will be slightly bigger than the size piped).

Bake in the oven for 10–12 minutes or until the cakes are cooked but still soft with a crust formed underneath. Use a palette knife to carefully remove the cakes from the paper to a wire rack and leave them to cool completely. Once the whoopie cakes cool down, they will have a bit of a crunch on the outside and the inside will be cakey and soft.

Make the chocolate glaze. I usually make this once the whoopie cakes have gone into the oven, as the glaze should have cooled down slightly but should still be runny and not completely set when you decorate the cakes. Soak the gelatine in cold water until it has softened. Place the caster sugar, measured cold water and cream in a small saucepan and bring to the boil over a high heat, then boil rapidly for 2 minutes. Stir in the cocoa powder and boil over a high heat for a further 1 minute. Remove from the heat.

Squeeze the gelatine gently to remove the excess water, then add the gelatine to the hot cocoa mixture and stir until dissolved. Transfer the mixture to a small bowl and set aside to cool until the mixture reaches about 20°C–22°C and it becomes a thick but still reluctantly runny consistency. You can put it over ice to speed the cooling process, if you like, but stir it to prevent the mixture from setting in a hard lump. This thicker glaze will be easier to apply to the whoopie cakes – if the glaze is too warm or runny it will run off the cakes and not coat them, but if it's too cold and set it will not spread and glaze the cakes evenly.

Pair up the whoopie cakes so that for each pair you have 2 cakes that are of a similar size. Place 1 whoopie cake from each pair on a wire rack, flat-side down. Spoon the chocolate glaze over these whoopie cakes, covering the cakes completely, then immediately sprinkle with your chosen decorations. Transfer the glazed tops to the fridge for 10–15 minutes so that the glaze sets. Remove them from the fridge as soon as the glaze is set.

Pipe the chilled salted peanut cream cheese filling on to the flat side of the remaining whoopie cakes. Sandwich the glazed cake tops with the cream cheese-topped cake bottoms, pressing each pair together gently. You now have your 12–14 whoopie pies. Enjoy!

The whoopie pies are best eaten on the day they are made and soon after they have been assembled.

Cook's Note

The salted peanut cream cheese filling and the chocolate glaze will both keep (separately) in airtight containers in the fridge for up to 3 days.

The British Larder | *May*

May provides plenty of green vegetables for our mealtimes with delicious fresh broad beans, peas and lettuces making a welcome appearance. Nasturtium and borage flowers are also coming into season, along with wild mint and marsh samphire. The long-awaited English asparagus and strawberry seasons are finally upon us and Pick Your Own farms will begin to bustle this month.

Mr P. goes elderflower picking

Sea bass, lemon sole, John Dory and lobsters are plentiful. Sardines and mackerel also make a welcome return to the dining scene. The season starts with plenty of fish supplies from the slightly warmer waters of the south coast, then slowly the supplies from the east coast up to Scotland will be available once the season is in full swing. New season lamb is succulent and tasty and as the price for lamb eases off, it makes it perfect for early summer dining.

The arrival of various wild foods in the English countryside is a pleasant sight with the elderberry shrubs/trees in full bloom and fresh young nettles and wild garlic growing in the hedges and woodlands. So, there is plenty for the enthusiastic foraging cook to pick and choose from. Our coastal shorelines are also bearing superb fruits at this time of year with the samphire from Norfolk and Suffolk at its best and sea purslane that tastes like salt and vinegar crisps. We are spoilt for choice.

I'm a selective gardener and when I get the time and urge, then I dig and plant. Every year about mid-spring, I get the urge. Every spring the wasteland at the back of the pub is turned into a tiny... no, let's rephrase that... a minute organic kitchen garden. It's obviously not by any means enough to provide the restaurant with all the fresh produce we need, but at least it provides inspiration for the team to pick a few edible flowers, herbs and strawberries. As well as other local suppliers, we rely heavily on the gluts of seasonal produce provided by locals' gardens to keep our fridges filled with a whole variety of produce.

I get seriously excited when I discover a local producer making, growing or rearing something truly British. It has influenced me to such an extent that I keep my own small kitchen garden at home. Doing so, taught me so much about food, I have this newly found respect for how long it takes to grow fruit and vegetables. To my shame, I previously did not know how many of the different fruit and vegetables grow and what the growing plants look like. As a chef, fruit and vegetables are delivered to us in a box, perhaps wrapped in plastic bags and with the outer leaves removed. The natural state of the produce has often been completely stripped away and it leaves you uninformed on the plant's life cycle. One example of this was kohlrabi. It was only after I planted kohlrabi, I realised that it's not a root vegetable but one that grows on top of the soil like many other members of the Brassicaceae family, of which it's a member. I was also unaware of the wonderful flowers that many of the plants produce. I hate to admit this, but as ignorant young chefs, we used to give the suppliers a hard time when the produce arrived with flowers on – we used to say it meant the vegetables or herbs were old and past it... now that is definitely ignorant! Thankfully, I am a little older and wiser now and I fully appreciate all the wonderful seasonal ingredients that are available to us in Britain.

Season's best during May...

Artichokes, Asparagus, Bananas, Borage Flowers, Broad Beans, Broccoli, Carrots, Chervil, Chives and Chive Flowers, Cod, Crab, Dill, Elderflowers, Herrings, Jersey Royal New Potatoes, John Dory, Lamb, Lettuce, Mackerel, Mangoes, Mint, Nasturtium Flowers, Nettles, New Potatoes, Parsley, Plaice, Pollack, Prawns, Radishes, Rhubarb (outdoor), Rocket, Rosemary, Salad/ Spring Onions, Salmon, Samphire, Sardines, Sea Bass, Sea Beet, Sea Purslane, Sea Trout, Sorrel, Spinach, Tarragon, Watercress, Whelks, Whitebait, Wild Garlic, Wild Mushrooms (spring), Woodpigeon.

My culinary rituals for May...

Homemade elderflower cordial is wonderful: now is the time of year to make it, but you need to be well organised. Identify elderberry shrubs/trees near your home, selecting ones away from the road (to avoid contamination from exhaust fumes, etc) and away from the main paths (as these will be the trees that people are most likely to strip bare first), get some suitable bottles washed and ready, and purchase some citric acid. Enjoy the beautiful sight of the apple and cherry orchards in blossom, if you are lucky enough to have them in your local area. Savour the scent from the blossoms and make a mental note for when the cherries arrive in June and the apples start trickling in from late September. Venture to the coast in search of edible delights such as sea purslane and samphire during low tide.

Plant salad leaves in shallow trays this month and leave them outside on a garden table or bench. Remember to water them regularly, and then, hey presto!, you should have a good crop of pick-your-own salad leaves by mid-June.

So, seize the day, or rather seize the season, and enjoy making a batch of refreshing **Homemade Elderflower Cordial** (see page 167). Or, try your hand at making fresh buffalo curd cheese with my simple but delicious **Fresh Buffalo Curd Seasonal Salad** (see page 176). Indulge in smoked foods from your local smokehouse this month and try my tempting recipes for **Warm Treacle and Cider-Cured Smoked Ham Hock Spring Barley Salad** (see page 179) or **Pan-Fried Mackerel with Smoked Mackerel Patties and Crushed Garden Pea Salad** (see page 184).

British Larder Heroes

Asparagus

Asparagus is a spring-flowering perennial plant from the lily family, so it is not, strictly speaking, a vegetable. Asparagus comes in several varieties, the main types being green, white and wild. The most common type we eat in Britain is the familiar green asparagus. The white and wild varieties tend to be grown and eaten on the continent, although a select few British farmers do now grow some white asparagus, but it tends to be in much smaller quantities. White asparagus is cut below the soil when the tips are about 5cm above it and green asparagus is cut at soil level when the spears or shoots are about 15cm long. It's not particularly easy to grow asparagus and a crown typically takes 2 years to mature before it bares any fruit. Most people still class asparagus as a delicacy, with British asparagus considered as some of the best. When the British asparagus season starts, asparagus features with pride on most restaurant menus. Select asparagus with firm, thin stems and tips and avoid any that look wilted or woody. Later on in the season asparagus can become woody (the stems become thicker) and the taste changes. Asparagus should be eaten as fresh as possible and preferably on the day it is picked. As with fresh peas and broad beans, as soon as asparagus is picked, the natural sugars turn to starch and within only a couple of days or so the asparagus does not taste nearly as delicious. I usually find the freshest and tastiest asparagus is bought from roadside stalls, farmers' markets or local farm shops. Asparagus requires very little preparation or cooking. To prepare fresh asparagus spears, trim off the woody part (bottom) of the stems (or bend the lower end of each stem until it snaps – this will be the point where the stem begins to toughen) and rinse. Cook the asparagus briefly in a large saucepan of boiling salted water (or in a special asparagus pan if you have one) for 3–4 minutes or until tender (the cooking time will vary a little depending on the thickness of the stems). Drain the asparagus, then season with salt and pepper and serve with a drizzle of olive oil, or with melted butter or Hollandaise sauce.

Asparagus

For a tasty supper with a difference, try my recipe for **Asparagus and Goat's Cheese En Croûte**. Preheat the oven to 200˚C/Gas Mark 6. Lightly grease a baking tray and set aside. Roll out 250g chilled fresh all-butter puff pastry to about 2mm thickness and cut out two 10cm squares, then brush the top surfaces all over with beaten egg yolk. Trim the woody ends from 12 thin fresh asparagus spears, and then chop the stems into thin slices, leaving the asparagus spears 8cm long. In a bowl, mix 100ml cold Thick Béchamel Sauce (see page 19) with 2 finely chopped spring onions, 50g crumbled goat's cheese, a couple of gratings of fresh nutmeg and the asparagus slices, then season to taste with sea salt and freshly cracked black pepper. Spoon the mixture into the centre of each puff pastry square, dividing it evenly. Toss the asparagus spears in 1 teaspoon olive oil, season with salt and pepper, then lay 6 asparagus spears over each portion of the béchamel mixture. With each pastry square, fold 2 opposite corners of pastry over the asparagus so that the pastry joins in the centre and press the corners together to seal (the filling will not be completely enclosed in the pastry). Brush the unglazed pastry with beaten egg yolk and sprinkle with poppy seeds or linseeds. Place the croûtes on the prepared baking tray and bake in the oven for 22–25 minutes or until the pastry is cooked, golden brown and crisp. Serve immediately with buttered boiled Jersey Royal new potatoes and a mixed leaf salad. Serves 2 as a supper.

Borage

Borage is an edible hardy annual herb and both its flowers and leaves are enjoyed in cooking. The flowers are traditionally used in the classic British drink, Pimms, as the flowers complement the fresh cucumber and mint in this refreshing and popular drink. The leaves especially are cucumber-flavoured. Borage is also known for its medicinal and cosmetic uses and borage oil or starflower oil is one of the most common commercial products produced from borage. In the kitchen garden, borage is used for companion-planting (pest control), as it lures the pest insects away from other food plants such as spinach, strawberries and tomatoes.

Try this delicious recipe for **Pimms with Borage Flowers**. Quarter-fill a 1 litre glass serving jug with ice cubes, then measure 8 x 25ml Pimms No.1 over the ice. Add 4 fresh orange slices, 4 fresh apple slices, 4 cucumber slices, the juice of 1 lime, 4 strawberries, quartered, 2 large fresh mint sprigs lightly bruised with your fingers and 10–12 fresh borage flowers. Fill the jug to the top with chilled lemonade, then stir and serve. Serves 4.

British smokehouses

The tradition of smoking meat and fish has been an integral part of British culture for many centuries. Originally food was smoked for preservation purposes, but nowadays the tradition lives on mainly for the enjoyment of the taste and texture of smoked foods, which are often considered to be a bit of a delicacy. Smoked fish and meat form part of our daily British diet and nearly every supermarket or delicatessen sells a good range of smoked fish and meat products. Some British seaside towns will have their own smokehouse or two (originally, and sometimes still, linked to the local fishermen and fishing trade) and some inland towns may also have a smokehouse. In 2009, Grimsby Traditional Smoked Fish was awarded Protected Geographical Indication (PGI) status by the European commission, as Grimsby is where the largest fishing port in the world was located during the 1950s and where many developments in smoking fish took place. During the 1970s, the collapse of the fishing industry in England meant that by the 1980s, the smoked fish industry had significantly declined. However, in the case of Grimsby, the fishing port re-established itself and the industry now continues to thrive, which has meant that the surviving smokehouses are still trading successfully today. Also, with smoked foods enjoying a comeback as part of the current food trends, old local smokehouses are doing better than ever before. Some restaurants, pubs and other establishments have also taken to building their own smokehouses in their back yards, to enable them to create their very own special smoked foods and delicacies. Smoked fish such as mackerel, herring, salmon, cod, haddock, halibut, eel and trout is regularly available, as is smoked meat such as beef, duck and chicken and pork to make smoked bacon and hams. Sausages, cheese and garlic are also smoked. There are two methods of smoking – hot smoking and cold smoking. For hot smoking, the food must be cold-smoked first to ensure that the 'smoke flavour' is retained in the food. The key to success with smoking all foods is to use prime, fresh, top quality ingredients. At the British Larder, we are well known for our popular 'Smokehouse Experience'. This is a large wooden platter of edible smoked delights that is ideally served for 2 people to share as a starter. The platter includes smoked salmon garnished with caper berries, lemon and slivers of freshly shaved radish, **Smoked Trout and Horseradish Pâté** (see page 72) served with plenty of freshly baked sourdough bread from Pump Street Bakery, and finally, the pièce de résistance, two Smoked Salmon Scotch Eggs (one for each person).

To make my delicious **Smoked Salmon Scotch Eggs**, soft-boil 2 eggs in a pan of boiling water for 6–7 minutes, then drain and immediately place in iced water to stop them cooking further. Once cool, drain the eggs, then peel them and set aside. Put 150g skinless, boneless salmon fillet, 100g smoked salmon, ½ egg white, the finely grated zest and juice of ½ lemon, 1 teaspoon chopped fresh mixed herbs (such as tarragon, chives and chervil) and sea salt and freshly cracked black pepper in a blender and pulse-blend until it all just comes together and is mixed, but be careful not to over blend. Transfer the mixture to a bowl, then cover and leave to rest in the fridge for about 10 minutes. Put 1 tablespoon plain flour in a small bowl and season with salt and pepper. Put 1 tablespoon fresh or dried breadcrumbs in another small bowl, then whisk together 1 egg with 1 tablespoon cold water in a third small bowl. Roll each peeled egg in the seasoned flour. Divide the salmon mixture in half, then mould each portion of salmon mixture around an egg, covering each egg completely. Roll each salmon-covered egg in the flour again, then roll in the beaten egg and finally roll in the breadcrumbs to coat all over. Place the coated eggs on a plate and chill in the fridge for 10 minutes. Meanwhile, heat some sunflower oil in an electric deep-fat fryer or in a deep frying pan to a temperature of 160°C (or until a small piece of bread browns within 20 seconds in the hot oil). Once the oil is hot enough, deep-fry the breadcrumbed eggs in the hot oil for 6–7 minutes or until golden brown and crisp all over. Using a slotted spoon, remove and drain the deep-fried eggs on kitchen paper. Season with salt and pepper and serve immediately. Serves 2 as a snack or as a starter if served as part of a platter.

Broad beans

Broad beans, also known as fava beans, are an annual plant that is easy to grow. They are also used by farmers as cover-crops – crops that are not planted to harvest but are planted to put nutrients such as nitrogen back into the soil, so acting as a natural fertiliser. Broad beans grow quickly and produce these valuable nutrients, making them an ideal crop for natural fertilization. Chefs treasure broad beans, but many find them a bit of a nightmare to prepare as it is hard work to double pod them. Double podding means to remove the beans from the green pods they grow in, blanch the beans in boiling water for a couple of minutes, then drain and plunge them into iced water. The beans are drained again and then the tender, bright green beans are popped out of their outer, thick, grey skins by squeezing gently. But, all this hard work is rewarded once the sweet, kidney-shaped, bright green, tender beans are revealed. Broad beans can be eaten with their grey/green outer skins left on, especially when they are young, small and tender, but as they get older, the outer skins do become thicker and tougher. Like fresh peas, broad beans are best eaten as soon as they are harvested. The smaller the beans the sweeter and more tender they are.

Try my tempting recipe for **Broad Bean Tempura with Chilli Salt**. Put 20g cornflour, 75g self-raising flour, a pinch of sea salt and a grinding of black pepper, 1 egg yolk and 125ml sparkling water in a bowl and whisk together to form a smooth batter. In a separate grease-free bowl, whisk 2 egg whites until they form soft peaks. Fold the whisked egg whites into the batter and then set aside for 10 minutes. Mix a large pinch of crushed dried chillies and 1 tablespoon sea salt together in a small bowl and set aside. Meanwhile, heat some sunflower oil in an electric deep-fat fryer or in a deep frying pan to a temperature of 160°C (or until a small piece of bread browns within 20 seconds in the hot oil). Once the oil is hot enough, dip 500g fresh broad beans (shelled weight) in the tempura batter and deep-fry the battered broad beans in the hot oil for about 2 minutes or until golden and crisp all over – you will need to deep-fry the broad beans in four batches. Using a slotted spoon, remove and drain the broad bean tempura on kitchen paper. Serve immediately sprinkled with the chilli salt. Serves 4 as a snack at a drinks or cocktail party or as a snack with pre-dinner drinks.

Broad beans

Elderflowers

Elderflowers are the white creamy flowers of the elderberry shrub (a shrub-like tree) that grow in clusters and appear in late spring. Towards early autumn, the flowers turn into clusters of small, shiny, dark purple round elderberries. Elderberry shrubs/trees are often found in hedgerows and gardens and they deliver plenty that can be used for the natural British larder as both the flowers and berries can be used in the kitchen (the berries should be cooked before eating). The flowers can be used to make cordials and Champagne, they can be dipped in batter and deep-fried, used to add fragrant flavour to jellies, tart fillings and sorbets, or they can simply be used as a decoration. The petals can be made into infusions such as fragrant tea, and the berries can be made into elderberry wine, elderberry liqueur, jam, syrup and fruit pies.

The ever-popular elderflower cordial (see page 167) is ideal served chilled at a village fete or jazzed up in a fancy cocktail at a city bar. It also makes delicious jellies and works a treat in sorbets and ice creams. Alternatively, try my wonderful recipe for **Elderflower and Lime Slush**. Put 3 large handfuls of ice into a food processor or blender, along with 200ml elderflower cordial, finely grated zest and juice of 4 limes and 8 fresh mint leaves, then use the pulse button to crush the ice and turn the mixture into a slush. Transfer the slush to a serving jug and top it up with chilled sparkling water (or, for a grown-up party drink, add a few shots of vodka or some St. Germain elderflower liqueur, to taste, just before serving). Pour into glasses and serve immediately. Serves 4.

Mackerel

Although classed as a humble sea creature, Atlantic mackerel is an exceptionally good-looking and sustainable fish with its shiny blue and silver striped skin and creamy-coloured flesh. The oily flesh is packed with vitamin B12 and essential omega-3 fatty acids, making it a healthy choice of fish to eat. Due to its rich and oily firm flesh, fresh mackerel is ideal for various cooking methods and the thin skin crisps up beautifully when pan-fried, grilled or barbecued. It is an excellent fish for smoking and is also suitable for marinating or pickling. Mackerel has a strong and distinctive taste and so it pairs easily with other strong flavours such as spices, citrus fruits and mustard.

For a tasty recipe, ideal for a light lunch, try these **Aromatic Fresh Mackerel Cakes**. Place 600g mackerel fillets (skin on) in a saucepan (it doesn't matter if the fillets overlap slightly), add a pinch of saffron and sea salt and freshly cracked black pepper and then cover the fish with cold water. Cover the pan with a lid and bring to the boil over a low-medium heat, then simmer for 2 minutes. Remove from the heat and let the fish sit in the water for a further 5 minutes, then drain. Remove and discard the skin and any pin bones, flake the flesh and set aside. Use a pestle and mortar to pound together 1 peeled clove garlic, 25g peeled fresh root ginger, 1 fresh green chilli (deseeded, if you like) and the juice of 1 lime to make a paste. Put the paste mixture and the flaked fish in a mixing bowl, then add 300g cold mashed potatoes, 4 tablespoons chopped fresh mixed herbs (such as tarragon, coriander and parsley) and salt and pepper and mix well. Dampen your hands and form the mixture into 8 equal patties. Place the fishcakes on a plate and chill in the fridge for 30 minutes. Spread 3 tablespoons sesame seeds out on a plate and then carefully press the mackerel cakes into the seeds to coat them completely. Heat 2 tablespoons sunflower oil in a large, non-stick frying pan and fry the fish cakes, 4 at a time, over a medium heat for 3–4 minutes on each side or until cooked, golden and crispy. Remove and drain the cooked fishcakes on kitchen paper and keep hot while you cook the second batch. Serve hot with lime wedges and a fresh cucumber salad. Serves 4 as a light lunch.

Wild mint

Wild mint is just one variety of a large group of hardy herbaceous perennial plants. It grows easily, and with its distinctive blue-purple flowers, it can be seen growing in fields and meadows, marking a pleasant sign that summer is approaching. The leaves of wild mint are smaller than those of common mint but the flavour is twice as strong. Make sure that if you do pick wild mint from the edges of fields that you avoid fields where livestock has been grazing. Wild mint can be used to make delights such as fresh mint tea, mint sauce and mint butter. Add the leaves to garden salads or Pimms, and use wild mint to add flavour to desserts such as mint chocolate ice cream, or to marinades for meats such as lamb.

This recipe for **Homemade Mint Sauce** is perfect served with roast lamb, or it can be tossed with warm boiled new potatoes or added to lamb meatballs. If you make a large batch, keep it in a sealed, sterilised jar in the fridge and use within 1 month. Once opened, use within 3 days. If you cannot find wild mint, just use common garden mint for this recipe. Use a pestle and mortar to finely grind together ½ teaspoon coriander seeds and 1 clove. Add the ground spices to 40g (half a small bunch) finely chopped fresh mint leaves (stripped from their stalks) in a small bowl. Add 2 teaspoons caster sugar, pour over 1 tablespoon boiling water and stir to dissolve the sugar. Add 2 tablespoons cider vinegar and season with sea salt and freshly cracked pepper, then stir. Chill in the fridge for 20 minutes before using, to let the flavours develop. Makes about 100ml, serving 6 as a condiment.

Mackerel

Homemade Elderflower Cordial

This is one of my most popular recipes at this time of year and the one that I am often asked for during the months of May and June. I should take it as a compliment as it must mean that the recipe is easy to use and is a great success!

By the beginning of May, as I drive to work and back, I am usually on the look out for sources of elderflowers, spotting bridle paths and footpaths that lead into fields with hedgerows containing elderberry shrubs/trees, but it all depends on how warm a spring we've had as to when the flowers will be ready for picking.

As well as finding a source of fresh elderflowers, you will need to buy the other ingredients required to make the cordial, citric acid being one of those and one that is not always easy to find. Citric acid used to be readily available from most high street chemists, but it is harder to find nowadays. Buying it online is the easiest solution, but make sure you buy it from reputable companies and only buy food-safe citric acid.

Makes about 2 litres elderflower cordial

Serves 20–25

1.1 litres cold water
900g caster sugar
2 lemons
2 limes
250g freshly picked elderflowers
50g citric acid

Pour the water into a large saucepan and bring it to the boil over a high heat, then reduce the heat and simmer for 30 seconds. Remove from the heat and pour the boiling water over the sugar in a large mixing bowl. Stir to dissolve the sugar. Wash the lemons and limes and cut into quarters, then add them to the hot syrup. Set aside and leave to cool completely.

Meanwhile, pick over the elderflowers and remove any dead bits and leaves. Place the elderflowers in a colander and wash under cold running water. Let the elderflowers drain while the syrup cools.

Add the elderflowers and citric acid to the cooled syrup mixture and stir to mix. Place a piece of cling film directly on the surface of the mixture and place in the fridge. Leave the cordial to infuse in the fridge for 48 hours, stirring a couple of times during this period.

Pass the cordial through a fine sieve and pour into sterilised bottles, then seal. Keep refrigerated and use within 6 weeks. To serve, dilute the cordial with either chilled sparkling, still or soda water and serve in tall glasses with plenty of ice. Alternatively, add a dash of cordial to Champagne for a refreshing Champagne cocktail.

Cook's Notes

If you add the elderflowers to the syrup while it's still boiling hot, you will scorch the flowers and it will change the taste and colour of the cordial. I have made this mistake in the past and the end result is not pleasant.

Instead of keeping the cordial in bottles in the fridge, you can pour the cordial into ice cube trays and freeze, then simply defrost and dilute as needed. The frozen cubes of cordial will keep in the freezer for up to 3 months.

Asparagus Soup

The arrival of the British asparagus season is a joyous time. British asparagus is classed as some of the finest in the world and our national consumption figures show that we have a healthy appetite for these delicate stems.

The season normally runs from May until June, but it is largely dependent on the weather. A mild winter and a warm spring will bring the asparagus season forward, whereas a late, cold winter and a chilly spring will delay the season.

East Anglia provides some of the country's best asparagus crops and we are delighted to be right in the heart of it all. Asparagus, like peas, broad beans and Brussels sprouts, should be eaten as soon as it's harvested. We are lucky enough to have one of the region's largest asparagus producers nearby us in Suffolk and, even better, is the fact that they deliver freshly picked asparagus every day to many local restaurants, cafés and farm shops, including ours. It's amazing that we can readily buy such fresh asparagus and that we can serve asparagus at lunchtime in our restaurant that's only been harvested that same morning.

There are many classic asparagus recipes and a few ingredients that are synonymous with asparagus, such as eggs, mayonnaise and ham. Asparagus requires care and attention when cooking and it needs to be cooked quickly to prevent overcooking (which will spoil the taste and cause discolouration).

The method for this soup is straightforward. I cook the soup base with plenty of onions, sliced potatoes, white wine and stock, and then once the soup base is ready, I quickly pan-fry the asparagus stems and heads in olive oil, then blend it all together with a dash of double cream. I use as much of the asparagus spear as possible, the only part that is not edible is the very end of the stem that is woody and tough.

Serves 4 as a starter or light lunch

For the crisp asparagus filo rolls
16 thin asparagus spears
2 sheets of chilled fresh or frozen (defrosted) filo pastry (each sheet about 40 x 30cm)
2 tablespoons unsalted butter, melted
about 1 teaspoon ground sumac, to season
about 1 teaspoon ras el hanout, to season

For the asparagus soup
1 tablespoon unsalted butter
1 large onion, sliced
1 large potato, finely sliced
200ml dry white wine
750ml vegetable or white chicken stock
100ml double cream
2 tablespoons olive oil
250g asparagus spears, trimmed and chopped
sea salt and freshly cracked black pepper

To serve
rapeseed oil, for drizzling
8 teaspoons fresh curd cheese
1 teaspoon fresh thyme leaves

First, make the asparagus filo rolls. Shorten the asparagus into 8cm long spears and set aside. Reserve the trimmed stems and use them in the soup. Cut the filo pastry into sixteen 5 x 12cm strips, lightly brush each strip with melted butter and then sprinkle each strip with a pinch of sumac and a pinch of ras el hanout.

Place an asparagus spear on one end of one strip of filo, leaving the tip exposed, and then roll up the spear in the filo pastry to make a roll. Repeat with the remaining filo strips and asparagus spears to make 16 asparagus filo rolls. Place on a plate and chill in the fridge while cooking the soup (see Cook's Notes).

For the soup, melt the butter in a large saucepan, add the onion, potato and salt and pepper, then cover and sweat over a low heat for 8–10 minutes or until the vegetables are softened but not coloured at all. Pour the wine into the pan and let it bubble, stirring and scraping the base of the pan with a wooden spoon to deglaze it. Cook over a high heat for 5–7 minutes or until the wine is reduced by half of its original volume and it becomes syrupy. Add the stock, bring back to a simmer, then cover and simmer gently for about 20 minutes or until the potatoes are cooked. Add the cream and simmer for a further 5 minutes, then remove from the heat.

Heat the olive oil in a large, non-stick frying pan and sauté the chopped asparagus (together with the reserved trimmed stems from the asparagus filo rolls), with salt and pepper added, for 3–4 minutes or until the asparagus has softened slightly.

Carefully transfer the soup to a blender, add the sautéed asparagus and purée until smooth. Return the soup to the pan and reheat gently, then taste and adjust the seasoning, if necessary. Keep hot until you are ready to serve.

Meanwhile, preheat the oven to 180°C/ Gas Mark 4 and line a baking tray with non-stick baking paper. Place the asparagus filo rolls on the prepared baking tray and bake in the oven for 15–18 minutes or until crisp and golden.

To serve, ladle the hot soup into bowls. Garnish with a drizzle of rapeseed oil, then top each portion with 2 teaspoons curd cheese and a few thyme leaves.

Serve immediately with the crisp asparagus filo rolls on the side (serve 4 asparagus rolls per portion).

Cook's Notes

The asparagus filo rolls can be made up to 2 days in advance, but do not bake them until needed. Store them in an airtight container in the fridge. Once baked, they are delicious served hot or cold.

The asparagus soup is equally delicious served cold. If serving cold, it's important to chill the soup as quickly as possible as it will quickly discolour and lose its bright green colour. Once made and blended, pour the soup into a suitable container and place the container in iced water. Once cool, chill the soup in the fridge over ice for at least 2 hours before serving.

Smoked Mackerel Garden Salad with Smoked Ham Cakes and Dill Crème Fraîche

The inspiration for this dish came from our first visit to Orford in Suffolk many years ago. Orford is a beautiful seaside village with two smokehouses. One of these smokehouses is situated in a little alleyway down a hill overlooking the sea, and you can't really miss it because the inviting aroma of the smoke greets you as you walk through the village. Every day they smoke treacle- and cider-cured ham knuckles and they are still warm when you buy them. The smell is wonderful and I fall for it every time. In fact, I can't get back to the car without having a nibble of the warm smoked ham hock!

This dish is simple, but be sure to use the best seasonal, and in this case, regional, ingredients that you can buy.

Serves 6 as a starter or light lunch

For the smoked ham and rocket cakes
600g Desiree potatoes, roughly diced
200g treacle and cider-cured smoked ham hock, flaked
2 spring onions, finely sliced
1 egg yolk
25g rocket leaves, roughly chopped
1 teaspoon wholegrain mustard
1 tablespoon rapeseed oil
sea salt and freshly cracked black pepper

For the dill crème fraîche
200g crème fraîche
1 tablespoon lemon juice
2 teaspoons chopped fresh dill
1 clove garlic, crushed

For the smoked mackerel garden salad
2 lemons, each cut into 3 thick slices
2 bunches of asparagus spears (200–250g per bunch), trimmed
200g fresh (or frozen) broad beans (shelled weight)
4 radishes, finely sliced
a large handful of a selection of baby or mini/micro salad leaves
1 teaspoon extra virgin olive oil
1 large whole smoked mackerel or 2 smaller ones (350–400g total weight)

First, make the ham and rocket cakes. Cook the potatoes in a pan of boiling salted water for 20–25 minutes or until soft. Drain well, then mash the potatoes using a potato ricer or potato masher. Put the mashed potatoes in a bowl, add the ham hock, spring onions, egg yolk, rocket and mustard and mix well. Season to taste with salt and pepper.

Divide the mixture into 12 equal portions and shape each one into a round patty or cake, about 3–4cm in diameter. Place on a plate or tray and chill in the fridge until you are ready to cook them (see Cook's Note).

Make the dill crème fraîche. Place all the ingredients for the dill crème fraîche in a bowl and mix together, then season to taste with salt and pepper. Cover and set aside in the fridge for about 20 minutes to allow the flavours to infuse and develop.

Meanwhile, make the smoked mackerel garden salad. First, caramelise the lemon slices. Heat a non-stick frying pan over a high heat, add the lemon slices to the hot, dry pan and cook for 5–6 minutes or until golden and caramelised on both sides. Remove them to a plate.

Cook the asparagus spears in a large saucepan of boiling salted water for 3–4 minutes or until just tender. Drain well, then refresh in iced water and drain again. Meanwhile, blanch the broad beans in a separate pan of boiling salted water for a couple of minutes, remove with a slotted spoon and refresh in iced water, then drain again. Pop the tender, bright green beans out of their outer grey skins by squeezing gently. Discard the outer grey skins.

Put the cold asparagus into a serving bowl with the cold broad beans, radishes and salad leaves and toss to mix. Drizzle over the olive oil, season with salt and pepper and toss to mix. Set aside.

Remove and discard the bones, head and fins from the mackerel (leave the skin on) and then cut the mackerel fillets into 6 even-sized pieces. Set aside.

When you are ready to serve, cook the ham and rocket cakes. Heat the rapeseed oil in a large, non-stick frying pan and pan-fry the cakes over a medium heat for about 4 minutes on each side or until cooked and golden brown, turning occasionally.

To serve, place the hot ham and rocket cakes on serving plates, serving 2 per portion. Spoon the dill crème fraîche into small dipping pots and place next to the cakes. Divide the salad between the plates, then place a piece of smoked mackerel and a caramelised lemon slice alongside. Serve immediately.

Cook's Note
The ham and rocket cakes can be made up to 2 days in advance and kept in the fridge. Store in an airtight container in the fridge.

Asparagus with Cheddar Brûlées

Late spring/early summer is a wonderful time of the year, especially as it brings us the taste of fresh asparagus. Early on in the season the asparagus is at its sweetest and most tender. The British asparagus season is short but when it's here we truly embrace it! Simplicity is key when serving asparagus and for me, a humble soft-boiled egg is the best companion, be it a hen or duck egg, served with plenty of sea salt and freshly cracked black pepper.

This recipe for Cheddar brûlées is one of the simpler recipes that highlights the fantastic taste of fresh asparagus. It's easy to prepare and is impressive to serve, providing some extra 'wow' factor at the dining table.

You will need to make the brûlées the day before you want to serve them.

Serves 6 as a starter or light lunch

200ml double cream
4 eggs, lightly beaten
40g mature Cheddar cheese, finely grated (I like to use a strong Cheddar like Montgomery or Keens, but perhaps choose one locally produced in your region)
36 thin asparagus spears, trimmed
2 tablespoons Sorrel Pesto (see page 135)
1 tablespoon demerara sugar
sea salt and freshly cracked black pepper
fresh chive flowers, to garnish (optional – see Cook's Notes)

First, prepare the Cheddar brûlées. Place 6 x 150ml swing-top glass jars (or ramekins) on a tray in the fridge. Half-fill a saucepan with water and bring up to a gentle simmer, then choose a heatproof mixing bowl that will sit comfortably over the saucepan without slipping down inside the pan (you also want to make sure that the bottom of the bowl does not come into contact with the simmering water underneath).

Place the cream, eggs, cheese and salt and pepper in the heatproof bowl and whisk together briefly until well mixed. Place the bowl over the pan of simmering water. Heat gently, stirring continuously with a wooden spoon, until the mixture starts to thicken, then continue to cook gently for about 14 minutes or until the mixture thickens enough to coat the back of the spoon; do not allow the mixture to boil or it will curdle. Once cooked, remove from the heat and immediately pour the brûlée mixture into the chilled serving jars, dividing evenly. Carefully return the brûlées to the fridge and leave to set overnight.

The next day, once the brûlées are set and ready to serve, cook the asparagus spears. Cook in a large saucepan of boiling salted water for 2–3 minutes or until the spears are just tender, then drain. Place the asparagus in a large bowl, add the sorrel pesto and toss to mix, then divide between serving plates and set to one side.

Sprinkle the sugar over the top of the brûlées and use a blowtorch to caramelise the sugar (see Cook's Notes). Serve immediately with the warm asparagus spears, then scatter over the chive flowers to garnish, if you like.

Cook's Notes

If you have a double boiler, you can use this to cook the mixture for the Cheddar brûlées, if you like.

If you don't have a blowtorch, simply place the sugar-sprinkled brûlées under a preheated hot grill and grill for 1½–2 minutes or until the sugar has caramelised.

Fresh chive flowers are a beautiful, bright purple-blue colour and they make a striking garnish. Not only are they edible and pretty to look, if planted in the garden, they attract bees, encouraging pollination, and they are also planted to repel and control some unwanted insects and pests. I love using them in my recipes, as they are so pretty and taste wonderful, but don't be fooled as they are quite potent and strong-tasting too, so use sparingly.

Carpaccio of East Coast Cod with Shallot, Ginger and Soy Vinaigrette

Living by the coast has some magnificent advantages, such as the regular availability of fresh fish. Fresh cod is very special – the skin has an almost transparent green tint and the flesh is opaque with the essence and smell of freshly squeezed lime.

Large, thick fillets are the best for this carpaccio recipe, but I would only recommend eating fish raw in this way if it's super fresh. If the fish is a few days old then it's best to be cooked and used for another recipe. The vinaigrette in this recipe is also one of my favourites and has been with me for many years, although, as with many of my recipes, it has evolved slightly from the original. It's easy to make and is another one of those 'shake-it-altogether-in-a-jar' recipes that I'm fond of – simply measure all the ingredients into a jar, seal the lid, shake, use, then seal and keep any leftovers for the next day (see Cook's Note). Wonderful!

For the cod carpaccio, I normally serve 60–80g raw cod per portion for a starter.

Serves 4 as a starter or light lunch

For the shallot and soy vinaigrette
3 banana shallots, finely diced
1 clove garlic, crushed
20g fresh root ginger, peeled and finely minced
50ml soy sauce
100ml toasted sesame oil
100ml groundnut oil or sunflower oil
50ml sherry vinegar
juice of 1 lemon
sea salt and freshly ground black pepper

For the cod carpaccio
320g skinless cod fillet (make sure the fish is super fresh)
1 tablespoon groundnut oil or sunflower oil

To serve
finely grated zest of 1 lemon
a sprinkling of ground sumac (optional)
fresh mustard cress

First, make the vinaigrette. Select a clean jar with a tight-fitting screw-top lid. Place all the vinaigrette ingredients in the jar, except the salt and pepper (remember that soy sauce is salty), shake the jar vigorously, then taste and add salt and pepper, if needed. Chill in the fridge for at least 1 hour before using to let the vinaigrette flavours infuse (see Cook's Note).

To prepare the cod carpaccio, first place 4 serving plates in the fridge to chill. Slice the raw cod into wafer thin slices using a sharp knife. Arrange the cod slices on the chilled plates, dividing evenly and leaving 2–4mm spaces between each slice for the marinade. Carefully brush the groundnut oil over the fish and season with salt. Shake the vinaigrette and use a teaspoon to spoon some vinaigrette over the cod on the plates.

Garnish the cod with a scattering of lemon zest, a sprinkle of sumac, if you like, and a scattering of mustard cress. Serve immediately with freshly baked rye or sourdough bread.

Cook's Note
The vinaigrette is at its best after a day or two, as the flavours will infuse and develop in this time. It will keep in a screw-top jar in the fridge for up to 7 days. The leftover vinaigrette also makes a delicious stir-fry sauce, so try stirring it into a beef stir-fry with udon noodles, for a tasty supper.

Fresh Buffalo Curd Seasonal Salad

I have always had an interest in making cheese, but have never really got around to trying it. As a young commis chef, I had this dream to give up my job for a year and travel through France, visiting the cheese-making regions (which is most of France!) and doing voluntary work for the small artisan cheese-makers. So far that has remained a dream, as I was never motivated enough to learn French nor to save enough money to give up my job and take a year out. Perhaps one day in the future I might fulfil this dream...

English cheeses were pretty much overlooked in my previous workplaces, mainly because these were establishments and restaurants specialising in modern French cuisine and it was not fashionable to serve English produce back then. It's really only relatively recently that British produce started enjoying a renaissance and I'm very privileged and proud to be in the thick of things, enjoying and serving the best of British produce.

Laverstoke Park Farm in Hampshire has a wonderful herd of water buffalo, which enables them to make English buffalo mozzarella. I found their milk on sale in a local supermarket and I was inspired to make my own fresh buffalo curd. It's actually quite easy to make and all you need is a bit of time and an understanding of the process.
It was a bit of trial and error for me at first, but once I had mastered the technique, I made it like a pro and it has the most amazing fresh taste.

When I make curd cheese and it's ready to eat, I put it into a clean sterilised jar, place fresh thyme leaves and sprinkle coarse sea salt on the top and cover the cheese surface with a glug of good extra virgin olive oil. This locks in the freshness and helps to retain the quality and the curd cheese will then keep in the fridge for up to 5 days. I have made this curd cheese with buffalo, goat and cows' milk, and each type has its own characteristic and delicious flavour.

The quantity of milk given in this recipe makes about 500g fresh buffalo curd cheese (though this depends on the richness and amount of cream in the milk). You will need to start this recipe the day before you want to serve it. Please note that you will need a kitchen thermometer for this recipe.

Serves 4 as a starter or light lunch

For the fresh buffalo curd cheese
2 litres fresh buffalo milk
150ml freshly squeezed lemon juice
1½ teaspoons table salt

For the lemon oil
60ml freshly squeezed lemon juice
60ml extra virgin olive oil
sea salt and freshly cracked black pepper

For the seasonal salad
1 kohlrabi (about 100g unprepared weight)
2 new-season courgettes, trimmed
4 asparagus spears, trimmed
120g fresh peas (shelled weight)
a small handful of mixed seasonal baby or mini/micro salad leaves
2 sprigs of fresh thyme (preferably purple thyme), leaves only
1 teaspoon ground sumac

To make the curd cheese, rinse a saucepan with cold water, then measure the buffalo milk, lemon juice and table salt into the dampened pan, stir and then set aside for 20 minutes.

Over a very low heat, gently bring the milk mixture up to 80°C, stirring occasionally, but only if you need to prevent the milk from burning – do not disturb the milk too much. Once the milk reaches the correct temperature, remove the pan from the heat and set aside to cool at room temperature for 3 hours.

Line a sieve with muslin cloth and carefully pour the curdled milk through the muslin into a bowl underneath, then leave it to drain naturally for 1 hour. Hang the muslin in the fridge (with a bowl underneath to catch any drips) and leave to drain further overnight.

The following day, discard the whey (runny, milky liquid) and transfer the fresh curd cheese to a clean container, then cover and keep it refrigerated. The fresh curd is now ready to use and it will keep in an airtight container in the fridge for up to 5 days.

Make the lemon oil. Place the lemon juice, olive oil and salt and pepper in a clean jar with a tight-fitting screw-top lid, shake vigorously and then taste and adjust the seasoning, if needed. Set aside.

For the seasonal salad, peel the kohlrabi, then use a mandolin to finely slice it. Cut the slices into 1cm strips, then dunk these in a bowl of iced water to crisp. Drain and set aside. Use a vegetable peeler to slice the courgettes into long ribbons. Use a sharp knife to cut through the asparagus spears lengthways to create long thin strips.

Blanch the peas in a pan of boiling salted water for 1½–2 minutes or until tender, then drain, refresh in iced water and drain again. Place the peas in a small bowl, add a teaspoon of the lemon oil and season to taste with salt and pepper, then lightly crush the peas. Wash and drain the salad leaves.

Place the strips of kohlrabi, courgette and asparagus on a large flat tray, season with salt and pepper and drizzle with the lemon oil (reserving a little for the garnish) then leave for 5 minutes to marinate.

To serve, fashion a quenelle (or a simple spoonful) of the fresh buffalo curd on a serving spoon, season with salt and pepper, add a few drops of the remaining lemon oil and some of the thyme leaves, then position the spoon on a serving plate. Repeat for each serving. Arrange the marinated vegetables on the plates, add some crushed peas, then garnish each plate with the salad leaves and a few more drops of the lemon oil. Sprinkle each portion with a little sumac and serve immediately.

Warm Treacle and Cider-cured Smoked Ham Hock Spring Barley Salad

It's mid-May and the height of spring, but with the occasional chill in the air, one might sometimes question the season we are in. This dish meets the seasons halfway. The barley salad is served warm and is full of the goodness and brightness of the seasonal bounty that this month provides. This recipe is a farmers' market one, as most of these ingredients should be easily available at a typical farmers' market during May. The treacle and cider-cured smoked ham hock is again from my local smokehouse, but if you cannot find it or anything similar, use plain smoked ham instead.

Serves 6 as a starter or 4 as a lunch

50ml light olive oil
1 onion, diced
1 clove garlic, crushed
2 sticks celery, diced
150g pearl barley
100ml real ale (I use Adnams, but choose your own local favourite)
400ml white chicken stock
2 smoked spicy chorizo or Spanish sausages (120–150g total weight)
a bunch of asparagus (200–250g), trimmed
120g treacle and cider-cured smoked ham hock, flaked
120g fresh (or frozen) broad beans (shelled weight)
120g fresh (or frozen) peas (shelled weight)
1 tablespoon unsalted butter
finely grated zest and juice of 1 lemon
a handful of fresh parsley, chopped
sea salt and freshly cracked black pepper
fresh pea tops or pea shoots, to garnish

Heat the olive oil in a large saucepan and sauté the onion, garlic and celery over a medium heat for about 6 minutes or until the vegetables are transparent and are starting to take on colour – cover the pan with the lid for the first 2 minutes, then remove the lid for the remaining time. Add the pearl barley and cook for 2 minutes.

Pour the ale into the pan and let it bubble, stirring and scraping the base of the pan with a wooden spoon to deglaze it. Cook over a high heat for 4–5 minutes or until the pearl barley has absorbed the ale, stirring regularly. Add the stock, bring back to a simmer (do not add any salt at this stage as it will make the barley tough – add seasoning towards the end of the cooking time), then cover and simmer gently for about 30 minutes or until the barley is tender, stirring occasionally. After about 20 minutes cooking time you can then add a little salt and pepper.

Meanwhile, cut the chorizo sausages into 1cm slices and pan-fry in a non-stick frying pan over a high heat for 5–6 minutes or until cooked and golden brown. Remove from the heat, set aside and keep hot.

Prepare the asparagus spears. Cut off the tips in 3–4cm lengths and reserve, then cut the stems into 2–3mm-thick slices and reserve.

Once the barley is cooked, remove the lid and increase the heat to a rapid boil. Add the ham, broad beans, peas and asparagus tips and stems and cook for about 5 minutes or until the remaining liquid is absorbed. Turn the heat off and stir in the butter, taste and adjust the seasoning, if needed, and then add the lemon zest and juice and chopped parsley. Stir in the cooked chorizo slices.

Serve the warm salad in bowls and garnish with pea tops. Serve with warm freshly baked bread rolls.

Pickled Seasonal Carrots with Cured Salmon and Borage Flowers

Pickling, smoking, curing and preserving have always played a huge part in my cooking. I love squirrelling away as much as possible and preserving the season's finest for as long as I possibly can. Sometimes we cure foods, such as bacon and salmon, not necessarily for keepsakes, but rather to create a new flavour or ingredient that we can then enjoy in recipes.

These pickled carrots, with their slightly spicy flavour and crunchy texture, are the perfect accompaniment for the mellow, soft flesh of the cured salmon. I like using edible flowers in recipes too, though I find some are a bit garish and perhaps old-fashioned, but borage flowers are one of the 'cooler' ones around. I use them for their taste and what they bring to recipes, and in this dish, the fresh cucumber taste of the borage flowers, compliments the rest of the ingredients perfectly.

You will need to start curing the salmon a couple of days before you want to serve it.

Serves 6 as a starter or light lunch

For the cured salmon

700g piece of super fresh salmon fillet, skin on and pin bones removed (there will be some weight loss after curing)
80g table salt
80g caster sugar
finely grated zest of 1 orange
4 tablespoons chopped fresh dill

For the pickled seasonal carrots

4 large carrots
1 teaspoon table salt
1 large fresh red chilli, deseeded and cut into thin matchstick (julienne) strips
1 star anise
1 clove garlic, lightly crushed
1 teaspoon black mustard seeds
1 tablespoon grated (peeled) fresh root ginger
2 tablespoons soy sauce
100ml freshly squeezed orange juice
100g caster sugar
100ml white wine vinegar
1 cinnamon stick
sea salt and freshly cracked black pepper

To serve

12 fresh borage flowers
a handful of seasonal baby salad leaves
1 tablespoon olive oil, for drizzling

To make the cured salmon, rinse the salmon, then pat it dry with kitchen paper. Mix the salt, sugar, orange zest and 2 tablespoons of the dill together and spread half of this mixture over the base of a deep white plastic tray or dish for the salmon to cure in – make sure the length of the fish fits in the dish, as it should remain flat at all times. Place the salmon, skin-side down, on to the salt mixture, then spread the rest of the salt mixture over the salmon. Cover the salmon directly with cling film and then place something heavy directly on to the salmon to weigh it down. Place the salmon in the fridge and leave to cure for 2 days, turning it over each day.

Make the pickled seasonal carrots. Using a mandolin, slice the peeled carrots on an angle into 2mm slices, then place in a dish, sprinkle with the table salt and set aside for 1 hour.

Place the rest of the ingredients for the pickled carrots in a saucepan. Heat gently, stirring until the sugar has dissolved, then increase the heat, bring to the boil and cook for about 10 minutes or until the mixture reduces and becomes syrupy.

Wash the carrots under cold running water to remove the salt and drain. Add the carrots to the boiling syrup, bring back to the boil and boil for 2 minutes. Remove from the heat and let the carrots cool for a few minutes, then spoon the carrots, syrup and spices into hot, sterilised jars. Cover with vinegar-proof lids and seal. Leave to cool, then label and store in the fridge. Use immediately or store for 1 week before using to let the carrots mature a bit. The unopened jars of pickled carrots should keep well in the fridge for up to 3 months. Once opened, keep in the fridge and use within 1 week. This recipe will make 2 x 200g jars of pickled carrots.

Once the salmon is cured, remove it from the dish and rinse under cold running water, then pat the salmon dry with kitchen paper and place on a clean tray or dish, skin-side down. Cover the flesh side with the remaining dill, then cover with cling film and refrigerate until needed. The cured salmon will keep for up to 5 days in the fridge.

Chill the serving plates for 20 minutes before serving (the chilled plates will help to keep the salmon cool on a hot day). To serve, use a sharp knife to cut the salmon into wafer thin slices – I usually serve about 80–90g of salmon per person. Divide the salmon between the serving plates, laying it flat to cover the base of the plates. Arrange some drained pickled carrots (reserving the pickling liquor), the borage flowers and salad leaves on the plates. Drizzle with the pickling liquor and olive oil and serve.

Pan-seared Woodpigeon with English Asparagus and Broad Bean and Wild Mint Hummus

The distinct earthy and robust taste of the woodpigeon in this recipe is tamed beautifully by the milder and sweeter tones of the English asparagus and broad beans. The mint then gives the whole dish a refreshing lift.

If wild mint is not easily available where you are, then use common fresh garden mint. I get the thyme flowers from the thyme plants in my garden, but pea tops are a good substitute and they are regularly available from good supermarkets.

Serves 4 as a starter or 2 as a main course

For the broad bean and wild mint hummus
400g fresh (or frozen) broad beans (shelled weight)
100g cooked chickpeas (drained weight, if using canned)
1 tablespoon tahini
1 clove garlic, crushed
a large handful of fresh wild mint leaves (or use common fresh garden mint), washed and patted dry
finely grated zest and juice of 1 lemon
1 teaspoon ground sumac (optional)
50ml rapeseed oil
sea salt and freshly cracked black pepper

For the woodpigeon and asparagus salad
2 heads of baby gem lettuce, washed, drained and each cut into quarters through to the root (to keep it together)
4 boneless (skin on) woodpigeon breasts (70–90g each)
½ teaspoon coriander seeds, crushed
1 clove garlic, crushed
1 teaspoon chopped fresh thyme
2 tablespoons unsalted butter
a bunch of asparagus (200–250g)
1 teaspoon olive oil

fresh thyme flowers and/or pea tops, to garnish (optional)

First, make the hummus. Cook the broad beans in a large pan of boiling salted water for a couple of minutes, then drain, refresh in iced water and drain again. Pop the tender, bright green beans out of their outer grey skins by squeezing gently. Discard the outer grey skins and reserve the inner bright green beans. Place half of the peeled broad beans in a covered container in the fridge ready for the salad. Place the rest of the peeled broad beans, along with all the remaining ingredients for the hummus, in a food processor and process until smooth. Taste and adjust the seasoning, if needed. Transfer the hummus to a bowl, then cover and chill in the fridge until needed (see Cook's Notes).

For the woodpigeon salad, season the baby gem lettuce quarters with salt and pepper and set aside. Season the woodpigeon breasts with salt and pepper, then scatter over the crushed coriander seeds, garlic and chopped thyme and rub into the breasts. Melt 1 tablespoon of the butter in a non-stick frying pan and once the butter starts to foam, place the pigeon breasts, skin-side down, in the pan and pan-fry over a high heat for 2 minutes. Flip the breasts over and pan-fry for another 2 minutes or until golden brown on the outside and pink on the inside, turning the heat down to medium if the pan is getting too hot. Remove the pigeon breasts to a plate and leave to rest, uncovered, for 4 minutes. Meanwhile, wipe the pan clean using kitchen paper, then return the pan to a high heat, add the remaining butter and once it has melted, pan-fry the baby gem quarters for 2 minutes or until golden, turning once.

In the meantime, remove and discard the thick ends of the asparagus stems – you just want the tender part of the stems and the tips. Blanch the asparagus in a large pan of boiling salted water for 2–3 minutes or until al dente, then drain and place in a dish. Drizzle over the olive oil and season with salt and pepper.

To serve, spoon some broad bean hummus on to each serving plate, then flatten this with your spoon (this is called a swipe or swirl in chef terms). Arrange the pan-fried baby gem quarters with the warm asparagus and remaining chilled broad beans on the plates, then add the warm pigeon breasts. Scatter over the thyme flowers and/or pea tops, if you like. Spoon over the pan juices and serve.

Cook's Notes
The hummus can be made in advance, as it will keep in an airtight container in the fridge for up to 3 days.

Do not be tempted to overcook the woodpigeon, otherwise it can become tough, it will look grey and will taste livery – not appetising at all. The secret is to leave the pan-fried meat to rest – this allows the residual heat to spread throughout the breasts, the cooked meat will relax and you will be left with succulent and tender pieces of pigeon.

Pan-fried Mackerel with Smoked Mackerel Patties and Crushed Garden Pea Salad

Mackerel is delicious and versatile and can be served hot or cold, smoked, raw or cooked. Due to its rich oily flesh, mackerel works best with strong, often acid flavours, such as saffron, lemon, lime, tomato, orange, fennel, chilli, ginger and wasabi.

My philosophy about mackerel is to keep it simple – over-complicating a recipe incorporating mackerel is doing no one any favours! The combination of using fresh and smoked mackerel together adds a different dimension to this dish.

Serves 4 as a starter or 2 as a main course

For the smoked mackerel patties

100g cold mashed potatoes
50g skinless smoked mackerel fillet, flaked
1 teaspoon finely sliced spring onion
1 tablespoon chopped fresh mixed herbs (such as dill, tarragon, mint, chervil and chives)
1 teaspoon capers, drained and chopped
½ teaspoon wholegrain mustard
finely grated zest and juice of ½ lemon
sea salt and freshly cracked black pepper

For the pan-fried mackerel salad

4 mackerel fillets (75–95g each), with skin on and pin bones removed
200g fresh or frozen (defrosted) peas (shelled weight)
1 tablespoon rapeseed oil
1 teaspoon chopped fresh tarragon
1 teaspoon chopped fresh mint
1 fennel bulb, trimmed and finely shaved into 2–3mm-thick slices (using a mandolin)
juice of 1 lemon
100g green beans, trimmed
20 Semi-dried Cherry Tomatoes, or use larger Semi-dried Tomatoes (see page 242), cut into pieces, if you like
12 caper berries, halved
a large handful of fresh pea shoots or any small fresh seasonal salad leaves of your choice

2 tablespoons rapeseed oil, for cooking patties and fish

First, make the smoked mackerel patties. Put the mashed potatoes, smoked mackerel, spring onion, chopped herbs, capers, mustard and lemon zest in a bowl and mix together well. Season to taste with lemon juice and salt and pepper. Divide the mixture into 8 equal portions and shape each one into a round patty or cake, about 2cm in diameter. Place on a plate or tray and chill in the fridge until you are ready to cook them.

For the pan-fried mackerel salad, cut the mackerel fillets into diamond shapes – you want about 2 diamonds per portion, each diamond measuring about 5cm long. Score the skin using a sharp knife, but do not cut all the way through the flesh. Set aside until you're ready to cook them.

Lightly crush the fresh peas in a bowl using a potato masher (or using a pestle and mortar), or, if using frozen peas, simply crush the defrosted peas using a fork. Add the rapeseed oil to the crushed peas, together with the tarragon, mint and one-third of the shaved fennel and then season with salt, pepper and lemon juice. Mix well, then set aside to allow the flavours to develop while you finish the salad and cook the patties.

Blanch the green beans in a pan of boiling salted water for about 2 minutes or until just tender. Drain, refresh in iced water, then drain again. Place the green beans, semi-dried tomatoes, caper berries, pea shoots (reserving a few for garnish) and the rest of the fennel in a bowl, season with salt, pepper and lemon juice, then set aside until you are ready to serve.

When you are ready to serve, heat 1 tablespoon rapeseed oil in a large, non-stick frying pan and fry the patties over a high heat for about 2 minutes on each side or until golden. Drain on kitchen paper and keep warm. Season the pieces of fresh mackerel fillets with salt and pepper. Heat the remaining 1 tablespoon rapeseed oil in the same pan, place the pieces of mackerel fillets, skin-side down, in the pan and cook over a medium heat for about 2 minutes or until the skin is crisp, then flip the fish over and cook for a further 1 minute or until the flesh turns opaque. Remove from the heat.

To serve, divide the salad between 4 serving plates (if serving as a starter). Place 2 pan-fried patties on top of each portion of salad. Spoon the crushed peas on to the plates, then place 2 diamonds of pan-fried mackerel on top of each portion. Serve immediately, garnished with the reserved pea shoots.

Chicken Escalopes with New-season English Asparagus Salad

I am particularly passionate about only using happy, free-range chickens, and so here at the British Larder we have joined the Freedom Food's Simply Ask restaurant scheme. The reason for this is that we want all our customers to know that we are true to our word and that we only use ethically-reared produce. We proudly only buy free-range eggs and chicken and Freedom Foods-approved pork and salmon.

As we are located in Suffolk, we buy Sutton Hoo chickens. This is a family-run business owned by the Nash Family and they produce the best and tastiest chickens in Suffolk. Interestingly, but not surprisingly, free-range chickens have a slightly coarser and flakier, almost stringy texture (might not sound appetising, but this is real chicken!), but sadly our palates have been primed to like woolly and sometimes pappy-textured chicken. If you buy organic or free-range chickens, expect your chicken to have a natural texture and not a mass-manufactured texture you so often find with many of the chickens sold in supermarkets. I would encourage you to buy organic or free-range chicken from reputable sources and also to support local butchers when you can, as it's good for the local economy, good for the end user and good from an ethics point of view.

This recipe uses some fantastic new-season ingredients, such as new potatoes, fresh asparagus and oregano from my garden... well, technically the oregano is from Lin's allotment (Lin is a customer and friend of ours), but she gave me a large chunk of her plant that was slightly overgrown, so we then transferred it to my kitchen garden where it grows happily.

This recipe is easy to prepare and super quick too, if you are organised. You can even prepare the chicken a day in advance, let it rest in the fridge overnight, and then cook it the following day.

Serves 2 as a main course

2 organic or free-range skinless, boneless chicken breasts (Sutton Hoo chicken or from a reputable source in your region), 120–150g each
50g coarse fresh breadcrumbs
1 tablespoon chopped fresh flat-leaf parsley
1 teaspoon chopped fresh oregano
finely grated zest and juice of 1 lemon
30g Hawkstone cheese (Suffolk hard cows' milk cheese), grated, or finely grated fresh Parmesan cheese
a pinch of cayenne pepper
a bunch of asparagus (200–250g), trimmed
125g fresh (or frozen) broad beans (shelled weight)
3 tablespoons unsalted butter
3 tablespoons extra virgin olive oil
1 clove garlic, crushed
2–3 tablespoons rapeseed oil
6 cooked cold new potatoes, halved
sea salt and freshly cracked black pepper
a bunch of watercress, washed and drained, to garnish

Butterfly the chicken breasts. To do this, place each breast flat on a chopping board. Place one hand on top of a breast to hold it in place and then with the other hand, carefully insert a sharp knife through the thickest part of the breast and slice it horizontally in half without cutting all the way through (stop cutting about three-quarters of the way through). Open out the breast so that it looks like a butterfly or open book. Repeat with the second breast. Place each butterflied chicken breast in a small polythene food bag and use a mallet or rolling pin to flatten the breast slightly. For the breadcrumb mixture, combine the breadcrumbs, parsley, oregano, lemon zest, grated cheese and cayenne pepper in a bowl and season lightly with salt and pepper. Set aside.

Blanch the asparagus and broad beans together in a large pan of boiling salted water for 1½–2 minutes or until the asparagus is al dente. Drain, refresh in iced water and drain again. Set the asparagus aside. Pop the tender, bright green broad beans out of their outer grey skins by squeezing gently. Discard the outer grey skins and reserve the inner bright green beans. Set aside.

Heat the butter and olive oil in a small saucepan until the butter has melted, then add the garlic, lemon juice and salt and pepper. Remove from the heat. Dip each chicken escalope into the melted butter mixture, then roll it in the bread-crumb mixture to coat it all over. Use your hands to press the crumbs on firmly.

Heat 1 tablespoon rapeseed oil in a non-stick frying pan and pan-fry the coated chicken escalopes over a medium heat for 12–15 minutes or until thoroughly cooked and golden brown all over, turning them regularly and adding another 1 tablespoon rapeseed oil to the pan partway through cooking, if needed. Drain the chicken escalopes on kitchen paper.

Meanwhile, heat the remaining 1 tablespoon rapeseed oil in a separate non-stick frying pan and sauté the new potatoes for 7–8 minutes or until golden. Add the blanched asparagus and reserved peeled broad beans and cook for a further 1 minute, then remove from the heat.

Serve the hot chicken escalopes with the warm potato salad and garnish with the watercress.

New Season Lamb Rumps with Lamb Shoulder Croquettes, Warm Pickled English Asparagus, Radishes and Kohlrabi

This is the perfect al fresco dish for sharing with friends and family. The warm pickled vegetables have a slight crunch and the acidity cuts through the richness of the lamb. Rump of lamb has a bit more texture than rack of lamb – the fibres are coarser and the fat is lovely and thick. My mouth is watering just writing about the smell of lamb cooking; the fat smells amazing too and if it is rendered correctly then it's delicious.

The croquettes might seem like hard work but they really are worth every moment spent in the kitchen. I make a large batch of these croquettes and freeze them. When needed, I defrost the croquettes in the fridge overnight and then coat them in the breadcrumb mixture just before cooking them. They are great fun and can be served as a canapé or served as part of this dish. The textures and flavours of this dish are wonderful and memorable.

Serves 4 as a main course

For the lamb shoulder croquettes

1 shoulder of lamb (1–1.5kg with bone), deboned
8 tablespoons rapeseed oil
a sprig of fresh thyme, leaves only
1 clove garlic, crushed
1 large onion, peeled
250ml cold water
8 banana shallots, finely diced
2 tablespoons chopped fresh mixed soft herbs (such as chives, tarragon, chervil and thyme)
1–2 tablespoons plain flour, seasoned with salt and pepper
2 eggs, lightly beaten
2–4 tablespoons fresh breadcrumbs
sea salt and freshly cracked black pepper
sunflower oil, for deep-frying

For the lamb rumps

2 whole lamb rumps (about 250g each)
1 tablespoon olive oil
1 clove garlic, lightly bruised
leaves from a sprig of fresh thyme, finely chopped
1 tablespoon unsalted butter

For the warm pickled asparagus, radishes and kohlrabi

200g Puy lentils
50g caster sugar
½ teaspoon mustard powder
50ml white wine vinegar
100g cold unsalted butter, diced
1 kohlrabi (80–100g unprepared weight), peeled and cut into batons, each about 4cm x 5mm
12 baby leeks, trimmed and cut into 4cm lengths
12 French breakfast radishes (or whatever radishes are available), trimmed and halved
a bunch of asparagus (200–250g), trimmed and cut into 4cm lengths

First, prepare the lamb shoulder croquettes. Preheat the oven to 140°C/Gas Mark 1. Season the lamb with salt and pepper, then rub it all over with 2 tablespoons rapeseed oil, the thyme leaves and garlic. Cut the onion into 4 thick, even slices and place them in the centre of a roasting tin to form a bed for the lamb. Place the lamb on top, add the water and cover the tin with foil. Cook in the oven for 4 hours, then remove the foil and cook for a further 1 hour or until the fat has turned golden brown and the meat is succulent, moist and flaky.

Remove from the oven and leave the lamb to cool completely. Do not refrigerate the lamb – let it cool naturally to room temperature or until it is cold enough to touch without burning your fingers. Remove and discard as much fat as possible and then finely flake the cooked meat into a bowl and set aside. Discard the onion.

Heat the remaining rapeseed oil in a small saucepan, add the shallots and salt and pepper, then cover and sweat over a low heat for about 8 minutes or until the shallots are transparent and soft, but make sure they don't take on any colour.

Add the shallots and cooking oil to the flaked shoulder meat, along with the chopped herbs, and mix well, then season with salt and pepper. Take a heaped tablespoonful of the mixture and shape it into a croquette shape, then place on a plate or tray. Repeat with the remaining mixture to make about 18–20 croquettes. Chill in the fridge for 30 minutes to firm up.

Put the seasoned flour, beaten eggs and breadcrumbs into 3 separate shallow bowls. Once the croquettes are firm, dip each one first into the seasoned flour, then into the beaten eggs, and then finally roll in the breadcrumbs to coat all over. Place on a plate or tray and chill in the fridge for at least 30 minutes before cooking. Keep chilled until you are ready to cook them (see Cook's Notes).

Cook the lamb rumps. Preheat the oven to 200°C/Gas Mark 6. Season the lamb generously with salt and pepper, drizzle over the olive oil and then rub the meat all over with the bruised garlic and chopped thyme. Melt the butter in a non-stick frying pan and once it starts to foam, place the lamb rumps, fat-side down, into the pan and cook over a medium heat for about 8 minutes or until the fat is golden brown and crisp. Do not turn the lamb over until the fat is golden. Turn the lamb over and cook for 1 minute on the reverse side, then remove from the heat and transfer the lamb to a baking tray. Cook in the oven for 4–6 minutes for medium-rare (or cook to your liking). Remove from the oven and let the lamb rest for about 10 minutes before serving.

Meanwhile, prepare the warm pickled vegetables and lentils. Put the Puy lentils in a small saucepan and cover with cold water. Cover the pan and bring to a gentle simmer, then cook for about 15 minutes or until the lentils are soft and cooked. Season with salt, then drain, set aside and keep hot until you are ready to serve.

In the meantime, put the sugar, mustard powder and white wine vinegar in a separate small saucepan and heat gently until the sugar has dissolved. Remove from the heat, then whisk the cold butter into the warm mixture and season to taste with salt and pepper. Set aside. Blanch all the prepared vegetables in a large pan of boiling salted water for 2 minutes or until al dente, then drain (see Cook's Notes). Put the blanched vegetables into a dish and pour over the warm vinegar mixture, then cover and set aside at room temperature for 10 minutes or so before serving.

Meanwhile, cook the croquettes. Heat some sunflower oil in an electric deep-fat fryer or in a deep frying pan to a temperature of 160°C (or until a small piece of bread browns within 20 seconds in the hot oil). Once the oil is hot enough, deep-fry 4 of the croquettes in the hot oil for 4–5 minutes or until cooked, golden brown and crisp all over (see Cook's Notes – you only need to cook 4 croquettes for this recipe, so store the leftover croquettes as directed and deep-fry them when required). Using a slotted spoon, remove and drain the cooked croquettes on kitchen paper.

To serve, slice the lamb into 1cm slices. Arrange the warm lentils and pickled vegetables on serving plates with the lamb and then place a croquette on each plate. Drizzle a little of the pickling liquor over the lamb and enjoy!

Cook's Notes

The leftover (uncooked) croquettes will keep in an airtight container in the fridge for up to 3 days. Alternatively, they can be frozen for up to 1 month. If frozen, defrost thoroughly in the fridge overnight and deep-fry the next day.

The leftover cooked croquettes can be deep-fried and served as canapés at a drinks party, or they can be served with a fresh garden salad and minted yogurt sauce as a starter or light lunch (serving 3–4 croquettes per portion).

The blanched vegetables can be char-grilled on a hot griddle pan, just before the vinegar mixture is poured over, if you like. Simply toss the blanched vegetables in 1 teaspoon olive oil, preheat a ridged griddle pan over a high heat until very hot, then add the blanched vegetables in a single layer and cook for about 1 minute on each side or until grill marks appear, turning once. You'll probably need to griddle the vegetables in batches. Transfer the griddled vegetables to a dish, then pour over the warm vinegar mixture and continue as the recipe directs.

New Season Lamb Rumps with Lamb Shoulder Croquettes, Warm Pickled English Asparagus, Radishes and Kohlrabi, page 188

Chocolate and Fresh Mint Parfaits

This recipe may sound quite challenging, but in fact it's fairly straightforward and it just requires a bit of forward thinking and planning. Prepare all the different components a day or two in advance and then you are ready to just serve it on the day, when needed. I like to use fresh wild mint, but common fresh garden mint will work just as well. My top tip is to serve the parfaits on chilled plates.

You will need to start this recipe the day before you want to serve it.

Serves 6

For the chocolate mint parfaits
6 egg yolks
200g caster sugar
3 egg whites
15 large fresh chocolate mint leaves (see Cook's Notes) or fresh garden mint leaves
250ml whipping cream

For the chocolate cinnamon biscuits
80g unsalted butter, softened
250g soft dark brown sugar
125g cocoa powder
1 teaspoon bicarbonate of soda
1 teaspoon ground cinnamon
2 egg whites
100g natural yogurt
1 teaspoon vanilla extract
300g plain flour

For the mint oil
20g fresh chocolate mint leaves or fresh garden mint leaves
½ teaspoon caster sugar
25ml groundnut oil

For the crystallised mint leaves
caster sugar, for dusting
1 egg white
12 fresh chocolate mint leaves or fresh garden mint leaves (stalks removed)

Make the chocolate mint parfaits. Half-fill a saucepan with water and bring up to a gentle simmer. Choose a heatproof mixing bowl that will sit comfortably over the saucepan without slipping down inside the pan (you also want to make sure that the bottom of the bowl does not come into contact with the simmering water underneath).

Put the egg yolks and 100g of the caster sugar into the bowl and place the bowl over the pan of simmering water. Using a balloon whisk or an electric hand-held whisk, whisk together until pale, thick and creamy – when you lift the whisk it should leave a visible trail on the surface (this is called the thick ribbon stage or sabayon). Remove from the heat, remove the bowl from the pan and set aside to cool slightly.

In a separate bowl, whisk the egg whites until foaming, then add the remaining caster sugar and whisk together until the mixture forms soft peaks.

Put the mint leaves and half of the cream into a blender and blend until smooth, then transfer the mixture to a bowl. Add the remaining cream and whip the cream until it forms soft peaks.

Fold the meringue, sabayon and whipped cream together until well combined. Pour the mixture into a shallow plastic white tray or plastic container measuring 25 x 12 x 7cm and freeze for about 12 hours or until completely set.

Make the chocolate cinnamon biscuits. Cream the butter and brown sugar together in a bowl until light and fluffy. Add the cocoa powder, bicarbonate of soda and cinnamon and mix well. Add the egg whites, yogurt and vanilla extract and stir to mix. Add the flour, mixing to make a soft dough. Gather the dough into a ball, then wrap it in cling film and refrigerate for 4 hours or until firm.

Preheat the oven to 180°C/Gas Mark 4 and line 2 baking trays with non-stick baking paper.

Roll out the biscuit dough between 2 sheets of non-stick baking paper to 2–3mm thickness. Cut out twenty-four 4 x 4cm square shapes and place them on the prepared baking trays. Bake in the oven for 8–10 minutes or until crisp, but not too hard. Remove from the oven and let the biscuits cool for 1 minute on the baking trays, then transfer them to a wire rack to cool completely (see Cook's Notes).

For the mint oil, blend the mint leaves, sugar and groundnut oil together in a small blender until smooth. Pass the oil through a fine sieve into a small bowl and then set aside until needed.

To make the crystallised mint leaves, preheat the oven to 120°C/Gas Mark ½. Line a baking tray with non-stick baking paper and heavily dust the paper with caster sugar.

Lightly whisk the egg white in a bowl until foaming. Dip each mint leaf into the foaming egg white, then place each leaf on to the caster sugar tray, presentation-side up, and dust with more caster sugar. Put the baking tray in the oven for 5–6 minutes to dry the leaves out, watching carefully to make sure the leaves don't burn and the sugar doesn't caramelise too much. Carefully transfer the crystallised mint leaves to a wire rack and leave to cool and crisp.

To serve, chill the serving plates in advance. Cut the parfait into 12 squares, cutting them to the same size as the biscuits, then remove from the tray.

Sandwich each parfait square between a pair of biscuits, to make 12 parfait 'sandwiches'. Place 2 parfait 'sandwiches' on each serving plate and decorate each portion with 2 crystallised mint leaves and a few drops of the mint oil. Serve immediately.

Cook's Notes

Chocolate mint is a variety of fresh mint. The upper part of the leaves is green and the underside and stalks are a chocolate brown colour. The leaves are smaller than those of common garden mint and the flowers are usually white. The taste and smell is reminiscent of after-dinner mints. Chocolate mint is easy to grow at home. Keep the leftover mint oil in an airtight container in the fridge and use within 1 week. The biscuits can be made in advance as they will keep in an airtight container in a cool, dry cupboard for up to 1 week.

Elderflower and Wine Jellies with Elderflower Cream

I find making elderflower cordial is very therapeutic and it gives me the feeling that I have achieved something great. I like to pick the flowers early on to capture their lovely fragrance (which is similar to the fragrance of freshly picked green almonds that I remember from my childhood), otherwise they become too mature and are past their best. I believe that elderflowers should be picked before the late spring rain, because once it has rained, the flowers then drop and this encourages the fermentation process, which in turn changes the flavour of the flowers.

For this recipe, I use English white wine. We have some wonderful, award-winning wines produced in England and we should be proud and use them as much as possible. If you prefer a bit of fizz, choose an English sparkling wine instead of a still one.

Remember that the jellies need time to set, so I suggest making them the day before you want to serve them.

Serves 6

For the jellies
4 leaves of gelatine
200ml Homemade Elderflower Cordial (see page 167)
300ml English white wine (use a still or sparkling wine)
150ml cold water

For the toasted almonds and elderflower cream
60g flaked almonds
1 teaspoon icing sugar
284ml double cream (a medium-sized pot)
2 tablespoons Homemade Elderflower Cordial (see page 167)
1 tablespoon crème fraîche

First, make the jellies. Soak the gelatine in cold water until it has softened. Mix the elderflower cordial, wine and the measured cold water together, then pour one-third of the liquid into a small saucepan. Heat until just before boiling point and then remove from the heat.

Squeeze the gelatine gently to remove the excess water, then add the gelatine to the warm liquid and stir until dissolved. Stir in the remaining liquid and then pour the mixture into 6 serving glasses, dividing evenly. Carefully place the glasses in the fridge and leave to set for at least 6 hours or preferably overnight.

To toast the flaked almonds, preheat the grill to medium. Scatter the almonds over a baking tray and dust with half of the icing sugar. Place under the grill for 2–3 minutes or until golden and lightly toasted, stirring or shaking regularly to prevent them from burning. Once toasted, remove from the grill and dust with the remaining icing sugar. Leave to cool completely.

For the elderflower cream, whip the cream and elderflower cordial together in a bowl until soft peaks form. Gently fold the crème fraîche into the whipped cream. Spoon the cream on top of the jellies, decorate with the toasted flaked almonds and serve.

The British Larder | *June*

The month of June brings basketfuls of colourful fruit and vegetables to the dining table. Fresh British strawberries are at their best – sweet and packed with flavour. Runner beans, French beans, bobby (dwarf) beans and peas are all being harvested in their droves. Sardines, mackerel, herrings, lobster and langoustines are all perfect for the early summer dining table too.

At this time of year, allotments, vegetable patches and kitchen gardens are bursting with plenty of wonderful, seasonal, early summer delights, such as peas, broad beans, courgettes and strawberries. The herbs are also doing very well and it's pleasing to see the return of the summer savory, chocolate and pineapple mints, borage, nasturtiums, garlic chives, wild English yarrow, lemon verbena, lemon balm and angelica.

Wild foods in our countryside are plentiful, providing us with ingredients such as the prolific, tender young nettles that can add an interesting and delicious twist to a classic British asparagus soup.

The sea purslane and Norfolk samphire are ready to be collected, and chickweed and wild watercress can now be

The beautiful Suffolk countryside

found in the barely damp fields that used to be waterlogged during the winter months. Although the month of June can still bring with it some sombre and grey rainy days, the rain can be a good thing to ensure that the fields and gardens do not dry out too much.

Season's best during June...

Artichokes, Asparagus, Aubergines, Beetroot, Blackcurrants, Borage Flowers, Broad Beans, Broccoli, Carrots, Cherries, Chervil, Chives and Chive Flowers, Cod, Courgettes, Crab, Dill, Elderflowers, Fennel, Gooseberries, Green Beans, Herrings, Lamb, Langoustines, Lettuce, Lobster, Mackerel, Mangoes, Mint, Nasturtium Flowers, Nettles, New Potatoes, Onions, Oregano, Parsley, Peas, Plaice, Pollack, Prawns, Radishes, Redcurrants, Rocket, Rosemary, Runner Beans, Salad/Spring Onions, Salmon, Samphire, Sardines, Sea Bass, Sea Beet, Sea Purslane, Sea Trout, Sorrel, Spinach, Strawberries, Tarragon, Thyme, Tomatoes, Watercress, Whelks, Whitebait, Woodpigeon.

My culinary rituals for June...

Keeping the kitchen garden watered and weeded is an all-important job. Taking long walks in the countryside and choosing bridleways away from the roads will be time well spent, as you will find plenty to harvest. This is the month for me to bake my own birthday cake – as Mr. P will probably forget! – and I love cake! I will also continue with my preserving motto and make some delicious seasonal jams, chutneys and preserves.

Visit local Pick-Your-Own farms and come home with basketfuls of wonderful, fresh seasonal ingredients. I like to visit PYO farms that grow unusual varieties of produce as this feeds my curiosity and gives me something new to think and talk about.

June is the month that kick-starts the festivals and village fetes, as well as the all-important picnics. Dig out the picnic basket and start planning those wonderful gatherings with friends in the fresh air and warm sunshine. As I have a particular interest in Victorian kitchen gardens, I like to visit as many as possible during the summer, but even if you only get to visit one or two, enjoy your time there as they bare wonderful secrets and are inspirational too.

Experience a whole new array of interesting dishes by bringing the barbecue back to life and enjoying some seasonal outdoor cooking and eating with family and friends. Try out new barbecue recipes, such as my South African-inspired recipe for **Curried Lamb and Apricot Kebabs** (see page 216), accompanied by the tasty **Sesame Toasted Basmati Rice and Broad Bean Salad** (see page 222), and make the most of the opportunity of being outside and enjoying the early summer weather, assuming it's not raining, of course!

To enjoy al fresco and summer entertaining at its best, prepare the delicious **Chilled Pea Soup with Cheddar Cream and Soft-boiled Quail's Eggs** (see page 210).

Fennel and chive flowers

If you do pick too many strawberries, then make my tasty **Strawberry, Lime and Almond Chutney** (see page 205), or for a classic dessert, try my luscious recipe for **Strawberry Arctic Roll** (see page 224), guaranteed to make you smile and be popular with the whole family.

British Larder Heroes

Aubergines

Native to East India, the aubergine is a fruit with many names. Related to potato and tomato plants (and a member of the Solanaceae family), it's also known as brinjal, eggplant, garden egg, melongene and Guinea squash. The fruit is botanically classified as a berry and contains many edible seeds, which are bitter as they contain nicotinoid alkaloids (the aubergine is a close relative to the tobacco plant). I have successfully grown aubergines organically in planters on my patio here in Britain, and I would encourage you to give it a go as they are beautiful plants with pretty purple flowers. Remember to plant them in fresh compost, water them well and leave in a sunny, sheltered spot, then watch them grow. Remember aubergines are one of those vegetables that have to be cooked very well, otherwise the taste is bitter and can make your mouth itch. During the early 1990s, when I worked at Kensington Place, we made aubergine caviar (aubergine seeds look like caviar, hence the unusual name) and I loved it. It tastes amazing and has a wonderful texture.

To make **Aubergine Caviar**, preheat the oven to 200°C/Gas Mark 6. Cut 2 aubergines (250–350g each) in half lengthways and use a sharp knife to score the flesh but do not cut all the way through to the skin. Crush 2 cloves garlic and spread over the aubergine halves, dividing evenly. Halve 2 canned (drained) anchovy fillets and place half an anchovy fillet on each aubergine half. Season with sea salt and freshly cracked black pepper, then bruise 4 sprigs of fresh rosemary and 4 sprigs of fresh thyme and place one of each on each of the aubergine halves. Drizzle 2 tablespoons good quality olive oil over each aubergine half, then sandwich the aubergine halves back together and wrap each aubergine in foil. Place on a baking tray and bake in the oven for about 50 minutes or until the aubergines are completely soft and cooked all the way through (they will collapse slightly when touched), then remove from the oven and leave to cool in the foil. Once cold, unwrap the aubergines and then, using a spoon, scoop out the flesh on to a chopping board. Discard the herb stalks. Use a sharp knife to finely chop the flesh, but do not blend it as you don't want a purée. Heat 4 tablespoons olive oil in a small saucepan over a medium heat, then gently fry the chopped aubergine flesh for about 5 minutes or until lightly toasted, stirring continuously. Adjust the seasoning to taste, if needed, then stir in 2 tablespoons chopped fresh mixed herbs (such as chervil, basil and coriander). Serve either hot or cold with freshly baked cheese straws or hot toast. Serves 4–6 as a snack, served with plenty of fresh toast, crisp breadsticks or cheese straws.

British cherries

Before the war, the British cherry industry was booming, with over 40,000 acres of farmland devoted to beautiful cherry orchards. However, sadly, over the past 50 years, the cherry industry has collapsed as imports are cheaper and the nation has simply fallen out of love with this wonderful crimson red fruit. But in recent years, the British cherry industry has started to enjoy a revival and cherries are once again being grown in the UK, much to my and others' delight. The British cherry season is short and it usually spans a 4-week period from mid-June to mid-July. Cherries are mainly grown in Kent and Herefordshire, where the typical weather in those regions provides the perfect growing conditions for the cherry trees to flourish. National Cherry Day takes place in July at Brogdale Farm in Kent which has around 350 cherry varieties in their National Fruit Collection. An organisation called FoodLovers Britain Ltd has also established a CherryAid campaign to save the British cherry. This campaign, which was launched a few years ago, highlights the reasons why it is so important to save the British cherry. It's reported that in the last fifty years, Britain has lost 90% of its cherry orchards, and we currently import 95% of the cherries we buy and consume in the UK. With the steep decline in the number of commercial cherry trees grown in the UK, it's important that we preserve our heritage and recreate the cherry orchards, as they are an important part of our culture, originally dating back to the 1st Century when they were introduced to Britain by the Romans.

For a lovely recipe using fresh British cherries, try these tempting **Cherry and Almond Cupcakes with Mascarpone Frosting**. Preheat the oven to 200°C/Gas Mark 6 and line a baking tray with non-stick baking paper. Wash and drain 400g fresh cherries, then cut them in half and remove the stones. Spread the cherry halves out on the prepared baking tray, then sprinkle with 100g caster sugar, the juice of 1 lemon and 1 teaspoon ground cinnamon. Stir gently to mix, then roast in the oven for 25–30 minutes or until the mixture is jammy and soft,

Aubergines

Cherries

stirring once or twice during cooking. Remove from the oven and leave the cherries to cool at room temperature. To make the cupcakes, preheat the oven to 180°C/Gas Mark 4 and line a 12-cup muffin tin with paper muffin cases. Sift 150g plain flour, 1 teaspoon baking powder, ½ teaspoon bicarbonate of soda and a pinch of table salt into a large mixing bowl, then stir in 150g ground almonds and the finely grated zest of 1 lemon. In a separate bowl, cream together 100g caster sugar and 50g softened unsalted butter, then add 2 eggs and beat well until creamy. Stir in 1 tablespoon Disaranno (or Amaretto) almond liqueur, if you like. Gently fold the sifted flour mixture into the egg mixture, but do not overwork the cake mixture. Spoon a large tablespoonful of the cake mixture into each muffin case, add a teaspoonful of the baked cherries on top, then top this with the remaining cake mixture, dividing evenly. Bake in the oven for about 25 minutes or until well risen, cooked and golden brown. Transfer to a wire rack and leave to cool completely. Meanwhile, make the frosting. In a bowl, cream together 60g softened unsalted butter, 80g icing sugar and the seeds scraped from ½ a split vanilla pod, until light and fluffy, then fold in 0g mascarpone. Cover and chill until needed. Spread some frosting over the top of each cupcake, then spoon the remaining baked cherries on top to decorate, dividing evenly. Store in an airtight container in the fridge for up to 2 days. Makes 12 cupcakes.

British lamb

From May to June, British lamb is at its most tender, and as the season progresses, the taste develops, producing a richer, more flavourful meat. Lambs become hoggets (juvenile sheep) after 12 months of age, and then once the adult sheep get to over 2 years of age, they become mutton. British lamb and mutton is produced to some of the highest animal welfare standards in the world. Admittedly, this does come at a cost, but I believe that we must stick by and support the British lamb farmers. The wonderful taste of new-season British lamb is a fantastic reminder of spring and early summer, with the taste and texture of the meat differing from region to region as not all breeds taste the same.

Try my recipe for **Maddy's Roast Leg of Lamb**. Ask your butcher to remove the bone from a 2kg leg of lamb, and also ask to keep the bone. Using a pestle and mortar, crush together

4 cloves garlic, the leaves from 2 large sprigs of fresh rosemary, 1 teaspoon sea salt, 1 teaspoon mustard powder, 1 tablespoon apricot jam, finely grated zest and juice of 1 lemon, 4 each of black and white peppercorns and 1 teaspoon coriander seeds to form a paste. Open up the leg of lamb and smear the paste on the inside, then roll the meat up and tie with kitchen string. Preheat the oven to 200°C/Gas Mark 6. Place the lamb bones in the centre of a large roasting tin. Cut 2 large onions into 1.5–2cm-thick slices and place them in the tin to form a platform for the leg of lamb to sit on. Add a couple of chopped carrots, ½ leek and 2 celery sticks, chopped, and 250ml dry white wine. Place the leg of lamb on top of this bed of ingredients, season the outside with more sea salt, then make a few incisions in the meat and poke extra sprigs of fresh rosemary inside each hole. Roast in the oven for about 1¼ hours or until the outside of the lamb is caramelised and the inside is still pink, basting the meat a couple of times during cooking (if you prefer your lamb a bit more well done, then roast it for a further 15 minutes or so). After 50 minutes cooking time, brush the leg with 2 tablespoons apricot jam, then return to the oven and continue to roast. Once cooked, remove the leg of lamb from the roasting tin to a board or plate, cover with foil and leave to rest for 20 minutes, while you finish the sauce. Add 2 tablespoons apricot jam to the roasting tin, along with 500ml lamb or chicken stock and place on the hob over a medium heat. Bring this all to a gentle simmer, stirring to dissolve the jam, then simmer for 10–12 minutes or until the liquid is reduced by half. Pass the juices through a fine sieve into a jug and discard the solids. Serve the sauce with the roast lamb and all the trimmings (roast potatoes, roasted shallots, minted garden peas and homemade mint sauce). Serves 6–8 as a main course.

British organic and free-range chicken

Chicken is the most common type of poultry reared for human consumption. Over the years, various methods have been developed and adopted to increase production and speed up growth, in a quest to meet the ever-rising demand for a cheaper end product, and this sadly is still very evident today in the rearing conditions and methods used by a lot of poultry farmers. As consumers, we are able to choose what food we eat, how it's reared and where it comes from. When it comes to poultry in particular, I'm a firm believer that British is best, and I only buy organic or free-range birds. There is a clear difference in the superior texture and taste of these birds, and at the same time, I have a clear conscience, because supporting high animal welfare practices and good husbandry methods are both very important to me. Part of our ethos at the British Larder is that we try to support the local economy as much as possible, and we consciously buy local whenever we can. However, if I cannot buy a food product, such as chickens, that I know have had a good life and were cared for in a humane manner from start to finish, then I'd rather go without and not purchase them at all. It's amazing how many meals can be prepared from one organic or free-range chicken – one 1.6–1.8kg chicken can provide 2 adults with up to 3 hearty meals. You can: separate the legs from the crown, then roast the crown and serve the breasts as part of a roast dinner; make a delicious soup with the bones and wings and lots of vegetables; bake the legs with a variety of root vegetables and serve with a suitable sauce. There you have your 3 hearty meals and, in my opinion, that really is great value for money.

Cod's cheeks

Waste not, want not! Cod's cheeks, along with monkfish cheeks, have plenty of good meat and these delicious, sweet, plump pieces of muscle provide a superb and interesting alternative ingredient to use in cooking. Most fishmongers will throw the heads of the cod in the waste bin or sell them for stocks. The truth is you will probably not easily find a lot of fresh cod's cheeks to buy, although they are becoming increasingly popular, so perhaps demand will mean that they become more readily available. Cod's cheeks almost look like scallops – not entirely, but they are the size of a large scallop and can be breadcrumbed, battered or pan-fried.

When you can get hold of some fresh cod's cheeks, try my delicious recipe for **Cod's Cheek Stir-fry with Sesame and Courgette Ribbons**. Cut 8 fresh cod's cheeks (320–480g total weight) in half and place them in a dish. Make a marinade by grinding together a small knob of peeled fresh root ginger, 1 clove garlic, 1 tablespoon soy sauce, 1 teaspoon clear honey and 1 tablespoon sesame seeds using a pestle and mortar. Spoon the marinade over the cod's cheeks and set aside while you prepare the courgettes. Cut 2 courgettes into long, thin ribbons using a potato peeler. Heat 1 tablespoon sesame oil in a wok over a high heat until hot, then add the marinated cod's cheeks and stir-fry for about 3 minutes or until pale golden. Add the courgette ribbons, along with a tiny sprinkling of sea salt and a grinding of freshly cracked black pepper, and stir-fry for a further minute or so. Sprinkle over 1 tablespoon sesame seeds and 150g beansprouts and stir-fry to mix, then serve immediately with steamed rice or cooked egg noodles. Serves 2 as a main course.

Fennel

Florence fennel, or finocchio, refers to the swollen base of the leaves of a variety of plant, which form a tight, bulb-like crisp vegetable. Florence fennel has a pleasant, mild aniseed flavour and it can be eaten raw or cooked. The whole fennel plant is edible – the leaves are often used as a herb in salads and the bulb can be served in a variety of ways, such as raw in salads, or baked, steamed, sautéed, pan-fried or pickled, or in soups and purées. Fennel is also a herb, indigenous to the Mediterranean, and the dried seeds, with their aniseed flavour, are used widely in Mediterranean cookery in dishes such as porchetta. Florence fennel is also one of the three main ingredients used to make absinthe, an anise-flavoured, strong alcoholic spirit.

This tasty recipe for **Baked Fennel with Anchovies and Pernod** is ideal served as a side dish with roast leg of lamb or roasted whole sea bass. Preheat the oven to 200°C/Gas Mark 6 and grease a small roasting tin or ovenproof serving dish with 1 tablespoon unsalted butter. Cut 2 fennel bulbs in half lengthways, and then cut each half into 3 right through to the root, but keep them together at the base. Place them in the prepared roasting tin, then season lightly with sea salt and freshly cracked black pepper. Finely chop 4 canned (drained) anchovy fillets and scatter over the fennel, then sprinkle over 4 tablespoons Pernod, 4 tablespoons water or vegetable stock and ½ teaspoon crushed fennel seeds. Cover with foil and bake in the oven for 25 minutes. Remove the foil and sprinkle over 2 tablespoons grated Hawkstone (Suffolk hard cows' milk cheese) or extra mature Wensleydale cheese (or use finely grated fresh Parmesan or Pecorino cheese) and 1 slice of sourdough bread ripped into small pieces, then return to the oven for 10–12 minutes or until the cheese has melted and the bread has turned golden brown. Serve immediately. Serves 2–4 as a side dish.

Fresh garden herbs

One of my food obsessions is fresh garden herbs. They are easy to grow either in the garden or on the windowsill in your kitchen. Some herbs are annuals, others are perennials, but all are seasonal, and spring going into summer is the time when we get the best from fresh herbs growing in our gardens. Using fresh herbs in recipes can transform a fairly standard recipe into something much more interesting and flavourful, and herbs will add extra taste and appeal to many dishes. Herbs can generally be divided into two groups. Hard herbs, such as bay, lavender, rosemary, savory and thyme, are usually perennials that grow as shrubs, bushes or small trees. Soft herbs, such as basil, chervil, chives, dill, marjoram, mint, oregano, parsley, sage and tarragon, are usually annuals (that need to be planted every year) that grow as small plants. Chopping herbs releases their essential oils, but remember to chop fresh herbs just before using them and use a very sharp knife. If your knife is blunt, it will bruise the herbs and the taste will be different. For basil and larger-leaf herbs, such as parsley and sage, use kitchen scissors to snip the herbs, or simply tear the leaves into pieces. You can also toss whole herb leaves into a simple leafy salad for an interesting taste sensation. My three favourites are parsley, tarragon and thyme.

Parsley is wonderful because it's so versatile. It can be used with fish, meat, poultry and many different vegetables. Parsley also counteracts the flavour of garlic – eat a few parsley leaves after a garlic-rich supper and it can help to neutralise the garlic smell. Stir a handful of chopped fresh parsley into a cooked Bolognese sauce just before serving and the parsley will lift the sauce and add freshness to this classic dish.

At first I had a love-hate relationship with tarragon, but the older I get, the more I understand and enjoy the complexity of this fairly strong, aniseed-tasting herb. Although traditionally tarragon pairs well with chicken and other poultry, it also works wonders with fish, especially oily fish, such as mackerel, trout and salmon. Or, try adding a tablespoon of chopped fresh tarragon to an uncooked fishcake mixture for an interesting, extra taste. Tarragon is also the ingredient used in hollandaise sauce to make it into a béarnaise sauce, which is traditionally served as part of the French classic, steak frites and béarnaise.

Because there are over 100 varieties of thyme that are all edible and each have their own character, you have the ultimate choice on which type of thyme to use in your recipes. I like lemon thyme as the citrus tones work beautifully with both sweet and savoury dishes, and it pairs wonderfully with chicken, duck, turkey, hake, cod, aubergines and cauliflowers. Add a teaspoon of chopped fresh lemon thyme to a standard shortbread biscuit dough for something different but utterly delicious, or poach apricots in a sugar syrup with fresh thyme for a lovely thyme-scented fruit dessert.

Kohlrabi

This rather unusual vegetable is a member of the Brassicaceae family and is a cultivar of the cabbage. Selected for its swollen stems, kohlrabi is not a fussy plant and can grow almost anywhere. It's easy to get confused and think that kohlrabi is a root vegetable, but it's not – kohlrabi has a shallow root and the edible part sits on top of the soil. They are two main types of kohlrabi – the more common green variety, and the purple variety that is slower growing, hence it is harder to find. Kohlrabi is a versatile vegetable with a crisp, crunchy texture and mild flavour and it can be eaten raw or cooked.

Try my recipe for **Kohlrabi Remoulade**, which is a delicious alternative to standard coleslaw. Serve the remoulade in a sandwich on granary bread with honey roast ham or mature Cheddar cheese, or serve it with pan-fried mackerel, grilled sardines or leftover cold roast chicken. For the remoulade, trim and peel 1 kohlrabi (80–100g unprepared weight), then coarsely grate it into a bowl. Add 1 tablespoon good-quality mayonnaise and 1 tablespoon wholegrain mustard and stir to mix, season to taste with sea salt and freshly cracked black pepper, then stir in a squeeze of fresh lime juice. Serve immediately (this is preferable) or cover and chill before serving (but serve within 1 hour of making). Serves 2 as an accompaniment.

Peas

Nothing beats freshly picked and shelled peas. Their natural sweetness and crispness makes them a fantastic seasonal treat, but they need to be eaten as soon as possible after harvesting. Even fresh peas in their pods that are only a week old will not taste nearly as good as when they are picked and eaten straightaway. This is because an enzyme in the peas soon causes deterioration and taints the taste, which eventually becomes bitter, eliminating the natural sweetness. Freshly shelled peas are delicious eaten either raw or cooked very quickly in a pan of rapidly boiling salted water. Frozen peas are available all year round and are the best substitute if you cannot find freshly-picked peas. I'm not much of an advocate for frozen foods, but there are a few ingredients that are excellent if frozen and peas are one of these. As the farmers harvest the peas, the peas get frozen very quickly to capture the freshness and prevent the enzymes from kicking in, hence frozen peas are a great nutritious and tasty vegetable to keep in your freezer.

I love classic recipes cooked with a slightly contemporary twist and this **Braised Gem Lettuce and Fresh Garden Peas**

Kohlrabi

Peas

dish is simplicity at its best. If it's cooked well, it is superb and will blow everyone away. Preheat the oven to 200°C/Gas Mark 6. Spread 80g softened unsalted butter over the bottom of a casserole (with a lid) and set aside. Wash and drain 2 baby Gem lettuces, then cut each one into quarters, cutting through just to the root to keep them together. Heat 1 tablespoon unsalted butter in a non-stick frying pan, then add the lettuces and cook over a high heat for 5–7 minutes or until golden all over. Season lightly with sea salt and freshly cracked black pepper, then transfer to the prepared buttered casserole and set aside. Return the same frying pan to the heat, add 1 tablespoon unsalted butter, 1 finely sliced large onion and 1 crushed clove garlic and sauté over a medium-high heat for 7–8 minutes or until golden brown. Add 100ml dry white wine and let it bubble, stirring and scraping the base of the pan with a wooden spoon to deglaze it. Cook over a high heat for 6–8 minutes or until the wine is reduced and becomes syrupy. Season lightly with salt and pepper, then spoon this mixture over the lettuces. Scatter over 300g (shelled weight) fresh garden peas, season lightly with salt and pepper, dot over 20g cold unsalted butter, then pour over 125ml white chicken stock. Place a piece of dampened non-stick baking paper directly on to the peas and lettuce, place the lid on top of the casserole and bake in the oven for 30 minutes or until the lettuces are soft and the liquid has thickened. Remove from the oven, remove the lid and paper lid and then scatter over 1 tablespoon combined shredded fresh mint and fresh basil. Serve immediately. Serves 2 as an accompaniment. Serve with roast chicken, baked haddock, pan-fried cod, roast lamb or poussins or pan-fried pork chops.

Strawberries

For many years, the British strawberry used to mark the welcome start of the summer season, but nowadays strawberries are also grown in polytunnels, hence an extended strawberry season in the UK. Sun-ripened strawberries bursting with fragrance and delicious flavour bring a fantastic splash of red colour to our summer dining tables. There are plenty of different strawberry varieties to choose from, Elsanta being the one that is most commonly grown and sold commercially. If you can, try less well-known varieties from your local Pick-Your-Own farm, as well as some greengrocers, farmers markets and larger supermarkets, or try growing your own strawberries at home, selecting more unusual varieties from your local nursery or garden centre. If you are lucky enough to find fraises des bois, better known as alpine strawberries, they are the ultimate when it comes to strawberries as they have a wonderful, exquisite flavour, but they do come at a price.

For a chutney with a difference, try my delicious **Strawberry, Lime and Almond Chutney**. Put 1 finely chopped large onion into a preserving pan, along with 200ml raspberry cider vinegar (see page 238), 200g caster sugar, 100ml cold water, 2 crushed cloves garlic, 1 teaspoon sea salt, 1 star anise, 4 toasted green cardamom pods, 4 cloves, 1 cinnamon stick, 60g peeled and grated fresh root ginger and 2 finely sliced large fresh red chillies. Cook over a medium heat, stirring until the sugar has dissolved, then increase the heat and bring the mixture to the boil, stirring. Boil vigorously over a high heat for about 10 minutes or until the syrup has thickened, then add 500g hulled and quartered fresh strawberries. Bring the chutney back to a gentle simmer and cook for a further 10 minutes or until the mixture is reduced to a thick consistency, and no excess liquid remains, stirring occasionally. Stir in 60g toasted flaked almonds and the finely grated zest and juice of 1 lime. Remove the pan from the heat and leave to cool for 10 minutes, then spoon the chutney into hot, sterilised jars. Cover with vinegar-proof lids and seal. Leave to cool, then label and store in a cool, dry cupboard. Store for at least 1 week before using. Unopened jars should keep well for up to 3 months. Once opened, store in the fridge and use within 1 week. Makes about 3 x 250g jars.

Strawberry, Lime and Almond Chutney

Roasted Aubergine Soup with Dry-roasted Almonds

Aubergines are funny vegetables and I think you either like them or loathe them. To cook aubergines in oil you need to make sure your pan is really hot and cook the aubergines in batches, keeping them moving to colour them evenly and cook them thoroughly. This will ensure that the aubergines don't absorb too much of the oil during cooking and then leave an unpleasant greasy mouthfeel. There is nothing worse than undercooked or greasy aubergines.

I got the inspiration for this lovely soup from a Middle Eastern dish called Imam Bayaldi that we used to make when I worked at a three-star Michelin restaurant in London. We served the rich and dark aubergine purée as a canapé in pretty little silver pots with slices of wafer-thin crispy ficelle (or toast, to you and me).

This recipe makes a generous amount of thick, smooth soup and even though I add no cream, the soup tastes rich and velvety. If you prefer a slightly thinner soup, you can thin it down with a little extra vegetable stock. I also like to garnish the soup with dry-roasted almonds and a swirl of natural yogurt.

Serves 6 as a starter or light lunch

2 large aubergines (250–350g each), cut into 2cm dice
table salt, for sprinkling, if needed
40g golden sultanas (or use regular sultanas if you wish)
1 bay leaf
100ml boiling water
3 tablespoons olive oil
1 red onion, sliced
1 clove garlic, crushed
1 teaspoon ras el hanout
½ teaspoon ground cumin
1 teaspoon clear honey
300g chopped fresh tomatoes
750ml vegetable stock
2 tablespoons flaked almonds
2 tablespoons natural yogurt
2 spring onions, sliced
sea salt and freshly cracked black pepper

If you choose to salt your aubergines, then do so (see Cook's Note). Put the diced aubergines into a colander and sprinkle with table salt, then leave them for 30–60 minutes. Rinse well and pat dry before sautéing them.

Meanwhile, put the golden sultanas and bay leaf in a bowl, pour over the boiling water and leave to soak for 15–20 minutes. Drain before use.

Heat 1 tablespoon olive oil in a large, non-stick frying pan and sauté half of the aubergines, with salt and pepper added, over a high heat for 10–12 minutes or until the aubergines are very dark in colour – not burnt but very well caramelised. Drain the aubergines in a colander. Cook the remaining aubergines the same way, adding another 1 tablespoon oil to the pan. Set aside.

Heat the remaining oil in the same pan, add the onion, garlic, ras el hanout and cumin and sauté over a high heat for 8–10 minutes or until the onion is golden brown. Stir in the honey and soaked (drained) sultanas and bay leaf.

Transfer the caramelised aubergines and onion mixture to a large saucepan and then add the tomatoes and stock. Bring the soup to a gentle simmer and then cook over a low heat, partly covered, for 25–30 minutes or until cooked and thickened. If you boil the soup too fast, the flavours will not develop and the liquid will evaporate, so a gentle simmer is perfect.

Remove and discard the bay leaf. Carefully transfer the soup to a blender and purée until smooth. Return to the pan and if the soup is a bit too thick for your liking, add a little more vegetable stock. Reheat gently, then taste and adjust the seasoning, if necessary.

Meanwhile, heat a small, non-stick frying pan over a medium heat, then dry-roast the flaked almonds in the hot pan for 1–2 minutes or until they have a golden tint. Remove from the heat.

Serve the hot soup in bowls. Garnish each portion with a swirl of natural yogurt, a sprinkling of spring onions and a scattering of the dry-roasted almonds.

Cook's Note

Should you salt aubergines before cooking, or not? I suppose that's the million-dollar question. Well, it works as follows: if you have young and very fresh aubergines like mine, that are harvested and cooked on the same day, then there is no need to salt. If they are a bit old, they might be bitter and will require salting. Aubergines are salted to draw out the bitterness. Remember not to over season your soup if you have chosen to salt beforehand. I didn't need to salt my aubergines for this recipe, so I added a generous amount of seasoning while sautéing them, to achieve the right depth of flavour.

Wild Boar and Lemon Thyme Popcorn

How much fun could you expect to have making popcorn? Well, in this case, a lot! This recipe might be slightly challenging but, hey, life is boring enough, so why not take a chance and have some fun? If you cannot find wild boar bacon, then I suggest using smoked pork bacon instead. The wild boar I use comes from a local Suffolk producer. Thyme is one of my favourite herbs and I like growing all the different types, because not only do they make pretty plants for the garden, but they are compatible with lots of different ingredients. For this recipe, I use lemon thyme, but if you cannot find this particular type, then ordinary thyme will do.

Make this recipe for a picnic or your local summer fete, or try serving it at a drinks party. It's perhaps a bit sophisticated for the little ones, but the grown-ups will love it.

Serves 6–8 as a snack

3 rashers wild boar back bacon
2 tablespoons chopped fresh lemon thyme
2 tablespoons sunflower oil
80g popcorn kernels
sea salt, to taste

Preheat the grill to medium. Place the bacon rashers on a baking tray (or on a rack in a grill pan) and grill for 7–9 minutes or until dry and very crisp, turning once or twice and checking the bacon regularly so that it does not burn. Remove from the grill, transfer the bacon to a wire rack and pat dry with kitchen paper, then leave to cool. Reserve the bacon dripping.

Once the bacon is cold, break it up into even-sized pieces. Using a food processor or blender, blend the cooled crisp bacon with the lemon thyme to make a fine crumb mixture. Set aside.

Heat the sunflower oil and reserved bacon dripping in a large saucepan over a medium heat, then add the popcorn kernels and place the lid on the pan. Shake the pan a couple of times and then once the popcorn starts to pop after about 7–9 minutes, turn the heat off and leave the saucepan on the hob, undisturbed, until you can no longer hear the corn popping.

Remove the lid, add the finely crumbed bacon mixture to the warm popcorn and mix well. Taste and add a little salt, if needed. Serve warm or cold.

Cook's Notes

This bacon-flavoured popcorn should be eaten on the same day it is made and kept in an airtight container once cool. I do not recommend that you keep it for any longer.

Use any bacon of your choice, but if you are going to use streaky bacon it would be best to double the number of rashers.

Chilled Pea Soup with Cheddar Cream and Soft-boiled Quail's Eggs

The season for peas is short, and preserving the flavour and colour of peas is very important when creating a dish such as this one. My top tip is to work as quickly as possible to capture and retain the freshness of the peas.

When fresh garden peas appear on market stalls and my home-grown peas are ready to be harvested, it's a wonderful reminder that the British summer is in full swing. Freshly picked peas taste sweeter and better than those that are even just a few days old. For this reason, frozen peas are as close as one can get to the real thing, unless you have your own kitchen garden. In fact, peas are very easy to grow as they do not need a lot of space and they are not prone to diseases.

I thoroughly enjoy a good chilled soup and this one is really packed with freshness and flavour.

Serves 4 as a starter or light lunch

For the Cheddar cream
400ml milk
150ml vegetable stock
50g unsalted butter
50g plain flour
40g extra mature Cheddar cheese, grated
60ml double cream
sea salt and freshly cracked black pepper

For the chilled pea soup
30g unsalted butter
1 large banana shallot, finely sliced
300g fresh garden peas (shelled weight)
a sprig of flowering fresh thyme, leaves only
50ml dry vermouth or dry white wine
300ml hot vegetable or white chicken stock
100ml double cream

To serve
4 tablespoons (shelled) fresh garden peas
2 quail's eggs
extra virgin olive oil, for drizzling
fresh pea tops and a selection of edible flowers (such as mizuna, nasturtium and thyme flowers)
finely grated fresh Parmesan cheese, for sprinkling

First, make the Cheddar cream. Bring the milk and stock to the boil in a saucepan, then remove from the heat. Melt the butter in a separate saucepan, stir in the flour and cook for 1 minute, stirring continuously, then season with salt and pepper. Keep the pan over a medium heat and gradually add the hot milk mixture, a ladleful or so at a time, stirring continuously, until all the milk mixture has been added and you have a smooth, thickened sauce. Cook over a medium heat for 6 minutes, stirring.

Remove from the heat, add the Cheddar cheese and cream and stir until smooth. Carefully transfer the mixture to a blender and blend until the sauce is really smooth. Pass the Cheddar cream through a fine sieve and then pour it into a cream whipper (see page 17 for more details on a cream whipper). Charge with 2 gas pellets, shake vigorously, then refrigerate for 2–3 hours so that the mixture thickens and chills completely.

Make the soup. Melt the butter in a large saucepan, add the shallot, then cover and sweat over a low heat for 7–8 minutes or until tender but not coloured. Add the peas, thyme leaves and salt and pepper and cook over a medium heat for a couple of minutes or so.

Increase the heat to high, then add the vermouth to the pan and let the liquid bubble, stirring and scraping the base of the pan with a wooden spoon to deglaze it. Boil rapidly over a high heat for 5–7 minutes or until the vermouth turns syrupy and coats the vegetables. Add the hot stock and cream, bring back to the boil and boil for about 2 minutes or until the peas are cooked and tender.

Carefully transfer the soup to a blender and purée until smooth. Quickly pass the soup through a fine sieve into a bowl set over ice. You want to chill the soup as quickly as possible to keep the bright green colour. Once cool, cover and chill in the fridge until you are ready to serve – you will need to chill the soup for at least 2 hours or until it is completely cold.

While the soup is chilling, prepare the peas and eggs for serving. Blanch the peas in a small pan of boiling salted water for about 2 minutes or until tender. Drain, refresh in iced water and drain again. Add the quail's eggs to a separate covered pan of boiling water and boil for 2½ minutes or until soft-boiled. Drain, refresh in cold water, then drain again and leave to cool completely. Peel the shells from the cold eggs, then halve them lengthways and season with salt and pepper.

To serve, lightly crush the blanched peas with a fork, season with salt and pepper and add a drop or two of olive oil. Divide the crushed peas between 4 chilled soup bowls, then carefully place a soft-boiled egg half on top of each portion, placing it slightly off centre. Pour the chilled soup around the egg halves. Shake the cream whipper vigorously and squirt some Cheddar cream next to each egg half (see Cook's Note). Garnish with the pea tops, flowers, Parmesan cheese and a few drops of olive oil. Serve.

Cook's Note

Any leftover Cheddar cream can be kept in the cream whipper in the fridge and used within 2 days. Serve with poached eggs and steamed asparagus spears for a tasty starter or light lunch.

A Cheeky Sandwich – Cod Cheeks with Fennel Slaw and Roasted Aubergine Chips

Cod cheeks are ideal bite-sized, boneless muscles that are very meaty indeed. They are also easy to use and as they are already small, they require very little preparation.

Mr. P loves fish finger sandwiches and not for love nor money will I let him purchase a certain well-known brand of pre-made frozen fish fingers, so this cheeky sandwich is just for Mr. P – isn't he a lucky bloke?!

For this recipe, the cod cheeks are coated in a batter and then deep-fried. Biting through the crisp batter into the soft, flaky fish inside makes these little gems rather delicious. It's a challenge for us to sell dishes such as this one as most people find the thought unappetizing, but perseverance and creative thinking has paid off and these cheeks are now a favourite choice on our British Larder menu.

Serves 4 as a lunch

For the roasted aubergine chips
2 large aubergines (250–350g each), trimmed
1 clove garlic, crushed
1 teaspoon ras el hanout
a sprig of fresh thyme, leaves only
3 tablespoons olive oil
sea salt and freshly cracked black pepper

For the fennel and kohlrabi slaw
1 fennel bulb, preferably with the tops (leaves)
1 kohlrabi (80–100g unprepared weight), trimmed and peeled
olive oil, for drizzling
finely grated zest and juice of 1 lemon

For the crispy battered cod cheeks
150g self-raising flour
40g cornflour
a pinch of sea salt and freshly cracked black pepper
1 egg yolk
250ml local real ale
2 egg whites
12 fresh cod's cheeks (480–720g total weight)
sunflower oil, for deep-frying

4 floury white baps, to serve

First, prepare the roasted aubergine chips. Preheat the oven to 200°C/Gas Mark 6. Cut the aubergines in half lengthways and scoop out and discard the soft seeds, leaving about a 1.5cm-thick layer of white flesh attached to the skin. Cut the prepared aubergine halves into long fingers, each about 5mm wide. In a large mixing bowl, mix together the aubergine fingers, garlic, ras el hanout, thyme leaves, olive oil and salt and pepper, tossing to coat the aubergines. Spread the aubergine fingers in a single layer on a baking tray and bake in the oven for about 15 minutes or until golden. Remove from the oven and keep hot.

Meanwhile, prepare the fennel and kohlrabi slaw. Cut the tops from the fennel and finely chop them. Using a mandolin, finely slice the fennel and kohlrabi, then mix with the fennel tops in a bowl. Season well with salt and pepper and then add olive oil, lemon zest and lemon juice to taste. Set aside.

In the meantime, make the batter for the cod's cheeks. In a bowl, mix together the flour, cornflour, salt and pepper, egg yolk and ale to form a smooth paste. In a separate bowl, whisk the egg whites until fluffy, stopping before they reach the soft peak stage. Fold the egg whites into the batter and then leave to stand for 5 minutes.

Prepare the cod's cheeks. Remove the skin from the cod's cheeks, then wash and pat them dry on kitchen paper.

Meanwhile, heat some sunflower oil in an electric deep-fat fryer or in a deep frying pan to a temperature of 160°C (or until a small piece of bread browns within 20 seconds in the hot oil). Once the oil is hot enough, dip the cod's cheeks in the batter and then deep-fry them (in two batches) in the hot oil for 3–4 minutes or until crisp and golden brown all over. Cooking time will depend on the size of the cheeks. Using a slotted spoon, remove and drain the deep-fried cod's cheeks on kitchen paper. Season with salt and serve immediately.

In the meantime, cut the 4 baps in half and toast both sides of each bap half. For each sandwich, place the bottom half of a toasted bap on to a serving plate and spoon some fennel and kohlrabi slaw on top. Arrange 3 crispy deep-fried cod's cheeks on top, then place the top half of the toasted bap on top. Repeat to make 4 'toasted' sandwiches. Serve the sandwiches with the warm roasted aubergine chips on the side.

Rare Roast Lamb Neck Fillets with Cucumber and Yogurt Salad and Homemade Pitta Pockets

Each season brings a variety of fun recipes and I particularly love eating and cooking dishes that include various elements and textures. You might find lamb neck fillets a strange choice for a quick-cook recipe, but as we are still at the beginning of the new British lamb season, the lamb neck fillets are lovely and tender and so are the perfect choice. Substitute the lamb neck fillets for pencil fillets, if you like (ask your local butcher for these, but they could be pricey and are fairly small).

Have you ever thought of making your own pitta bread? Well, now you can and here is the know-how. It's easy, fun and you can involve the whole family.

Serves 4 as a lunch

For the homemade pitta breads
500g strong white bread flour
15g fresh yeast or 7g dried yeast (do not use fast-action dried yeast)
1 teaspoon sea salt
2 tablespoons extra virgin olive oil, plus extra for brushing
300ml hand-hot (lukewarm) water

For the rare roast lamb neck fillets
4 lamb neck fillets (about 120g each)
2 tablespoons olive oil
finely grated zest and juice of 1 lemon
a pinch of ground sumac
sea salt and freshly cracked black pepper

For the cucumber yogurt salad
1 cucumber
1 small clove garlic, crushed
2 spring onions, chopped
a large handful of fresh mint leaves, shredded
finely grated zest and juice of 1 lemon
1 teaspoon chopped (drained) preserved lemons
150g natural yogurt or Greek-style natural yogurt

To serve and garnish
a large handful of seasonal salad leaves
sliced cucumber and chopped spring onions
a pinch or two of ground sumac

First, make the pitta breads. Place the flour in a large bowl, then rub in the fresh yeast until it resembles fine breadcrumbs (or, if you are using dried yeast, simply stir it into the flour). Add the salt, 2 tablespoons olive oil and the water and gradually work the liquid into the flour using a flexible plastic scraper, to form a soft dough.

Turn the dough on to a lightly floured work surface and knead for 7–8 minutes or until the dough becomes silky smooth and elastic. Shape the dough into a ball and place it in a lightly oiled bowl, then cover with a clean dry tea towel or cling film and leave the dough to prove (rise) in a warm place for 45–60 minutes or until it is doubled in size.

Lightly flour 2 baking trays and set aside. Turn the dough on to a lightly floured work surface and divide into 8 equal portions, then roll each portion into a ball. Use your fingertips to then gently flatten and stretch each ball of dough to an even thickness to make a flat, oval pitta shape (it doesn't matter if, by accident, you make a few holes in the dough as this will add to the character of the pitta breads!). Place the pitta breads on the prepared baking trays, leaving space between each one, then cover with clean dry tea towels and leave to prove in a warm place for 15–20 minutes or until doubled in size.

Prepare the lamb while the pitta breads are proving. Drizzle 1 tablespoon olive oil and a few drops of the lemon juice over the lamb neck fillets in a dish, then sprinkle over the lemon zest, sumac and salt and pepper and rub all the ingredients into the lamb. Leave the lamb to marinate in the fridge for 20 minutes before cooking.

Prepare the cucumber and yogurt salad while the lamb is marinating. Cut the cucumber in half lengthways and use a teaspoon to scoop out the seeds (discard the seeds), then slice the cucumber. Combine the cucumber and all the remaining salad ingredients in a serving bowl and season to taste with salt and pepper. Cover and chill in the fridge until you are ready to serve.

Meanwhile, to cook the pitta breads, preheat the oven to 220°C/Gas Mark 7. Heat a ridged griddle pan over a high heat until smoking hot (this will take 6–8 minutes), then gently lift the pitta breads on to the hot pan and griddle them for 1 minute on each side, so you can see the griddle marks on the pittas.

Transfer the pitta breads back to the baking trays and then bake in the oven for 5–7 minutes or until cooked, puffed up and starting to crisp (once cooked, the pitta breads will sound hollow when you tap them). Remove from the oven, brush each pitta bread with olive oil, then leave to cool slightly on a wire rack until needed.

Reduce the oven temperature to 200°C/ Gas Mark 6. To cook the lamb fillets, heat the remaining 1 tablespoon oil in a non-stick frying pan until hot, then add the marinated lamb fillets and cook over a high heat for 5–6 minutes or until golden brown and sealed all over. Transfer the lamb fillets to a roasting tin and roast in the oven for 5–8 minutes or until browned on the outside but still pink on the inside. Remove from the oven and let the lamb rest for 3 minutes.

To serve, cut each warm pitta bread in half and arrange some salad leaves on top. Slice the lamb fillets into slices and place on top of the salad, then garnish each portion with some sliced cucumber, chopped spring onions and a small pinch of sumac. Allow 2 filled pitta breads per portion. Spoon the cucumber yogurt salad into small bowls and serve alongside the pitta breads. Serve immediately.

Curried Lamb and Apricot Kebabs

The warmer weather in June often marks the beginning of the barbecue season in the UK. This recipe is my version of the South-African classic lamb dish called Sosaties, meaning lamb on a skewer (or kebabs). Traditionally, Sosaties are made with fatty shoulder and leg of lamb meat that is cubed and then marinated in a rich, thick, fruit-based curry marinade for up to 3 days. However, if you can't wait that long, marinate the meat overnight and hope for the best.

There is a predominantly Cape Malay influence in the history of the traditional cookery of Cape Town. Malay is the 'name' given to immigrants that came to South Africa from North Africa, Malaysia and anywhere in between. These immigrants made Cape Town their home and over the years, they gradually merged their different cooking styles, resulting in the classic Cape Malay cooking style and traditions as we know them today. Sosaties is one of those adapted Cape Malay-influenced dishes that has been passed on from generation to generation.

I always make a good-sized batch of the marinade, then put some in a sealed jar and keep it in the fridge (see Cook's Note). It forms the perfect base for my homemade curries, and a tablespoon stirred in with cooked chicken and crème fraîche, makes a lovely coronation chicken sandwich too!

You will need to start this recipe at least 2 days before you want to serve it.

Serves 6 as a main course

For the curry marinade

1 tablespoon coriander seeds
4 cloves
1 teaspoon turmeric
1 teaspoon garam masala
1 tablespoon mild Madras curry powder
1 clove garlic, crushed
40ml olive oil
2 large onions, chopped
3 sticks celery, chopped
1 bay leaf
3 tablespoons demerara sugar
2 fresh red chillies, chopped
175ml cider vinegar
2 tablespoons Worcestershire sauce
150g peach or mango chutney
150ml cold water
sea salt and freshly cracked black pepper

For the lamb kebabs

600g shoulder of lamb (boned weight)
200g Curry Marinade (see above)
12 large ready-to-eat dried apricots
12 bay leaves

First, make the marinade. Put the coriander seeds and cloves in a small pan and lightly toast over a low heat for 1½–2 minutes. Remove from the heat and then crush using a pestle and mortar, along with the ground spices, garlic, a small splash of olive oil and salt and pepper, mixing well.

Heat the remaining oil in a saucepan and add the onions and celery, together with the crushed spice mix, and sauté over a high heat for 7–8 minutes or until golden brown. Add the bay leaf, sugar and chillies and sauté for a further 2 minutes. Add the cider vinegar and Worcestershire sauce to the pan and let the liquid bubble, stirring and scraping the base of the pan with a wooden spoon to deglaze it. Boil rapidly over a high heat for 6–8 minutes or until the liquid has reduced and thickened to a syrup.

Add the chutney and water and bring to the boil. Reduce the heat to a gentle simmer, then cover and cook the marinade for about 30 minutes or until thickened and glossy, stirring occasionally to prevent the marinade from catching.

Remove from the heat and remove and discard the bay leaf. Use a stick blender to pulse-blend the marinade until it forms a spreadable paste – it's your choice if you want a smooth or a slightly coarse marinade. Transfer the marinade to a suitable container and let it cool, then cover and chill in the fridge for at least 24 hours before use, to let the flavours blend and develop (see Cook's Note).

Make the kebabs. Remove the excess fat and sinew from the lamb, then roughly cut the lamb into large cubes (I work on using about 6 pieces of lamb per skewer). Measure the quantity of marinade needed and then mix the diced lamb with the marinade in a bowl. Transfer the lamb and marinade to an airtight container and chill in the fridge for at least 1 day before cooking, or for up to 3 days for maximum taste.

Soak 6 bamboo skewers in cold water about 30 minutes before you are ready to assemble the kebabs. By now, your barbecue should be hot enough to use. Alternatively, preheat your griddle pan or grill.

For each kebab, skewer 2 pieces of marinated lamb with 1 dried apricot and a bay leaf, then skewer 2 more pieces of lamb, another dried apricot and another bay leaf, then finish with 2 more pieces of lamb. Repeat with the remaining pieces of marinated lamb, dried apricots and bay leaves to make the 6 kebabs.

Cook the kebabs on the barbecue over medium-hot coals or medium heat for 10–12 minutes or until the lamb is caramelised on the outside but is still pink on the inside, turning regularly. Alternatively, cook the kebabs on a hot, ridged griddle pan over a high heat for about 6 minutes on each side, turning regularly, or cook them under a preheated medium grill for about 6 minutes on each side, turning occasionally.

Remove the kebabs from the heat and leave to rest in a warm place for about 6 minutes before serving. Serve with potato salad or Sesame Toasted Basmati Rice and Broad Bean Salad (see page 222).

Cook's Note

Store the leftover marinade in a sealed, sterilised jar in the fridge and use within 1 month. Once opened, keep refrigerated and use within 1 week.

Garden Herb-marinated Half Roast Chicken with Kohlrabi, Fennel and Peanut Slaw

Cooking chicken on the bone helps to keep the delicate flesh moist and gives it that extra injection of flavour. With this recipe, the coconut, lime and coriander marinade also works its magic on the chicken.

As it's summer, you can either cook the chicken in the oven or you can barbecue it. If you decide to barbecue, I would definitely recommend that you part-cook the chicken in the oven first for at least 30 minutes, to ensure that the skin does not burn and that you are not left with raw meat on the bones. I tend to cook these half chickens in a fairly low oven; not only does this result in moist and tender meat, but it ensures that the marinade does not burn and become bitter. The marinade becomes sweet as it gently caramelises and the coconut toasts and becomes nutty.

This is a perfect holiday recipe for me and it reminds me of a relaxing lazy day in the warm sunshine, enjoying a lovely glass of chilled rosé wine, sitting under the parasol on the patio reading the newspaper. Bliss!

Serves 4 as a main course

For the half roast chicken

1 organic or free-range chicken (1.6–1.8kg)
a large bunch of fresh mixed garden herbs (such as tarragon, parsley, lemon thyme, coriander, chervil and mint), roughly chopped
2 cloves garlic, crushed
20g desiccated coconut
½ teaspoon turmeric
2 tablespoons sunflower oil
finely grated zest and juice of 2 limes
½ teaspoon madras curry powder
2 tablespoons clear honey
1 teaspoon fish sauce (nam pla)
1 tablespoon flaked almonds
sea salt and freshly cracked black pepper

For the sauce

2 tablespoons coconut cream
150ml natural yogurt
1 tablespoon chopped fresh mixed garden herbs (such as tarragon, parsley, lemon thyme, coriander, chervil and mint)
finely grated zest and juice of 1 lime
1 clove garlic, crushed

For the kohlrabi, fennel and peanut slaw

1 kohlrabi (80–100g unprepared weight), peeled and coarsely grated
1 fennel bulb, trimmed and finely sliced
¼ red cabbage, finely sliced or shredded
¼ white cabbage, finely sliced or shredded
100g beansprouts
50g fresh sprouting mung beans, plus extra to garnish
40g toasted peanuts, roughly chopped, plus extra to garnish
finely grated zest and juice of ½ lime
1 tablespoon sesame oil
1 teaspoon clear honey
1 tablespoon rice wine vinegar
1 teaspoon soy sauce

First, prepare the chicken. Wash the chicken and pat dry with kitchen paper. Cut the chicken in half through the breastbone. Flatten the two halves and remove the wing tips, then slash the thigh and legs with a sharp knife about 3 or 4 times. This will allow the meat to cook all the way through and let the marinade penetrate the flesh.

Mix all the remaining ingredients for the chicken together in a bowl (it doesn't matter if the almonds get crushed), seasoning the marinade mixture lightly with salt and pepper. Spread the marinade all over the chicken, rubbing it in well using your hands. Place the chicken in a dish and leave to marinate in the fridge for 1 hour before cooking.

Preheat the oven to 160°C/Gas Mark 3. Place the 2 marinated chicken halves on a baking tray lined with non-stick baking paper. Roast the chicken in the oven for about 1¼ hours or until the chicken is cooked throughout and the skin is crispy and golden brown (slow cooking will ensure moist chicken and a delicious, crispy skin).

While the chicken is roasting, prepare the sauce. Mix all the sauce ingredients together in a bowl and season with salt and pepper. Cover and chill in the fridge for 30 minutes before serving.

Meanwhile, prepare the slaw. In a mixing bowl, mix all the ingredients for the slaw together and season with salt and pepper to taste. Cover and chill in the fridge until you are ready to serve.

Once the chicken is ready, remove it from the oven and leave to rest in a warm place for about 10 minutes.

To serve, slice the chicken, then arrange it on serving plates with the kohlrabi, fennel and peanut slaw and serve the sauce on the side. Garnish with extra sprouting mung beans and chopped peanuts and serve immediately.

Aubergine, Goat's Cheese and Tomato Bake

After successfully growing my own aubergines in a sheltered sunny spot on my patio, without a cold frame or fleece to protect it from potential frosty nights, I felt obliged to cook something special with these wonderful home-grown vegetables. It's a great feeling of satisfaction to achieve something as good as growing your own vegetables. I try growing as many different fruit, vegetables and herbs as I possibly can, concentrating on the ones I like. After having some successes and some failures, I have a newfound respect for farmers, growers and allotment keepers, as it takes time, attention and a lot of patience to grow your own, with no guarantee of a successful harvest at the end!

The tomato sauce in this recipe is also made using home-grown tomatoes, but if you don't grow your own, during the peak season, fresh ripe tomatoes should be in plentiful supply at a good price at local farmers' markets.

This recipe is based on a classic Italian recipe called Aubergine Parmigiana, which means aubergines baked in a tomato sauce with cheese. For me, tomato sauce and melted cheese is the ultimate comfort food combination. You can make this recipe in individual serving pots or bake it in one larger dish. Serve as a main course with a seasonal side salad.

Serves 4 as a main course

600ml Tomato Sauce For Keeps (see page 242)
1 cinnamon stick
2 star anise
2 aubergines (250–350g each), trimmed
8 large field mushrooms, stalks removed
4 tablespoons olive oil
sunflower oil, for frying
4 large sprigs of fresh basil, leaves only
8 large leaves of cavolo nero (black cabbage), shredded
320g mild soft goat's cheese, crumbled
2 thick slices sourdough bread or wholegrain bread, crusts removed and bread ripped into small pieces to make coarse breadcrumbs
200g grated hard cow's milk cheese (I like to use a local cheese called Shipcord, but you can find your own suitable cheese or fresh Parmesan cheese will also do)
2 sprigs of fresh oregano, leaves only
sea salt and freshly cracked black pepper

Lightly grease 4 individual round ovenproof serving dishes (each about 10 x 5cm), or a large ovenproof dish (about 25 x 18cm), then place the dishes (or dish) on a baking tray and set aside.

Put the tomato sauce into a large saucepan with the cinnamon stick and star anise and bring to the boil over a high heat, then reduce the heat, cover and simmer for 8 minutes, stirring occasionally to prevent it from catching. Remove from the heat and set aside to infuse while preparing the aubergines and mushrooms.

Preheat the oven to 200°C/Gas Mark 6. Heat a griddle pan over a high heat for 6–8 minutes or until very hot. Slice the aubergines widthways into 5mm-thick slices, then lay them and the field mushrooms in a single layer on 2 baking trays, season on both sides with salt and pepper and then brush them with the olive oil. Griddle the aubergines and mushrooms in batches on the griddle pan for 3–4 minutes on each side or until dark griddle marks appear, then return them to the baking trays (you will probably need to griddle the vegetables in 3 or 4 batches, depending on the size of your griddle pan). Bake the griddled aubergines and mushrooms in the oven for about 15 minutes or until cooked and golden brown. Remove from the oven and set aside. Reduce the oven temperature to 180°C/Gas Mark 4.

Meanwhile, pour some sunflower oil, about 1cm deep, into a small saucepan and heat gently over a medium heat for 6–7 minutes or until hot (the oil is hot enough when a small piece of bread browns within 30 seconds in the hot oil). Carefully add 12 of the basil leaves to the hot oil and fry for 30–40 seconds or until crispy on both sides and bright green, stirring gently. Using a slotted spoon, remove and drain the fried basil leaves on kitchen paper, then season with salt and pepper and leave to cool.

Blanch the cavolo nero in a pan of boiling salted water for 2 minutes or until just softened, then drain. Remove and discard the cinnamon stick and star anise from the tomato sauce.

To assemble the bake, either in the individual dishes or in the larger dish, using half of the ingredients, start with a layer of the tomato sauce, followed by a layer of aubergines, top this with some crumbled goat's cheese, coarse breadcrumbs, cavolo nero, mushrooms and grated hard cheese, then top this with the remaining fresh basil leaves and the oregano and season with black pepper. Repeat the layers with all the remaining ingredients, finishing the second series of layers with some aubergine slices on top, then sprinkle over the remaining grated hard cheese. You will need to push the ingredients down in the dish(es) to ensure they all fit in (if you don't pack it all in well, then once cooked, the ingredients will sink considerably and your dishes will be half empty).

Bake in the oven for 30–35 minutes for the individual dishes, or for 40–45 minutes for the larger dish or until the top is golden and crisp. Remove from the oven and leave to rest for 5 minutes before serving. Garnish with the crispy fried basil leaves and serve with a seasonal side salad.

Sesame Toasted Basmati Rice and Broad Bean Salad

This recipe is another one that simply makes me smile. As with peas, I love broad beans and they are just as easy to grow. I do have a complete obsession with having to shell broad beans and I'm not talking about taking them out of their outer pods, I'm referring to double-podding them or popping them out of their outer grey skins, revealing the tender, bright green beans inside. You might think this is cheffy nonsense, but I encourage you to try it and to experience the difference in taste.

For this recipe, I'm cooking the rice in a slightly unusual way, but trust me, it's deliberate and the results are delicious! First, I toast half of the basmati rice in toasted sesame oil in a saucepan until the rice is dark brown and looks nearly burnt, then the remaining rice and water are added to the pan and cooked until tender.

This dish is lovely eaten hot or cold. It's one of those dishes that tastes even better the following day, so it's a good idea to make a little extra and keep it chilled in the fridge.

Serves 6 as a side dish

2 tablespoons toasted sesame oil (make sure you use toasted sesame oil as some brands of sesame oil are not toasted and do not have the flavour you are looking for)
200g white basmati rice
650ml cold water
1 tablespoon olive oil
100g chestnut mushrooms, sliced
100g leeks, washed and sliced
100g celery, diced
100g broad beans (shelled weight)
2 spring onions, sliced
1 tablespoon golden linseeds, toasted
1 tablespoon sesame seeds, toasted
sea salt and freshly cracked black pepper

Heat the sesame oil in a large saucepan over a medium heat until hot (don't use too high a heat level as the sesame oil will burn easily). Add half of the dry basmati rice and salt and pepper to the pan and cook over a medium heat for 8–10 minutes or until the rice is deep golden brown and toasted, stirring continuously as the rice will catch and burn easily.

Once the rice is toasted, add the rest of the rice and the water to the pan, then cover and bring to the boil. Reduce the heat and simmer for 7 minutes, then remove from the heat and leave the rice to rest in the covered pan for about 20 minutes or until all the water has been absorbed. Holding the lid firmly in place, give the saucepan a good shake to fluff up the rice.

Heat the olive oil in a non-stick frying pan and sauté the mushrooms, leeks and celery over a high heat for 5–6 minutes or until the mushrooms are golden. Season to taste with salt and pepper, then remove from the heat.

Meanwhile, cook the broad beans in a pan of boiling salted water for a couple of minutes, then drain, refresh in iced water and drain again. Pop the tender, bright green beans out of their outer grey skins by squeezing gently. Discard the outer grey skins and reserve the inner bright green beans.

If you are serving the dish hot, add the hot sautéed mushroom mixture, spring onions and peeled broad beans to the hot fluffy toasted rice, adjust the seasoning to taste, and then sprinkle the golden linseeds and sesame seeds over the salad. Serve immediately.

Alternatively, if you wish to serve the dish cold, let the cooked rice cool completely before you add the rest of the ingredients (let the sautéed mushroom mixture cool too before adding this to the cold rice), then chill in the fridge until you are ready to serve.

Strawberry Arctic Roll

I love strawberries and everything about them – their colour, fragrance and flavour. When I close my eyes and smell a sun-ripened strawberry, it brings back memories of my childhood and visits to the PYO farm with my family. My dad especially used to love eating strawberries, with a sprinkling of sugar and lots of sweetened whipped cream.

Creating recipes and dishes to serve at the British Larder is something we take seriously and I try to put as much thought into it as possible and to consider our ethos and what we stand for. Cooking for us is also all about food that tastes fantastic, makes us smile and stimulates conversation (and often some great memories too), not only for the staff but also for the customers. This recipe is dedicated to two of our regular customers – Gloria and Dennis Lee. When I first served this arctic roll for Gloria, the look of sheer joy on her face is imprinted on my mind. I shall never forget that moment because this recipe obviously brought back many happy memories to Gloria – she didn't have to say anything – her face said it all!

This recipe is a perfect way to use flavourful British strawberries and the added beauty of this fantastic retro dessert is that everything can be made in advance – up to 3 days in advance, if you like – making it a perfect dessert for either casual dining or for a special occasion.

You will need to start this recipe at least one day before you want to serve it.

Serves 8

For the strawberry ice cream
250ml fresh strawberry purée (see Cook's Note)
150ml double cream
75ml milk
70g caster sugar
150g fresh strawberries, hulled and quartered

For the strawberry jam
125g fresh strawberries, hulled and quartered
125g jam sugar (see page 16)
juice of ½ lemon

For the sponge
3 eggs
50g caster sugar, plus extra for sprinkling
40g plain flour, sifted twice
finely grated zest of 1 lemon

To serve and decorate
8 small thimbles filled with double cream
hulled fresh strawberries

First, make the strawberry ice cream. Place the strawberry purée, cream, milk and sugar in a bowl and whisk together until well mixed. Cover and leave to rest in the fridge for 2 hours. Pour the mixture into an ice-cream maker and churn until frozen (following the manufacturer's instructions for your particular model). Alternatively, pour the chilled mixture into a shallow, freezer proof container, cover with a lid and freeze until firm, whisking the mixture 3 or 4 times during freezing (every hour or so) to break down the ice crystals and ensure an even-textured result.

If you have made the ice cream by hand, remove it from the freezer about 10 minutes or so before using in this next stage to allow it to soften a little (you won't need to do this if you have made the ice cream using an ice-cream maker, as it will be soft enough already). Lay 4 pieces of cling film on a clean, cold work surface. Spoon a quarter of the ice cream on to each piece of cling film in a straight line, then arrange a row of strawberry quarters on top of each portion of ice cream. Roll up each portion of ice cream in the cling film, enclosing the strawberries inside each roll of ice cream, to make 4 sausage shapes or logs, each about 10cm long and 4cm in diameter. Place the ice cream logs in the freezer overnight to set.

Meanwhile, make the strawberry jam. Place the strawberries in a heavy-based saucepan, sprinkle over the sugar and then the lemon juice and leave to stand for 30 minutes.

Cook the strawberry mixture over a low heat, stirring to dissolve the sugar, then increase the heat and bring the mixture to the boil. Boil rapidly for 10–12 minutes or until the jam reaches a temperature of 105°C (setting point), stirring every now and then to prevent it from catching and skimming off any scum from the surface. If you don't have a jam thermometer, check to see if setting point has been reached by spooning a little of the jam on to a chilled small plate. Push a finger across the jam; if the surface wrinkles and it is beginning to set, it has reached setting point. If not, boil it for a further 5 minutes or so and test again. Pour the jam into a heatproof bowl and leave to cool completely. Once cool, cover and refrigerate.

The following day, prepare the sponge and finish the arctic rolls. For the sponge, preheat the oven the 190°C/Gas Mark 5 and line a large baking tray (about 36 x 28cm) with non-stick baking paper. Put the eggs and 50g caster sugar in a bowl and, using a hand-held electric mixer, whisk together until pale, thick and doubled in volume – this will take 8–10 minutes. Gently fold in the flour and lemon zest until well incorporated.

Using a palette knife, spread half of the sponge mixture over the whole sheet of prepared baking paper to about 5mm thickness. Bake in the oven for 5–6 minutes or until pale golden and evenly risen. Meanwhile, sprinkle a second sheet of non-stick baking paper with caster sugar. Remove the baked sponge from the oven and invert it on to the sheet of sugar-dusted baking paper. Roll up the sponge from a short side (rolling the paper up inside) like a Swiss roll, then place, seam-side down, on a wire rack and leave to cool completely. Repeat with the remaining sponge mixture and fresh non-stick baking paper to make a total of 2 rolls of sugar-dusted cooked sponge cake.

To assemble the arctic rolls, unroll the sponge cakes and discard the paper. Cut each sponge in half widthways. For each arctic roll, spread some of the strawberry jam (reserving a little for serving) on the pale (non sugar-dusted) side of a piece of sponge, unwrap a strawberry ice cream log (discard the cling film) and place the log along one edge of the sponge, then roll the sponge up tightly, enclosing the ice cream log in the sponge. Trim and neaten the sponge where the two edges meet. Wrap the arctic roll in fresh cling film and return to the freezer for about 4 hours or until set. Repeat the process with the remaining pieces of sponge cake, strawberry jam and ice cream logs to make 4 arctic rolls.

To serve, slice each arctic roll in half widthways using a warm, sharp knife to cut through the frozen ice cream logs. Spread (or swipe) some of the reserved strawberry jam on each serving plate, arrange a piece of arctic roll on top and serve each portion with a small thimble of cream and some strawberries alongside to decorate.

Cook's Note

Make your own strawberry purée by blending 500g over-ripe hulled strawberries in a blender until smooth. Pass the purée through a fine sieve and measure the 250ml required for this recipe. If you have any leftover strawberry purée, keep it in an airtight container in the fridge and use within 3 days. Serve the purée as a sauce or coulis to accompany other desserts such as chilled cheesecake or mixed fresh berries, or serve it for breakfast with natural yogurt, fruit or muesli and toasted flaked almonds.

Chocolate Fudge Cakes with Cherries in Red Wine

Cherries, red wine and chocolate are all favourite foods of mine, and served separately or together, they are fantastic ingredients, providing they are all good quality. I recommend using dark bitter chocolate with either 85% or 70% cocoa solids for this recipe – the darker and more bitter the chocolate, the better.

I bake the chocolate fudge cakes in small individual cake moulds as they are rich and are best served in small portions. The cakes are equally delicious served warm or cold, but if served warm, the centres will be wonderfully soft, like fondant. I then finish off these sumptuous desserts with a small quenelle (spoonful) of chocolate ganache and a spoonful of British cherries in red wine alongside. Pure chocolate indulgence and deliciousness at its best!

I normally make the ganache a day in advance to ensure that it sets completely. The cherries in red wine can also be made a day in advance.

Serves 6

For the chocolate ganache
200ml double cream
100g dark bitter chocolate (85% cocoa solids), roughly chopped

For the cherries in red wine
50ml red wine
50g caster sugar
½ vanilla pod, split in half lengthways and seeds scraped out
200g fresh cherries, halved and stoned

For the chocolate fudge cakes
25g cocoa powder, plus extra for dusting
150g unsalted butter
150g dark bitter chocolate (85% cocoa solids), roughly chopped
2 eggs
200g caster sugar
75g plain flour
a pinch of sea salt

First, make the ganache. This can be done a day in advance and kept refrigerated until needed. Pour the cream into a small saucepan and bring to the boil, then remove from the heat and add the chocolate, stirring continuously until the chocolate has completely melted. Pour the smooth chocolate ganache into a small bowl and leave to cool completely, then cover and refrigerate for 4–6 hours or until completely set.

Prepare the cherries in red wine (it's best to make these a day in advance too). Put the wine, sugar and vanilla seeds into a small saucepan and bring to the boil over a low heat, then simmer for 4–5 minutes or until the mixture is reduced by half and becomes thickened and syrupy. Pour the hot syrup over the prepared cherries in a dish and set aside at room temperature for 1 hour. If you are making these a day in advance, let them cool, then cover and refrigerate until ready to serve (see Cook's Note).

For the chocolate fudge cakes, preheat the oven to 180°C/Gas Mark 4. Grease six individual 8 x 3cm round cake moulds or tins and dust them with cocoa powder. Melt the butter in a small saucepan, then remove from the heat, add the chocolate and stir until the chocolate is completely melted. Set aside to cool for 10 minutes.

Put the eggs and sugar into the bowl of an electric stand mixer and whisk together for 7–8 minutes or until pale, thick and fluffy. With the mixer running on a low speed, add the cooled melted butter and chocolate mixture and whisk for 2 minutes. Sift the flour, 25g cocoa powder and the salt together. Gently fold the sifted flour mixture into the egg and chocolate mixture until well incorporated.

Spoon the cake mixture into the prepared moulds, dividing it evenly, then place the moulds on a baking tray. Bake in the oven for 10–12 minutes or until the cakes are just cooked – I like to ensure they have a moist fudgy centre. The cakes will rise during cooking, but once you remove them from the oven they will sink slightly. If they are very gooey and undercooked they might even collapse with a hole in the centre, but this is not a problem as I like to serve mine warm. Remove from the oven, transfer to a wire rack and leave the cakes to cool slightly in the moulds before turning them out.

To serve, carefully turn each warm cake out on to a serving plate. Place a spoonful of the cherries on top of each cake, place a small quenelle (spoonful) of the chocolate ganache on top of the cherries and drizzle with a little of the red wine syrup. Serve immediately.

Cook's Note
You can make a large jarful of the cherries in red wine, if you like, and keep them in the fridge. Simply increase the quantities of the ingredients used and follow the recipe as directed (you may need to increase the cooking time a little when reducing the liquid to a thick syrup). Spoon the hot cherry mixture into a sterilised jar, then cover, seal and cool. Store the jar of cherries in the fridge and use within 1 week. Serve the cherries in red wine with crème fraîche and shortbread biscuits for an easy dessert, or serve with freshly made pancakes and mascarpone for a tempting brunch or dessert.

Goat's Milk Puddings with Cherry Sherbet-dusted Doughnuts

I have a slight love affair with cherries and they are one of my favourite summer fruits. This recipe uses cherries in three ways – raw in a superb, fresh-tasting salad, cooked to create a delicious and flavourful compôte, and dried and used to make a fizzy sherbet to coat the hot, crisp doughnuts.

All the cherry flavours work incredibly well together when served with this very light, softly set goat's milk pudding, which is best served in small glasses. The goat's milk pudding has its own unique and natural fresh taste and is almost jelly-like in texture. If you make the goat's milk puddings and want to turn them out to serve, remember to add a little more gelatine to ensure that they do not collapse. This recipe is for a soft set pudding that is served in glasses rather than being turned out.

If cherries are not available and you really fancy making this recipe, you can use other fresh berries and seasonal stone fruits such as blueberries, blackberries, apricots or plums instead.

The goat's milk puddings are best made the day before you want to serve them as they need to chill and set in the fridge for several hours before serving. You will also need to dry the cherries for the cherry sherbet sugar the day before.

Serves 6

For the goat's milk puddings
2½ leaves of gelatine
275ml double cream
275ml goat's milk (see Cook's Notes)
70g caster sugar
1 vanilla pod, split in half lengthways and seeds scraped out (reserve the pod)

For the cherry sherbet sugar
200g fresh cherries, halved and stoned (see Cook's Notes)
¼ teaspoon citric acid (see Cook's Notes)
1 teaspoon bicarbonate of soda
120g caster sugar

For the bite-sized doughnuts
60g strong white bread flour
190g plain flour
15g fresh yeast or 7g dried yeast (do not use fast-action dried yeast)
100ml goat's milk
30g unsalted butter
40g caster sugar
1 teaspoon table salt
2 egg yolks
sunflower oil, for deep-frying

For the cherry compôte
200g fresh cherries, stoned
180g caster sugar
juice of ½ lemon

For the cherry salad
100g fresh cherries, stoned
finely grated zest of 1 lemon

Make the goat's milk puddings (I suggest making these the day before you want to serve them). Select 6 small serving glasses and place them in the fridge to chill. Soak the gelatine in cold water until it has softened.

Place the cream, milk, sugar and vanilla seeds and pod in a saucepan and bring just to the boil, then remove from the heat and leave to infuse for 6 minutes. Squeeze the gelatine gently to remove the excess water, then add the gelatine to the warm cream mixture and stir until dissolved. Pass the mixture through a fine sieve into a bowl and leave to cool for 10 minutes, then pour it into the chilled glasses. Return the glasses to the fridge and leave to set for a minimum of 6 hours.

For the cherry sherbet sugar, drying the cherries can take up to 6 hours. Preheat the oven to 110°C/Gas Mark ¼. Lay the cherries out in a single layer on a baking tray lined with non-stick baking paper and place in the oven for 3 hours. See if the cherries are dry enough after this time and if not, continue drying them in the oven until they are completely dry and shrivelled – this can take up to 6 hours and it all depends on the size and sweetness of the cherries.

Remove from the oven and let the cherries cool completely at room temperature. Once cold, put the dried cherries, citric acid and bicarbonate of soda into a food processor and process to a fine powder. Stir this powder into the sugar in a bowl (or airtight container), then cover and keep until you are ready to cook the doughnuts.

To make the doughnuts, put both flours in a bowl, then rub in the fresh yeast until it resembles fine breadcrumbs (or, if you are using dried yeast, simply stir it into the flours). Place the milk, butter, sugar and salt in a saucepan and heat together until the butter has melted, then remove from the heat and cool the mixture to blood temperature. Mix the egg yolks into the milk mixture. Make a well in the centre of the dry ingredients, then pour in the warm milk mixture and mix with a palette knife to form a soft dough.

Turn the dough on to a lightly floured work surface and knead for about 5 minutes or until the dough becomes silky smooth and elastic. Shape the dough into a ball and place it in a lightly oiled bowl, then cover with a clean dry tea towel or cling film and leave the dough to prove (rise) in a warm place for about 1 hour or until it is doubled in size.

Meanwhile, prepare the cherry compôte. Place the cherries and sugar in a small, heavy-based saucepan and set aside for 30 minutes.

Gently heat the cherry mixture over a medium heat and bring to the boil, stirring to dissolve the sugar, then increase the heat and boil rapidly for 10–12 minutes or until the mixture reaches a temperature of 102°C, skimming off any scum from the surface. If you don't have a thermometer, to test if the mixture is ready, place a small plate in the freezer to chill, then spoon a few drops of the compôte on to the cold plate and run your finger through it – it should be thickened, not runny. Remove the pan from the heat, stir in the lemon juice, then transfer the compôte to a bowl and set aside to cool.

Shape the proved doughnut dough. Divide the dough into 20–25 portions and roll each portion into a smooth, walnut-sized ball. Place the balls of dough on a shallow plastic tray or baking tray, cover with a clean dry tea towel and leave to prove in a warm place for 10–15 minutes or until doubled in size.

Meanwhile, prepare the cherry salad. Cut the cherries into quarters and place them in a bowl, then stir in the lemon zest. Set aside until you are ready to serve.

To cook the doughnuts, heat some sunflower oil in an electric deep-fat fryer or in a deep frying pan to a temperature of 160°C (or until a small piece of bread browns within 20 seconds in the hot oil). Deep-fry the balls of dough in the hot oil (do this in about 4 batches) for 2–3 minutes or until they are puffed up, golden brown and crisp.

Using a slotted spoon, remove and drain the deep-fried doughnuts on kitchen paper, then roll each one in the cherry sherbet sugar and serve immediately following the instructions below.

To serve, place a glass of goat's milk pudding on each serving plate and spoon some of the cherry compôte and cherry salad on top or alongside. Thread a doughnut on to each of 6 wooden cocktail sticks, then balance a threaded doughnut over each pudding and serve immediately. The rest of the doughnuts in a bowl in the centre of the table for your guests to help themselves to extra, if they like. Otherwise, serve the leftover doughnuts another time (see Cook's Notes).

Cook's Notes

Goat's milk is much easier to digest than cow's milk and it has a unique, natural fresh and slightly acidic taste – you will be pleasantly surprised as it does not taste goaty at all and it's nothing like any goat's cheese I have ever tasted being mellow and light. There are some wonderful goat's milk and cheese producers around the British Isles, and with many supermarkets and delis selling goat's milk, it's now much more readily available.

For the cherry sherbet sugar, instead of drying your own cherries, you can use freeze-dried cherries instead. They are often found in good health food shops and you will need about 25g freeze-dried cherries for this recipe.

Citric acid is used to make recipes such as elderflower cordial. See page 167 for more information on where to buy citric acid.

Once deep-fried and cooled, any leftover doughnuts will keep in an airtight container in a cool, dry cupboard for up to 2 days.

The British Larder | *July*

The month of July leads the British summer to its peak with soft fruits, berries and stone fruits coming into their own. Gooseberries, blueberries and the different varieties of currants are at their best during July.

From the ocean, the warmer waters bring plenty of sardines, mackerel and herrings, along with the season's best delicacies, such as lobsters and langoustines. Freshwater crayfish are also to be found in rivers and streams across the country. Wild edible seashore plants such as sea purslane and samphire (also known as sea asparagus) can also be found.

Artichokes

Lettuces of all varieties, along with courgettes and beetroot are plentiful and at their best. The herb garden is also doing well at this time of the year, and if you remembered to plant the herbs during April and May, then they should be thriving now and many will be in bloom. Fresh thyme and rosemary flowers taste exceptionally good, as do chive and borage flowers.

Green walnuts are ready to be harvested towards the end of July, and if you fancy a labour of love, then pickling your own walnuts is not an easy task but it's definitely a rewarding one.

British honey is also at its very best now as the bees are hard at work and have plenty of flowering fruits and plants to collect their nectar from. The most enjoyable sight is to watch them working away and pollinating the flowers that will produce fruits for us to enjoy later on in the season.

Season's best during July...

Apricots, Artichokes, Aubergines, Beetroot, Blackberries, Black Cabbage (Cavolo Nero), Blackcurrants, Blueberries, Borage Flowers, Broad Beans, Broccoli, Carrots, Cherries, Chives and Chive Flowers, Cod, Courgettes, Crab, Crab Apples, Crayfish (freshwater), Cucumbers, Dover Sole, Fennel, Garlic (new season), Gooseberries, Green Beans, Greengages, Haddock, Halibut, Herring, Kohlrabi, Lamb, Langoustines, Lettuce, Lobster, Loganberries, Mackerel, Mint, Mulberries, Nasturtium Flowers, New Potatoes, Onions, Oregano, Parsley, Peaches, Peas, Peppers, Plaice, Pollack, Potatoes (main crop), Prawns, Rabbit, Radishes, Raspberries, Redcurrants, Rocket, Rosemary, Runner Beans, Sage, Salad/Spring Onions, Salmon, Samphire, Sardines, Scallops, Sea Bass, Sea Beet, Sea Plantain, Sea Purslane, Sea Trout, Sorrel, Strawberries, Swiss Chard, Tarragon, Thyme, Tomatoes, Walnuts (green), Watercress, Whelks, Whitebait, Woodpigeon.

My culinary rituals for July...

Summer is coming to its peak and Pick-Your-Own farms are bustling with happy customers foraging for the best produce. I'm particularly looking out for gooseberries, blueberries, raspberries and all the currant varieties. Walking the dogs by the coast can also turn into a lucrative foraging trip, searching for fresh sea purslane and samphire. For a tasty starter or light lunch for 2, why not try my recipe for **Seashore Extravaganza** (see page 240)?

Making fruit cordials, jams, preserves and pickles is the order of the day this month. It's time to harvest tomatoes and if you find boxes of inexpensive over-ripe tomatoes for sale, buy them and use the glut to make some of my tasty tomato recipes, including chutney, semi-dried tomatoes and fresh tomato sauce, all of which can be stored and enjoyed during the cooler months to come.

Make the most of all the fresh, seasonal produce on offer during July and try my preserving recipes for **Star Anise and Cinnamon-Pickled Beetroot** (see page 234), **Tomato, Ginger and Sultana Chutney** (see page 242) or **Mulberry Jam** (see page 238).

Enjoy al fresco dining this month and explore different ways of cooking, including barbecuing, grilling and quick-cook recipes. For some tempting recipes to eat outdoors, try **Courgette-Wrapped Chicken Skewers** (Spiedini Toscana) (see page 253) or **Picnic in a Jar** (see page 256).

Finally, if your sweet tooth needs some satisfying, try my delicious **Chocolate and Raspberry Meringue Sandwich Cookies** (see page 262) or **Gooseberry Flapjacks** (see page 236).

British Larder Heroes

Artichokes

Globe artichokes and baby artichokes (small immature globe artichokes with the tips of the bracts cut off, otherwise known as artichoke hearts) not only provide us with a delicious ingredient in the culinary world, they are also beautiful structural plants in gardens or in a flower arrangement. They are more difficult to grow than Jerusalem artichokes (though they are not related at all) as they require a lot of patience. The plants do not normally bear any fruits worthy of culinary use in the first year, but in the second year you should get a good supply of quality artichokes. They are also usually in plentiful supply during the summer months growing wild along the coastlines of Devon and Cornwall. Artichokes thrive in soil with a high salt content and it's thought that seaweed is the best fertiliser for these plants. Globe and baby artichokes (both grown on the same plant) are the fruits of plants of the thistle family, thought to be native to North Africa, South Asia and the Mediterranean. The cultivated artichoke is a descendant of a wild cardoon. The word 'artichoke' is used as the name of the fruits for three very different plants, but they are no relation to each other at all – as well as the globe artichoke, the two other types are Jerusalem artichokes and French crosnes (or Chinese artichokes), both of which are tubers.

How to Prepare Globe or Baby Artichokes
Preparing artichokes is a time-consuming but ultimately rewarding activity. It has tested my patience as a chef over the years but, intriguingly, it's one of the most satisfying and gratifying jobs to do. Bizarrely, I cannot put my finger on it as it's hard work and if you're not careful the sharp spikes at the tops of the leaves can easily stab you, and yes, you end up with stained, sticky hands. I do not really like wearing gloves but for this task I highly recommend that you do! Be organised and prepare as much as possible in advance before you make the first cut. Artichokes oxidize (discolour) as soon as you cut into the flesh and therefore the artichokes should be dipped in a solution of ice-cold water and lemon juice or white wine vinegar (or vitamin C powder) to prevent discolouration. Therefore, have ready a large bowlful of acidulated ice-cold water to submerge the prepared artichokes in while you finish the rest. To prepare artichoke bottoms or hearts for cooking, using a serrated knife, for each artichoke, cut off most of the stem leaving about a 5cm length in place if you are preparing baby artichokes (the stems at this stage are still tender and edible). Alternatively, cut off the stalk flush with the base if preparing larger, fully grown artichokes. Remove the tough outer leaves by pulling them off with your fingers, then once you can see the base, use the knife to trim it further into a round shape following the artichoke's natural shape. Use a paring knife to neaten the bottom, trimming off all the remaining leaves, following the natural curves and trimming the base so that it sits flat. Cut off the top of the artichoke to reveal the flowery bits (hairy fibres), and if you are cutting the artichoke in half for cooking (or leaving it

whole), scoop out the choke with a small spoon, taking care to remove all of the hairy fibres (if serving whole, you can scoop out the hairy 'choke' after cooking, if you prefer). Dip the artichoke regularly in the acidulated water to prevent it from discolouring. Once all the artichokes are prepared, place them in a pan of fresh cold water and add the juice of 1 lemon, then add the squeezed-out lemon halves to the pan too. Add 1 teaspoon sea salt to the water, place a cartouche (a circle of greaseproof paper) on top of the artichokes and weigh them down with a small plate that just fits inside the saucepan. Cover the pan with the lid. Bring to the boil, then reduce the heat gently and simmer for 8–10 minutes or until the artichokes are just tender. Remove from the heat and let the artichokes cool completely in the cooking liquid. Once cool, transfer the artichokes and cooking liquid to an airtight container and store in the fridge. Use within 3 days. Most importantly, enjoy every single one!

Preparing globe artichokes to cook and serve whole
To trim globe artichokes to serve them whole, cut off the tough tips from the artichoke leaves using kitchen scissors. Using a large, sharp knife, cut off the stalk flush with the base to give the artichoke a flat bottom, then cut off the pointed top. The artichoke is now ready to be cooked whole. Cook in a pan of boiling salted water (or steam) for 25–35 minutes or until you can pull a leaf out easily. To eat cooked whole artichokes, pull off the leaves one by one, dip them in a dressing (such as mayonnaise or hollandaise sauce), then suck off the fleshy part. Slice off and discard the hairy 'choke' and then eat the tender base with a knife and fork. Allow 1 whole artichoke per person as a starter or light lunch.

Beetroot

Beetroot is another seasonal favourite of mine that is incredibly versatile. Beet is the generic name for members of the Beta family and includes beetroot, Swiss chard and sugar beet (used in sugar production). Beetroot is a biennial plant that is cultivated as an annual and it is easy to grow. The whole plant is edible – the tender small beetroot leaves make an interesting addition to a salad, and once they have grown larger, the leaves are delicious lightly sautéed with a little unsalted butter and seasoned with sea salt. The swollen, bulbous root (which grows at ground level) of this familiar vegetable, with its characteristic deep red colour (though other colours of beetroot, such as pink, yellow/golden, white and stripy varieties, are also available), come in two main forms – globe-shaped and long. Beetroot can be eaten raw (usually grated or marinated in salads), cooked (including steamed, boiled or baked) or pickled, and it goes well with seafood, meat and poultry and can even be used to make a delicious and interesting chocolate and beetroot cake.

For a tasty seasonal pickle, try this recipe for **Star Anise and Cinnamon-Pickled Beetroot**. Remove and discard the leaves from 500g raw small beetroots, then wash them in cold water. Place the beetroots in a large saucepan with fresh cold water and 1 tablespoon sea salt and bring to the boil, then cover and cook over a fairly high heat for 15–18 minutes or until tender. Drain well and let the beetroots cool slightly, then scrape off the skins with a small sharp knife (the skins will come off very easily). Be careful, as beetroot will stain anything remotely white. If the beetroots are large, cut them into smaller wedges, otherwise keep them whole, then set aside. Wash, then sterilise jam jars in a low oven while you make the pickling liquid. Put 180g caster sugar into a saucepan with 180ml malt vinegar, 50ml balsamic vinegar, 1 cinnamon stick, 4 star anise, 4 cloves, 30ml extra virgin olive oil, 1 teaspoon coriander seeds and 1 teaspoon sea salt. Bring to the boil, then reduce the heat and simmer for 5 minutes. Add the cooked beetroots to the pickling liquid and bring back to the boil, then cook over a high heat for 1 minute. Remove from the heat and cool the beetroots slightly before spooning them into the sterilised jars. Pour the pickling liquid over the beetroots to cover them completely. Pour a layer of extra virgin olive oil (about 1cm in depth) into the top of each jar of hot pickled beetroot to keep the oxygen out (the pickling liquid combined with the olive oil makes a delicious vinaigrette). Cover the jars with vinegar-proof lids and seal tightly, then cool completely before refrigerating. You can eat the pickled beetroots immediately, but I highly recommend leaving them for at least 1 week before using them. The unopened jars of pickled beetroot will keep in the fridge for up to 1 month. Once opened, keep refrigerated and use within 1 week. Makes about 2 x 300g jars. Serve the pickled beetroots with cooked sliced cold meats, such as turkey or ham, or serve as part of a ploughman's lunch. They also go well with pan-fried herrings or grilled sardines, served with horseradish crème fraîche.

Courgettes

Courgettes are perhaps one of the easiest vegetables to grow, and with their high demand for water, the British Isles with its typically high summer rainfall, is just the place to grow them. If you are planting courgettes, then

Crayfish

my recommendation is that two plants will be plenty for a household of four. Plant them in a sunny spot, giving them plenty of space to grow as their leaves do grow pretty big. They do require a lot of water, but if watered regularly, you will be the lucky harvester of a healthy supply of courgettes throughout the summer. Courgette flowers are not only pretty and the bearer of the fruits, but they are also edible. They are delicious stuffed, then steamed or deep-fried and served as a starter with plenty of lightly dressed summer salad leaves. Remember to remove the stamens and lightly brush the flowers clean with a pastry brush before using – do not wash the flowers as the water will ruin them. Cook the courgette flowers on the same day that they are picked. Courgettes are the small juvenile or immature fruits of the marrow vegetable (summer squash) and they are usually green, but yellow varieties are obtainable too. Round courgettes and baby courgettes are also readily available. The smaller the courgette, the sweeter and less seedy it will be. The larger, more swollen courgettes can become quite watery, so with these courgettes it's best to cut them into quarters and remove the soft seedy parts before cooking. For a wonderful recipe using freshly picked courgette flowers, try my recipe for **Crispy Battered Crab-Stuffed Courgette Flowers**. Select 4 fresh courgette flowers with small courgettes attached, then remove the stamens and gently brush the flowers clean, being careful not to snap the flowers from the courgettes attached. Set aside. Make the beer batter. Place 75g self-raising flour in a bowl with 1 tablespoon cornflour, ½ teaspoon baking powder and a pinch of sea salt and freshly cracked black pepper. Add 1 egg yolk and 125ml real ale (I use Adnams, but choose a local ale from your region) and beat together to make a smooth batter. In a separate bowl, whisk 1 egg white to form soft peaks, then fold into the batter. Leave to rest for 10 minutes. Meanwhile, heat some sunflower oil in an electric deep-fat fryer or in a deep frying pan to a temperature of 160°C (or until a small piece of bread browns within 20 seconds in the hot oil). In the meantime, make the crab stuffing. In a bowl, combine 3 tablespoons white crab meat with 1 tablespoon brown crab meat, 2 tablespoons cream cheese or full-fat soft cheese (such as Philadelphia), 1 teaspoon snipped fresh chives, 1 teaspoon chopped fresh chervil, finely grated zest and juice of 1 lemon and a small pinch of cayenne pepper or a few drops of Tabasco sauce. Season with sea salt and freshly cracked black pepper. Use a teaspoon to carefully spoon the mixture into the courgette flowers, dividing the mixture between the 4 flowers and stuffing them well. Take the end of each flower and carefully twist it to close, but be careful not to break the flower. Carefully roll the courgette flowers in 1 tablespoon plain flour seasoned with salt and pepper, and then dip each flower and attached courgette in the batter. Deep-fry the stuffed courgette flowers with the courgettes attached in the hot oil for 6–8 minutes or until golden brown and crisp. Using a slotted spoon, remove and drain the deep-fried courgettes and flowers on kitchen paper. Season with salt and serve immediately. Serve with a lightly dressed mixed leaf salad and lemon wedges. Serves 2 as a starter or light lunch.

Freshwater crayfish

Freshwater crayfish are crustaceans that look like miniature lobsters, which they are related to. The White-Clawed Crayfish is Britain's only native crayfish and it is endangered by the American Red Signal Crayfish, which was introduced to the waters of the British Isles during the 1970's. The American Red Signal Crayfish is now caught in the rivers and waterways around the UK as part of a conservation project to save the native White-Clawed Crayfish. The White-Clawed Crayfish is now a protected species in the UK.

For a delicious starter or light lunch using freshwater crayfish, try my recipe for **Crayfish Cocktail with Buttered Brown Bread**. Half-fill 2 martini glasses with shredded Little Gem lettuce that has been dressed with Classic Vinaigrette (see page 19) and seasoned with sea salt and freshly cracked black pepper. Set aside. Next, make a Marie Rose sauce. In a small bowl, mix together 2 tablespoons mayonnaise, 8 drops of Tabasco sauce, 2 splashes of Worcestershire sauce and 1 teaspoon brandy and season with salt and pepper. Set aside. Bring a large pan of water to a rolling boil, then place 10 fresh whole crayfish (800g–1kg in total) in the boiling water and boil for 5 minutes. Remove them from the pan to a plate using a slotted spoon and leave to cool. Repeat the procedure with another 10 fresh whole crayfish (another 800g–1kg in total). Carefully remove the tails from the bodies of the cooked crayfish while they are still slightly warm, then peel off the shells. Leave the crayfish tails to cool completely, then add them to the Marie Rose sauce. (Keep the shells for making a bisque.) Spoon the crayfish tails in the Marie Rose sauce on to the shredded lettuce, squeeze over the juice of 1 lemon and serve immediately with buttered brown bread. Serves 2 as a starter or light lunch.

Gooseberry Flapjacks

Gooseberries

Native to Europe, north-west Africa and south-west Asia, the gooseberry is one of our nation's favourite fruits with its firm, typically yellowish-green flesh (although red and yellow varieties are also available later in the season) and hairy (occasionally smooth), green striated skin and sharp taste. Most gooseberries must be cooked to make them palatable, but dessert gooseberries, which are green to light brown in colour, can be eaten raw when ripe.

For a tempting sweet treat, try my sumptuous recipe for **Gooseberry Flapjacks**. Preheat the oven to 200°C/Gas Mark 6. Grease and line a 32 x 22 x 3.5cm baking tin with non-stick baking paper and set aside. Spread 30g sunflower seeds, 30g pumpkin seeds and 50g whole hazelnuts over a baking tray and roast in the oven for 5–6 minutes or until golden brown and lightly toasted, but not burned or too dark – remember nuts and seeds burn very quickly. Remove from the oven and set aside. Reduce the oven temperature to 160°C/Gas Mark 3. Put 250g unsalted butter, 150g caster sugar and 150g golden syrup into a large saucepan and melt over a low heat, stirring until the mixture is melted and combined. Remove from the heat. Top, tail and wash 300g fresh gooseberries and add to the melted mixture, together with 500g jumbo oats, a pinch of table salt and the toasted seeds and hazelnuts, mixing well to combine. Spoon the mixture into the prepared baking tin, pressing level with the back of a spoon. Bake in the oven for 35–40 minutes or until golden brown. The warm flapjack mixture will still be slightly soft when you press it with your finger, but it will become firmer as it cools. Remove from the oven and leave to cool completely in the tin, then turn out and cut into 18 bars. Store in an airtight container in a cool, dry cupboard for up to 1 week. Makes 18 flapjacks.

Lobster

Classed as a delicacy and typically commanding high prices, lobster should not be taken for granted. It takes the average lobster about 8 years to reach maturity, hence the strict controls in place that ensure lobsters must measure at least 10cm from between the eyes to where the tail is attached to the body, before they can be caught and killed. Lobsters are the largest sea crustaceans and there are several types that are caught on both sides of the Atlantic and in Europe. The most common types used in cooking in the UK are the (usually larger) Canadian or North American lobster and the European lobster (which tends to be slightly smaller). Lobsters have eight legs, two forward-facing strong crushing claws, a muscular tail and several antennae. Lobsters are usually a blue-grey or green-blue colour when alive and they turn a reddish-orange colour when cooked. They feed at the bottom of the sea and generally move fairly slowly, but if they need to flee, they swim backwards and can cover an area of up to 5 metres per second. Lobsters are like spiders and snails in that they have blue blood due to the presence of haemocyanin, a blue copper-containing respiratory pigment. As with crayfish, langoustines and crabs, the meat (and, to some extent, the shells) of lobsters is highly prized and sought after. A wonderful **Lobster Bisque** (see page 248) can be made using the lobster shells once the meat is removed. On the subject of lobsters, one question beckons – how do you kill a lobster humanely? When killing a lobster, I always try very hard to ensure that things are done correctly and that the creature does not suffer in the process, especially as I prepare food for enjoyment. To kill lobsters humanely you must work fast and be precise. You might be slightly cautious, but if you do not work quickly and confidently, the creatures might suffer. If you have a very lively lobster then place it on a chopping board, holding on to the tail with one hand, and stroke the lobster between the eyes – you will find it calms the lobster and they, in effect, 'go to sleep', though technically they don't. Turn the lobster on its back and hold it firmly, then with a large, heavy cook's knife, position the point of the knife just behind but between the eyes (you will have to judge this as best you can as you cannot see the eyes because the lobster is on its back) and quickly push the blade down, cutting through the head and down to where the head and body join the tail section, working quickly to cut through the central nervous system. By severing along the centre line of the whole body in this way, starting at the head end, this will instantly kill the lobster without it suffering. Plonking a live lobster or crab in a pan of boiling water is cruel and so is ripping the

Lobster

tail from the body while it is still alive. Once you have successfully and humanely killed the lobster, use the lobster for your chosen recipe or cook it as follows. Bring a large saucepan of water to the boil. Remove the tail and claws from the lobster. Cook the tail in the pan of boiling water for 3 minutes or until it has turned red, then remove using a slotted spoon, refresh it in iced water, drain and set aside. Cook the claws in the same pan of boiling water for at least 7 minutes (cooking time will depend on the size of the claws) or until they too have turned red, then drain, refresh in iced water and drain again. Crack open the claws using the back of a heavy knife or a wooden meat hammer/mallet and remove the meat from inside. Using a sharp knife, split the lobster tail in half lengthways, then remove the meat. Place the meat on a plate, cover and chill until you are ready to use it, then chop or slice it before use. Use the shells and meat to make the wonderful **Lavish Lobster Macaroni Bake** (see page 248), or add the cooked meat to recipes such as salads, stir-fries, soups or pasta fillings. To make lobster thermidor, you will need to cook the whole lobster in a pan of boiling water (allowing about 10 minutes cooking time per 500g). Once cooked, drain the lobster and let it cool slightly, then remove the claws, crack them open and remove the meat. Cut the lobster in half lengthways and remove and reserve the tail meat, then clean the main body of the lobster and reserve the shells for serving. Finish and serve as the recipe directs.

Mulberries

Mulberries are small, soft, sweet, juicy berries, similar in appearance to blackberries, that grow on dome-headed trees. There are two main varieties, black and white (or slightly pink), and they can be eaten raw or cooked in recipes such as ices, jams, sauces or fruit vinegars. Mulberries contain natural colouring pigments that are used in the medicine, clothing and food manufacturing industries and the leaves from the mulberry tree are a common food for silk worms. Mulberry trees grow to about 10m and the older the tree, the more droopy the branches become, almost like an umbrella. The trees bear the fragile, perishable fruit once a year for a very short period of time, and they naturally lose their leaves in the winter.

To make **Mulberry Jam**, combine 400g fresh mulberries with 400g caster sugar and 50ml cold water in a saucepan. Cook the mulberry mixture over a low heat, stirring to dissolve the sugar, then increase the heat and bring to the boil. Boil rapidly for 10–15 minutes or until the jam reaches a temperature of 105°C (setting point), stirring every now and then to prevent it from catching and skimming any scum off the surface. If you don't have a jam thermometer, check to see if setting point has been reached by spooning a little of the jam on to a chilled small plate. Push a finger across the jam; if the surface wrinkles and it is beginning to set, it has reached setting point. If not, boil it for a further 5 minutes or so and test again. Once the jam has reached setting point, stir in the juice of 1 lemon, then remove from the heat and allow the jam to cool slightly. Carefully pour the jam into hot, sterilised jars, cover with wax discs (wax-side down) and seal. Once cold, label and store in a cool, dry cupboard. The jam should keep well for a year or so. Once opened, keep in the fridge and use within 1 month. Makes about 3 x 200g jars.

Raspberries

The raspberry plant is a hardy perennial shrub or rambling plant with a woody stem (cane) and soft light red fruit with a sweet, slightly acidic and perfumed fruity flavour. Raspberries are a member of the rose (rubus) family and most varieties are thorny climbers or ramblers that require training either on to walls or wire fences. Raspberries grow well in cool, damp climates and are cultivated so they produce new, relatively short canes each year. The most common type is the red raspberry, but black, yellow/golden and white varieties are also available. Look for large plump fruit and, once picked, use them as quickly as possible, as raspberries tend to soften and go mouldy easily. If you have too many to use them all up quickly, raspberries are perfect for home freezing. Raspberries can be eaten both raw and cooked and they add delicious flavour and colour to many dishes, especially desserts. Another of my preserving tips is that I love making flavoured fruit vinegars and fresh raspberries are perfect for this. I make fruit vinegars when the fruit is in season and store it for later use. Homemade fruit vinegars make fantastic Christmas or birthday gifts too.

For my wonderful **Raspberry Cider Vinegar**, rinse 120g ripe or very ripe raspberries (removing any mouldy bits) and

Mulberry Jam

drain. Place the raspberries in a non-metallic bowl and use a fork to lightly mash them. Add 350ml cider vinegar (or white wine vinegar) and stir to mix, then cover and refrigerate for 5 days, stirring twice. At this stage, you can either pass the vinegar through a fine sieve into sterilised bottles or it can be bottled as it is, retaining the raspberries. However, if the raspberries are retained, the fruit may, over time (about 3 months or so), lose its attractive red colour, so at this point pass the vinegar through a fine sieve or muslin cloth to preserve the colour, and then re-bottle in clean, sterilised bottles. Cover and seal the bottles, then label and store in a cool, dry cupboard for up to 1 year. Once opened, keep in the fridge and use within 1 week. Makes about 2 x 200ml bottles (if you are bottling the raspberries in the vinegar as well, then the volume will be more).You can go wild and make all sorts of flavoured fruit vinegars by applying the same method above to other fresh fruits. Alternative fruits that are suitable for making fruit vinegars include fresh ripe mulberries, tayberries, rowanberries, strawberries, blackberries, blackcurrants or gooseberries. For a special touch, you can also add a few sprigs of fresh herbs or whole spices to your fruit vinegars to add extra flavour and appeal.

Sardines

Named after the island of Sardinia, sardines are found in abundance throughout the Atlantic and Mediterranean. Also known as young pilchards, and related to herrings, sardines are oily fish with silver-blue skins. Sardines are rich in omega-3 fatty acids and are a good source of vitamin D, calcium and vitamin B12. Since March 2010, under the EU law, Cornish Sardines now have Protected Geographical Status (PGS). Fresh sardines are great for grilling or pan-frying and they are also commonly available in cans.

For a simple but delicious snack or light lunch, try my recipe for **Sardines on Toast**. Place 6 small skin-on sardine fillets (350–400g total prepared weight), scaled and pin bones removed, on a plate, season with sea salt and freshly cracked black pepper and splash over 1 tablespoon olive oil. Heat a non-stick frying pan over a medium heat for a few minutes or until hot, then place the sardines, skin-side down, in the pan, sprinkle over 1 deseeded and finely sliced fresh green chilli and 2 finely sliced spring onions and add another dash of olive oil, if needed. Cook for 3 minutes, then flip the sardines over and cook for a further minute on the flesh side or until the flesh has turned opaque and is flaky and moist. Meanwhile, toast 2 thick slices of sourdough bread on both

Sardines

sides, then rub one side of each piece of toast with ½ clove garlic and some olive oil. Transfer the sardines to the slices of warm toast (garlic and oil side up), dividing them evenly between the 2 slices, drizzle over the pan juices, then sprinkle and squeeze over the finely grated zest and juice of 1 lemon. Place a handful of lightly dressed and seasoned fresh rocket leaves on top of or alongside each portion and serve immediately. Serves 2 as a snack or light lunch.

Sea bass

The sea bass found in our British coastal waters is also known as the European sea bass, with its characteristic two dorsal fins, silver-grey sides and white belly and delicately flavoured firm white flesh. As well as sea bass, the name bass also refers to other varieties of fish in the same species, including freshwater bass (though there are no freshwater bass in Britain). Wild sea bass is one of the many species that has suffered from intensive fishing and high demands, but extensive conservation projects that have been put in place over recent years, have meant that we can now enjoy the return of the locally caught sea bass from around the British coast. Sea bass is also successfully farmed in the UK and this helps to keep wild stocks replenished. It's a true delight to walk along the beaches and around the harbours along the Suffolk coast, typically at places such as Southwold, Orford and Aldeburgh, and find freshly landed sea bass, skate and cod, all of which have benefited from the intensive conservation projects.

Sea bass is even more delicious when it is cooked on the bone, and is perfect for informal dining with friends and family. For a fantastic barbecue lunch or supper to enjoy al fresco this month, try my recipe for **Barbecued Sea Bass in Foil**. Preheat the barbecue to a medium heat level. Select a whole sea bass (1.5–1.8kg) that has been gutted and scaled, with the dorsal fins removed. Wash the fish, then pat it dry with kitchen paper. Take a large piece of double-thickness foil and rub the inside of the foil with 1 tablespoon olive oil. Quarter 4 ripe plum tomatoes and place them in the centre of the foil, then season with sea salt and freshly cracked black pepper. Sprinkle over 1 tablespoon sherry vinegar, 1 tablespoon pitted black olives and a large handful of chopped fresh mixed herbs (such as basil, parsley and oregano). Trim a bunch of spring onions, then place them on top of the tomatoes. Score the fish several times on both sides with a sharp knife and place it on top of the spring onions and tomatoes. Season with more salt and then splash over 2 tablespoons olive oil. Close the foil around the fish, but do not wrap the foil too tightly. Place the foil parcel over the barbecue and cook for 25–30 minutes or until the fish is cooked and the flesh is opaque, flaky and moist. Depending on the fierceness of the barbecue, you may need to move the fish to a cooler spot after a little while, or you may prefer to cook the fish over a lower heat for a longer period of time. When the fish is cooked, the flesh should be soft and flaky and the tomatoes should have broken down and become juicy along with the herbs and spring onions. Remove from the heat. Carefully undo the foil and then remove the fish from the bone by cutting along each side of the backbone from head to tail. Carefully remove the fillet from each side of the backbone to a plate. Turn the fish over and do the same on the other side. Discard the head and backbone and serve 1 fish fillet per portion. Serve immediately with a wild rice salad, couscous salad or warm potato and samphire salad, and enjoy! Serves 4 as a lunch or supper. If you don't have a barbecue, preheat the oven to 200°C/Gas Mark 6. Prepare the recipe as directed above and place the foil-wrapped fish on a baking tray. Bake in the oven for 25–30 minutes or until the fish is cooked and the flesh is opaque, flaky and moist. Serve as directed.

Sea purslane

Sea purslane

Sea purslane is a fantastic wild coastal plant that you can forage for along our shorelines. It has a matt green colour and slightly swollen leaves and the taste is interesting – it almost tastes like salt and vinegar crisps. Sea purslane is mainly found on salt marshes that are flooded at high tide. When the leaves are freshly picked early in the morning they are still crispy with a lovely salty taste of the sea. Sea purslane is particularly delicious used as an ingredient in dishes containing seafood and it can be served raw or cooked. It is also good as an addition to salads. If you are lucky enough to find salt marsh lamb, then sea purslane will make a fantastic companion to create a spectacular dish.

For a delicious recipe using sea purslane, try my **Seashore Extravaganza**. Buy 4 large scallops in their shells (480–550g total weight in shell) and ask the fishmonger to open them for you, then, once you get home, remove the roe (or coral) and gut string, discard the guts and wash the roe. Clean and reserve 2 of the 4 shells and use them for serving. Place the scallops and roe on a plate. Butterfly 2 large fresh prawns (80–120g total whole/unpeeled weight) – to butterfly the prawns, remove the shells, leaving the tails in place, and remove the black veins, then cut deep into the body of each prawn along its length, being careful not to cut all the way through, then flatten the prawn, pushing the meat apart, to make a butterfly prawn. Season the scallops, roe and prawns lightly with sea salt and freshly cracked black pepper and drizzle over 1 tablespoon olive oil. Heat a large, non-stick frying pan over a medium heat for a few minutes or until hot, then add 1 finely diced rasher smoked back or streaky bacon to the pan and sauté over a medium heat for 2–3 minutes or until cooked and golden. Increase the heat, add 1 tablespoon olive oil and then place the roes in the pan first, followed by the scallops and prawns, and sauté for 2 minutes on each side or until cooked and starting to turn golden brown. Add a dash of dry vermouth to the pan and let it bubble over a high heat, stirring and scraping the base of the pan with a wooden spoon to deglaze it. Meanwhile, blanch a handful of fresh samphire in a pan of boiling water for about 1 minute or until al dente, then drain. Remove the pan containing the scallops from the heat, then add a handful of fresh sea purslane to the pan, together with the blanched samphire, 6 halved cherry tomatoes and a handful of double-podded broad beans (see page 164 for more information on double-podding broad beans) and stir to mix. Adjust the seasoning to taste, then divide the mixture equally between the 2 reserved scallop shells. Serve immediately with buttered sourdough or brown bread. Serves 2 as a starter or light lunch.

Heirloom tomatoes

Tomatoes in general

Perhaps lesser known as love apples, tomatoes are fruits that grow on annual herbaceous plants. Tomatoes are available all year round and we successfully grow them in hot houses here in the UK throughout the year. However, there is a huge difference in the flavour of hot house tomatoes and sun-ripened tomatoes, with tomatoes ripened on the vines in the sun producing a more intense and superior flavour (the longer the tomatoes are left on the vine to ripen in the sun, the better the flavour they will have). There are plenty of tomato varieties available on the market and with an increasing interest in growing heirloom or heritage tomatoes, the older and less well-known varieties such as the yellow, orange, black and white tomatoes are making a comeback. So, it's out with the perfectly round-shaped fruits and in with the odd-shaped tomatoes of yesteryear. Tomatoes are easy to grow, but how good your harvest will be is another question. I have planted tomatoes every year for the past 4 years and some years I have had a better harvest than others (though every year I seem to make the same silly mistake of planting them too close to each other). When you plant baby tomato plants, plant them in good compost, making sure you give them enough space, position them in a sunny spot and water them regularly.

Heirloom tomatoes

Also known as heritage tomatoes, heirloom tomatoes are an open-pollinated (non-hybrid) heirloom cultivar of tomato, often passed down through several generations of family. They come in all shapes, sizes and colours, as well as an array of tomato flavours. These earlier varieties of tomatoes have never made the grade for mass production and were almost forgotten in years gone by, but with the growing popularity of grow-your-own and the rediscovery of heritage varieties of all kinds, the heirloom tomato has leapt back into favour in recent years and has fast become the choice for the dining table and market place. Have you ever wondered what to do with a glut or surplus of tomatoes? Well, if you have, there are three simple but excellent recipes to follow which show you how to use them up and preserve them for use later in the year. Try one or all of the following delicious recipes using fresh tomatoes – Tomato, Ginger and Sultana Chutney, Tomato Sauce for Keeps or Semi-dried Tomatoes.

To make **Tomato, Ginger and Sultana Chutney**, wash, then sterilise jam jars in a low oven while you make the chutney. Put 150ml white wine vinegar in a preserving pan with 150g caster sugar, 4 toasted green cardamom pods, 1 finely sliced large fresh red chilli (deseeded, if you like), 1 diced large onion, 50g finely grated (peeled) fresh root ginger, 1 crushed clove garlic, 1 teaspoon coriander seeds and sea salt and freshly cracked black pepper. Cook over a low heat, stirring until the sugar has dissolved, then increase the heat and bring to the boil, stirring. Boil vigorously over a high heat for about 10 minutes or until the syrup has thickened. Stir in 500g chopped ripe tomatoes (skinned first, if you prefer), 3 tablespoons tomato purée, 80g sultanas, 1 bay leaf, 1 teaspoon black onion seeds and 1 teaspoon chopped fresh thyme, then reduce the heat to a gentle simmer and cook for a further 12–15 minutes or until the mixture is reduced to a thick consistency, and no excess liquid remains, stirring occasionally. Remove from the heat and leave to cool for 10 minutes, then spoon the chutney into the hot, sterilised jars. Cover with vinegar-proof lids and seal. Leave to cool, then label and store in a cool, dry cupboard. Store for at least 1 week before using. The unopened jars of chutney should keep well in a cool, dry cupboard for up to 3 months. Once opened, store in the fridge and use within 1 week. Makes about 3 x 200g jars. Serve the chutney with homemade curry or with freshly baked cheese and tomato scones. The chutney is also delicious served in a smoked ham and salad sandwich or as an accompaniment to cheese. For an extra flavour boost, stir a spoonful or two of the chutney into an uncooked minced meat meatball mixture (before shaping the mixture into balls), or stir a few spoonfuls into a beef stew towards the end of the cooking time.

To make **Tomato Sauce for Keeps**, heat 50ml olive oil in a large saucepan, add 4 diced large onions, 5 crushed cloves garlic, 2 bay leaves and sea salt and freshly cracked black pepper and sauté over a high heat for 8–10 minutes or until the onions are golden brown and caramelised. Add 3 tablespoons tomato purée and 2 tablespoons caster sugar and cook for a further 5 minutes, stirring. Add 250ml dry white wine and let it bubble, stirring and scraping the base of the pan with a wooden spoon to deglaze it. Cook over a high heat for 5–6 minutes or until the wine is reduced and becomes thick and syrupy. Cut 1.5kg very ripe tomatoes in half and add them to the pan with 200ml cold water. Cover and bring to the boil, then reduce the heat to a gentle simmer and cook for about 30 minutes or until the mixture is rich and glossy, stirring occasionally. Place a food mill over a clean saucepan and pass the tomato sauce through the food mill, then discard the skins. (If you don't have a food mill, pass the mixture through a sieve instead.) Bring the sauce back to the boil over a medium heat, then reduce the heat and simmer for 10 minutes or until the sauce has reduced further and the colour has deepened. Place several sprigs of fresh oregano and thyme into sterilised glass jars or bottles, then pour the sauce into the jars or bottles, cover, seal and leave to cool. Once cool, label and store in a cool, dry cupboard. The sauce can be used straightaway, but it is best if stored for at least 1 week before using. The unopened jars or bottles of tomato sauce should keep well in a cool, dry cupboard for up to 3 months. Once opened, store in the fridge and use within 3 days. Makes about 2 litres tomato sauce. The tomato sauce can be used in recipes such as **Aubergine, Goat's Cheese and Tomato Bake** (see page 220) or when making dishes such as moussaka or Bolognese sauce. For a simple light meal, turn the tomato sauce into a cream of tomato soup – bring the tomato sauce gently to the boil in a saucepan, then add some hot vegetable stock to thin it down a little and heat until hot. Stir in a dash or two of double cream and then serve with crusty bread.

To make **Semi-dried Tomatoes**, preheat the oven to 110°C/Gas Mark ¼ and place 2 large wire cooling racks on 2 large baking trays. Set aside. Cut 2kg ripe tomatoes into halves or quarters, depending on their size. Arrange them, cut-side up, in a single layer on the prepared wire racks. Scatter over 3 finely sliced cloves garlic and the finely chopped leaves from 2 sprigs of fresh thyme, then season with sea salt and freshly cracked black pepper. Place the baking trays in the oven for about 4 hours or until the tomatoes look shriveled and dry but still retain a bit of moisture/juiciness (i.e. they are semi-dry, not completely dry). The length of time that you dry the tomatoes for partly depends on the size you have cut them to and how dry you want them. I check them after about 2 hours, and then increase the drying time, if necessary, to suit my needs. Once the tomatoes are dried sufficiently, remove them from the oven and leave to cool completely on the wire racks.

Once cool, transfer them to an airtight container and either store them in the fridge and use within 3 days, or freeze and use within 3 months (defrost in the fridge overnight, before use). Makes about 750g semi-dried tomatoes. Alternatively, you can preserve the semi-dried tomatoes in oil. To do this, place the semi-dried tomatoes in hot, sterilised jars (filling each jar about three-quarters full), then top up the jars with warmed olive oil or sunflower oil. Cover, seal and cool, then store in the refrigerator for up to 3 months. Once opened, keep refrigerated and use within 1 month. Use the oil for salad dressings. Makes about 4 x 250g jars preserved semi-dried tomatoes in oil. Use the semi-dried tomatoes in garden salads or roughly chop and stir them into cooked hot pasta with fresh rocket leaves and cooked spicy Italian sausages. Semi-dried tomatoes also make a great garnish served with steak, chips, fried field mushrooms and béarnaise sauce. Or, use them to top macaroni or cauliflower cheese, then sprinkle over some extra grated cheese before baking or grilling. You can semi-dry and preserve cherry tomatoes in the same way as the standard tomatoes above. Simply halve 3kg cherry tomatoes and then follow the directions above for drying and storing the tomatoes. With cherry tomatoes, 2 hours drying time in total will probably be long enough.

Tomato, Ginger and Sultana Chutney

Beetroot Tarte Tatins with Frozen Broad Bean Crème Fraîche

I can hear the true traditionalists shrieking and screaming at me, how dare I ruin a classic! Well, this is my version of a savoury tarte tatin. For me, a tarte tatin is a fruit or vegetable tart with a puff pastry disc that is cooked upside-down. The fruit or vegetables are initially cooked with sugar and butter to help them caramelise, then they are topped with puff pastry and baked. Once baked, the tart is inverted so that the pastry forms the base and the caramelised fruit or vegetables sit proudly on top.

Savoury tarte tatins are one of my culinary trademark dishes. People who know me well know my mushroom and taleggio tarte tatin that I serve as a canapé at drinks parties. That recipe is the inspiration for this beetroot tarte tatin. When I first created this recipe, I had a beetroot pickle in mind made using my homemade Raspberry Cider Vinegar (see page 238), and the fruity vinegar works perfectly, giving the pickled beetroot a mysterious deliciousness.

Serves 4 as a starter or light lunch

For the frozen broad bean crème fraîche

100g fresh broad beans (shelled weight)
100g crème fraîche
sea salt and freshly cracked black pepper

For the beetroot tarte tatins

2 tablespoons unsalted butter, plus extra to grease the moulds
350g raw beetroots, peeled, plus 1 extra raw whole beetroot
300g red onions, finely sliced
2 tablespoons dark muscovado sugar
50ml Raspberry Cider Vinegar (see page 238)
1 teaspoon chopped fresh thyme
240g good quality chilled fresh all-butter puff pastry

baby or mini/micro salad leaves, to serve

For the frozen broad bean crème fraîche, cook the broad beans in a small pan of boiling salted water for a couple of minutes, then drain, refresh in iced water and drain again. Pop the tender, bright green beans out of their outer grey skins by squeezing gently. Discard the outer grey skins and reserve the inner bright green beans.

Weigh 50g broad beans into a small bowl (reserve the remaining broad beans for the garnish) and use a fork to lightly crush the beans, then season to taste with salt and pepper. Stir in the crème fraîche, then transfer the mixture to a freezer proof container, cover and freeze for 2–3 hours or until the mixture is firm enough to scoop.

For the beetroot tarte tatins, grease four 8 x 2cm round tart moulds or tins with the extra butter and set aside.

Coarsely grate the peeled raw beetroots. Melt the remaining 2 tablespoons butter in a saucepan, add the grated beetroot, onions and salt and pepper, then cover and sweat over a medium heat for 10–15 minutes or until the mixture starts to caramelise, stirring regularly. Add the sugar and stir until dissolved.

Add the raspberry cider vinegar to the pan and let it bubble over a high heat for 1–2 minutes, stirring and scraping the base of the pan with a wooden spoon to deglaze it, then cover and cook over a medium heat for a further 15–20 minutes or until the pickle is glossy and thickened but is not too dry. Once the pickle is ready, remove from the heat, stir in the thyme, then set aside to cool. While the pickle is cooling, cook the remaining whole beetroot in a pan of boiling salted water for 20–25 minutes or until tender (the cooking time will depend on the size and age of the beetroot). Once cooked, drain, refresh in cold water and drain again, then peel the beetroot.

Slice the cooked beetroot into 5mm slices and place a slice in the centre of the base of each prepared mould (reserve any remaining slices for the garnish). Spoon a generous amount of beetroot pickle on top of the beetroot slices, dividing it evenly between the moulds, then press it down firmly with a spoon.

Roll out the puff pastry on a lightly floured work surface to 2–3mm thickness. Cut out four 9cm rounds. Place a round of pastry on top of each beetroot-filled mould, tucking the pastry in around the edges to encase the beetroot. Leave them to rest in the fridge for 30 minutes before baking. Preheat the oven to 200°C/Gas Mark 6. Place the tarte tatins on a baking tray and bake in the oven for about 30 minutes or until the pastry is cooked, well-risen and golden brown.

Remove from the oven and let the tarts cool in the moulds for a few minutes before carefully turning them out on to serving plates (you may need to loosen them around the edges with a butter knife). It's important that you turn the tarts out while they are still hot, otherwise they will stick to the moulds. Serve the tarte tatins hot or warm. Spoon a quenelle (spoonful) of the frozen broad bean crème fraîche and some baby salad leaves alongside each tart tatin. Garnish with the reserved broad beans and any remaining cooked beetroot slices (chopped, if you like) and serve immediately.

Crayfish Popcorn with Seashore Salad and Crayfish Ketchup

This is a spectacular dish with bags of flavour and texture. The crayfish ketchup is a combination of roasted crayfish shells and homemade tomato ketchup. The whole dish is refreshing and light with added fun-factor.

Serves 6 as a starter or light lunch

For the crayfish ketchup
2kg fresh live medium-sized crayfish
50ml rapeseed oil
1 large onion, sliced
1 fennel bulb, trimmed and sliced
2 sticks celery, sliced
50g fresh root ginger, peeled and sliced
2 cloves garlic, crushed
1 fresh red chilli, deseeded and chopped
2 tablespoons coriander seeds
1 teaspoon fennel seeds
a small bunch of fresh oregano, stalks and all, chopped
200ml red wine vinegar
50ml brandy
80ml Worcestershire sauce
80g tomato purée
80g soft dark brown sugar
500ml cold water
1kg very ripe or over-ripe plum tomatoes, quartered, seeds removed
500g canned chopped tomatoes
sea salt and freshly cracked black pepper

For the seashore salad and crayfish popcorn
300g fresh broad beans (shelled weight)
250g fresh peas (shelled weight)
200g fresh samphire
100ml rapeseed oil
70g popcorn kernels
a good pinch of ras el hanout
a large handful of fresh pea shoots
120g fresh sea purslane leaves, rinsed
120ml Classic Vinaigrette (see page 19)

juice of 1 lemon
blanched crayfish tails (from the Crayfish Ketchup – see recipe above)
1 tablespoon chopped fresh dill

For the crayfish ketchup, first, cook the crayfish. Preheat the oven to 200°C/ Gas Mark 6. Blanch the crayfish in a large pan of boiling water for 1 minute, then drain, dip into iced water and drain again. Remove the tails from their shells and place on a plate, then leave to cool and refrigerate. The tails will be used in the popcorn. Place the crayfish tail shells and the crayfish heads in a roasting tin and roast in the oven for about 30 minutes or until they are cooked and have turned pink. Remove from the oven and lightly bash the shells and heads with a rolling pin to break them up into smaller pieces. Set aside.

While the shells are roasting, heat the rapeseed oil in a large saucepan, add the onion, fennel, celery, ginger, garlic, chilli, coriander and fennel seeds and salt and pepper, then cover and sweat over a medium heat for about 10 minutes or until golden brown, stirring regularly. Add the oregano, red wine vinegar, brandy, Worcestershire sauce, tomato purée and sugar and cook for 5 minutes.

Add the roasted crushed crayfish shells, the water and the fresh and canned tomatoes and stir to mix. Bring to the boil, then reduce the heat to a gentle simmer, cover and cook for about 30 minutes or until the mixture is reduced and thickened and is a rich, deep red colour, stirring occasionally.

Put the mixture through a food mill or pass it through a fine sieve. Discard the solids and transfer the tomato ketchup to a clean saucepan. Bring to a gentle simmer and then cook, uncovered, for 15–20 minutes or until the mixture is reduced to half of its original volume – you are looking for a slightly thickened, glossy coating consistency. Remove from the heat, pour the ketchup into a bowl and leave to cool, then cover and chill in the fridge until needed (see Cook's Notes).

Prepare the seashore salad. Cook the broad beans in a pan of boiling salted water for a couple of minutes, then drain, refresh in iced water and drain again. Pop the tender, bright green beans out of their outer grey skins by squeezing gently. Discard the outer grey skins and reserve the inner bright green beans. Blanch the peas and samphire together in a separate pan of boiling salted water for 1½–2 minutes or until just tender. Drain, refresh in iced water and drain again. Set aside.

Meanwhile, cook the crayfish popcorn. Heat half of the rapeseed oil in a large saucepan over a medium heat, then add the popcorn kernels and place the lid on the pan. Shake the pan a couple of times and then once the popcorn starts to pop after about 7–9 minutes, turn the heat off and leave the pan on the hob, undisturbed, until you can no longer hear the corn popping. Remove the lid, add the ras el hanout and salt and pepper to taste.

In the meantime, finish the salad and cook the crayfish. Put the broad beans, peas, samphire, pea shoots and sea purslane in a large bowl. Whisk the vinaigrette and lemon juice together, then add to the salad and toss to mix. Divide the dressed salad between serving plates or bowl plates and set aside.

Heat the remaining oil in a non-stick frying pan until hot, then sauté the blanched crayfish tails over a high heat for about 2 minutes on each side or until cooked and golden. Season with salt and pepper, then stir in the dill. Mix the sautéed crayfish tails with the cooked popcorn and serve on top of the lemon-dressed salad. Serve each portion with some chilled crayfish ketchup on the side. Serve immediately.

Cook's Notes

The recipe for crayfish ketchup makes about 500ml in total, so you will have some leftover. Store the leftover ketchup in an airtight container in the fridge and use within 3 days.

If you like, for a tasty light lunch, reheat the leftover crayfish ketchup in a saucepan over a low heat until piping hot, then toss it with cooked hot pasta, a spoonful or two of crème fraîche, some chopped fresh tomatoes and chopped fresh oregano and serve.

Lavish Lobster Macaroni Bake

Macaroni cheese is one of my mother's specialties and she used to make it for us on a Saturday evening. I remember sitting in front of the oven watching the cheese bubbling in the glass dish. The best bit was the cold leftovers; dad and I loved eating it cold – ooh, the cold melted cheese and tomatoes always tasted so good!

This particular macaroni bake has nothing ordinary or simple about it, but it has that luxurious comfort food feel to it, just the kind of food that Mr. P and I love to eat.

When I cook this dish, I enjoy every moment as it takes me right back to the years when I used to cook lobsters every day to make the exquisite lobster raviolis for the restaurant where I used to work. It was a daily task performed early in the morning and it was my job to cook the lobsters, pull them apart and prepare the meat for the raviolis. I have a mild allergy when I touch cooked lobsters – my fingers swell up and they itch fiercely. I remember how the boys used to call me a 'pansy' for wearing the yellow marigolds, as they thought I could not stand the pain when the sharp bits of shell pierced my fingers, but it was in fact due to my mild allergy.

Lobster is still classed as a delicacy and it commands incredibly high prices. Lobster should not be taken for granted and for that reason I use the whole lobster to make this wonderful lavish dish.

Serves 4 as a main course

For the lobster bisque

2 x 450g live lobsters
1 tablespoon olive oil
2 banana shallots, sliced
½ fennel bulb, trimmed and sliced
1 carrot, sliced
2 sticks celery, sliced
2 cloves garlic, lightly crushed
4 white peppercorns
1 teaspoon coriander seeds
1 bay leaf
a large handful of fresh herbs (such as parsley and thyme)
a pinch of cayenne pepper
100g tomato purée
6 large ripe plum tomatoes, roughly diced
200ml brandy
300ml dry vermouth
1 litre fish stock
500ml brown chicken stock
200ml double cream
sea salt and freshly cracked black pepper

For the lavish lobster macaroni

300g raw macaroni
about 300ml Lobster Bisque (see recipe above)
150g mascarpone
100g finely grated fresh Parmesan cheese
2 spring onions, finely sliced
6 egg yolks
2 tablespoons chopped fresh mixed soft herbs (such as basil, oregano, chives and chervil)
cooked lobster claws from making the Lobster Bisque (see recipe above)
cooked lobster tails from making the Lobster Bisque (see recipe above)
1 tablespoon unsalted butter
20–24 Semi-dried Cherry Tomatoes (see page 242)
12 large or 24 small fresh basil leaves, fried (see page 221 for instructions on how to fry basil leaves)

For the lobster bisque, first humanely kill then cook the lobsters to obtain the meat. Bring a large pan of water to a rapid boil. Put a sharp knife through the head of each lobster to ensure they are killed humanely (see more detailed instructions on how to kill a lobster humanely on page 237). Remove and reserve the tails and claws and set the heads aside.

Cook the tails first in the pan of boiling water for 3 minutes or until they have turned red, then drain, refresh in iced water and drain again. Next, cook the claws in the same pan of boiling water for at least 7 minutes (cooking time will depend on the size of the claws) or until they too have turned red, then drain, refresh in iced water and drain again. Keep 2 of the 4 claws whole, then remove the meat from the other 2 and dice it (reserve the shells). Keep the lobster tails whole, but trim off any raggedy bits to tidy them up and chop this meat. Remove the shells from the 2 tails, then reserve the whole tails and 2 whole claws, place them on a plate and refrigerate. Combine the diced claw meat and chopped tail trimmings in a dish, then cover and refrigerate – this meat will be used for the macaroni and the whole tails and whole claws will be used for serving and the garnish. Reserve all the shells for the bisque.

Preheat the oven to 200°C/Gas Mark 6. Put the lobster heads, along with the reserved shells, in a roasting tin and roast in the oven for 45 minutes or until deep golden brown. Remove from the oven and lightly crush the shells using a rolling pin.

Heat the olive oil in a large stockpot and sauté the shallots, fennel, carrot, celery, garlic, peppercorns and coriander seeds, with a little salt and pepper added (be conservative with the salt as the bisque can easily become salty), over a medium heat for about 10 minutes or until golden brown. Add the herbs, cayenne pepper, tomato purée, diced tomatoes and roasted crushed lobster shells.

Add the brandy to the pan and let it bubble, stirring and scraping the base of the pan with a wooden spoon to deglaze it, then cook over a high heat for 5–6 minutes or until the brandy is reduced and becomes syrupy. Add the vermouth to the pan and cook over a high heat for 7–8 minutes or until the vermouth is reduced and becomes syrupy. Add the fish and chicken stocks, then bring to a gentle simmer and cook for 40 minutes, removing any scum from the surface with a ladle.

Remove from the heat and carefully pour the mixture into a blender and blend until smooth. Pass the mixture through a fine sieve, then return the liquid to a clean saucepan (discard the solids in the sieve). Bring the bisque to the boil over a medium heat, then simmer for 15–18 minutes or until reduced, thickened, glossy and dark golden copper brown in colour.
Stir in the cream and simmer for 5 minutes, then remove from the heat and taste and adjust the seasoning, if necessary. Measure the 300ml lobster bisque needed for the macaroni and keep it hot, then cool and chill the leftover bisque (see Cook's Note for instructions on how to cool, store and reheat the leftover lobster bisque).

Make the lavish lobster macaroni. Preheat the oven to 200°C/Gas Mark 6. Lightly grease an ovenproof serving dish and set aside. Cook the macaroni in a large pan of boiling salted water for 8–10 minutes or until al dente, then drain well.

Place the cooked macaroni in a large mixing bowl, then add the measured lobster bisque, a ladleful at a time, stirring to mix and adding just enough until you have a nice juicy pasta mixture that isn't too sloppy. Stir in 100g of the mascarpone, 50g of the Parmesan cheese, the spring onions, egg yolks, chopped herbs and the diced lobster meat (from the 2 claws and tail trimmings), mixing well. Season to taste with salt and pepper.

Spoon the lobster macaroni into the prepared ovenproof dish, spoon the rest of the mascarpone on top in small dollops and then sprinkle over the remaining Parmesan cheese. Bake in the oven for about 25 minutes or until golden brown on top and bubbling.

Remove from the oven and leave to rest for 10 minutes while you sauté the reserved lobster tail meat and the 2 whole claws. Melt the butter in a non-stick frying pan, then add the whole (shelled) lobster tails and the 2 whole claws and sauté over a fairly low heat for 5–7 minutes or until hot throughout.

To serve, spoon the lobster macaroni on to serving plates. Cut the sautéed lobster tails into 5mm-thick slices and carefully cut the sautéed claws in half. Arrange the sliced lobster meat on top of the macaroni, garnish each portion with half a lobster claw, then finish with the semi-dried cherry tomatoes and fried basil leaves. Serve immediately.

Serve with a simple mixed seasonal green leaf or garden salad, tossed with a little Classic Vinaigrette (see page 19), if you like.

Cook's Note

Once you have measured the 300ml hot lobster bisque that you need for the macaroni, pour the remaining lobster bisque into a suitable bowl and cool it rapidly over ice. Once cool, pour the lobster bisque into an airtight container and chill in the fridge, then use within 3 days. Alternatively, freeze for up to 3 months, then defrost in the fridge overnight (once defrosted, you may have to thin the bisque down a little with some stock). Reheat the lobster bisque in a saucepan over a low heat until piping hot and then serve as a light lunch with buttered brown bread.

'Tinned' British Sardines with Heirloom Tomato and Onion Salad

This recipe is dedicated to my late father, Harlan. He loved tinned sardines served with thickly sliced tomatoes and raw onion, seasoned with lots of freshly cracked black pepper and salt. As a child, it made me cringe as I didn't like the smell of tinned sardines, but as I grew older the smell reminded me of dad, and nowadays I find it less off-putting as it brings back fond memories.

I have prepared my own 'sardines in a tin' by selecting really small fresh sardines for this recipe, and the accompanying tomato salad features heirloom tomatoes. Go on, be inspired and make your own version of this classic combination!

You will need to start this recipe the day before you want to serve it as the 'tinned' sardines are left to marinate for 12 hours. Ideally, like me, you would serve this recipe in new sardine tins, which you can buy from some good cookshops, specialist chef's equipment companies or online (see Cook's Notes).

Serves 6 as a starter or light lunch

1kg fresh small sardines (total/ unprepared weight), descaled, filleted and pin bones removed (keep skin on)
½ teaspoon coriander seeds
¼ teaspoon fennel seeds
a pinch of crushed dried chillies
1 star anise
¼ teaspoon black peppercorns
200ml dry white wine
200ml white wine vinegar
100ml crustacean oil or olive oil (see Cook's Notes)
2 bay leaves
½ teaspoon sea salt
1 clove garlic, lightly crushed
250g fresh samphire
100g fresh sea purslane leaves
2 heirloom tomatoes
2 spring onions, sliced
2 small round shallots, sliced
6 thin slices wholegrain bread
sea salt and freshly cracked black pepper

For the 'tinned sardines', wash the sardine fillets and pat dry, then place them, skin-side up, in a single layer in a wide, flat, white plastic tray or non-metallic container and set aside.

Lightly toast all the spices in a small dry saucepan over a medium heat for 2–3 minutes – once you hear the seeds pop, they are ready. Add the wine and white wine vinegar to the pan, then bring to the boil over a high heat and simmer for 2 minutes. Remove from the heat and add the crustacean or olive oil, bay leaves, salt and garlic. Set aside to cool to about 37°C (blood temperature) – if you can comfortably hold your finger in the mixture, then it's the right temperature. Pour the mixture over the prepared sardine fillets in the tray, covering them completely, then cover and refrigerate for 12 hours or overnight.

The next day, prepare the salad. Bring a large saucepan of water to the boil. Blanch the samphire in the boiling water for 1 minute, then remove using a slotted spoon, dunk in iced water, drain, pat dry and set aside. Do the same with the sea purslane, blanching it for 20 seconds only, then dunk in iced water, drain and pat dry. Divide the blanched samphire and sea purslane between 6 new sardine tins or suitable dishes (see Cook's Notes), then divide the marinated sardine fillets between the tins and drizzle over some of the marinating liquid. Discard any leftover marinating liquid.

Slice the tomatoes and divide them between 6 serving plates, then scatter the spring onions and shallots over the tomatoes and season with salt and pepper. Toast the bread on both sides and place on the serving plates. Serve a 'tin of sardines' on each plate alongside the tomato salad and toast. Serve immediately.

Cook's Notes

Ideally, you would serve this recipe in brand new sardine tins, which you can buy from some good cookshops, specialist chef's equipment companies or online. You will need six new sardine tins, each about 11.4 x 6.9 x 3cm in size. Alternatively, you can simply serve the salad and 'tinned' sardines in suitable small shallow dishes, serving bowls or ramekins.

To make crustacean oil, preheat the oven to 200°C/Gas Mark 6. Put 80–100g leftover shells from fresh crayfish, lobsters or crabs in a roasting tin and roast in the oven for 30 minutes or until deep golden brown. Remove from the oven and crush the shells with a rolling pin, then mix the hot crushed shells with 250ml sunflower oil or groundnut oil in a bowl. Cover and refrigerate for at least 24 hours before use and for up to 5 days (the longer it's left, the better the flavour and colour will be), then pass the oil through muslin cloth or a fine sieve into an airtight container, cover and keep refrigerated until needed. Use within 2 weeks. This crustacean oil also makes the basis of wonderful dressings for seafood salads.

Courgette-wrapped Chicken Skewers (Spiedini Toscana)

This recipe is dedicated to the Italian holidays many of us enjoy each year. I love the Italians' way of thinking when it comes to cooking, and I simply adore their food. Their philosophy is to grow fresh fruit and vegetables, eat them when they're at their best and keep their recipes simple. They celebrate their own regions, they are patriotic and they believe their locality is the best. In this recipe, I've tried to capture this ethos and a little bit of their passion too.

The direct meaning of spiedini is cubes or balls of meat on a skewer and it derives from the word spiedie that means 'spit roast'. For my delicious take and version of spiedini, I'm using diced chicken thighs dipped in a garlic-infused lemon butter, which are then dipped in breadcrumbs laced with Parmesan cheese, parsley and lemon zest. After that, the chicken cubes are wrapped in wafer-thin slices of courgette, before cooking them. The chicken retains its moisture and the fresh lemon zest provides a zingy flavour for the taste buds to enjoy with every bite.

This dish shouts summer to me! I cook these spiedini over a coal barbecue and it's truly delicious. You might think that the breadcrumbs will burn but they don't, they become crispy and golden, and the courgettes act as a blanket and help to steam the chicken inside.

This dish is a simple affair, but it looks pretty and impressive and it tastes magnificent!

Serves 4 as a main course

500g organic or free-range skinless, boneless chicken thigh fillets (see Cook's Notes)
50g coarse fresh breadcrumbs
2 tablespoons coarsely chopped fresh flat-leaf parsley
1 teaspoon coarsely chopped fresh oregano
finely grated zest of 2 lemons
30g finely grated fresh Parmesan cheese
40g unsalted butter
3 tablespoons extra virgin olive oil
1 small clove garlic, crushed
juice of 1 lemon
2 courgettes, trimmed
sea salt and freshly cracked black pepper

Preheat the barbecue. I like to use a coal barbecue but gas barbecues work just as well. I tend to cook the chicken skewers over a cool barbecue, so if you are planning to barbecue other food, then I would suggest that you cook the chicken skewers towards the end once the coals have cooled slightly (see Cook's Notes).

Cut the chicken thighs into large (3–4cm) dice and set aside. For the breadcrumb coating, put the breadcrumbs, parsley, oregano, lemon zest and Parmesan cheese in a bowl and mix together. Set aside.

Put the butter and olive oil in a saucepan and heat gently until the butter is melted. Remove from the heat and add the garlic, lemon juice and salt and pepper.

Dip each piece of chicken into the melted garlic butter, then roll in the breadcrumb mixture to coat completely, using your hands to press the breadcrumb mixture on firmly. Lay the chicken pieces on a baking tray lined with non-stick baking paper and leave to rest in the fridge for about 10 minutes. Meanwhile, slice the courgettes lengthways into 2mm-thick slices or long ribbons using a mandolin.

Wrap each piece of breadcrumbed chicken in a courgette ribbon and gently roll up. Thread about 4 pieces of courgette-wrapped chicken on to each skewer (use metal or soaked wooden skewers); 1 skewer then makes a good portion. Cook the chicken skewers over a cool barbecue for 18–20 minutes or until cooked all the way through and golden brown all over, turning them regularly. Serve immediately. Serve with Star Anise and Cinnamon-Pickled Beetroot (see page 234) or with a fresh tomato, rocket and Pecorino salad, if you like.

Cook's Notes

Use chicken breast fillets instead of chicken thighs, if you prefer, as the crumb and courgette coating protects the chicken and you will still retain the meat's moisture.

If you don't have a barbecue, this recipe works just as well if cooked in the oven. Preheat the oven to 200°C/Gas Mark 6. Place the chicken skewers on a baking tray lined with non-stick baking paper and roast in the oven for 16–18 minutes or until cooked all the way through and golden brown all over, turning once.

Orford-landed Sea Bass with Crispy Potatoes, Bacon and Sea Purslane

Orford is a fantastic place, though getting to it is slightly tricky as it requires manoeuvring down narrow country lanes, but the 'pot of gold at the end of the rainbow' is fantastic. A true gem in its own right, the village has lots of character and wonderful 'olde worlde' seaside charm.

Small coastal villages such as Orford, home to the local fishing trade, can be found all along Britain's coastline. It's up to each and every cook out there to go and rediscover these small villages and buy freshly caught fish to support the local economy.

Sea purslane is a fantastic wild coastal foraging find with its matt green, slightly swollen leaves and an interesting, salty taste of the sea. It combines well with sea bass and adds a lovely flavour to this special dish.

Serves 4 as a main course

For the seaweed vinaigrette

a large handful of baby spinach leaves (about 40g)
2 dark green sheets nori (paper-thin toasted sheets of seaweed)
2 teaspoons mirin
2 teaspoons warm water
juice of 1 lime
2 tablespoons sunflower oil or groundnut oil
sea salt and freshly cracked black pepper

For the pan-roasted sea bass and warm smoked bacon, broad bean and sea purslane salad

8 new potatoes (480–520g total weight), washed but left unpeeled
20 fresh sea purslane leaves
2 French breakfast radishes, trimmed
3 tablespoons olive oil
2 rashers smoked back bacon, cut into strips
125g fresh broad beans (double-podded weight – see page 164 for instructions on how to double-pod broad beans)
4 sea bass fillets (150–180g each), skin on, pin bones removed
sea salt and freshly cracked black pepper

For the broad bean and sea purslane tempura

75g self-raising flour
20g cornflour
a pinch of sea salt
1 egg yolk
125ml sparkling water
2 egg whites
sunflower oil, for deep-frying
50g fresh broad beans (double-podded weight – see page 164 for instructions on how to double-pod broad beans)
20 fresh sea purslane leaves, rinsed and patted dry

First, make the seaweed vinaigrette and then refrigerate it to allow the flavours to develop. Put the baby spinach leaves, nori sheets, mirin, warm water, lime juice and salt and pepper in a blender and blend together until smooth. With the motor running, slowly add the sunflower oil until it is all incorporated. Taste and adjust the seasoning, if necessary. Pour the vinaigrette into a bowl, then cover and refrigerate for a minimum of 20 minutes before using.

Meanwhile, prepare the potatoes for the salad to accompany the sea bass. Cook the new potatoes in a pan of boiling salted water for 15–18 minutes or until tender. Drain, refresh in cold water, then drain again. Peel the potatoes, then break them into irregular, bite-sized chunks. Set aside at room temperature.

Next, make the batter for the broad bean and sea purslane tempura. Put the flour, cornflour, salt, egg yolk and sparkling water into a bowl and mix together to form a smooth paste. In a separate grease-free bowl, whisk the egg whites until they form soft peaks. Fold the whisked egg whites into the batter and then set aside for 5 minutes.

Finish the salad. Rinse the sea purslane leaves and pat dry, then finely shred them. Finely slice the radishes using a mandolin. Set aside. Heat 2 tablespoons olive oil in a large, non-stick frying pan until hot, then sauté the potato chunks and bacon strips over a high heat for 5–6 minutes or until golden brown. Stir in the shredded sea purslane and the broad beans and sauté for a further 1–2 minutes or until heated through, then taste and adjust the seasoning, if necessary. Remove from the heat, stir in the radishes and keep warm. Meanwhile, finish the tempura, heat some sunflower oil in an electric deep-fat fryer or in a deep frying pan to a temperature of 160°C (or until a small piece of bread browns within 20 seconds in the hot oil). Once the oil is hot enough and you are ready to serve, first dip the broad beans in the tempura batter and deep-fry them in the hot oil for about 2 minutes or until golden and crisp all over. Using a slotted spoon, remove and drain the broad bean tempura on kitchen paper, season with salt and keep hot. Next, dip the sea purslane leaves in the tempura batter and deep-fry them in the hot oil for 1½–2 minutes or until golden and crisp all over. Using a slotted spoon, remove and drain the sea purslane tempura on kitchen paper, season with salt and keep hot.

In the meantime, cook the fish. Heat the remaining 1 tablespoon olive oil in a large, non-stick frying pan until hot. Season the fish fillets with salt only, then place the fillets, skin-side down, in the pan and cook over a high heat for about 2 minutes (depending on the thickness of the fillets) or until golden brown. Turn the fillets over and cook on the flesh side for about 1 minute or until the fish is cooked and golden brown.

Serve the warm salad on serving plates, place the sea bass fillets on top, then drizzle the vinaigrette over and around. Garnish with the tempura broad beans and sea purslane. Serve immediately.

Picnic in a Jar

I'm like a dog with a bone. Once I get an idea into my head I will not let it go without trying it at least once. I love this fabulous idea of a picnic in a jar. I know it's not revolutionary as the lunchbox was invented before I even existed, but hey, it's making me feel good!

The pasta that I use in this recipe is little pieces of pasta called orzo pasta. It's now regularly available from most supermarkets, but a few years ago that was not the case. When on holiday in other countries, Mr. P and I like to visit their supermarkets to look for unusual ingredients that we might not get here. We brought a packet of orzo pasta back from the Greek island of Santorini a few years ago and learned the lesson that you can find culinary inspiration wherever you go.

This recipe is perfect for a picnic (or lunch boxes) and al fresco dining, so simply pack it all in jars, take some spoons and enjoy it with your friends!

Fills 10 x 350ml glass jars with metal clip tops

For the meatballs

1 slice white or wholemeal bread
50ml milk
350g lean minced beef
1 small red onion, finely chopped
1 clove garlic, crushed
1 egg
1 teaspoon cumin seeds, crushed
1 teaspoon coriander seeds, crushed
2 tablespoons pine nuts, toasted and chopped
2 tablespoons chopped fresh mixed soft herbs (such as parsley, chervil and oregano)
1 teaspoon wholegrain mustard
1 tablespoon sunflower oil
sea salt and freshly cracked black pepper

For the pasta and roasted tomato salad

600g ripe tomatoes, roughly chopped
2 orange peppers, deseeded and roughly chopped

2 fresh red chillies, deseeded and chopped
2 tablespoons tomato purée
2 tablespoons balsamic vinegar
3 tablespoons extra virgin olive oil
1 clove garlic, crushed
2 bay leaves
200g orzo pasta (or use any small pasta of your choice)
4 spring onions, chopped
a small bunch of fresh coriander, chopped
finely grated zest and juice of ½ lemon
4 tablespoons Roasted Tomato Mayonnaise (see recipe below)

For the roasted tomato mayonnaise
100g roasted tomato mixture (from the salad recipe above)
2 egg yolks
1 teaspoon Dijon mustard
1 teaspoon creamed horseradish
200ml sunflower oil or groundnut oil

To finish
200g feta cheese
3 tablespoons pine nuts, toasted
3 tablespoons pitted kalamata olives, chopped

First, make the meatballs. Place the bread in a shallow dish, pour over the milk and leave to soak for about 10 minutes. Place the soaked bread, minced beef and all the remaining ingredients for the meatballs, except the sunflower oil, in a large mixing bowl. Season with salt and pepper. I like to get my hands dirty so give it all a good mix together using your hands. Divide the meatball mixture into 30 equal portions, then roll each portion into a walnut-sized ball. Place the meatballs on a large plate and leave them to rest in the refrigerator for 30 minutes.

Heat the sunflower oil in a large, non-stick frying pan until hot, then pan-fry the meatballs over a medium heat for 12–14 minutes or until golden brown all over and cooked through, carefully turning them regularly (see Cook's Notes). Remove the cooked meatballs to a plate and leave to cool completely. Once cool, cover and refrigerate until needed.

Next, prepare the pasta and roasted tomato salad. Preheat the oven to 200°C/Gas Mark 6. Put the tomatoes, peppers, chillies, tomato purée, balsamic vinegar, 2 tablespoons olive oil, the garlic and bay leaves in a deep casserole and mix together. Cover and roast in the oven for 50 minutes or until the mixture is reduced, glossy and a deep red colour. Remove from the oven and leave to cool completely, then weigh out 100g of the mixture for the mayonnaise and keep it separate. Refrigerate both portions of the roasted tomato salad.

Cook the orzo pasta in a pan of boiling salted water for 8–10 minutes or until cooked or al dente. Drain, refresh in cold water, then drain again. Toss the cold pasta in the remaining 1 tablespoon olive oil.

Put the cold pasta in a bowl, add the spring onions, coriander, lemon zest and juice and the chilled roasted tomato salad mixture and mix well, then set aside at room temperature while you make the mayonnaise.

Make the roasted tomato mayonnaise. Put the reserved 100g roasted tomato mixture, the egg yolks, mustard, horseradish and salt and pepper in a small blender and blend together until smooth. With the motor running, gradually and slowly add the sunflower oil until the mixture forms an emulsion and the mayonnaise is thick. If the mayonnaise becomes a bit too thick before you have added all the oil, whisk in 1 tablespoon hot water, then continue slowly adding the oil until it is all incorporated. Taste and adjust the seasoning, if necessary.

Measure 4 tablespoons of the roasted tomato mayonnaise, add it to the pasta and roasted tomato salad and toss to mix.

To assemble the picnic pots, divide the pasta and roasted tomato salad evenly between the glass jars with metal clip tops, filling each one about half full. Place 3 cold cooked meatballs into each jar, then to finish, crumble the feta cheese over the meatballs and top with a sprinkling of the pine nuts and olives. Finish each portion with a small dollop of the roasted tomato mayonnaise, then cover the jars and refrigerate. Keep refrigerated and use within 3 days. Take the filled picnic pots along with you on a picnic or serve instead of packed lunches, remembering to pack teaspoons or small forks and a few napkins for serving.

Cook's Notes
Instead of pan-frying the meatballs, place them on a large baking tray in a single layer and roast in a preheated oven at 200°C/Gas Mark 6 for 12–14 minutes or until cooked and golden brown. Cool, then refrigerate, as directed.

Put any remaining roasted tomato mayonnaise into an airtight container, store in the fridge and use within 3 days. Combine the leftover mayonnaise with cold cooked peeled prawns and use as a filling for a sandwich, or toss the mayonnaise with cold cooked new potatoes and serve with slices of cold cooked ham, hard-boiled eggs and some cheese for a light lunch or supper.

Roasted Rumps of Lamb with Baby Artichokes, Baby Beets and Fennel Purée

This dish is a combination of lots of ingredients I simply adore – artichokes, beetroot, lamb and fennel. For this recipe, I make a purée with the fennel, the baby beets are cooked then marinated and I even use the beetroot leaves. To finish, the rumps of lamb are roasted and the artichokes are sautéed to create this really special seasonal main course. Preparing artichokes is a time-consuming activity, but ultimately a rewarding one.

Serves 4 as a main course

For the baby beets

a bunch of raw baby beetroots (about 16 baby beets – 900g–1kg total weight)
1 teaspoon sea salt
1 tablespoon olive oil
1 teaspoon sherry vinegar
1 teaspoon coriander seeds, crushed
1 clove garlic, crushed
a sprig of fresh thyme
1 bay leaf

For the fennel purée

1 tablespoon unsalted butter
1 fennel bulb, trimmed and sliced
60ml white wine
80ml chicken stock
sea salt and freshly cracked black pepper

For the roasted rumps of lamb

8 baby artichokes, prepared and cooked (left whole with leaves and 'chokes' removed – see page 233 for instructions on how to do this)
2 tablespoons unsalted butter
2 lamb rumps (160–180g each)
100g fresh broad beans (shelled weight)
about 120g baby beetroot leaves, reserved from the baby beets above (select the smallest and most tender leaves)
60g fresh buckler leaf sorrel, rinsed and patted dry, to garnish

First, prepare the baby beets. Trim the tops off the baby beetroots, reserving the smallest leaves for the roasted rumps of lamb. Place the baby beets in a large saucepan, cover with cold water and add the salt. Cover, then bring to the boil over a medium-high heat and cook for 20–25 minutes or until tender. Once cooked, drain the baby beets, refresh in cold water and drain again, then peel them, keeping them whole.

Place the baby beets in a suitable container, add the olive oil, sherry vinegar, coriander seeds, garlic, thyme and bay leaf and stir to mix, then cover and refrigerate for 1 hour. (Just before reheating and serving, remove and discard the thyme sprig and bay leaf.)

Prepare the fennel purée. Melt the butter in a saucepan and once the butter starts to foam, add the fennel and salt and pepper, then cover and sweat over a medium heat for 8–10 minutes or until the fennel starts to turn transparent, stirring occasionally.

Add the wine to the pan and let it bubble, stirring and scraping the base of the pan with a wooden spoon to deglaze it. Cook over a high heat for 1–2 minutes or until the wine is reduced and becomes syrupy. Add the stock, then cover and cook over a low heat for about 10 minutes or until the fennel is tender. Remove the lid and cook over a high heat for a further 5–6 minutes or until all the stock has evaporated.

Remove from the heat, then carefully transfer the mixture to a blender and blend until smooth. Return the fennel purée to a clean saucepan and reheat gently until hot, then keep warm until you are ready to serve.

For the roasted rumps of lamb, preheat the oven to 200°C/Gas Mark 6. Cut the prepared and cooked artichokes into quarters and set aside. Melt 1 tablespoon butter in a non-stick frying pan, season the lamb rumps with salt and pepper, then add them to the pan and cook over a high heat for about 3 minutes on each side or until browned and sealed all over. Transfer the lamb to a roasting tin and roast in the oven for about 8 minutes for medium-rare. Remove from the oven, then transfer the lamb rumps to a wire rack, cover with foil and leave to rest for 5 minutes.

While the lamb is resting, sauté the artichokes. Use kitchen paper to wipe clean the frying pan used to seal the lamb. Melt the remaining butter in the frying pan and sauté the artichokes, with salt and pepper added, over a high heat for 5–6 minutes or until golden brown. Drain on kitchen paper.

In the meantime, reheat the baby beets in their juices in a small saucepan over a high heat for 4–5 minutes or until piping hot throughout. Blanch the broad beans and beetroot leaves in a pan of boiling salted water for 1–2 minutes or until tender, then drain. Spoon the warm fennel purée on to the serving plates, then arrange the artichokes, baby beets, broad beans and beetroot leaves on the plates. Carve the roast lamb into slices and serve the equivalent of half a lamb rump per portion. Garnish with the sorrel and serve immediately.

Gooseberry Curd and Brown Sugar Meringue Mess with Garibaldi Biscuits

I like making and eating fruit curds and I believe there is a fruit curd for all seasons. The natural tartness of the gooseberries in this recipe works well with the sweetness of the crushed brown sugar meringues.

Early on in the season the green gooseberries will produce a green-coloured curd, but later on look out for the red variety that will make a curd with a slight pink tinge to it. Any leftover gooseberry curd will keep in the fridge for up to 3 days and it is ideal for filling cooked pastry tartlet cases for afternoon tea.

The Garibaldis are great. This recipe is very trustworthy as we use it in the pub every day and have made hundreds of Garibaldi biscuits over the years. I make a large batch of the biscuit dough, then roll it into logs, wrap it in cling film and keep it in the freezer. When I need to bake some biscuits, I simply defrost a log of the dough in the fridge overnight, then cut the biscuits the next day and bake them. Once baked, the garibaldis and meringues will both keep well in separate airtight containers for up to 1 week.

Serves 6

For the mini brown sugar meringues (makes about 5–50 mini meringues)

6 egg whites
200g soft dark brown sugar
200g caster sugar
a pinch of table salt

For the Garibaldi biscuits (makes about 24 biscuits)

150g unsalted butter, softened
150g icing sugar
1 egg
200g plain flour
200g currants
50g caster sugar

For the gooseberry compôte

350g caster sugar
50ml St. Germain elderflower liqueur
1 vanilla pod, split in half lengthways and seeds scraped out
500g fresh gooseberries, topped and tailed, rinsed and drained

For the gooseberry curd

400g cooked Gooseberry Compôte (from recipe above)
50ml freshly squeezed lemon juice
2 whole eggs
2 egg yolks
125g chilled unsalted butter, cut into small pieces

First, make the mini brown sugar meringues. Preheat the oven to 110°C/ Gas Mark ¼ and line 2–3 large baking trays with non-stick baking paper.

Place the egg whites, both sugars and the salt in a large saucepan. Put on a clean pair of disposable gloves to cover your hands. Place the saucepan over a very low heat to gently heat the egg whites and dissolve the sugar. Put one of your hands into the egg white and sugar mixture and stir it continuously to help dissolve the sugar. By using your hand, you can control the heat, as you do not want to heat the mixture above 37°C (blood temperature). Once the mixture has reached 37°C (this will take about 5 minutes), remove the pan from the heat and continue stirring with your hand for another minute. Transfer the mixture to an electric stand mixer fitted with a balloon whisk and whisk for 6–8 minutes or until the mixture becomes very thick and glossy. Transfer the meringue mixture to a piping bag fitted with a medium plain nozzle, then pipe 45–50 small peaked rounds (each about the size of a small walnut, with a peaked top) on to the prepared baking trays, spacing them well apart.

Bake the mini meringues in the oven for about 1 hour or until they are dry. Check that they are cooked by touching their outsides – if they are firm on the outside but still slightly gooey in the centre they are done. Remove from the oven, then carefully peel the meringues off the paper and transfer to a wire rack to cool completely. Store the mini meringues in an airtight container in a cool, dry cupboard and use within 1 week.

Next, make the Garibaldi biscuits. Cream the butter and icing sugar together in a bowl until pale and fluffy. Add the egg and beat until well mixed. Sift the flour over the creamed mixture and add the currants, then mix it all together but do not overwork the mixture. Divide the mixture into 3 equal portions, then place each portion on to a sheet of cling film and roll it up in the cling film to form a sausage or log shape, each one measuring about 10–12cm in length and 3–4cm in diameter. Refrigerate the logs of biscuit dough for at least 1 hour before cutting and baking (see Cook's Notes).

To bake the Garibaldi biscuits, preheat the oven to 180°C/Gas Mark 4 and line 2 large baking trays with non-stick baking paper. Unwrap the logs of chilled biscuit dough (discard the cling film) and cut each one into 8 even thick slices. Place the slices on the prepared baking trays, leaving a little space between each one. Bake in the oven for 12–15 minutes or until golden brown and crisp. Remove from the oven and immediately sprinkle the biscuits with the caster sugar, then transfer them to a wire rack and leave to cool completely. Store the Garibaldi biscuits in an airtight container in a cool, dry cupboard and use within 1 week.

Make the gooseberry compôte. Put the sugar, elderflower liqueur and vanilla seeds in a saucepan and cook over a low heat, stirring until the sugar has dissolved, then increase the heat, bring to the boil and boil for 5 minutes. Add the gooseberries and then cook rapidly, uncovered, for 5–8 minutes or until the first berries start to burst. Remove from the heat, transfer the compôte to a bowl and leave to cool completely, then cover and chill until needed (see Cook's Notes).

For the gooseberry curd, weigh 400g of the gooseberry compôte into a blender and blend until smooth (set the remaining compôte aside). Add the lemon juice, whole eggs and egg yolks and blend together, then pass the mixture through a sieve and transfer to a heatproof mixing bowl. Place the bowl over a pan of simmering water (making sure that the bottom of the bowl does not come into contact with the simmering water underneath) and heat gently, stirring continuously with a wooden spoon, until the mixture starts to thicken, then continue to cook gently for a further 10–12 minutes or until the gooseberry curd thickens enough to coat the back of the spoon; do not allow the mixture to boil or it will curdle.

Remove the pan from the heat (but leave the bowl set over the pan) and gradually but quickly whisk the cold butter into the gooseberry curd, a few pieces at a time, until the butter is completely melted and incorporated – by this stage you should have a rich, creamy and glossy gooseberry curd. Pour the warm curd into a clean bowl, place a piece of cling film directly on the surface to prevent a skin forming, cool and then refrigerate for up to 3 days. If you are making the gooseberry curd to serve another time, pour the warm curd into hot sterilised jars (the gooseberry curd will make about 3 x 200g jars). Cover with wax discs (wax-side down) and seal. When cold, label, then store in the fridge and use within 2–3 weeks. Once opened, keep in the fridge and use within 3 days.

To assemble the desserts, select 6 suitable large serving glasses. For each dessert, spoon 1½ tablespoons of the remaining gooseberry compôte into the base of each glass, crush 2 mini brown sugar meringues over the compôte and then spoon 1½ tablespoons of the gooseberry curd on top. Repeat these layers once more for each dessert.

Decorate each dessert with 3 mini brown sugar meringues and serve each one with 2 Garibaldi biscuits alongside. Serve immediately.

Cook's Notes

The wrapped logs of unbaked Garibaldi dough will keep in the fridge for up to 3 days. They can also be frozen for up to 3 months. If frozen, when required, simply defrost a log of dough in the fridge overnight, then cut and bake as directed above.

The gooseberry compôte can be stored in an airtight container in the fridge for up to 3 days. It can also be used as a filling for pre-baked pastry tartlet cases or for filling a freshly baked sponge cake, if you like. Alternatively, for a tempting dessert, serve the gooseberry compôte hot or cold with custard or cream and some shortbread biscuits.

Serve any leftover mini meringues with coffee for an after-dinner sweet treat.

If you are making the meringues to serve them as a simple dessert, sandwiched together in pairs with whipped cream, you can make larger, standard-size meringues instead of mini meringues, if you like. Simply pipe the meringue mixture into 6–8cm rounds or ovals on the prepared baking trays, spacing them well apart. Bake in the oven for 2–3 hours or until the meringues are crisp and dry. Cool and store as directed above.

Chocolate and Raspberry Meringue Sandwich Cookies

These spiced chocolaty biscuits with soft naughty centres are outrageously delicious! The blend of flavours is bold, but I think the raspberry, chocolate, cinnamon and coffee combination really works well!

The meringue disc centres are both crispy and chewy and are laced with fragrant homemade raspberry jam. They are sandwiched between the chocolate and cinnamon crackle cookies to create these fabulous sweet treats.

These little beauties are packed with flavour and are definitely a grown ups' tea party temptation!

Makes 15 sandwich cookies

For the raspberry jam
150g fresh raspberries
150g caster sugar
juice of ½ lemon

For the chocolate and cinnamon crackle cookies
80g unsalted butter, softened
250g soft dark brown sugar
125g cocoa powder
2 teaspoons instant coffee granules
1 teaspoon bicarbonate of soda
1 teaspoon ground cinnamon, plus extra for dusting
2 egg whites
100g natural yogurt
1 teaspoon vanilla extract
300g plain flour
150g Raspberry Jam (see recipe above), to assemble

For the meringue discs
3 egg whites
200g caster sugar
½ teaspoon white wine vinegar

First, make the raspberry jam. Place the raspberries in a heavy-based saucepan and add the sugar. Cook over a low heat, stirring to dissolve the sugar, then increase the heat and bring the raspberry mixture to the boil. Boil rapidly for 10–12 minutes or until the jam reaches a temperature of 105°C (setting point), stirring every now and then to prevent it from catching and skimming off any scum from the surface. If you don't have a jam thermometer, check to see if setting point has been reached by spooning a little of the jam on to a chilled small plate. Push a finger across the jam; if the surface wrinkles and it is beginning to set, it has reached setting point. If not, boil it for a further 5 minutes or so and test again. Stir in the lemon juice, then pour the jam into a heatproof bowl and leave to cool completely. Once cool, cover and refrigerate until needed (see Cook's Notes).

Next, make the cookie dough. Cream the butter and brown sugar together in a bowl until light and fluffy. Add the cocoa powder, coffee granules, bicarbonate of soda and 1 teaspoon cinnamon and mix well. Add the egg whites, yogurt and vanilla extract and mix well, then stir in the flour, mixing to form a soft dough. Divide the cookie dough into 3 equal portions, then place each portion on to a sheet of cling film and roll it up in the cling film to form a sausage or log shape, each one measuring about 10–12cm in length and 3–4cm in diameter. Refrigerate the logs of cookie dough for at least 1 hour before cutting and baking (see Cook's Notes).

While the cookie dough is chilling, make the meringue discs. Preheat the oven to 110°C/Gas Mark ¼ and line 2 large baking trays with non-stick baking paper. I normally mark the underside of the paper with 5cm circles (you will need a total of 15 thin meringue discs) to indicate the size of the meringues I will be piping.

Place the egg whites, caster sugar and white wine vinegar in a saucepan. Put on a clean pair of disposable gloves to cover your hands. Place the saucepan over a very low heat to gently heat the egg whites and dissolve the sugar. Put one of your hands into the egg white and sugar mixture and stir it continuously to help dissolve the sugar. By using your hand, you can control the heat, as you do not want to heat the mixture above 37°C (blood temperature). Once the mixture has reached 37°C (this will take about 5 minutes), remove the pan from the heat and continue stirring with your hand for another minute.

Transfer the mixture to an electric stand mixer fitted with a balloon whisk and whisk for 6–8 minutes or until the mixture becomes very thick and glossy. Transfer the meringue mixture to a piping bag fitted with a small plain nozzle, then pipe fifteen 5cm discs, each about 5mm-thick (it is important that the meringue discs are thin), on to the prepared baking trays, spacing them well apart.

Bake the meringue discs in the oven for 30–45 minutes or until they are dry. Check that they are cooked by touching their outsides – if they are firm and dry on the outside but are still slightly gooey and chewy in the centre, they are done. Remove from the oven, then carefully peel the meringue discs off the paper and transfer to a wire rack to cool completely.

To bake the cookies, preheat the oven to 180°C/Gas Mark 4 and line 2 baking trays with non-stick baking paper. Unwrap the logs of chilled cookie dough (discard the cling film) and cut each one into 10 even slices (you need a total of 30 cookies).

Place the slices on the prepared baking trays, leaving space between each one, then press each one out to form a 5cm round (so they are the same size as the meringue discs). Bake in the oven for 10–12 minutes or until golden brown and crisp on the outside. I like the cookies to be slightly soft, but you can bake them for a further couple of minutes or so, if you prefer them to be crispy. Remove from the oven and let the cookies cool on the baking trays for 1 minute, then transfer them to a wire rack and leave to cool completely.

To assemble the sandwich cookies, use 2 cookies and 1 meringue disc for each one. For each sandwich cookie, spread ½ teaspoon of the chilled raspberry jam on one side of a cookie, then place a meringue disc on top of the jam. Spread a second cookie with ½ teaspoon of the raspberry jam and then sandwich it to the other side of the meringue disc to make a sandwich cookie. Repeat with the remaining cookies, raspberry jam and meringue discs to make 15 sandwich cookies in total. Lightly dust the sandwich cookies with ground cinnamon and serve immediately (see Cook's Notes).

Cook's Notes

Any leftover raspberry jam will keep in an airtight container in the fridge for up to 1 week. Serve it with freshly baked scones or stir a spoonful or two into cooked porridge for breakfast. The wrapped logs of unbaked cookie dough will keep in the fridge for up to 3 days. They can also be frozen for up to 3 months. If frozen, when required, simply defrost a log of dough in the fridge overnight, then cut and bake as directed above.

Once assembled, serve the sandwich cookies on the same day and within about 4 hours of assembling.

If you would like to keep some sandwich cookies for the following day, store the cookies and meringue discs in separate airtight containers, keep the jam in the fridge and then assemble the sandwich cookies the next day.

Left: Chocolate and Raspberry Meringue Sandwich Cookies, page 262
Right: Mulberry and Gin Bakewell Tart, page 266

Mulberry and Gin Bakewell Tart

Mulberries are fruits from my childhood. Mum has a large mulberry tree in her front garden and it came in handy when I had silk worms, as the leaves were perfect food for them. Dad disliked the mulberry tree as the birds got a bit fruity and decorated the drive rather unpleasantly! Mulberries are fragile, perishable fruits and they start to deteriorate as soon as they are picked. I too have a tree in our garden at home here in the UK and as soon as the fruits ripen, I pick and freeze them immediately to make sure they don't get wasted in any way. Our generous customers at the pub often bring us some wonderful fresh produce and mulberries are one of those. Our bartering or exchange system (see page 12 for more details on this) is definitely working and it's heart-warming to get the whole community involved.

Serves 6–8

300g Sweet Shortcrust Pastry (see page 18)

For the bakewell mixture
150g unsalted butter, softened
150g caster sugar
1 tablespoon gin
4 eggs
finely grated zest and juice of 1 lemon
170g ground almonds
160g Mulberry Jam (see page 238)
50g fresh mulberries
20g flaked almonds

For the glaze
50g icing sugar
1 teaspoon gin
juice of 1 lemon

Roll out the pastry on a lightly floured work surface to about 2mm thickness and use it to line a (loose-bottomed, if you like) 35 x 10 x 2.5cm fluted oblong flan tin (leaving a slight overhang of pastry). Leave to rest in the fridge for 30 minutes.

Preheat the oven to 160°C/Gas Mark 3. Prepare the bakewell mixture. Cream the butter and caster sugar together in a bowl until pale and fluffy, add the gin, then add the eggs, 1 at a time, beating well after each addition. Add the lemon zest and juice, then fold in 150g of the ground almonds until well mixed.

Spread the mulberry jam evenly over the base of the chilled pastry case, then sprinkle over the remaining ground almonds. Spoon the bakewell mixture over the top, spreading it evenly, then scatter over the mulberries and flaked almonds. Bake in the oven for about 45 minutes or until the filling is well-risen and golden brown.

Remove from the oven to a wire rack and leave the tart to cool completely in the tin before trimming the pastry and pouring over the glaze. Once cold, trim the overhanging pastry from the top edges of the tart with a small, serrated knife.

For the glaze, sift the icing sugar into a small bowl, stir in the gin, then gradually stir in enough lemon juice, mixing to make a smooth, pourable glaze that is not too runny in consistency. Pour the glaze evenly over the cold tart and leave to set. Once the glaze has set, carefully remove the tart from the tin and cut it into slices. Serve with either whipped cream, crème fraîche, vanilla ice cream or custard.

My Grandmother's Gooseberry Ginger Beer

My late maternal grandmother was a wonderful cook and she kept the most amazing recipe book. This precious book is now in the hands of my very lucky mother. When visiting me a few years ago, mum brought this book with her. We had a wonderful trip down memory lane, leafing through the book, and amongst the tears, there was a lot of laughter as we came across some of the most bizarre recipes you could possibly imagine in my grandmother's collection. There were recipes for making soap and homemade golden syrup, through to ginger beer, atjar (a South African chutney), spiced sausages, tripe, brawn and many more interesting delights.

With freshly picked gooseberries sitting in a basket on the kitchen table one day, I was inspired to make ginger beer. We found three recipes for ginger beer in my grandmother's recipe book. One was unusable as it called for crystals – we are still wondering today exactly what kind of crystals she was referring to. We eventually settled for the third recipe, and after a bit of tweaking, the end result was this wonderful recipe for gooseberry ginger beer.

I will be making this recipe for many years to come, remembering that glorious Sunday afternoon in the kitchen with my mum, granny's recipe book and the gooseberries.

Makes about 2 litres gooseberry ginger beer

Serves 8–10

300g fresh gooseberries, topped and tailed
400g caster sugar
1 teaspoon ground ginger
50g fresh root ginger, peeled and finely chopped
100g sultanas
juice of 2 lemons
2 litres cold water
1 sachet (7g) fast-action/easy-blend dried yeast

Preheat the oven to 200°C/Gas Mark 6 and line a large baking tray with non-stick baking paper. Set aside. Rinse the gooseberries, then drain. Put the gooseberries in a large mixing bowl with the sugar and ground ginger and stir to mix. Transfer the gooseberry mixture to the prepared baking tray, spreading it out evenly, then roast in the oven for 30 minutes or until tender. By this stage, the gooseberries will have started to burst and some will probably have started to go golden brown.

Transfer the roasted gooseberry mixture to a food processor, scraping in all the syrupy bits, then add the root ginger and sultanas and blend until smooth. Transfer the mixture to a large saucepan, add the lemon juice, plus the squeezed-out lemon halves, then add the water. Bring to a gentle simmer, then cook for 2 minutes. Remove from the heat and set aside until the mixture is cool enough for you to be able to hold your finger comfortably in it (about 37°C or blood temperature). Stir in the yeast until dissolved. Cover the pan with cling film and refrigerate overnight.

The next day, pass the ginger beer through a fine sieve or muslin cloth into a clean bowl, then pour it into sterilised bottles to about three-quarters full. Cover and seal the bottles, but do not tighten them too tightly, otherwise they may have the potential to explode. Refrigerate for 2 days before serving to allow the mixture to ferment, and then use within 1 week (after a few days or so the ginger beer will start to lose its fizz).

The British Larder | *August*

270

It's the height of the British summer this month and farmers all over the country are preparing for harvest time. The British summer berry season is coming to an end with blueberries, raspberries and currants going out of season, but other berries such as blackberries and hedgerow brambles are in full fruit. Stone fruits such as apricots, peaches and plums are also at their best now.

Beans of all varieties are perfect at this time of year with fresh borlotti, runner, green and bobby (dwarf) beans ready to be picked and enjoyed. Grey mullet, herring and monkfish, to name just a few of the wonderful delights from the sea, are delicious and tasty during August; a great reminder that summer is here.

The Suffolk coast

The game season is kicking off yet again for another season this month with the glorious grouse starting the season on the 12th August.

August signifies the height of the pickling and preserving season, when fresh produce is in abundance and the urge to savour the season's finest is at its peak. During August, look out for the beautiful greengages and the early dark purple damsons and bullaces and other wild plums.

Fresh cobnuts and small, young, soft green walnuts (ideal for pickling) both have short seasons, so pick them now and store them correctly (or pickle the walnuts) to enjoy later in the year.

Season's best during August...

Apricots, Artichokes, Aubergines, Beetroot, Blackberries, Black Cabbage (Cavolo Nero), Blueberries, Borage Flowers, Borlotti Beans, Broad Beans, Broccoli, Carrots, Celery, Chard, Chives, Cobnuts, Cod, Coley, Courgettes, Crab, Crab Apples, Crayfish (freshwater), Cucumbers, Damsons, Dover Sole, Duck, Fennel, Flounder, Garlic, Green Beans, Greengages, Grey Mullet, Grouse (from 12th August), Haddock, Halibut, Herring, Kohlrabi, Lamb, Langoustines, Lettuce, Lobster, Loganberries, Mackerel, Mint, Monkfish, Onions, Oregano, Parsley, Peaches, Peppers, Plaice, Plums, Pollack, Potatoes (main crop), Prawns, Pumpkins, Rabbit, Radishes, Raspberries, Redcurrants, Rocket, Rosehips, Rosemary, Runner Beans, Sage, Salmon, Samphire, Sardines, Scallops, Sea Bass, Sea Beet, Sea Plantain, Sea Purslane, Sorrel, Summer Savory, Sweetcorn, Swiss Chard, Tarragon, Thyme, Tomatoes, Walnuts (young green ones, for pickling), Watercress, Whelks, Whitebait, Wild Plums (Bullaces, Mirabelles), Woodpigeon.

My culinary rituals for August...

For me, there is a preserve, pickle and/or jam for every season, but August is the month where these activities are crucial, with produce in abundance and the urge to savour the season's best taking over. Try my recipes for **Sweet and Sour Pickled Green Beans** (see page 270) or **Plum Cheese** (see page 284). Our hedgerows in the countryside are the perfect place to look for wild foods to feast on. Apart from making jams, chutneys and preserves, my flavoured vinegar collection is also starting to take shape at this time of year, with a range of flavours including my **Bramble and Rosemary Vinegar** (see page 273).

Harvest and collect the fruits, nuts and vegetables from the garden and tidy and replenish the ground for the winter vegetables that require planting. Try my delicious seasonal vegetable and fruit recipes such as **Roasted Heritage Carrot Soup** (see page 281), **Fresh Borlotti Bean, Prawn and Chorizo Bake** (see page 288), **Mustard Seed-smoked Beef with Soft-boiled Duck Eggs and Cobnuts** (see page 286) or **Plum and Blackberry Jelly with Plum Sorbet** (see page 294).

Fresh garden herbs will be coming to an end soon, so savour them by picking large bunches of rosemary, lavender and thyme, tie them in bunches and hang them in a cool, dark, well-ventilated room or garage to dry out. Once dried, shake the branches and capture the dried leaves/flowers and keep them in clean glass jars to be used in soups, sauces and stews during the winter months to come.

The game season is also about to start, so make friends with local gamekeepers, meet up with acquaintances and book those all-important shooting days.

British Larder Heroes

Apricots

Related to the plum, apricots are round, striking orange-yellow and pink-blushed stone fruit with an aromatic flavour, soft flesh and a velvety skin. There are many varieties of apricot and although apricots are native to continental climate regions with cold winters, it's relatively easy to grow them in the UK. The apricot tree is hardier than the peach tree and can tolerate erratic weather changes more easily. Fresh apricots can be eaten raw or cooked and are ideal stewed, baked or poached or used in sorbets and flans or pies; apricots can also be made into a lovely jam. Apricot kernels or seeds, with their distinctive almond flavour, are sometimes used as a substitute for almonds, but they are more commonly used to flavour the almond liqueur, amaretto. Dried apricots and ready to eat dried apricots are also readily available in several varieties.

To make **Rosemary-Roasted Apricots**, preheat the oven to 200°C/Gas Mark 6 and line a baking tray with non-stick baking paper. Wash, halve and stone 6 fresh apricots and place the apricot halves in a mixing bowl. Add 1 tablespoon caster sugar, 1 tablespoon clear honey, the roughly chopped leaves from a sprig of fresh rosemary and a pinch of table salt. Mix together and then spread the apricots out in a single layer on the prepared baking tray. Bake in the oven for 20 minutes, by which time the apricots should have collapsed slightly and the sugar caramelised. Remove from the oven and leave to rest for 10 minutes before serving warm with a scoop of vanilla ice cream for dessert. Alternatively, transfer to a bowl, leave to cool completely, cover and chill in the fridge, then serve chilled for breakfast with natural yogurt and toasted almonds. Serves 2 for dessert or breakfast.

Beans – borlotti beans

Fresh borlotti beans are also known as cranberry beans. The beautiful pink-speckled pods enclose the most wonderful and pretty pinkish-brown oval-shaped beans, speckled/streaked with dark red. If you grow your own, don't be tempted to pick them too early as they need to be fully ripe before harvesting. If you open a pod and the beans are still green inside, they are not ready – they need to be pinkish-brown and speckled with dark red to be ready for harvesting. Borlotti beans have a pale flesh with a smooth and creamy texture and an earthy, slightly sweet flavour. They are used in soups, stews, casseroles and salads and are popular in Italian cooking. To cook fresh borlotti beans, simply cook them in a pan of boiling salted water for about 15 minutes or until tender. Borlotti beans are also readily available as canned beans or dried beans. If using dried beans, soak the dried beans overnight in plenty of cold water, then rinse and drain them before cooking the beans. Boil them rapidly in fresh, unsalted water for 10 minutes, then reduce the heat and simmer for about 1½ hours or until tender (the cooking time will depend on the age of the dried beans). Remember not to add salt to the water at the beginning, as salt will toughen the bean skins; add salt 10 minutes before the end of the cooking time.

Borlotti beans

Beans – green beans

There are around 130 varieties of green beans, so it's understandable why they have so many different names. Some call them common green beans, others call them string beans or dwarf beans, but the most common variety is the finer, thinner French bean. These are easy to grow in the UK and they produce a good yield. Here in the UK, we also grow the bobby bean, which is the fatter variety of the green bean, with its fleshy texture and sweet flavour. The green bean season is long and stretches for most of the summer months; many gardeners often manage to plant two crops of green beans per season. Green beans are best eaten when they are young and tender and are usually eaten whole or cut into short lengths and lightly steamed or boiled. Once cooked, green beans can be served hot, warm or cold. If serving them cold, once cooked, refresh them in iced water to ensure they keep their bright green colour. They are often served as an accompaniment, but are also used in salads, soups and other dishes.

Green beans are one of the essential ingredients for a Niçoise salad, so try my tasty recipe for **Roasted Chicken and Green Bean Niçoise**. First, make the dressing. Put 3 tablespoons olive oil, 1 teaspoon wholegrain mustard, 1 tablespoon cider vinegar, 1 crushed small clove garlic, 1 teaspoon chopped fresh parsley and sea salt and freshly cracked black pepper to taste in a small, clean, screw-top jar. Put the lid on and shake vigorously to mix, then set aside. Soft-boil 2 duck eggs in a pan of boiling water for 7 minutes, drain, refresh in iced water and drain again, then peel and set

Blackberries

aside. Cook 80g fresh green beans in a pan of boiling water for about 2 minutes or until al dente, then drain, refresh in iced water and drain again. Put the cooked green beans into a large bowl, then add 1 tablespoon pitted black olives, 2 quartered tomatoes, 10 cold cooked new potatoes, halved, 6 canned (drained) anchovy fillets, ripped into small pieces, 2 handfuls of mixed seasonal salad leaves and the flaked meat from 2 cold roasted chicken legs. Toss to mix, then drizzle over the dressing to taste. Divide the salad between 2 serving plates, cut the duck eggs in half, and serve 2 egg halves on each plate. Season with salt and pepper and serve with fresh crusty bread. Serves 2 as a lunch or supper.

Blackberries and brambles

Blackberries are plump, dark blue-black soft berries that are a relative of the rose and raspberry and there are several varieties, some of which are cultivated and others that grow wild and are a common sight in our hedgerows at this time of the year. Blackberries, also often referred to as brambles, are a popular edible fruit in Britain. Wild blackberries are normally smaller in size with a highly perfumed fragrance and taste but, when cultivated, blackberries tend to have a larger and sometimes more elongated shape with a slightly diluted taste. Like loganberries, raspberries, boysenberries, dewberries (a smaller relative of the blackberry) and tayberries, blackberries and brambles grow on long, rambling thorny canes or bushes. Once picked, they should be used as quickly as possible as they spoil easily. Blackberries can be eaten raw or cooked, and in cooking they work well with most game and poultry, such as the classic combination of pheasant and blackberries. In fact, many wild birds feast on brambles too, as they are very nutritious. Blackberries also pair well with apples and are ideal for pies, crumbles, jams and jellies.

For a lovely fruit vinegar, try my recipe for **Bramble and Rosemary Vinegar**. Sterilise one 250ml bottle with a lid and set aside. Place 10 fresh brambles or blackberries in a small bowl, then sprinkle over 1 teaspoon caster sugar and crush with a fork. Spoon this mixture into the prepared bottle, add a sprig of fresh rosemary and then top the bottle up with red wine vinegar. Seal, label and store the vinegar in a cool, dry cupboard for up to 12 months. Once opened, store in the fridge and use within 1 week. Use the vinegar for making salad dressings or as an ingredient when pickling vegetables, such as beetroot. The vinegar can also be used as an ingredient when making chutneys or when making marinades for meats such as beef or venison. Makes about 250ml.

Carrots

Carrots are very common sweet root vegetables from a biennial plant, primarily known for their familiar orange colour, but other colours such as purple, white and yellow carrots are also available. They are members of the parsley family (and are related to parsnips, fennel and celery) and they come in a range of shapes and sizes. Carrots are an excellent source of beta-carotene (which the body converts into vitamin A and which gives the carrot its typical orange colour), as well as vitamin C, potassium and fibre. Carrots be eaten raw or cooked and can be used in a wide variety of savoury and sweet dishes, including salads, juices, purées or as crudités, and also in soups, casseroles, burgers, halva and carrot cake.

My delicious carrot cake recipe is easy to make and although it requires a bit of labour at first, once all the ingredients are in the bowl, it's just a case of stir and bake. For **Maddy's Ultimate Carrot Cake**, preheat the oven to 160°C/Gas Mark 3 and grease and line a 24–25cm springform cake tin. Warm 50ml dry cider in a small pan over a high heat for a few minutes or until it just starts to boil, then remove from the heat, pour over 100g sultanas in a bowl and set aside for 15–20 minutes. Sift 300g plain flour, 1 teaspoon baking powder, 1 teaspoon bicarbonate of soda and a pinch of table salt into a large mixing bowl. Add 350g soft dark brown sugar, 80g roughly chopped (shelled) pistachio nuts, 80g toasted sunflower seeds, 125g grated (cored but unpeeled) eating apples and 250g grated carrots (preferably with their skins on – wash well and pat dry before grating). Measure 250ml rapeseed oil into a measuring jug, then add 4 eggs and lightly whisk together. Add the egg mixture and the soaked sultanas and cider to the flour mixture and stir together lightly with a wooden spoon until combined. Transfer the mixture to the prepared tin and level the surface. Bake in the oven for about 1 hour or until risen and deep golden brown and a skewer inserted into the centre of the cake comes out clean. Remove from the oven and leave the cake to cool in the tin for 10 minutes, then carefully turn it out on to a wire rack and leave to cool completely. Once cold, dust the cake heavily with icing sugar and serve in slices with crème fraîche or clotted cream. Serves 8–10. The carrot cake will keep in an airtight container in a cool, dry cupboard for up to 3 days. This cake also freezes well – wrap the cold cake in a double layer of foil or cling film and freeze for up to 3 months. Defrost at room temperature overnight before serving.

Carrots

Cobnuts

Cobnuts are a type of hazelnut (also known as filbert), although unlike hazelnuts, we tend to eat cobnuts fresh and do not generally store them throughout the year. There are several varieties of cobnuts that grow in Britain, but they are mainly grown in the southern county of Kent in the UK, hence they are often known as Kentish cobnuts. Cobnuts are green when they are young and they become golden as they mature. They can be eaten fresh and raw at this time of the year, or they can be dried or processed for use at a later date and eaten on their own, or roasted and used whole or ground in desserts, baking and confectionery.

For a lovely sweet treat to enjoy with a mug of tea or coffee, try my recipe for **Cobnut Shortbread Biscuits**. Shell

Cobnuts

enough cobnuts (350–400g with shells) so that you have 200g cobnuts (shelled weight), then roughly chop them and set aside. Cream 125g softened unsalted butter and 55g caster sugar together in a bowl until pale and fluffy. Sift 150g plain flour, 30g cornflour and a pinch of table salt over the creamed mixture. Add the cobnuts and gently mix together until the dough just comes together. Shape the dough into a log or sausage shape, about 4cm in diameter and wrap in cling film, then refrigerate for 2 hours. Preheat the oven to 180°C/ Gas Mark 4 and line 2 baking trays with non-stick baking paper. Unwrap the log of dough (discard the cling film) and cut the log into about twenty-four 1cm-thick slices, then place the slices on the prepared baking trays, leaving a little space between each one. Bake in the oven for 15–18 minutes or until cooked but still pale in colour. Remove from the oven and immediately sprinkle over plenty of caster sugar, then leave the biscuits to cool on the baking trays for 5 minutes before transferring them to a wire rack to cool completely. The biscuits will keep in an airtight container in a cool, dry cupboard for up to 1 week. Makes about 24 biscuits.

Duck eggs

Duck eggs are larger than hen's eggs (about twice the weight), but the taste is quite similar. The white of a duck egg is more gelatinous and the yolk is a striking, deep yellow colour and tastes richer than those of hen's eggs. The richness of duck eggs makes them ideal for baking cakes as the yolks provide a rich yellow sponge. Duck eggs have now become more fashionable to eat here in the UK, whereas in Asia they have been a delicacy for many centuries. In that part of the world, particularly in China, the 1000-year-old egg, also known as the 'century egg' or Chinese preserved egg, is a popular choice. These preserved eggs are raw duck (or hen's) eggs that are covered with a paste (typically made from salt, wood ash, garden lime and black tea or rice husks) and left to ferment in earth or earthenware containers for a period of time (usually several months – typically for 100 days, despite their main name) before they are then washed, shelled and eaten as an appetiser.

Try my **Duck Egg Mayo Sandwich** for a tasty snack or lunch. Bring a small pan of water to a rapid boil, carefully place 2 duck eggs into the boiling water, then bring back to the boil and boil for 9 minutes. Remove from the heat and drain, then immediately run cold water over the eggs to cool them quickly. Drain, then peel the eggs while still warm. In a small bowl, mash the hard-boiled eggs with a fork, then season with sea salt (or celery salt, if you have it to hand) and plenty of freshly cracked black pepper. Stir in 1 tablespoon good quality mayonnaise, a squeeze of fresh lemon juice and a sprinkling of snipped fresh chives (you can add a few chive flowers too, if they're available). Butter one side of each of 2 thick slices of dark rye bread. Spoon the egg mixture on to one of the buttered slices, top with plenty of freshly cut mustard cress and then place the other slice of bread on top. Eat immediately while the egg mixture is still slightly warm. Serves 1.

Herrings

Herrings are oily fish that are rich in protein, vitamins and omega-3 fatty acids. North Atlantic and North Sea herrings are plentiful, moving about in large shoals, though due to some over-fishing and ecological factors, they are less widely available than they once were. These relatively small, slender fish, with their steel blue skin and silvery white undersides, are mainly food for larger predators such as halibut, tuna and salmon, as well as humans. Herrings have a rich, firm flesh and they can be eaten fresh and cooked whole or filleted (they have many tiny bones), either grilled, pan-fried, barbecued or poached, or coated with oatmeal and fried. They can also be preserved in several ways, including pickled, smoked, salted, marinated and soused. Herrings are commonly eaten in the UK for breakfast in the form of kippers, whereas in other European and Scandinavian countries they are more popular pickled as fillets and served as rollmops.

Kippers are herrings that have been split, gutted and cold-smoked. For a seasonal supper, try my **Kipper Rice Salad**. First, make the vinaigrette. Measure 3 tablespoons olive oil, 1 teaspoon Dijon mustard, 1 teaspoon mild curry powder and 1 tablespoon cider vinegar into a small, clean, screw-top jar, then add the finely grated zest and juice of 1 lemon, a pinch of caster sugar, and sea salt and freshly cracked black pepper to taste, then put the lid on and shake vigorously to mix. Set aside. Preheat the grill to medium and line a baking tray with foil, then butter the foil. Place 2 kippers (450–500g total weight) on the prepared baking tray, brush them with melted butter and grill for about 2 minutes on either side or until the skin is crispy and the kippers are hot throughout. Remove from the heat and cool slightly, then remove the skin and bones from the fish and flake the flesh into a bowl. Add 300g cooked mixed brown, white and wild rice to the fish, together with 1 sliced small round shallot, 1 sliced spring onion, 1 diced celery stick, a handful of fresh watercress, 1 tablespoon chopped (drained) capers and 1 tablespoon chopped (drained) gherkins and stir to mix. Give the dressing a quick shake, then drizzle it over the rice salad and toss to mix. Adjust the seasoning to taste. Serve the kipper rice salad in a large bowl and top with 2 cold hard-boiled eggs, shelled and cut into quarters. Garnish with a little more fresh watercress and finely grated lemon zest. Serve immediately. Serves 2 as a light lunch or supper.

Herring

Plums

Victoria plums are said to be the queen of plums. First cultivated in Sussex in 1840, Victoria plums quickly became the nation's favourite. There are now over 300 cultivated plum varieties available in Britain, plus the various wild plums, such as damsons, greengages, bullaces, sloes, mirabelles and cherry plums. Plums vary in size and colour from blue-black to golden yellow to purple-red. Dried plums are known as prunes. We all love to get something for free and at this time of the year be on the look out for wild plums in the hedgerows, as you are bound to find something useful. Plums freeze well so you can keep them for the colder months when stone fruits are less readily available. Most plums can be eaten either raw or cooked and they are ideal for stewing, poaching or baking, or for use in pies, tarts, crumbles, batter puddings, cobblers, fools and ices. Due to their high pectin content, plums are also ideal for making jams and jellies. They are not only synonymous with sweet recipes, but are also equally good for use in savoury dishes and they work wonderfully with rich meats such as duck.

Try my tasty savoury recipe for **Grilled Goat's Cheese Salad with Cobnuts and Plum Sauce**, which uses plums to make a lovely sauce. First, make the plum sauce. Melt 1 tablespoon unsalted butter in a saucepan, then add 1 finely diced onion, 1 crushed clove garlic and sea salt and freshly cracked black pepper and sauté over a medium heat for 5–6 minutes or until softened. Add 5 stoned and thinly sliced fresh plums (such as Victoria, Opal or Jubilee plums, greengages or bullaces), then add 1 teaspoon caster sugar, 2 tablespoons cider vinegar, 2 tablespoons white wine, 1 cinnamon stick and 2 cloves and cook over a medium heat for 10–15 minutes or until the mixture is thickened and jam-like, stirring regularly. Remove from the heat. While the plum sauce is cooking, preheat the grill to high. Put four 1cm-thick slices of soft goat's cheese (each slice weighing about 40g and taken from a log of soft goat's cheese with rind on) on a greased baking tray, sprinkle over 1 teaspoon roughly chopped fresh thyme leaves, splash over a drizzle of olive oil, then grill the cheese for 2–3 minutes or until it starts to brown and bubble. To serve, spoon a tablespoon of the plum sauce on to each serving plate, followed by 2 slices of grilled goat's cheese. Add a handful of lightly dressed seasonal salad leaves to each portion and then scatter over a sprinkling of toasted fresh (shelled) cobnuts. Serve immediately. Serves 2 as a light lunch or supper or serves 4 as a starter (serving 1 slice of grilled goat's cheese and a small handful of salad leaves per portion). Cool any leftover plum sauce, store it in an airtight container in the fridge and use within 3 days. Use in a duck and sugar-snap pea stir-fry and serve with cooked rice noodles, or serve the plum sauce cold in a sandwich with sliced smoked ham and peppery salad leaves.

Savory

Summer savory is an annual herb with lilac-coloured elongated flowers and slightly larger, more rounded, soft green leaves than the winter variety, which is a perennial herb. Both types of savory have a pungent, robust, peppery flavour (a bit like a mixture of rosemary and thyme with a hint of pepper), though the winter savory is slightly milder in flavour than the summer variety. Summer savory is at its best between July and September and it goes very well with chicken, turkey, duck, lamb, celeriac and potatoes and it works particularly well with squashes and pumpkin.

Both types of savory are good with fresh green beans and dried beans, as well as in hearty soups and meaty stews and casseroles. If, like me, you are quite fond of this herb, you can pick and tie the fresh summer savory into bunches, then hang and leave it to dry in a cool, dark, well-ventilated place. Once it is dry, remove the leaves from the stalks and then keep it in a sealed jar in a cool, dry cupboard. Add the dried herb to dishes such as shepherd's pie or Bolognese sauce.

For some herby scones to serve with soup, try my recipe for **Summer Savory Scones**. Preheat the oven to 220°C/ Gas Mark 7 and line a baking tray with non-stick baking paper. Set aside. Sift 225g self-raising flour and 1 teaspoon baking powder into a mixing bowl, then rub in 50g diced cold unsalted butter until the mixture resembles fine breadcrumbs. Stir in 100g grated mature Cheddar cheese, 1 teaspoon mustard powder, 2 tablespoons chopped fresh summer savory and sea salt and freshly cracked black pepper to taste. Add 80ml buttermilk and 1 egg and mix gently to form a soft dough. Turn the dough on to a lightly floured work surface and knead lightly, then gently roll the dough out to about 2cm thickness. Use a 5cm round plain cutter to cut out about 9 scones. Place on the prepared baking tray and brush the tops with beaten egg yolk, then sprinkle with linseeds or poppy seeds and season with a little extra sea salt. Bake in the oven for 8–10 minutes or until the scones are well risen and golden brown. Transfer to a wire rack and leave to cool. Serve warm with homemade soup such as Roasted Heritage Carrot Soup (see page 281). Makes about 9 scones.

Plums

Apricot and Thyme Soda

This soda drink recipe is refreshing and perfect for a hot summer's day. Serve it ice-cold, diluted with chilled soda water or sparkling mineral water and, if you're in the mood, add a 25ml measure of gin to each glass. You will need to start this recipe the day before you want to serve it, to allow enough time for the apricot mixture to infuse overnight.

Makes about 600ml

Serves 6

450g fresh ripe apricots
250g caster sugar
250ml cold water
3 large sprigs of fresh thyme, plus a few extra sprigs (lightly crushed), to serve
finely grated zest and juice of 1 lemon
chilled soda water or sparkling mineral water and ice cubes, to serve

Wash, halve, stone and roughly chop the apricots, then combine them with the sugar, water and 3 large thyme sprigs in a saucepan. Cook over a low heat, stirring until the sugar has dissolved, then bring to the boil and simmer for 4–5 minutes or until the apricots are softened. Remove from the heat and transfer the mixture to a bowl, then stir in the lemon zest and juice. Leave to cool, then cover and leave to infuse in the fridge for at least 12 hours or overnight.

The next day, pass the mixture through a fine sieve or muslin cloth. Keep the apricot pieces for another use (see Cook's Notes), discard the thyme and pour the apricot syrup into a clean container, then cover and keep refrigerated until needed. The apricot syrup will keep in an airtight container in the fridge for up to 3 days.

Dilute the chilled apricot syrup to taste with chilled soda water or sparkling mineral water and serve with plenty of ice. Decorate with extra lightly crushed thyme sprigs (see Cook's Notes) and serve immediately.

Cook's Notes

Store the reserved apricot pieces in an airtight container in the fridge and use within 3 days. Serve the apricot pieces with Buttermilk Ice Cream (see page 119) for a lovely dessert. Alternatively, serve them with bircher muesli for breakfast, or blend the apricot pieces with natural yogurt, milk and a tablespoon or so of rolled oats for a tasty breakfast smoothie.

To lightly crush fresh thyme sprigs, gently rub them between your hands to lightly bruise them and release the essential oils.

Sweet and Sour Pickled Green Beans

Summer is the season of plenty and many keen gardeners will have a glut of something, whether it's beans, raspberries, plums or perhaps courgettes. This recipe is one answer if you have a surplus of green beans. Cooking these sweet and sour pickled green beans is not difficult and is actually very quick, but the preparation is time-consuming.

I find that a glass of wine, a chair, a chopping board and a sharp knife do the trick and, of course, if you have a friend to gossip with even better; the time passes by quickly and before you know it, the beans are prepared and all that is left to do is the cooking.

These sweet and sour pickled green beans are tasty served hot or cold and they will brighten up a picnic hamper beautifully. Serve them as a salad at a barbecue or as an accompaniment to a delicious homemade ham terrine with toasted sourdough bread. I like a large spoonful of these pickled beans on a slice of freshly baked bread with thick slices of Montgomery Cheddar and a cup of tea – a perfect lunch fit for a queen!

Makes 4 x 250g jars

600g green beans (such as French beans, runner beans, bobby beans – whatever type of green beans you have a glut of)
225ml malt vinegar
15g cornflour
225g soft light brown sugar
225g onions (peeled weight), finely diced
1 clove garlic, crushed
1 tablespoon golden syrup
1 tablespoon curry powder (I like Sharwoods' mild curry powder)
1 teaspoon turmeric
1 teaspoon mustard powder
1 teaspoon sea salt
freshly cracked black pepper, to taste

Top and tail the beans, then cut them diagonally into 2–3mm-thick slices in short lengths. Blanch the beans in a large saucepan of boiling salted water for 1 minute, then drain and immediately plunge them into a bowl of iced water. Set aside.

In a separate saucepan, combine the malt vinegar and cornflour, stirring until smooth. Add the rest of the ingredients and then bring the mixture to the boil, stirring. Reduce the heat to a gentle simmer and cook for about 5 minutes or until thickened, stirring.

Drain the green beans, then add them to the simmering mixture. Cover and bring the mixture back to the boil, then simmer for 1 minute. Remove from the heat and taste and adjust the seasoning, if necessary.

Spoon the pickled beans into hot, sterilised jars, then cover with vinegar-proof lids and seal. Leave to cool, then label and store in a cool, dry cupboard. Store for at least 1 week before using to allow the flavours to develop. The unopened jars of pickled green beans should keep well in a cool, dry cupboard for up to 6 months. Once opened, store in the fridge and use within 1 week.

These pickled green beans are delicious served hot or cold. If you want to serve them hot, simply empty a jar of the pickled beans into a small saucepan and heat gently for a few minutes or until piping hot before serving.

Borlotti Bean and Courgette Hummus

280

This recipe is by no means a classic hummus, but it does have the fundamentals of a hummus-style dish. I'm using fresh borlotti beans and courgettes for this earthy and delicious seasonal dish. For this recipe, it's important to choose a really good quality olive oil that has a fruity taste. Serve with plenty of breadsticks or toasted pitta bread.

Makes about 500g hummus

Serves 4 as a starter

250g fresh borlotti beans (shelled weight) (see Cook's Notes)
1 bay leaf
½ teaspoon sea salt
4 tablespoons extra virgin olive oil
1 onion, finely diced
4 cloves garlic, crushed
250g courgettes, trimmed and sliced
1 tablespoon tahini (see Cook's Notes)
1 teaspoon ground sumac
juice of ½ lemon
sea salt and freshly cracked black pepper

Place the borlotti beans in a saucepan with the bay leaf and cover with cold water. Cover and bring to the boil, then reduce the heat and simmer gently for about 15 minutes or until the beans are cooked and tender. Add the measured salt to the beans for the last 5 minutes of the cooking time. Drain the beans, discard the bay leaf and set the beans aside to cool completely.

Meanwhile, heat 1 tablespoon olive oil in a non-stick frying pan until hot, then add the onion, garlic and a little salt and pepper and sauté over a medium heat for about 8 minutes or until the onion is just starting to caramelise. Add the courgettes and sauté for a further 5–6 minutes or until the courgettes are tender and starting to colour. Remove from the heat.

Place the borlotti beans, onion and courgette mixture, tahini, three-quarters of the sumac, the lemon juice and salt and pepper in a food processor or blender. Blend together until smooth, then taste and adjust the seasoning, if necessary. Spoon the hummus into a serving dish, drizzle over the remaining olive oil and sprinkle with the remaining sumac to garnish. Serve immediately with breadsticks or toasted pitta bread, torn into pieces.

Cook's Notes

Canned borlotti beans can be substituted for the fresh beans, if you like. Use 250g (rinsed and drained weight) canned borlotti beans. There is no need to cook the canned beans, so simply blend the rinsed and drained beans with the onion and courgette mixture, etc, to make the hummus. Alternatively, you can use canned butter beans or chickpeas instead of the borlotti beans.

What is tahini? Tahini is a thick, creamy paste made from ground sesame seeds. It is readily available in jars or plastic tubs from most large supermarkets, health food shops or delicatessens. It reminds me of peanut butter as it is similar in texture, but it is made from sesame seeds not peanuts. Open the jar of tahini and stir it well before use. Once opened, keep it refrigerated and use within 1 month. I love adding a teaspoon or two of tahini to marinades, salad dressings or soups. It also adds an extra dimension if you add 1 tablespoon tahini to uncooked flapjack and cookie mixtures before baking.

The hummus can be made in advance. Store it in an airtight container in the fridge and use within 3 days. Remove the hummus from the fridge about 10 minutes or so before serving to allow the flavours to come through.

Roasted Heritage Carrot Soup

Carrots are humble vegetables of the earth that are common all over the world. Using heritage carrots when making something as simple as a carrot soup adds a different dimension to this popular recipe. Using very fresh or freshly dug carrots gives a more intense and pure flavour. If you can't lay your hands on these funky carrots, then use standard fresh organic carrots instead.

Serves 6 as a starter or light lunch

1kg orange heritage carrots, trimmed and washed (peel left on)
1 purple heritage carrot (80–100g), trimmed and peeled
1 yellow heritage carrot (80–100g), trimmed and peeled
2 tablespoons rapeseed oil, plus extra for the garnish
2 cloves garlic, unpeeled
50g unsalted butter
2 banana shallots, sliced
1 teaspoon coriander seeds, crushed
1.5 litres vegetable stock
sea salt and freshly cracked black pepper
a little chopped fresh flat-leaf parsley, to garnish

Preheat the oven to 200°C/Gas Mark 6 and line 2 baking trays (one of which should be large) with non-stick baking paper. Set aside. Cut the prepared orange carrots into 5mm slices/rings. Cut the prepared purple and yellow carrots into 5mm slices/rings and set aside.

Spread the orange carrot slices out on the prepared large baking tray, add 1 tablespoon of the rapeseed oil and salt and pepper and stir to mix, then roast in the oven for about 1 hour or until the carrots are very soft and golden, stirring once or twice to prevent them from burning (at the end of the cooking time, if there are a few dark carrots, that's absolutely fine). At the same time, toss the purple and yellow carrot slices in the remaining 1 tablespoon oil, season with salt and pepper, then spread them out on the second prepared baking tray. Roast in the oven for 40 minutes, stirring once or twice, then add the garlic cloves and roast for a further 20 minutes or until the carrots are soft and golden. Remove both trays of roasted carrots from the oven, set aside and keep hot.

Meanwhile, just before the carrots are ready, melt the butter in a large saucepan and once it starts to foam, add the shallots and sauté over a high heat for 5–6 minutes or until they start to turn golden brown. Add the coriander seeds and sauté for 1 minute, then add the roasted orange carrots. Pop the roasted garlic flesh out of its skin, add to the pan and sauté for a further minute. Add the stock and bring the soup to a gentle simmer, then cover and cook for 10 minutes or until slightly thickened.

Remove from the heat, then carefully transfer the soup to a blender and blend until smooth. Return to the pan and if the soup is a bit too thick for your liking, add a little more stock or water. Reheat gently until hot, then taste and adjust the seasoning, if necessary.

To serve, ladle the hot soup into soup bowls and garnish each portion with the roasted purple and yellow carrot slices, a drizzle of rapeseed oil and a sprinkling of flat-leaf parsley and freshly cracked black pepper. Serve immediately with fresh crusty bread or warm herb scones, such as Summer Savory Scones (see page 277).

Left: Borlotti Bean and Courgette Hummus, page 280
Right: Roasted Heritage Carrot Soup, page 281

Plum Cheese

This is a most delicious and highly concentrated fruit jelly that is best served with savoury food such as cheese or roast pork, duck or game. Substitute the plums for damsons, mixed wild plums, blackberries and apples or quinces. This plum cheese will keep in a sealed jar in the fridge for up to 1 month.

Makes about 1 x 250g jar

400g fresh ripe plums (of your choice)
100ml cold water
50g caster sugar
2 leaves of gelatine
½ teaspoon agar agar powder (see page 16)

Wash the plums and cut them in half, but leave the stones intact, then place them in a saucepan with the water and sugar. Heat gently, stirring to dissolve the sugar, then cover the pan and bring the mixture to a simmer over a medium heat. Remove the lid, reduce the heat and, stirring regularly, simmer for about 25 minutes or until the mixture is soft, pulpy, reduced and thickened. Remove the pan from the heat, then cover and set aside for 30 minutes.

While the fruit mixture is resting, soak the gelatine in cold water until it has softened.

Pass the plum mixture through a sieve, discard the stones and then pour the plum purée into a small saucepan. Stir the agar agar powder into the plum purée, bring to the boil over a low heat, stirring constantly, then simmer for 2 minutes, stirring. Remove from the heat.

Squeeze the gelatine gently to remove excess water, then add the gelatine to the hot plum purée and stir until dissolved.

Pour the plum cheese into a hot, sterilised jar. Cover with a wax disc (wax-side down) and seal, then leave to cool for about 2 hours and try not to move the jar until the mixture has set. When cold, label, then store in the fridge and use within 1 month. Once opened, keep in the fridge and use within 1 week.

Herring Escabeche

This herring escabeche is like a portion of sunshine on a plate and it reminds me of hot sunny days and holidays in France. The beauty is that you can make the salad early in the morning or even the day before, and when it comes to serving the dish, it's then perfectly pickled. I like the simplicity and purity of this recipe as it's not at all complicated. I serve this dish with Sweet and Sour Pickled Green Beans (see page 279) and plenty of buttered brown bread – and the pickled vegetables are just as delicious as the escabeche.

Herring is a very bony fish and it's not easy to remove all the bones, but the richness of the oily flesh makes it perfect for pickling. Alternatively, you can use sardines or mackerel instead of herrings – I sometimes use the really small sardines, but again you end up with a bone problem.

You will need to start this recipe the day before you want to serve it, to allow enough time for the fish to marinate.

Serves 6 as a starter or light lunch

6 herring fillets with skin on (360–480g in total), pin bones removed
3 tablespoons olive oil
1 bay leaf
a sprig of fresh summer savory (or you can use a sprig of fresh thyme instead)
1 teaspoon coriander seeds, lightly crushed
2 star anise
1 onion, finely sliced
½ fennel bulb, trimmed and finely sliced
1 carrot, finely sliced
1 clove garlic, lightly crushed
1 teaspoon caster sugar
a pinch of saffron strands
200ml white wine
75ml cider vinegar
sea salt and freshly cracked black pepper
Sweet and Sour Pickled Green Beans (see page 279), to serve

First, prepare the fish. Wash the herring fillets and pat dry, then cut them in half widthways and lightly score the skin. Place the fish pieces, skin-side up, in a wide, shallow, non-metallic container and smear the fish with half of the olive oil, then add the bay leaf and summer savory and set aside.

Heat a saucepan until hot, then toast the coriander seeds and star anise in the hot dry pan over a high heat for 1–2 minutes. Remove from the heat and carefully add the remaining oil to the pan, along with the onion, fennel, carrot and garlic, then return the pan to the heat, cover and sweat over a low heat for 7–8 minutes or until the onion turns transparent. Season lightly with salt and pepper, then stir in the sugar and saffron.

Add the wine and cider vinegar to the pan and bring the mixture to the boil, then reduce the heat and simmer for 2 minutes or until the liquid has reduced and thickened slightly. Remove from the heat and let the mixture cool for 5 minutes or so (see Cook's Note).

Season the herrings with sea salt, then ladle the pickling liquid over the fish. Leave the mixture to cool completely, then cover and leave the fish to marinate in the fridge for at least 12 hours or overnight before serving, to allow the flavours to develop. The herrings can be left in their pickling liquid in the fridge for up to 2 days before serving, if you like.

To serve, drain and reserve the herrings and then reserve a little of the pickling liquid and some of the pickled onion, fennel and carrot slices; discard the rest. Arrange 2 pieces of pickled herring fillets on each serving plate and garnish each portion with a few of the reserved pickled vegetable slices. Drizzle a teaspoon or so of the reserved pickling liquid over each portion, spoon some pickled green beans on to the plates and serve immediately with buttered brown bread.

Cook's Note
Let the pickling liquid mixture cool slightly before pouring it over the fish, otherwise the heat will cause the skin of the fish to curl up.

Mustard Seed-smoked Beef with Soft-boiled Duck Eggs and Toasted Cobnuts

The 'quick-smoke method' is one that has been used by chefs for many years. It's easy and requires no special equipment, in fact, the older the roasting tin you use, the better. When smoking with mustard seeds and rice, the rice is the smoking medium and the mustard seeds provide the flavour. The sugar and salt marinade beforehand makes the beef firm and tightens the muscles, and the seasoning also penetrates into the beef, adding extra delicious flavour.

Serves 6 as a starter or light lunch

For the mustard seed-smoked beef
750g beef fillet
2 tablespoons yellow mustard seeds
1 teaspoon coriander seeds
100g caster sugar
100g sea salt
300g white basmati rice
100ml cold water
1 tablespoon sunflower oil
5 black peppercorns
1 tablespoon unsalted butter
100g fresh cobnuts (shelled weight)
6 duck eggs
2 teaspoons olive oil
a large handful of fresh watercress, rinsed and patted dry

For the watercress emulsion
100g fresh watercress, rinsed and patted dry
6 fresh mint leaves
1 teaspoon Dijon mustard
1 teaspoon sherry vinegar
100ml sunflower oil
sea salt and freshly cracked black pepper

For the mustard seed-smoked beef, trim the beef into an even barrel shape and set aside. Using a pestle and mortar, lightly crush 1 tablespoon of the mustard seeds with the coriander seeds, then mix this with the sugar and salt in a bowl. Cover the beef completely with this curing mixture, then place the coated beef in a suitable container or white plastic tray, cover with cling film and refrigerate for 4 hours.

Place 200g of the rice in a bowl, add the water and leave to soak for 30 minutes. Remove the beef from the fridge, wash it under cold running water and pat dry, then rub the beef all over with the sunflower oil.

Once you are ready to smoke the beef, you will need to make a smoker using a deep roasting tin, a wire cooling rack and some foil. Line the roasting tin with a layer of foil, then spread the soaked rice (water and all, if the rice has not soaked up all the water) over the foil and sprinkle over the remaining mustard seeds and the peppercorns. Sprinkle the remaining 100g dry (unsoaked) rice over the top, then position the wire rack over the rice mixture.

Place the roasting tin on the hob over a high heat and start the smoking process. Heat until the rice starts to smoke, then place the beef on to the wire rack. Remove from the heat, cover the whole thing with a tent of foil and leave the beef to smoke for 30 minutes – by this stage, the outside of the beef will look cooked and the surface will have dried out slightly (the smoking process will also give the beef a very slight yellowish colour). Uncover and remove the beef to a plate and leave to cool. Discard the rice and spices.

Melt the butter in a non-stick frying pan over a high heat and once it starts to foam, roll the beef in the hot pan for about 1 minute on each side or until sealed all over and caramelised. Remove the beef from the pan and drain on kitchen paper. Leave to cool, then wrap the beef in cling film and re-shape it into a barrel shape. Refrigerate until cold, then transfer the beef to the freezer for at least 2 hours (and for a maximum of 4 hours) to firm up. Place the serving plates in the fridge to chill.

Toast the cobnuts. Preheat the oven to 200°C/Gas Mark 6. Spread the shelled cobnuts over a baking tray, then roast in the oven for 2 minutes. Shake the baking tray, then roast the nuts for a further 2 minutes or until they are lightly toasted. Remove from the oven and leave to cool, then lightly crush the nuts with the back of your hand or a rolling pin. Set aside.

Meanwhile, cook the duck eggs. Bring a pan of water to a rapid boil, carefully place the duck eggs into the boiling water, then bring back to the boil and boil for 7 minutes. Remove from the heat and drain, then immediately run cold water over the eggs to cool them quickly. Drain, then peel them. Keep the peeled eggs in a bowl of cold water in the fridge until you are ready to serve (this will prevent the soft-boiled eggs from breaking and spilling their yolks when you serve them).

In the meantime, prepare the watercress emulsion. Put the watercress, mint leaves, mustard and sherry vinegar into a small blender and purée together until smooth. With the motor running, slowly add the sunflower oil to form an emulsion. Season to taste with salt and pepper, then pour into a small bowl, cover and chill in the fridge until needed (see Cook's Note).

To serve, use a sharp knife to slice the beef into 2–3mm-thick slices. Place about 4 slices of beef on to each chilled plate and rub the surface of the beef slices with olive oil. Set aside at room temperature for about 5 minutes before serving. Drain the peeled duck eggs, pat them dry, then cut each one in half. Place 2 duck egg halves on top of each portion of beef and season the yolks with salt and pepper. Drizzle each portion with 1 tablespoon of the watercress emulsion. Garnish with the toasted cobnuts and watercress and serve immediately.

Cook's Note

Keep any leftover watercress emulsion in an airtight container in the fridge and use within 3 days. Serve as a salad dressing or serve drizzled over boiled new potatoes and sprinkle with a pinch or two of chopped fresh mint. Alternatively, toss the watercress emulsion with hot pasta shells, add some flaked poached salmon and serve for a light lunch or supper.

Fresh Borlotti Bean, Prawn and Chorizo Bake

Farmers' markets and local suppliers is what the British Larder's ethos is all about, but it's also about recognising that we do live in a multicultural society with people from all walks of life, and with them they have brought ideas, dishes, traditions, ingredients and recipes. There is one fresh food market in London that I absolutely adore and like to visit as often as I possibly can and that is Borough Market.

When I lived closer to London it used to be a Saturday ritual to go 'foraging' at the market and come home with all sorts of weird and wonderful things. Amongst all of the glory of Borough Market there is a fantastic Spanish restaurant and shop called 'Brindisa'. They sell what I consider to be some of the best chorizo sausage and smoked paprika available in the UK.

Combining these two ingredients with prawns and fresh produce straight from my summer garden, this wonderful dish emerged. This is my take on posh baked beans! If you do not have fresh borlotti beans, then simply use canned ones as they work just as well. I make this dish in small individual ovenproof dishes, but you can bake it in one large terracotta-style dish, if you like, as it's perfect for sharing.

Serves 4 as a main course

4 red onions, peeled
100ml olive oil
1 fresh red chilli, deseeded and finely sliced
300g chorizo, cut into 1cm dice
1 clove garlic, crushed
1 tablespoon red wine vinegar
300ml chicken stock
400g can plum tomatoes
½ teaspoon caster sugar
250g fresh borlotti beans (shelled weight) (see Cook's Note)
1 teaspoon chopped fresh thyme
1 teaspoon chopped fresh oregano
finely grated zest and juice of 1 lemon
2 red peppers, halved lengthways and deseeded (I keep the green stalks on purely because they look pretty)
20 cherry tomatoes
12 raw tiger prawns, peeled and deveined
2 slices ciabatta or white bread
sea salt and freshly cracked black pepper
a little extra chopped fresh thyme and oregano, to garnish

Preheat the oven to 200°C/Gas Mark 6. Dice 2 of the onions and then cut each of the remaining 2 onions into 8 wedges. Set aside.

Heat 80ml of the olive oil in a saucepan over a medium heat for a minute or two until hot. Add the diced red onions, the red chilli, chorizo, garlic and salt and pepper and sauté over a medium heat for 8–10 minutes or until the onions start to colour. Add the red wine vinegar, stock, canned tomatoes and sugar and bring to the boil, then reduce the heat to a gentle simmer. Add the borlotti beans, thyme and oregano, then cover and simmer for about 15 minutes or until the beans are cooked and tender and the sauce becomes rich and slightly thickened, stirring regularly. Remove from the heat and stir in the lemon zest and juice.

Meanwhile, start the peppers. If you would like to bake this recipe in 4 individual dishes like I do, then choose 4 suitable individual ovenproof dishes and put a pepper half, cut-side up, into each one, or use 1 large ovenproof terracotta dish and place the pepper halves, cut-sides up, in the dish. Lightly drizzle the remaining oil over the peppers and season with salt and pepper. Bake in the oven for 15 minutes or until they start to colour and soften. Remove from the oven.

Ladle the borlotti bean and chorizo mixture into and around the part-baked peppers. Divide the cherry tomatoes and onion wedges between the peppers, then bake in the oven for a further 20 minutes for the individual dishes and for 30 minutes for one larger dish, until the sauce is reduced and thickened.

Arrange the prawns on top of the borlotti bean mixture and peppers, then rip the bread into pieces and scatter over the top. Return to the oven and bake for a further 10–12 minutes (same cooking time for both size of dishes) or until the prawns are cooked and the bread pieces are crisp and golden brown. Garnish with a little thyme and oregano and serve immediately on its own or with plain boiled white or brown rice.

Cook's Note

Canned borlotti beans can be substituted for the fresh borlotti beans, if you like. Simply use 250g (rinsed and drained weight) canned borlotti beans, add them to the hot tomato and chorizo mixture (there is no need to cook the canned beans first) and heat through, then continue as the recipe directs.

Warm Carrot, Puy Lentil and Summer Savory Salad

My attempts to grow my own fruit and vegetables and to keep an organic garden had been a success, until I had to decide whether or not to use pesticides. At times, the pests have pushed my patience to the limit and I could not bear to watch the pesky caterpillars and ants destroying my crops. My strawberries suffered and so did my Cavolo nero. Ants made their home in half of my broad beans and I was nearly in tears when a slug nibbled right through one of my courgette plants! Mr. P adamantly did not want me to spray or use any sort of pesticides on my crops, but I must admit I was tempted to after a personal struggle seeing my fruit and vegetables being destroyed. But after some disagreement (and a near divorce!), Mr. P finally won the battle and I decided not to spray.

So, I have experienced a rollercoaster of emotions with my garden, but I was so thrilled when I pulled my first carrots from the soil. Admittedly, they were all different shapes and sizes, some very misshapen and some really small, but hey, that's alright, because they are my very own home grown carrots and they deserve a lovely recipe to be created just for them… and here it is!

Serves 4 as a side dish

For the honey nuts

1 tablespoon olive oil
20g pecan halves
15g sunflower seeds
15g pumpkin seeds
2 tablespoons clear honey

For the carrot and Puy lentil salad

100g Puy lentils
400g small organic carrots or Chantenay carrots, with tops and roots intact
1 tablespoon extra virgin olive oil
1 orange pepper, deseeded and cut into long strips
1 clove garlic, crushed
1 tablespoon clear honey
finely grated zest and juice of ½ orange
1 tablespoon soy sauce
1 teaspoon grated (peeled) fresh root ginger
½ teaspoon nigella seeds (also known as black onion seeds or kalonji seeds)
1 tablespoon chopped fresh summer savory (or you can use chopped fresh thyme or rosemary instead)
sea salt and freshly cracked black pepper

For the honey nuts, line a baking tray with non-stick baking paper and set aside. Heat the olive oil in a non-stick frying pan until hot, then add the pecan halves and sunflower and pumpkin seeds. Toast the nuts and seeds over a medium heat for 2–3 minutes or until they start to turn golden, stirring continuously to prevent the nuts from burning. Add the honey and keep heating and stirring for a further 1–2 minutes or until the nuts are a deep golden colour. Transfer the honey nuts to the prepared baking tray, then set aside and leave to cool completely.

For the carrot and Puy lentil salad, place the Puy lentils in a small saucepan, cover with plenty of cold water and bring to a gentle simmer, then cook, uncovered, for 15–20 minutes or until the lentils are cooked and tender. Season with salt, then drain well, place in a bowl, set aside and keep warm.

Meanwhile, wash the carrots, then remove the top green leaves but leave the long roots on as they look pretty. If the carrots are very fresh, there is no need to peel them, otherwise, you can peel them, if you prefer. Cook the carrots in a pan of boiling salted water for 8–10 minutes or until cooked and tender (cooking time will depend on their size). Drain well, then mix with the cooked Puy lentils, set aside and keep warm.

Heat the olive oil in a large, non-stick frying pan until hot, then add the strips of pepper and the garlic and sauté over a medium heat for 3–4 minutes or until softened and starting to turn golden brown. Season with salt and pepper, then add the combined cooked Puy lentils and carrots and cook for a further 2 minutes or until heated through. Add the honey, orange zest and juice, soy sauce and ginger and cook for 2 minutes or so, until the liquid thickens and starts to coat the carrots.

Transfer the cooked carrot mixture to a serving dish, then fold in the nigella seeds, toasted honey nuts and summer savory and serve immediately. Serve as a side dish with roast chicken, pan-roasted duck or confit duck leg, grilled pork chops, crisp turkey escalopes or homemade chicken Goujons.

Left: Fresh Borlotti Bean, Prawn and Chorizo Bake, page 288
Right: Warm Carrot, Puy Lentil and Summer Savory Salad, page 289

Old Fashioned Jam Tartlets

There is nothing remotely complicated about this recipe, it's just a good (and delicious!) reminder of simplicity. Any jam can be used, but making your own with seasonal fruit is best. The basic sweet pastry (see page 18) is brilliant as you can make it in advance and freeze the dough in blocks or portions to then defrost when needed. Just roll the pastry, bake the tartlet cases and then fill them with your own homemade jam.

I usually bake a load of these pastry tartlet shells and keep them in an airtight container in a cool, dry place for up to 1 week. In fact, you will be surprised how well they keep, as they remain crispy and are very handy to have as a standby to be filled with a dollop of jam, ready for an unexpected visitor or two.

Makes 24 jam tartlets

For the greengage jam
250g fresh greengages
200g caster sugar
1 tablespoon cold water
juice of ½ lemon

For the jam tartlets
300g Sweet Shortcrust Pastry (see page 18)
icing sugar, to dust

First, make the greengage jam. Wash the greengages, then cut into quarters and remove the stones. Place the greengages, sugar and water in a heavy-based saucepan. Cook over a low heat, stirring to dissolve the sugar, then increase the heat and bring the greengage mixture to the boil. Boil gently over a medium heat for 15–18 minutes or until the jam reaches a temperature of 105°C (setting point), stirring every now and then to prevent it from catching (I do not cook this particular jam over a high heat as I find that it catches much more easily than the berry jams I also make). If you don't have a jam thermometer, check to see if setting point has been reached by spooning a little of the jam on to a chilled small plate. Push a finger across the jam; if the surface wrinkles and it is beginning to set, it has reached setting point. If not, boil it gently for a further 5 minutes or so and test again.

Remove from the heat, stir in the lemon juice, then pour the jam into a heatproof bowl and leave to cool completely. Once cool, cover and refrigerate until needed (see Cook's Note). If you are making the greengage jam to serve another time, pour the hot jam into hot, sterilised jars (the greengage jam will make about 2 x 200g jars). Cover with wax discs (wax-side down) and seal. When cold, label, then store in a cool, dry cupboard. The jam should keep well for a year or so. Once opened, keep in the fridge and use within 1 month.

For the jam tartlets, preheat the oven to 200°C/Gas Mark 6. Lightly grease two 12-hole shallow bun tins and set aside. Roll out the pastry on a lightly floured work surface to about 2mm thickness. Cut out twenty-four 5.5cm rounds using a fluted pastry cutter, then line the prepared bun tins with the pastry rounds and leave to rest in the fridge for 20 minutes.

Prick the pastry rounds all over with a fork, then place a paper cake case filled with baking beans inside each one and bake blind in the oven for 8–10 minutes. Remove the beans and paper cases, then return the pastry cases to the oven and bake for a further 5 minutes or until cooked, golden brown and crisp. Remove from the oven and carefully transfer the pastry cases to a wire rack. Leave to cool completely before filling with the greengage jam.

When you are ready to serve, fill each pastry tartlet case with a generous dollop of jam, then dust with icing sugar and serve immediately.

Cook's Note
If you have made the jam fresh and have poured it into a heatproof bowl to cool (rather than potting it into jars for later use), any leftover greengage jam will keep in an airtight container in the fridge for up to 1 week. Serve it with freshly baked scones for afternoon tea, or with toasted teacakes or crumpets for breakfast. The greengage jam also makes a great filling for a Victoria sponge cake.

Plum and Blackberry Jelly with Plum Sorbet

As a child I really liked jelly and, as an adult, I love it even more. My father loved jelly too, especially when it was served with ice cream. Dad quite liked a pudding on a Sunday and if mum had not planned to make a dessert, it was dad's job to make a jelly. He used packets of jelly and set it with sliced bananas in, then served it with ice cream. I remember the expression on his face as if it were yesterday. Dad would lie down after Sunday lunch for a nap and then when he woke up it was time to eat the jelly. He would fill his bowl to the brim and he enjoyed every single mouthful! This recipe is a dedication to dad's love of jelly and ice cream.

Victoria plums are simply luscious and when they are super-ripe they are just bursting with flavour. I make the most of their short season by halving and stoning the plums and freezing them for use later in the year. The frozen plums also make a wonderful sorbet.

You will need to start this recipe the day before you want to serve it, to allow the fruit mixture to stand overnight in the fridge, and also to allow enough time for the jelly mixture to set.

Serves 6

For the plum and blackberry jelly

600g fresh ripe plums (preferably Victoria)
300g fresh blackberries
150ml cold water
100g caster sugar
1 vanilla pod, split in half lengthways and seeds scraped out
juice of ½ lime
25g clear honey
5 leaves of gelatine

For the plum sorbet

500g fresh ripe plums (preferably Victoria)
100g caster sugar
100ml cold water
50ml freshly squeezed lime juice

To serve and decorate

2 tablespoons chopped pistachio nuts
12 fresh blackberries
about 1 teaspoon rapeseed oil

First, make the plum and blackberry jelly. Wash the plums, cut into quarters and remove the stones. Place the plums, blackberries, water, sugar, vanilla seeds, lime juice and honey into a heatproof bowl and cover tightly with cling film. Place the bowl over a pan of simmering water (making sure that the bottom of the bowl does not come into contact with the simmering water underneath) and leave to cook for about 30 minutes or until the fruits have completely softened and released all their juices, stirring once or twice. Remove from the heat and remove the bowl from the pan, then set aside to cool. Once cool, place in the fridge and leave to chill overnight.

The following morning, pass the chilled plum and blackberry mixture through a fine sieve or pour it into a piece of suspended muslin cloth and leave it to drain over a bowl for about 1 hour. Discard the fruit pulp and keep the fruit juice. Measure 500ml of the juice into a bowl and set aside.

Soak the gelatine in cold water until it has softened. Pour 100ml of the remaining juice (see Cook's Notes) into a saucepan and heat until just before boiling point, then remove from the heat. Squeeze the gelatine gently to remove excess water, then add the gelatine to the hot juice and stir until dissolved. Add the gelatine mixture to the measured juice in the bowl and stir to mix, then pour the jelly into 6 individual jelly moulds, each measuring about 8 x 3cm. Chill in the fridge for about 6 hours or until set.

Meanwhile, make the plum sorbet. Wash the plums, cut into quarters and remove the stones, then set aside. Put the sugar and water in a small saucepan and heat gently, stirring until the sugar has dissolved. Bring to the boil and boil for 2 minutes, then remove from the heat and stir in the lime juice. Place the plums in a blender or food processor, add the hot syrup and blend together until smooth, then pass the plum purée through a sieve. Cover and leave to rest in the fridge for 1 hour, then pour the chilled mixture into an ice-cream maker and churn until frozen (following the manufacturer's instructions for your particular model). Alternatively, pour the chilled mixture into a shallow, freezer proof container, cover with a lid and freeze until firm, whisking the mixture 3 or 4 times during freezing (every hour or so) to break down the ice crystals and ensure an even-textured result. Allow the sorbet to soften slightly at room temperature or in the fridge before serving (see Cook's Notes).

Place 6 serving plates in the fridge to chill before serving.

For each serving, briefly dip a jelly mould into hot water, give it a light shake to loosen, then carefully unmould the jelly on to a chilled plate. Sprinkle 1 teaspoon chopped pistachios over the top, then place a small quenelle (spoonful) of plum sorbet on top. Repeat for the remaining 5 jellies.

Decorate each jelly with 2 blackberries and then decorate each plate with a few drops of rapeseed oil. Serve immediately.

Cook's Notes

If there is any leftover juice, use it to make a Victoria Plum and Champagne Bellini – measure a shot of plum juice into a Champagne glass, top up with chilled Champagne and enjoy a seasonal cocktail.

Transfer any leftover plum sorbet to an airtight, freezer proof container and store in the freezer. Use within 1 month. Serve the plum sorbet with plum tarte tatin or plum frangipane tart, or make a plum milkshake by blending together a few scoops of the plum sorbet and some milk.

Victoria Plum and Blackberry Frozen Ice Cream Slices

With the summer season peaking, we can make the most of some warm and sunny days that are perfectly suited for gardening, barbecues and enjoying lunch on the patio.

These delicious and indulgent fruity ice cream slices are the perfect seasonal treat to bid farewell to the summer and welcome early autumn with a smile. If you like the sound of this dessert but do not have Victoria plums, any fruit that can be puréed would be a perfect substitute.

You will need to start this recipe the day before you want to serve it, to allow enough time for the ice cream to set in the freezer. The next day, I recommend that you place the serving plate and bowls in the freezer for 30 minutes before serving, as this will help to prevent the ice cream from melting quickly in the summer sun.

Serves 6–8

For the Victoria plum and blackberry purée

150g fresh Victoria plums
100g fresh blackberries
25g caster sugar

For the ice cream

2 fresh Victoria plums
50g fresh blackberries
3 egg yolks
2 tablespoons cold water
100g caster sugar
2 egg whites
125ml double cream
125g chilled Victoria Plum and Blackberry Purée (see recipe above)
additional fresh blackberries and fresh mint leaves, to decorate

First, make the Victoria plum and blackberry purée. Wash both types of fruit and drain. Cut the plums in half and remove the stones. Place the plums and blackberries in a small saucepan with the sugar, then heat gently, stirring to dissolve the sugar. Increase the heat and bring the fruit mixture to a gentle simmer, then cook, uncovered, for about 10 minutes or until the plums are softened and have broken down and the mixture has thickened slightly.

Remove from the heat and cool slightly, then transfer the fruit mixture to a blender and blend until smooth. Pass the fruit purée through a fine sieve into a bowl and leave to cool. Once cool, measure out the 125g purée needed for the ice cream and keep the rest separate (if there is any leftover). Cover and chill both portions of purée in the fridge until needed.

Make the ice cream. Line a 20 x 10cm (or 450g) loaf tin with a double layer of cling film, leaving an overhang of cling film around the rim (see Cook's Note). Wash the plums and blackberries. Cut each plum into 6 wedges and remove the stones. Arrange the plum wedges and blackberries in the bottom of the lined tin. Set aside.

Half-fill a saucepan with water and bring up to a gentle simmer. Choose a heatproof mixing bowl that will sit comfortably over the saucepan without slipping down inside the pan (you also want to make sure that the bottom of the bowl does not come into contact with the simmering water underneath).

Put the egg yolks, water and 50g of the sugar into the heatproof bowl and place the bowl over the pan of simmering water. Using a balloon whisk or an electric hand-held whisk, whisk together until the mixture is pale, thick and creamy – when you lift the whisk it should leave a visible trail on the surface (this is called the thick ribbon stage or sabayon). Remove from the heat, remove the bowl from the pan and set aside to cool slightly.

In a separate bowl, whisk the egg whites until foaming, then add the remaining sugar and whisk together until the mixture forms soft peaks. Put the cream and the measured chilled Victoria plum and blackberry purée in another bowl and whisk together until the mixture forms soft peaks. Fold the whipped cream mixture into the sabayon, then gently fold in the meringue until well combined.

Pour the ice cream mixture evenly over the prepared fruit in the tin. Fold the overhanging cling film over to cover completely and then place the loaf tin in the freezer for a minimum of 8 hours (but preferably overnight) or until the ice cream is completely set.

The next day, place a large serving plate and the serving plates in the freezer about 30 minutes before serving.

To serve, turn the ice cream out of the loaf tin on to the chilled serving plate and remove the cling film. Slice the ice cream loaf into 6–8 slices using a sharp knife dipped in hot water, then place a slice onto each chilled serving plate. If there is any leftover fruit purée, drizzle it around the plates, then decorate the desserts with blackberries and ripped mint leaves and serve immediately.

If you're not going to serve the dessert immediately, then place the serving plates (containing the portions of dessert) back in the freezer until you're ready to serve.

Cook's Note

Lining a loaf tin with a double layer of cling film can be a little tricky at the best of times. I have a helpful tip that works every time. Wipe a clean kitchen work surface with wet kitchen paper and lay a piece of cling film on top of the damp area. Take a clean, dry tea towel and wipe over the cling film to flatten it and remove any bubbles. Wipe the cling film with the wet kitchen paper, lay another piece of cling film over the first one and flatten it with the tea towel to remove any bubbles.

Dampen the loaf tin by rinsing it with water, then shake it to remove as much water as possible. Lift and position the double layer of cling film over the loaf tin, then using your fingers, carefully push the cling film down into the corners of the tin and press it over the base and up the sides, leaving an overhang of cling film around the rim. And, hey presto, you have a perfectly lined tin! It's really easy but it does take a bit of practice and, most importantly, patience.

The British Larder | September

Autumn is slowly settling in and the game season has started. A snap of cooler weather is now required to encourage the partridges and pheasants to eat well and fatten up quickly.

Damsons, sloes, rowanberries, wild plums, crab apples and rosehips are ready to be picked and turned into wonderful jams, pickles, vinaigrettes or jellies for the winter months to come. English apples and pears are plentiful, and as with damsons and blackberries. Pick them quickly before the dampness turns them soggy, otherwise they will quickly start to rot.

September is another month that is ideal for pickling and preserving the last of the late summer's gluts of fresh produce. It's the perfect time to put your jam, jelly and chutney-making skills to the test. Hopefully, the summer will have been good to us with a balance of rain showers and sunshine, producing lots of seasonal produce and goodies, but now it's time for Mother Nature to wind down during autumn and enjoy a well-earned winter of rest. The farmers are working all hours against the clock to gather their crops in from the fields, and the arable farmland and nearby country lanes are heaving with harvesting activity.

Collecting the day's shoot

The beginning of autumn is the perfect time to forage for wild foods and fruit. After a good downpour and a bit of humidity, wild mushrooms start popping up everywhere with varieties such as giant puffballs, chanterelles, slippery jack, cauliflower fungus, fairy rings, ceps, beefsteak mushrooms and large, flat field mushrooms all potentially on offer.

From around our coast there is also plenty to choose from, including sea beet, sea plantain, sea aster, sea purslane and sea blight, all of which are crisp and varying shades of green. They benefit from quick cooking, either blanched briefly in a pan of boiling water or lightly sautéed in a drop of olive oil.

Squash are ready to be harvested too, from butternut squash and acorn squash all the way through to green hubbard, red kuri and spaghetti squash. They all look and taste different and it's well worth trying these seasonal treasures.

As the season is changing, ingredients such as lettuces, courgettes, crab and peaches are all coming to an end.

Season's best during September...

Apples, Artichokes, Aubergines, Beetroot, Blackberries, Black Cabbage (Cavolo Nero), Borlotti Beans, Broccoli, Butternut Squash, Cabbages, Carrots, Celery, Chard, Chives, Clams, Cobnuts, Cod, Coley, Courgettes, Crab, Crab Apples, Crayfish (freshwater), Cucumber, Damsons, Dover Sole, Duck, Elderberries, Fennel, Figs, Flounder, Garlic, Golden Plover, Goose, Grapes, Grey Mullet, Grouse, Guinea Fowl, Haddock, Halibut, Hawthorn Berries, Herring, Horseradish, John Dory, Kale, Kohlrabi, Lamb, Langoustines, Leeks, Lemon Sole, Lettuce, Lobster, Mackerel, Marrow, Medjool Dates, Mint, Monkfish, Onions, Oregano, Parsley, Parsnips, Partridge, Peaches, Pears, Peppers, Plaice, Plums, Pollack, Potatoes (main crop), Prawns, Pumpkins, Rabbit, Radishes, Rocket, Rosehips, Rosemary, Rowanberries, Runner Beans, Sage, Salmon, Samphire, Sardines, Scallops, Sea Bass, Sea Beet, Sea Plantain, Sea Purslane, Squid, Sweetcorn, Swiss Chard, Teal, Thyme, Tomatoes, Turbot, Turnips, Venison, Walnuts, Watercress, Whelks, Whitebait, Wild Mushrooms (autumn), Wild Plums (bullaces, mirabelles),Winkles, Woodpigeon.

My culinary rituals for September...

With autumn arriving, the hustle and bustle of pickling and preserving is still going strong. Apart from frantically turning everything into jams, chutneys and flavoured vinegars, I'm experimenting with making fruit cheeses, fruit pastilles, fruit candy and fruit leathers to keep for the leaner months to come.

The colours of autumn are luxurious, rich and lavish, the burnt oranges, reds and shades of purple are a delight to the eye and they provide a seasonal feast for us to enjoy. Squash are ready to be harvested this month, and then we wait for the pumpkins to ripen. Harvest damsons this month and keep an eye on the elderberries, making sure you pick the hedgerow produce at its peak and before it is lost to the wildlife or even the weather. My tempting recipe for **Hedgerow Fruit Pastilles** (see page 331) makes perfect use of seasonal hedgerow fruits.

Damsons come and go quickly during the season and, depending on the weather, the harvest may be bountiful one year and not so good the next, so keep a sharp eye open for them and harvest them as soon as they are ripe. Damsons are perfect for making jams, jellies and wines, but do try my wonderful recipe for **Pickled Damsons** (see page 304) for something a bit different that you can then enjoy later in the year. If you are in search of something sweet, try my delicious recipe for **Damson and Bramble Plate Pie** (see page 328).

If the wild mushrooms are plentiful, dry the glut in a cool oven and keep the dried mushrooms in a clean airtight jar (see page 127 for more information on drying mushrooms). Take extra care when harvesting wild mushrooms and if you are in any doubt, then don't pick them and only harvest the ones that you can identify with ease. If you're in need of a hearty lunch, try my tasty recipe for **Field Mushroom and British Chorizo Minestrone** (see page 317), or if you are looking for a tempting main course, try the recipe for **Crisp Crusted Puffball with Woodland Mushroom Ragoût and Fried Duck Eggs** (see page 319).

For me, autumn means that it's time to dust off the pie dishes and casseroles. Hearty food is very much the order of the day with plenty of delicious and warming roasts, soups and bakes. Tempting recipes to tantalise your taste buds this month include **Slow-cooked Belly of Pork with Crab Apple Jelly and Caramelised Damsons** (see page 321), **Poached Roasted Chicken with Butternut Squash Anna** (see page 322) or **Elderberry and Apple Muffins** (see page 304).

British Larder Heroes

Autumn wild mushrooms

The main edible wild mushroom season occurs during the autumn, apart from the St George's mushrooms and morels, which appear during mid to late spring. Read more about morels on page 132 in the April chapter. Ceps, puffballs, chanterelles (also known as girolles), horn of plenty (also known as black trumpets or trompette de la mort) and plenty of other fantastic varieties of fresh wild mushrooms are available during the autumn and, if the conditions are right, they will be growing in abundance in woods and forests all over Britain, from Scotland in the north to Cornwall in the south-west. It's important to remember that before you set off to forage for wild mushrooms in a specific area, you will need to check that you are allowed to do so. Some woods, forests and other areas require a licence or permission officially granted. For wild mushrooms to grow, they require a good downpour, a bit of humidity and mild weather. If you do go foraging, my recommendation is always that unless you are absolutely certain and confident that you can identify edible mushrooms correctly, then leave it to the experts and don't take any risks yourself. Some wild mushrooms and fungi are inedible and can be deadly. I buy fresh wild mushrooms only from reputable suppliers. I do like to look for them in the forests too and have a go at identifying them, but I still prefer to buy them instead of foraging for them. As well as the highly prized morels, ceps (or porcini as the Italians call them – they are also called penny buns elsewhere) hold a similar status. Ceps are meaty and fleshy and they pair perfectly with earthy flavours such as game, beef and duck and meaty fish such as turbot and halibut. In the kitchen, we have a bit of fun with puffballs and even though they are fairly tasteless, they provide a good basis for interesting vegetarian dishes.

If you have too many fresh wild ceps and wish to preserve them for use another time, dry them out and keep the dried mushrooms in rice in a jar – the filled jar will make a fantastic foodie gift if wrapped up beautifully. To make your own jar of **Dried Ceps in Rice**, select 4–5 fresh large ceps, then use a pastry brush and some damp kitchen paper to clean them, removing as much forest debris by dusting and wiping them. Do not place the mushrooms in water as they are like sponges and will absorb the water and become ruined. Preheat the oven to 110°C/Gas Mark ¼ and line 2 baking trays with non-stick baking paper. Use a sharp knife and cut the mushrooms lengthways into 2mm slices. (Please be aware that maggots and worms also love ceps, so if you find that they've made a home inside a mushroom, you will have to throw it away and select another one for drying.) Lay the mushroom slices in a single layer on the prepared baking trays, then place in the oven to dry for about 3 hours, turning them once halfway through. To test if the mushrooms are dry, remove 1 slice from the oven, wave it in the air to cool it quickly and, once cold, feel how crispy it is. It must be very dry and crisp; if it's still slightly bendy, then return to the oven and leave to dry for a bit longer. The mushrooms will have shrivelled and shrunk significantly, and indeed you might wonder to yourself what's the point of drying them, but dried mushrooms contain an enormous amount of delicious concentrated flavour and once re-hydrated they will pack a real flavour punch. Once the mushrooms are all sufficiently dried, remove them from the oven, transfer to a wire rack and leave to cool completely. Put the dried mushrooms into a bowl, add a few scoops of dried (raw) arborio or carnaroli rice, then transfer the mixture to a clean, dry jar, seal, label and store in a cool, dry cupboard until needed (alternatively, you could simply layer up the rice and dried mushrooms attractively in the jar). Use within 6 months. Before use, separate the mushrooms from the rice and rehydrate them, then use the dried rice and rehydrated mushrooms to make a delicious risotto to serve on its own or as an accompaniment to roast chicken or pan-fried turbot or halibut.

British pork

British pork is classed as some of the best in the world, not only because of the variety of species available, but also the important fact that the pork reared by most British pig farmers is produced to some of the highest welfare standards in the world. However, with plenty of pork to choose from in our supermarkets, markets and butchers, it's sometimes difficult to identify the best products on the market. With the information now available on carcass traceability, the best option is to have a conversation with the butcher or seller, asking if the pork they supply is carrying one of the following three labels or logos: Red Tractor Pork, Freedom Food or the Quality Standard Mark, and if it does, then that is the pork to buy. Using the whole pig carcass for cooking and serving is a fantastic challenge and in recent years we have seen an increased growth in the use of non-prime cuts, such as pig's head, trotters, cheeks and belly, which are used to create some truly delicious dishes.

For one such tasty dish, do give my recipe for **Crispy Pig's Ears** a try. Once you have tasted it, you'll never look back! Carefully scrape the hairs from 6 pig's ears (80–100g each) using a sharp razor blade, then wash and pat them dry. Place the prepared pig's ears in a large saucepan and cover with plenty of cold water. Cover the pan and bring to the boil, then reduce the heat and simmer for about 5 minutes or until any scum has risen to the surface. Drain and rinse the ears in a colander, then return them to the pan and cover with plenty of fresh cold water. Add ½ teaspoon sea salt, ½ roughly diced onion, 1 roughly diced carrot, 1 roughly diced stick of celery, 1 teaspoon coriander seeds, 1 bay leaf, 2 lightly bruised, peeled cloves garlic, a sprig of fresh rosemary and a sprig of fresh thyme. Cover and bring to the boil, then reduce the heat and simmer for about 2 hours or until the ears are cooked and tender, topping up the water once or twice during this period, if necessary. Remove the pan from the heat and leave the ears to cool in the liquid at room temperature. After about 1 hour, drain the mixture, reserving the pig's ears and discarding the cooking liquid and vegetables, herbs and spices. Slice the ears into 3–4mm slices. Put 2 tablespoons plain flour into a bowl and season with sea salt and freshly cracked black pepper. Toss the ear strips in the seasoned flour, coating them completely, then shake off any excess flour and place them on a plate. Meanwhile, heat some sunflower oil in an electric deep-fat fryer or in a deep frying pan to a temperature of 160°C (or until a small piece of bread browns within 20 seconds in the hot oil). Once the oil is hot enough, deep-fry the pig's ear strips (you'll need to do this in 3–4 batches) in the hot oil for 3–4 minutes or until golden brown and crisp all over, shaking the basket or stirring them to prevent the strips from sticking together. Using a slotted spoon, remove and drain the deep-fried pig's ear strips on kitchen paper. Season with salt and serve immediately. Serves 6 as a snack. Alternatively, use the crispy pig's ear strips as a garnish for dishes such as slow-cooked pork belly (instead of crackling), or serve as a garnish on a fresh salad with apples, to accompany pork rillettes or pâté.

Crab apples

Primarily grown as ornamentals, crab apples are the wild versions of the apple and they can be found growing in hedgerows as small trees or shrubs. Crab apples are small, crisp apples with an extremely tart or sour flavour that makes them inedible when raw, but they do have a high natural pectin content and are therefore ideal for making a wonderful sweet fruit jelly to accompany rich meats such as pork and game. Some cider makers use a small quantity of crab apples to add an interesting and unique flavour to their cider. Crab apple trees are also planted among domestic apple trees to act as pollenisers in the apple orchards.

If you are lucky enough to find some crab apples in hedgerows near you, do try my recipe for **Crab Apple Jelly (Wild Apple Jelly)**. Wash and scrub 1kg fresh crab apples, cut them in half, place in a large saucepan and cover with plenty of cold water. Place a plate on top to weigh the apples down, then cover the pan with a lid and bring to the boil over a high heat. Once the mixture is boiling, remove the lid, then reduce the heat to a gentle simmer and cook for about 30 minutes or until the apple mixture is completely softened and pulpy. Remove from the heat, then pour the hot apple mixture into a jelly bag suspended over a bowl, or pour into a large sieve lined with muslin cloth placed over a bowl, and let the mixture drip overnight (preferably in the fridge). The following day, discard the solids and measure the apple juice into a clean saucepan, then add enough preserving sugar (see page 16), using the ratio of 10 parts apple juice to 7 parts preserving sugar. Cook gently, stirring to dissolve the sugar, then increase the heat to high, bring to the boil and boil rapidly for about 30 minutes or until the apple mixture reaches a temperature of 105°C (setting point) on a jam thermometer, skimming off any scum from the surface. If you don't have a jam thermometer, check to see if setting point has been reached by spooning a little of the jelly on to a chilled small plate. Push a finger across the jelly; if the surface wrinkles and it is beginning to set, it has reached setting point. If not, boil it gently for a further 5 minutes or so and test again. Once the jelly has reached setting point, stir in the juice of 1 lemon. Remove the pan from the heat and leave the jelly to cool slightly, then carefully pour it into hot, sterilised jars. Cover with wax discs (wax-side down) and seal. When cold, label, then store in a cool, dry cupboard. The crab apple jelly should keep well for a year or so. Once opened, store in the fridge and use within 1 month. Serve the crab apple jelly with roast pork, venison or cheese. Makes about 2 x 250g jars.

Damsons

These small, oval stone fruit with their dark blue to purple skins and yellow-green flesh are a type of plum. Damsons or damson plums are also sometimes known as Damask plums. Raw damsons have a very sour taste so they need to be cooked before eating and are ideal stewed (with plenty of sugar!) or cooked and used to make pies and other desserts. Damsons are naturally high in pectin, making them perfect for preserves such as jams and jellies. Damson gin and damson wine are two other traditional uses of this fruit, but I am including another recipe with a difference. My Pickled Damsons are delicious served with pan-roasted salmon, partridge or pheasant or stirred into a game casserole.

To make **Pickled Damsons**, rinse 380–400g fresh damsons, then remove and discard the stones (you need 300g prepared damsons). Place the prepared damsons in a saucepan with 100ml cold water, 120ml red wine vinegar and 120g caster sugar. Add a pinch of crushed dried chillies, a pinch of sea salt, 1 cinnamon stick, 2 star anise, 5 whole cloves, 1 lightly bruised (peeled) clove garlic, 1 teaspoon lightly crushed coriander seeds and some freshly cracked black pepper. Cook over a low heat, stirring until the sugar has dissolved, then increase the heat and bring to the boil. Boil rapidly for 2 minutes, then remove from the heat and transfer the damsons and pickling mixture to hot, sterilised jars. Cover with vinegar-proof lids and seal, leave to cool, then label and store in a cool, dry cupboard. Store for at least 1 week before using to allow the flavours to mellow. The unopened jars of pickled damsons should keep well for up to 6 months. Once opened, store in the fridge and use within 1 week. Makes about 2 x 200g jars.

Figs

Elderberries

Earlier in the year, during late spring/early summer we enjoy picking elderflowers (see page 164 for more details on elderflowers and elderberry shrubs) and making delights such as **Homemade Elderflower Cordial** (see page 167). Later on in the year towards early autumn, the flowers turn into clusters of small, shiny, dark purple round elderberries. Raw elderberries should be washed well and cooked before using as the raw berries contain a poisonous alkaloid that becomes harmless once cooked.

For a tasty bake, try my recipe for **Elderberry and Apple Muffins**. Preheat the oven to 200°C/Gas Mark 6 and grease a 12-hole muffin tin. Sift 300g self-raising flour, a pinch of table salt and 1 teaspoon baking powder into a mixing bowl. Add 100g soft dark brown sugar, 2 tablespoons rolled oats, 1 large coarsely grated (cored) eating apple and 80g washed and drained fresh elderberries (removed from their stalks). Stir to mix, then make a well in the centre. Measure 200ml milk into a measuring jug, add 2 eggs and whisk together, then add 80g melted unsalted butter and whisk to mix. Pour the egg mixture into the centre of the flour mixture, then stir until the ingredients are just combined; do not over mix. Divide the mixture equally between the prepared muffin holes, then sprinkle the tops with some extra rolled oats. Bake in the oven for 15–20 minutes or until well risen and golden brown. Remove from the oven and let the muffins cool in the tin for 5 minutes, then transfer to a wire rack. Serve warm or cold. These muffins are best eaten on the day they are made. Makes 12 muffins.

Figs

Figs are the fruit of large trees that grow in warm and semi-tropical regions, including Southern Asia and the Mediterranean, but they can also be successfully grown in the UK, although they need plenty of warmth and sunshine to ripen the fruits. Fresh figs vary in shape from round to squat pear-shaped and they have a soft skin that varies in colour from purple and black to green and gold. Inside the flesh is a sweet, sticky seedy pulp, which ranges from pale pink to deep red. Both the skin and the flesh can be eaten and they are easy to peel, if required. Figs can be eaten raw (they should be eaten very fresh, as they spoil quite easily) and they are also readily available dried or canned. Fresh figs are often cut into quarters and served with Parma ham for a simple starter, or they are served as a dessert. They can also be poached or baked. Dried figs are sweet, sticky and golden or dark brown in colour and they can be eaten as a snack or used in desserts, cakes, bakes and fruit compotes.

Fresh fig leaves are also packed with flavour and are ideal for making panna cotta or ice cream. Try my delicious recipe for **Fig Leaf Ice Cream**. Select 6 large fresh fig leaves (dark green ones are the best), rinse and pat them dry, then leave them to air-dry until they are completely crisp (this will take about 1 week, especially if the air is dry and warm). To dry the leaves, place them on a wire rack on a baking tray and cover them loosely with kitchen roll to prevent them from getting dusty. Place in an airing or boiler cupboard or in a warm, dry room and leave to dry. Once the leaves are completely dry and crisp, place them in a food processor with 150g caster sugar and blend together to make a fine powder. Pass the sugar mixture through a fine sieve to remove any large pieces of leaf – the sieved mixture should be a combination of fine green powder and white sugar. Pour 600ml double cream into a saucepan and heat gently until it just starts to boil, then remove from the heat. Meanwhile, put the fig leaf sugar and 6 egg yolks in a bowl and whisk together to mix. Gradually whisk in the hot cream, then pour the mixture back into the pan. Cook over a low heat, stirring constantly, for 7–8 minutes or until the mixture has thickened enough to coat the back of the wooden spoon; do not allow the mixture to boil, otherwise it may curdle. Remove from the heat, then pass the mixture through a fine sieve into a bowl and leave to cool. Pour the cold mixture into an ice-cream maker and churn until frozen (following the manufacturer's instructions for your particular model). Alternatively, pour the cold mixture into a shallow, freezer proof container, cover with a lid and freeze until firm, whisking the mixture 3 or 4 times during freezing (every hour or so) to break down the ice crystals and ensure an even-textured result. Allow the ice cream to soften slightly at room temperature or in the fridge before serving. Serve with natural yogurt panna cotta or with freshly baked brandy snaps or shortbread biscuits. Serves 6–8.

Flounder

Flounder are sustainable, bottom-dwelling, small flat sea fish that are found in oceans around the world, including the North Atlantic and Pacific Oceans, and they are readily caught off the coasts around the UK, especially the east and north east coasts. Flounder are similar in appearance to plaice and the white flesh has a fairly mild flavour, which is felt to be inferior to plaice. As flounder are small fish, it's best to cook them whole on the bone to keep the flesh moist. If flounder are filleted, be sure to cook the fillets quickly in a hot pan for a short period of time. Flounder can be grilled, pan-fried, steamed or coated and deep-fried.

For a tasty dish using whole flounder, try this recipe for **Whole Baked Flounder with Squash and Red Onion**. Preheat to oven to 200°C/Gas Mark 6. Grease a large, shallow, ovenproof dish (such as a lasagne dish) with 1 tablespoon softened unsalted butter and set aside. Cut 1 red onion into 2mm-thick slices and cut 250g (peeled and deseeded weight) butternut squash flesh (or another variety of squash of your choice) into 2cm dice. Mix the onion and squash together and spread over the base of the prepared dish. Season with sea salt and freshly cracked black pepper, then sprinkle over 1 teaspoon chopped fresh oregano. Pour over 125ml white wine, squeeze over the juice of 1 lemon, then add the squeezed lemon halves to the dish. Cover with foil and bake in the oven for 15 minutes, then remove from the oven, remove the foil and stir. Wash a whole (gutted) flounder (about 1.2kg gutted weight, skin left on) and pat dry, then season with salt and pepper and place the fish on top of the onion and squash mixture. Melt 1 tablespoon unsalted butter and brush it over the fish, then scatter over 1 tablespoon pumpkin seeds and a pinch of crushed dried chillies. Bake in the oven for 25–30 minutes or until the vegetables are golden brown and the fish is cooked, moist and flaky. Remove from the oven and leave to rest for 5 minutes before serving. Serve with a dressed fresh garden salad and buttered boiled new potatoes. Serves 2 as a main course.

Langoustines

Langoustines are a relative of the lobster and they look like pink shelled mini lobsters. They are also known as Norwegian lobsters or Dublin Bay prawns, but they are not related to prawns. They are found along the coasts of the Atlantic, Mediterranean and Adriatic and they are widely fished off the coast of Ireland and around the UK, and Scottish langoustines are superb. Langoustines are best bought very fresh and still alive, if possible, as they go off quickly. Because of this they are very often frozen at sea by the fishermen before transporting them back to the fishing ports to be sold. Langoustines have tender, sweet and succulent flesh that makes them a popular shellfish to eat. They can be grilled, boiled, poached or baked or added to recipes such as paella and risotto. Shelled langoustines coated in breadcrumbs and deep-fried are known as scampi – a well-known and popular British dish (scampi is in fact the Italian word for langoustine). Cook langoustines in their shells as you would cook lobsters – in a pan of rapidly boiling water for 2–3 minutes or until they are cooked and have turned pink. Alternatively, bake them in their shells in a preheated oven at 200°C/Gas Mark 6 for 5–6 minutes or until the shells are roasted and the flesh is cooked, soft and moist. As with lobsters and crab, once you have retrieved the sweet succulent meat, the shells can be roasted and turned into a delicious bisque.

For an easy finger-licking dish, try my recipe for **Langoustine, Fennel and Apple Parcel**. Preheat the oven to 200°C/ Gas Mark 6. Place 6 whole fresh langoustines (600–800g total weight) on a large piece of foil, then finely grate 1 trimmed fennel bulb over the top. Add 1 finely sliced (cored) seasonal eating apple (such as Cox's Orange Pippin or Egremont Russet) and a handful of shredded Cavolo nero (black cabbage) leaves. Season with sea salt and freshly cracked black pepper. In a small bowl, combine 2 tablespoons soft unsalted butter, 2 crushed cloves garlic, a pinch of chopped fresh rosemary leaves and some salt and pepper. Dot knobs of the butter over the langoustines and vegetables, then gather the foil over the ingredients and seal to make a parcel. Place on a baking tray and bake in the oven for 12 minutes or until the langoustine shells have turned pink and the fennel and apple have softened. Meanwhile, preheat the grill to high. Remove the parcel from the oven and leave it on the baking tray, then open the foil and place the open parcel under the grill for about 5 minutes or until golden brown and caramelised. Divide the cooked langoustines, fennel, apple and cabbage between 2 serving plates and drizzle over the juices. Serve immediately with plenty of buttered rye bread. Serves 2 as a starter or light lunch.

Red onions

Red onions are distinctive with their purple/dark red papery skins. They have a crisp white flesh that is tinged with deep red and they have a mild, slightly sweeter flavour than standard white onions. Because of this, they are often used raw in salads, salsas and marinated dishes, but they are also wonderful baked, roasted or made into marmalade.

Red Onion Marmalade is a delicious way to preserve red onions. Peel 1kg red onions, then thinly slice them (preferably using a mandolin). Place the sliced onions in a large, heavy-based saucepan and add 4 crushed cloves garlic, 6 cloves (finely ground using a pestle and mortar), 200g cold unsalted butter, cut into 6 cubes, 250g golden caster sugar, 1 tablespoon chopped fresh thyme, 1 teaspoon sea salt, plenty of freshly cracked black pepper, 250ml red wine vinegar, 250ml red wine and 100ml port. Stir to mix, then place a cartouche (a circle of greaseproof paper) directly on the surface of the mixture and place a small plate on top to weigh it down. Cover the pan with a lid and place over a very low heat. Let the onion mixture slowly come to the boil and then, once boiling, remove the lid and stir. Continue cooking, uncovered, over a very low heat for about 30 minutes, stirring occasionally. Once the onion marmalade is cooked and ready, the onions will be completely soft and the liquid will be sticky and thick. Taste and adjust the seasoning, if necessary. Remove from the heat and transfer the mixture to hot, sterilised jars, then cover with vinegar-proof lids and seal. Leave to cool, then label and store in a cool, dry cupboard. The unopened jars of red onion marmalade should keep well in a cool, dry cupboard for up to 6 months. Once opened, store in the fridge and use within 1 week. Makes about 4 x 250ml jars. Serve the red onion marmalade with ripe cheese such as Stinking Bishop or Tunworth or with sliced baked gammon on a ploughman's platter.

Rosehips

With their orange to dark red appearance, rosehips are a pretty sight in our hedgerows at the beginning of autumn. Rosehips are the seedpods or fruits of the rose, which appear once the flowers have died off. They are rich in vitamin C and can be turned into syrups, jellies, wine and herbal teas.

To make **Rosehip Syrup** full of hedgerow goodness, wash 500g ripe rosehips (topped and tailed), then place them in a food processor with 500g caster sugar and blend together to

Rosehips

make a thick pulp. Scrape the contents into a large saucepan and then add 1.2 litres boiling water. Cook gently, stirring to dissolve the sugar, then bring to a rolling boil over a medium heat and cook for about 10 minutes or until the rosehip mixture has reduced and thickened. Remove the pan from the heat and set aside to infuse for about 30 minutes. Pour the mixture into a jelly bag suspended over a bowl, or pour into a large sieve lined with muslin cloth placed over a bowl, and leave to drip for about 1 hour. Discard the solids, then pour the liquid into a clean pan, add the juice of 1 lemon and bring the mixture back to a simmer over a medium heat. Increase the heat and boil rapidly for 18–20 minutes or until the mixture is reduced by about half its original volume to form a slightly thickened syrup, skimming off any scum from the surface – you should be left with about 500ml syrup and it will have turned a deep orange-red colour. Remove from the heat and pour the hot syrup into sterilised bottles or jars. Cover and seal the bottles or jars, then cool, label and store in a cool, dry cupboard for up to 3 months. Once opened, keep in the fridge and use within 1 week. Makes about 2 x 250ml bottles or jars. Serve the rosehip syrup as a cordial – simply dilute it to taste with chilled sparkling water and serve with plenty of ice and some fresh mint. Alternatively, pour the rosehip syrup over vanilla ice cream, or pour the chilled syrup over a warm, freshly baked Madeira cake, leave to cool and then liberally dust with icing sugar before serving for afternoon tea.

Rosemary

Rosemary is a perennial herb with woody stems and thin pointed green leaves that look a bit like pine needles. Rosemary grows in temperate and Mediterranean climates and so it grows well in gardens around Britain. During the summer months this attractive evergreen shrub produces pretty purple-blue flowers. Both the leaves and flowers of this robust herb can be eaten and its strong, pungent flavour is traditionally used with meats such as lamb, pork, sausages and rabbit, as well as in hearty bean and vegetable soups and stews. Rosemary is also used to flavour breads such as focaccia and it will impart a pleasant flavour to poached fruits, fruit salads or sorbets. Remove the leaves (or flowers) from the woody stalks before use (the woody stalks make perfect fragrant 'skewers' for chicken or prawn kebabs). Use rosemary flowers as a garnish for starters or serve a few scattered over a roast leg of lamb just before serving, or add to a seasonal garden salad.

Try this tasty recipe for **Rosemary and Sea Salt Oatcakes**. Place 100g rolled oats, 1 teaspoon sea salt, 2 teaspoons chopped fresh rosemary leaves, some freshly cracked black pepper and ¼ teaspoon bicarbonate of soda in a food processor and blend together until the oats have become finely ground. Tip this mixture into a large mixing bowl, then add another 75g rolled oats and 1 heaped tablespoon pumpkin seeds. Make a well in the centre, add 2 tablespoons rapeseed oil and 4 tablespoons boiling water, then mix together to form a sticky dough – if it's feeling a bit dry, add another spoonful of boiling water. Cover with cling film and leave to rest in the fridge for 30 minutes so that the oats absorb the water and the mixture binds together. Preheat the oven to 180°C/Gas Mark 4 and line 2 baking trays with non-stick baking paper. For each oatcake, take a heaped tablespoon of the oat mixture, roll it into a ball and place on the prepared baking tray, leaving a 5cm gap between each one. Press down on each ball to make a 5mm-thick round. Repeat for all the oatcakes. Bake in the oven for 20–25 minutes or until cooked, crisp and lightly golden. Remove from the oven and cool slightly on the baking trays, then transfer the oatcakes to a wire rack and leave to cool completely. Store in an airtight container and use within 1 week. Makes about 20 oatcakes. Serve the oatcakes with Stilton or any other good cheese and homemade chutney, or serve with poached pears, roasted walnuts, chicory and crumbled blue cheese as a starter. Alternatively, serve the oatcakes with homemade chicken liver parfait.

Sea beet and sea plantain

These are two superb edible coastal plants that can be found growing wild on our British seashores and sea walls. Sea beet, also called sea spinach, is a species of wild beet and is a native perennial plant with a sprawling habit, which flowers in the summer. The leaves have a pleasant taste and can be eaten raw or cooked like spinach. Sea plantain is a native herbaceous perennial plant that grows in sandy soils or cliffs around our coasts. The green leaves are fleshy and can also be eaten raw or cooked.

Try this lovely recipe for **Pan-Seared Scallops with Cobnuts, Sea Beet and Sea Plantain**. First, in a bowl, mix together 1 tablespoon softened unsalted butter, 1 tablespoon crushed roasted (shelled) cobnuts (or ground roasted hazelnuts), ½ crushed clove garlic, 1 teaspoon chopped fresh chervil and sea salt and freshly cracked black pepper and set aside. Season 6 shelled fresh scallops (150–200g total shelled weight) with salt and pepper and set aside. Heat a dash of rapeseed oil in a large, non-stick frying pan until hot, then place the scallops in the pan and sauté over a high heat for about 2 minutes or until golden brown and caramelised on the underside. Wash and drain a generous handful of sea beet (stalks removed) and a generous handful of sea plantain (stalks removed) and rip both into even-sized pieces. Flip the scallops over, then add the prepared butter and the sea beet and sea plantain to the pan and cook for a further 2 minutes or until the scallops are just cooked and are golden brown on the outside and moist and succulent on the inside. Remove the scallops from the pan and keep hot, then toss the sea vegetables in the melted butter to coat them all over. Divide the sea vegetables between 2 serving plates, then place 3 scallops on each plate, spoon the pan juices over and serve immediately with buttered brown bread, if you like. Serves 2 as a starter or light lunch.

Sea beet

Squash (general)

Squash are members of the Cucurbitaceae family and are divided into two main groups – summer squash and winter squash. Squash are the fruits of the species, though in culinary use they are considered to be vegetables. Summer squash are harvested as immature fruits, so they have softer, more tender edible skins and include vegetables such as courgettes, marrows and patty pans. Summer squash do not keep fresh for very long and are at their best if eaten soon after they have been picked. They can be eaten whole/unpeeled and the flowers of courgettes can also be eaten (see pages 234–235 for more information on courgettes). Summer squash are usually cooked before eating, but some varieties such as courgettes can be eaten both raw and cooked. Winter squash are the fruits that are harvested when they are more mature or fully ripe, so the skins have hardened into tough rinds. Most varieties of winter squash store well for use during the winter and they are usually cooked before eating. Winter squash need to be peeled and deseeded before cooking and they include several different varieties, including butternut, acorn, little gem, onion, hubbard, kabocha, turk's cap and pumpkins. Winter squash are typically used in savoury recipes, such as soups and risottos, and they are equally delicious roasted, pan-fried or steamed. Pumpkin pie is a popular dessert, especially in the USA and Canada. To prepare winter squash, peel, halve and scoop out the seeds, then cut the flesh into chunks or slices before cooking, depending on the recipe. Some winter squash can also be stuffed, either whole (with the top removed to form a 'lid') or in halves, with the seeds scooped out, and then oven-baked or roasted. Winter squash seeds, like pumpkin seeds, can be toasted or roasted and served as a tasty and nutritious snack. The seeds are also pressed and turned into oil for use in cooking and for salad dressings.

Squash (butternut squash)

Butternut squash is one of the most popular of all the winter squash. It is a bulbous, pear- or club-shaped squash with a pale yellow or creamy beige skin and a firm, orange-coloured flesh. Butternut squash is especially delicious roasted or baked, but the flesh can also be chopped or sliced and used in recipes such as soups, stews and risottos or simply pan-fried, steamed or stir-fried. Like other winter squash, the skin is tough so unless you are roasting butternut squash in halves (plain or stuffed), it needs to be peeled and deseeded before use. The seeds are also delicious if roasted and seasoned with coarse sea salt and ground spices and they can be served as a snack or sprinkled over salads and soups for extra texture and interest.

Butternut squash is also ideal for making a tasty chutney, so do try my recipe for **Spiced Butternut Squash Chutney**. Put 1 quartered onion, 2 deseeded large fresh red chillies, 50g peeled fresh root ginger and 2 cloves garlic into a food processor and blend together until minced and combined. Transfer the minced mixture to a large, heavy-based saucepan, then add 200g caster sugar, 200ml cider vinegar, 1 cinnamon stick, 3 toasted and crushed green cardamom pods, 1 star anise and sea salt and freshly cracked black pepper and cook over a gentle heat, stirring to dissolve the sugar. Bring to a gentle simmer over a medium heat, then cook, uncovered, for about 8 minutes or until the mixture has reduced and thickened to a syrup. Add 200g (peeled, deseeded weight) diced butternut squash flesh, 50g golden sultanas,1 peeled, cored and diced cooking apple (180–200g unprepared weight – you need about 150g prepared apple flesh), and 2 skinned and diced plum tomatoes and bring the mixture back to the boil, stirring occasionally. Cook the mixture, uncovered, over a medium heat for 18–20 minutes or until the mixture is reduced to a thick consistency, and no excess liquid remains, stirring occasionally. Taste and adjust the seasoning, if necessary. Remove the pan from the heat and leave to cool for 10 minutes, then spoon the chutney into hot, sterilised jars. Cover with vinegar-proof lids and seal. Leave to cool, then label and store in a cool, dry cupboard. Store for at least 1 week before using to allow the flavours to develop. The unopened jars of chutney should keep well for up to 12 months. Once opened, store in the fridge and use within 1 week. Makes about 2 x 250g jars. Serve this chutney with roast venison or pork (serve the meat hot or cold), or serve it in a sandwich with cold roast pork or pulled venison shoulder. Alternatively, try serving the chutney with cheese or smoked salmon.

Spiced Butternut Squash Chutney

Spiced Pickled Eggs and Pork Scratchings

These two recipes are a must-have for any pub's blackboard menu. I must say that at first the thought of pickled eggs was slightly, well, off-putting, but they are in fact delicious, so do give them a try! The challenge for me was to come up with a traditional and ultimate bar snack menu with a contemporary British Larder twist, and pickled eggs and pork scratchings are two quintessential British snacks that really complement a glass of real ale.

There is a very true saying that all good things take time to create and nurture. Well, these two recipes will certainly test your patience – and they did test mine – but they will be well worth all the effort, I can assure you! The eggs are really easy to make, but you do then have to wait 2 weeks for them to be pickled. The pork scratchings require a little more work and they also need 2 days of salting. The pickled eggs are kept in a pickling mixture that is laden with spices, so the pork scratchings had to follow suit and they also include a nice bit of spice.

I highly recommend both of these recipes and I prepare them with pride at the British Larder, but they must come with the following health warning: "Consume responsibly in small quantities as sensitive teeth might suffer, and a slightly tired heart and well-lived body might feel the strain if consumed in large, lavish quantities." Or, if you have a life motto like mine: "Eat and enjoy, because you only live once!"

Makes 20 pickled eggs and plenty of pork scratchings (enough to serve about 20)

For the spiced pickled eggs

2 litres cider vinegar (preferably Aspall organic cyder vinegar)
15g black peppercorns
2 star anise
2 cinnamon sticks
1 teaspoon crushed dried chillies
4 cloves
2 teaspoons fennel seeds, lightly toasted
2 teaspoons coriander seeds, lightly toasted
20 eggs

For the pork scratchings

2kg pork (pig's) skin, with as much fat removed as possible (see Cook's Notes)
2 star anise
5 black peppercorns
1 tablespoon coriander seeds
100g coarse sea salt
4 bay leaves
1 lemon, cut in half
sea salt, for dipping

For the pickled eggs, sterilise a very large glass jar (or 2 or 3 smaller jars) with a tight-fitting lid (see page 16 for more information on sterilising jars). Pour the cider vinegar into a saucepan, add all the spices and bring to the boil over a high heat, then reduce the heat and simmer for 2 minutes. Remove from the heat and set aside to cool for about 10 minutes.

Meanwhile, bring a separate large pan of water to a rapid boil, carefully place the eggs into the boiling water, then bring back to the boil and boil for 9 minutes. Remove from the heat and drain, then immediately place the eggs in a bowl of iced water to cool them quickly. Drain, then peel the eggs. Place the cold hard-boiled eggs into the sterilised jar, then pour the slightly cooled pickling liquid over the eggs, ensuring the eggs are completely covered with the vinegar mixture. Cover, seal and cool, then refrigerate for 2 weeks before serving. To serve, simply remove the eggs from the pickling liquor and drain. Once opened, keep the jar of pickled eggs in the fridge and use the eggs within 1 month.

For the pork scratchings, start by removing as many hairs as possible from the pork skin by carefully using a sharp razor blade or a very sharp knife (alternatively, briefly singe the hairs using a chef's blowtorch, then use a sharp knife to scrape the singed hairs off).

Grind the star anise, peppercorns and coriander seeds together using a pestle and mortar, then rub this mixture into the pork skin on both sides.

Spread half of the coarse salt in a layer over a deep white plastic tray (or a large ceramic lasagne dish), put the bay leaves on top, then lay the pork skin on top and cover with the remaining coarse salt. Cover with cling film and refrigerate for 2 days.

After 2 days, wash the salt off the pork skin, then pat dry and place it on a large baking tray. Boil a kettleful of water and pour this over the skin. Leave for 5 minutes, then remove the pork skin from the water, pat it dry and then lay it out on a clean white plastic tray (or a large ceramic lasagne dish). Place, uncovered, in the fridge and leave overnight. The following day, pat the pork skin dry with kitchen paper.

Preheat the oven to 180°C/Gas Mark 4. Place the pork skin on a wire rack positioned over a roasting tin. Dip the lemon halves in sea salt, then rub them all over the pork skin. Cook the pork skin in the oven for 30 minutes, then

carefully remove it from the oven, turn it over and use a spoon to scrape away and discard any obvious bits of fat (this fat can also be reserved and used for roast potatoes, if you like – see below and Cook's Notes).

Return the pork skin to the oven and cook for a further 20–30 minutes or until it is golden brown and crisp all over – keep a close eye on it to make sure it doesn't burn. Remove from the oven and test the pork skin to see if it's crispy – the fat should have rendered and dripped into the roasting tin (use the fat to make delicious roast potatoes – see Cook's Notes).

Leave the pork skin to cool completely, then use a sharp knife to cut it into bite-sized pieces or simply snap it into small pieces using your hands, and enjoy! Store the pork scratchings in an airtight container in a cool, dry cupboard for up to 5 days.

Cook's Notes

Pork or pig's skin is available from many butchers – ask your butcher in advance to keep the pork skin for you and they should happily put it to one side for you to collect.

Transfer the rendered fat to a sealed jar or a covered container and leave to cool, then store in the fridge and use within 3 days. As well as roast potatoes, the rendered fat can be used to fry eggs for breakfast.

Oven-roasted Acorn Squash with Salt-baked Beetroots and Rosehip and Elderberry Vinaigrette

Using a glut from the garden means that recipes can be adapted and changed as required, as different ingredients become available. If you do not have acorn squash, then use any of the many other different squash varieties, such as butternut or hubbard. The beetroot baked in salt gives it a concentrated and intense earthy taste, which works beautifully with the rosehip and elderberry vinaigrette. For the vinaigrette, use the Rosehip Syrup recipe on page 306.

This dish is best eaten at room temperature, so make all the components in advance and let them cool before serving.

Serves 4 as a starter

For the salt-baked beetroots

4 whole fresh beetroots (480–500g total weight), leaves trimmed off
200g coarse sea salt

For the oven-roasted acorn squash

1 acorn squash (900g–1kg total weight), cut in half lengthways, peeled and deseeded
2 tablespoons olive oil
2 teaspoons ras el hanout
sea salt and freshly cracked black pepper

For the roast cauliflower and soft-boiled eggs

½ head cauliflower, cut into small florets and thick stalk discarded (about 450g prepared florets)
2 tablespoons olive oil
1 tablespoon cider vinegar
1 teaspoon ras el hanout
2 eggs

For the rosehip and elderberry vinaigrette

4 tablespoons Rosehip Syrup (see page 306)
1 tablespoon cold water
1 tablespoon cider vinegar
1 tablespoon fresh elderberries (stalks removed), washed and patted dry
2 tablespoons olive oil

mixed seasonal baby salad leaves, to garnish

First, cook the salt-baked beetroots. Preheat the oven to 160°C/Gas Mark 3. Wash the beetroots and place in a roasting tin, then pack the coarse salt around them. Bake in the oven for about 2 hours or until cooked and tender. To test if the beetroots are ready, insert a metal skewer into each one – if it glides in and out with ease it's ready, but if there is a bit of resistance, continue cooking until tender. Remove from the oven and leave to cool. Remove the beetroots from the salt, rub the skins off and cut the beetroots into 3–4cm dice. Set aside.

While the beetroot is cooling, roast the squash. Increase the oven temperature to 200°C/Gas Mark 6. Cut the squash flesh into 5–6cm dice, then place in a bowl, add the olive oil, ras el hanout and salt and pepper and toss together to mix well. Transfer the squash to a baking tray, spreading it out evenly, then roast in the oven for 25–30 minutes or until cooked, tender and golden brown. Remove from the oven and leave to cool.

While the squash is roasting, roast the cauliflower at the same time. Put the cauliflower florets in a bowl, add the olive oil, cider vinegar and ras el hanout and toss together to mix well. Spread the cauliflower mixture out on a baking tray and roast in the oven for 10–12 minutes or until the cauliflower is tender but still retains a little bit of crunch. Remove from the oven and leave to cool.

Meanwhile, soft-boil the eggs. Bring a small saucepan of water to a rapid boil, carefully place the eggs into the boiling water, then bring back to the boil and boil for 7 minutes. Remove from the heat and drain, then immediately place the eggs in a bowl of iced water to cool them quickly. Drain, then peel the eggs and set aside.

In the meantime, to make the vinaigrette, place the rosehip syrup, water, cider vinegar, elderberries and salt and pepper in a small saucepan. Bring to a gentle simmer over a low heat, then cook for 2 minutes, stirring occasionally. Remove from the heat and stir in the olive oil, then leave to cool. Season to taste with salt and pepper.

To serve, cut the soft-boiled eggs in half and season each half with salt and pepper. Arrange the squash, beetroot and cauliflower with the egg halves on serving plates, season with salt and pepper and spoon some vinaigrette over (see Cook's Notes). Garnish each portion with some baby salad leaves and serve.

Cook's Notes

If you have any of the vinaigrette leftover, store it in an airtight container in the fridge and use within 1 week. Serve the vinaigrette with roast partridge and roast parsnips, or drizzle it over warm pan-fried mackerel and sea beet.

This dish can also be served as an accompaniment to poached salmon or whole baked grey mullet.

Fig and Caramelised Red Onion Tarts with Goat's Cheese and Pink Peppercorn Vinaigrette

This dish is pretty as a picture. Fresh figs and goat's cheese work wonderfully together and adding a dash of fragrant crushed pink peppercorns to the vinaigrette completes the dish. The caramelised red onions can be made in advance, if you like, as they will keep in an airtight container in the fridge for up to 3 days. Serve the tarts slightly warm so that the cheese starts to relax and almost soften.

Serves 4 as a starter or light lunch

For the fig and caramelised red onion tarts

30g unsalted butter, plus extra to grease the tins
600g red onions
1 clove garlic, crushed
30g light muscovado sugar
50ml Raspberry Cider Vinegar (see page 238)
1 teaspoon chopped fresh thyme
240g good quality chilled fresh all-butter puff pastry
6 large fresh ripe figs
sea salt and freshly cracked black pepper

For the pink peppercorn vinaigrette

1 teaspoon English mustard
100ml rapeseed oil
2 tablespoons cider vinegar (preferably Aspall organic cyder vinegar)
1 clove garlic, crushed
juice of ½ lemon
1 tablespoon clear honey
¼ teaspoon pink peppercorns, crushed

To serve

120g soft goat's cheese
a large handful of baby or mini/micro salad leaves

For the fig and caramelised red onion tarts, grease four 8 x 2cm round tart tins with butter and set aside. Peel and finely slice the onions.

Melt the remaining 30g butter in a saucepan, add the onions, garlic and salt and pepper, then cover and sweat over a medium heat for 10–15 minutes or until the onions are golden brown and caramelised, stirring regularly. Add the sugar and stir until dissolved, then add the raspberry cider vinegar and cook over a high heat for 8–10 minutes or until the vinegar is reduced and the onions are tender and coated in the thickened syrup (keep an eye on the mixture to make sure it doesn't catch or burn). Stir in the thyme, then remove the pan from the heat and set aside to cool.

Meanwhile, roll out the puff pastry on a lightly floured work surface to 2–3mm thickness. Cut out four 9cm rounds, place them on a tray and leave to rest in the fridge for 20 minutes or so.

Wash the figs and pat dry, then cut them into quarters. Arrange 6 fig quarters over the base of each prepared tin. Spoon a generous amount of the caramelised onions on top of the figs, press down firmly, then top with more onions, packing them in to ensure a firm layer. Place the pastry discs on top, tucking each one in around the edges to encase the caramelised onions. Transfer the tarts to the fridge and leave them to rest for 30 minutes before baking.

Meanwhile, preheat the oven to 200°C/Gas Mark 6.

Bake the tarts in the oven for about 30 minutes or until the pastry is cooked, well risen and golden brown. Remove from the oven and let the tarts cool in the tins for a few minutes before carefully turning them out and inverting them on to serving plates (you may need to loosen them around the edges with a butter knife). It's important that you turn the tarts out while they are still hot, otherwise they will stick to the tins. The tarts are best served warm.

Meanwhile, to make the vinaigrette, measure all the ingredients for the vinaigrette into a clean jam jar with a tight-fitting lid, cover with the lid and shake vigorously until mixed. Season to taste with salt.

To serve, crumble the goat's cheese over the warm tarts and garnish with the salad leaves. Drizzle over some pink peppercorn vinaigrette (see Cook's Note) and serve immediately.

Cook's Note

If you have any of the vinaigrette leftover, store it in an airtight container in the fridge and use within 1 week. Serve with a mixed seasonal salad, or toss the vinaigrette with cooked hot pasta and slithers of cooked duck for a tasty light meal.

Field Mushroom and British Chorizo Minestrone

The word minestrone means a 'big soup' that is substantial and is made with plenty of mixed chunky vegetables, usually with the addition of pasta, rice or beans. Minestrone soup forms the cornerstone of Italian cuisine and there is no real set recipe as it varies from region to region. It's mainly cooked with whatever vegetables are to hand, with the addition of either pasta or rice, but meat is optional. Well, I suppose it all comes down to whatever leftovers are available. This kind of recipe is right up my street as our dinners normally consist of whatever needs using up. At home we call it a 'fridge special' instead.

I'm fond of good chorizo that is chewy and spicy and it's brilliant to cook with, so when I discovered that there are a few producers here in Britain making British chorizo with British Freedom Food-approved pork, I was one happy foodie. The word chorizo refers to the recipe and style of sausage used – but everything else about these amazing sausages is, well, British!

In this recipe, the chorizo adds a smoky, rich flavour to my soup, but you can substitute it for a more traditional sausage if you do not have chorizo to hand. I have used pasta 'rice' known as orzo pasta, but you could use short macaroni or long grain white rice instead or simply break spaghetti into small pieces.

Serves 6 as a hearty lunch

2 tablespoons olive oil
2 onions, sliced
3 cloves garlic, crushed
2 baking potatoes, such as Desiree (200–250g each), peeled and diced
2 sticks celery, finely diced
300g field mushrooms or mixed fresh wild mushrooms, cleaned and sliced
150g chestnut mushrooms, sliced
200g chorizo, cut into 1cm pieces
½ teaspoon smoked paprika
100g orzo pasta (or use short macaroni, long-grain white rice or spaghetti broken into small pieces)
200ml dry white wine or dry sherry
1.2 litres vegetable or chicken stock
sea salt and freshly cracked black pepper
1 tablespoon snipped fresh chives, to garnish

Heat the olive oil in a large saucepan, add the onions, garlic, potatoes, celery, all the mushrooms, the chorizo, smoked paprika and salt and pepper and sauté over a medium heat for 8–10 minutes or until golden brown. The lower the heat you use (a medium heat is perfect), the more even golden brown colour you will get, and the most flavour will be extracted from the meat and vegetables. Avoid a fierce, high heat, stir regularly and do not be tempted to add more oil.

Once you are happy with the colouring of the vegetables and meat, add the orzo pasta to the pan and mix well, then add the wine and let it bubble, stirring and scraping the base of the pan with a wooden spoon to deglaze it. Cook over a high heat for 8–10 minutes or until all the wine is absorbed.

Add the stock, cover the pan and bring the mixture to a gentle simmer over a low heat, stirring frequently to prevent the pasta from sticking, then continue to simmer gently for about 25 minutes or until the pasta is cooked and the soup is thickened, stirring occasionally.

Ladle the hot soup into bowls and garnish each portion with a sprinkling of snipped chives. Serve with warm freshly baked bread on the side.

Cook's Note

This soup tastes even better the following day, so if you like you can make it a day in advance and keep it refrigerated for the next day. Simply make the soup as directed, then remove from the heat and leave it to cool. Once cool, store in an airtight container and use within 3 days. When you are ready to serve, reheat the soup gently in a saucepan until piping hot. The soup will have thickened in the fridge, so when reheating it, add a little extra stock or some water to thin it down.

Pan-fried Flounder and Langoustines with Sea Beet and Sea Plantain Salad and Apple and Caper Vinaigrette

Flounder are sustainable white flat fish. Combined in this recipe with succulent sweet langoustines, its flavour is set off beautifully by the sweet and sour combination from the apple and caper vinaigrette. The sea beet and sea plantain make this dish a really special seasonal delight.

Serves 4 as a starter or 2 as a main course

For the apple and caper vinaigrette
2 small cooking apples (about 400g total weight), left whole
100ml unsweetened apple juice
200g capers (drained weight), drained
25ml olive oil
sea salt and freshly cracked black pepper

For the pan-fried flounder and langoustines
¼ teaspoon mild curry powder
½ teaspoon sea salt
1 large fresh flounder (about 1.5kg total weight), skinned and filleted
12 fresh langoustine tails (600–720g total weight), peeled
2 tablespoons olive oil

For the sea beet and sea plantain salad
1 tablespoon olive oil
4 fresh sea beet leaves (about 80g in total), stalks removed
12 fresh sea plantain leaves (60–80g in total), stalks removed

First, prepare the apple and caper vinaigrette. Preheat the oven to 180°C/Gas Mark 4. Score each cooking apple around the centre, then place them on a baking tray and bake in the oven for 35 minutes or until cooked and tender. Remove from the oven and leave the apples to cool slightly, then once they are cool enough to handle, cut off the tops, scoop out the cooked apple flesh and discard the skins and cores.

Place the cooked apple flesh in a blender, add the apple juice, capers, olive oil and salt and pepper and blend together until very smooth. Pass the mixture through a fine sieve into a bowl – you should be left with a fairly thick vinaigrette rather than a runny one. Cover and refrigerate until needed (see Cook's Note).

For the pan-fried flounder and langoustines, mix the curry powder and salt together, then season the flounder fillets and langoustine tails lightly with the curried salt.

Heat the olive oil in a large, non-stick frying pan until hot, then add the flounder fillets and langoustine tails and cook over a high heat for 2 minutes. Flip them over and cook for a further 2 minutes on the other side or until cooked and golden brown. Drain on kitchen paper and keep hot while you prepare the salad.

For the sea beet and sea plantain salad, wipe out the pan used for the fish with kitchen paper. Add the olive oil to the pan and heat until hot, then add the sea beet and sea plantain leaves and sauté for about 2 minutes or until cooked and softened. Season with salt and pepper, then drain on kitchen paper.

To serve, arrange the sautéed sea beet and sea plantain salad on serving plates. Dot some of the apple and caper vinaigrette around each plate, then place the pan-fried flounder fillets and langoustine tails on the plates. Serve immediately.

Cook's Note
If you have any of the vinaigrette leftover, store it in an airtight container in the fridge and use within 1 week. Serve the vinaigrette with pan-fried scallops or homemade battered coley fish fingers.

Crisp Crusted Puffball with Woodland Mushroom Ragoût and Fried Duck Eggs

The woodlands and forests of Great Britain provide plenty for us to enjoy, including wild mushrooms. Puffball mushrooms can be quite tasteless and some people ask why we would even consider cooking them, but I disagree. In this recipe, the crisp exterior of the crusted puffball slices adds texture and interest, and the lemon zest, herbs and cheese add delicious flavour, so it proves to be a winning combination and a delightful dish all round.

Serves 4 as a main course

For the crisp crusted puffball and duck eggs

1 tablespoon chopped fresh flat-leaf parsley
1 teaspoon chopped fresh oregano
100g coarse fresh breadcrumbs
finely grated zest and juice of 1 lemon
30g finely grated Hawkstone cheese or fresh Parmesan cheese
80g unsalted butter
80ml extra virgin olive oil
2 cloves garlic, crushed
4 x 2cm-thick slices (each slice 100–120g) fresh puffball mushroom
3 tablespoons rapeseed oil
4 duck eggs
sea salt and freshly cracked black pepper

For the woodland mushroom ragoût

100g unsalted butter
1 onion, diced
1 clove garlic, crushed
300g mixed field and fresh wild woodland mushrooms, cleaned and sliced
80ml Madeira
250ml double cream
2 tablespoons chopped fresh flat-leaf parsley

For the crisp crusted puffball, put the flat-leaf parsley, oregano, breadcrumbs, lemon zest and grated cheese into a bowl with some salt and pepper and mix together. Set aside.

Put the butter and olive oil into a small saucepan and heat until melted, then remove from the heat and stir in the garlic, lemon juice and salt and pepper. Dip each slice of puffball mushroom into the melted butter mixture, then roll it in the breadcrumb mixture to coat all over. Use your hands to press the breadcrumb mixture on firmly. Place on a plate and set aside while making the ragoût.

For the woodland mushroom ragoût, melt the butter in a saucepan and once it is foaming, add the onion, garlic and salt and pepper and sauté over a high heat for 6–7 minutes or until golden brown. Add the mushrooms and sauté for a further 10 minutes or so until they turn golden brown. Add the Madeira to the pan and let it bubble, stirring and scraping the base of the pan with a wooden spoon to deglaze it. Cook over a high heat for 6–7 minutes or until all the Madeira is absorbed. Add the cream and bring to the boil, then remove from the heat. Stir in the parsley, then taste and adjust the seasoning, if necessary. Keep warm while you cook the puffball slices and eggs.

To cook the puffball slices you will probably need to cook them in 2 batches. For each batch, heat 1 tablespoon rapeseed oil in a large, non stick frying pan until hot, then add the coated puffball slices and fry over a medium heat for about 4 minutes on each side or until cooked and golden all over, turning once. Drain on kitchen paper and keep hot. Repeat to cook the remaining 2 puffball slices.

Once the crisp puffball slices are cooked, wipe the frying pan clean and then heat the remaining 1 tablespoon rapeseed oil in the pan until hot. Carefully crack the eggs into the hot pan, then fry the eggs over a medium heat for 3–3½ minutes or until the whites are set and the yolks are still soft and runny (or cook them to your liking). Season the yolks with salt and pepper.

Spoon the warm mushroom ragoût on to serving plates, place a slice of pan-fried crisp crusted puffball on top of each portion, followed by a fried duck egg. Serve immediately on its own or serve with steamed seasonal greens or a green side salad.

Slow-cooked Pork Belly with Crab Apple Jelly and Caramelised Damsons

Pork belly has become a hugely popular cut of meat during the birth and boom of the gastropub. It used to be classed as the underused cut and one that butchers could not get rid of, but my, how things have changed over recent years!
The secret to the success of a delicious pork belly meal depends on the length of time that the belly is cooked for and the temperature that it's cooked at.
My theory is long, slow and low.

The wonderful Crab Apple Jelly recipe can be found on page 303 and the acidic damsons are a perfect accompaniment to serve with pork belly, as they cut through the richness of the meat and balance the dish.

Serve this dish with either creamy mashed potatoes or boiled new potatoes and plenty of seasonal vegetables. I should warn you now though that this pork belly recipe is missing the crackling (the low temperature that the pork slowly cooks at would prevent it crisping up). I know, I know, it's a crime, but if you really must, then use the pork skin that is removed from the belly to make the delicious crispy Pork Scratchings on pages 310–311.

Serves 4 as a main course

For the slow-cooked pork belly

1kg pork belly, skin removed and fat trimmed off evenly
30ml clear honey
2 cloves garlic, crushed
1 teaspoon coriander seeds, crushed
a sprig of fresh rosemary
2 bay leaves
1 tablespoon sunflower oil
1 onion, roughly diced
2 carrots, roughly diced
1 stick celery, roughly diced
½ leek, washed and roughly diced
1 cinnamon stick
2 star anise
40ml soy sauce
200ml red wine
100ml port
500ml white chicken stock
1 teaspoon chilled unsalted butter
sea salt and freshly cracked black pepper

For the caramelised damsons

1 tablespoon unsalted butter
12 fresh damsons (240–300g unprepared weight), washed, then halved and stones removed
1 tablespoon caster sugar mixed with 1 clove, freshly ground (using a pestle and mortar)

Crab Apple Jelly (see page 303), to serve

For the slow-cooked pork belly, preheat the oven to 160°C/Gas Mark 3. Lay the pork belly on a chopping board and rub all over with a generous amount of salt and black pepper, the honey, garlic and crushed coriander seeds. Place the pork belly in a large, deep roasting tin, insert the rosemary and bay leaves underneath the pork, then set aside at room temperature while preparing the vegetables.

Heat the sunflower oil in a non-stick frying pan, add the onion, carrots, celery and leek and sauté over a high heat for about 10 minutes or until golden brown. Add the cinnamon and star anise towards the end of the cooking time. Add the soy sauce, red wine and port to the pan and let the mixture bubble, stirring and scraping the base of the pan with a wooden spoon to deglaze it, then bring to the boil. Immediately pour the mixture over the pork belly in the roasting tin. Return the pan to the heat, add the stock and bring to the boil, then pour the hot stock over the pork. Cover the roasting tin with foil and bake in the oven for 3 hours or until the pork is flaky, tender and succulent.

Remove from the oven and increase the oven temperature to 200°C/Gas Mark 6. Carefully remove the pork from the roasting tin to a large plate, pour the sauce off into a bowl and then return the pork to the tin. Return the pork to the oven and cook for a further 45 minutes or until it is cooked and golden brown. Remove from the oven and let the pork rest for 10 minutes.

Meanwhile, pass the sauce through a fine sieve into a small saucepan. Bring to the boil, then boil rapidly over a high heat for 5–6 minutes or until the sauce is reduced, thickened and almost syrupy. Remove from the heat and stir the cold butter into the sauce to give it a gloss.

In the meantime, for the caramelised damsons, melt the butter in a non-stick frying pan until it is foaming. Toss the damsons in the sugar and ground clove, then add the damson mixture to the foaming butter and sauté over a high heat for 3–4 minutes or until golden brown and caramelised (do not overcook the damsons as you want them to retain their shape). Season lightly with salt and pepper.

To serve, slice the pork belly and arrange the slices on serving plates, then spoon over the caramelised damsons. Serve immediately with the hot sauce and crab apple jelly served in the centre of the table so that everyone can help themselves.

Poached Roasted Chicken with Butternut Squash Anna

We all love a good roast on a Sunday, but my main concern with roast chicken is that the meat can sometimes become dry if you are roasting the whole bird on the bone.

For my take on a classic roast chicken, I remove the legs from a large organic or free-range chicken and use them for another meal, then I'm simply left with the crown – basically this is just the breast meat on the bone. I then part-roast the chicken on the bone, and once this is done, I take the breasts off the bone and poach them in chicken stock until cooked. This ensures two moist and tender roasted chicken breasts with maximum flavour. This may sound a little complicated, but really it's not at all.

I serve this delicious chicken with butternut squash Anna. Classically and traditionally, pommes Anna is a French dish made with layers of thinly sliced potatoes, melted butter and seasoning, oven-baked together in a dish. So, I use thinly sliced butternut squash instead of the potatoes to create my delicious seasonal twist for this lovely recipe (see also Cook's Notes).

Serves 2 as a main course

For the butternut squash Anna

400g butternut squash flesh (peeled and deseeded weight) (see Cook's Notes)
100g unsalted butter
sea salt and freshly cracked black pepper

For the roasted then poached chicken crown

1 chicken crown from a 1.6–1.8kg organic or free-range corn-fed chicken, skin left on
1 tablespoon sunflower oil
1 tablespoon unsalted butter
300ml white chicken stock
a large sprig of fresh thyme

Make the butternut squash Anna first and leave them to cool while the chicken is cooking, then reheat them (alongside the chicken) before serving with the hot chicken.

For the butternut squash Anna, preheat the oven to 200°C/Gas Mark 6. Place four 6.5cm-high (4.5cm width) metal dariole moulds on a baking tray and set aside.

Thinly slice the squash into 2mm-thick slices (preferably using a mandolin), then use a 4cm round cutter to cut the squash into discs. Keep the trimmings to use for making a butternut squash purée for another dish or for a soup base.

Melt the butter in a saucepan over a medium heat until it starts to bubble, then remove from the heat. In a bowl, mix together the melted butter, squash discs and salt and pepper. Pour a teaspoon of the melted butter into each dariole mould, then divide the butternut discs between the 4 moulds, layering the slices in the moulds and packing them in until each mould is nearly full, then cover with the remaining melted butter. Bake in the oven for 15 minutes or until cooked all the way through and the tops are starting to turn golden brown. Remove from the oven and let the butternut squash Anna cool in the moulds while you cook the chicken.

For the roasted chicken, preheat the oven to 200°C/Gas Mark 6. Season the chicken crown generously all over with salt and pepper. Heat the sunflower oil and butter in a large, non-stick frying pan until melted, then add the seasoned chicken crown to the pan, skin-side down, and cook over a high heat for 2–3 minutes on each breast or until the skin turns golden brown. Remove the pan from the heat and transfer the chicken crown to a roasting tin. Roast in the oven for 15 minutes, then remove from the oven and leave to rest for 5 minutes. Remember the chicken will only be partly cooked, but this is correct at this stage.

Remove the breasts from the bone, then place the 2 breasts, flesh-side down, in a deep roasting tin or casserole. (Reserve the carcass to make some stock later.) Bring the stock to the boil in a saucepan, then carefully pour it around the chicken so that it just covers the bottom of the roasting tin or casserole but doesn't cover the skin of the chicken. Add the sprig of thyme. Return the chicken to the oven and cook for a further 18–20 minutes or until the chicken is cooked and hot all the way through.

When you are ready to serve, reheat the butternut squash Anna in the oven for 8–10 minutes or until hot (reheat them at the same temperature and at the same time as the chicken is poaching so that they are then ready together). Meanwhile, drain the cooking juices from the chicken into a small pan, then bring the juices to the boil and boil over a high heat for about 5 minutes or until reduced slightly. Season to taste with salt and pepper. The reduced juices can then be served as a light gravy with the chicken.

To serve, remove the butternut squash Anna from the oven and carefully turn them out on to a chopping board, drain off the excess butter, then carefully transfer them to serving plates. Serve the cooked chicken breasts alongside and serve with cooked Chantenay carrots and broccoli. Pour over the light gravy to taste and serve immediately.

Cook's Notes

When making the butternut squash Anna, take most of the flesh from the solid top part of the squash (which doesn't contain any seeds) if you can, so that you can then easily cut it into nice round slices.

Traditionally, pommes Anna is made with potatoes. I have used butternut squash for this recipe as it cooks faster than potatoes, so you will need to adjust the cooking time if you choose to use potatoes or celeriac instead. Turnips, swede and carrots would also make lovely alternative Anna, but again you will need to adjust the cooking time accordingly.

Goat's Curd Marrow Bakes

A trip to London is not complete without stopping at the fabulous Borough Market. When walking through the market with a shopping list in hand, it's pretty normal for me to let my emotions take over and my radar (or foodar, as I call it!) goes haywire when I detect all those wonderful ingredients. Before you know it, I have spent more than anticipated and have not bought a single item from my list.

Just stopping at the famous Neal's Yard cheese shop can result in near bankruptcy for me! I tell myself every time to stay focused and purchase just what's needed... but it's much easier said than done! Their goat's curd works perfectly in this recipe.

As the marrow I used when creating this recipe was incredibly fresh and the skin still very tender, I grated the whole marrow, skin and all, and I like the resulting texture as it does not go completely mushy but still retains some coarseness. So, select very fresh marrow if you can, but if the skin is tough, peel the marrow and discard the skin. I flavour the marrow with a little garam masala as it works well with the strong goat's curd. If goat's curd is not available, you can use ricotta or even Stilton instead (see Cook's Notes).

This bake is ideal served as a vegetarian main course. You can make four individual bakes or one larger one, whichever you prefer.

Serves 4 as a main course

500g marrow (trimmed weight), washed and patted dry
2 eggs
50ml double cream
50g plain flour
1 teaspoon garam masala
1 teaspoon caster sugar
1 teaspoon baking powder
200g goat's curd
1 large thick slice white bread, crusts removed
2 tablespoons coarsely chopped fresh flat-leaf parsley
1 clove garlic, crushed
sea salt and freshly cracked black pepper

Preheat the oven to 200°C/Gas Mark 6 and grease 4 individual round ovenproof dishes (each about 10 x 5cm) or 1 large ovenproof dish (about 25 x 18cm). Set aside.

If the marrow is very fresh and the skin is tender, then there is no need to peel it, but if the skin is tough and thick, peel the marrow and discard the skin. Coarsely grate the marrow and set aside.

Put the eggs, cream, flour, garam masala, sugar, baking powder and salt and pepper into a mixing bowl and whisk together to make a thick smooth batter. Add the grated marrow and fold together to mix. Spoon the marrow mixture into the prepared dishes (or dish) dividing it evenly between the dishes, then top each portion with 50g goat's curd (or if you are using one larger dish, spoon over all of the goat's curd), placing it in small dollops or dots over the top.

Bake the individual dishes in the oven for about 20 minutes (or bake the larger dish for 30–35 minutes) or until cooked and golden brown on top – the bakes will rise or soufflé slightly during baking, but once they are removed from the oven they will sink back into the dishes as they start to cool.

While the marrow bakes are cooking, put the bread, parsley and garlic into a food processor and process until the mixture resembles fine breadcrumbs. Set aside.

Remove the cooked marrow bakes from the oven, sprinkle the garlic crumbs over the top and serve immediately. Serve with buttered cooked seasonal greens, steamed broccoli or a dressed mixed seasonal salad.

Cook's Notes

If you like the sound of this recipe but do not have marrow available, substitute the marrow with courgettes, butternut squash, pumpkin or even sweet potatoes.

The goat's curd can be substituted with soft goat's cheese, ricotta, mascarpone or Stilton, or it can be omitted altogether, if you prefer.

If you make one larger bake, this recipe can also be served as a side dish to serve 6. Serve with slow-cooked pork belly or grilled lamb Barnsley chops.

Sautéed Black Cabbage and Roasted Butternut Squash with Ewe's Milk Cheese Shavings

Warm autumn salads are a terrific substitute for the lighter leafier ones that we love so much during the summer. I can eat salad all year round as it makes the perfect accompaniment to grilled or roasted meat, fish and poultry.

Use the tender interior leaves of the black cabbage (also known as Cavolo nero) for this recipe and keep the larger outer leaves for adding to a risotto or soup (see Cook's Notes). These young, tender leaves benefit from being cooked quickly in a dash of olive oil and a tiny amount of unsalted butter. I believe firmly in adding a knob of butter when cooking cabbages of all varieties as the nutty flavour perfectly matches the cabbage. The roasted butternut squash adds a lovely sweet flavour with a creamy texture.

Finish this wonderful salad with shavings of ewe's milk cheese and a drizzle of honey and wholegrain mustard vinaigrette from the fridge.

Serves 4 as a side dish

For the salad

1 butternut squash (800–900g total weight), peeled
6 white carrots, peeled (or use heritage carrots – see Cook's Notes)
3 tablespoons olive oil
200g (prepared weight) young black cabbage (Cavolo nero) leaves (stalks removed), washed, drained and left whole or roughly shredded (see Cook's Notes)
1 teaspoon unsalted butter
50g hard ewe's milk cheese (choose one from your local region, if possible – see also Cook's Notes)
sea salt and freshly cracked black pepper

For the honey and wholegrain mustard vinaigrette

1 tablespoon balsamic vinegar
1 tablespoon wholegrain mustard
3 tablespoons extra virgin olive oil
1 teaspoon clear honey
1 clove garlic, crushed

First, for the salad, roast the butternut squash. Preheat the oven to 200°C/ Gas Mark 6. Cut the peeled butternut squash in half lengthways and remove the seeds, then slice the flesh widthways into 3–4mm slices and spread them out on a large baking tray. Cut the white carrots into quarters lengthways and add them to the baking tray, then season with salt and pepper and drizzle over 2 tablespoons of olive oil.

Roast in the oven for 20–25 minutes or until cooked and tender. Test to see if the squash and carrots are cooked by inserting a metal skewer into them; if it glides in and out easily then they're cooked; if there is a bit of resistance, then roast for an extra 5 minutes or so until cooked. Remove from the oven and keep hot.

While the squash is roasting, prepare the vinaigrette. Place all the ingredients for the vinaigrette, plus salt and pepper, into a small, clean jam jar with a tight-fitting lid, then seal and shake vigorously. Taste and adjust the seasoning, if necessary, then cover and refrigerate until needed.

Once the squash is nearly cooked, heat the remaining 1 tablespoon olive oil in a large, non-stick frying pan until hot, then add the black cabbage and salt and pepper and sauté over a high heat for 2–3 minutes or until wilted and slightly softened but still al dente. Reduce the heat, add the butter, then let the butter melt and turn golden, stirring to mix well. Drain the cabbage on kitchen paper, then mix it with the roasted butternut squash and white carrots. Add a tablespoon of the vinaigrette and toss to mix. Transfer the mixture to serving plates and use a vegetable peeler to shave the ewe's milk cheese over the top. Serve immediately with grilled pork chops, grilled lamb cutlets or baked whole John Dory.

Cook's Notes

I have chosen to only use the very tender and young black cabbage leaves for this recipe. However, do not throw the tougher outer leaves away as they will be perfect shredded and boiled in a pan of boiling salted water for 6–7 minutes or until tender. Drain, then stir the cooked leaves through creamy mashed potatoes, risotto or soup, just before serving.

The leftover vinaigrette will keep well in a sealed jar in the fridge for up to 1 week. Toss it with warm boiled new potatoes and serve with baked ham, or serve the vinaigrette tossed with a salad of baby spinach, cooked crispy smoked bacon, chopped hard-boiled eggs and croûtons.

White carrots are typically available from farmers' markets or specialist greengrocers. If you can't find white carrots, use heritage carrots of your choice, or try using small parsnips in place of the carrots.

Other hard or semi-hard cheeses such as Cornish Yarg, Berkswell, fresh Parmesan or Pecorino can be substituted for the ewe's milk cheese, if you like.

Damson and Bramble Plate Pie

I love this concept. The idea is that you make and bake the pie on the same plate that you will serve it on – superb! Just my kind of thing as I do not like too many dirty dishes.

This is the ultimate family pie. Place the whole pie on the table with a big jug of steaming custard and everyone can dive in and help themselves. When I first made this recipe, the damsons came from our garden and the brambles (blackberries) from the nearby hedgerows. If you do not have damsons, you could use plums instead.

I get so excited about the seasonal fruit that I dare not let any go to waste, so if you have plenty of damsons to spare, freeze them for a later date.

Serves 6

450g Sweet Shortcrust Pastry (see page 18)
100g fresh brambles or blackberries
150g (prepared weight) fresh damsons, quartered and stones removed
20g pecan halves, roughly chopped
20g ground almonds
50g golden caster sugar
a pinch of table salt
a pinch of ground ginger
1 egg yolk, lightly beaten with ½ teaspoon caster sugar

Preheat the oven to 200°C/Gas Mark 6 and select a suitable round enamel or ceramic plate (about 20cm in diameter) to make the pie on. Set aside.

Roll out the pastry on a lightly floured work surface to about 5mm thickness. Cut out two rounds, both 22cm in diameter. Line the plate with one round of pastry, place the other round on a baking tray and then place both rounds of pastry in the fridge to rest while you make the filling.

Put the brambles, damsons, pecans, ground almonds, sugar, salt and ground ginger in a mixing bowl and stir to mix. Pile the fruit mixture on to the lined plate, brush the edge of the pastry with water, then gently lay the second round of pastry over the top and press the edges together to seal. Use a knife to trim off any excess pastry, then crimp around the edges of the pastry. Pierce or slash 3 steam holes in the top of the pie using a metal skewer or sharp knife. Brush the top of the pie with the egg yolk mixture.

Bake the pie in the oven for 15 minutes, then reduce the oven temperature to 180°C/Gas Mark 4 and bake for a further 20–25 minutes or until the pastry is cooked and golden brown. Remember to place a baking tray on the shelf underneath the pie in the oven as the pie is bound to leak some sugary fruit juices.

Remove from the oven and let the pie rest for 10 minutes before serving. Serve with hot custard, clotted cream, crème fraîche or vanilla ice cream.

Cook's Notes

You could make your own filling and just use the concept for this pie, if you like. Instead of the damsons, try using diced (peeled and cored) cooking or eating apples or pears, and instead of the brambles, you could use raspberries or (stoned) cherries.

The ground almonds are there to soak up some of the juiciness of the brambles and damsons and the ginger adds a little spice. The ginger can be substituted with freshly grated nutmeg, ground cinnamon or ground mixed spice, if you like.

Hedgerow Fruit Pastilles

Making fruit pastilles is really just as easy as making jam and you will require similar basic tools, including a jam thermometer. You also need to be well prepared and have all your tools in place, as the mixture thickens incredibly fast once it is ready, so line your chosen tray with cling film in advance and leave it in an easy-to-reach spot.

Remember, once the pastilles are made and set, do not refrigerate them, otherwise they will get damp and will start to dissolve. They are best kept in an airtight container in a cool, dry cupboard and eaten within 3 days.

Although stone fruits and berries contain a decent amount of pectin, they don't contain quite enough to set these pastilles sufficiently, so a little extra pectin is added for that reason. Powdered pectin is available from most good supermarkets or health food shops. The liquid glucose gives the sweets a lovely chewiness and it can be found in the baking ingredients section of most supermarkets.

Ideally, you will need to start this recipe the day before you want to serve the pastilles, as the mixture is best left to set overnight and then cut into sweets the next day.

Makes 24 fruit pastilles

360g (unprepared weight) fresh wild plums such as bullaces
100g (prepared weight) fresh elderberries, stalks removed
400g fresh brambles or blackberries
100ml cold water
180g liquid glucose
300g caster sugar
20g powdered pectin
demerara sugar, for coating

Line a 21 x 14 x 1.5cm sturdy white plastic tray (or a shallow ceramic dish of the same size) with a double layer of cling film (see Cook's Note on page 297 for information on this) and set aside.

Wash and drain the plums, elderberries and brambles, then cut the plums in half and remove the stones (you need 300g prepared plums). Place the prepared plums and stones (the stones contain pectin and for that reason you should boil them together with the fruit) and the elderberries and brambles in a saucepan with the water and bring the mixture to the boil over a very low heat, stirring occasionally. Simmer the fruit mixture, uncovered, for about 30 minutes or until it is completely softened and pulpy. Remove from the heat and pass the fruit mixture through a sieve into a bowl. Discard the stones and any solids.

Measure 500ml of the purée (see Cook's Notes) into a clean saucepan and add the glucose. Bring to the boil, then reduce the heat to a gentle simmer and boil gently for 10–15 minutes or until the mixture reaches a temperature of 105°C (setting point) on a jam thermometer, stirring a couple of times to prevent it from catching. Add the caster sugar and pectin, stirring until the sugar has dissolved, then bring the mixture back to a simmer and cook for a further 10 minutes or so until it reaches a temperature of 105°C for a second time.

Remove from the heat and immediately pour the boiling mixture into the lined tray, then leave at room temperature until it is completely set. I find leaving it to set overnight usually works best. Once it is cold, it's also best to cover the mixture with a tray or something that covers it but doesn't touch the surface (if you use cling film to cover, then it will stick to the surface of the fruit jelly and will ruin all your efforts).

Once it is completely set, cut the fruit jelly mixture into 24 squares, roll each jelly square in demerara sugar and then serve the pastilles. Store the fruit pastilles in an airtight container (with non-stick baking paper between each layer) in a cool, dry cupboard and use within 3 days.

Cook's Notes

If you have any leftover fruit purée, leave it to cool, then store in an airtight container in the fridge and use within 3 days. Serve the fruit purée with ice cream for a dessert, or serve it with muesli and natural yogurt for breakfast.

To make Mirabelle Fruit Pastilles, simply follow the recipe as directed above, but replace the wild plums, elderberries and brambles with 900g mirabelle plums (unprepared weight). Wash and drain the plums, cut them in half and remove the stones (you need 750g prepared plums), then continue as the recipe directs.

Damson and Rosemary Jelly

Making jelly does not require very much skill, but what you do need is some know-how, patience and perseverance. I must admit that my first attempt at making jelly worked a treat, as I hadn't done it before and I was on full alert and followed my recipe to the letter. The next attempt was a disaster though, because of two simple things – the first was that I was over-confident, and the second was that I was trying to make a huge batch all at once, so the resulting jelly set but it looked cloudy instead of clear. I learnt my lesson, so my message to you is don't be over-confident, follow the recipe and definitely don't attempt to make the jelly in large batches.

You can make the first stage in a large batch if you like, but when it comes to the second boiling stage with the sugar, I suggest you cook that in smaller batches as I have done in this recipe. It cooks faster and the results are much better.

Makes 3 x 250ml jars

800g fresh damsons
2 large sprigs of fresh rosemary
about 700g preserving sugar (see page 16)
juice of 1 lemon

Wash and drain the damsons, then cut them in half, but leave the stones intact. Place the prepared damsons in a large saucepan with enough cold water to cover the fruit, then bring the mixture to the boil. Reduce the heat, carefully place a plate on top of the damsons to weigh them down and simmer over a low heat for about 30 minutes or until they are completely softened and pulpy. Add the rosemary sprigs for the last 10 minutes of the cooking time.

Remove the pan from the heat, then pour the hot damson mixture into a jelly bag suspended over a bowl, or pour into a large sieve lined with muslin cloth placed over a bowl, and let the mixture drip overnight (preferably in the fridge). This stage is important, as the stones contain all the natural pectin and this will help the jelly to set.

The following day, discard the stones and solids, measure the damson juice into a clean saucepan and then work out how much preserving sugar is needed. Use the ratio of 10 parts damson juice to 7 parts preserving sugar, so for 1 litre juice (about how much this recipe will make) use 700g preserving sugar.

Add the measured sugar to the juice in the pan and cook over a gentle heat, stirring to dissolve the sugar, then turn the heat up and bring to the boil. Boil rapidly for about 30 minutes or until the damson mixture reaches a temperature of 105°C (setting point) on a jam thermometer, skimming off any scum from the surface. If you don't have a jam thermometer, check to see if setting point has been reached by spooning a little of the jelly on to a chilled small plate. Push a finger across the jelly; if the surface wrinkles and it is beginning to set, it has reached setting point. If not, boil it gently for a further 5 minutes or so and test again.

Once the jelly has reached setting point, stir in the lemon juice. Remove the pan from the heat and leave the jelly to cool slightly, then carefully pour it into hot, sterilised jars. Cover with wax discs (wax-side down) and seal. When cold, label, then store in a cool, dry cupboard. The jelly should keep well for a year or so. Once opened, keep in the fridge and use within 1 month.

Serve the jelly with roast pork, venison or pheasant or with cheese. Alternatively, enjoy it simply spread on buttered crusty bread, hot toasted crumpets or freshly baked scones.

The British Larder | *October*

What an incredible time of year. The forests and landscape are covered in the most glorious shades of orange, red, brown and deeper shades of green and with the cold snaps coming and going and occasional warmer days in between, there is plenty of activity to deliver an abundant and grand selection of seasonal produce. The game season is in full swing – venison, partridges, pheasants and wild ducks are plentiful – and this makes autumn cooking interesting and exciting.

Rainbow chard

Enjoy wild blackberries only until the 11th of October as British folklore suggests that on this date – 'old Michaelmas' – the devil was banished from heaven and fell into a blackberry bush, cursing, stamping and spitting on the fruit, making it unfit to eat. The cooler weather will encourage mould growth and make blackberries unpalatable, so I harvest as many as I can, preferably before the rain sets in, then either pickle, preserve or freeze them for a rainy day. Blackberries and game make a delicious partnership.

After a few cold nights and a touch of frost, the sloes are ready to be picked and turned into the all-important sloe gin, to be stored for next season's shooting expeditions. There is plenty to harvest in the hedgerows, including rosehips and elderberries, so prepare, store and preserve them while the abundance is still available. Chestnuts and walnuts are ready to be collected and add extra texture and protein to the season's dishes, and there should be plenty of good quality wild mushrooms to forage after the autumn rain.

Brill, sea bass, skate and squid are superb this month, but we are seeing the end of the lobster season.

Season's best during October...

Apples, Artichokes, Aubergines, Beetroot, Blackberries, Black Cabbage (Cavolo Nero), Brill, Broccoli, Butternut Squash, Cabbages, Carrots, Celeriac, Celery, Chard, Chestnuts, Chickweed, Chives, Clams, Cobnuts, Cod, Coley, Crab, Crab Apples, Duck, Elderberries, Fennel, Figs, Flounder, Garlic, Golden Plover, Goose, Grapes, Grey Mullet, Grouse, Guinea Fowl, Haddock, Hake, Halibut, Hare, Hawthorn Berries, Horseradish, Jerusalem Artichokes, John Dory, Kale, Kohlrabi, Lamb, Langoustines, Leeks, Lemon Sole, Lettuce, Lobster, Mackerel, Mallard, Marrow, Medjool Dates, Medlars, Mint, Monkfish, Mussels, Onions, Oysters, Parsnips, Partridge, Peaches, Pear, Peppers, Pheasant, Plaice, Pollack, Potatoes (main crop), Prawns, Pumpkin, Quinces, Rabbit, Radishes, Rocket, Rosehips, Rosemary, Rowanberries, Sage, Scallops, Sea Bass, Shallots, Skate, Sloes, Squid, Swede, Swiss Chard, Teal, Thyme, Truffles (black), Tufted Duck, Turbot, Turnips, Venison, Walnuts, Watercress, Widgeon, Wild Mushrooms (autumn), Winkles, Woodcock, Woodpigeon.

My culinary rituals for October...

The colder weather brings a yearning for heartier, slow-cooked food. Invite family and friends for a classic Sunday roast and fill your home with pleasure, laughter and love. Brush up your pie-making skills and try out different recipes for soups and casseroles.

Keep an eye out for woodland mushrooms, especially after a good downpour. Varieties such as puffballs, girolles and ceps will be lurking among the brown and orange leaves covering the forest floor. The glorious flavour of these autumn mushrooms is a perfect partner for other autumn favourites, such as game and chestnuts. Try my delicious recipes for **Pan-fried Partridge with Caramelised Figs and Fig Vinaigrette** (see page 351), **Pan-roasted Teal with Pearl Barley and Damson Vinaigrette** (see page 358) or **Puy Lentil-stuffed Roasted Golden Plover with Sloe Gin Grapes** (see page 361).

Halloween and bonfire night are approaching. Be inspired by the apple harvest and make toffee apples to add a lovely homemade touch to the celebrations.

And even though Christmas is still two months away, it's the perfect time to start preparing your festive fare. Try my wonderful **Luxury Sweet Mincemeat** (see page 432) and **My Ultimate Christmas Pudding** (see page 436) recipes from the December chapter. By making them both now, you'll allow the flavours plenty of time to mature and develop and the results will be even tastier.

My Christmas puddings are particularly well received. My secret – although a secret no more! – is the local ale and sourdough breadcrumbs I use. Select your own favourite ale and, if possible, use sourdough bread as I believe this is truly my secret ingredient – it adds depth of flavour and gives the pudding a completely different texture to a shop-bought version: the pudding is lighter and almost cake-like. Make, steam and store the pudding, then feed it with brandy every now and then, as described in the recipe. Come Christmas, the pudding will be matured and simply scrumptious.

British Larder Heroes

Brill

Brill is a flat fish closely related to turbot, but its skin is smoother and in general it is slightly smaller and a little more oval-shaped than the diamond-shaped turbot. Brill has a delicate, slightly sweet taste and is highly valued for its meaty flesh, which is an excellent source of protein. It is, however, priced slightly more affordably than its expensive cousin the turbot. As with turbot and halibut, the skin is fairly thick and leathery and while I generally cook brill in its skin to lock in moisture, I prefer to remove it before serving. As with turbot and halibut, brill bones make an excellent fish stock.

To make my tasty recipe for **Oven-baked Brill with Rosemary, Butternut Squash and Fennel**, preheat the oven to 200°C/Gas Mark 6 and grease an ovenproof dish with 1 tablespoon unsalted butter. Cut 200g (peeled and deseeded weight) butternut squash flesh into wedges. Trim 1 fennel bulb and cut into 8 wedges, then scatter the butternut squash and fennel wedges over the base of the prepared dish. Season with sea salt and freshly cracked black pepper, then scatter over 1 tablespoon chopped fresh rosemary and 1 sliced clove garlic. Cover the dish with foil and bake in the oven for 15 minutes. Remove the foil and place 2 skinless, boneless brill fillets (100–120g each), seasoned with salt and pepper, on top of the baked vegetables. Place a small knob of unsalted butter on top of each piece of fish, then sprinkle over ½ teaspoon chopped fresh rosemary. Return the dish to the oven and bake for about 10 minutes or until the fish is flaky, moist and pale golden. Serve immediately with buttered seasonal greens. Serves 2 as a main course.

British apples

The apple tree is a deciduous tree from the rose family, which includes roses, strawberries, raspberries, apricots, plums and pears. It is one of the most widely cultivated fruit trees in the world: in Britain alone over 2300 apples varieties are grown and cultivated and they come in many different shapes, sizes, colours, tastes and textures. Cox's Orange Pippins and Egremont Russets are among the favourite varieties, and are also some of the most widely available, but do look out for unusual or locally-grown apple varieties at your local farmers' markets. There are two kinds of apple: cooking and eating. Cooking apples, such as Bramleys, are too acidic to be eaten raw but are excellent for cooking when a softer texture is required, as they quickly become mushy once cooked. Cooking apples, such as Bramleys, need to be sweetened and they are perfect for using in crumbles and pies. They also have a lovely fluffy texture when baked. Eating or dessert apples have sweet flesh, making them suitable for eating raw, but they can also be used for cooking, as they tend to hold their shape well and are ideal for desserts such as French-style apple tarts. Choose apples that are firm with taught unbroken skins. Many varieties have naturally freckled or dull surfaces, but the odd blemish or two is nothing to worry about. The British apple season runs from late September through to January.

For a delicious pudding or teatime treat, try this recipe for **Apple and Spelt Slice**. I have chosen to use Egremont Russet apples, but I encourage you to experiment and choose an apple variety of your liking. First, make a baked apple butter. Preheat the oven to 200°C/Gas Mark 6. Wash 4 Egremont Russet apples, place in a roasting tin and bake in the oven for about 30 minutes or until cooked, soft and bursting from their skins. Remove from the oven and leave to cool for about 10 minutes, then scoop out the flesh (discarding the cores and skin) and place it in a small saucepan. Add 2 tablespoons caster sugar, 1 tablespoon clear honey and a pinch of table salt and bring to a simmer over a low heat, stirring to dissolve the sugar. Simmer for 5 minutes, then remove the pan from the heat and quickly stir in 3 teaspoons cold unsalted butter. Set aside. To make the spelt pastry, put 225g spelt flour, 100g cornflour, 100g icing sugar, 1 teaspoon ground cinnamon, a pinch of table salt and 225g diced unsalted butter into a large mixing bowl. Using your fingertips, rub the butter into the flour to form a firm dough. Gather the dough into a ball, wrap in cling film and chill in the fridge for 20 minutes. Preheat the oven again to 200°C/Gas Mark 6. Grease and line a 35 x 11 x 2.5cm baking tin with non-stick baking paper. Roll out the pastry on a lightly floured work surface to the same size as the base of the tin and to 1cm thickness, then transfer the pastry to the

Apple and Spelt Slice

prepared tin. Spread the apple butter evenly over the pastry. Core 2 even-sized Egremont Russet apples, leaving the skin on, then thinly slice the apples on an angle into 2mm slices (preferably using a mandolin). Arrange the apple slices, overlapping each other, over the apple butter, then sprinkle with 1 tablespoon caster sugar. Bake in the oven for about 30 minutes or until the pastry is cooked and the apples are golden brown. Remove from the oven and immediately drizzle over 1 tablespoon clear honey. Dust with icing sugar, then scatter over 1 tablespoon chopped pistachio nuts. Serve warm or at room temperature with cream, vanilla ice cream or custard. Serves 6.

Chard

Chard is a large leafy vegetable, in the same family as the beetroot, which both descend from sea beet. Swiss chard, rainbow chard, red chard and silver beet are all variations of chard and different varieties will have different coloured leaves and/or stalks, including red, yellow, pink or white. The earthy, 'iron' flavour of chard is a good match for wild duck, pheasant and other game, so for a simple vegetable accompaniment, blanch chard leaves in a pan of boiling salted water for 1–2 minutes or until tender, then dress with olive oil and season with sea salt and freshly cracked black pepper.

For tasty **Chard and Feta Filo Fingers**, wash 350g fresh chard in cold water, then remove the stalks from the leaves. Finely shred the leaves and finely dice the stalks. Heat 1 tablespoon olive oil in a non-stick frying pan over a medium heat and add 2 crushed cloves garlic, 1 finely diced onion, 4 sliced spring onions, the chard stalks, a pinch of turmeric and a sprinkling of sea salt and freshly cracked black pepper. Sauté for 8 minutes or until the vegetables are tender, soft and golden brown. Add the chard leaves and sauté for a further minute, then remove the pan from the heat. Put the pan contents into a colander set over a bowl to drain. Transfer the vegetables to a mixing bowl, then add a few gratings of fresh nutmeg, 1 teaspoon each chopped fresh parsley and fresh oregano and 1 beaten egg. Crumble over 100g feta cheese and gently mix together, then cover and refrigerate for 1 hour. Preheat the oven to 200°C/Gas Mark 6 and line a baking tray with non-stick baking paper. Lay 1 sheet of filo pastry (about 40 x 30cm in size) on a clean work surface, brush lightly with melted unsalted butter, then cut the filo sheet in half widthways. Place 1 tablespoon of the chilled mixture at one end of each piece of filo in a sausage shape, fold the sides over and roll up the mixture in the filo pastry to make two separate fingers. Brush with more melted butter and sprinkle with sesame seeds. Repeat the process with a further 5 sheets of filo pastry (of a similar size) to create 12 fingers in total. Place the filo fingers on the prepared baking tray, leaving a 2cm gap between each, and bake in the oven for 18-20 minutes or until crisp and golden. Transfer to a wire rack and either serve warm or at room temperature on the day they are made. Serves 4 as a snack or as a light lunch with salad, or serves 12 as a canapé.

Medlars

Medlars are a very intriguing fruit. They resemble apples, and indeed are from the same family, but when ripe and harvested they are very hard and acidic and require 'bletting' – ripening – before they are ready to be eaten or cooked. Bletting means that the fruit needs to ripen to the point where the flesh starts to decay and ferment and the medlars darken and become very soft.

Medlars

To make delicious **Medlar and Apple Jellies**, place 6 serving glasses in the fridge. Peel 500g British eating apples, then core and roughly chop them into 2cm dice. Wash and chop 500g very ripe medlars into 2cm dice, then place both fruits in a large saucepan with the juice of 1 lemon, 400g caster sugar and 2 litres cold water. Bring to the boil over a medium heat, stirring occasionally to dissolve the sugar, then reduce the heat, cover and simmer for about 45 minutes or until the liquid becomes pink in colour and the fruits are completely soft. Remove the pan from the heat and remove the scum from the surface using a ladle. Pour the hot fruit mixture into a jelly bag suspended over a bowl, or pour into a large sieve lined with muslin cloth placed over a bowl, and let the mixture drip for about 10 minutes. Reserve the liquid and discard the solids. Soak 5 leaves of gelatine in cold water until softened. Measure 600ml of the reserved hot fruit liquid into a bowl or large jug (discard any leftover liquid). Squeeze the gelatine gently to remove the excess water, then add to the hot liquid and stir until dissolved. Pour the jelly into the chilled serving glasses, dividing evenly. Carefully transfer the glasses to the fridge and leave to set completely – this will take 4–6 hours. Once set, serve with a scoop of clotted cream or vanilla ice cream. Serves 6.

Parsnips

Parsnips are a root vegetable from the umbelliferae family, which includes carrots, fennel and celeriac. They rely on the frost to develop their distinctive sweet, earthy flavour. They are easy to grow and maintain, hence their popularity among gardeners. Parsnips are a good source of dietary fibre and are rich in vitamins and minerals, particularly potassium. Parsnips are very versatile and can be used in plenty of savoury and sweet dishes – in fact, before sugar was widely available they were used as a sweetener. They can be boiled, steamed, roasted or pan-fried and they also make an interesting alternative to traditional mashed potatoes.

Try my lovely recipe for **Maple-glazed Parsnips and Giant Couscous Salad**. Place an Assam tea bag in a measuring jug, pour over 100ml boiling water and add 50g raisins. Leave to steep for 10 minutes, then remove the tea bag and set the raisins aside to continue to steep. Bring a saucepan of salted water to the boil, then once boiling, add 150g giant couscous and 1 teaspoon ground turmeric and stir. Cover and bring back to the boil, then remove the lid, reduce the heat to a gentle simmer and simmer for about 20 minutes or until the couscous is tender. Drain, refresh in cold water, then drain again and transfer to a bowl. Stir in 1 tablespoon olive oil and set aside. While the couscous is cooking, peel 1 large parsnip (80–100g) and 1 large courgette (80–100g). Use a melon baller to scoop out balls of flesh (or simply cut the vegetables into 1–1.5cm dice). Melt 1 tablespoon unsalted butter in a large non-stick frying pan and once it is foaming, add the parsnip balls and sea salt and freshly cracked black pepper and sauté over a medium heat for about 8 minutes or until golden brown. Add 80ml cold water, bring to the boil, then cover and cook for 7–8 minutes or until the parsnips are tender. Remove the lid and add 2 tablespoons maple syrup. Increase the heat to high, then add the courgette balls and cook for about 5 minutes or until tender.

Drain the raisins and add them to the parsnip mixture along with 50g roughly chopped pecan nuts. Remove from the heat and add to the bowl of cooked couscous. Stir in 1 teaspoon each chopped fresh savory and fresh chives and 2 tablespoons pomegranate seeds. Taste and adjust the

Maple-glazed Parsnips and Giant Couscous Salad

seasoning, if necessary. Serve slightly warm or chill in the fridge until needed, then bring to room temperature before serving. The salad will keep in the fridge for up to 2 days. Serves 4 as a light lunch or supper.

Partridge

Partridge are non-migrational birds from the pheasant family and they are in season from September until February. In the UK, there are two types of partridge: the very precious native grey-legged partridge, and the red-legged partridge, which was originally brought here from Europe. Grey-legged partridge has a distinctive red face and is smaller than the red-legged partridge. Red-legged partridges have white necks and chins. The meat on both birds has a delicate flavour, which becomes richer and stronger as the season progresses. As they are small birds, partridge are ideal for starters or light lunches, typically serving one bird per person. Alternatively, serve two birds per person for a main course.

For a delicious twist on a classic, try this recipe for **Partridge, Stilton and Walnut Wellingtons**. Melt 1 tablespoon unsalted butter in a non-stick frying pan and once it is foaming, add 1 finely diced large onion, 1 crushed clove garlic, 2 finely diced smoked back bacon rashers and sea salt and freshly cracked pepper. Sauté over a medium heat for 8 minutes or until golden brown. Remove from the heat, transfer the mixture to a mixing bowl and leave to cool for 15 minutes. Select 4 skinless, boneless partridge breast fillets (240–320g total weight) and use a sharp knife to butterfly each breast (see page 187 for instructions on how to butterfly chicken breasts and use the same method for the partridge breasts). Set aside. Dice 80g Stilton cheese and add to the cooled bacon mixture, then add 2 teaspoons finely chopped fresh thyme leaves and 50g chopped toasted walnuts and stir to combine. Divide the bacon mixture in half then, using your hands, press one half on to a butterflied partridge breast, then place another butterflied breast on top and enclose the filling. Repeat with the other two partridge breasts and remaining filling, then wrap each partridge parcel in a slice of Parma ham, so that the main part of the partridge is covered. Line a baking tray with non-stick baking paper. On a lightly floured work surface, roll out 200g chilled fresh all-butter puff pastry to 3–4mm thickness and cut out two 18 x 12cm rectangles, then brush the top surfaces all over with beaten egg. Place a partridge parcel at one end of a pastry rectangle, then fold the pastry around the parcel to cover the partridge completely. Crimp the edges to form a sealed parcel. Repeat with the other partridge parcel and pastry. Brush the wellingtons with a little more beaten egg, sprinkle with poppy seeds or linseeds and place on the prepared baking tray. Leave to rest in the fridge for 30 minutes. Meanwhile, preheat the oven to 200˚C/Gas Mark 6. Bake the wellingtons in the oven for about 25 minutes or until the pastry is cooked, golden brown and crisp. Remove from the oven and leave to rest for 5 minutes, then serve with buttered seasonal greens. Serves 2 as a main course.

Partridges

Quinces

Related to apples and pears, ripe quinces are a bright yellow, slightly lumpy, fragrant-scented fruit and the largest of the three. Like medlars, quinces need to be 'bletted' (see page 339) before they are ready to be used, as their hard, acidic flesh is sour and not suitable to be eaten raw. Quince flesh has a unique grainy texture, which is retained regardless of how long you cook it. Quinces oxidise as soon as their skin is peeled away, so to prevent discoloration you can put them into acidulated water. The flesh also colours as they cook, turning a varying shade of pink, depending on the cooking time. Quinces suit both savoury and sweet dishes – from pickles and chutneys to serve alongside roast meats, to crumbles and pies as puddings. They are most commonly used to make membrillo, a traditional Spanish recipe, which is served as an accompaniment to cheese.

Quinces

For a deliciously creamy and comforting autumn pudding, try my **Quince Crème Brûlée Tarts**. Preheat the oven to 180°C/Gas Mark 4. Grease six 10 x 2cm fluted round tart tins. Roll out 250g Sweet Shortcrust Pastry (see page 18) to about 2mm thickness and use it to line the prepared tins. Transfer the lined tins to the fridge and leave to rest for 20 minutes. Prick the pastry cases all over with a fork, then line each one with greaseproof paper and fill with baking beans. Bake blind in the oven for 15–20 minutes or until almost cooked. Remove the baking beans and paper, brush the pastry cases with beaten egg, then return them to the oven and bake for a further 5 minutes or until cooked, golden brown and crisp. Remove from the oven and carefully transfer the pastry cases to a wire rack to cool. While the pastry is baking, prepare the quince cream. Peel, core and dice 260g fresh ripe quinces. Place in a small saucepan with 500ml cold water, then cover and bring to the boil over a medium heat. Reduce the heat to a gentle simmer, place the lid on an angle and simmer for 20 minutes or until tender and soft. Remove from the heat and transfer the quinces and their poaching liquid to a blender, add 100g caster sugar and purée together until smooth, then add 2 eggs and blend until creamy. Transfer the mixture to a small saucepan and heat gently, stirring continuously with a wooden spoon, until the mixture starts to thicken, then continue to cook gently for 5 minutes or until the mixture thickens enough to coat the back of the wooden spoon; do not allow the mixture to boil or it will curdle. Remove from the heat and whisk in 3 teaspoons cold unsalted butter, then spoon the quince cream into the tart cases and dust heavily with icing sugar. Use a blowtorch to caramelise the sugar, taking care not to burn the pastry (see Cook's Note on page 172 for what to do if you don't have a blowtorch). Serve immediately as these tarts won't keep as the tops will dissolve and become runny. Serves 6.

Sloes or blackthorn berries

Sloes are the small, dark purple/blue-black fruit of the blackthorn bush or tree. They look like small plums and have tough skins and acidic flesh. Blackthorn bushes or trees are found across the British Isles and they are deciduous, with thick, thorny branches, thus they make excellent hedges, often used to contain livestock such as sheep and goats in their fields. Sloes ripen from October to December but are best picked after the first frost, as this softens the berries' skin and helps them to release their juices.

Do try my recipe for **Sloe Gin**. It's a must for this time of year, and once you have made a bottle or two, you might find yourself hooked. Sloe gin also makes a wonderful gift for loved ones. I find it best to first semi-freeze the sloes by putting them in the freezer for 2–3 hours, until hard but not completely frozen (if they are completely frozen they will be harder to burst later). Place 600g semi-frozen fresh sloes in a polythene freezer food bag and use a rolling pin or wooden mallet to beat them lightly, enough to split the skins but not to make a purée. Sterilise a 750ml glass bottle with a cap (see page 16 for more details on sterilising bottles), then open two 750ml bottles of good quality gin and pour one third of each bottle into the sterilised bottle. Divide the beaten sloes evenly between the 3 bottles, then add 125g caster sugar to each bottle, replace the bottle tops and shake well. Keep the bottles in a cool, dry cupboard for 3 months, shaking the bottles gently every 2 weeks. Strain the sloe gin through a fine sieve into clean, sterilised bottles and seal (discard the contents of the sieve), then store the bottles of sloe gin in a cool, dry cupboard for up to 1 year. Makes about 1.5 litres. Serve the sloe gin chilled or at room temperature and serve over plenty of ice. You can also add a teaspoon of sloe gin to Champagne or Prosecco for an interesting cocktail.

Thyme

Thyme is a hardy evergreen low-growing herb, with tiny leaves and pale lilac flowers. It has a distinct, strong, aromatic flavour, which works well with many different foods, particularly red meat, oily fish, game, chicken and tomatoes, and it is especially popular in Mediterranean cooking. It can also be used in bouquet garni and makes a good flavouring for stocks, soups and stews. During the winter, the plants stop growing, so harvest only lightly throughout the colder months if you have plants in your garden. Thyme can also be picked during the summer or early autumn (this month will probably be your last opportunity to do so) and then dried or frozen for later use. There are many different varieties of thyme available, the most common types in the UK being garden thyme (also known as common thyme) and lemon thyme. Lemon thyme has a slightly subtler, lemony flavour that goes well with fish, veal and egg dishes. Thyme is grown not only for culinary purposes, but also for its medicinal and antiseptic qualities, for example, thymol is commonly used in the making of mouthwash.

Walnuts

Fresh or 'wet' walnuts become available just as the Kentish cobnut season is drawing to a close. Walnuts have two lives, the first being a green walnut that flourishes at the end of July/beginning of August; the second being the wet walnut, which appears towards the end of autumn. Wet walnuts have a pale ivory colour and a wonderful milky texture and sweet flavour. Wet walnuts are delicious eaten fresh but they have a short life because they go mouldy quickly, so to prevent this they need to be dried. Once dried, the essential oils in the walnut become more potent, creating a stronger flavour and this is how walnuts are most commonly used in cooking. As dried walnuts contain a lot of natural oils, they also go stale or rancid easily. Store them in the fridge in a sealed jar or alternatively, in a cool, dry cupboard. Never keep dried

Sloe Gin

Walnut and Cracked Wheat Salad

walnuts for longer than 1 year. If you manage to get your hands on wet walnuts, keep them in the shell covered with a damp cloth in the fridge for up to two weeks.

To make my tasty recipe for **Walnut and Cracked Wheat Salad**, place 200g quick-cook cracked wheat in a sieve and rinse under cold running water. Place the wheat in a saucepan, cover with cold water and add sea salt to taste. Cover and bring to a gentle simmer over a medium heat, then cook for 12–15 minutes or until the cracked wheat is cooked and tender. Drain and set aside. While the wheat is cooking, melt 1 teaspoon unsalted butter in a non-stick frying pan and once it is foaming, sauté 100g shelled fresh walnuts over a medium heat for 5–8 minutes or until golden brown and toasted. Remove from the heat and set aside to cool. Put the drained cracked wheat in a serving bowl and add 200g finely diced celery, the finely grated zest and juice of 1 lemon, 50g finely chopped spring onions, the seeds of 1 pomegranate, 4 tablespoons finely chopped fresh flat-leaf parsley, 2 tablespoons finely chopped fresh mint, 2 tablespoons olive oil and sea salt and freshly cracked pepper to taste. Mix well, then serve immediately or keep in an airtight container in the fridge for up to 2 days. Serves 4–6 as a light lunch.

Wild duck

Mallard is the largest and most common wild duck. An ancestor of the domestic duck, mallard has a strong flavour and rich meat. Mallard should be eaten pink: if you overcook it, the meat becomes chewy and tastes livery. One mallard will serve 2. Golden plover is a wild wading bird that feeds on crustaceans and insects. These small birds are a delicacy and are rich and strong in taste. Like mallard, golden plover need to be cooked quickly, to medium-rare, for the best result, otherwise they will be come tough and taste livery. I serve 2 birds per person as a main course. Teal is a small dabbling duck. Its meat is dark in colour, rich in flavour and has a slightly more gamey taste than mallard. As teal graze on wetlands, the meat might also have a slight fishy taste. The breast is best cooked quickly to rare, to keep it tender, and then served immediately. I serve 1 bird per person. Tufted duck is a diving duck. It grazes on marshes and areas close to the seashore. This species is quite lean, but the breast meat is flavoursome and if you mix it with other meats such as chicken livers, which mellow the flavour, it is great for making pâtés or for adding to a pie. Wild ducks are less fatty than their farmed counterparts, so if you are roasting the whole bird they will cook more quickly. Care needs to be taken to prevent them from drying out.

Golden plover

Mallard

Red Wine-poached Quinces and Goat's Cheese Open Filo Tarts with Salted Caramel Walnuts

This recipe is dedicated to our local community: regular customers and staff who bring quinces to the British Larder every season without fail. Since we first arrived in Suffolk, we have been overwhelmed by the 'quince brigade'. Volunteers come in their droves and we welcome them with open arms. The first year, a slight panic set in as we worried about what we would do with all the quinces, but Mr. P set to work turfing the junk out of one of our sheds and this became their store. Mr. P carefully manages the quinces' ripening process, turning them, then checking which ones are ready to be used and which ones need to go in the compost bin. The quince project has been a great community experience and a labour of love.

Savoury and sweet, from chutneys and purées to crumbles, curds and jellies, quinces feature in anything and everything on our menu. We even managed to create a seasonal cocktail we called a 'Quince Collins', which is a quince vanilla purée mixed with gin and topped with soda water and plenty of ice. This recipe has become one of my favourites.

You will need to start this recipe the day before you want to serve it, as the poached quinces are refrigerated overnight.

Serves 6 as a starter or light lunch

For the red wine-poached quinces
600ml red wine
1 cinnamon stick
2 star anise
2 cloves
2 black peppercorns
10 coriander seeds
2 tablespoons caster sugar
5 fresh ripe quinces (750–850g total weight)

For the spiced filo sheets
1 star anise
3 sheets of chilled fresh or frozen (defrosted) filo pastry (each sheet about 40 x 30cm)
2 tablespoons unsalted butter, melted

For the salted caramel walnuts
1 tablespoon unsalted butter
200g walnuts
50g caster sugar
25g sea salt

For the whipped goat's cheese
250g strong soft goat's cheese, plus 80g extra to serve
75g mascarpone
½ teaspoon ground cinnamon
50ml double cream
sea salt and freshly cracked black pepper

a handful of mixed fresh cress, to garnish

For the red wine-poached quinces, first prepare the poaching liquid before peeling the quinces as they discolour quickly. Place the wine, cinnamon, star anise, cloves, peppercorns, coriander seeds and sugar in a saucepan. Bring to the boil over a medium heat, then lower the heat and simmer for 5 minutes or until the mixture reduces and becomes syrupy.

Peel and core the quinces, then cut the flesh into 2cm dice. Add the quince flesh to the poaching liquid, then place a cartouche (a circle of greaseproof paper) on the surface of the liquid and cover the pan with a lid. Reduce the heat to low and poach the quince for 15–18 minutes or until it is soft but still retains its shape. Once the quince is cooked, remove from the heat and set aside to cool for 1 hour.

Drain half of the poached quince through a fine sieve, reserving the other half and all the poaching liquid separately. Put the drained quince and a splash of the poaching liquid into a blender and blend to form a smooth purée. Transfer the purée to a bowl, then cover and refrigerate overnight. Transfer the reserved (un-blended) quince and poaching liquid to a covered container and refrigerate overnight. Just before serving, drain the poached quince pieces and reserve (discard the poaching liquid).

Meanwhile, prepare the spiced filo sheets. Preheat the oven to 200°C/Gas Mark 6 and lightly grease a baking tray. Put the star anise into a spice grinder or use a pestle and mortar and grind it to a fine powder. Cut each sheet of filo pastry in half widthways to make

6 smaller sheets. Lightly brush 1 smaller sheet of filo pastry with melted butter and sprinkle with a pinch or two of ground star anise. Place another sheet of filo on top, brush with melted butter and sprinkle with ground star anise, and then continue in the same way until all 6 smaller sheets of filo pastry are stacked on top of each other, but leave the top sheet free of star anise. Use a sharp knife to cut the filo stack into six 5 x 20cm strips.

Place the filo stack strips on the prepared baking tray and bake in the oven for 5–8 minutes or until crisp and golden. Remove from the oven, transfer to a wire rack and leave to cool, then store in an airtight container until needed (see Cook's Notes).

Next, prepare the salted caramel walnuts. Melt the butter in a non-stick frying pan and once it starts to foam, add the walnuts, sugar and salt and sauté over a medium heat for 6–8 minutes or until the nuts are golden brown and caramelised. Remove from the heat, transfer the walnuts to a baking tray lined with non-stick baking paper and leave to cool completely, then store in an airtight container until needed (see Cook's Notes). Before serving, gently break the walnuts into pieces. For the whipped goat's cheese, put the 250g goat's cheese, the mascarpone, cinnamon and salt and pepper into a bowl and use a balloon whisk to whisk together until creamy. Add the cream and whisk together until the mixture thickens – when you lift the whisk it should leave a visible trail on the surface. Transfer the whipped cheese to a covered container and refrigerate for 20 minutes.

To serve, spread (or swipe) some of the puréed quince on each serving plate, crumble the remaining goat's cheese and scatter half of it over the purée, then place the spiced filo stack strips on top. Arrange the poached quince pieces around the goat's cheese and then place a quenelle (or spoonful) of whipped goat's cheese on to each filo stack strip. Garnish with the remaining crumbled goat's cheese, the salted caramel walnuts and mixed cress. Serve immediately.

Cook's Notes

The filo stack strips can be made up to 3 days in advance. Store them in an airtight container in a cool, dry cupboard.

The salted caramel walnuts can also be made up to 3 days in advance. Store them in an airtight container in a cool, dry cupboard.

You can substitute the quinces with pears and the goat's cheese with a creamy blue cheese, if you like.

Tufted Duck and Chicken Liver Parfait with Red Wine Jelly and Pickled Walnuts

Our 'deer' friend and local game expert, David Grimwood, often comes to see us bearing gifts. Over the years, he has brought us a wonderful array of game, including some fabulous tufted ducks. Every time David comes we learn something new, and the inspiration for this recipe came from his recommendation that tufted ducks are only good for pâtés.

After a good look and a prod, I realised there is not much meat on tufted ducks, but the breast meat can be bulked out with items such as chicken livers, which in turn mellow the strong game flavour.

I serve this rich and flavoursome parfait with the red wine-poached quinces from my Red Wine-poached Quinces and Goat's Cheese Open Filo Tarts with Salted Caramel Walnuts recipe (see page 346), accompanied by pickled walnuts from one of our wonderful customers, Professor Baker. The combination of textures and flavours works a treat. Do remember just to serve small amounts of this parfait, as it's incredibly rich, and accompany it with plenty of toasted sourdough bread.

To make the tufted duck and chicken liver parfait, you will need to start a day in advance. You can prepare the jelly either on the day you wish to serve the parfait or the day before, but note that it takes about 2 hours to set.

Serves 8–10 as a starter or light lunch

For the tufted duck and chicken liver parfait

550g unsalted butter, plus extra, melted, for greasing the terrine mould
150g banana shallots, finely diced
1 clove garlic, crushed
1 teaspoon chopped fresh thyme leaves
60ml brandy
1 teaspoon coriander seeds, crushed
200g tufted duck breast meat, cut into 2cm pieces
450g chicken livers
sea salt and freshly cracked black pepper

For the red wine jelly

200ml red wine
30g caster sugar
¼ teaspoon agar agar powder (see page 16)

To finish and serve

8–10 thin slices baguette
300g Red Wine-poached Quinces (see page 346), cut into 1cm wedges not dice
100g (drained weight) pickled walnuts, drained and diced
a handful of baby or mini/micro salad leaves
rapeseed oil

Make the tufted duck and chicken liver parfait. Preheat the oven to 150°C/Gas Mark 2. Melt 50g of the butter in a non-stick frying pan, add the shallots and salt and pepper, then cover and sweat over a low heat for about 8 minutes or until the shallots are transparent but with no colour. Stir in the garlic, thyme, brandy and coriander seeds, then remove from the heat. Melt the remaining butter in a separate pan, then add it to the shallot mixture and leave to cool slightly.

Place the duck meat and chicken livers in a blender and slowly purée together until very smooth (see Cook's Notes). With the motor running, slowly add the cooled shallot and butter mixture and salt and pepper and blend to form an emulsion.

Grease a 28 x 12 x 11cm terrine mould with melted butter and transfer the blended duck meat mixture to the mould. Place the mould in a deep roasting tin and pour in enough warm water to come two-thirds of the way up the sides of the mould. Cover the terrine mould with its lid, or cover with non-stick baking paper and then foil to keep the paper in place. Cook in the oven for 45 minutes or until the parfait still has a slight wobble in the middle when shaken gently. Remove the terrine mould from the roasting tin and cool over ice for 30 minutes, then transfer to the fridge to set overnight.

The next day, put the parfait into a blender and blend until silky smooth, then transfer to an airtight container and refrigerate for 1 hour before serving (see Cook's Notes).

Meanwhile, make the red wine jelly. Combine all the jelly ingredients in a small saucepan and bring to the boil over a medium heat, stirring, then reduce the heat and simmer for 1 minute, stirring. Remove from the heat and pour the hot liquid into a sturdy shallow white plastic tray, about 21 x 14cm in size (or a suitable container of a similar size) and leave to set completely at room temperature (don't move the tray again until the mixture is set) – this will take about 2 hours. Once the jelly has set, refrigerate until you are ready to assemble the dish (see Cook's Notes).

To finish and serve, toast both sides of the baguette slices and place a slice on to each serving plate. Top each baguette slice with a quenelle (or spoonful) of parfait. Decorate the plates with teaspoonfuls of red wine jelly, the red wine-poached quinces and pickled walnuts. Finish with a few baby salad leaves and a drizzle of rapeseed oil. Serve immediately.

Cook's Notes

When blending the duck meat and chicken livers, you need to be careful that the friction from the blender doesn't heat the mixture, so it's best to blend it in short bursts or in small quantities.

To store any leftover tufted duck and chicken liver parfait, put a piece of non-stick baking paper directly on to the surface of the parfait to preventing it from discolouring. Cover the container with a tight-fitting lid, then place in the fridge and use within 3 days.

Store any leftover red wine jelly in an airtight container in the fridge and use within 3 days.

Pan-fried Partridge with Caramelised Figs and Fig Vinaigrette

The combination of partridge, figs, lentils and fresh walnuts is a joy for the palate – the array of different textures and tastes means that every mouthful is interesting and has a story to tell. Throw in a drop of fig vinaigrette and it becomes a fantastic sight for the eye too. This dish is one you wish would never end.

Serves 4 as a starter or light lunch

For the fig vinaigrette
100g fresh ripe figs, roughly chopped
200ml cold water
2 teaspoons sherry vinegar
1 teaspoon Dijon mustard
100ml rapeseed oil
a pinch of caster sugar
sea salt and freshly cracked black pepper

For the pan-fried partridge and caramelised figs
2 oven-ready partridges (about 250g each)
3 tablespoons olive oil, plus 1 teaspoon for roasting the partridge legs
200g Puy lentils
3 banana shallots, finely diced
100g horn of plenty mushrooms (trompette de la mort), brushed clean and ripped lengthways into strips
1 teaspoon chopped fresh thyme leaves
1 tablespoon unsalted butter
2 fresh ripe figs, each cut into 6 wedges
2 tablespoons fresh or 'wet' walnuts, peeled and roughly chopped, to serve
a handful of cress salad leaves, to serve

First, make the fig vinaigrette. Put the figs and water into a small saucepan and bring to the boil over a high heat. Boil for about 8 minutes or until the figs are soft and the water has nearly evaporated. Remove from the heat and add the rest of the vinaigrette ingredients to the pan, then transfer the mixture to a blender and blend until smooth. Adjust the seasoning to taste, then transfer the vinaigrette to a bowl, cover and refrigerate until needed (see Cook's Note).

For the pan-fried partridge, preheat the oven to 200°C/Gas Mark 6. Remove the breasts from the partridges using a sharp knife (leave the skin on), then place them in a covered container and refrigerate until needed. Remove the legs from the birds, rub them all over with 1 teaspoon olive oil and season with salt and pepper (discard the carcasses or use them for making stock at a later date – see page 22 for Roasted Game Stock). Place the legs in a roasting tin and roast in the oven for about 25 minutes or until the skin is golden brown and the meat is tender. Remove from the oven and leave to rest for 10 minutes. Flake the partridge leg meat while it is still hot, then set aside and keep hot. Discard the bones.

While the partridge legs are roasting, put the Puy lentils in a saucepan and cover with cold water. Bring up to a gentle simmer over a medium heat, then add a pinch of salt and cook, uncovered, for 15–20 minutes or until the lentils are cooked and tender. Drain, set aside and keep warm.

Heat the remaining olive oil in a non-stick frying pan until hot, then add the shallots, mushrooms and a little salt and pepper and sauté over a medium heat for 5–6 minutes or until golden brown. Add the leg meat and lentils and sauté for a further 30 seconds, then taste and adjust the seasoning, if necessary. Add the thyme and 1 tablespoon of the fig vinaigrette. Remove from the heat, transfer the mixture to a bowl and keep warm.

Meanwhile, to cook the partridge breasts and make the caramelised figs, melt the butter in a non-stick frying pan over a high heat and once it starts to foam, season the breasts with salt and pepper and place in the butter, skin-side down. Cook for 5–6 minutes or until the skin is golden brown and caramelised. Turn the breasts over and cook for a further 6 minutes or until cooked through and golden brown. Add the figs to the pan 2 minutes before the end of the cooking time and caramelise on both sides. Remove the pan from the heat and let the partridge rest for 5 minutes. Drain the figs and partridge and slice each partridge breast.

To serve, spoon a portion of the lentil mixture on to each serving plate and place a sliced partridge breast on top. Arrange the caramelised figs and fresh walnuts around the plates, then drizzle with some fig vinaigrette. Garnish with cress salad leaves and serve immediately.

Cook's Note
Store any leftover fig vinaigrette in an airtight container in the fridge and use within 1 week. Serve the vinaigrette with salt-baked beetroot and crumbled goat's cheese, or serve it with pan-fried grey mullet, roasted figs and toasted cobnuts.

Creamy Parsnip Soup with Partridge Sausage Rolls

This recipe has a level of sophistication that lends itself to a show-off starter. The partridge sausage rolls are to die for! Partridge meat is combined with pork mince and smoked bacon to give extra character and body to the traditional sausage roll. Serve a few of the rolls alongside a large bowl of this soup and the recipe can easily become a hearty suppertime meal. Sausage rolls also make a lovely change from the usual soup accompaniment of bread and butter.

I roast the bones from the partridge to make a stock that forms the base of this soup. Soups are pretty simple to make, but they are a type of dish where shortcuts and laziness can really stand out. When you cook a soup, it's very important to start seasoning from the very beginning and to do it in stages. It's easy to add too much salt, yet also very noticeable if you do not season the soup at all and then add the salt on serving. All you will taste is surface salt and you won't have achieved the layers of flavour that should have been carefully built up throughout the cooking process.

Michel Roux Jr. always said that whatever touches the pan must be accompanied by seasoning. I shall never forget his wise words but I would suggest this is done within reason. I have made plenty of mistakes during my career as a chef, and I shall never forget an incident when I was a commis chef and made 20 litres of leek and potato soup that was only good enough for the drain. Surface salt and too much pepper were the obvious causes of its ruin and I still hang my head in shame when I think about it.

Serves 6 as a starter or 4 as a main course

For the partridge sausage rolls

2 oven-ready partridges (about 250g each)
200g minced pork
60g smoked streaky bacon rashers, finely diced
50g parsnip (prepared weight), grated
½ onion, finely diced
1 teaspoon ground coriander
1 tablespoon chopped fresh flat-leaf parsley
2 eggs
300g good quality chilled fresh all-butter puff pastry
1 tablespoon golden linseeds
sea salt and freshly cracked black pepper

For the creamy parsnip soup

50g unsalted butter
1 leek, washed and roughly sliced
1 stick celery, roughly diced
1 onion, roughly diced
2 cloves garlic, crushed
1 bay leaf
a sprig of fresh thyme, leaves only
1 teaspoon coriander seeds, crushed
2 black peppercorns, crushed
1.2 litres cold water
700g parsnips, peeled and sliced
200ml dry white wine
100ml double cream
1 tablespoon rapeseed oil

Start by roasting the partridge bones to make the stock for the soup. Preheat the oven to 200°C/Gas Mark 6. Remove the skin from the birds, then remove the breasts and leg meat from the bones and set aside. Place the bones in a roasting tin and roast in the oven for 30 minutes or until dark golden brown. Remove from the oven and set aside.

While the bones are roasting, prepare the sausage rolls. Cut the partridge breast and leg meat into 1cm dice, then place in a large mixing bowl and add the minced pork, bacon, parsnip, onion, ground coriander, parsley and 1 egg. Season lightly with salt and pepper and mix well.

Whisk the remaining egg in a small bowl and set aside. Divide the puff pastry in half and roll out each half on a lightly floured work surface to a rectangular shape, about 18 x 8cm in size and 2–3mm thickness. Divide the meat mixture in half and roll each portion into a long sausage shape, about 3cm in diameter. Place one half of the sausagemeat on to the centre of a pastry rectangle and brush the pastry edges with the beaten egg, then fold one half of the pastry over to cover the sausage and press the long edges together to seal, to form one long sausage roll. Turn the sausage roll over so that the joined edge is underneath. Repeat with the remaining pastry rectangle and sausage. Brush the 2 long sausage rolls with the beaten egg and sprinkle over the linseeds. Transfer the sausage rolls to a baking tray lined with non-stick baking paper and leave to rest in the fridge for about 30 minutes.

Meanwhile, make the parsnip soup. Melt half the butter in a large saucepan and once it starts to foam, add the leek, celery, onion, garlic, bay leaf, thyme, coriander seeds and peppercorns. Season with salt and pepper and sauté over a medium heat for about 10 minutes or until the leek and onion are golden brown and soft. Add the roasted partridge bones to the pan and use a wooden spoon to break them up gently. Add the water and bring to a simmer, then reduce the heat to low and simmer gently, uncovered, for 20 minutes, skimming off any scum from the surface. Remove from the heat and pass the mixture through a fine sieve, discarding the vegetables, herbs and bones. Transfer the stock to a clean saucepan and keep warm over a low heat.

Rinse the large saucepan and return it to a medium heat with the remaining butter. When the butter starts to foam, add the parsnips and salt and pepper, then cover with a lid and sweat for about 10 minutes or until the parsnips are softened, stirring occasionally to prevent the parsnips taking on too much colour. Remove 3 tablespoons of the parsnips to use as a garnish and set aside until needed. Add the wine to the pan and let it bubble, stirring and scraping the base of the pan with a wooden spoon to deglaze it. Boil rapidly over a high heat for about 5 minutes or until the liquid has reduced by half. Add 800ml of the warm partridge stock and bring the soup to a gentle simmer. Cook, uncovered, over a low heat for about 15 minutes or until the parsnips begin to soften and break up. Add the cream and bring back to the boil, then remove from the heat. Carefully transfer the soup to a blender and blend until smooth. Taste and adjust the seasoning, if necessary, then pour the soup back into the pan, cover and set aside until you are ready to serve. Before serving, reheat the soup over a medium heat until piping hot.

To cook the sausage rolls, preheat the oven to 200°C/Gas Mark 6 and line 2 baking trays with non-stick baking paper. Cut the sausage rolls into 3cm lengths and place them on the prepared trays, leaving at least a 3cm gap between each one. Bake in the oven for 20–25 minutes or until cooked, risen and golden brown. Remove from the oven and transfer the sausage rolls to a wire rack, then leave to rest for 5 minutes before serving.

While the sausage rolls are resting, reheat the soup as directed. Heat the rapeseed oil in a small, non-stick frying pan, add the reserved parsnip garnish and sauté over a medium heat for about 5 minutes or until golden and heated through. Serve the hot soup in bowls, garnish with the sautéed parsnips and serve with the hot sausage rolls.

Cook's Note

Cool any leftover sausage rolls, then store them in an airtight container in the fridge and use within 3 days.

Partridge with Pastillas, Parsnips and Barley

With the richest foods on offer, I almost feel that autumn and winter have the most to give. Wow, what a bold statement to make! For me to feel spoiled does not mean that my food has got to cost the earth; I can feel like a 'rich man' after enjoying a truly wonderful rich dish.

This recipe is one we love and our regulars love it too. Partridge breast meat is poached gently then roasted and partnered with pastry-encased crispy partridge leg meat. Preparing the parsnips in three ways brings contrasting tastes and textures to the palate. Velvety parsnip purée adds richness, the roasted parsnip wedges bring character and a hearty, roasted flavour, while the diced truffled parsnip brings depth of flavour and a touch of luxury.

If you can and want to splash out, you can throw in a few shavings of fresh truffle for good measure.

Serves 4 as a starter or 2 as a main course

For the partridge
a sprig of fresh thyme
1 teaspoon coriander seeds, lightly crushed
5 black peppercorns, lightly crushed
2 oven-ready partridges (about 250g each)
1 teaspoon olive oil
1 tablespoon unsalted butter
sea salt and freshly cracked black pepper

For the pastillas
60g unsalted butter
100g leeks, washed and finely sliced
1 banana shallot, finely diced
1 clove garlic, crushed
2 tablespoons chopped fresh mixed herbs (such as parsley, chervil, chives and tarragon)
2 sheets of chilled fresh or frozen (defrosted) filo pastry (each sheet about 40 x 30cm)
1 tablespoon ground sumac (see page 151)

For the parsnip purée
2 large parsnips (about 160g total weight)
1 tablespoon unsalted butter
200ml milk

For the parsnips and barley
100g kale, stalks removed
200g pearl barley
4 large parsnips (about 320g total weight)
4 tablespoons unsalted butter
a few drops of truffle oil
50ml olive oil
2 sprigs of fresh thyme, leaves only, chopped

fresh black or summer truffle, to serve (optional)

First, prepare the partridge. Preheat the oven to 200°C/Gas Mark 6. Place the thyme, coriander seeds and peppercorns in a large saucepan, fill with water, cover with a lid and bring to the boil over a high heat.

Meanwhile, remove the legs from the partridges and place them in a roasting tin with the olive oil and some salt and pepper. Roast in the oven for 25 minutes or until the skin is golden brown and the meat is tender. Remove from the oven and leave to rest for 5 minutes. Flake the partridge leg meat while it is still hot, then set aside 100g for the pastillas and keep the remainder warm.

In the meantime, place the partridge crowns in the pan of boiling water (containing the herbs and spices) and boil for 1 minute. Remove the pan from the heat, remove the partridge crowns to a wire rack and leave to rest for 5 minutes (discard the cooking water). Remove the breasts from the bone, transfer them to a covered container and refrigerate until needed. Discard all the bones or use them for making stock at a later date – see page 22 for Roasted Game Stock).

Make the filling for the pastillas. Melt 20g of the butter in a non-stick frying pan and once it is foaming, sauté the leeks, shallot and garlic, with salt and pepper added, over a medium heat for 7–8 minutes or until the leeks and shallot are soft and transparent. Remove from the heat and transfer to a mixing bowl. Add the reserved 100g cooked leg meat and the herbs, mix well, then cool slightly, cover and chill in the fridge for 1 hour.

Next, prepare the parsnip purée. Peel and chop the parsnips into 2cm dice. Melt the butter in a saucepan and once it is foaming, sauté the parsnips, with salt and pepper added, over a medium heat for about 8 minutes or until they start to turn golden and are nearly tender. Add the milk and continue to cook over a medium heat for 15–20 minutes or until the parsnips are soft, then remove from the heat. Immediately use a hand-held stick blender to purée the mixture to a smooth but thick consistency. Taste and adjust the seasoning, if necessary, then transfer to a bowl and leave to cool. Cover and refrigerate until you are ready to serve, then reheat gently in a saucepan until piping hot.

Meanwhile, prepare the parsnips and barley. Blanch the kale in a large pan of boiling salted water for 2–3 minutes or until just tender. Drain, refresh in iced water, then drain again thoroughly. Roughly chop the blanched kale, then place in a large mixing bowl and set aside. Rinse the pearl barley under cold running water, then place in a large saucepan and cover with plenty of fresh cold water. Cover the pan and bring to the boil over a high heat, then boil rapidly for 25–30 minutes or until the barley is cooked and tender. Add a little salt 2 minutes before the end of the cooking time. Remove from the heat and drain, then place the barley in the bowl with the kale, stir to mix and keep warm.

While the pearl barley is cooking, peel and chop 2 of the parsnips into 1cm dice. Melt 2 tablespoons butter in a large, non-stick frying pan and once it's foaming, sauté the parsnips, with salt and pepper added, over a medium heat for 8–10 minutes or until they turn golden brown. Reduce the heat to low and cook for a further 8–10 minutes or until the parsnips are soft and caramelised but not mushy. Remove from the heat and add to the bowl of barley and kale. Add the truffle oil and remaining flaked partridge leg meat to the bowl, mix well and adjust the seasoning, if necessary. Set aside and keep warm.

In the meantime, peel the 2 remaining parsnips and cut each one lengthways into 6 wedges. Place the parsnip wedges in a non-stick roasting tin, season with salt and pepper, then add the olive oil and mix well. Roast in the oven at 200°C/Gas Mark 6 for 10–12 minutes or until golden and tender. Remove from the oven, scatter the thyme over the parsnips, then transfer to a plate and keep warm until needed. Meanwhile, to finish the pastillas, line a baking tray with non-stick baking paper and melt the remaining 40g butter. Brush 1 sheet of filo pastry with melted butter, then place the second sheet on top and brush this with melted butter. Sprinkle over the sumac, then cut the filo stack widthways into ten 4cm-wide strips. Place a small spoonful of the filling mixture on to one corner of each filo stack strip, dividing the filling mixture evenly between each one, then fold each filo stack strip up and over several times to make a triangular shape like a samosa. Place the pastillas on the prepared baking tray and brush each one with melted butter. Bake in the oven for 12–15 minutes or until crisp and golden brown. Remove from the oven, then set aside at room temperature until you are ready to serve.

Once you are ready to serve, reheat the parsnip purée as directed, and pan-fry the partridge breasts. Melt the butter in a non-stick frying pan and once it is foaming, season the breasts with salt and pepper, then place in the pan, skin-side down, and cook for 5–6 minutes or until caramelised. Flip over and continue cooking for a further 5–6 minutes or until still moist but cooked through and golden brown.

To serve, spread the parsnip purée on to 4 serving plates, then spoon a portion of the parsnip and barley mixture into the centre of each plate. Top with roast parsnips and a partridge breast, then place 1–2 pastillas alongside. You could also shave over a few slivers of fresh black or summer truffle, if you like. Serve immediately.

Cook's Note
Store any leftover pastillas in an airtight container in the fridge for up to 3 days. You could serve them as a light lunch with a simple salad or as an interesting accompaniment to a bowl of soup. They would also be perfect as a snack or pre-dinner nibble with a glass of something special.

Pan-fried Brill and King Prawns with Creamy Caper Vermouth Sauce and Aromatic Lentils

This delicious recipe brings sophisticated flavours together. The brill is simply pan-fried in butter and served with warm aromatic Puy lentils and a delicious creamy but strong-flavoured caper and vermouth sauce. Finally, a few slivers of raw crispy fennel add a touch of crunchiness. A taste and texture extravaganza in one dish!

Serves 4 as a main course

For the fennel
1 small fennel bulb, trimmed
1 teaspoon rapeseed oil
finely grated zest and juice of ½ lemon
sea salt and freshly cracked black pepper

For the aromatic lentils
300g Puy lentils
1 teaspoon unsalted butter
3 rashers smoked streaky bacon, finely diced
1 banana shallot, finely diced
1 clove garlic, crushed
1 carrot, finely diced
1 tablespoon sherry vinegar

For the caper vermouth sauce
1 teaspoon unsalted butter
1 small banana shallot, finely chopped
75ml dry vermouth or dry white wine
200ml fish stock
200ml double cream
2 tablespoons small capers, drained

For the pan-fried brill and king prawns
4 skinless brill fillets (100–120g each)
4 raw king prawns, peeled and deveined
1 tablespoon rapeseed oil
1 teaspoon cold unsalted butter
1 tablespoon chopped fresh mixed herbs (such as chervil, fennel tops or dill, flat-leaf parsley and chives)

First, prepare the fennel. Cut the fennel into slithers or thin slices, preferably using a mandolin, and place in a bowl. Season with salt and pepper, then add the rapeseed oil and lemon zest and juice and toss to mix. Set aside at room temperature until you are ready to serve.

For the aromatic lentils, put the Puy lentils in a saucepan and cover with cold water. Bring up to a gentle simmer, then add a pinch of salt and cook, uncovered, over a medium heat for 15–20 minutes or until the lentils are cooked and tender, then drain and set aside.

Melt the butter in a non-stick frying pan and once it starts to foam, add the bacon, shallot, garlic and carrot. Season with salt and pepper and sauté over a medium heat for about 8 minutes or until the shallot turns opaque and the bacon caramelises. Add the cooked lentils, then add the sherry vinegar and let it bubble, stirring and scraping the base of the pan with a wooden spoon to deglaze it. Remove from the heat and keep the lentils warm.

Meanwhile, to make the caper vermouth sauce, melt the butter in a small saucepan and sauté the shallot over a medium heat for about 5 minutes or until it starts to caramelise. Add the vermouth to the pan and let it bubble, stirring and scraping the base of the pan with a wooden spoon to deglaze it. Cook over a high heat for a further 5 minutes or until the vermouth has reduced by half. Add the stock and cream and season with salt and pepper to taste (go easy on the salt as the capers might be quite salty). Bring the sauce to the boil, then reduce the heat and simmer for about 8 minutes or until the sauce is slightly thickened, stirring occasionally. Taste the capers and if they are very vinegary and salty, rinse them under cold water, then pat dry. Stir the capers into the sauce, then remove from the heat and keep warm.

In the meantime, cook the brill and prawns. Season the brill and prawns with salt and pepper. Heat the rapeseed oil in a large, non-stick frying pan until hot but not smoking, then place the fish fillets in the pan and fry over a medium-high heat for 3 minutes. Turn the fillets over and then add the prawns and butter to the pan. Cook the fish and prawns for a further 3 minutes or until the fish is golden brown and cooked but still moist and the prawns have turned pink. Turn the prawns halfway through the cooking time to make sure they are cooked on both sides. Drain the fish and prawns on kitchen paper, then leave to rest for 1 minute before serving.

To serve, spoon a portion of lentils on to each serving plate, place a pan-fried brill fillet on top, followed by a pan-fried prawn, then top with the marinated fennel. Spoon the caper sauce around the lentils and garnish with the chopped herbs. Serve immediately with wilted spinach or steamed broccoli on the side.

Cook's Note
The brill could be substituted with halibut, sea bass, turbot, lemon sole or sea trout. It's quite an expensive and elaborate dish, so the prawns are optional or, if you're feeling flush, substitute the prawns for lovely meaty fresh shelled scallops. The scallops, brill and aromatic lentils would make a fantastic combination too.

Pan-roasted Teal with Pearl Barley and Damson Vinaigrette

We are situated in a part of the British Isles where game is enjoyed by young and old. The tradition of shooting is passed down through the generations and with it comes the appreciation and enjoyment of eating and cooking game. Teal is one of the wild ducks that is plentiful throughout the shooting season, which lasts from September to the end of January.

This dish is autumn on a plate: the woodland taste of the wild girolles and the damson vinaigrette work beautifully with the teal, as the fruitiness cuts through the gamey duck, and the barley adds substance to the whole dish. I serve a whole teal per person for a deliciously rich main course.

Serves 4 as a main course

For the pan-roasted teal and pearl barley

4 whole teals, plucked and gutted (about 250g each)
2 tablespoons rapeseed oil
1 teaspoon fresh thyme leaves
300g pearl barley
1 tablespoon unsalted butter
2 banana shallots, finely diced
200g fresh girolles, cleaned
2 tablespoons golden linseeds
finely grated zest and juice of 1 lemon
sea salt and freshly cracked black pepper

For the damson vinaigrette

200g (prepared weight) fresh ripe damsons, stones removed
200ml cold water
75g caster sugar
20ml sherry vinegar
100ml rapeseed oil
1 teaspoon coriander seeds, crushed

fresh thyme leaves, to garnish

First, prepare the pan-roasted teal. Preheat the oven to 190°C/Gas Mark 5. Remove the legs from the teals and place in a roasting tin, season with salt and pepper, then drizzle over 1 tablespoon rapeseed oil and scatter over the thyme leaves. Roast in the oven for about 25 minutes or until the skin is crisp and the meat is tender. Remove from the oven and leave to rest for 5 minutes, then flake the meat from the bones. Transfer the meat to a plate, set aside and keep warm. Discard the bones.

Meanwhile, to make the damson vinaigrette, place the damsons, water and sugar in a small saucepan and bring to the boil, then simmer over a medium heat for about 10 minutes or until the damsons are cooked and soft. Carefully transfer the damsons to a blender, add the rest of the vinaigrette ingredients, then blend together until smooth. Season to taste with salt and pepper, then transfer to an airtight container, cover and refrigerate for at least 30 minutes before serving to allow the flavours to develop (see Cook's Note).

Meanwhile, cook the pearl barley. Rinse the barley under cold running water, then place in a large saucepan and cover with plenty of fresh cold water. Cover the pan and bring to the boil over a high heat, then boil rapidly for 25–30 minutes or until the barley is cooked and tender. Add a little salt 2 minutes before the end of the cooking time. Remove from the heat and drain, then transfer the barley to a bowl, set aside and keep warm.

Melt the butter in saucepan and once it is foaming, add the shallots and girolles and sauté over a medium heat for about 6 minutes or until softened and golden brown. Remove from the heat and add them to the bowl of warm barley, along with the flaked leg meat and linseeds and toss to mix. Taste and adjust the seasoning, then add the lemon zest and juice to taste. Set aside at room temperature.

Reduce the oven temperature to 180°C/Gas Mark 4. To cook the teal crowns, heat the remaining rapeseed oil in a non-stick frying pan until hot. Season the teal crowns with salt and pepper and add them to the pan, then cook over a high heat for about 2 minutes on each breast or until golden brown. Transfer the teal crowns to a roasting tin and roast in the oven for 10 minutes for rare or 12 minutes for medium. Remove from the oven and let the teal rest for 5 minutes, then remove the breasts from the crowns, leaving the skins on the breasts. Discard the bones.

To serve, spoon the barley mixture on to serving plates and place the teal breasts on top. Serve immediately with a drizzle of damson vinaigrette and a scattering of thyme leaves to garnish.

Cook's Note

Keep any leftover damson vinaigrette in an airtight container in the fridge and use within 1 week. Serve the vinaigrette over pan-fried monkfish or mackerel with roasted golden or red beetroots, or stir it through a warm salad of roasted beetroot, feta and cress.

Pot-roasted Mallard with Cider Apples and Celeriac Mash

This is a dish I would typically cook for friends. It's quite a lot of work to make it just for two, but invite a couple of friends over for supper, crack open a bottle of your finest Barolo and you've got the perfect excuse to make a bit more of an effort and have a superb evening.

The celeriac mash is gutsy and yummy, slightly informal but sophisticated enough to be served with the roasted mallard. The apples in cider bring a sharp fruitiness to the dish that cuts through the richness of the mallard.

Serves 4 as a main course

For the celeriac mash
1 celeriac (400–500g)
2 tablespoons unsalted butter
200ml dry white wine
200ml chicken stock
100ml double cream
sea salt and freshly cracked black pepper

For the pot-roasted mallard
2 whole mallards, plucked and gutted (about 1.4kg total weight)
1 tablespoon softened unsalted butter
1 large onion, sliced
1 carrot, sliced
1 stick celery, roughly chopped
a sprig of fresh thyme
250ml red wine
1 tablespoon redcurrant jelly or homemade Crab Apple Jelly (see page 303)
250ml chicken stock

For the apples cooked in cider
1 tablespoon unsalted butter
2 eating apples (preferably Cox's Orange Pippin), peeled, cored and cut into wedges
200ml apple cider

For the celeriac mash, peel and chop the celeriac into 2cm dice. Melt the butter in a saucepan and once it starts to foam, add the celeriac and salt and pepper and sauté over a medium heat for about 8 minutes or until the celeriac starts to turn golden brown. Add the wine to the pan and let it bubble, stirring and scraping the base of the pan with a wooden spoon to deglaze it. Boil rapidly over a high heat for 5 minutes, then add the stock and bring back to the boil. Reduce the heat, cover the pan and cook for about 12 minutes or until the celeriac is soft and falling apart. Remove from the heat, add the cream and mash together until smooth using a potato masher. Keep warm.

Meanwhile, cook the pot-roasted mallard. Preheat the oven to 220°C/Gas Mark 7. Season the mallards with salt and pepper, then rub them all over with the butter. Heat a casserole over a high heat, then add the mallards and cook for 1 minute on each breast or until golden brown. Remove the birds from the casserole to a plate, reduce the heat to medium, then add the onion, carrot, celery and thyme to the casserole and sauté for about 5 minutes or until the vegetables start to turn golden brown. Add the wine, redcurrant jelly and stock, increase the heat to high and stir to dissolve the jelly.

Remove from the heat, then return the mallards to the casserole, placing them on top of the vegetables. Roast in the oven, uncovered, for 15 minutes, then reduce the oven temperature to 180°C/Gas Mark 4 and continue roasting for a further 15 minutes or until the mallards are golden brown and the flesh is still lightly pink. Remove from the oven and transfer the mallards to a plate to rest. Pass the sauce through a fine sieve and set aside until needed. Discard the vegetables. Just before you are ready to serve, gently reheat the sauce until piping hot.

While the mallards are roasting, prepare the apples cooked in cider. Melt the butter in a non-stick frying pan, add the apple wedges and cook over a high heat for about 6 minutes or until golden, stirring. Add the cider to the pan and let the liquid bubble, stirring and scraping the base of the pan with a wooden spoon to deglaze it. Reduce the heat to low and cook for about 8 minutes or until the juices have caramelised and become syrupy and the apples are tender but not falling apart. Remove from the heat.

To serve, remove the legs and breasts from the roast mallards using a sharp knife. Spoon the warm celeriac mash and cider apples on to serving plates. Top each portion with 1 roasted mallard breast and leg, spoon over the hot sauce and serve immediately with cooked broccoli and chard.

Puy Lentil-stuffed Roasted Golden Plover with Sloe Gin Grapes

Golden plover are rich, strong-tasting wild ducks, but they are small, so serve two per portion for a main course. The delicate birds require light cooking as overcooking will result in a livery taste. To protect the delicate breast meat, wrap a rasher of streaky bacon around the breast – this will protect the meat from direct harsh heat and keep it succulent and moist. For this lovely recipe, I stuff the birds with cooked Puy lentils; the juices of the bird will then run into the lentils and give them that extra gamey flavour.

Serves 2 as a main course

For the roasted golden plover
250g Puy lentils
6 unsmoked streaky bacon rashers
2 tablespoons unsalted butter
1 banana shallot, finely diced
1 clove garlic, crushed
1 small carrot, finely diced
1 stick celery, finely diced
4 whole golden plovers, plucked and gutted (400–500g total weight)
sea salt and freshly cracked black pepper

For the sloe gin grapes
80g dried muscat grapes or golden sultanas
2 tablespoons Sloe Gin (see page 343)

For the vegetable medley
1 small swede (about 300g), peeled and cut into 2cm dice
½ celeriac (about 300g), peeled and cut into 2cm dice
16 baby carrots, cleaned
200g Savoy cabbage, roughly shredded
2 tablespoons unsalted butter
6 shallots, cut in half
4 large fresh ceps (300–350g total weight), cleaned and quartered

Start by cooking the lentils for the roasted golden plover. Put the Puy lentils in a saucepan and cover with cold water. Bring up to a gentle simmer, then add a pinch of salt and cook, uncovered, over a medium heat for 15–20 minutes or until the lentils are cooked and tender. Drain and set aside.

Next, prepare the sloe gin grapes. Place the grapes and sloe gin in a small saucepan and heat gently for about 10 minutes so that the grapes plump up and absorb the gin. Remove from the heat and set aside.

To prepare the roasted golden plover, preheat the oven to 200°C/Gas Mark 6. Dice 2 of the bacon rashers. Melt 1 tablespoon of butter in a saucepan and once it is foaming, add the diced bacon, the shallot, garlic, carrot, celery and salt and pepper and sauté over a medium heat for about 8 minutes or until golden brown and soft. Remove from the heat, then add the cooked lentils to the pan and mix well. Taste and adjust the seasoning, if necessary.

Fill the cavities of the plovers with the lentil mixture, dividing it evenly between the birds. Place one bacon rasher over each plover's breast and tie the legs together with kitchen string. Place the plovers in a roasting tin. Melt the remaining butter in a small saucepan, then brush the plovers all over with the melted butter. Roast in the oven for 15–20 minutes or until the skin is golden brown and the meat is tender. Remove from the oven and leave to rest for 5 minutes.

Meanwhile, for the vegetable medley, cook the swede, celeriac and carrots in a large pan of boiling salted water for 4–5 minutes or until tender. Remove from the heat and transfer the vegetables to a bowl using a slotted spoon, then bring the water back to the boil and cook the cabbage for 2 minutes or until just tender. Drain the cabbage and mix with the rest of the vegetables.

Melt the butter in a large, non-stick frying pan and once it starts to foam, add the shallots, ceps, cooked vegetables and salt and pepper and sauté over a high heat for 6–8 minutes or until golden brown and cooked through. Add the sloe gin grapes to the pan and sauté for a further 30 seconds, then remove from the heat.

To serve, divide the sautéed vegetables between serving plates. Place the roasted plovers on top (serving 2 per portion) and serve immediately with steamed broccoli.

Poached Quinces and Twice-baked Hazelnut Crumbles with Quince Custard

Quinces represent a special childhood memory for me. My grandmother used to poach quinces in syrup and keep them in big glass jars in her walk-in larder. The quince poaching syrup turned a light pink colour and I remember how pretty it was. My grandmother used to open a jar or two after Sunday lunch, warm the fruit and serve it with thick sweet custard. The quinces were not only pretty but they were fragrant too and I loved the soft but grainy texture against the roof of my mouth.

This crumble recipe really takes me back. I have chosen to serve individual crumbles in little espresso cups as they look pretty and sophisticated – perfect for a special occasion. The beauty of this recipe is that you can prepare everything in advance and simply pop the crumbles in the oven while you enjoy your main course, then reheat the custard to serve.

Serves 8

For the poached quinces
500g caster sugar
500ml cold water
1 vanilla pod, split in half lengthways and seeds scraped out
1 bay leaf
a sprig of fresh rosemary
juice of 1 lemon
600g fresh quinces

For the hazelnut crumble mixture
100g plain flour
a pinch of table salt
75g unsalted butter, diced
50g soft dark brown sugar
25g golden syrup
50g jumbo or porridge oats
20g blanched hazelnuts (skins removed), chopped

For the quince custard
200ml poaching syrup from the Poached Quinces (see above)
100ml single cream
3 egg yolks
1 tablespoon caster sugar

For the poached quinces, first prepare the poaching liquid before peeling the quinces as they discolour quickly. Place the sugar, water, vanilla pod and seeds, bay leaf, rosemary and lemon juice in a large saucepan. Bring the mixture to the boil over a medium heat and boil for 2 minutes to form a syrup, while you prepare the quinces.

Peel and core the quinces, then chop the flesh into 1cm pieces. Add the chopped quince flesh to the hot syrup, then place a cartouche (a circle of greaseproof paper) on the surface of the syrup and cover the pan with a lid. Reduce the heat to low and poach the quince for 20–25 minutes or until it is soft but still retains its shape. Once the quince is cooked, remove from the heat and set aside.

While the quince is poaching, prepare the hazelnut crumble mixture. Preheat the oven to 180°C/Gas Mark 4 and line a baking tray with non-stick baking paper.

Sift the flour and salt into a mixing bowl, then add the butter and use your fingertips to rub the butter into the flour until the mixture resembles coarse breadcrumbs. Add the sugar, golden syrup, oats and hazelnuts and mix everything together, then transfer the crumble mixture to the prepared baking tray and spread it out evenly. Bake in the oven for about 20 minutes or until pale golden, stirring once during the cooking time. Remove from the oven and set aside.

Place 8 espresso cups or ramekins on a baking tray. Drain the poached quince through a fine sieve, reserving the quince and syrup separately. Discard the vanilla pod and herbs. Spoon the drained quince into each cup, dividing it evenly between the cups and filling each one about three-quarters full. Spoon 2 tablespoons of the poaching liquid into each cup, then fill to the top with the baked crumble mixture. You can set the crumbles aside at this point (see Cook's Notes) until you're ready to serve, or bake them immediately.

Bake the crumbles in the oven for 15–18 minutes or until the tops are golden brown and the quince syrup is bubbling up around the edges of the cups.

Meanwhile, make the quince custard. Measure the 200ml of poaching syrup needed, then set the rest aside (see Cook's Notes). Place the measured poaching syrup and cream in a saucepan and bring to the boil over a low heat. Whisk the egg yolks and sugar together in a bowl, then whisk a little of the hot cream mixture into the egg mixture. Gradually whisk in the remaining hot cream mixture, then strain back into the pan. Cook over a low heat, stirring continuously, for 8–10 minutes or until the custard thickens enough to coat the back of a wooden spoon; do not allow the mixture to boil or the custard may curdle. Serve the custard with the baked crumbles (see Cook's Notes).

Remove the crumbles from the oven and leave to cool for 5 minutes before serving with the custard.

Cook's Notes

You can make the crumbles up to 3 days in advance. Once made, store the crumbles in the fridge, then bring to room temperature before baking and bake as directed.

Keep any leftover poaching syrup from the quince in an airtight container in the fridge and use within 1 week.
You can re-use it to poach another batch of quinces, or you could serve it with other poached fruits, such as pears, either chilled or by reheating it gently in a pan until piping hot.

The custard will have a grainy texture due to the natural texture of the quinces. If you prefer a smoother custard, simply substitute the poaching syrup for milk.

The custard can also be made in advance, if you like. Make the custard as directed, then pour it into a bowl and cover the surface with a disc of dampened greaseproof paper (to prevent a skin forming). Leave to cool, then refrigerate for up to 3 days. Reheat the custard in a saucepan over a low heat until hot, making sure it does not boil.

Apple Snow with Warm Honey Madeleines

We are fortunate to have been inundated with the most glorious varieties of apples from our lovely customers as part of our bartering system (see page 12 for more details on this). The apples come in dribs and drabs over the season and we get hugely inspired by the many different varieties, which include some local Suffolk ones as well as the more mainstream Bramleys.

This is a traditional recipe and one that is very simple, but the quality of the eating apples used is what makes it a taste sensation. Choose your apple variety carefully; remember the apple must be the hero of this dish (see Cook's Notes).

I do love a Madeleine. I think it's the rich nutty flavour of the butter, combined with almonds and lemon that makes me drool over these little cakes. I often refer to them as 'mini me', and while I do not think the world could cope with more than one Madalene, a freshly baked honey Madeleine is a different matter altogether! In this recipe, the warm Madeleines set the pudding off beautifully.

Madeleines are easy to make but do not make them if you are in a rush! The secret to successful Madeleines is to allow them to rest for at least 12 hours. If you try and fast-track this part of the process, you're in for a disaster – the normally light, fluffy texture of the cakes will be heavy and dense.

You will need to start this recipe the day before you want to serve it to allow the Madeleine batter to rest. The compôte for the apple snow is also best if made the day before to allow the flavours time to develop.

Serves 6

For the warm honey Madeleines

125g unsalted butter
1 tablespoon clear honey
finely grated zest and juice of 1 lemon
100g icing sugar
40g plain flour, plus extra for dusting
40g ground almonds
2 egg whites
a pinch of table salt

For the apple snow

1 tablespoon unsalted butter
300g eating apples (see Cook's Notes), peeled, cored and cut into 1cm dice
2 tablespoons clear honey
2 tablespoons Cognac or apple brandy
100ml fresh unsweetened apple juice
3 egg whites
100g caster sugar, plus extra if needed
100ml double cream
1 vanilla pod, split in half lengthways and seeds scraped out

First, prepare the honey Madeleines batter. Turn the butter to beurre noisette (see Cook's Notes) by melting it in a small saucepan over a medium heat, stirring occasionally. Once it starts to foam, reduce the heat to low, stir, and continue cooking for about 5 minutes or until the solids start to turn golden brown, then remove from the heat. Stir in the honey and lemon juice and leave to cool completely.

Sift the icing sugar and flour into a mixing bowl, then stir in the ground almonds. In a separate bowl, whisk the egg whites and salt together to form soft peaks. Add the beurre noisette and lemon zest to the sifted flour mixture and stir gently. Fold the egg whites into the mixture, then cover the bowl, transfer to the fridge and leave to rest for 12 hours (see Cook's Notes).

To prepare the compôte for the apple snow, melt the butter in a non-stick frying pan and once it starts to foam, add the apples and honey and sauté over a medium heat for 6–8 minutes or until light golden. Add the Cognac to the pan and let it bubble over a high heat for 2 minutes, stirring and scraping the base of the pan with a wooden spoon to deglaze it, then add the apple juice and return to a gentle simmer. Cook over a medium heat for about 5 minutes or until the apples are soft but haven't lost their shape. Taste and add a little caster sugar, if necessary, according to your taste (see Cook's Notes). Remove from the heat, transfer the mixture to a bowl and leave to cool completely, then cover and refrigerate, preferably overnight, until ready to serve.

To bake the Madeleines, preheat the oven to 190°C/Gas Mark 5. Grease a tray of Madeleine moulds with melted butter (I use a baking tray with 12 standard Madeleine moulds – see Cook's Notes) and dust lightly with flour. Stir the rested batter, then spoon it into the prepared moulds, filling each one three-quarters full (do not overfill, otherwise the batter will spill over the edges while cooking). Bake in the oven for 12–14 minutes or until the Madeleines are crisp with an even, golden brown exterior. Carefully turn out on to a wire rack and leave to cool slightly (see Cook's Notes).

While the Madeleines are baking, finish the apple snow. Place the egg whites and caster sugar in a saucepan. Put on a clean pair of disposable gloves to cover your hands. Place the saucepan over a very low heat to gently heat the egg whites and dissolve the sugar. Put one of your hands into the egg white and sugar mixture and stir it continuously to help dissolve the sugar. By using your hand, you can control the heat, as you do not want to heat the mixture above 37°C (blood temperature). Once the mixture has reached 37°C (this will take about 5 minutes), remove the pan from the heat and continue stirring with your hand for another minute. Transfer the mixture to an electric stand mixer fitted with a balloon whisk and whisk for 6–8 minutes or until the mixture becomes very thick and glossy.

In a large mixing bowl, whisk the cream with the vanilla seeds until it forms soft peaks. Fold the meringue mixture, cream and 6 tablespoons of the apple compôte together.

To serve, spoon the remaining apple compôte into the bottom of 6 serving glasses, dividing it evenly. Spoon the meringue and cream mixture over the top and use a blowtorch to colour the tops (see Cook's Notes). Serve immediately with the warm honey Madeleines.

Cook's Notes

I would recommend using a fairly acidic eating apple for this recipe, such as Cox's Orange Pippin, as the 'snow' is sweet. You may need to adjust the sugar levels to complement your apple's natural sweetness.

A 'beurre noisette' is the French term for 'brown butter' (literally 'hazelnut butter') – butter that has been cooked until golden or brown; some would even describe it as 'burnt'.

The Madeleine batter can be made up to 3 days in advance, if kept covered and stored in the fridge.

A true Madeleine is defined by its all-important scallop/shell shape, which is achieved by baking the cakes in specially designed baking trays of Madeleine moulds. You can get different sizes of moulds, but please note that I have used the standard size in a 12-hole baking tray. The perfectly cooked Madeleines have a crisp, even, golden brown exterior with a fluffy, crumbed interior. They are best eaten freshly baked, straight from the oven.

If you don't have a blowtorch, simply place the meringues under a preheated hot grill and grill for about 20 seconds or until the tops are lightly caramelised. However, please note that you will need to use thick serving glasses if you are putting them under the grill, as thin glasses may crack.

The British Larder | *November*

Winter is really settling in now and the frosts and chillier weather have arrived. A light frost is good news for British root vegetables, such as parsnips, celeriac and swede, as the cold helps to sweeten them.

Cabbages of all varieties are plentiful, from red, white and Savoy cabbage to pointed (sweetheart) cabbage. Brussels sprouts are arriving and quinces and medlars are slowly coming to an end, making way for the new season's pears. Pumpkins are taking over from squashes, and the last of the rosehips and elderberries should be harvested before they're lost to the cold and wind.

Pheasants and partridge are plentiful, and wild rabbit, woodcock, hare and teal are dominating menus around the country as we all celebrate the game season.

Mussels are sweet and plump, while pollack, sea bass, halibut and hake give us plenty else from the sea for our menus at this time of year.

The beautiful colours of Autumn

Season's best during November...

Apples, Artichokes, Beetroot, Brill, Brussels Sprouts, Cabbages, Celeriac, Celery, Chard, Chestnuts, Chickweed, Chicory, Clams, Clementines, Cod, Coley, Crab Apples, Cranberries, Duck, Elderberries, Flounder, Golden Plover, Goose, Grouse, Guinea Fowl, Haddock, Hake, Halibut, Hare, Hazelnuts, Horseradish, Jerusalem Artichokes, John Dory, Kale, Kohlrabi, Langoustines, Leeks, Lemon Sole, Lobster, Mallard, Medjool Dates, Medlars, Monkfish, Mussels, Oysters, Parsnips, Partridge, Passion Fruit, Pears, Pheasant, Plaice, Pollack, Pomegranates, Potatoes (main crop), Pumpkin, Quinces, Rabbit, Rosehips, Salsify, Scallops, Sea Bass, Shallots, Skate, Squid, Swede, Teal, Truffles (black and white), Tufted Duck, Turbot, Turkey, Turnip, Venison, Walnuts, Widgeon, Wild Mushrooms (autumn), Winkles, Woodcock, Woodpigeon.

My culinary rituals for November...

Celebrate bonfire night with a few delicious recipes from my collection, such as my sumptuous **Pheasant Kiev** (see page 373) followed by my mother's **Pumpkin Fritters with Cinnamon Sugar** (see page 375). Alternatively, enjoy other tempting recipes including **Crown Prince Pumpkin and Chestnut Soup** (see page 378) or **Turnip, Apple and Cheddar Soup** (see page 376), both of which are great warming soups, ideal for sharing with friends on a chilly evening.

Collecting fresh chestnuts from the forest is an activity I enjoy immensely at this time of year. It's my time to be alone and to think and reflect as I collect these beauties. All I need is a few essentials: a basket, thick gloves, a decent pair of shoes or boots and a warm jumper. I do not pick the chestnuts from the trees, I simply collect the fallen ones, as it's once the pods are ripe that the chestnuts burst open and fall to the ground. Be careful though as there is a distinct difference between sweet, edible chestnuts (from the sweet chestnut tree) and the poisonous nuts (conkers) from the horse chestnut tree. The husk or casing of the sweet chestnut has lots of long, fine, prickly, needle-like hairs, whereas the fleshy exterior of the horse chestnut nut has fewer shorter and coarser spikes. And while sweet chestnuts themselves are slightly conical, the horse chestnut nut is rounded at both ends. Another word of warning though, the forest's residents might have taken the fabulous sweet chestnuts before you arrive, leaving the outer casings empty, but I suppose that's simply nature and a case of first come, first served. This is also a perfect time to absorb the tranquillity of the woods and forests and to observe the pheasants prancing about, plus, if you're lucky, a few fallow or muntjac deer might be seen bouncing past. Carefully move the crisp leaves about on the forest floor and you may be surprised to find some amazing hidden gems. If it's not too cold but still damp you may be lucky enough to find wild woodland mushrooms, such as chanterelles and ceps.

So do savour the game season and enjoy the abundance of pheasants and other small birds, rabbits and venison on offer this month. Even though ready-plucked game is available from butchers, it's definitely a humbling experience to try plucking a bird yourself. It's a messy and feathery job but the meal will be appreciated even more because you have done it yourself.

With the shorter days and longer nights, cooking becomes slower as we embrace comforting stews and hearty roasts. Try my wonderful recipe for **Pheasant Forestière** (see page 394), guaranteed to bring you warmth and comfort at this time of year.

Pomegranates and medjool dates from the Middle East are in season, and these are both readily available from good delicatessens and supermarkets, so why not be adventurous and try something exotic? Add medjool dates to a lamb stew to thicken and sweeten it naturally, then stir a few pomegranate seeds through boiled wild rice to accompany the meal. Finish the meal with my delicate **Rose and Pomegranate Blancmanges** (see page 370).

Pomegranates

With the prospects of a cold, grey autumn going into winter, this wonderful fruit with its orange-red-blushed skin and its beautiful pearled pink-red edible seeds is enough to brighten up the dullest of days. Pomegranates are imported and come mainly from the Middle East, America and south and east Asia. They are said to have health benefits as they contain a high level of antioxidants and are a good source of vitamin C and fibre. Choose fruits with hard, shiny, unblemished skin, which feel heavy for their size, as these will be the most juicy. How do you remove pomegranate seeds? Let's face it, this is a messy job! The best tip I can give you is to make sure you are wearing your oldest clothing. Take the pomegranate in both hands and give it a bit of a squeeze to loosen the seeds; you will feel them moving about inside. Roll the pomegranate on a chopping board as you would a lemon or orange before juicing them, then cut it in half. Place a deep bowl in an empty sink, then hold each pomegranate half over the bowl, cut-side down, and use a wooden spoon to hit it so that the seeds fall into the bowl. You might get splashed a little with the juice but this method is fairly effective. Once all the seeds are out (remove any seeds left behind with a teaspoon), remove any bitter white pith that is stuck to the seeds and drain the juice using a fine sieve. Both the seeds and juice are now ready to be used.

These delicate **Rose and Pomegranate Blancmanges** make the perfect dessert for a sophisticated dinner party. Rinse/dampen the insides of eight individual 6 x 5cm round moulds (each mould about 85ml volume) with cold water,then place them in the fridge on a baking tray. Soak 2 leaves of gelatine in cold water until it has softened. Combine 335ml milk and 2 tablespoons caster sugar in a saucepan and bring to the boil over a medium heat, stirring to dissolve the sugar, then simmer for 1 minute. Remove from the heat, squeeze the gelatine gently to remove excess water, then stir the gelatine into the hot milk until dissolved. Add 325ml natural yogurt, 2 tablespoons rose water (or to taste) and 1 teaspoon pomegranate molasses (optional – see Cook's Note) to the milk and stir to combine. Pour the mixture into the chilled moulds, dividing it evenly, then chill in the fridge for about 4 hours or until completely set. While the blancmanges are setting, make a pomegranate jelly by soaking 2 leaves of gelatine in cold water until it has softened. Place 200ml pomegranate juice in a small saucepan and bring to the boil over a high heat, stirring continuously, then boil for 30 seconds. Remove from the heat, squeeze the gelatine gently to remove excess water, then stir the gelatine into the hot juice until dissolved. Pour the jelly into a 21 x 14 x 1.5cm white plastic tray and leave to cool, then refrigerate for about 3 hours or until completely set. To serve, dip each blancmange mould in warm water, shake gently, then turn out on to a serving plate. Cut the pomegranate jelly into small cubes and place some alongside each blancmange, then decorate with fresh pomegranate seeds. Serve immediately. Serves 8. Pomegranate molasses, also known as pomegranate syrup, is a dark, thick, concentrated syrup made by simmering pomegranate juice until it reduces to a sticky syrupy consistency. It has a tangy, sweetly tart flavour (it has an undertone of sweetness) and can be used in sweet and savoury dishes. Pomegranate molasses is especially popular in Mediterranean and Middle Eastern cooking. It is available in many supermarkets, health food shops or delicatessens, or on-line.

Rose and Pomegranate Blancmanges

British Larder Heroes

Cabbages

Cabbage is the most common member of the Brassica family. There are many different types of cabbage of varying shapes, sizes and colours and they can be eaten raw, cooked or preserved. Savoy cabbage is one of the best-known varieties and it is beautiful and somewhat rustic-looking with its crinkled leaves and superb flavour. It is versatile and is often viewed as the king of cabbages for cooking. Savoy cabbage benefits from being cooked quickly and this not only gives the best flavour, it also helps to retain its vibrant green colour. Red and white cabbages can be eaten raw (for example, in coleslaw and salads) or cooked, and red cabbage in particular benefits from long, slow cooking by braising or baking. Red cabbage braised with apples, onions, vinegar, sultanas and spices is a popular sweet and sour accompaniment. Red cabbage is also ideal for pickling and white cabbages are suitable for making the well-known fermented cabbage dish from Germany called

Savoy cabbage

Chestnuts

sauerkraut. Choose cabbages that are heavy and firm with bright, unblemished leaves and with crisp outer leaves (watch out for cabbages where the outer leaves are removed by retailers to make cabbages look more attractive – this simply causes them to lose their freshness more quickly).

For a perfect accompaniment to slow-roasted pork, try my recipe for **Braised Red Cabbage with Apples and Sultanas**. It is one of my favourite late autumn recipes, and what's more the flavour improves if left overnight, so leftovers are definitely to be encouraged! Preheat the oven to 150°C/Gas Mark 2. Melt 2 tablespoons unsalted butter in a large casserole and once it is foaming, add 1 roughly chopped onion, 2 crushed cloves garlic and 2 cinnamon sticks and sauté over a medium heat for about 6 minutes or until the onion starts to turn golden brown. Add 500g shredded red cabbage, 50g sultanas, ¼ teaspoon ground cloves, ¼ teaspoon ground nutmeg, 2 tablespoons soft dark brown sugar, 3 tablespoons cider vinegar, 250ml apple cider, 100g (prepared weight) peeled, cored and finely diced Bramley apple, the finely grated zest and juice of 1 orange and sea salt and freshly cracked black pepper. Bring the mixture to a gentle simmer and simmer for 5 minutes, then remove from the heat. Cover with a tight-fitting lid and cook in the oven for about 2 hours or until tender, stirring at least once during the cooking time. Remove from the oven, then taste and adjust the seasoning, if necessary. Serves 6 as an accompaniment. If you have any leftovers, transfer to an airtight container and leave to cool, then store in the fridge and use within 3 days.

Chestnuts

Chestnuts are the edible fruit of the sweet chestnut tree, originally native to western Asia, but now very much native in southern Europe, and they are used in both sweet and savoury dishes. They are available to buy in many different forms, from fresh, dried, vacuum-packed, canned, frozen and ground, to sweetened or unsweetened puréed versions, as well as chestnut flour. Sweet chestnuts (once they are removed from their hairy outer casings) are covered in a shiny brown, leathery skin and they contain a higher amount of starch than other nut varieties, as well as less fat and protein. They are always eaten cooked and fresh roasted chestnuts are delicious incorporated into or shaven over desserts, as this shows off their true character beautifully. For a fabulous sweet treat, do give my **Bitter Chocolate and Chestnut Truffle Cake with Candied Chestnuts** recipe a try (see page 400). I promise you won't be disappointed!

The smell of roasting chestnuts sends a warming and comforting smell through the house, and these **Roasted Chestnuts** are the perfect snack to enjoy around the fire with a glass of mulled wine or cider. Preheat the oven to 200°C/Gas Mark 6. Using a sharp paring knife, cut a small cross into the shell of each of 800g–1kg chestnuts, then place in a roasting tin. Roast in the oven for 25–30 minutes or until the nuts are tender and the shells and skins lift away easily. Transfer to a serving dish, then cover with foil and leave to cool for 10 minutes before serving, otherwise the chestnuts will be too hot to handle. Serves 4–6 as a snack.

Pears

Like the apple, the pear is a deciduous tree from the rose family. However, unlike its cousin, the flavour of pears actually improves after they're picked, and, in fact, the grainy texture of its flesh is more reminiscent of a quince than an apple. Choose pears that are slightly underripe as the delicate flesh can bruise easily when ripe, then store them in a cool place to ripen at home. Once they're ripe, it's best to refrigerate pears to prevent further ripening, but eat them as soon as possible. Pears can be eaten raw or cooked and are ideal for poaching whole in syrup or red or white wine. Pears can also be cooked in pies, tarts, crumbles and cakes. They go very well with salty cheeses and have a natural affinity with chocolate. Pears can also be preserved in syrup, brandy or wine, made into chutneys or pickles or sliced thinly and dried. For a very impressive and grown-up dessert using pears, try my recipe for **Pear Parfait with Liquorice Jelly and Spice-poached Pears** (see page 397).

The cultivation of pears goes back about 4000 years and references to pear trees being used as boundary markers can be found in the Domesday Book of 1086. The number of pear varieties grown in Britain peaked during the late nineteenth century and today there are about 1,000 varieties. Sadly, despite there being so many British varieties, few of them are actually available to buy and 80% of the pears we consume in Britain are imported, meaning that we are in danger of losing our native varieties forever. Although the Conference, Packham's, Comice and Rocha might be the most familiar to you, try seeking out other interesting British varieties at farmers' markets. Fortunately, there is some excellent work being done in Britain to try and protect our native fruits and prevent older varieties from dying out. Brogdale Farm in Kent, home to the National Fruit Collection, which is supported by the government's Department for Environment, Food and Rural Affairs (Defra) and other groups, is one such organisation. Brogdale Farm is devoted to the conservation of fruit and has one of the largest fruit collections in the world, which includes over 3500 samples of different varieties of fruit. To visit the site is a humbling experience and the work they do there should ensure that the future of our native fruits, including pears, is safe.

For an attractive and tasty dessert, try these lovely **Pear Tarts**. Preheat the oven to 200°C/Gas Mark 6 and line a large baking tray with non-stick baking paper. On a lightly floured work surface, roll out 240g good quality chilled fresh all-butter puff pastry to 3–4mm thickness. Cut out four 16cm squares, then brush the top surfaces with 1 beaten egg yolk mixed with 1 teaspoon caster sugar. Place the puff pastry squares on the prepared baking tray and chill in the fridge

Pears

while you make the pastry cream. Combine 100ml milk and the seeds scraped from ½ a split vanilla pod in a small saucepan. Heat over a medium heat and as soon as the milk starts to boil, remove from the heat. Meanwhile place 1 egg yolk, 1 tablespoon caster sugar and 1 tablespoon plain flour in a small mixing bowl and whisk together to form a smooth paste. Pour half of the hot milk over the egg mixture, stirring to mix well, then return the egg mixture to the remaining hot milk in the pan. Cook over a low heat, stirring continuously, until the mixture comes to a gentle simmer, then simmer for about 5 minutes or until the mixture has thickened, stirring. Remove the pastry cream from the heat and whisk in 2 teaspoons unsalted butter until completely incorporated. Place a piece of cling film directly on the surface of the pastry cream and leave to cool at room temperature. while you prepare the pears. Place 150ml cold water, 150g caster sugar and the juice of 1 lemon in a saucepan and stir over a low heat until the sugar has dissolved, then bring to the boil over a high heat and boil for about 3 minutes or until thickened slightly. Peel, quarter and core 2 ripe pears (about 120g each, unprepared weight), then cut each quarter in half lengthways. Add the pears to the hot syrup, reduce the heat to low, then place a cartouche (a circle of greaseproof paper) on top of the pears, and place a small plate on top to weigh them down. Poach the pears in the syrup for 6–8 minutes or until they are soft but still retain their shape. Drain the pears and discard the syrup. Remove the puff pastry squares from the fridge. Spoon the pastry cream into the centre of each square, dividing it evenly. Flatten the cream slightly, leaving 1cm clear around the edges of the pastry. Place the pear pieces on top of the pastry cream in a line, dividing them equally, then bake the tarts in the oven for 25 minutes or until the pastry is cooked, golden brown and crisp. Transfer to a wire rack and leave to cool for 10 minutes before serving with vanilla ice cream or crème fraîche. Serves 4.

Pheasants

Pheasants are beautiful, large, long-tailed game birds. Officially, the pheasant season starts on 1st of October, but rarely does anyone ever shoot them before the end of October as a good snap of cold weather is needed to encourage the birds to eat so that they become plump. Pheasants are normally plentiful by mid-November at which time they become cheaper – the price of pheasant can plummet by up to 50% when the glut kicks in. The males (cocks) are the larger, more colourful birds with the bottle-green head, red wattle and the very long tail; the females (hens) are the smaller, mottled brown birds. Pheasant are normally sold in a pair (or brace), with one male and one female. The leg meat is normally very tough and in most cases inedible unless the legs have been cooked for a long period of time at a low temperature. The breasts are the prime cuts on a pheasant as they are flavoursome, juicy and rich. There is very little fat on a pheasant so you need to be careful not to let the meat dry out. When cooking the breasts, I generally recommend that you keep the skin on in order to retain the moisture and keep them succulent and tender. Pheasant, particularly older birds, is well suited to more moist cooking methods including braising, casseroling and pot-roasting, though younger birds can successfully be barded with bacon and roasted.

For a delicious twist on the classic chicken version, try this recipe for **Pheasant Kiev**. Preheat the oven to 200°C/ Gas Mark 6 and line a baking tray with non-stick baking paper. Remove the skin from 4 pheasant breasts (100–120g each) and use a sharp knife to make an incision horizontally across the thickest part of each breast, but do not cut all the way through. Set aside. Place 150g soft unsalted butter,

Pheasant

2 crushed cloves garlic, 1 tablespoon chopped fresh parsley, the finely grated zest of 1 lemon and sea salt and freshly cracked black pepper in a small bowl and mix together to form a smooth, spreadable paste. Transfer the mixture to a piping bag fitted with a plain nozzle (about 4mm diameter), then pipe it into the cavity in the pheasant breasts, dividing it evenly between them. I pipe rather than spoon the mixture into the breasts as it is easier to get a good quantity of herb butter into each one successfully. It also prevents me having to make such a large opening – if the opening is too large, the herb butter will simply leak out. Put 1 tablespoon plain flour in a small bowl and season with salt and pepper. Put

Pheasant Kiev, page 373

100g fresh breadcrumbs in another small bowl, then whisk together 1 egg and 1 tablespoon cold water in a third small bowl. Roll each stuffed pheasant breast in the flour, then in the egg and then finally roll it in the breadcrumbs to coat all over. Place the coated breasts on a plate and chill in the fridge for 10 minutes. Heat 1 tablespoon unsalted butter and 1 tablespoon sunflower oil in a large, non-stick frying pan until hot, then fry the kievs over a high heat for about 2 minutes on each side or until golden. Transfer the kievs to the prepared baking tray and cook in the oven for about 15 minutes or until cooked, golden brown and crisp. Remove from the oven and leave to rest for 2 minutes, then serve with a generous helping of Creamed Savoy Cabbage (see page 384) and mashed potatoes. Serves 4 as a main course.

Pumpkins

Pumpkins are a member of the Cucurbitaceae family, which also includes squashes, courgettes, marrows, melon and cucumber. In Britain, the pumpkin season runs from October–December. There are plenty of different pumpkin varieties, ranging from large pumpkins with thick skins, to small, single-serving varieties. As they vary in size, they also vary in colour, and can be orange, yellow, green or grey. The skin is tough and can be difficult to remove, so you may need to cut the pumpkin into pieces first to enable you to get your knife underneath the skin more easily. It's worth the effort, though, because the bright orange flesh beneath is sweet and delicate and is rich in antioxidants and vitamins. Pumpkin is very versatile and its velvety texture and sweetness works well in both savoury and sweet dishes, from silky soups and hearty stews and tagines, to the classic and popular American dessert, pumpkin pie.

Pumpkin Seeds are just as nutritious and delicious – simply toss them with 1 teaspoon olive oil and sea salt, spread them out on a baking tray and roast in a preheated oven at 180°C/ Gas Mark 4 for about 10 minutes or until lightly toasted, stirring once or twice. Serve the roasted seeds as a snack, or add to salads for a lovely bit of crunch.

Pumpkin is another of my favourite vegetables. I was brought up on pumpkin and my mother used to roast it to accompany our Sunday meal. Any leftovers were used the next day and were often turned into pumpkin fritters served with cinnamon sugar – a quick and delicious after-dinner treat. To make my mother **Dalene's Pumpkin Fritters with Cinnamon Sugar**, choose a dense variety of pumpkin with a firm, dry flesh, such as Crown Prince. Melt 1 tablespoon unsalted butter in a large saucepan and once it starts to foam, add 500g (prepared weight) peeled, deseeded and finely sliced pumpkin, a pinch of sea salt and 125g caster sugar, mix well, then cover the pan with a lid. Cook over a medium heat for 10 minutes, stirring occasionally, then add 100ml cold water, bring to a simmer and cook, uncovered, for a further 10 minutes or until the pumpkin is completely soft and all the liquid has evaporated (it's important that the cooked pumpkin is dry). Remove from the heat. Meanwhile, mix 1 teaspoon ground cinnamon with 2 tablespoons caster sugar in a small bowl and set aside. Transfer the pumpkin to a mixing bowl and use a fork to mash it until smooth. Add 125g plain flour, 2 eggs, 1 teaspoon baking powder, 1 teaspoon ground cinnamon and a couple of gratings of fresh nutmeg, then mix well to form a thick batter. Heat 1 tablespoon sunflower oil in a non-stick frying pan until hot, then spoon heaped tablespoonfuls of the batter into the hot oil and fry each fritter for about 2 minutes on each side or until golden brown. You will need to fry them in batches, adding 1 extra teaspoon oil to the pan for each batch. Drain on kitchen paper, then cover and keep warm until all the

Pumpkin

fritters are cooked. Serve immediately with the cinnamon sugar and lemon wedges. Serves 4.

Turnips

The humble turnip is a member of the Brassicaceae family. Turnips are usually round and slightly flattened in shape and grow protruding just above the ground. They are a creamy colour and the upper part is often blushed with pink-purple, red or green. There are two optimum times for harvesting turnips. Sweet baby turnips, which are about the size of radishes, are available in early summer and can be eaten raw or cooked. They have a distinctive peppery, slightly sweet flavour and a crisp texture. Winter turnips, which have a slightly milder flavour and a coarser texture, are at their best from October–February and they need to be peeled and cooked before eating. Turnip leaves or turnip tops can also be eaten and have a mustardy flavour, not dissimilar to mustard greens.

Roasting turnips with your Sunday joint is a great way of serving them, but for something a little bit different try this delicious recipe for **Turnip, Apple and Cheddar Soup**. Melt 2 tablespoons unsalted butter in a large saucepan and once it starts to foam, add 1 diced onion, 2 crushed cloves garlic, 400g (prepared weight) peeled and finely sliced turnips, 100g (prepared weight) peeled and finely sliced potatoes, 150g (prepared weight) peeled, cored and finely diced Bramley apple, and sea salt and freshly cracked black pepper and sauté over a high heat for 5–6 minutes or until golden brown. Add 125ml dry sherry, then reduce the heat to medium and cook for a further 2 minutes. Add 1 litre vegetable stock, cover the pan with a lid and bring the soup to a gentle simmer, then simmer for about 20 minutes or until the turnips begin to soften and break up. Add 100ml double cream and 80g grated mature Cheddar cheese and bring back to a simmer, then remove from the heat. Carefully transfer the mixture to a blender and blend until smooth, then return to the pan and taste and adjust the seasoning, if necessary. Reheat the soup gently and serve piping hot with plenty of fresh crusty bread and extra grated Cheddar cheese for sprinkling. Use a blue cheese if you prefer, it will be equally delicious. Serves 4 as a starter, light lunch or supper.

Turnips

Wild rabbit

The rabbit is a member of the Leporidae family, which also includes the hare. Wild rabbit has a mild gamey taste, but with hanging, the flavour becomes stronger. Unlike its farmed counterpart, which has pale and tender meat, wild rabbit meat is darker and tends to be a little tougher and it can easily become dry and tasteless if overcooked. The legs can be tough, so they require long, slow cooking at a low temperature to tenderise them, while the saddle (loins) should be cooked quickly at a high temperature to prevent it from drying out. Both farmed and wild rabbit meat is low in fat and cholesterol. Wild rabbit are available all year round, but their flavour and size are better from August to late December. The larger the rabbit, the older and tougher they are likely to be, so choose rabbits that are smaller than 1kg. This size should serve 2. Wild rabbits are especially good for braises, casseroles and stews or to add to pie fillings. There is a significant difference between wild rabbits and hares. Wild rabbits are altricial and their young are born hairless and blind, whereas hares are precocial and generally their young are born with hair and can see. Wild rabbits live underground in burrows, whereas hares live above ground in a 'nest' (or a small depression formed in the ground among long grass) known as a 'form'. Hares are larger than wild rabbits and have longer ears and hind legs. Hare meat is also darker, richer and more strongly flavoured than wild rabbit. Young hare (or leveret) is best for eating and ideal for roasting as saddle of hare, but older hare can also be eaten and is best for long, slow cooking such as in casseroles and stews. Jugged hare is a traditional British recipe.

This wonderful **Potted Wild Rabbit** is one of the recipes we prepare during the game season as part of **The British Larder's Famous Tasting of Game** (see pages 380–381). Preheat the oven to 160˚C/Gas Mark 3. Season 4 wild rabbit legs (380–400g total weight) with sea salt and freshly cracked black pepper. Heat 1 tablespoon sunflower oil in a casserole until hot, then add the seasoned rabbit legs and cook over a high heat for about 3 minutes on each side or until golden brown. Add a large sprig of fresh thyme, 2 bay leaves, 1 clove crushed garlic and 1 litre chicken stock. Bring the stock to the boil and boil for 4 minutes, then remove from the heat. Cover the pan with a lid, then transfer to the oven and cook for about 1 hour or until the rabbit is tender. Remove from the oven and leave to cool in the stock for 30 minutes. Meanwhile, lightly grease four 8 x 5cm ramekins. While the rabbit is cooling, heat 1 teaspoon goose fat in a small saucepan. Add 2 finely diced banana shallots and 1 crushed clove garlic, then cover the pan and sweat over a low heat for 8–10 minutes or until soft and transparent. Remove from the heat. Drain the rabbit legs, reserving the stock (you can either cool, then freeze the stock in a covered freezer proof container for up to 3 months, or store it in an airtight container in the fridge and use within 3 days). Flake the rabbit meat into a mixing bowl (discard the bones). Add the cooked shallots, 1 teaspoon finely chopped fresh thyme leaves, 1 tablespoon finely chopped gherkins, 1 tablespoon finely chopped capers, 6 drops of Tabasco sauce, ½ teaspoon Worcestershire sauce, 3 tablespoons melted goose fat and salt and pepper and mix well. Divide the mixture evenly between the prepared ramekins, packing it in well using the back of a spoon. Chill in the fridge for 30 minutes. Melt 3 tablespoons goose fat and pour it on top of the chilled rabbit mixture, dividing it evenly between the ramekins. Return the potted rabbit to the fridge for a further 30 minutes before serving (the potted rabbit will keep in the fridge for up to 3 days). Bring back to room temperature to serve and accompany with plenty of toast and lightly dressed salad leaves. Serves 4 as a starter.

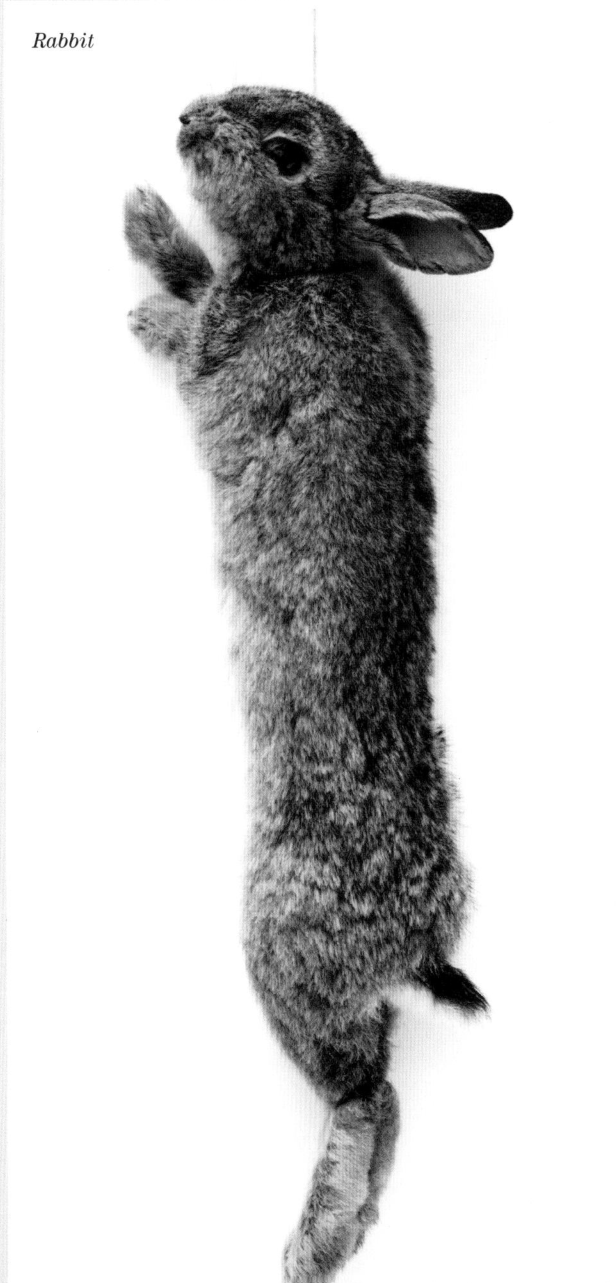
Rabbit

Crown Prince Pumpkin and Chestnut Soup

Vibrant pumpkin soup has some magical memories for me. I used to work in one of Britain's toughest kitchens and we served pumpkin soup every day. The leftovers from the previous day were given to staff for lunch and I remember it as if it were yesterday. Back then I considered the meal to be liquid gold. The chestnuts lend the soup a rounded nutty flavour and give it a wonderful velvety texture. Roast the pumpkin's seeds and use them for the garnish.

Serves 4 as a starter or light lunch

500g (prepared weight) Crown Prince pumpkin (see Cook's Note), peeled, deseeded and diced (reserve the seeds)
1 teaspoon olive oil
2 tablespoons unsalted butter
1 cinnamon stick
100ml dry white wine
1 litre white chicken stock or vegetable stock
50g (prepared weight) Roasted Chestnuts (see page 372), peeled
sea salt and freshly cracked black pepper

Preheat the oven to 180°C/Gas Mark 4 and line a baking tray with non-stick baking paper.

Wash the pumpkin seeds and remove any membrane that is still clinging to them. Pat dry using kitchen paper, then spread the seeds out on the prepared baking tray. Season with salt and pepper and drizzle with the olive oil, then toss gently to mix. Roast in the oven for about 10 minutes or until the seeds are lightly toasted, stirring halfway through the cooking time. Remove from the oven and set aside to cool.

Melt the butter in a large saucepan and once it is foaming, add the pumpkin flesh, cinnamon stick and salt and pepper. Cover the pan with a lid and cook over a low heat for 10 minutes, stirring occasionally to prevent it from catching. Remove the lid and increase the heat to medium, then add the wine, bring to the boil and cook for 2 minutes. Add the stock and bring to the boil, then reduce the heat to a gentle simmer, cover and simmer for about 20 minutes or until the pumpkin begins to soften and break up. Add half of the chestnuts, simmer for a further 10 minutes, then remove the pan from the heat. Remove and discard the cinnamon stick.

Carefully transfer the soup to a blender and purée until very smooth. Return to the pan and if the soup is a bit thick for your liking, stir in a little more stock. Reheat gently until hot, then taste and adjust the seasoning, if necessary. While the soup is reheating, roughly chop the remaining chestnuts.

Serve the hot soup in bowls, garnished with the chopped chestnuts and roasted pumpkin seeds. Serve with plenty of fresh crusty bread.

Cook's Note
Crown Prince pumpkins have grey-blue skin and a rich orange flesh and they are a little more unusual than the orange-skinned varieties you will be used to seeing. I'd highly recommend seeking them out. They are especially prized for their flavour, which is particularly sweet in comparison with other varieties of pumpkin. Look out for them at farmers' markets, or why not try growing your own?

The British Larder's Famous Tasting of Game

This dish is possibly the one that gave the British Larder its real identity. I'm not particularly fond of the term 'signature dish', but if the glove fits... Once this dish was created and served, we had customers returning regularly to enjoy it time and again. That was when we knew we'd established the style of food we wanted to be serving, and it was a pretty special moment. This dish has been such a success that when the game season of that first year came to an end, we were almost slightly lost. For days we debated about what the 'summer version' was going to be. In the end, we came up with our 'pork tasting', which follows the same formula, and fortunately it became just as popular.

The idea of the dish is to make up a platter with small morsels of gamey goodness and serve part of it hot and part cold. To complete this dish, you will need to add the Potted Wild Rabbit (see page 377) and the Cauliflower and Shallot Piccalilli (see page 85).

You will need to start this recipe at least 1 day before you want to serve it, to allow the terrine time to set.

Serves 6 as a starter or light lunch

For the game terrine

1 ham hock (about 1.2kg with bone)
2 mallard duck legs (100–120g each)
1 clove garlic, crushed
a large sprig of fresh thyme, leaves only, finely chopped
2 mallard duck breasts (120–140g each)
1 teaspoon unsalted butter
50g horn of plenty mushrooms (trompette de la mort), brushed clean and finely chopped
50g Savoy cabbage, finely shredded
3 leaves of gelatine
sea salt and freshly cracked black pepper

For the venison Scotch eggs

3 eggs
300g venison sausages
2 tablespoons finely chopped fresh mixed soft herbs (such as parsley, chervil and chives)
1 tablespoon plain flour, seasoned with salt and pepper
1–2 eggs, lightly beaten
150g fresh breadcrumbs
sunflower oil, for deep-frying

For the partridge, prune and bacon sausages

50g dried stoned prunes, chopped
2 tablespoons Armagnac
1 oven-ready partridge (about 250g)
2 tablespoons olive oil
100g Cumberland sausagemeat
1 banana shallot, finely diced
2 tablespoons chopped fresh mixed soft herbs (such as parsley, chervil and chives)
6 rashers smoked streaky bacon, cut in half widthways
200g Puy lentils

Potted Wild Rabbit (see page 377), to serve
Cauliflower and Shallot Piccalilli (see page 85), to serve

To allow the terrine time to set, you will need to start a day in advance. For the game terrine, place the ham hock in a large saucepan, cover with plenty of cold water, place a lid on the pan, then bring to the boil over a high heat. Once boiling, remove the lid and remove any scum from the surface with a ladle. Reduce the heat to low and simmer the ham, uncovered, for about 3½ hours or until the meat falls away easily from the bone (you may need to occasionally top up the water). Remove from the heat and leave the ham to cool in the stock for 1 hour.

Remove the ham from the stock and flake the cooked meat into a bowl. Pass the stock through a fine sieve, then measure out 250ml. Place the measured quantity of stock in a small saucepan, bring to the boil and keep hot (see Cook's Notes).

Meanwhile, while the ham is cooling in the stock, cook the mallard duck legs and breasts. Preheat the oven to 160°C/Gas Mark 3 and line a 14 x 4 x 5cm terrine mould with a double layer of cling film (see page 297 for the best way of doing this), then place the mould in the fridge. Place the duck legs on a baking tray and rub in the garlic, thyme and salt and pepper. Cook in the oven for 30–35 minutes or until the duck is cooked and the meat comes away easily from the bone. Remove from the oven and leave to cool for 20 minutes, then remove and discard the skin and flake the meat into a small bowl. Set aside until the ham is ready. Increase the oven temperature to 200°C/Gas Mark 6.

Heat a non-stick frying pan over a high heat until hot, then add the duck breasts, fat-side down, and cook for about 5 minutes or until the fat is golden brown and crisp. Remove from the heat and transfer the duck breasts to a roasting tin, fat-side up. Roast in the oven for about 6 minutes for medium-rare (or cook to your liking). Remove from the oven and let the duck breasts rest for 10 minutes. Once rested, cut the breasts lengthways into 1cm strips.

Melt the butter in a non-stick frying pan and once it starts to foam, add the mushrooms and cabbage and sauté over a high heat for about 5 minutes or until softened. Remove from the heat and drain on kitchen paper. Soak the gelatine in cold water until it has softened, then squeeze it gently to remove excess water. Add the gelatine to the measured hot ham stock and stir until dissolved, then set aside to cool for 10 minutes.

Assemble the terrine by ladling a third of the ham stock into the mould. Place a layer of the flaked ham on top, followed by a few strips of the duck breast, then a layer of the mushroom and cabbage mixture, then a layer of the flaked duck leg meat. Add another third of the stock and repeat the layers until all the layering ingredients are used up and the terrine mould is full to the top. Fold the overhanging cling film over to cover completely and place the mould on a baking tray. Place a few light weights on top to press the terrine down, then chill in the fridge overnight.

The next day, prepare the venison Scotch eggs. Cook the eggs in a covered saucepan of boiling water for 6–7 minutes, then remove the eggs using a slotted spoon and place them in a bowl of iced water to cool them quickly. Once cold, peel the eggs carefully.

Meanwhile, remove the skins from the venison sausages, place the sausagemeat in a bowl with the herbs and mix well. Divide and shape the mixture into 3 equal balls. Press each ball of venison mixture flat, place a peeled boiled egg in the centre of each one and then wrap the venison mixture around the egg, enclosing each egg completely. Place the balls on a plate and chill in the fridge for 10 minutes.

Put the seasoned flour, beaten eggs and breadcrumbs into 3 separate shallow bowls. First, roll a venison-covered egg in the seasoned flour, tapping off the excess flour, then roll it in the beaten egg and then finally in the breadcrumbs, making sure it is evenly coated all over. Repeat this process with the other 2 venison-covered eggs. Return to the plate and chill in the fridge for 15–20 minutes to rest and firm up.

Meanwhile, prepare the partridge, prune and bacon sausages. Preheat the oven to 180°C/Gas Mark 4. Put the prunes into a small bowl, pour over the Armagnac and leave to soak for 10–15 minutes. In the meantime, place the partridge in a roasting tin, season with salt and pepper and rub all over with 1 tablespoon olive oil. Roast in the oven for about 30 minutes or until the skin is golden brown and the meat is tender. Remove from the oven and leave to rest for 10 minutes. Remove the legs and breasts and discard their skin, then remove the meat from the bones (discard the bones and carcass or use them for making stock at a later date – see page 22 for Roasted Game Stock). Flake the leg and breast meat into a bowl, then add the soaked prunes, along with the sausagemeat, shallot and herbs. Mix well, then add salt and pepper to taste.

Divide the sausage mixture into 12 equal balls, then roll each one into a sausage shape, about 2cm in diameter. Wrap a piece of bacon around each sausage, securing the ends together with a wooden cocktail stick. Place the sausages on a baking tray and cook in the oven at 180°C/Gas Mark 4 for 12–15 minutes or until the sausages are cooked and brown and the bacon is crisp. Remove from the oven and keep warm until you are ready to serve.

While the sausages are cooking, put the Puy lentils in a saucepan and cover with cold water. Bring up to a gentle simmer over a medium heat and cook, uncovered, for 15–20 minutes or until the lentils are cooked and tender. Add a pinch of salt towards the end of the cooking time. Drain the lentils, then add the remaining 1 tablespoon olive oil and salt and pepper to taste and mix well. Set aside and keep warm.

When you are ready to serve, finish the venison Scotch eggs. Heat some sunflower oil in an electric deep-fat fryer or in a deep frying pan to a temperature of 160°C (or until a small piece of bread browns within 20 seconds in the hot oil). Once the oil is hot enough, deep-fry the breadcrumbed eggs in the hot oil for 6–7 minutes or until cooked, golden brown and crisp all over. Using a slotted spoon, remove and drain the cooked eggs on kitchen paper. Cut each venison Scotch egg in half just before serving.

To serve, cut the terrine into 6 generous slices and place on serving plates or simply place on a wooden board or platter. Remove the potted wild rabbit from the ramekins and divide equally between the serving plates (see Cook's Notes). Place half a venison Scotch egg on each plate, then spoon a portion of the warm lentils alongside the egg and top with 2 partridge sausages. Serve immediately with the piccalilli on the side.

Cook's Notes

The leftover ham stock will keep for up to 3 days in the fridge and for up to 3 months in the freezer. (The total amount of ham stock you make will depend on the size of pan you use and how much water you add.)

The Potted Wild Rabbit recipe serves 4, but for this recipe it will serve 6 – we spoon the potted rabbit out of the ramekins and then divide it between 6 smaller glass jars to serve on this tasting platter, serving one smaller jarful per person (or you can spoon the potted rabbit on to the serving plates or wooden board/platter, dividing it evenly into 6 smaller portions).

Left: The British Larder's Famous Tasting of Game, pages 380–381
Right: Rabbit en Croûte with Creamed Savoy Cabbage and Turnip Purée, pages 384–385

Rabbit en Croûte with Creamed Savoy Cabbage and Turnip Purée

This is an ideal dinner party meal. The beauty of cooking 'en croûte' is that you can prepare the pastry parcels up to 3 days in advance and keep them refrigerated until you're ready to cook the dish. On the day, all you will need to do is make the turnip purée and creamed cabbage.

I use the whole rabbits, but cook the legs and loins separately to ensure all the meat remains moist and succulent.

Serves 4 as a main course

For the rabbit en croûte

2 whole wild rabbits (about 600g each), skinned and cleaned
1 tablespoon sunflower oil
2 cloves garlic, crushed
2 large sprigs of fresh thyme
1 teaspoon coriander seeds, lightly crushed
5 black peppercorns, lightly crushed
1 litre white chicken stock
1 tablespoon unsalted butter
250g mixed fresh wild mushrooms, cleaned and sliced
1 skinless, boneless chicken breast (120–150g), roughly diced
1 egg white
200ml double cream
2 tablespoons chopped fresh mixed soft herbs (such as tarragon, chives and chervil)
1 teaspoon truffle oil
400g good quality chilled fresh all-butter puff pastry
1 egg, lightly beaten
poppy seeds, for sprinkling
sea salt and freshly cracked black pepper

For the turnip purée

1 tablespoon unsalted butter
400g (prepared weight) turnips, peeled and roughly diced
150ml white chicken stock
100ml double cream

For the creamed Savoy cabbage

200g Savoy cabbage, finely shredded
8 baby turnips (about 200g total weight), peeled
1 tablespoon unsalted butter
2 rashers smoked back bacon, diced
1 carrot, finely diced
1 large turnip (80–100g), peeled and finely diced
50ml dry white wine
100ml white chicken stock
100ml double cream

Start by preparing the rabbit en croûte. Preheat the oven to 160°C/Gas Mark 3. Joint each rabbit into 5 portions (2 front legs/shoulders, 2 back legs and 1 saddle that is then boned and halved into 2 loins). To do this, remove the front legs/shoulders and back legs, then remove the saddle from the bone and cut it in half so you have 2 loins – you end up with 6 portions per rabbit (see Cook's Notes). Transfer the 4 loins to a covered container and store in the fridge until needed (discard the carcasses or use them for making stock at a later date – see page 22 for Roasted Game Stock).

Season all the rabbit legs with salt and pepper. Heat the sunflower oil in a large casserole until hot, then add all the rabbit legs and cook over a high heat for about 3 minutes on each side or until golden brown. Add the garlic, thyme sprigs, coriander seeds, black peppercorns and stock to the pan, then bring to the boil. As soon as it boils, remove from the heat, cover the casserole with a lid, then transfer it to the oven and cook for about 1 hour or until the rabbit legs are tender. Remove from the oven and let the rabbit legs cool in the cooking liquid for 30 minutes. Remove the rabbit legs from the stock and discard the stock, then remove and discard the skin from the legs and flake the meat into a bowl (discard the bones). Cool, then chill in the fridge until needed.

Melt the butter in a non-stick frying pan and once it is foaming, sauté the mushrooms, with salt and pepper added, over a high heat for 5–6 minutes or until golden brown. Remove from the heat and drain the mushrooms on kitchen paper, then set aside to cool.

Place the chicken breast in a food processor along with the egg white and blend together until just combined. Add the cream and a sprinkling of salt and pepper and pulse for 10 seconds. Do not overwork the mixture as the cream can separate. Transfer the mixture to a mixing bowl and use a spoon to finish blending the cream with the chicken purée, then stir in the herbs, truffle oil, cooled sautéed mushrooms and chilled rabbit leg meat. Cover the bowl and refrigerate for 30 minutes.

To assemble the rabbit en croûte, roll out the puff pastry on a lightly floured work surface to about 2mm thickness and cut out four 15 x 10cm rectangles. Set aside. Line a baking tray with non-stick baking paper.

Remove the 4 rabbit loins from the fridge and cut each one in half widthways to make 8 loin halves in total. For each en croûte, place 2 tablespoonfuls of the rabbit leg mixture into the centre of each pastry rectangle, then top with 2 loin halves. Brush the pastry edges with a little of the beaten egg, then fold the long sides into the middle so that they overlap slightly (you should have a tube shape). Repeat with the remaining pastry rectangles, rabbit leg mixture and rabbit loin halves to make 4 en croûtes in total.

Turn the en croûtes over so that the joins are underneath, then crimp the edges of the open ends to form sealed parcels. Brush the unglazed pastry with the remaining beaten egg and sprinkle with poppy seeds. Place the en croûtes on the prepared baking tray and leave to rest in the fridge for 30 minutes, or until you are ready to cook them (see Cook's Notes).

When you are ready to serve, preheat the oven to 200°C/Gas Mark 6. Bake the en croûtes in the oven for 22–25 minutes or until the pastry is cooked, crisp and golden brown.

Meanwhile, prepare the turnip purée. Melt the butter in a saucepan and once it starts to foam, sauté the turnips, with salt and pepper added, over a medium heat for about 5 minutes or until they start to turn golden. Add the stock and bring to the boil, then reduce the heat to low, cover and simmer gently for about 12 minutes or until the turnips are soft and the stock has nearly all evaporated. Add the cream, bring back to a simmer and simmer gently for 2 minutes. Remove from the heat, carefully transfer the mixture to a blender and blend to a smooth purée. Return the turnip purée to a clean saucepan and reheat gently until hot. Taste and adjust the seasoning, if necessary, then keep warm until you are ready to serve.

In the meantime, for the creamed Savoy cabbage, bring a saucepan of salted water to a rapid boil over a high heat. Blanch the shredded cabbage in the boiling water for 3–4 minutes or until tender, then remove using a slotted spoon, drain well and set aside. Bring the water back to a rapid boil and add the baby turnips. Cover the pan and cook for about 6 minutes or until the turnips are tender, then remove from the heat and drain. Transfer the baby turnips to a bowl, then set aside and keep warm until you are ready to serve.

Meanwhile, melt the butter in a clean saucepan and once it starts to foam, sauté the bacon, carrot and diced turnip over a high heat for 7–8 minutes or until golden. Add the wine and let it bubble, stirring and scraping the base of the pan with a wooden spoon to deglaze it. Cook over a high heat for about 2 minutes or until the wine is reduced by half, then add the stock. Bring back to the boil, then reduce the heat and simmer for about 6 minutes or until the stock is reduced by half. Add the blanched cabbage and the cream, bring back to a simmer and simmer for 2 minutes. Remove from the heat, taste and adjust the seasoning, if necessary, then keep warm until you are ready to serve.

To serve, spoon some warm turnip purée on to each serving plate, followed by a generous portion of the warm creamed Savoy cabbage. Place a rabbit en croûte on top, then spoon the warm baby turnips alongside. Serve immediately.

Cook's Notes

If you do not feel confident jointing the rabbits yourself, you can ask your butcher to do it for you.

The rabbit en croûtes can be made up to 3 days in advance, but do not bake them until needed. Once made, store the en croûtes in a covered container in the fridge, then bring to room temperature before baking, and bake as directed.

Pulled Pork and Pumpkin Pies

These are exceptionally delicious pies. Marinating the pork shoulder overnight using cinnamon, sugar and smoked paprika gives the meat an incredible fragrance, and by cooking it slowly in a low oven for about 4½ hours, it remains beautifully tender and the porky goodness is locked in. They are topped with buttery mashed pumpkin that is cooked in the oven alongside the meat. You will need to start this recipe the day before you want to serve it, to allow time for the pork to marinate.

Serves 6 as a main course

For the pulled pork pies
80g soft dark brown sugar
1 tablespoon sea salt
1 teaspoon smoked paprika
1 cinnamon stick
1 tablespoon mustard powder
a large pinch of crushed dried chillies
1 tablespoon coriander seeds
1 clove garlic, crushed
20g fresh root ginger, peeled and finely chopped
1 shoulder of pork (about 1.2kg with bone), deboned and fat left on
700ml fresh unsweetened apple juice
250ml cold water
500g Shortcrust Pastry (see page 18)
freshly cracked black pepper, to taste

For the pumpkin mash
1 pumpkin (900g–1kg total weight)
freshly grated nutmeg, to taste
2 teaspoons soft light brown sugar
50g unsalted butter
sea salt, to taste

First, make the marinade for the pulled pork pies. Use a pestle and mortar to grind together the dark brown sugar, salt, smoked paprika, cinnamon stick, mustard powder, crushed dried chillies, coriander seeds, garlic, root ginger and some black pepper, to form a spreadable paste. Spread the spice paste all over the pork shoulder, rubbing it in well with your hands. Place the pork in a dish, cover with cling film and leave to marinate in the fridge overnight.

The next day, finish making the pulled pork pies. Preheat the oven to 150°C/Gas Mark 2. Place the marinated pork, fat-side up, on a wire rack positioned over a roasting tin, then pour the apple juice and water into the tin and loosely cover the whole thing with a tent of foil (it's a good idea to rub a little butter on the inside of the foil to prevent it from sticking to the meat). Cook in the oven for about 4½ hours or until cooked and tender.

Meanwhile, prepare the pumpkin mash. Cut the pumpkin in half and remove and discard the seeds. Place the pumpkin halves on a large piece of foil. Season the cut sides with salt and pepper and nutmeg, then sprinkle over the light brown sugar. Divide the butter in half and place one half in the centre of each pumpkin half. Fold the edges of the foil over the top and seal together to make a parcel, then transfer to a baking tray. Roast the pumpkin in the same oven as the pork for the last 50 minutes of the pork's cooking time, or until the pumpkin is soft.

Remove the pumpkin from the oven and let it cool for 5 minutes, then use a spoon to scrape out all the flesh from the skin into a bowl, and mash the flesh well with a fork until smooth (discard the skin). Taste and adjust the seasoning, if necessary, then set aside and keep warm.

Remove the pork from the oven and then increase the oven temperature to 200°C/Gas Mark 6. Remove the foil, then pour the pork's cooking liquid into a bowl and set aside. Transfer the pork to a clean baking tray and return to the oven for about 30 minutes or until the fat has turned golden brown and the meat is succulent, moist and flaky. Remove from the oven and leave the pork to rest for 20 minutes, then, using 2 forks, finely flake the cooked meat into a bowl.

Meanwhile, lightly grease six 10 x 8cm round moulds (each mould about 300ml volume) – I find small pudding basins work best. Roll out the shortcrust pastry on a lightly floured work surface to 3–4mm thickness and cut out six 16cm rounds, then use them to line the prepared moulds. Leave to rest in the fridge for about 30 minutes or until needed.

To finish the pies, combine the pulled pork meat with its reserved cooking liquid and taste and adjust the seasoning, if necessary. Spoon the pork mixture into the pastry-lined moulds, filling each mould about three-quarters full. Spoon the warm mashed pumpkin on top of the pulled pork mixture, dividing it equally between the moulds.

Bake the pies in the oven for 25–30 minutes or until the pastry is cooked through and the pumpkin tops are golden brown. Remove from the oven and let the pies rest in the moulds for 10 minutes, before carefully turning them out on to serving plates (you may need to loosen them around the edges with a butter knife). Serve immediately with buttered new potatoes and teamed seasonal greens.

Cook's Notes
You can replace the pumpkin mash with a buttery potato mash if you prefer.

You could make a single crustless pie, if you prefer. Place the pulled pork mixture in a 30 x 21 x 8cm ovenproof dish, cover the pork mixture with the warm mash of your choice, then bake as directed – you will need to increase the baking time to 35–40 minutes for a single pie.

Roasted Pheasant Breasts with Pickled Mushrooms in Red Wine Vinaigrette

Pheasant is one of my seasonal favourites as it is lean, healthy and plentiful. The individual ingredients in this dish all have quite bold flavours, yet they work in harmony to create something really rather delicious. The pickled mushrooms add acidity to the dish and balance out the sweetness of the griddled leeks and the richness of the roasted pheasant breasts beautifully.

Serves 4 as a main course

For the pickled mushrooms in red wine vinaigrette

5 tablespoons olive oil
100g mixed fresh wild mushrooms, cleaned and sliced
1 clove garlic, crushed
½ teaspoon coriander seeds, lightly crushed
1 teaspoon caster sugar
25ml walnut oil or hazelnut oil
1 teaspoon Dijon mustard
1 tablespoon red wine vinegar (choose Cabernet red wine vinegar, if possible)
1 bay leaf
sea salt and freshly cracked black pepper

For the roasted pheasant breasts

1 tablespoon unsalted butter
4 boneless (skin on) pheasant breasts (90–120g each)
finely grated zest and juice of 1 lemon

For the griddled leeks and the mushroom purée

2 thin leeks, trimmed and washed (140–200g trimmed weight)
1 tablespoon olive oil
1 tablespoon unsalted butter
100g chestnut mushrooms, sliced
50ml dry sherry
50ml double cream
a sprig of fresh thyme, leaves only

150g kale, stalks removed, to serve

First, make the pickled mushrooms. Heat 1 tablespoon of the olive oil in a small saucepan, add the mushrooms, garlic and coriander seeds, then cover and sweat over a medium heat for about 5 minutes or until the mushrooms have wilted, but make sure they don't take on any colour. Remove the pan from the heat and add the remaining pickled mushrooms ingredients, including the rest of the olive oil, mix well and then transfer to a covered container. Set aside at room temperature to allow the flavours to develop, while you prepare the rest of the dish.

For the roasted pheasant breasts, preheat the oven to 200°C/Gas Mark 6. Melt the butter in a non-stick frying pan and once it is foaming, place the pheasant breasts, skin-side down, in the pan and fry over a high heat for 2 minutes. Flip the breasts over and fry for a further 2 minutes or until golden brown. Transfer the pheasant breasts to a roasting tin and roast in the oven for about 8 minutes or until the skin is crispy. Remove from the oven, then sprinkle the lemon zest and juice over the pheasant. Leave the pheasant breasts to rest for 5 minutes, then slice each one just before serving.

Meanwhile, prepare the griddled leeks. Cut the leeks to the length of your serving plates, making the cut at the leaf (top) end rather than at the base. Bring a large saucepan of salted water to a rapid boil over a high heat. Add the whole leeks and cook for 4–5 minutes or until tender, then drain and cut the leeks in half lengthways. Preheat a ridged griddle pan over a high heat until very hot. Season the leeks with salt and pepper and drizzle with the olive oil. Griddle the seasoned leeks for about 1 minute on each side or until grill marks appear, turning once. Remove from the heat and keep warm until you are ready to serve.

In the meantime, make the mushroom purée. Melt the butter in a non-stick frying pan and once it starts to foam, add the chestnut mushrooms and salt and pepper and sauté over a high heat for about 6 minutes or until golden brown. Add the sherry to the pan and let the liquid bubble, stirring and scraping the base of the pan with a wooden spoon to deglaze it, then boil rapidly over a high heat for about 2 minutes or until the liquid becomes syrupy but has not completely evaporated. Stir in the cream and thyme leaves, then bring the mixture to a gentle simmer for 30 seconds. Remove from the heat, carefully transfer the mixture to a blender and blend to form a smooth purée, then return the purée to the pan and reheat gently.

When you are ready to serve, blanch the kale in a pan of boiling salted water for about 1 minute or until tender, then drain. Drain the pickled mushrooms, reserving the red wine vinaigrette.

To serve, spoon the warm mushroom purée on to serving plates. Place a leek half and a portion of kale on to each plate, then place a sliced pheasant breast on top of each leek half. Scatter over the drained pickled mushrooms and serve immediately with a good drizzle of the red wine vinaigrette.

Pheasant Ravioli with Chestnut Sauce

I used to be known as 'the ravioli queen' in one of the London restaurants where I worked. I have small hands so I was nominated to make the ravioli, twice a day, every day! It was a task and a half as the chef was very particular about his ravioli, so I could not risk getting it wrong.

In this recipe, I serve one large raviolo per person – it looks like a plump pillow sitting on your plate and makes the dish pretty and refined. It's the perfect show-off starter. This dish does require a bit of work, but the satisfaction and sense of achievement when you've finished it, make it well worth all the effort.

Serves 6 as a starter or light lunch

For the fresh egg pasta
225g type '00' pasta flour
1 tablespoon olive oil
a pinch of sea salt
2 egg yolks
2 eggs

For the pheasant ravioli
1 oven-ready pheasant (about 500g)
1 tablespoon olive oil
1 clove garlic, crushed
a sprig of fresh thyme, leaves only
1 egg white
60ml double cream
1 tablespoon chopped fresh mixed soft herbs (such as parsley, chives, chervil and tarragon)
1 egg, lightly beaten
200g kale, stalks removed
sea salt and freshly cracked black pepper

For the chestnut sauce
1 tablespoon unsalted butter
1 leek, washed and sliced
1 banana shallot, sliced
1 clove garlic, crushed
150g vacuum-packed whole chestnuts, chopped
100ml dry sherry
300ml chicken stock
150ml double cream

100g Kale Pesto (see page 32), to serve

Start by making the fresh egg pasta dough using a food processor. Some people might find this method unconventional, but provided you don't overwork the dough and you process it in short bursts, the result is just as good as making the dough by hand.

Place the flour, oil and salt into the bowl of a food processor and pulse 2 or 3 times, until the oil and flour are just combined. With the motor running, add the egg yolks one at a time, followed by the whole eggs and blend for about 1 minute or until the dough forms a ball.

Turn the dough on to a lightly floured work surface and knead for about 4 minutes or until the dough becomes silky smooth and elastic. Shape the dough into a ball, then wrap it in cling film and chill in the fridge for 1 hour.

Meanwhile, prepare the pheasant for the pheasant ravioli. Preheat the oven to 180°C/Gas Mark 4. Remove the legs and breasts from the bird using a sharp knife, then remove and discard the skin from the breasts (discard the carcass or use it for making stock at a later date – see page 22 for Roasted Game Stock). Cut the breast meat into 1cm dice and refrigerate until needed. Season the pheasant legs with salt and pepper, then rub them all over with the olive oil, garlic and thyme leaves. Transfer to a roasting tin and roast in the oven for about 25 minutes or until the meat is cooked and flaky and the skin is golden brown. Remove from the oven and leave to rest for 10 minutes, before flaking the meat from the bone. Discard the bones and skin, transfer the meat to a bowl, then cover and chill in the fridge.

While the leg meat is chilling, make the chestnut sauce. Melt the butter in a saucepan and once it starts to foam, sauté the leek, shallot, garlic and chestnuts over a high heat for 6–7 minutes or until golden brown. Add the sherry to the pan and let it bubble, stirring and scraping the base of the pan with a wooden spoon to deglaze it, then boil rapidly over a medium heat for about 2 minutes or until the sherry becomes syrupy but has not completely evaporated. Add the stock, cover and bring to the boil, then reduce the heat to a gentle simmer, remove the lid and simmer for about 12 minutes or until the sauce has thickened slightly. Add the cream, bring the sauce back to a gentle simmer and simmer for 1 minute, then remove from the heat. Transfer the sauce to a blender and blend until smooth. Set the sauce aside while you make the ravioli, then reheat it gently before serving (see Cook's Notes).

To prepare the ravioli filling, place half the diced pheasant breast meat and the egg white in a food processor and blend together until smooth. Add the cream and salt and pepper and pulse until just combined. Do not overwork the mousse as the cream can separate. Transfer the mousse to a mixing bowl and fold in the remaining diced pheasant breast meat, the chopped herbs, the cooled flaked pheasant leg meat and another sprinkling of salt and pepper. Divide the mixture into 6 equal balls, then place on a plate and chill in the fridge for 30 minutes.

Continue making the ravioli. Roll out the rested ravioli dough using a pasta machine. Start with the machine at its thickest setting and pass the dough through the rollers. Repeat this process several times, decreasing the roller setting and dusting the pasta with flour between each pass to prevent it from sticking to the rollers. For ravioli, I take the pasta down to the penultimate setting, about 1.5mm thickness. You should end up with a silky sheet of dough.

Place the dough on a lightly floured work surface. Cut out twelve 10cm rounds. Place a chilled pheasant ball on to 6 of the rounds, brush the edges of the pasta with the beaten egg and place another pasta round over the top of each ball of filling. Dust your hands with flour and then, using your fingers, press down firmly around each ball of filling to push out any trapped air. Pinch the edges of the pasta rounds together to seal the filling inside, to make 6 large ravioli in total.

To cook the ravioli, bring a large pan of salted water to a rapid boil over a high heat. Blanch the kale in the boiling water for 1 minute, then remove with a slotted spoon, drain it well, transfer to a bowl and keep warm. Add the ravioli, all at once, to the pan, then return the water to a rapid boil. Cook for about 6 minutes or until the ravioli float to the surface. Carefully remove the ravioli with a slotted spoon and drain on kitchen paper. While the ravioli are cooking, bring the chestnut sauce back to a gentle simmer.

To serve, divide the warm kale between the serving plates, making a nest on which to sit the ravioli. Place a raviolo on top of each kale nest, spoon the warm chestnut sauce over the ravioli (see Cook's Notes) and serve immediately with the kale pesto spooned alongside.

Cook's Notes

The chestnut sauce can be made in advance, if you like. Make it as directed, then pour the sauce into a bowl and leave to cool. Once cool, cover and refrigerate for up to 3 days. When you are ready to serve, gently reheat the sauce in a saucepan until piping hot.

If you're serving the sauce at a dinner party, or simply want to make it that extra bit special, you can serve it as a foam. Reheat the sauce in a deep saucepan, then use a stick blender to aerate it. I find it aerates best if the sauce is just below boiling point. If the sauce is too thick, it will not foam, so if this is the case, add a dash more double cream to thin it down slightly. I also find adding a small knob of cold unsalted butter does the trick as fatty components help the sauce to aerate. As soon as the sauce is aerated and foamy, serve it immediately.

Matfer 100
Made in France

Left page: top-left: the rolled-out pasta dough; top-right: cutting out the ravioli rounds; bottom-left: pinching the edges of the rounds together to seal in the filling; bottom-right: the finished ravioli, ready for cooking
Right: Pheasant Ravioli with Chestnut Sauce, pages 390–391

Pheasant Forestière

This casserole is one of those homely one-pot wonders that is like a huge hug of comforting warmth. 'Forestière' translates as 'foods from the forest' and the combination of wild mushrooms and pheasant are a reminder of the two living alongside each other in the wild. Serve with creamy mashed potatoes or boiled brown rice.

Serves 2 as a main course

1 oven-ready pheasant (about 500g)
2 rashers smoked streaky bacon
2 tablespoons unsalted butter
150g small round onions or shallots, peeled
150g mixed fresh wild mushrooms and field mushrooms, cleaned and sliced
150g celery, diced
1 clove garlic, crushed
100ml dry sherry or dry white wine
50ml brandy or Cognac
250ml chicken stock
100ml double cream
1 teaspoon chopped fresh thyme leaves
sea salt and freshly cracked black pepper

Preheat the oven to 180°C/Gas Mark 4. Remove the legs and breasts from the pheasant, then remove and discard the skin from the breasts (discard the carcass or use it for making stock at a later date – see page 22 for Roasted Game Stock). Wrap a rasher of bacon around each pheasant breast. Season the pheasant legs with salt and pepper.

Melt half of the butter in a large casserole and once the butter starts to foam, add the pheasant legs and breasts and cook over a high heat for about 3 minutes on each side or until golden brown all over. Remove the legs and breasts to a plate.

Return the casserole to a medium heat, add the remaining butter and once it starts to foam, add the onions, mushrooms, celery and garlic and sauté for about 8 minutes or until golden. Pour the sherry and brandy into the pan and let the liquid bubble, stirring and scraping the base of the casserole with a wooden spoon to deglaze it, then cook over a medium heat for about 2 minutes or until the liquid has thickened slightly. Return the browned meat to the casserole, then add the stock and bring to a gentle simmer. Place a piece of non-stick baking paper directly on to the surface of the stock and cover with the lid. Transfer the casserole to the oven and cook for about 35 minutes or until the pheasant is cooked and tender.

Remove from the oven and carefully remove the pheasant breasts and legs from the stock, then set them aside and keep warm, while you finish the sauce. Place the casserole over a medium heat, add the cream and bring the sauce to a gentle simmer, then simmer for 5 minutes. Stir in the thyme, then taste and adjust the seasoning, if necessary.

Serve 1 pheasant leg and 1 pheasant breast per portion with plenty of sauce. Serve immediately with mashed potatoes or boiled brown rice and steamed seasonal greens.

Cook's Note

If you like the sound of this dish but aren't able to buy a pheasant or are not keen on its gamey flavour, you can substitute it for partridge, chicken or even rabbit – the cooking times will be the same.

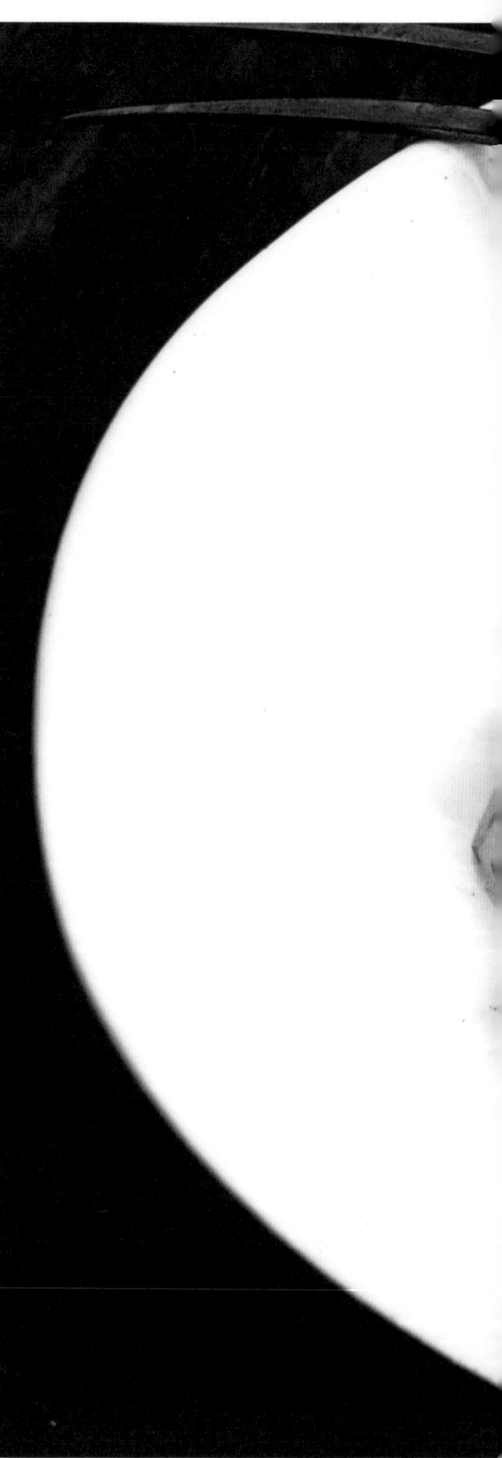

Turnip, Bacon and Cider Gratin

The humble turnip is a widely underused vegetable in the UK, but with a bit of thought and a few choice ingredients to accompany it, the turnip can be transformed into an interesting and delicious meal. This tasty gratin makes a wonderful side dish to accompany roast chicken or pork, but it is fairly rich so serve it in modest portion sizes.

Serves 4 as a side dish

6 rashers smoked streaky bacon
1 tablespoon unsalted butter
2 banana shallots, finely sliced
200ml apple cider
1 tablespoon grated fresh horseradish (or substitute ready-grated horseradish from a jar or creamed horseradish, if you like)
1 tablespoon wholegrain mustard
400ml white chicken stock or vegetable stock
200ml double cream
1kg turnips, peeled
2 tablespoons grated mature Cheddar cheese (I like to use a strong Cheddar like Montgomery or Keen's, but perhaps choose one locally produced in your region)
2 tablespoons coarse fresh breadcrumbs
1 teaspoon finely chopped fresh flat-leaf parsley
sea salt and freshly cracked black pepper

Preheat the oven to 180°C/Gas Mark 4. Cut 2 of the bacon rashers into thin strips and set aside. Heat a large, non-stick frying pan until hot, then add the remaining 4 whole bacon rashers to the pan and cook over a high heat for 2–3 minutes on each side or until golden. Remove from the heat and set aside to drain on kitchen paper.

In the same pan, melt the butter and once it starts to foam, sauté the bacon strips and shallots over a high heat for 7–8 minutes or until golden brown. Pour the cider into the pan and let it bubble, stirring and scraping the base of the pan with a wooden spoon to deglaze it. Cook over a medium heat for 1 minute, then add the horseradish, mustard and stock. Bring to the boil, then reduce the heat and simmer for 8–10 minutes or until the stock has reduced by half. Stir in the cream, then bring the mixture to a gentle simmer and simmer gently for 2 minutes. Remove from the heat and add salt and pepper to taste.

Slice the turnips into 2–3mm-thick slices (preferably using a mandolin) and place in a large mixing bowl. Add the cream sauce and mix well. Transfer the mixture to a shallow, ovenproof dish and sprinkle over the grated cheese. Bake in the oven for about 25 minutes or until the turnips are cooked and tender.

Remove the dish from the oven, lay the cooked bacon rashers on top of the cheese and then sprinkle over the breadcrumbs and parsley. Return the gratin to the oven for a further 5 minutes or so, until the breadcrumbs are golden brown and crisp and the liquid is bubbling. Serve immediately.

Pear Parfait with Liquorice Jelly and Spice-poached Pears

This is a very grown-up dessert. Liquorice is not to everyone's taste, yet the combination of pears and liquorice works very well and might convince even the most ardent of liquorice haters to rethink. I certainly hope so! I like the grainy texture of pears, and in this recipe the graininess of the poached pears provides an interesting contrast to the silky smooth sorbet and parfait and the firm, quivering jelly. The whole dish is an exciting mouthful of different sensations.

It's not easy to make parfait in small quantities, so this quantity of parfait is enough to serve 12. You can keep the parfait in the freezer and serve it at a later date (see Cook's Notes) – a lifesaver when you need a dessert in a hurry. The parfait sits on a delicate sponge base. Don't worry if the sponge looks very thin – it's supposed to be. The sponge is really just providing a firm base on which you then sit the parfait.

You will need to start this recipe at least 1 day before you want to serve it, to allow the different components time to set. However, it might be easier to start preparing the components a few days in advance and then you are ready to just serve the dessert when needed.

Serves 12

For the pear parfait
800g ripe pears, peeled, cored and finely sliced
350g caster sugar
225ml cold water
2 eggs
40g plain flour, sifted
6 egg yolks
500ml double cream
2 tablespoons pear liqueur, such as Poire William eau de vie

For the liquorice and pear sorbet
160ml cold water
160g caster sugar
2 tablespoons liquid glucose
juice of 1 lemon
500ml chilled pear purée from the Pear Parfait (see above)
40ml liquorice essence (see Cook's Notes)

For the liquorice jelly
2 leaves of gelatine
65g caster sugar
200ml cold water
40ml liquorice essence (see Cook's Notes)
½ teaspoon agar agar powder (see page 16)

For the spice-poached pears
500g caster sugar
500ml cold water
2 liquorice roots, lightly crushed (see Cook's Notes)
1 cinnamon stick
2 star anise
finely grated zest and juice of 2 lemons
6 firm ripe pears, peeled, halved and cored

Start by making a pear purée for the pear parfait (and the pear sorbet). Combine the pears, 175g of the caster sugar and 200ml of the water in a large saucepan and bring to the boil. Cook the pears over a medium heat for 8–10 minutes, stirring occasionally, until the pears are soft and almost forming a purée. Remove from the heat, carefully transfer the mixture to a blender and blend until smooth, then transfer the purée to a bowl. Leave to cool, then cover and chill in the fridge.

Next, prepare the sponge for the base of the pear parfait. Preheat the oven to 180°C/Gas Mark 4 and grease, then line a large baking tray (about 36 x 28cm in size) with non-stick baking paper. Set aside. Put the eggs and 50g of the remaining sugar into the bowl of an electric stand mixer and whisk together until pale, thick and creamy – when you lift the whisk it should leave a visible trail on the surface (this is called the thick ribbon stage or sabayon). Gently fold in the flour using a large metal spoon until well incorporated.

Using a palette knife, spread the sponge mixture to about 2mm thickness on the prepared baking tray. Bake in the oven for 5–6 minutes or until the sponge is pale golden but not crisp. Remove from the oven and transfer to a wire rack to cool (leaving the sponge on the paper). Place a rectangular metal frame (28 x 18 x 4cm in size) on top of the sponge and press it down, cutting the sponge to size (see Cook's Notes). Discard the excess sponge, then place the sponge-filled metal frame with the baking paper beneath it on a clean baking tray and chill in the fridge.

Set aside 500ml of the chilled pear purée for the liquorice and pear sorbet and keep it chilled in the fridge, then keep the rest for the pear parfait.

Next, finish the pear parfait. Half-fill a saucepan with water and bring up to a gentle simmer. Choose a heatproof mixing bowl that will sit comfortably over the saucepan without slipping down inside the pan (you also want to make sure that the bottom of the bowl does not come into contact with the simmering water underneath). Put the egg yolks, the remaining 125g sugar and the remaining 25ml water into the bowl and place the bowl over the pan of simmering water. Using a balloon whisk or an electric hand-held whisk, whisk the ingredients together until

(continued on page 399)

(continued from page 397)

pale, thick and doubled in volume – when you lift the whisk it should leave a visible trail on the surface (again, this is called the thick ribbon stage or sabayon). Remove from the heat, remove the bowl from the pan and set aside to cool slightly.

Put the remaining chilled pear purée (you should have about 200ml) in a clean bowl. Add the cream and pear liqueur and whisk together until the mixture forms soft peaks. Fold the cream into the sabayon until well combined and then immediately pour the parfait mixture evenly into the metal frame over the chilled sponge base. Freeze for about 12 hours or until completely set.

Meanwhile, make the liquorice and pear sorbet. Put the water, sugar, glucose and lemon juice into a small saucepan and bring to a simmer over a medium heat, stirring until the sugar has dissolved, then simmer for 5 minutes. Remove from the heat. Stir the reserved 500ml chilled pear purée into the hot syrup, along with the liquorice essence. Transfer the mixture to a bowl and leave to cool, then cover and chill in the fridge for about 30 minutes. Pour the chilled mixture into an ice-cream maker and churn until frozen (following the manufacturer's instructions). Alternatively, pour the chilled mixture into a shallow, freezer proof container, cover with a lid and freeze until firm, whisking the mixture 3 or 4 times during freezing (every hour or so) to break down the ice crystals and ensure an even-textured result.

Allow the sorbet to soften slightly at room temperature or in the fridge before serving (see Cook's Notes).

Next, make the liquorice jelly. Soak the gelatine in cold water until it has softened. Put the sugar, water, liquorice essence and agar agar powder into a small saucepan and bring to the boil over a medium heat, stirring. Boil for 2 minutes, then remove from the heat. Squeeze the gelatine gently to remove excess water, then add the gelatine to the hot liquid and stir until dissolved. Pour the hot liquid into a small sturdy white plastic tray, about 21 x 14 x 1.5cm in size, (or use a shallow ceramic dish of the same size) and leave to set completely at room temperature (don't move the tray again until the mixture is set) – this will take about 2 hours. Once the jelly has set and is cold, cover with a lid (or with something that covers it but doesn't touch the surface, such as a tray – don't use cling film as this will stick to the surface) and refrigerate (see Cook's Notes).

Prepare the spice-poached pears. Place the sugar, water, liquorice roots, cinnamon stick, star anise and lemon zest and juice in a large saucepan. Bring the mixture to the boil over a medium heat, stirring until the sugar has dissolved, then lower the heat and simmer for about 10 minutes or until the mixture is slightly reduced and syrupy. Add the pears to the hot syrup, then place a cartouche (a circle of greaseproof paper) on the surface of the syrup and place a small plate on top to weigh the pears down, then cover the pan with a lid. Poach the pears over a low heat for 15–18 minutes or until tender. Remove from the heat and leave the pears to cool in the syrup. Once cool, transfer the pears and syrup to a bowl, then cover and refrigerate until needed (see Cook's Notes). Remove and discard the whole spices before serving. Place serving plates in the fridge to chill before serving.

To serve, cut the jelly into 5mm squares. Remove the metal frame from the parfait by using a blowtorch to slightly warm the frame to release it (see Cook's Notes), then carefully lift it off. Using a sharp knife dipped in hot water, cut the parfait into slices and place a slice on each serving plate, along with half a poached pear and a small scoop of the sorbet. Decorate the plates with squares of liquorice jelly and serve immediately.

Cook's Notes

Transfer any leftover parfait to a freezer proof container, then cover and store in the freezer for up to 2 weeks. Any leftover liquorice and pear sorbet can be transferred to a freezer proof container, then cover and store in the freezer for up to 2 weeks. And any leftover liquorice jelly can be stored in an airtight container in the fridge and used within 3 days.

Liquorice essence and liquorice roots are available from many health food shops or on-line.

I use a metal frame rather than a conventional baking tin because it's easier to turn the parfait out and the cut portions are neater. If you don't have a frame or don't want to buy one, then you can use a similar-sized baking tin lined with non-stick baking paper instead.

The poached pears and syrup can be stored in an airtight container in the fridge for up to 3 days. You can reheat them gently or simply serve them chilled with ice cream, cream or custard, and any leftover liquorice and pear sorbet.

If you don't have a blowtorch, use a sharp knife dipped in boiling water to remove the parfait from the metal frame. Carefully insert the knife between the edge of the metal frame and the parfait to 'melt' the parfait slightly and thus release it from the frame, then carefully lift off the frame.

Bitter Chocolate and Chestnut Truffle Cake with Candied Chestnuts

I use a combination of freshly roasted chestnuts and chestnut purée for this delicious truffle cake. It's rich, sweet and ever so naughty, but definitely worth every mouthful! The inspiration for this recipe came from years of living in London. Walking along Oxford Street in November and December in the cold and damp, there was always a strong smell of roasted chestnuts combined with candied peanuts, which the street vendors used to sell. Whether I was hungry or not, I had a desire to eat them. Now, when I collect chestnuts in the forest on a chilly day, the memory of the sweet smell of roasted and candied nuts often returns. This recipe is created from those memories.

Using the best chocolate you can find is essential to ensuring the deepest, richest flavour. I recommend using a chocolate with 70% cocoa solids for the best results, as the contrast between its bitterness and the natural sweetness of the chestnuts works beautifully.

Serves 10–12

For the bitter chocolate and chestnut cake base

100ml dark rum
125g Roasted Chestnuts (see page 372), peeled and roughly chopped
5 eggs, separated
100g caster sugar
225g dark bitter chocolate (70% cocoa solids), broken into pieces
125g unsalted butter, diced
50g ground almonds

For the bitter chocolate and chestnut mousse

2 leaves of gelatine
2 tablespoons cold water
225g dark bitter chocolate (70% cocoa solids), broken into pieces
175g unsweetened chestnut purée
4 eggs, separated
60ml dark rum
50g caster sugar
200ml double cream

For the candied chestnuts

250g Roasted Chestnuts (see page 372), peeled
1 tablespoon unsalted butter
200g caster sugar

For the chocolate glaze

2 leaves of gelatine
110g caster sugar
100ml cold water
100ml double cream
40g cocoa powder

First, prepare the cake base. Preheat the oven to 180°C/Gas Mark 4 and grease, then line a 28 x 18 x 4cm baking tin with non-stick baking paper. Set aside. Place the rum and chestnuts in a small saucepan and bring to the boil over a medium heat, then simmer for about 1 minute – just long enough to warm the nuts and help them to absorb the rum flavour. Remove from the heat and set aside for 10 minutes.

Put the egg whites into a bowl and whisk until foaming, then add the sugar and whisk together until the mixture forms soft peaks. Set aside.

Half-fill a saucepan with water and bring up to a gentle simmer. Choose a heatproof mixing bowl that will sit comfortably over the saucepan without slipping down inside the pan, and place the bowl over the pan (you also want to make sure that the bottom of the bowl does not come into contact with the simmering water underneath). Put the chocolate and butter into the bowl and stir gently until melted and combined. Remove from the heat and remove the bowl from the pan, then stir in the soaked chestnuts and rum and the egg yolks. Using a large metal spoon, fold in the ground almonds and meringue.

Spoon the cake mixture into the prepared baking tin and level the surface. Bake in the oven for 18–20 minutes or until well risen but still soft and a skewer inserted into the centre of the cake comes out clean. Remove from the oven to a wire rack and leave the cake to cool completely in the tin. The cake will sink slightly, so use the back of a spoon to gently flatten it and even it out. Once cool, refrigerate the cake base (leaving it in the tin), while you make the mousse.

To prepare the bitter chocolate and chestnut mousse, soak the gelatine in cold water until it has softened. Squeeze the gelatine gently to remove excess water, then place the gelatine in a small heatproof bowl with the measured cold water. Place the bowl over a small pan of simmering water and stir the gelatine until it has dissolved, then remove from the heat. Meanwhile, melt the chocolate in a separate heatproof mixing bowl set over a pan of simmering water (as above). While the chocolate is melting, place the chestnut purée, egg yolks and rum in another mixing bowl and use a wooden spoon to combine. Add the dissolved gelatine and melted chocolate to the chestnut purée mixture and stir to mix.

In a separate bowl, whisk the egg whites until foaming, then add the sugar and whisk together until the mixture forms soft peaks. Whip the cream in another bowl until it forms soft peaks. Fold the meringue and whipped cream into the chocolate mixture using a metal spoon, until well combined, then spoon the mousse evenly over the chilled cake base in the tin and level the surface. Refrigerate for about 6 hours or until completely set, before glazing.

Meanwhile, make the candied chestnuts. Line a baking tray with non-stick baking paper and set aside. Cut the chestnuts into quarters. Melt the butter in a non-stick saucepan and once it starts to foam, add the sugar and chestnuts and heat gently, stirring to dissolve the sugar. Increase the heat and boil the mixture until it turns a golden brown caramel colour and is thick and sticky, stirring regularly (stirring will encourage crystallisation and a fudge-like texture). Pour the candied crystallised chestnuts on to the prepared baking tray. Leave to set and cool completely at room temperature, then break the candied chestnuts into smaller pieces and store in an airtight container until needed (see Cook's Notes).

Make the chocolate glaze. Soak the gelatine in cold water until it has softened. Place the sugar, water and cream in a small saucepan and heat gently, stirring to dissolve the sugar, then bring to the boil over a high heat and boil rapidly for 2 minutes. Stir in the cocoa powder and boil over a high heat for a further 1 minute. Remove from the heat and set aside to cool at room temperature, until the glaze is considerably thickened and nearly set, then pour it evenly over the set mousse. Return the cake to the fridge for about 30 minutes to allow the glaze to set completely.

To serve, cut the cake into slices using a warm, sharp knife, then carefully remove from the tin. Place a slice on to each serving plate and decorate with the candied chestnuts. Serve immediately with cream or crème fraîche.

Cook's Notes

The candied chestnuts can be made up to 3 days in advance. Store them in an airtight container in a cool, dry cupboard.

Any leftover truffle cake can be stored in an airtight container in the fridge for up to 3 days.

The British Larder | *December*

December is the month for celebrating with family and friends and eating well. From a seasonal point of view, December is the bearer of rich, sumptuous foods, which in turn inspires lavish meals made from luxurious ingredients.

Turkey and goose supplies are starting to flow and fresh cranberries are plentiful. And although there's still plenty of game in season, grouse and wild rabbit are coming to an end for another year.

Brussels sprouts are reaching their peak and root vegetables such as turnips, parsnips, swede and celeriac are tasting sweeter after the recent frosts. Exotic fruits, such as pomegranates and medjool dates, are used in our festive meals as our home grown fruits become limited. However, remember that you can still dig into your store cupboard for the goodies that were squirrelled away during the seasonal gluts.

From the oceans, scallops, oysters, sea bass and turbot add to the lavishness of what December has to offer.

Season's best during December...

Apples, Beetroot, Brill, Brussels Sprouts, Cabbages, Cauliflower, Celeriac, Celery, Chestnuts, Chickweed, Chicory, Clams, Clementines, Cod, Coley, Crab Apples, Cranberries, Duck, Flounder, Golden Plover, Goose, Grouse, Guinea Fowl, Haddock, Hake, Halibut, Hare, Hazelnuts, Horseradish, Jerusalem Artichokes, John Dory, Kale, Langoustines, Leeks, Lemon Sole, Mallard, Medjool Dates, Monkfish, Mussels, Oysters, Parsnips, Partridge, Passion Fruit, Pears, Pheasant, Pineapple, Plaice, Pollack, Pomegranates, Potatoes (main crop), Pumpkin, Rabbit, Salsify, Scallops, Sea Bass, Shallots, Skate, Swede, Teal, Truffles (black and white), Turbot, Turkey, Turnips, Venison, Walnuts, Widgeon, Winkles, Woodcock, Woodpigeon.

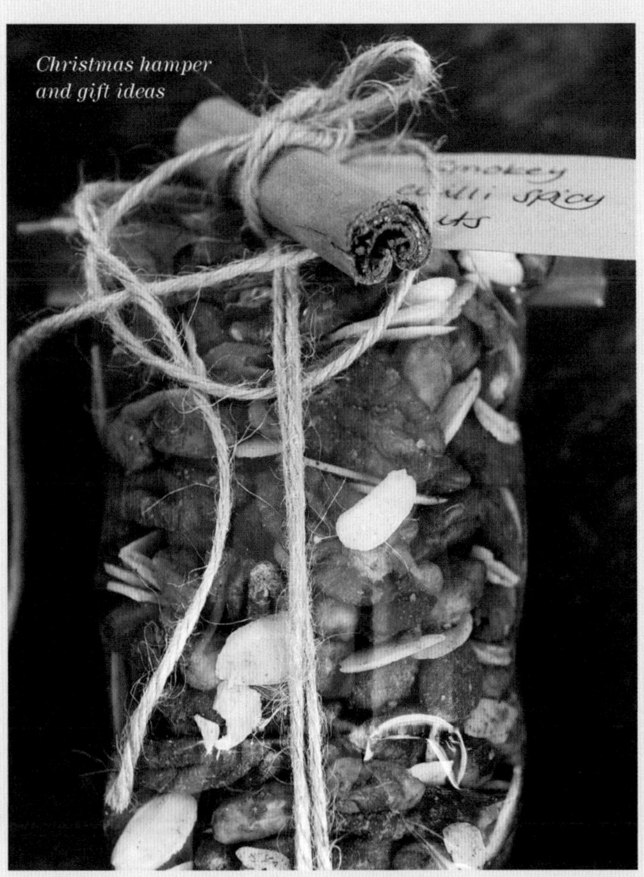

Christmas hamper and gift ideas

My culinary rituals for December...

The end of the year and time to celebrate everything that has been achieved over the past twelve months. There's that feeling of winding down and of all the festive celebrations beginning. Hopefully my recipes might inspire confidence in you to organise your own gathering or two. **My Rustic Game Terrine** (see page 420) is a perfect party piece. It's not only spectacular, it's also perfect for sharing, and as it can be prepared in advance, it's ready for serving when your guests arrive.

I've developed this month's recipes so that they can be adapted to serve larger numbers and many of them can also be prepared or partly prepared in advance. Try my delicious recipe for **Roasted Goose with Goose and Cranberry Faggots and Brussels Sprouts Purée** (see page 418). It's a show-stopping dish, but it's pretty hassle-free for you as so much of it can be prepared a day or two in advance.

Christmas is on my mind throughout December. The endless planning and preparations are dominating my thoughts. Making edible homemade gifts, such as jars of my **Luxury Sweet Mincemeat** (see page 432), or my very tempting **Medjool Date and Rum Bonbons** (see page 413), or the luxurious **Chocolate and Cranberry Salami** (see page 434) are high on my agenda too. I love making homemade gifts and I'm the self-confessed hamper queen! I love that sense of achievement when creating something special like a hamper; taking the time to plan it, collect the ingredients, make it and pack it with tender loving care. Seeing the look on the recipient's face is a very special moment and I hope that you might give edible gifts a try.

I'd made my **Luxury Sweet Mincemeat** (see page 432) in October, but now is the time to use it, turning it into wonderful festive offerings for party food and gifts. Make my tasty **Luxury Bite-size Mince Pies** (see page 433), or for something a little different, try my **Festive Power Bars** (see page 435). And if you haven't yet made your Christmas pudding, all is not lost – be quick and make it now. Ideally, the longer it's left the better it will taste, but if you make **My Utimate Christmas Pudding** (see page 436) at the start of this month, you've still got time to feed it several times with brandy before Christmas Day and it will still taste delicious. Just remember to feed it generously!

Finally, of course, there is Christmas Day itself to prepare for. Pre-order your turkey now and plan what trimmings you're going to make – for me, the Christmas Day meal is all about the trimmings! I've given you lots of ideas to start you off, including **My Best Ever Roast Potatoes** (see page 430) and **Suffolk Warriors in Blankets** (see page 431). Not everyone is a fan of Brussels sprouts, so to try and encourage those who don't get as excited about them as I do, try my recipe for **Orange and Honey Caramelised Sprouts** (see page 408) and see if I can convert you into a sprout eater!

Homemade cranberry sauce tastes so much better than bought, and making it provides another opportunity to take time and care over something special, so I urge you to try my luxurious **Cranberry and Port Sauce** (see page 410). It's also the perfect accompaniment to several of my other recipes this month.

As the dust settles after Christmas Day, and you realise you've got enough food to feed a small army, be inspired to use up your leftovers with my tasty recipe for **Jersey Royal New Potato and Pig Hash** (see page 139); it makes the perfect Boxing Day brunch. Simply substitute the Jersey Royal new potatoes for leftover roast potatoes, add a few shredded Brussels sprouts and flake in any leftover turkey and ham meat instead of the pork. Delicious!

British Larder Heroes

British game season

There is a certain natural beauty and treasured national tradition about taking game from the wild. As a chef, I automatically tend to think of the wonderful products we enjoy as a result of game shooting, but it is primarily a sport and the food that is generated from it is actually a 'by-product' of the activity. Despite the controversy that often surrounds killing wild animals, game shooting is an acceptable sport that also has environmental and economical benefits in helping to sustain rural economies. As with any sport, however, there are rules that govern its practice and these rules need to be observed to ensure that we, as consumers of game, can continue to enjoy it in the years to come. Like all natural ingredients, most game animals need a time of year when they are left alone to reproduce, so a system has evolved – the game season – which defines exactly when you are allowed to shoot certain animals. The 'open' season refers to the period during which you are allowed to shoot game, and the 'closed' season refers to the period during which you are not. These seasons apply throughout the British Isles but may differ between countries, so you will need to check the local guidelines before you shoot anything that might have a closed season. A few species, such as rabbits and woodpigeons, do not have a closed season, as they are plentiful, so they are available all year round. However, most wild game does have a closed season and it therefore can, and should, only be bought in season unless it is frozen. Farmed game, on the other hand, is not subject to the seasons and can often be bought all year round. At the British Larder, we only buy game from reputable suppliers where we can be sure of its provenance and how the animal was killed, and I would urge you to do the same. You can buy game with its fur or feathers, in which case you'll have to skin or pluck the meat yourself, or as oven-ready game. If you buy oven-ready game, look for moist cuts with fresh-smelling meat; also make sure the skin is not dried out. To counteract the toughness of the meat, game is 'hung' after shooting to help tenderise it and encourage the flavours to develop. The longer the meat is hung, the stronger and richer its flavour. Some people prefer their game well hung (for long periods) but we prefer not to hang our game and so keep the flavour milder. Game is something that many people are wary of eating – for many reasons, but often because of the strong flavour – so we like to introduce people to it gently and encourage them to eat this lean, tasty and healthy source of natural protein.

British turkey

Although it's not on everyone's menu, turkey is associated with this time of the year as the quintessential centrepiece for the Christmas feast. Indeed, if the birds are reared following traditional farming methods, turkey should only be eaten from November until the end of January, when the birds are at their most plump. Sadly, intensive turkey farming has become common, so the value of this delicacy has decreased and cut-price turkey is regularly available all year round. As with all poultry, sourcing and traceability are vital to ensure that your turkey has had a humane life and also to guarantee you a better quality of meat. The type of feed the birds were raised on, how much access they had to the outdoors and the age at which they were slaughtered, all have a huge bearing on the flavour and quality of the meat, so it's really important to investigate the provenance of your turkey. At the British Larder we always buy free-range or organic turkey. Turkey farming took shape and became established during the 17th century in East Anglia and some of the most prized breeds are originally from this part of the world, including the Norfolk Black, Norfolk Bronze and Cambridge Bronze. These are still some of the most popular breeds today, and along with Kelly Bronze, are seen as the superior breeds for the festive meal because of the careful way they are reared. Black turkeys are generally not as plump as bronze (white) varieties, so they have less fat on them and a stronger, gamier flavour. Although they were the strain of turkey that was first raised in Britain, black turkeys went out of favour for a while because their black feathers, and the marks these left once the birds had been plucked, were considered unsightly. Yet in the 16th century, the Norfolk Black was the luxury breed enjoyed by Henry VIII. If you like a slightly stronger flavour to your turkey, then it's really worth trying one of these birds.

For the perfect Christmas turkey
For the traditionalists among us that still value the turkey as the main event at our celebratory meal, these tips will ensure you and your family have a stress-free Christmas and a deliciously moist, perfectly cooked bird.

* Order your turkey as early as possible to ensure you get the size and breed you're after. Know the dimensions of your oven, so that you can make sure the turkey will actually fit in it before you order it. As a rough guide, a 3kg turkey will serve 6 people and a 6kg turkey will serve 12 people.
* Check that you've cleared enough space in the fridge so that your turkey will fit into it and collect the bird as close to the day as possible. Turkey will keep for up to 3 days in the fridge.
* If your turkey is frozen, then defrost it at least 3 days in advance in the fridge. The bigger the bird, the longer it will take to defrost – it won't cook properly unless it is thoroughly defrosted.
* Request to keep the giblets (heart, liver and kidneys) as they make wonderful gravy. They need to be removed from the cavity of the turkey and stored separately in a covered container in the fridge.
* The turkey needs to be at room temperature before it goes in the oven, so make sure you take it out of the fridge at least 2 hours before you need to start cooking it.
* Calculate the cooking time for your bird (if you are stuffing the bird, remember to weigh it once it has been stuffed). Calculate the cooking time, allowing 25–30 minutes per kilogram of raw weight. Roast the turkey in the oven at 220°C/Gas Mark 7 for 30 minutes, then reduce the oven temperature to 180°C/Gas Mark 4 and roast the turkey for the calculated time or until it is thoroughly cooked.
* To test if your turkey is cooked, push a long metal skewer into a thick fleshy part until it touches the bone, leave it there for 30–60 seconds, then remove the skewer and if the skewer is hot and the juices run clear, the turkey is cooked. If not, put the turkey back in the oven and cook for another 20 minutes, then test again.
* Once the turkey is cooked, remove it from the oven, then cover it loosely with foil and leave the bird to rest for 20 minutes before serving.

Brussels sprouts

Love them or loathe them, even just a token Brussels sprout is a must on every festive plate! Brussels sprouts are a member of the Brassicaceae family. They grow on a thick vertical stalk and when they are ready to harvest, they are plump and bright green. Brussels sprouts look like miniature

Brussels sprouts

cabbages and have a sweet, nutty flavour. If possible, buy sprouts that are still attached to the stalk as these are fresher and will taste the best, then trim off any loose or damaged leaves. Look for small, firm sprouts that have tightly wrapped leaves and avoid any with yellowing leaves. There is much debate over whether you should cut a cross in the bottom of sprouts before cooking them. Some people think it makes them cook more evenly, but personally I think this is an old wives' tale. If you think it makes a difference, then please don't let me stand in the way of tradition. Brussels sprouts are usually boiled or steamed, but they can also be braised or used in stir-fries.

These **Orange and Honey Caramelised Sprouts** are delicious served on Christmas Day with a roast turkey or goose. Cook 400g (prepared weight) trimmed and halved Brussels sprouts in a pan of boiling salted water for about 3 minutes or until just tender. Transfer to a colander using a slotted spoon, then shake to remove as much water as possible. While the sprouts are cooking, melt 1 tablespoon goose fat in a large, non-stick frying pan, then add 100g diced smoked streaky bacon rashers and 1 cinnamon stick and sauté over a high heat for 3–4 minutes or until the bacon turns golden. Add the drained sprouts, along with 1 tablespoon clear honey, 50g roughly chopped hazelnuts (or fresh shelled sweet chestnuts) and some sea salt and freshly cracked black pepper. Sauté for a further 1 minute to heat the sprouts all the way through, then reduce the heat to medium, add the finely grated zest and juice of 1 orange and cook for 10 seconds. Transfer to a serving dish (discard the cinnamon stick) and serve immediately. Serves 4 as an accompaniment. You can cook the sprouts a day in advance, then drain, cool and keep them in an airtight container in the fridge. As the turkey is about to be carved, sauté the sprouts with the rest of the ingredients, as directed above, until hot, then serve. Cooking them in advance makes life a lot easier and less stressful and there is no difference in the taste – trust me!

For another tasty accompaniment and an alternative way to serve Brussels Sprouts, try my recipe for **Creamed Brussels Sprouts with Bacon**. Melt 1 tablespoon unsalted butter in a large, non-stick frying pan and once it starts to foam, add 100g diced smoked back bacon rashers and sauté over a medium heat for about 8 minutes or until golden brown. Add 300g (prepared weight) trimmed and shredded Brussels sprouts and season very lightly with sea salt and freshly cracked pepper. Sauté over a medium-high heat for about 8 minutes or until they start to take on some colour. Add 50ml dry white wine to the pan and let it bubble, stirring and scraping the base of the pan to deglaze it, then boil over a high heat for 1–2 minutes or until the wine becomes syrupy and coats the Brussels sprouts. Add 100ml double cream and bring to the boil over a medium heat, then simmer for 3–5 minutes or until the cream is reduced and thickened, stirring occasionally. Finally, add a few gratings of fresh nutmeg and then serve immediately. Serves 4 as an accompaniment. Serve with **Roasted Guinea Fowl Breasts with Cep and Herb Butter** (see page 415), or serve with roasted pheasant or grouse.

Celeriac

Celeriac is the large, swollen globular root of a wild form of the celery plant. It has a knobbly exterior with a thick skin and a smooth, pale creamy-white flesh, and, as one might expect, its flavour is similar to celery but it is milder, sweeter and has a distinctive nutty taste with an aniseed undertone. Like parsnips and swede, celeriac relies on the frost to develop its sweetness. The skin is very thick and coarse and can be quite tough to remove, so you may need to cut it away

Celeriac Soup with Steamed Prawns

with a sharp knife rather than simply using a peeler. Celeriac is a versatile vegetable and it can be roasted, steamed or boiled then mashed. It can also be eaten raw (grated or thinly sliced), such as in the classic French dish, celeriac remoulade. Celeriac is also ideal for adding to soups, stews and casseroles.

For an elegant starter over the festive period, try this tasty **Celeriac Soup with Steamed Prawns**. Melt 1 tablespoon unsalted butter in a large saucepan, add 400g (prepared weight) peeled and diced celeriac and some sea salt and freshly cracked black pepper, then cover and sweat over a medium heat for 8–10 minutes or until softened, stirring occasionally to prevent the celeriac taking on too much colour. Add 200ml dry white wine or dry vermouth to the pan and let it bubble, stirring and scraping the base of the pan with a wooden spoon to deglaze it. Boil rapidly over a high heat for about 5 minutes or until the liquid has reduced by half, then add 700ml white chicken stock and bring to a gentle simmer. Replace the lid and simmer gently for about 15 minutes or until the celeriac begins to soften and break up. Add 100ml double cream and bring back to the boil for 1 minute, then remove from the heat. Carefully transfer the soup to a blender and blend until smooth. Taste and adjust the seasoning, if necessary, then return the soup to the pan and reheat gently until hot. In the meantime, mix 12 peeled and deveined raw tiger prawns with 1 teaspoon rapeseed oil, a pinch of ras el hanout and salt and pepper. Place a steaming basket over a saucepan of rapidly boiling water and steam the prawns for about 2 minutes or until they are cooked and have turned pink. Serve the hot soup in bowls and then float 3 steamed prawns in each portion of soup. Serves 4 as a starter or light lunch.

Cranberries

Cranberries are hard, shiny, bright red berries (related to the blueberry and bilberry) that are predominantly grown in northern Europe and North America and imported into the UK. The shrubs are traditionally harvested by flooding the plains with water; the harvesters then go past and scoop up the ripe fruits that float to the surface. Even though cranberries are imported, they are a traditional accompaniment to roast turkey. They have a sour, tangy flavour, so even in savoury

Celeriac

Cranberries

Cranberry and Port Sauce

dishes they need to be sweetened. Because of their high pectin content, they are good for making preserves such as cranberry jelly, and they are also made into cranberry sauce or added to desserts such as pies, tarts, cakes and bakes. Dried cranberries are also readily available (and are often sweetened) and these are good to use in cakes and bakes, muesli and stuffings for poultry and meat.

I don't think a shop-bought version will ever taste as good as a homemade one, so I'd urge you to make your own cranberry sauce to serve over the Christmas period. Try my delicious recipe for **Cranberry and Port Sauce**. Put 225g fresh cranberries, 1 finely diced onion, 1 minced clove garlic, 50g peeled and minced fresh root ginger, 250g caster sugar, 100ml red wine vinegar, 100ml port, the finely grated zest and juice of 1 orange, 4 cloves, 1 cinnamon stick and sea salt and freshly cracked black pepper into a saucepan (choose a pan with a wide base, if you can). Bring the mixture to a gentle simmer over a medium heat, stirring to dissolve the sugar, then reduce the heat to low and simmer for about 20 minutes or until the sauce is reduced to a thick consistency (the cranberry sauce will continue to thicken as it cools), stirring occasionally. Remove from the heat and leave to cool for 10 minutes, then pour the sauce into a hot, sterilised jar. Cover with a wax disc (wax-side down) and seal. Once cold, label and store in a cool, dry cupboard. Store for at least a couple of days or so before using to allow the flavours to mingle and mature, but leave it for a couple of weeks before opening, if you can. The unopened jar of sauce should keep well for up to 3 months. Once opened, store in the fridge and use within 1 month. Makes 1 x 250g jar (serves 8–12). Discard the whole spices when serving. Alternatively, the cranberry and port sauce can be made up to 3 days before serving it on Christmas Day. Simply make it as directed, transfer to an airtight container and leave it to cool, then store in the fridge until needed. It can be served cold, or it can be gently warmed through in a saucepan before serving, if you like. Cranberry and port sauce is delicious added to cold turkey or goose sandwiches, served with plenty of watercress. Alternatively, stir a spoonful or two of cranberry and port sauce into a casserole (especially lamb or game) to enrich the flavour. It is also good served with oily fish, such as grilled mackerel or smoked trout or pan-fried rainbow trout.

Goose

Tradition has it that goose pre-dates turkey as the choice of bird for the Christmas meal, and it was only in Victorian times that turkey began to overtake goose as the 'luxury' choice for Christmas. Goose, however, remained unaffordable for all but the most wealthy, so it was during the 19th century that the working class created the idea of 'goose clubs', whereby members of the club could save up for a goose by putting money towards it each week and then sharing the bird when Christmas arrived. These days, the delicious flavour of goose meat is being rediscovered, and goose is making a return to the Christmas table. Geese reared in the UK are predominantly free-range or organic and they are in season from September to January. They are reared naturally and are allowed to graze outdoors, mostly on grass, which gives them a very rich, buttery taste. Like duck, goose has a thick layer of fat, although most of this is just under the skin rather than in the meat. When you cook a whole goose, it's important to prick the skin all over to allow this fat to render. If you're just cooking the breast, you need to put the breast, fat-side down, in a dry pan to facilitate this rendering process. This will guarantee a crisp golden layer of fat and the meat underneath it will be moist and tender. There can be quite a lot of mess involved in cooking and carving a whole goose as a result of all the fat that comes from it, so if you aren't keen on roasting the whole bird, then you can try my recipe for **Roasted Goose with Goose and Cranberry Faggots and Brussels Sprouts Purée** (see page 418), which uses just the breasts and giblets and is a lot less messy.

If you are a traditionalist, however, and like the spectacle of a **Whole Roasted Goose**, then cook it as follows. As a rough guide, a 4.5kg goose will serve 4–6 people and a 6kg goose will serve 8–10 people. Take the goose out of the fridge at least 2 hours before you want to cook it, to allow it to come to room temperature. Remember to weigh the goose (if you are stuffing the bird, weigh it once the bird has been stuffed) so that you can calculate the cooking time (see below). Preheat the oven to 220°C/Gas Mark 7. Remove the giblets from the goose, then prick the skin of the goose all over with a metal skewer, especially under the wings, which are particularly fatty, and season with sea salt and freshly cracked black pepper. Remove any excess fat from the inside (see Cook's Notes), then put the goose on a wire rack positioned over a large roasting tin. Roast in the oven for 30 minutes, then reduce the oven temperature to 180°C/Gas Mark 4 and roast the goose for the calculated time, allowing

Goose

20 minutes per kilogram of raw weight for medium-rare and 30 minutes per kilogram of raw weight for medium. Once the goose is cooked, remove it from the oven, then cover it loosely with foil and leave the bird to rest for 20 minutes before serving. Halfway through the cooking time, remove the roasting tin from the oven and pour as much of the fat from the tin as possible into a heatproof bowl (see Cook's Notes), then return the roasting tin and bird to the oven. Baste the goose at least twice during cooking to ensure it remains succulent and moist. Once rested, carve the bird and serve with **My Best Ever Roast Potatoes** (see page 430), **Creamed Brussels Sprouts with Bacon** (see page 408), steamed seasonal greens and **Cranberry and Port Sauce** (see page 410). The excess fat from the inside of the bird can be rendered by placing it in a small pan over a low heat and melting it very slowly. Pass the melted fat through a fine sieve into a sterilised jar, then cover, cool and keep in the fridge for up to 1 month. You can also reserve the fat that comes from roasting the bird. Pass it through a fine sieve into a sterilised jar, then cover, cool and keep in the fridge for up to 1 week. Goose fat is great for roasting potatoes as it gives them a fantastic flavour. Use your goose fat to make **My Best Ever Roast Potatoes** (see page 430).

Medjool dates

If you're faced with an excess of cooked goose meat, then this **Leftover Goose and Potato Pie** is a perfect way to use it up. In fact, it's great for any meaty leftovers, so you could substitute the goose meat for turkey or pheasant meat, if you like. Preheat the oven to 200°C/Gas Mark 6. Melt 1 tablespoon unsalted butter in a large saucepan and once it is foaming, add 1 sliced (washed) leek, 1 crushed clove garlic, 1 diced large onion, 200g diced leftover roast potatoes (or other cooked root vegetables, such as celeriac, parsnip or swede), 1 tablespoon mild curry powder and sea salt and freshly cracked black pepper and sauté over a medium heat for 6–8 minutes or until golden brown. Sprinkle over 1 tablespoon plain flour and stir well, then add 100ml dry sherry or dry white wine and cook for 4–5 minutes, stirring, until the sherry is reduced by half. Add 300ml chicken stock and bring to a gentle simmer, stirring occasionally. Once simmering, add 300g flaked cooked goose meat and 100g mango chutney and simmer for about 20 minutes or until the sauce is reduced, thickened and almost syrupy, stirring occasionally. While the filling is cooking, place 700g (peeled weight) peeled and diced potatoes in a large saucepan, cover with cold water and bring to the boil over a high heat. Cover and cook for 18–20 minutes or until tender. Remove from the heat and drain well, then add 200ml milk, 2 tablespoons unsalted butter and a few gratings of fresh nutmeg. Mash the potatoes with a potato ricer or potato masher and season to taste with salt and pepper. Spoon the cooked filling mixture into a shallow ovenproof serving dish, top with the mashed potato and sprinkle over 50g grated mature Cheddar cheese. Bake in the oven for 25–30 minutes or until golden brown and bubbling hot. Serve with buttered seasonal greens or a lightly dressed green salad. Serves 4 as a main course.

Medjool dates

Medjool dates are imported into the UK from the Middle East and North Africa. They are available all year round, but are particularly associated with this time of year because of the sense of luxury they bring to festive cooking. Medjool dates are a particularly large fleshy variety of date and their intense sweet flavour and soft, juicy texture make them an interesting ingredient to pair with game and other meats.

They can also simply be eaten on their own as a sweet snack, or they can be stoned and filled (with marzipan, walnut halves or sweetened mascarpone) and served as petit fours. For a savoury pre-dinner canapé, stuff the stoned dates with creamy, soft goat's cheese combined with chopped fresh thyme leaves and finely grated lemon zest. Medjool dates can also be added to stews and casseroles or chopped and added to salads.

These **Medjool Date and Rum Bonbons** make wonderful gifts to include in your festive hampers, or you could simply serve them at the end of a meal with coffee. Place 125g digestive biscuits in a small polythene food bag and use a rolling pin to lightly crush them into coarse crumbs. Melt 125g unsalted butter in a saucepan, then add 100g demerara sugar and 125g (prepared weight) stoned, chopped medjool dates. Bring the mixture to the boil over a medium heat, stirring continuously, then reduce the heat and simmer for about 5 minutes or until the sugar has dissolved and the mixture has combined and is thickened and sticky. Remove from the heat and stir in 1 teaspoon vanilla extract, 2 teaspoons dark rum and the crushed digestive biscuits. Mix well until the mixture comes together, then cover and set aside to cool for 30 minutes. Divide the mixture into about 30 equal portions, then roll each portion into a walnut-sized ball and immediately roll each ball in desiccated coconut to coat all over. Transfer the bonbons to a plate and refrigerate for at least 6 hours (but ideally overnight – I think they taste better if you leave them for longer to let the flavours develop) to allow them to set before serving. Once set, store the bonbons in an airtight container in a cool, dry cupboard and use within 1 week. Makes about 30 bonbons.

Swede

Better known as 'neeps' in Scotland, where it is a traditional accompaniment to haggis (along with 'tatties' or potatoes) on Burns night, swede is a root vegetable from the Brassicaceae family that is sometimes confused with the turnip. Swede is also known as rutabaga in the US. Swede is a large, swollen round root with a purple-tinged skin and dense yellow-orange flesh. It has an earthy, slightly sweet flavour and can be cooked in much the same way as other root vegetables, such as turnips, carrots and parsnips, although its flesh is very soft and it can start to disintegrate quickly, so make sure you don't overcook it. Smaller swedes will have a sweeter flavour and a softer texture, so they are best suited to being mashed with butter and salt and pepper to make an interesting side dish. Add diced larger swedes to hearty casseroles, stews and soups, but avoid the very large ones as the flesh can become woody and tough. Swede can also be cut into chunks and roasted with other root vegetables.

If you're as fanatical about food as I am, then you will understand how I relate certain recipes to specific people or events. I shall always associate Mr. P with this carrot and swede mash, which we serve on Christmas Day. For him, no Christmas meal is complete without **Ross's Famous Carrot and Swede Mash**. Melt 2 tablespoons unsalted butter in a large saucepan and once it starts to foam, add 350g (prepared weight) peeled and sliced swede, 350g (prepared weight) peeled and sliced carrots and sea salt and freshly cracked black pepper and sauté over a medium heat for 8–10 minutes or until softened, making sure the vegetables don't take on too much colour. Add 200ml dry white wine to the pan and let it bubble, stirring and scraping the base of the pan with a wooden spoon to deglaze it. Boil rapidly over a high heat for 5 minutes, then stir in 250ml chicken or vegetable stock and bring back to the boil. Reduce the heat, then cover the pan and simmer over a low heat for 18–20 minutes, stirring once or twice, until the swede and carrots are soft and almost falling apart and the liquid has evaporated. If there is still liquid in the pan, remove the lid, turn the heat up and cook until it has evaporated, without letting the vegetables catch or brown too much. Remove from the heat, add 2 tablespoons unsalted butter and mash together until smooth using a potato masher, then add the finely grated zest of 1 lemon, a few drops of freshly squeezed lemon juice and a few gratings of fresh nutmeg and stir to mix. Adjust the seasoning to taste and serve piping hot. Serves 4 as an accompaniment. This mash tastes even better the following day, so I'd advise making it a day in advance – you can make it up to 3 days in advance, if you like. Make it as directed and leave to cool, then transfer the mash to an airtight container and store in the fridge for up to 3 days. When you are ready to serve, gently reheat the mash in a saucepan over a medium heat until it is piping hot.

Creamy Brussels Sprouts Soup with Puffed Stilton and Walnut Beignets

This soup is a true taste of Christmas and makes an elegant starter or light lunch over the festive period. You can make the Stilton and walnut batter for the beignets a day in advance and keep it refrigerated until you're ready to cook and serve the dish, if you like.

Serves 4 as a starter or light lunch

For the puffed Stilton and walnut beignets

100ml milk
50g unsalted butter
¼ teaspoon sea salt
80g plain flour
a pinch of cayenne pepper
2 eggs
60g Stilton, crumbled into small pieces
30g walnuts, roughly chopped
sunflower oil, for deep-frying

For the creamy Brussels sprouts soup

1 tablespoon unsalted butter
150g (prepared weight) leeks, trimmed, washed and finely shredded
100g peeled potatoes, finely sliced
600ml white chicken stock
300g (prepared weight) Brussels sprouts, trimmed and finely shredded
100ml double cream
sea salt and freshly cracked black pepper

First, prepare the beignet batter (see Cook's Note). Put the milk, butter and salt into a saucepan and heat gently until the butter has melted, then bring the mixture to a gentle simmer. Remove the pan from the heat and immediately sift the flour and cayenne pepper into the milk mixture, then beat vigorously with a wooden spoon until the mixture is smooth and leaves the sides of the pan to form a ball. Return to a very low heat and cook gently for 5 minutes, stirring continuously, then remove from the heat.

Transfer the dough to an electric stand mixer fitted with a paddle attachment. Turn the mixer on and add the eggs to the dough, one at a time, beating well after each addition. Beat until the mixture becomes silky, smooth and shiny. If you don't have an electric mixer, gradually add the beaten eggs to the dough, beating well with a wooden spoon until you have a smooth and shiny mixture. Add the Stilton and walnuts and mix well, then cover and refrigerate the batter until the soup is cooked and you are ready to serve.

Make the creamy Brussels sprouts soup. Melt the butter in a large saucepan and once the butter starts to foam, add the leeks, potatoes and salt and pepper and sauté over a medium heat for 6–8 minutes or until slightly softened and lightly coloured. Add the stock and bring to the boil, then lower the heat, cover and simmer gently for 8 minutes. Add the Brussels sprouts and bring back to the boil, then simmer for a further 3–4 minutes or until the potatoes are tender. Add the cream, then bring the soup back to the boil and simmer for 2 minutes.

Remove from the heat, then carefully transfer the soup to a blender and purée until smooth. Return to the pan and reheat gently until hot, then taste and adjust the seasoning, if necessary. Keep the soup hot until you are ready to serve.

To cook the beignets, heat the sunflower oil in an electric deep-fat fryer or in a deep frying pan to a temperature of 160°C (or until a small piece of bread browns within 20 seconds in the hot oil). Once the oil is hot enough, spoon heaped teaspoons of the batter into the hot oil and deep-fry the beignets (in two batches) for about 2 minutes or until golden brown and crisp all over. Using a slotted spoon, remove and drain the cooked beignets on kitchen paper, season with salt and serve immediately.

To serve, ladle the hot soup into bowls and serve with the Stilton and walnut beignets alongside.

Cook's Note

The Stilton and walnut beignet batter can be made a day in advance and kept refrigerated until you're ready to use it the following day. Often resting the batter for a day actually improves the flavour and makes the finished beignets lighter and puffier.

Roasted Guinea Fowl Breasts with Cep and Herb Butter

Ceps hold wonderful memories for me of working in a Michelin-starred kitchen. At this time of year, when the game, dried wild mushrooms and truffles came in through the back door, the smells in the kitchen became intense and almost forest-like. Now, if I close my eyes, the smell of ceps soaking brings back the sights and sounds of that kitchen and for a split second I can hear "deux covers at table cinq" – the delightful mixture of French and English as somebody called out an order to the chef. In my heart, I still have a strong desire to be a part of that world, but my head and body tell me that those days are behind me. This recipe is a tribute to all my years of hard graft in restaurant kitchens.

I love guinea fowl as it's a lot meatier and more flavoursome than chicken, but not as gamey as you might expect it to be. You do need to be careful not to let it dry out during cooking, but wrapping it in bacon, as I've done, should keep it beautifully succulent and moist. Served with a decadent mushroom and herb butter and a rich helping of one of the season's best – creamed Brussels sprouts – this recipe is what my foodie dreams are made of. It's luxurious, creamy and delicious. What's more, if you dried your own ceps a little earlier in the year during the autumn wild mushroom season (see page 302), this recipe is a fantastic opportunity to show them off.

This is another wonderful dish for entertaining, as it looks very impressive and you can prepare it up to three days in advance and then simply roast the guinea fowl when needed.

Serves 4 as a main course

30g dried ceps
100ml boiling water
50g unsalted butter, softened, plus 1 tablespoon unsalted butter
3 cloves garlic, crushed
1 tablespoon chopped fresh mixed herbs (such as tarragon, flat-leaf parsley and lemon thyme)
4 guinea fowl breasts (about 100–125g each), with skin and bone, French trimmed
8 rashers smoked streaky bacon or 8 slices smoked pancetta
sea salt and freshly cracked black pepper

Creamed Brussels Sprouts with Bacon (see page 408), to serve

Soak the dried ceps in the boiling water for 30 minutes. Drain and squeeze to remove the excess water, then finely chop the ceps (discard the soaking water).

Melt the 1 tablespoon butter in a non-stick frying pan and once it starts to foam, add the chopped soaked mushrooms, the garlic and salt and pepper and sauté over a medium heat for 7–8 minutes or until golden brown and soft. Remove from the heat and drain on kitchen paper, then leave to cool slightly.

In a small bowl, mix the remaining 50g softened butter with the drained, cooked mushrooms, the herbs and a little salt and pepper. Transfer the flavoured butter to a piping bag fitted with a small plain nozzle and set aside.

Prepare the guinea fowl breasts. Preheat the oven to 200°C/Gas Mark 6. Line a baking tray with non-stick baking paper and set aside. Trim off any excess fat and then carefully loosen the skin on the breasts. Gently insert the nozzle of the piping bag between the guinea fowl flesh and skin. Pipe a quarter of the flavoured butter under the skin of each breast, then use your fingers to flatten and spread the butter under the skin, being careful not to let it come out or to split the skin.

Place the breasts on a chopping board, skin-side up. Take the tip of each breast and pull it around to the bone to form a circular shape, then sit the breasts on the chopping board, with the bone pointing upwards, and wrap 2 bacon rashers around the bottom of each breast, where the skin and flesh meet. Tie a piece of kitchen string around the bacon to secure it, then place the guinea fowl breasts on the prepared baking tray. (If you are preparing these in advance, cover and refrigerate until you are ready to cook them – see Cook's Note.)

Roast the guinea fowl breasts in the oven for 20–22 minutes or until the guinea fowl is cooked and the bacon is crispy. Remove from the oven and leave to rest for 5 minutes before serving. Remove the kitchen string before serving.

Serve 1 guinea fowl breast per portion with the creamed Brussels sprouts alongside. Serve immediately with My Best Ever Roast Potatoes (see page 430) or roasted mixed root vegetables.

Cook's Note
The prepared raw guinea fowl breasts can be prepared up to 3 days in advance, then stored in an airtight container in the fridge until you are ready to cook and serve them. Roast them in the oven, as directed, allowing a few extra minutes cooking time, as the breasts will be chilled when they go into the oven.

Smoked Haddock Kedgeree with Soft-boiled Quail's Eggs and Curried Mayonnaise

Technically, this is not a traditional kedgeree as the rice I'm using is risotto rice instead of long-grain, and the cooked rice mixture is then made into balls and deep-fried like the Italian dish, arancini. However, the flavours of a kedgeree are present, so I like to think of this dish as my twist on a classic, just presented in a slightly different way.

We serve this dish as a pretty lunchtime starter, but you could serve it as a hearty lunch for two by making the rice balls slightly bigger, if you like.

Serves 4 as a starter or 2 as a hearty lunch

300g skinless undyed smoked haddock fillet
250ml milk
1 bay leaf
3 black peppercorns, lightly crushed
½ teaspoon coriander seeds, lightly crushed
200ml fish stock
1 tablespoon unsalted butter
2 banana shallots, finely diced
2 teaspoons ras el hanout
1 teaspoon mild curry powder
100g arborio or carnaroli rice
125ml dry white wine
1 lemon
80g dried breadcrumbs
4 tablespoons mayonnaise
6 quail's eggs
sunflower oil, for deep-frying
sea salt and freshly cracked black pepper

a large handful of a selection of baby or mini/micro salad leaves, to serve
rapeseed oil, for drizzling

First, prepare the haddock. Place the haddock in a saucepan with the milk, bay leaf, black peppercorns and coriander seeds, cover and bring to a gentle simmer over a low heat, then simmer gently for 2 minutes. Remove from the heat and set aside, covered, for about 8 minutes or until the fish is cooked and flaky. Meanwhile, bring the stock to the boil in a separate small saucepan, then reduce the heat and keep it warm over a very low heat.

Remove the haddock from the milk, then remove and discard any stray bones. Flake the flesh into a bowl, then cool, cover and refrigerate. Meanwhile, pass the milk through a fine sieve into a bowl, measure out 200ml and stir this into the warm fish stock (discard the remaining milk), then remove the pan from the heat.

To cook the rice, melt the butter in a saucepan and once it starts to foam, add the shallots, 1 teaspoon ras el hanout, ½ teaspoon curry powder and a pinch of salt and pepper. Cover the pan with a lid and sweat the shallots over a medium heat for 8–10 minutes or until softened and transparent.

Add the rice to the pan and cook, uncovered, for about 3 minutes, stirring continuously, to toast the rice. Add the wine to the pan and let it bubble, stirring and scraping the base of the pan with a wooden spoon to deglaze it, then boil rapidly over a high heat for 7–8 minutes or until the wine has evaporated.

Reduce the heat to medium, then gradually add the warm milk and stock mixture, a ladleful or so at a time, stirring well after each addition and only adding more liquid once the previous ladleful has been completely absorbed by the rice. Keep adding the liquid until it is all used up and the rice is cooked. This should take about 18–20 minutes. You want the rice to be soft (slightly softer than if you were serving it as a risotto). If you run out of stock but need to cook the rice a little longer, just add a little boiling water. Remove the pan from the heat, then taste and adjust the seasoning, if necessary.

Finely grate the zest from the lemon, then cut the lemon in half and remove the segments. Squeeze out any juice left in the fruit halves (once the segments have been removed). Set aside. Stir the lemon zest and one-third of the chilled poached haddock into the rice mixture and mix well. Once it is cool enough to handle, divide and shape the rice mixture into 12 equal balls. Roll each rice ball in the dried breadcrumbs to coat it all over, using your hands to press the crumbs on firmly. Repeat until all the rice balls are coated, then place them on a plate and chill in the fridge for 1 hour to rest and firm up (see Cook's Notes).

While the rice balls are chilling, make the curried mayonnaise. In a small bowl, combine the mayonnaise with the reserved lemon juice, the remaining 1 teaspoon ras el hanout and ½ teaspoon curry powder and salt and pepper. Cover and refrigerate until needed (see Cook's Notes).

Cook the quail's eggs in a covered pan of boiling water for 2 minutes, then remove the eggs using a slotted spoon and place them in a bowl of iced water to cool quickly. Once cold, peel the eggs carefully and set aside at room temperature, or in the fridge if you are preparing the eggs in advance (see Cook's Notes).

When you are ready to serve, cook the rice balls. Heat some sunflower oil in an electric deep-fat fryer or in a deep frying pan to a temperature of 160°C (or until a small piece of bread browns within 20 seconds in the hot oil). Once the oil is hot enough, deep-fry the breadcrumbed rice balls in the hot oil for 4–5 minutes or until golden brown and crisp all over – you will need to deep-fry the balls in two batches. Using a slotted spoon, remove and drain the cooked rice balls on kitchen paper.

To serve (as a starter), mix the remaining chilled poached haddock with the salad leaves and lemon segments, then divide between 4 serving plates. Place 3 deep-fried rice balls on each plate and spoon the curried mayonnaise alongside. Cut the quail's eggs in half, season with salt and pepper, then place 3 egg halves on each plate. Drizzle a little rapeseed oil over each plate and serve immediately.

Cook's Notes

The uncooked rice balls can be made up to 3 days in advance and stored in an airtight container in the fridge.

The curried mayonnaise can be made up to 3 days in advance and stored in an airtight container in the fridge.

You can also cook the quail's eggs up to 3 days in advance and keep them in cold water in an airtight container in the fridge.

Roasted Goose with Goose and Cranberry Faggots and Brussels Sprouts Purée

This recipe is perfect if you don't want to tackle roasting a whole goose on the bone. It eliminates the risk of overcooking the goose and making it dry, it reduces the cooking time significantly and, frankly, avoids a lot of the mess involved in handling a whole goose. The faggots are an intriguing alternative to the traditional accompaniment of 'pigs in blankets', and they enable you to use the whole bird in a more sophisticated and interesting way.

Caul fat is the lace-like fatty membrane that encases the internal organs of animals such as pigs, sheep, etc. It comes in thin sheets and is naturally sticky so it is wonderful for wrapping and sealing meat, and as it cooks, the fat melts, leaving the meat inside it wonderfully moist. You can buy it from your butcher, but you'll need to pre-order it. Wash it thoroughly before use.

You can prepare the faggots up to 3 days in advance, if you like, and then just cook them on the day alongside the goose breasts, as directed. Serve the dish with my delicious homemade Cranberry and Port Sauce (see page 410).

Serves 4 as a main course

For the goose and cranberry faggots
2 tablespoons unsalted butter
2 banana shallots, finely diced
250g skinless, boneless goose leg meat (about 1 leg)
125g goose giblets (heart, liver and kidneys)
100g pork neck, cut into 2cm pieces
100g fresh cranberries, roughly chopped
1 tablespoon coarse fresh breadcrumbs
1 tablespoon chopped fresh mixed herbs (such as tarragon, chervil, chives, parsley and thyme)
100g caul fat, washed thoroughly
sea salt and freshly cracked black pepper

For the roasted goose
2 boneless (skin on) goose breasts (250–340g each)
1 teaspoon coriander seeds
5 cloves
a sprig of fresh thyme, leaves only
finely grated zest of 1 orange
1 tablespoon sea salt

For the Brussels sprouts purée
1 tablespoon unsalted butter
300g (prepared weight) Brussels sprouts, trimmed and finely shredded
50ml dry white wine
100ml double cream
freshly grated nutmeg, to taste

Cranberry and Port Sauce (see page 410), to serve
blanched Brussels sprouts leaves, to garnish (optional)

First, prepare the goose and cranberry faggots. Melt 1 tablespoon butter in a non-stick frying pan, add the shallots and salt and pepper, then cover and sweat over a medium heat for 7–8 minutes or until the shallots are transparent. Remove from the heat and set aside to cool completely.

Mince the goose leg meat, giblets and pork neck separately using a mincer or the mincer attachment for your electric stand mixer (see Cook's Notes). The meat needs to be coarsely minced so use the appropriate plate for your mincer. Transfer the minced meat mixture to a mixing bowl, add the cooled shallots, the cranberries, breadcrumbs and herbs and season lightly with salt and pepper. Mix together thoroughly, then taste and adjust the seasoning (see Cook's Notes). Cover and leave to rest in the fridge for 30 minutes.

Lay the caul fat out on a clean work surface. Dampen your hands and divide the faggot mixture into 8 equal portions, then shape each one into a ball. Place a faggot ball on the caul fat so that you can see how large you will need to cut the caul. You need to cut a square of caul fat that's large enough to be wrapped around each ball in a single layer. Use a sharp knife or pair of kitchen scissors to cut out an initial piece of caul fat, then cut out 7 more pieces of the same size. Carefully wrap each faggot ball tightly in a piece of caul fat. Transfer the balls to a plate, cover loosely with foil, then set aside in the fridge until you are ready to cook them (see Cook's Notes).

Next, prepare the roasted goose. Preheat the oven to 200°C/Gas Mark 6. Score the skin of the goose breasts using a sharp knife, being careful not to cut all the way through to the flesh. Heat a non-stick frying pan over a medium heat until hot, then toast the coriander seeds and cloves in the pan for 2 minutes, moving them constantly to prevent them from burning. Remove from the heat, then grind the warm toasted spices with the thyme, orange zest, salt and a sprinkling of black pepper using a pestle and mortar. Rub the spice mixture all over the goose breasts, massaging it into the meat and skin. Return the frying pan to a medium heat and once hot, place the goose breasts, skin-side down, in the pan and cook for 8–10 minutes or until the skin is golden brown and crisp (you do not need any extra fat in the pan as the goose skin is naturally fatty). Remove from the heat and pour the fat from the pan into a small heatproof bowl (see Cook's Notes). Turn the breasts over, then return the pan to a high heat and cook for about 2 minutes on the reverse side or until golden brown. Remove from the heat and transfer the goose breasts to a baking tray, skin-side up, then roast in the oven for 18–20 minutes or until cooked to medium. Remove from the oven and leave to rest for 5 minutes before serving.

Meanwhile, finish cooking the faggots. Line a roasting tin with non-stick baking paper and set aside. Wipe the frying pan (used for cooking the goose breasts) clean using kitchen paper, then return it to a high heat, add the remaining 1 tablespoon butter and once it is foaming, add the faggots and cook for 3–4 minutes or until browned all over. Transfer the faggots to the prepared roasting tin and cook in the oven (alongside the goose breasts) for 15–18 minutes or until fully cooked and golden brown. Remove from the oven and leave to rest for 5 minutes before serving.

While the goose breasts and faggots are cooking, prepare the Brussels sprouts purée. Melt the butter in a saucepan and as soon as it starts to foam, sauté the sprouts, with salt and pepper added, over a medium heat for about 6 minutes or until they are softened and are starting to take on colour. Add the wine to the pan and let it bubble, stirring and scraping the base of the pan with a wooden spoon to deglaze it, then boil rapidly over a high heat for 1–2 minutes or until the wine has evaporated.

Add the cream and season to taste with nutmeg, then reduce the heat and simmer for 4–5 minutes or until thickened, stirring occasionally. Remove from the heat, carefully transfer the mixture to a blender and blend until smooth. Transfer to a bowl and keep warm until you are ready to serve.

While the goose breasts and faggots are resting, gently warm the cranberry and port sauce in a small saucepan, if you like (the cranberry and port sauce can be served either warm or cold, whichever you prefer).

To serve, divide the Brussels sprouts purée between 4 serving plates, slice each goose breast into 4 and then place 2 slices on each plate. Serve 2 faggots per portion with the warmed cranberry and port sauce alongside. Garnish with blanched Brussels sprouts leaves, if you like, and serve immediately.

Cook's Notes

If you don't have a mincing device, you can use your food processor to mince the meat for the faggots. Process the meat in short bursts, until minced and combined. Be careful not to over process it – you need a coarse mixture.

To check you have added enough seasoning to your faggot mixture before cooking, place a teaspoonful of the mixture in a dry, non-stick frying pan over a high heat and fry for about 1 minute or until cooked. Taste, then adjust the seasoning in the mixture accordingly.

The prepared (uncooked) faggots can be made up to 3 days in advance and stored in an airtight container in the fridge until you are ready to cook them.

Transfer the rendered goose fat to a sealed jar or a covered container and leave to cool, then store in the fridge and use within 1 week. The rendered fat can be used to make My Best Ever Roast Potatoes (see page 430) and Orange and Honey Caramelised Sprouts (see page 408).

Rustic Game Terrine

The sheer size and splendour of a whole terrine make it a thing of great beauty. As a chef, I normally see this creation in its entirety only briefly, before it's then carved into slices, plated and garnished to be served to customers. A very talented chef taught me that when cooking and serving food, generosity should come naturally – "Never skimp Madalene, be generous". Those words have made me quite a lavish cook!

Present the terrine in a rustic manner – whole, on a wooden board with a generous amount of homemade chutney. Let guests carve as large a portion as they like and remember to provide plenty of warm toast and a freshly dressed salad to accompany the terrine.

You'll need to make this the day before you want to serve it, to allow the terrine time to chill and set overnight.

Serves 8–10 as a starter or light lunch

12 rashers smoked streaky bacon
2 tablespoons rapeseed oil
3 banana shallots, finely diced
3 cloves garlic, crushed
1 tablespoon chopped fresh thyme leaves
50ml Cognac
200g pork back fat
200g pork belly
500g mixed lean game meat (such as venison haunch and shoulder, pheasant breast and leg, partridge breast and rabbit loin)
150g chicken livers, cleaned and finely diced
1 tablespoon chopped fresh tarragon
1 tablespoon chopped fresh flat-leaf parsley
1 tablespoon snipped fresh chives
½ teaspoon ground cinnamon
½ teaspoon ground mace
½ teaspoon smoked paprika
2 skinless, boneless rabbit loins (about 100g each)
2 skinless, boneless partridge breasts (about 60g each)
sea salt and freshly cracked black pepper

Preheat the oven to 150°C/Gas Mark 2. Line a 32 x 11 x 7cm terrine mould or loaf tin with the bacon, leaving an overhang of bacon rashers around the rim. Set aside.

Heat the rapeseed oil in a small, non-stick frying pan until hot, then sauté the shallots, garlic and thyme, with salt and pepper added, over a medium heat for about 6 minutes or until they start to colour. Add the Cognac and bring to a simmer, then cook for a further 2–3 minutes or until reduced slightly. Remove from the heat, transfer the mixture to a small bowl and set aside to cool.

Mince the pork back fat, pork belly and game meat using a mincer or the mincer attachment for your electric stand mixer (see Cook's Notes). The meat needs to be coarsely minced so use the appropriate plate for your mincer.

In a large mixing bowl, combine the minced meat, the cooked shallot mixture, the chicken livers and all the herbs and spices, then season lightly with salt and pepper. Taste and adjust the seasoning (see Cook's Notes).

Dice the rabbit loins and partridge breasts into 4cm pieces and season lightly with salt and pepper.

To assemble the terrine, press a third of the minced meat mixture into the prepared terrine mould and press down firmly to compact the meat. Add a layer of half of the diced rabbit and partridge and press down firmly, then repeat these layers, pressing each layer down firmly. Finish with the last third of the minced meat mixture. Fold the overhanging bacon over to cover the meat completely. Cover the terrine mould with its lid or cover tightly with foil.

Place the terrine in a large, deep roasting tin and then pour boiling water into the tin to come halfway up the sides of the mould. Carefully place the roasting tin in the oven and cook for 1½–2 hours or until the terrine is cooked. To test whether your terrine is cooked, either insert a temperature probe into the centre of the terrine – it should read 68°C, or insert a metal skewer into the centre and leave it there for about 30 seconds – it should be piping hot when removed.

Carefully remove the terrine from the oven. For the best texture, your terrine then needs to be pressed as it cools. Remove the lid (or foil) and cover the meat with a double layer of fresh foil. Find a suitable flat piece of metal or sturdy plastic that fits neatly inside the top of the terrine mould and place weights (such as cans of food) directly on top to press the meat down. Leave to cool, then carefully transfer the mould to the fridge and leave to cool and set overnight.

The next day, remove the terrine from its mould. To do this, briefly dip the terrine mould in hot water, then give it a light shake to loosen it. Carefully turn the terrine out on to a serving plate or wooden board. Serve with homemade chutney or my Damson and Rosemary Jelly (see page 332), plus plenty of warm toast and a freshly dressed salad.

Cook's Notes

If you don't have a mincing device, you can use a food processor to mince the meat for the terrine. Process the meat in short bursts, until minced and combined. Be careful not to over-process it – you need a coarse mixture.

To check you have added enough seasoning to your terrine mixture before cooking, place a teaspoonful of the mixture in a dry, non-stick frying pan over a high heat and fry for about 1 minute or until cooked. Taste, then adjust the seasoning in the mixture accordingly.

Sage, Prune and Armagnac-stuffed Turkey Breast with Prune Sauce

If you wanted something a little bit different from the traditional roast turkey on Christmas Day, you could try this delicious alternative, but it's also perfect for a Sunday roast with the family throughout the turkey season.

If you don't feel confident enough to butterfly the turkey breast, you can ask your butcher to do it for you, keeping the two halves joined by the skin. Don't forget to ask your butcher for a turkey breast or leg bone too, as you will need it to make the sauce.

The prunes soaked in Armagnac give this dish a luxurious touch and add a lovely sweetness. Serve with My Best Ever Roast Potatoes (see page 430) and Ross's Famous Carrot and Swede Mash (see page 413).

Serves 4–6 as a main course

For the prune sauce

1 turkey bone (from your butcher)
1 tablespoon sunflower oil
80g peeled onions, roughly diced
80g (prepared weight) carrots, peeled and roughly diced
80g (prepared weight) leeks, trimmed, washed and roughly diced
2 sticks celery, roughly diced (about 80g prepared weight)
2 cloves garlic, crushed
1 teaspoon coriander seeds, lightly crushed
¼ teaspoon black peppercorns, lightly crushed
80ml Armagnac
250ml red wine
2 bay leaves
a large sprig of fresh thyme
700ml brown chicken stock
100g dried stoned prunes, chopped
1 tablespoon finely chopped fresh sage
sea salt and freshly cracked black pepper

For the sage, prune and Armagnac-stuffed turkey breast

5 cloves
½ teaspoon coriander seeds
1 tablespoon unsalted butter
80g smoked back bacon rashers, finely chopped
1 small onion, finely diced
50g celery, finely diced
2 cloves garlic, crushed
100g dried stoned prunes, chopped
80ml Armagnac
300g minced pork
2 tablespoons chopped fresh sage, plus 10 large fresh sage leaves
finely grated zest and juice of 1 lemon
1 boneless (skin on) turkey breast (1–1.2kg), butterflied (see page 187 for instructions on how to butterfly chicken breasts and use the same method for the turkey breast but make sure you keep the skin attached to the breast)
6 slices Parma ham
1 tablespoon sunflower oil

My Best Ever Roast Potatoes (see page 430), to serve
Ross's Famous Carrot and Swede Mash (see page 413), to serve

First, make the prune sauce. Preheat the oven to 230°C/Gas Mark 8. Place the turkey bone in a roasting tin and roast in the oven for about 30 minutes or until it is dark brown in colour. Remove from the oven and cool slightly, then lightly bash the bone with a rolling pin to break it into smaller pieces. Set aside.

Heat the sunflower oil in a saucepan until hot, then add the onions, carrots, leeks, celery, garlic, coriander seeds and black peppercorns and sauté over a high heat for 8–10 minutes or until golden brown. Add the crushed roasted turkey bone to the pan, then add the Armagnac and let it bubble, stirring and scraping the base of the pan to deglaze it. Cook over a high heat for about 5 minutes or until the Armagnac is reduced and becomes syrupy. Add the wine to the pan and cook over a high heat for 7–8 minutes or until the wine is reduced and becomes syrupy. Add the bay leaves, thyme sprig and stock and bring to the boil, then reduce the heat to medium and simmer for about 20 minutes or until the stock is reduced and the sauce has thickened slightly.

Remove from the heat and pass the sauce through a fine sieve into a clean saucepan, discard the solids, then add the prunes to the sauce in the pan and stir to mix. Set aside for 30 minutes so that the prunes soften. Taste and adjust the seasoning, adding salt and pepper, if necessary. Once cool, cover and refrigerate the sauce until you are ready to serve (at which point you'll reheat and add the sage).

Meanwhile, prepare the stuffing for the turkey breast. Heat a non-stick frying pan over a medium heat until hot, then toast the cloves and coriander seeds in the pan for 2 minutes, moving them constantly to prevent them from burning. Remove from the heat, then grind the warm toasted spices using a pestle and mortar.

Return the frying pan to a medium heat, add the butter and once it is foaming, add the bacon, onion, celery, garlic and ground spices and sauté for 8–10 minutes or until golden brown. Add the prunes and Armagnac and bring the mixture to a simmer, then simmer for about 8 minutes or until the Armagnac is completely absorbed, stirring occasionally. Remove from the heat, transfer the mixture to a bowl and set aside to cool for 30 minutes. Once the bacon mixture is cool, add the minced pork, chopped sage, lemon zest and juice and salt and pepper and mix well.

Preheat the oven to 180°C/Gas Mark 4. To stuff and wrap the turkey breast, open out the butterflied turkey breast, skin-side down, on a chopping board and season with salt and pepper. Place the stuffing mixture in the centre of the turkey breast and use your hands to shape the mixture into a log or sausage shape.

Lay 3 Parma ham slices next to each other horizontally (long edges slightly overlapping) on a clean work surface, then lay the remaining 3 Parma ham slices horizontally next to the first 3 slices, overlapping the short edges slightly, to make a rectangle of Parma ham (this will look like an open book). Place the whole sage leaves on top of the Parma ham. Carefully transfer the turkey breast, skin-side down, on to the centre of the Parma ham rectangle. Fold the breast over to enclose the filling, then fold the Parma ham over the stuffed turkey breast to cover as much of it as possible (you will have 2 open ends where the turkey breast is not covered by the Parma ham – the joint will look like a fat sausage). Tie the Parma ham-wrapped stuffed turkey breast tightly with kitchen string.

Flip the joint over and place it in a roasting tin with the seam underneath and Parma ham wrapping on top. Brush the sunflower oil over the turkey joint, then cover with foil and roast in the oven for 1 hour. Remove the foil and increase the oven temperature to 200°C/Gas Mark 6, then return the joint to the oven and roast for a further 30 minutes or until the turkey is thoroughly cooked, tender and moist and the Parma ham is golden brown and crispy. Test to see if the turkey is cooked by inserting a metal skewer into it; if the juices run clear then it's cooked. If not, put the turkey joint back in the oven and cook for another 10–15 minutes, then test again. Remove from the oven, then cover loosely with foil and let the turkey joint rest for 20 minutes before serving.

Just before serving, bring the prune sauce back to the boil over a medium heat and simmer for 1–2 minutes, then stir in the sage and serve.

To serve, remove the string from the rested turkey breast joint, then carve the joint and arrange the slices on serving plates. Serve immediately with the hot prune sauce, roast potatoes and carrot and swede mash served in the centre of the table so that everyone can help themselves. Serve with buttered Brussels sprouts too, if you like.

Cook's Note

You can also make smaller individual Sage, Prune and Armagnac-stuffed Turkey Parcels using this recipe, to serve 6 as a main course with accompaniments. Ask your butcher to cut you six 120–140g turkey escalopes. Place each escalope in a small polythene food bag and use a wooden mallet or rolling pin to flatten each escalope to 7mm thickness.

Make the stuffing following the recipe above, then divide the stuffing mixture between the 6 escalopes, spreading it out evenly. Fold each escalope around the filling, then wrap each one in a slice of Parma ham so that the main part of the turkey escalope is covered.

Place the Parma ham-wrapped turkey escalopes, seam-side down, in an ovenproof dish and bake in a preheated oven at 190°C/Gas Mark 5 for 25–30 minutes or until the turkey is thoroughly cooked and the Parma ham is crispy. Remove from the oven and leave the escalopes to rest for 5 minutes before serving.

Jerusalem Artichoke and Walnut Pithiviers with Cranberry and Port Sauce

A pithiviers is a rich round baked pie that is thought to have originated in the French town of the same name. It is made by sandwiching a filling between two rounds of puff pastry and the top is then usually decorated with an elegant Catherine-wheel pattern before baking, which gives it a very professional-looking finish. Originally the filling was almond-based and pithiviers were sweet, but now you can find both savoury and sweet incarnations of the dish.

This recipe makes a sumptuous and elegant vegetarian option on Christmas Day, but it also makes a delicious main course throughout the Jerusalem artichoke season.

The pithiviers can be made a day in advance: just bake them when you need to, leaving you with one less thing to worry about on the big day.

Serves 4 as a main course

80g golden sultanas (or use regular sultanas, if you wish)
120ml dry white wine
500g Jerusalem artichokes
50g unsalted butter, plus 1 tablespoon unsalted butter
4 banana shallots, diced
1 clove garlic, crushed
200ml vegetable stock
80g toasted walnuts, roughly chopped
500g good quality chilled fresh all-butter puff pastry
2 egg yolks, lightly beaten
1 tablespoon linseeds
juice of 1 lemon
4 salsify (about 160–200g total weight)
4 baby leeks (about 125g total weight), trimmed, washed and cut into 5cm lengths
80g kale, stalks removed
2 pickled walnuts, drained and finely sliced
sea salt and freshly cracked black pepper

Cranberry and Port Sauce (see page 410), to serve

Put the golden sultanas in a bowl. Heat the wine in a small saucepan until it just comes to the boil, then pour it over the sultanas and leave to soak for 15–20 minutes.

Meanwhile, peel and slice the Jerusalem artichokes. Melt the 50g butter in a large saucepan and once the butter starts to foam, add the shallots, garlic, Jerusalem artichokes and salt and pepper. Cover the pan and sweat over a low heat for 10–12 minutes or until the vegetables are softened but not coloured at all, stirring regularly to prevent the Jerusalem artichokes from catching.

Add the soaked sultanas and wine to the pan, then increase the heat to medium, bring to a simmer and simmer for 5 minutes. Add the stock and bring back to a simmer, then simmer, uncovered, for a further 12 minutes or until the Jerusalem artichokes are completely soft and all the liquid has evaporated. Use a fork to crush the artichokes as much as possible as this helps them to absorb more liquid. Remove the pan from the heat and stir in the toasted walnuts. Taste and adjust the seasoning, if necessary, transfer the mixture to a bowl, then cool, cover and chill in the fridge for 30 minutes.

Roll out the puff pastry on a lightly floured work surface to 5mm thickness and cut out four 10cm rounds and four 12cm rounds. Place the rounds on a large tray and leave to rest in the fridge for 20 minutes.

Line a large baking tray with non-stick baking paper and place the 4 smaller rounds of pastry on the prepared baking tray. Divide the Jerusalem artichoke mixture into 4 equal amounts and place a portion in the centre of each round, flattening it slightly and leaving about 15mm border around the edges. Brush the exposed pastry with the beaten egg yolks, then gently lay the larger pastry rounds over the top. Use your hands to press the pastry tops down around the filling to remove any air pockets and press the edges together to seal. Use a knife to trim off any excess pastry, then crimp around the edges of the pastry.

Using a sharp paring knife, score the tops of the pithiviers by running curved lines from the centre of the pastry to the edge in a Catherine-wheel pattern, being careful just to score it and not to cut through the pastry. Brush the tops with the beaten egg yolks and sprinkle over the linseeds. Return the pithiviers to the fridge and leave to rest for 30 minutes.

Meanwhile, preheat the oven to 200°C/Gas Mark 6. Bake the pithiviers in the oven for 22–25 minutes or until the pastry is cooked, golden brown and crisp.

Meanwhile, fill a bowl with cold water and add half of the lemon juice. Peel the salsify, dip it into the bowl of acidulated water (to prevent browning), then drain. Cut the salsify into 5–7cm batons, place it in a saucepan, cover with cold water, then add salt and the remaining lemon juice. Bring to the

boil, then reduce the heat and simmer for 8–10 minutes or until the salsify is tender, then drain. While the salsify is cooking, blanch the leeks in a separate pan of boiling salted water for about 2 minutes or until tender, then drain well.

Melt the remaining 1 tablespoon butter in a large, non-stick frying pan and once it starts to foam, add the drained salsify and leeks and sauté over a high heat for about 2 minutes or until golden brown, then remove from the heat and season with a sprinkling of salt and pepper. Meanwhile, blanch the kale in a pan of boiling salted water for about 2 minutes or until tender, then drain well.

To serve, divide the kale between 4 serving plates, place the hot baked pithiviers on top and then arrange the sautéed salsify and leeks and pickled walnuts around the pithiviers. Serve immediately with the cranberry and port sauce alongside.

Roasted Pheasant with Prunes, Creamed Celeriac, Pink Fir Fondant and Barley

The flavour combination of pheasant, celeriac and prunes is warming and full-bodied, like a well-aged Cognac. This dish is ideal for a party and festive celebrations as you can prepare most of the components in advance.

The pheasant is not served as you might expect roast pheasant to be served. To keep the pheasant breasts beautifully moist and tender, I brown them in butter, then finish the cooking by poaching them in hot stock. It might sound like additional work, but it's worth it, particularly at this time of year when you want to make meals that extra bit special. The meat from the pheasant legs is combined with prunes and made into irresistibly delicious sausages, which I wrap in bacon to keep them moist and add flavour during cooking.

Serves 4 as a main course

For the roasted pheasant
40g dried stoned prunes, finely chopped
2 tablespoons Armagnac
2 oven-ready pheasants (about 500g each)
1 tablespoon rapeseed oil, plus 1 teaspoon rapeseed oil
a sprig of fresh thyme, leaves only
1 clove garlic, crushed
80g pork sausagemeat
1 tablespoon chopped fresh mixed herbs (such as sage, parsley, rosemary, chives and chervil)
¼ teaspoon freshly grated nutmeg
2 rashers smoked streaky bacon, cut in half widthways
1 tablespoon unsalted butter
200ml brown chicken stock or roasted game stock
sea salt and freshly cracked black pepper

For the Pink Fir fondant
85g unsalted butter, plus 1 tablespoon unsalted butter
16 Pink Fir Apple potatoes (about 1kg total weight), washed well and drained
200ml cold water

For the barley
200g pearl barley
1 tablespoon rapeseed oil
1 tablespoon chopped fresh mixed herbs (such as rosemary, chives and chervil)

For the creamed celeriac
1 tablespoon unsalted butter
1 celeriac (400–500g), peeled and finely sliced
200ml white chicken stock
50ml double cream

200g purple sprouting broccoli, florets only

First, prepare the roasted pheasant. Preheat the oven to 180°C/Gas Mark 4. Line a baking tray with non-stick baking paper and set aside. Place the prunes in a small bowl, add the Armagnac and leave to soak for 10–15 minutes.

Remove the breasts from the pheasants using a sharp knife (leave the skin on), then place them in a covered container and refrigerate until needed. Remove the legs from the birds, rub them all over with 1 teaspoon rapeseed oil, the thyme leaves and garlic and season with salt and pepper (discard the carcasses or use them for making stock at a later date – see page 22 for Roasted Game Stock). Place the legs in a roasting tin and roast in the oven for about 25 minutes or until the skin is golden brown and the meat is tender. Remove from the oven and leave to cool for 30 minutes.

Remove and discard the skin from the legs, then flake the meat into a bowl. Measure out 80g of the flaked leg meat and place it in a mixing bowl with the sausagemeat, herbs, nutmeg and soaked prunes. Season lightly with salt and pepper and mix well (put the remaining leg meat into an airtight container and save for another recipe – see Cook's Notes). Divide the mixture into 4 equal balls and roll each portion into a sausage shape (about 2cm in diameter). Wrap a piece of bacon around each sausage, then transfer to the prepared baking tray and chill in the fridge for about 30 minutes to firm up (see Cook's Notes).

Next, prepare the Pink Fir fondant. Preheat the oven to 180°C/Gas Mark 4. Melt the 1 tablespoon butter in a casserole and sauté the potatoes over a high heat for 2–3 minutes or until golden, then season lightly with salt and pepper. Add the remaining 85g butter and the water to the casserole, stir to mix, then place a cartouche (a circle of greaseproof paper) directly on the surface of the liquid. Cover the casserole with a lid, transfer to the oven and cook for 20–22 minutes or until the potatoes are tender and most of the liquid has evaporated (the cooking time will depend on the size of the potatoes). Remove the potatoes from the pan using a slotted spoon, transfer to a bowl and keep warm until you are ready to serve (see Cook's Notes).

Meanwhile, prepare the barley. Rinse the pearl barley under cold running water, then place in a large saucepan and cover with plenty of fresh cold water. Cover the pan and bring to the boil over a high heat, then boil rapidly for 25–30 minutes or until the barley is cooked and tender. Add a little salt about 2 minutes before the end of the cooking time. Remove from the heat and drain, then stir in the rapeseed oil and herbs. Taste and adjust the seasoning, if necessary, then keep the barley warm (see Cook's Notes).

While the pearl barley is cooking, prepare the creamed celeriac. Melt the butter in a saucepan and once it starts to foam, add the celeriac and salt and pepper, then cover and sweat over a low heat for about 15 minutes or until softened but not coloured at all, stirring regularly to prevent the celeriac from catching. Add the stock, increase the heat to medium and bring the stock to a simmer, then cover and cook for a further 12 minutes, by which time the liquid should have evaporated – if not, remove the lid, turn the heat up and cook until all the liquid has evaporated. You want the celeriac to be fairly dry. Remove from the heat and carefully transfer the celeriac to a blender, add the cream and then purée until very smooth. Taste and adjust the seasoning, if necessary, then transfer to a bowl, cover and set aside until you are ready to serve (see Cook's Notes). Just before serving, gently reheat the creamed celeriac in a saucepan until piping hot. In the meantime, finish cooking the pheasant. Preheat the oven to 200°C/Gas Mark 6. Heat the butter and the remaining 1 tablespoon rapeseed oil in a non-stick frying pan, season the pheasant breasts with salt and pepper, then place them in the pan, skin-side down, and cook over a high heat for about 2 minutes or until golden brown. Flip the breasts over and cook for a further 2 minutes or until golden brown on the reverse side, then remove from the heat and transfer to a deep roasting tin, skin-side up.

Bring the stock to the boil in a saucepan, then carefully pour it around the pheasant breasts so that it just covers the bottom of the roasting tin but doesn't cover the skin of the pheasant. Cook in the oven for about 12 minutes or until the pheasant is cooked and hot all the way through. Remove from the oven and leave the breasts to rest in the stock for 5 minutes before draining and serving.

While the pheasant breasts are roasting, cook the pheasant sausages at the same time. Cook them in the oven for 12–15 minutes or until they are golden brown and cooked through.

While the pheasant breasts are resting, reheat the creamed celeriac as directed. Blanch the purple sprouting broccoli in a pan of boiling salted water for 2–3 minutes or until just tender, then drain.

To serve, spread the hot creamed celeriac on to 4 serving plates, then spoon a portion of the warm barley into the centre of each plate. Top with a pheasant breast and a pheasant sausage, then place the fondant potatoes and broccoli alongside. Serve immediately.

Cook's Notes

Store the leftover cooked pheasant leg meat in an airtight container in the fridge and use within 3 days. It's perfect for a pie, so you could use it as a substitute for the goose meat in my Leftover Goose and Potato Pie (see page 412).

The uncooked pheasant sausages can be made up to 3 days in advance, then stored in an airtight container in the fridge until you're ready to cook them.

The Pink Fir fondant can be made up to 3 days in advance, then cooled and stored in an airtight container in the fridge until needed. Reheat in a preheated oven at 180°C/Gas Mark 4 for 12–15 minutes or until hot throughout.

The barley can also be made up to 3 days in advance, then cooled and stored in an airtight container in the fridge until needed. Reheat in a saucepan over a low heat for 8–10 minutes or until hot throughout.

The creamed celeriac can be made up to 3 days in advance, then cooled and stored in an airtight container in the fridge until needed. Reheat as directed.

Beef and Oyster Pies

This classic combination of beef and oysters in a pie is hearty British cooking at its best, though my version of the pie is not served quite as you might expect. I fill the deeper (bottom) oyster shells with the beef mixture, cover them with pastry and bake them, then batter and deep-fry the oysters and serve it all on top of a bed of buttery kale. The oysters definitely add a bit of drama and a lovely texture if served this way.

The oyster juice is used to make the pastry, so for safety's sake you will need to use the pastry on the day it is made and not keep any leftovers. I use shin of beef for the pie filling because I love the lip-smackingly rich flavour you get from slow-cooking this cut of beef.

These delicious pies are perfect for a cold winter's evening, served with a bottle or two of good red wine in front of a roaring log fire.

Serves 4 as a main course

2 tablespoons rapeseed oil
500g boneless shin of beef, trimmed
80g (prepared weight) turnips, peeled and cut into 1cm dice
80g (prepared weight) celeriac, peeled and cut into 1cm dice
80g (prepared weight) swede, peeled and cut into 1cm dice
80g (prepared weight) carrots, peeled and cut into 1cm dice
80g banana shallots, finely diced
1 clove garlic, crushed
1 tablespoon chopped fresh thyme leaves
350ml stout
1 litre beef stock
8 large fresh oysters (in shell), washed thoroughly
1 dark green sheet nori (paper-thin toasted sheet of seaweed)
275g self-raising flour
120g cold unsalted butter, diced
1 egg yolk, lightly beaten
200g kale, stalks removed
sunflower oil, for deep-frying
sea salt and freshly cracked black pepper

First, make the pie filling. Preheat the oven to 150°C/Gas Mark 2. Heat 1 tablespoon rapeseed oil in a large casserole until hot, then place the beef in the casserole, season with salt and pepper and cook over a high heat for 7–9 minutes or until golden brown all over, turning regularly. Remove the beef to a plate.

Return the casserole to the heat, add the remaining rapeseed oil and once it is hot, sauté the turnips, celeriac, swede, carrots, shallots, garlic and thyme over a medium heat for about 6 minutes or until they start to colour. Return the beef to the casserole, add 250ml of the stout and bring the mixture to the boil, then boil rapidly for about 5 minutes or until the liquid is reduced by half. Add the stock and bring to a simmer, then remove from the heat.

Place a cartouche (a circle of greaseproof paper) directly on the surface of the stock and cover the casserole with a lid. Transfer the casserole to the oven and cook for about 3 hours or until the beef is tender, flaky and succulent. Remove the casserole from the oven and carefully remove the beef to a plate to rest for 10 minutes.

Meanwhile, place the casserole over a high heat and bring the stock to the boil, then cook for 6–8 minutes or until the sauce is reduced, thickened and almost syrupy, then remove from the heat. Flake the cooked beef, using 2 forks, then add the flaked meat to the casserole and mix well. Leave to cool, then cover and refrigerate until needed. While the beef is cooking, prepare the oysters. Shuck the oysters over a bowl to catch the juices, then pass the juices through a fine sieve into a bowl and set aside. Remove the oysters from the shells, then transfer them to a container, cover and refrigerate until needed. Rinse the deeper bottom shells well and remove any grit or barnacles (discard the flatter top shells). Set aside to dry.

Next, make the pastry. Using a pestle and mortar, grind the nori sheet to a fine powder, then place in a mixing bowl with 200g of the flour and a pinch of salt. Using your fingertips, rub 100g of the butter into the flour until the mixture resembles fine breadcrumbs, then add 2–3 tablespoons of the reserved oyster juices, mixing to form a firm dough. Gather the dough into a ball, wrap in cling film and chill in the fridge for 30 minutes.

Roll out the pastry on a lightly floured work surface to 3–4mm thickness. Cut out 8 pieces of pastry in the same shape as the oyster shells but slightly larger. Divide the beef mixture between the prepared oyster shells, then place a piece of pastry on top of each one. Press down lightly, then crimp the pastry around the edges. Brush the pastry with beaten egg yolk, then carefully transfer the pies to a tray and leave to rest in the fridge for 30 minutes.

Meanwhile, preheat the oven to 200°C/Gas Mark 6. Transfer the pies to a baking tray and bake in the oven for 18–20 minutes or until the pastry is cooked, golden brown and crisp.

While the pies are baking, finish the oysters and cook the kale. Put the remaining flour and stout in a bowl, season lightly with salt and pepper and then mix together to form a fairly thick batter. Set aside. Cook the kale in a large saucepan of boiling salted water for 2–3 minutes or until just tender. Drain, add the remaining 20g butter and mix well, then season with salt and pepper and keep warm.

Meanwhile, heat some sunflower oil in an electric deep-fat fryer or in a deep frying pan to a temperature of 160°C (or until a small piece of bread browns within 20 seconds in the hot oil). Once the oil is hot enough, dip each oyster into the stout batter, then deep-fry in the hot oil for 2–3 minutes or until golden brown and crisp all over (the cooking time will depend on the size of the oysters) – you will need to deep-fry the oysters in two batches. Using a slotted spoon, remove and drain the cooked oysters on kitchen paper.

To serve, divide the buttered kale between 4 serving plates, making a nest in which to sit the pies. Place 2 pies on each plate and season with salt and pepper, then top each pie with a battered oyster. Serve immediately.

All the Trimmings

For me, the Christmas day meal is all about the trimmings. If you do not get the roast potatoes, gravy, cranberry sauce and all the other bits and bobs right, the perfect roast turkey or goose can never be enjoyed as much. Well, that is my theory and I am sure many people would agree with me. The million-dollar question is then where do you stop?! For me, the festive meal is complete when I have the following trimmings on my plate:

My Best Ever Roast Potatoes (see below)
Suffolk Warriors in Blankets (see below)
Cranberry and Port Sauce (see page 410)
Ross's Famous Carrot and Swede Mash (see page 413)
Orange and Honey Caramelised Sprouts (see page 408)
Braised Red Cabbage with Apples and Sultanas (see page 371)

My Best Ever Roast Potatoes

It's a bit of a bold statement to call these my 'best ever' roast potatoes, but to my taste these roasties are really rather good – dare I say it, I think I've achieved the perfect recipe?! Perhaps it's boasting, but I think there is that same sense of pride in most of us when we feel we have done something well and have produced our best.

Suffolk is a county blessed with plenty of potato fields. But we buy our fresh King Edwards locally from James Foskett, a local legend in potato-growing circles, because I can't help but feel that his are the most flavoursome.

It goes without saying that cooking your potatoes in goose or duck fat is unrivalled in terms of the flavour they provide. I then simply add just a few carefully chosen aromatics to 'inject' the potatoes with a little extra taste and goodness. Don't be afraid to shake your potatoes really hard after parboiling them. The rougher you are with them, the more you will be rewarded with those delicious crunchy bits. It's a cook's prerogative to pinch the crispy bits!

You will need to start preparing the potatoes the day before you want to serve them, as they need to be parboiled, then left to dry out overnight.

Serves 4 as an accompaniment

1kg King Edward potatoes, peeled and cut into quarters if medium, or cut into 6 chunks if large
1 teaspoon sea salt, plus extra for seasoning
1 clove garlic, crushed
a large sprig of fresh thyme
1 bay leaf
200ml goose or duck fat

Start preparing the potatoes a day in advance. Place the potatoes in a large saucepan and cover with cold water, then add the teaspoon of salt, the garlic, thyme sprig and bay leaf. Cover and bring the potatoes to the boil over a medium heat, then cook for 8 minutes, until partially cooked.

Drain the potatoes in a colander (discard the thyme stalk and bay leaf), then shake the colander to roughen the edges of the potatoes and make the outsides fluffy. Spread the potatoes out on a baking tray that fits in the fridge, let them cool, then leave them uncovered in the fridge overnight to dry out.

The following day, preheat the oven to 200°C/Gas Mark 6 and put a large roasting tin in the oven to heat. Once hot, place the goose fat in the roasting tin in the oven for 10 minutes to melt and heat through, then remove the tin from the oven and carefully add the potatoes to the hot fat, using a spoon to baste them with the fat. Season with salt, then roast in the oven for 25 minutes.

Remove from the oven, turn the potatoes over, basting them again, then roast in the oven for a further 25 minutes or until cooked and crispy. The potatoes are ready when the outsides are golden brown and crispy and the insides are fluffy and white. The more times you turn and baste the potatoes during cooking, the crispier they will become.

Once cooked, season the roast potatoes with salt, then transfer to a serving dish using tongs or a slotted spoon and serve immediately.

Suffolk Warriors in Blankets

The Suffolk Warrior has become one of our trademarks at the British Larder, a name we're proud to have given this dish. If I had a penny for every time someone asked us what a Suffolk Warrior was, I think I'd have been able to buy us a shiny new cooker by now!

A standard Suffolk Warrior is a chipolata sausage roasted in the oven with clear honey and wholegrain mustard. For a festive addition, we wrap the chipolatas in bacon first, then roast them with the honey and mustard. We use Suffolk-reared Dingley Dell pork chipolatas, but you can create your own warriors using your regional variety of chipolatas.

Serves 4 as an accompaniment

12 rashers smoked streaky bacon
12 chipolata sausages
1 tablespoon rapeseed oil
2 tablespoons clear honey
1 tablespoon wholegrain mustard

Preheat the oven to 200°C/Gas Mark 6 and line a roasting tin with non-stick baking paper.

Wrap a rasher of streaky bacon around each chipolata sausage, then place them in the prepared roasting tin and drizzle with the rapeseed oil. Roast in the oven for 10 minutes, then remove from the oven, drizzle over the honey and add the mustard and mix carefully.

Return to the oven and roast for a further 10 minutes or until the bacon-wrapped chipolatas are cooked and the honey becomes sticky and coats them. Serve immediately.

Luxury Sweet Mincemeat

The wonderful thing about making your own mincemeat is that it's hugely satisfying but also very easy. This recipe is simple to prepare but it's one for a rainy weekend when you have a little bit more time on your hands, as the mixture needs to stand overnight and then be cooked the next day. The warm, sweet smell of the baking mincemeat will linger and fill your home with a wonderful aroma.

It's best to make this mincemeat at least six weeks before Christmas to allow the flavours to blend, mellow and mature.

I sometimes get a bit over-enthusiastic with the quantity of mincemeat that I make and end up with more than I know we're going to be able to eat. However, a jar of mincemeat makes a pretty gift and it does keep well, so you can still make my delicious Festive Power Bars (see page 435) long after Christmas is over. The bars make an indulgent breakfast or a perfect afternoon snack with a cup of tea.

Makes 3 x 250g jars

120g raisins
80g sultanas
80g currants
25g chopped mixed peel
25g dried stoned prunes, chopped
120g soft dark brown sugar
200g (prepared weight) cooking apples, peeled, cored and coarsely grated
80g shredded vegetable or beef suet
finely grated zest and juice of 1 orange
finely grated zest and juice of 1 lemon
25g flaked almonds, chopped
25g pecan halves, chopped
2 teaspoons ground mixed spice
1 teaspoon freshly grated nutmeg
50ml brandy

Place all the ingredients, except the brandy, in a mixing bowl and mix together thoroughly. Cover and leave to stand in a cool place overnight to allow the flavours to develop.

The next day, preheat the oven to 120°C/Gas Mark ½. Transfer the mincemeat mixture to a large, deep roasting tin and cover the tin with foil. Bake in the oven for 2 hours – by this time the grated apple will have broken down and the mixture will have become much darker in colour. Remove from the oven and leave the mixture to cool slightly, then stir in the brandy.

Spoon the warm mincemeat into hot, sterilised jars. Cover with the lids and seal. Once cold, label and store in a cool, dry cupboard. Store for at least 2 weeks (but preferably 6 weeks) before using. The unopened jars of mincemeat should keep well in a cool, dry cupboard for up to 6 months. Once opened, keep in the fridge and use within 1 month.

Luxury Bite-size Mince Pies

I love a mince pie and if it's homemade, it's even better. I also prefer small bite-size ones like these, as this way eating two will not make me feel so guilty! They also look lovely and pretty served at the end of a meal. I like serving mine slightly warm and dusted with caster sugar, with plenty of Brandy Butter (see page 437) or Brandy Cream (see Cook's Notes). You could also try making and baking these mini mince pies for friends – simply fill a cellophane bag with a few cold baked mince pies, then tie the bag with red string to seal and take it as a small gift when you are invited to parties over the festive period.

Makes 24 mini mince pies

250g Sweet Shortcrust Pastry (see page 18)
250g Luxury Sweet Mincemeat (see page 432)
24 pecan halves, to decorate
caster sugar, for dusting

Preheat the oven to 180°C/Gas Mark 4. Lightly grease a 24-hole mini muffin tin and set aside.

Roll out the pastry on a lightly floured work surface to about 2mm thickness. Use a 6–7cm plain or fluted cutter to cut out 24 pastry rounds, then line the prepared mini muffin tin with the pastry rounds and leave to rest in the fridge for 20 minutes.

Fill each pastry case with some mincemeat, then decorate the top of each mince pie with a pecan half, pressing it down gently. Bake the pies in the oven for 20–25 minutes or until the pastry is cooked, golden brown and crisp.

Remove from the oven and transfer the mince pies to a wire rack, then immediately dust them with caster sugar. Leave the mince pies to cool slightly, then serve them warm or at room temperature with cream, vanilla ice cream, Brandy Butter (see page 437) or Brandy Cream (see Cook's Notes).

Cook's Notes
To make Brandy Cream to serve with the mince pies, in a bowl, whip 200ml double cream with 25ml brandy and 1 teaspoon icing sugar until it forms soft peaks. Serve immediately or cover and refrigerate until needed. The brandy cream will keep in an airtight container in the fridge for up to 3 days. Serves 6–8. The quantity of brandy cream made above will also be ample to serve with the 24 mini mince pies.

Leftover mince pies can be stored in an airtight container in a cool, dry cupboard for up to 3 days. You can then warm them through in a preheated oven at 180°C/Gas Mark 4 for 4–5 minutes before serving. Alternatively, cooked mince pies can be frozen for up to 1 month. Reheat them from frozen in a preheated oven at 180°C/Gas Mark 4 for 10–12 minutes.

Chocolate and Cranberry Salami

This recipe definitely gets everybody talking! I serve the salami as a fun after-dinner treat with coffee; I simply put one on a plate with a knife and let everyone help themselves. I also put the salamis into the Christmas hampers I make for my family and friends (see Cook's Notes).

Makes 2 x 200g salamis

- 100g digestive biscuits
- 40g flaked almonds
- 40g dried cranberries
- 40g (shelled) pistachio nuts (left whole)
- 40ml port
- 40g unsalted butter
- 100g dark bitter chocolate (70% cocoa solids), roughly chopped
- 50g icing sugar
- a pinch of table salt
- 1 teaspoon vanilla extract
- 40g condensed milk
- 2 tablespoons cocoa powder

Place the digestive biscuits in a small polythene food bag and use a rolling pin to lightly crush them (you want to crush them into small pieces not crumbs). Transfer them to a mixing bowl, then add the almonds, cranberries, pistachios and port and mix well. Set aside at room temperature for 20 minutes to allow the flavours to mingle.

Melt the butter in a small saucepan, then remove the pan from the heat, add the chocolate and stir until the chocolate is completely melted and combined, then transfer to a mixing bowl. Add the icing sugar, salt, vanilla extract, condensed milk and the biscuit mixture and mix well. Set aside to cool for 20 minutes to allow the mixture to thicken slightly. As it starts to thicken, the mixture will become easier to work with, but don't let it sit for longer than 20 minutes or it will start to set and become too hard.

Divide the mixture in half, then place each portion on to a double layer of cling film and roll it up in the cling film to form a sausage or log shape, each one 12–15cm in length and 4–5cm in diameter. Refrigerate the salamis for at least 4 hours or overnight before serving (see Cook's Notes).

Remove the salamis from the fridge about 1 hour before serving. Unwrap the salamis (discard the cling film), then roll each one in the cocoa powder to coat all over. Serve on a plate at room temperature with a sharp knife for everyone to help themselves.

Cook's Notes

These salamis make a wonderful homemade gift. After they've been coated in the cocoa powder, I like to then wrap each one in greaseproof paper and tie the ends with string to mimic a real salami.

The salamis can be stored (wrapped in cling film or greaseproof paper) in the fridge for up to 1 week. They can also be frozen for up to 3 months. Simply defrost in the fridge overnight and then bring to room temperature before serving.

Festive Power Bars

A recipe borne from a desire to use up every last bit of sweet mincemeat that I had made one year. I thought it would be good to create some 'power bars' as an alternative to mince pies. These are perfect for when you need a quick snack or a pick-me-up with a cup of tea, or try one in the morning on your way to work when you don't have time to stop for breakfast – they make the perfect festive breakfast bar!

Makes 6–8 bars

For the pastry base and filling
85g plain flour, sifted
50g icing sugar, sifted
50g unsalted butter, diced
1–2 tablespoons ice cold water
250g Luxury Sweet Mincemeat (see page 432)

For the topping
25g plain flour
25g rolled oats
20g caster sugar
1 tablespoon semolina
1 teaspoon ground cinnamon
30g unsalted butter, diced
20g walnuts, roughly chopped
20g flaked almonds

Grease, then line a 22 x 12 x 7cm loaf tin with non-stick baking paper and set aside.

To make the pastry base, place the flour, icing sugar and butter into a mixing bowl. Using your fingertips, rub in the butter until the mixture resembles coarse breadcrumbs, then add enough water, mixing to form a firm dough. Gather the dough into a ball, wrap in cling film and chill in the fridge for 20 minutes.

Preheat the oven to 160ºC/Gas Mark 3. Roll out the pastry on a lightly floured work surface to the same size as the base of the loaf tin and to about 1cm thickness, then transfer the pastry to the prepared tin, gently pressing it into the base of the tin. Spread the mincemeat evenly over the pastry base, then refrigerate while you make the topping.

For the topping, place the flour, oats, caster sugar, semolina, cinnamon and butter in a mixing bowl. Using your fingertips, rub in the butter until the mixture resembles coarse breadcrumbs. Add the nuts and run your fingers through the mixture to combine thoroughly. Scatter the crumbly mixture evenly over the mincemeat and then press the topping down firmly with your hands. Bake in the oven for 35–40 minutes or until cooked and golden brown.

Remove from the oven to a wire rack and leave to cool completely in the tin. Once cold, turn the large bar out of the tin and then cut it widthways into 6–8 smaller bars or fingers (see Cook's Note). Serve each bar on its own for a delicious festive breakfast, or serve with Chantilly cream or vanilla ice cream for a lovely afternoon teatime treat.

Cook's Note
Once cooled and sliced, the bars can be stored in an airtight container in a cool, dry cupboard for up to 1 week.

My Ultimate Christmas Pudding

Making my own Christmas pudding – mixing, steaming, maturing and feeding it – is a wonderful way to capture the spirit and anticipation of Christmas. I love a good Christmas pudding and making my own has enabled me to perfect my recipe. I thought long and hard about everything that was great about puddings I've eaten in the past and everything I've not liked about them, and I have to say I think my recipe is now perfect (and a lot of our customers agree)!

I use a local ale, which provides a little bitterness, and I use Pump Street Bakery's sourdough bread (see page 120) to make the breadcrumbs. Most importantly, I leave my raw mixture to rest for two days before steaming the pudding. This helps all the flavours to combine and blend and allows the breadcrumbs to soak up as much liquid as possible. The mixed fresh apple and pear starts breaking down and the fruitiness blends into the mixture.

I also like to make my pudding a minimum of six weeks before Christmas so that I can gradually feed it with brandy, allowing the cooked pudding time to mellow and mature. However, if you suddenly find yourself with only a month to go and realise that you haven't made your Christmas pudding yet, then it's still perfectly OK to make this pudding then and feed it with brandy for four weeks rather than six – it will still taste wonderful on Christmas Day. Merry Christmas!

Serves 4–6

1 egg
1 tablespoon dark rum
75ml dark ale (I like to use our local ale, Adnams bitter, which has a strong flavour, but you might like to choose one locally produced in your region)
finely grated zest and juice of 1 orange
60g fresh coarse sourdough breadcrumbs
50g shredded vegetable or beef suet
2 tablespoons strong white bread flour
1 teaspoon baking powder
1 teaspoon ground mixed spice
a pinch of freshly grated nutmeg
½ teaspoon ground cinnamon
½ teaspoon ground ginger
115g soft dark brown sugar
50g sultanas
50g raisins
50g dried cranberries
100g currants
1 tablespoon chopped mixed peel
50g flaked almonds
100g (prepared weight) mixed cored apple and pear (leave skin on), coarsely grated
brandy, to feed the pudding

You will need to prepare the pudding mixture, then leave it to steep for 2 days before cooking it.

Place the egg, rum, ale and orange juice in a small bowl and use a fork to mix well. Place all the remaining ingredients, except the brandy, in a large mixing bowl, then stir in the ale mixture and mix thoroughly. Cover the bowl and refrigerate for 2 days.

After 2 days of resting the mixture, finish making the pudding. Grease a 1 litre pudding basin. Stir the pudding mixture well, then transfer it to the prepared pudding basin and level the surface, leaving a 4cm gap between the top of the mixture and the rim of the bowl. Cut a circle of non-stick baking paper and place it on top of the pudding mixture, cover the basin tightly with foil, then tie with kitchen string to keep the foil in place and keep the pudding watertight. Make a handle with the string to enable you to lift the pudding out of the steamer more easily.

Place the pudding in a steamer set over a pan of simmering water, cover the pan with a lid and steam the pudding for 4 hours (see Cook's Notes). Make sure you keep an eye on the water level in the pan and top it up with boiling water from the kettle if it starts getting too low.

Remove from the heat, then carefully remove the pudding from the steamer and leave it to cool completely. Once the pudding is cold, unwrap the foil and remove the baking paper, then make small holes in the top of the pudding using a metal skewer and spoon over 4 tablespoons brandy. Cover the pudding with a fresh circle of non-stick baking paper and wrap the basin tightly in fresh foil. Store the pudding in a cool, dry cupboard for at least 6 weeks before using, feeding the pudding with 1–2 tablespoons brandy once a week and resealing with fresh baking paper and foil each time.

To reheat your pudding on the day you want to serve it, cover the top of the pudding with a fresh circle of non-stick baking paper, wrap it in fresh foil and tie with kitchen string. Make a handle out of the string, then steam the pudding as above for at least 2 hours, to ensure it's hot all the way through.

To serve, remove the pudding from the steamer and carefully unwrap it, then turn the pudding out on to a serving plate. Heat 2 tablespoons brandy very gently in a small saucepan, then pour the warm brandy over the pudding and set it alight. Carefully carry the pudding to your guests in a darkened room for maximum 'wows' and pleasure. Serve immediately with a choice of Brandy Butter (see Cook's Notes), Brandy Cream (see page 433) and fresh custard.

Cook's Notes
You can also cook the pudding in a large saucepan. Place an inverted saucer into the bottom of the pan, sit the pudding basin on the saucer, then pour in enough boiling water to come halfway up the sides of the basin. Cover the pan and cook as above, topping up the hot water, as necessary.

To make a rich and delicious Brandy Butter to serve with your pudding, put 125g softened unsalted butter, 125g sifted icing sugar and the seeds scraped from ½ vanilla pod into a bowl and cream together until pale and fluffy. Stir in 1 tablespoon brandy until combined, then taste and add a little extra brandy, if needed. Serve the brandy butter at room temperature and use on the day of making. Serves 4–6.

Index

Thank you

And finally the time has come to thank people who have played such an integral part in our lives and careers, and those who helped making this book become a reality.

First of all, I thank my parents, Dalene and Harlan Hamel (my late father). Thank you for passing on your hard grafting working ethics, giving me the best chance in life, my education and upbringing. I will be in debt to you for the rest of my life.

A huge thank you to Ross Pike aka Mr.P, you're my work buddy, my lover, my soul mate and my best friend: thank you for being there every step of the way. Ross, you made me believe that I can achieve anything. Thank you for the endless hours, days, weeks, months and years whilst holding your full time job and then every Godsent hour spare you helped me with creating these wonderful dishes, supporting me with the website and working every hour there is in the kitchen at the British Larder Suffolk. Thank you to Roy and Linda Pike (Ross's parents) for your continuous support.

A big thank you to every chef I had the privilege to work with. I owe a special thank you to Rowley Leigh for imbedding the passion for seasonal British food in me. Gordon Ramsay for igniting the passion for perfection and desire to always do better. Fabien Ecuvillon (wonderful pastry chef and friend): you are one very special Frenchman, thank you for your support, friendship and everything you have ever taught me.

Thank you to Mike Smith and Peter Borg-Neil, you always believed in us, we both thank you for your continuous dedication, mentoring and support.

Thank you to Jon Croft, my Publisher, for believing enough in me to publish this wonderful book. Jon I shall never forget our first telephone conversation and meeting. I asked you to promise me that you will deliver for me a 'beautiful book' and you did. A special thank you to Matt Inwood, my Art Director, for putting up with me. Thank you for driving the project and keeping the dream alive. Thank you for your continuous words of encouragement when I doubt my own ability and photographic skills. Matt: thank you for creating this beautiful book.

A special thank you Anne Sheasby, my editor, for your editing support, I love the way you work and appreciate your careful attention to detail. Those e-mails gave me the confidence that we will get it right. It's a satisfying feeling, thank you. Thank you to Imogen Fortes who embraced the style of the book and being sympathetic towards the relationship and work already done by Anne by the time you joined the editing team, fairly later on in the book. Your contribution is special and heartfelt.

A special thank you to every website follower, British Larder Suffolk customer, supplier and team member. Without you we would not have had the encouragement to create the British Larder.

And a final thank you goes to my two beautiful boys, Hector and Mr Darcy, two very lively Springer Spaniels for keeping me sane.